DATE DUE

	DATE DUE		

THE OIL FOLLIES OF 1970–1980

Also by Robert Sherrill:

THE ACCIDENTAL PRESIDENT
GOTHIC POLITICS IN THE DEEP SOUTH
THE DRUGSTORE LIBERAL
MILITARY JUSTICE IS TO JUSTICE AS
MILITARY MUSIC IS TO MUSIC
THE SATURDAY NIGHT SPECIAL
THE LAST KENNEDY
WHY THEY CALL IT POLITICS
GOVERNING AMERICA

THE
OIL
FOLLIES
OF
1970–1980

*How the Petroleum Industry Stole the Show
(and Much More Besides)*

Robert Sherrill

ANCHOR PRESS/Doubleday, Garden City, New York
1983

Excerpt from *National Journal* article by Richard Corrigan reprinted
with permission from *National Journal*.

Library of Congress Cataloging in Publication Data

Sherrill, Robert.
   The oil follies of 1970–1980.

Includes bibliographical references and index.
1. Petroleum industry and trade—United States.
2. Petroleum industry and trade—Government policy—
United States. I. Title.
HD9565.S447 1983   338.2'7282'0973
ISBN: 0-385-18221-X
Library of Congress Catalog Card Number 82-45462

For my cartel: Peter, Holden,
Brooke, Charlie, Casey, Martin,
Melba . . . and Mary.

CONTENTS

"An honest and scrupulous man in the oil business is so rare as to rank as a museum piece."

HAROLD ICKES

A FEW WORDS ABOUT THIS BOOK

"It is automatically assumed that we are liars and connivers instead of trying to be decent citizens like newspaper people and senators are."

JOHN E. SWEARINGEN, *chairman, Standard of Indiana*

Half a billion years before Robert Kerr and Lyndon Johnson and Russell Long were sent to Congress to watch over the interests of the oil and gas industry, nature began preparing for their careers. In many parts of the earth where continents are today, there were oceans then; dead microorganisms and rotting vegetable matter drifted to the bottom of those ancient seas, and their graveyard was covered through the millennia by many layers of silt and sand. Under pressure and by a natural process that geologists still find mysterious, vast areas of the sedimentary seabeds were transformed into oil and gas.

And the seas receded, and man discovered these things.

And lo, after a suitable gestation period, an industry as colorful as it was corrupt was born. The first giant to emerge from that primordial corporate swamp was Standard Oil, and it begat other corporations of its own size and ethics, and they begat many imitators, big and small, and they all begat lots and lots of trouble down to the present day. Trouble, that is, for you and me—assuming you are not among the lucky ones who sank a drill bit into those transformed fossils—and for many millions of people around the world.

But wait: that is an ungrateful summation of history. The truth is, there was a sizable stretch of years when mankind, or at least that portion of mankind that could afford machinery, considered oilmen to be their benefactors. After all, they made it possible for us to transport ourselves via 350-horsepower machines burning 30-cent gasoline to such necessary destinations as Disneyland. America rolled to its destiny on cheap power, and we were offhandedly grateful to the oilmen for this, even though, having witnessed their rapaciousness in the marketplace and their duplicity in politics, we did not trust them. We had heard those tales of how the world's great oil moguls, while shooting grouse and drinking champagne at Achnacarry Castle, had carved up the world and made the first grand price-fixing alliance. Old magazines told of scandalous manipulations, as when California refineries created shortages by shipping gasoline from Los Angeles to northern parts of the state and then, after prices had jumped tenfold, bringing it back. History books recorded the embarrassment of Teapot Dome. But those things were long ago. Should we be concerned? We were all pretty well convinced that bribery and price fixing continued in many ways and under many guises, but we had grown accustomed to those things and were willing to accept them—so long as gasoline, natural gas, and heating oil were cheap.

Most Americans would probably have agreed with John Nance Garner's advice to Harold Ickes that ". . . we couldn't appeal to the consciences of those oil people because they didn't have any consciences." Most would have sympathized with Franklin Roosevelt's celebrated complaint that it was impossible to get along politically with, or without, oilmen. But these things all seemed so far removed from our lives; and so for many years we accepted, perhaps a bit sullenly, both the oilmen's dishonesty and lack of conscience and their political power, because, well, there just didn't seem to be much that the average citizen, or even the average politician (had he or she been so inclined), could do about such things. And besides, oil and gas *were* cheap, and the rest rooms in some of the filling stations were still reasonably clean. Why get involved?

And then, as the decade of the 1960s came to an end, something amazing happened. The truce suddenly ended too. A significant segment of the people got mad. Consumer groups and environmental groups and their smallish but vocal band of allies in Congress began to demand changes. These hotheads were no longer willing to forgive everything in return for cheap energy. Hell, they took cheapness for granted. Now they demanded social responsibility as well; they wanted the oil companies to start paying their share of taxes and show more concern for the safety of the environment and for the conservation of the nation's resources. They insisted on stiffer regulation of, and a closer accounting from, the oil companies. The Torrey Canyon spill, in 1967, the Santa Barbara spill, in 1969, the proposed pell-mell construction of the Alaska pipeline, the absurdly costly oil import program, the endlessly illogical oil depletion allowance—these were some of the things that aroused anger and fear.

Don't get the idea that a great many people were involved, for this was not the case—at least not at first. The impressive thing was that an organized pack of critics of *any* size had united. This was new, startling, almost anticapitalism, almost . . . un-American. Or so one would have thought from the panicky outcries of the oil industry and the pitiful complaints that it poured into the ear of the press.

"Oil, the nation's largest and most powerful industry," wrote the New York *Times* in 1969, "is being buffeted by the most severe and high-powered political gale it has ever known. If these winds of criticism develop into hurricanes of change, as well they might, the national economy as well as international politics may feel a major upheaval. Many billions of dollars in oil-company earnings, foreign exchange and taxes are in the balance. In addition, the nation's defense posture and political outlook are deeply involved."

This kind of wowy writing was not restricted to the eastern press. Across the continent, the Los Angeles *Times* was reporting the scene in the same shocked tones: "The U.S. oil industry is floating on a sea of troubles. From the Santa Barbara beaches to the halls of Congress, the industry is on the defense over issues, including pollution, import controls and cherished tax advantages. At the same time, oil companies are worrying about how to raise $200 billion needed for capital investment over the next 10 years to satisfy the nation's voracious appetite for petroleum products. Apprehension fills the air in executive suites. 'This is the worst year for attacks on the industry since I started in the oil business in 1933,' says W. E. Avery, a Texaco vice-president. Other officials say things haven't been so bad since the Teapot Dome Scandal of the 1920s . . ."[1]

It was highly ironic that 1969 should turn out to be so rough on the oil industry, for all signs at the beginning of the year had seemed to promise blue skies and an endlessly capricious orgy of expansion and riches. With the swearing in of Richard Nixon, the White House was occupied by the best friend oil had had since Eisenhower was President. In raising $35 million for the 1968 race (more than both major candidates had spent in 1964), Nixon depended heavily on oil money; indeed, oil gave him one tenth of his take, which was more than any other industry contributed. The size of some of the gifts indicated a true love affair. The Mellon family, Gulf Oil's major stockholders, for example, gave him $279,000. The Sun Oil family, of J. Howard Pew, gave $208,000. Robert Orville Anderson, top man at Atlantic Richfield (ARCO), gave more than $100,000.

Eager to show his gratitude, Nixon immediately upon taking office announced that although the Interior Department would continue to oversee much of the nation's oil and gas operations, oil *policy* would no longer be fashioned at Interior, as ostensibly had been done during the Kennedy and Johnson years, but within the White House itself. With Nixon's hand immersed in it.

He further conveyed his feelings by naming Peter M. Flanigan (who had raised much of the corporate money Nixon had been running on since 1966) to be his liaison with the oil industry. Prior to becoming Nixon's assistant, Flanigan had been a partner in Dillon Read & Co., an investment banking firm that helped such companies as Ashland, Superior, Texas Eastern, and Union Oil of California in mergers and stock un-

---

1. You'll see quite a few references to the Teapot Dome scandal in this book; it's everybody's favorite measuring stick for scandal. Look up the *TEAPOT DOME* entry in the Appendix for a brief history.

derwritings. At one time, Flanigan was chief executive officer of Barracuda Tanker Corporation, which was controlled by Union Oil, and he continued to hold stock in the company until a few days before Barracuda received an extraordinary shipping waiver worth an estimated $6.5 million; the waiver was rescinded only after the press began to build it into a scandal. Some said Union Oil president Fred Hartley had merely "lent" Flanigan to Nixon. If the witticism was justified, it did not make Flanigan unusual. Indeed, Nixon swept into office with a retinue that was as devoted as it was indebted to oil. And of course Congress was still dominated by men from states that were virtually owned by energy companies.

So there really was no good reason for the gloom that hung over oil's executive suites in 1969. But it was understandable. Accustomed as they were to skewering their enemies or buying them off with no trouble at all, industry's leaders were rattled by being confronted with so many varying problems at once, including some created by opponents who obviously could not be subjugated so easily by the usual pressure and sweetheart tactics. But the gloom was a passing mood, the product of momentary panic, a summer squall, no more. Although startled by the alarums, the oilmen were not about to be cowed. And when they bounced back, it was in a fighting mood. They, too, were fed up with the way things were going. They were tired of cheap energy being taken for granted. They wanted to work out an arrangement that would push prices much, much higher, and keep them there. They were not about to let the government remove the oil import quota—one of history's most successful price-fixing schemes—until some other arrangement was in place to suppress the oil supply. Industry was also ready to launch another major offensive to kill even the feeble government regulations that had dogged it for much of its existence, particularly the Federal Power Commission's control over natural gas prices. Now, *that* was a crusade the oilmen could really get zealous about. Directly or indirectly, the FPC entered into the lives of 42 million residential, commercial, and industrial users of gas. Indeed, the price it set for natural gas affected the price of all fuels. For years and years, the oil/gas crowd (three fourths of the natural gas is controlled by two dozen oil companies) had been trying to persuade Congress—sometimes with argument, sometimes with campaign contributions, sometimes with outright bribes—to free natural gas from price regulations. Now it was ready to exert itself in another strenuous effort to that end.

The 1970s were obviously destined to be a bloody battleground. As things turned out, most of the blood would be that of consumers. Still, the oil companies would bleed some too, for they would from time to time shoot themselves in the foot, or feet. If victory in the commercial world must include winning public approbation, then the oil companies

lost the war of the 1970s disastrously; they emerged from that decade
with hardly a shred of credibility still covering their affluence. Previously
they had sometimes been able to claim at least some grudging respect;
after the 1970s they were, it is fair to say, universally feared and despised. On the other hand, if victory can be measured only in new
wealth, then it must be said that the oil companies were victorious indeed, for never in modern history has so much wealth been transferred
from consumers to producers—with, let us add, so little justification. In
forcing this transfer, the oil companies received the incalculable assistance of the Organization of Petroleum Exporting Countries (OPEC).
It was history's best example of what can happen when thieves fall in.

And of course, the oil companies were abetted all the way by a majority of Congress and by every President who served during the 1970s. For
consumers, what happened during this decade must be counted the
greatest betrayal that they are likely ever to encounter.

It does make one wonder about our system. If a government is good
for anything, it is, second only to preserving the peace and liberties of
the people, supposed to be good for protecting a nation's nonreplenisha-
ble natural resources and using them in a wise fashion, and not permitting commercial groups, simply by spouting silly stuff about free enterprise, to corner these resources and sell them at harmful prices. Our
government, as I hope this book shows emphatically, abandoned these
responsibilities during the 1970s.

To be sure, we can and should blame the corporations and OPEC for
many of our troubles, but they were, after all, only doing what comes
naturally to corporations without a social conscience and to emerging nations and to other birds of prey. Our politicians and bureaucrats have no
such excuse; politics and civil service in America haven't yet sunk to the
point that their selling out is looked upon as a natural response to pressure. Of course, politicians have been selling out to oil companies since
the latter first saved enough money to buy political happiness (see Appendix entry on *MARK HANNA*). But fortunately, such is the naïve
hopefulness of Americans, they still look upon this as an unnatural act
upon the body politic; since that's my feeling too, you will notice some of
my naïve outrage spotting these pages. When one deals with the history
of oil politics and especially with the great betrayal of the 1970s, one
does tend to froth over a bit.[2]

---

2. I offer my froth in tribute to the reporters who did such a good job telling the story
of the sellout as it was happening; and most of them were doing it, I suspect, with no
more than a thimbleful of encouragement from their publishers, who, naturally, were
on the side of monopoly and profiteering—two characteristics that are as commonplace
in newspapering as in the oil world. From ignorance or forgetfulness, I will leave out
some who should be mentioned, but my personal pantheon of energy-reporting heroes
includes Morton Mintz, Stephen Aug, Roberta Hornig, J. P. Smith, Thomas O'Toole,

Perhaps the most impressive thing about the oil companies' victory in the 1970s is that it was built on such old, predictable techniques and was aimed at such old, predictable goals. Confidence men (which is basically what these corporations are) know that suckers never learn. They keep falling for the same old tricks, over and over. And that's what happened in the 1970s. Nothing the oilmen did, nothing they said, should have come as much of a surprise. Their con was perfected decades ago. If there is anything the oil industry has been, it is consistent—consistent in its pretension, its deceitfulness, its heavy-handedness, its arrogance, and the tactics that go with these characteristics. From time to time it may make technical changes; it may, for example, in one era seek its profits from production and in another era squeeze most of its profits from refining and marketing. And there have been many other technical or policy changes. But in basic matters, there's consistency, era after era. The industry has with stupefying regularity manipulated government— and most of the press—with the same discredited claims, the same unreliable data, the same vacuous forecasts, the same brutal undercutting of competition, the same perversions of law.

Talk about moss-encrusted techniques! The oldest in the oil industry's repertoire is the fright campaign—usually based on hysterical warnings that we are running out of energy and endangering our "national security." (Please see *EARLY FRIGHT CAMPAIGNS*, in the Appendix.) Whenever Big Oil has wanted Washington's assistance in breaking through cartel competition overseas, or in violating antitrust laws with impunity at home or abroad, or in juggling their foreign income records to evade U.S. taxes, or in throwing off statutory regulations without fear of punishment, or in imposing price-fixing restraints on independent competitors—it has always managed to come up with a supply crisis that, the oilmen insist, threatens the nation's very existence. The only solution is to let them do as they wish. The argument has always worked, because Washington officials just love to play straight men in the oil industry's little melodramas. Indeed, over the past seven decades, most U.S. foreign and domestic policies relating to oil have been created in response to an assortment of "crises" that the industry pulled from its hat. It continued pulling them throughout the 1970s.

And the most amazing thing about it all was that, stale and threadbare and predictable though their tactics were, the oilmen once again seemed to catch most of our officials (and most of the press) off guard. Oh, that's being much too kind. They weren't caught off guard; they were wide-eyed and very willing suckers, apparently only too happy to disre-

Peter Behr, Ronnie Dugger, Richard Corrigan, and the team of Donald L. Barlett and James B. Steele. There were, of course, a few feisty editors; those who helped me the most were Ned Chilton, Carey McWilliams, Hoc Noble, Phil Pochoda, and Jim Goode.

gard the long and notorious history of the industry's deceptions. Boy oh boy, were they stupid.[3]

Unfortunately, it is not the kind of stupidity that we pay for just once. Long after the politicians and bureaucrats who sold us out (and the publishers and editors who misled us) have retired on fat pensions and annuities, you and I will be paying for their blunders and their collusion with the oil crowd. And we'll go on paying, year after year, through one recession after another.

I have used the title *The Oil Follies* because it allows several levels of meaning. The book could have, for the same reason, been called *The Oil Scandals*. The decade was filled with excruciatingly foolish actions, to be sure, but it also was filled with a great deal of raw entertainment, the old-fashioned sort that Webster would define as a "lapse from strict propriety or sobriety." To thoroughly appreciate the oil crowd's wacky production, it is necessary to come to the theater with some awareness of what had gone on before, leading up to and including the dress rehearsal of 1969.

I've divided "The Great Dress Rehearsal" into the seven topics that are key to the action of the 1970s: The Company Cartel, OPEC, The Alaska Pipeline, The Mandatory Oil Import Control Program, The Surrender of the Federal Power Commission, Propaganda, and The Great Public Relations Gesture. The Rehearsal section extends over about fifty-five pages. When you consider how many topics I've crammed into that space, it's obvious that I have not tried to be definitive but instead have settled for the broad stroke and the crude gesture—which is only appropriate for this kind of entertainment.

As for the Follies themselves, they will come later on in chronological order, a chapter for each year, 1970 through "1980 Etc.," with every turn of the calendar offering our leaders in an abundance of farce, pratfalls, and juggling acts.

---

3. This was not true of the general public. Once again, the people showed they were light-years ahead of their leaders. Poll after poll throughout the 1970s indicated a majority of the people didn't believe a word the oil companies said about all those "crises" or of their desperate need for higher profits with which to save us from ourselves.

THE GREAT DRESS REHEARSAL THE '60S

> "We use 30 percent of all the energy . . . That isn't bad; that is good. That means that we are the richest, strongest people in the world . . . That is why we need so much energy, and may it always be that way."
>
> *President* RICHARD NIXON

THE COMPANY CARTEL

The history of oil in the 1970s is, in a way, simply another chapter in the posthumous life of John D. Rockefeller. The world of oil is much more densely populated than when he launched his Standard empire, but still the axis on which that world spins depends heavily on Rockefeller companies. At home and abroad. At home, four of the companies that were spun off by the alleged "breakup" of the Standard Oil Trust in 1911 still dominate the market in a total of forty-three states. Abroad, Rockefeller's dead hand has an equally impressive grasp of energy matters.

By the start of the seventies, there were more than forty large and medium-sized U.S. companies with significant foreign holdings. They had come on strong during the previous two decades. In the early 1950s, only the five largest of these companies—Standard of New Jersey (Exxon), Standard of California, Texaco, Mobil, and Gulf—had even 200 million barrels of proven foreign crude oil reserves. But twenty years later there were, in addition to the five, another thirteen U.S. companies that each owned more than 2 billion barrels of oil in foreign lands.

After a fashion, these "other" companies brought competition. They helped trigger the psychology of revenge that brought about the creation of OPEC. Their aggressiveness so upset the old order that it raised defensive restrictions against their oil imports. So the "other" companies that went exploring abroad were very important indeed.

Still, barrel for barrel, their influence has been inconsequential compared to the world's seven largest companies, the celebrated Seven Sisters, who are the five U.S.-based companies mentioned above plus British Petroleum and Royal Dutch-Shell. Three of the five U.S. sisters—the most influential of the three: Exxon, Standard of California, and Mobil—are children of Rockefeller's enterprise. As Exxon, the world's largest corporation, went, so went—or drifted—our energy fate.

At the end of the 1960s the Seven Sisters were producing about 40 percent of the oil in the United States and about 80 percent of the oil in the Middle East. Even today, though the tugging and scratching of the seventies has left it in a shocking state of dishabille, this great cartel retains the kind of naughty glory, "though changed in outward luster," that Milton saw in the Fallen Angel.

The story of how these five U.S. companies got their hands on some of the richest fields in the Middle East, particularly in Saudi Arabia and Iran, and participated in the cartel is well known but must be briefly told again here because the how and why of it relates directly to what happened in the seventies.

*

Standard Oil of California became, in 1933, the first wholly American-owned oil company with a permanent stake in the Middle East when it outbid other companies to win a large lease in the eastern part of the new kingdom of Saudi Arabia. This was the beginning (though the name would evolve later) of the Arabian American Oil Company—Aramco—which the world has come to know so well, and to suspect, and fear, and sometimes hate.

Socal had a problem. Even if there had been a demand for oil (the world was at the bottom of a depression), Socal did not have a marketing organization broad enough to handle any significant discovery. Texaco, however, did; so, in 1936, Socal brought in Texaco as a partner, for $3 million cash and $18 million on credit—one of the better bargains of the century.

In 1938, Aramco struck an enormous pool of oil, and the future looked rosy indeed. But not for long. In 1939, with the outbreak of World War II, Axis planes and submarines disrupted the shipment of oil across the Mediterranean, and the new and profitable partnership between the American oilmen and the Saudi Arabian Government fell on hard times. Except for its oil, Saudi Arabia had virtually nothing to sell. It had no industry and did little farming. Its nomadic population was often close to starvation. As if these burdens weren't enough, Saudi Arabia was led by Abdul-Aziz Ibn Saud, who was as wasteful as he was lusty (legend had it that he slept with a different woman every night of his adult life; he died in 1953, at the age of seventy-two). When the American oilmen arrived in Arabia, they found a kingdom that was—and would somehow manage to continue to be for most of Ibn Saud's life—disastrously in debt as a result of tribal wars, the king's whims, and government corruption.

Once the oil money began to flow his way, King Ibn Saud, spending it wildly, considered its increase to be absolutely as necessary and automatic as the sun's rising. So when World War II wiped out most of Aramco's market, and income, he was ominously unhappy. In January 1941, Ibn Saud informed Aramco that he wanted $6 million "as an advancement on oil royalties" and indicated that other requests for advancements would probably follow. Aramco did not want to pay, but neither did it want to risk losing its Arabian concession. So it followed the path so often followed by corporations: it unloaded its problem on the U.S. Government, and the U.S. Government, as it so often does, cheated a bit to help out. By that time, the United States had launched the lend-lease program to support England's war effort; the first "loan" would be for $400 million. President Roosevelt asked England to clip off $6 million and pass it along to King Ibn Saud. This was illegal, for lend-lease money was supposed to be spent only for the war effort.

Then Aramco got to worrying about this arrangement. If King Ibn Saud somehow got the impression that the money was coming from England, not the United States, might he not permit British oilmen to come in and start drilling? So Aramco persuaded Roosevelt to declare Saudi Arabia a national security ally, which he did, on February 18, 1943—"I hereby find that the defense of Saudi Arabia is vital to the defense of the United States"—a finding that was rather odd; the Allies were not at that moment receiving a single barrel of oil from Arabia. But the declaration did the trick: thereafter, the United States could give millions of dollars directly to King Ibn Saud and keep him happy so that Aramco could hang on to its lease.

During this period, some U.S. officials were genuinely worried about the way the war was draining U.S. oil reserves. Of the 7 billion barrels of oil burned by the United States and its allies between 1941 and 1945, nearly 6 billion of those barrels was pumped from U.S. fields.[1]

The largest international oil companies exploited this fear of rapid depletion, and added to it by supplying the government with shockingly low estimates of their U.S. oil reserves. In 1947, Standard Oil of New Jersey claimed its wells were drying up so fast in this country it might not be able to last beyond 1955; other companies sounded equally gloomy, and the gloom was echoed by their allies in government. Oil industrialists said the only hope of preserving America's way of life was to give private industry a free hand in the Middle East, unfettered by U.S. Government interference.

To give credence to the gloom, they announced a "shortage" and raised prices. Smelling something rotten, the Senate Small Business Committee investigated. In 1949 it concluded: "During the year and a half the committee has been investigating the oil industry, there never has been a real overall shortage of petroleum. Price increases on crude oil have been frequent and substantial, going from $1.25 per barrel at the

---

1. During this period, a strong effort was made by Commerce Secretary Harold Ickes and others to buy out part of Aramco to put the United States Government directly into the oil business, so that it could be sure of an adequate supply during military emergencies—in the same way that the British Government had bought into the Anglo-Iranian Oil Company during World War I. But the majors successfully fought off the plan. See the Appendix entry on *FEDERAL OIL AND GAS CORPORATION.*

end of 1945 to $2.65 per barrel in the spring of 1947, with several companies posting $3 per barrel as this report is written. At the time the consumers were feeling the greatest pinch in January and February 1947, there were 220 million barrels of crude oil in storage, mainly controlled by the larger units, which could have been distributed among independent refiners who were running under capacity."

In other words, the "shortage" was a fraud. But the crisis paid off just as the majors had hoped.

First of all, it helped win government approval of a cartel expansion scheme that would obviously be in violation of U.S. antitrust laws. The exploitation came about like this:

With the sea-lanes again open, and King Ibn Saud pressing harder than ever for money, Aramco pumped a hundred times more oil in 1946 than it had pumped in 1940. But it was confronted with the same problem Socal faced before bringing Texaco into Aramco: an insufficient market organization to handle so much oil. Aramco's solution was to expand by adding Standard Oil of New Jersey and Socony-Vacuum (Mobil) to the partnership. But such concentration of economic power was boggling. Even Socony-Vacuum's own lawyer, C. V. Holton, seemed perturbed. He pointed out to Socony president B. Brewster Jennings in October 1946 that the new Aramco arrangement—added to similar partnerships in Iraq and Iran, plus the majors' domination of the U.S. market —"would place practical control of crude reserves in the hands of seven companies." Five of those companies were based in the United States. Certainly the American public wouldn't stand for such concentration. "I cannot believe," Holton told Brewster, "that a comparatively few companies for any great length of time are going to be permitted to control world oil resources without some sort of regulation."

He was wrong. How could the American public prevent such concentration of ownership if their own government let them down? When, in March of 1947, the addition of Jersey Standard and Socony to the Aramco team was contracted, the Department of Justice made not the slightest complaint. (For more on the federal government's traditional failures of this sort, see the Appendix entry on *ANTITRUST*.) Although throughout 1946 State Department officials, knowing that the expanded merger was about to take place, had quibbled and furrowed their brows privately, they neither officially warned the oil companies that they might be lawbreakers nor pressed the Justice Department to take action. To the contrary, they made excuses for the new Aramco cartel. Using oil industry data, not independent data (this was standard procedure; the government has always depended on the industry's own figures), the chief of the State Department's Petroleum Division flatly stated that "sufficient oil cannot be found in the United States"; his implication was that any arrangement, however illegal, that could tap a bountiful foreign source, should be permitted. This fictional shortage was elaborated on two years later, when Interior Secretary Julius Krug, again using industry figures, said that the "end of the U.S. oil supply is almost in sight." National security, he implied, clearly called for the development of more overseas sources, and if it could be done only via illegal international oil cartels, that was just something the public would have to adjust to. After all, better an outlaw supply than none at all.

*

The use of "national security" to obtain a fabulous tax break occurred in 1949 when King Ibn Saud, still living it up and still heavily in debt, demanded that Aramco pump more and increase its royalty payments rate. Part of the king's unhappiness with Aramco came from the postwar appearance of adventurous, high-rolling "independents." In 1948 Aramco had paid the king only $28 million in royalties for a veritable river of oil, and yet in 1949 J. Paul Getty, one of the newcomers, had paid the king more than $10 million (the majors were horrified at the size of the down payment) *not* for any oil but just for the chance to *hunt* for oil in the Neutral Zone between Saudi Arabia and Kuwait. The king implied that Aramco was something of a piker.

Aramco saw a way to overcome these complaints without losing a dime. But again it would need the collusion of the United States Government. Aramco leaked its U.S. income tax records to Saudi officials, who saw that whereas—in return for their precious oil—they had received $38 million in royalties from Aramco in 1949, the U.S. Government—in return for no tangible quid at all—had received from Aramco $43 million in taxes. That didn't seem fair to the Saudis. Indeed, they felt they were being cheated, which, of course, is exactly the reaction Aramco had hoped they would have. So the Saudis asked Aramco—as an Aramco official later told a U.S. Senate committee—"Isn't there some way in which the income tax you pay to the United States can be diverted to us in whole or in part?" (Frederick A. Davies, testimony before the Senate's Joint Hearings on the Emergency Oil Lift Program and Related Oil Problems, 85th Cong., 1st sess., 1957) To which Aramco replied, in effect: Of course we will be happy to do exactly that, but you will have to persuade our government to let us do it.

Easing the way to that end, Aramco mentioned to Assistant Secretary of State George C. McGhee (who would later become a Mobil director) that the Saudis would be coming around to talk about the tax problem; and they told McGhee that they had to find a way to give the Saudis more money without costing themselves anything.

Fred Davies, then president of Socal's portion of Aramco, later recalled that McGhee was very "sympathetic"; and McGhee acknowledges that indeed he was sympathetic, because he felt that staying in good with Saudi Arabia was of paramount importance to our national security: "At that time, the Middle East was perhaps the most critical area in the world in the contest between ourselves and the Soviets . . . The Arab States were very hostile to us because of our involvement in the Israeli affair, as we know. Saudi Arabia, which is, I assume, the key country . . . was more tolerant than the others."

So, to win the hearts of the Saudi princes, the U.S. Treasury Department broke the law. Federal statutes require income taxes to be applied equally and uniformly to all businesses. But the Treasury's Internal Revenue Service ruled that, as of 1951, overseas royalty payments would be considered income taxes, even though this ruling would *exclusively* benefit oil companies. They were the only companies paying such royalties.

And since U.S. law forbids double taxation, these "taxes" (royalties) could be deducted, dollar for dollar, from taxes owed at home. So everybody—but the U.S. taxpayer—got what he wanted. The Saudis got their higher royalties at no extra cost to Aramco, which simply deducted the additional payments from their U.S. tax bills. Whereas Aramco had paid Saudi Arabia $60 million in royalties in 1950, it paid nearly twice that ($110 million) in "taxes" in 1951. In the same period, Aramco's payments to the U.S. Treasury dropped from $50 million to $6 million, a loss of $44 million that the U.S. taxpayer had to make up. Within four years, the taxpayer's subsidization of Saudi Arabia had risen to $154 million a year.

It was such a beautiful setup for the oil companies that, of course, it quickly spread. They and the State Department persuaded host countries everywhere to categorize company payments as income taxes, rather than royalties.

Thus encouraged, the U.S.-based giants began turning away from domestic exploration to developing their lush foreign fields. Why not? After all, an oil company that paid $1,000 in royalties to a landowner in Texas or Louisiana could deduct only $480 as business expenses. But an oil company that paid a foreign government (and most of the foreign oil lands were owned by governments, not by private persons) $1,000 in "taxes" could deduct the full $1,000. The foreign tax credit was sweet indeed.

***

Perhaps the cleverest use of a national-security scare came in the wake of an upheaval in Iran in 1951–53.

In 1951, that fiery, mystical, emotionally unstable and foolishly courageous politician Mohammed Mossadegh canceled the long-standing contracts with Anglo-Iranian Oil Company (British Petroleum), nationalized his country's oil industry, and ousted the Shah.

The Western press made Mossadegh seem a comical character. This gaunt old man, they said, would hold press conferences in his pajamas and sometimes spend half of the time weeping and babbling incoherently. They reported that when his nose leaked, which was often, he did not bother to wipe it. They made him out to be always naïve and sometimes simpleminded.

But in fact he was only a single-minded patriot whose country was not equipped to follow him, and who was attempting more than could be accomplished at that time. If he had made his bid twenty years later, he would have won.

But he didn't win, and there were several reasons:

In seizing the Anglo-Iranian Oil Company, Mossadegh also seized its Abadan refinery and banished the British technical staff. Unfortunately, there were no trained Iranian technicians to take their places, so the refinery had to close; thousands of Iranians lost jobs that were dependent on the refinery, and the nation's entire economy began to wither. Mossadegh might have been able to recruit enough technicians from friendly countries to get the refinery back in operation and keep it perking, but that wasn't the only problem. Western markets, controlled by the major international oil companies, boycotted Iranian oil. As the Iranian economy slumped, so did some of Mossadegh's popular support.

Those were the technical reasons for his failure. In addition, he was crushed by fright propaganda. The five major oil companies already entrenched in the Middle East—Jersey Standard, Standard of California, Texaco, Mobil, and Gulf—persuaded the Eisenhower administration (which wasn't difficult) that Mossadegh was going to let the U.S.S.R. get hold of Iran's oil—a transparent falsehood to anybody who knew Mossadegh's zealous anticommunism.

So the U.S. Government sent a CIA team into Iran to stir up a rebellion and overthrow Mossadegh. Leading the show, with a budget of $1 million (though he later claimed he spent only a tenth of that), was Kermit Roosevelt, a 37-year-old grandson of President Theodore Roosevelt, product of Harvard, veteran of OSS action in World War II. The coup was successful. Mossadegh went to jail; the Shah climbed back onto the Peacock Throne; and the West had its hands on Iran's oil once more.

With one big difference. Britain lost its monopoly hold on Iran. In its place came a consortium, divvying up the spoils 40 percent to the old Anglo-Iranian Oil Company, 40 percent to a group of American oil companies, 14 percent to Royal Dutch-Shell, and 6 percent to the Compagnie Française des Pétroles, which is the French state oil company.

And who were the American companies now involved in Iranian oil? The same old crowd: Gulf, Jersey Standard, Standard of California, Texaco, and Socony-Mobil. And the ironic part was, they were allowed to move into Iran despite the fact that, only two years earlier, the U.S. Justice Department had accused them of running an international cartel in violation of antitrust laws. Embarrassed by the obvious conflict of signals, President Truman ordered the Justice Department to back away from that suit. However, since these five companies represented a concentration of power both in the United States and in the Middle East that was outrageously in violation of antitrust, the government decided that it would shave off a tiny fragment (5 percent) of the Iranian spoils and let sixteen small companies divvy up that fragment. That was supposed to show that the U.S. Government believed in competition.

"Big oil . . . can even keep the sun from rising as an energy competitor."

S. DAVID FREEMAN

THE MATURING OF OPEC

Prior to the 1970s, foreign oil production had slight effect on the U.S. market, and this was particularly true of production in the Middle East. Practically speaking, we were self-sufficient, or could have been with a little extra effort; such help as we needed from foreign imports was gotten mostly from Venezuela and Canada. Only about 3 percent of our imports came from the Middle Eastern and North African countries, which left these countries vulnerable to abuse by the international oil cartel, made up of major companies largely based in the United States, the world's most gluttonous user of oil.[1] If we didn't really need their product, how could those countries force the majors to pay them more for their oil by threatening to withhold it from us? How, indeed, could they force an increase in prices by threatening to withhold oil from Europe, when, as proved during the 1957 and 1967 crises—during which the Middle Eastern output was sharply reduced to Europe—we made up the difference by increasing Texas' production and shipping it abroad?

The Middle Eastern producing nations also were easy to abuse because at that time they were woefully lacking in skilled personnel of their own to handle production. They also had little sophisticated knowledge about international marketing. For guidance in production and marketing, they were totally dependent on the majors.

So, naturally, the majors gypped them right and left. Whenever pained

---

1. "Major" oil company is a loose term. There are, by most counts, seventeen to nineteen "majors"; the list fluctuates, largely because of mergers. The basic characteristic of a major company is that it is "vertically integrated," meaning that it is equipped to handle everything from well to pump: production, shipping, refining, marketing. That's the main difference between a "major" company and an "independent" company, which, again, is a somewhat misleading term. Anyway, some of the larger independents are anything but minor.

observers suggested to the majors that the day might come when their host countries would balk and withhold their oil, the majors replied, "What are they going to do with it? Drink it?" That was a joke so long established as to be hackneyed in the boardrooms of Big Oil: "What are they going to do with it? Drink it?"

Of course, the world was changing in such a way that inevitably the host countries would have eventually gotten together and stuffed that joke back in the majors' collective throat. As it happened, however, this response was not the result of evolutionary change but of a sharp and bitter confrontation.

It was triggered by the cumulative ill will between the majors and Signor Enrico Mattei, the fiercely independent Italian who helped break the back of Big Oil's contractual arrangements in the Middle East. Before his death, in 1962—under mysterious circumstances—Mattei had taught the cartel that it should not underestimate the potential vengeance of the world's peasantry.

Mattei himself was of that peasantry. Of low Italian stock and relatively uneducated (at least he had no university degree), Mattei was shrewd, boundlessly inventive, and utterly without fear. He was head of Italy's state oil company, Ente Nazionale Idrocarburi (ENI), and its subsidiary, Azienda Generale Italiana Petroli (AGIP). Indeed, almost single-handedly Mattei built ENI into what *Fortune* grudgingly described as "a unique combination of private initiative and public enterprise—a structure without equal anywhere in the world. He wielded political power, wrote his own rules, and took bold risks in an almost visionary pursuit of an oil and petrochemical empire." While he lived, that empire was so powerful that Italians nicknamed it "the state within the state." To most Italians, he was a hero for taking on the multinational oil cartel and whipping it; but to the cartel he was an intolerable nuisance.

Having little in the way of fuel deposits of its own, Italy's postwar efforts at industrialization were successful only to the extent that it could obtain oil from others. This meant going to the Middle East, hat in hand, and dickering with the lords of that area, the multinational companies that had tied up the producing nations with long-term contracts.

Then, in 1951, Italy had its first big chance to deal with a Middle Eastern nation on a first-party basis. In that year, the impulsive Mossadegh nationalized the Anglo-Iranian Oil Company before he realized that there were not enough Iranians trained to operate the production end or, more important, trained to sell the oil they brought up (see the Appendix entry on the *SHAH OF IRAN*). So he sought desperately for outside help. Among those he turned to, in vain, was Mattei.

Surely Mattei must have been tempted to take on the job of marketing the Iranian oil. He was a marketing genius and probably would have been able to salvage Mossadegh's rapidly failing economy. If Mattei had done no more than use Iranian oil for Italy's needs, that alone might have saved Mossadegh.

But after meeting with Lord Strathalmond, chairman of Anglo-Iranian, Mattei announced that he was keeping his hands off the Iranian situation. Anglo-Iranian had warned that it would sue anyone who bought the nationalized oil, and Mattei, after talking with Strathalmond, said he was backing away in the face of that threat. (ENI had been buying most of its oil from Anglo-Iranian.) His excuse for not dealing with Mossadegh was hard to believe, for Mattei had never previously—nor did he ever again—display the slightest reluctance to trespass on what Big Oil considered to be its legal domain. More likely, Mattei decided to refuse Mossadegh's offer for the reason most commonly rumored at the time: that Strathalmond had promised to "take care of" Mattei's ENI in some very significant way.

If that was the promise, Mattei learned that the multinationals could not be trusted.

After Mossadegh was overthrown, and the Shah restored to power, the oil giants set about splitting up Iran's oil franchise once again. New companies were to be brought into the deal. Mattei clearly expected that ENI would be one of the new members of the consortium. But the Italian firm was rejected; in fact, it was never even seriously considered for membership. Mattei not only felt cheated, he felt insulted, and he set out on a program that was to realize more revenge than he could have dreamed possible.

He spent long hours with the Shah of Iran and with Iran's Petroleum Minister, Dr. Ali Amini, assisting them in working out the details of the Petroleum Act, which the Iranian parliament passed in 1957, dealing a hefty blow to the multinationals. Previously, the terms of the exploration and production contracts had given the foreign companies actual ownership of the oil as soon as they brought it out of the ground and paid Iran its royalties. The companies controlled the rate of extraction and the sale of the oil. That was the way it used to be—before Mossadegh, before the Shah learned arrogance, and before Mattei became vengeful. But now, with the Petroleum Act, Iran declared itself the owner of the oil throughout the production and sales process. It declared that the companies would from now on serve as its agents only. No longer would Iran be forced to stand to one side, humbly, and wait for the companies to produce and peddle the oil. Now it would have a true partnership role all the way.

Proving that he was willing to back his advice with action, Mattei stepped forward (in the corporate body of AGIP) and signed the very first contract with Iran under the new terms of the Petroleum Act. It was a contract such as the Mideast had never seen before. AGIP and the state-owned National Iranian Oil Company (NIOC) formed a separate company, the Iranian-Italian Oil Company (SIRIP); its chairman was Iranian (the first time foreigners submitted to native leadership), and its board was equally divided between Iranians and Italians. Moreover, the Italians took all the financial risk. Only after oil was discovered and ready for production would Iran have to share costs. And then Iran (NIOC) and the Italians (AGIP) would split the profits, the true profits, fifty-fifty. However, because SIRIP paid a 50 percent tax, half of which would of course come from AGIP's 50 percent share of the profits, Iran would actually wind up with 75 percent of the income: NIOC's 50 percent plus half of AGIP's 50 percent.

The generosity of the agreement was unique. And it spurred many producing nations—United Arab Republic, Sudan, Morocco, Tunisia, Somalia, Ghana, etc.—to sign up with Mattei.

ENI made such generous offers to India in 1961 for exploration rights that Stanvac, a subsidiary of Standard Oil of New Jersey, withdrew from the bidding.

It might seem odd that this competition from a middle-weight state oil company would upset the cartel very much, but stability in the oil world is always so precarious that it doesn't take much of a blow to result in significant reverberations. And Mattei's action was more than a slight blow. For one thing, it gave others the same idea; and here came Japan, not offering as good a deal as ENI but a much better deal than the cartel ever offered (Japan offered 57 percent of all net profits instead of the usual 50 percent), and here came even the first of a number of U.S. independent companies, Pan-American, a subsidiary of Standard of Indiana, adopting the Mattei technique.

That was the first crack in what had appeared an adamant shield against change. But ENI's actions had an even more shattering effect, for the old concession contracts wangled by the cartel contained a proviso that if the producing countries were ever offered better terms for their oil (back in the beginning of the cartel's reign in the Middle East, the companies were too cocky to think there could ever be serious competition they couldn't buy off), then the old contracts would be subject to renegotiation and revision. Thus Mattei had canceled out the past, and the Arabs quickly seized on the opportunity to start demanding that the oil giants live up to their promised renegotiations.

Mattei was enjoying his role and reputation as disturber of the peace, which he had earned by great effort. He was not without a sense of drama. *Time* magazine noted, July 21, 1961, "When rumors spread throughout the oil world from Baghdad to Manhattan last week that Iraq, out of pique at Britain, was planning to nationalize its oil industry [controlled by the cartel under the company name of Iraq Petroleum], worried oilmen instinctively turned their eyes to Rome, as Iraq's likeliest collaborator." Mattei did not disappoint them. The majors at first did not

take the threat very seriously, because they presumed that Iraq, the most
nettlesome and rebellious of the producing countries, would not be able
to find the technicians to operate the company. But Mattei made it a real
threat by promising to send five hundred engineers and technicians to
help Iraq, explaining that "ENI does not operate according to the obso-
lete pattern of the 19th century colonialist capitalism, but looks towards
financial coparticipation and joint technical and commercial management
on terms of perfect equality."

As if that weren't bad enough, Mattei next offended the international
oil giants by negotiating a deal with the Soviet Union whereby in return
for oil ENI would pay money, steel pipes, synthetic rubber, and other
goods. For Italy, the exchange was critically needed, but it was quite un-
forgivable to some U.S. politicians, who denounced the purchase of Soviet oil by NATO countries, such as Italy, as a sure way of undercutting
the security of the West. An investigation of such trade was launched, in
July 1962, in the Senate Subcommittee on Internal Security.

Soviet oil output was becoming troublesome. The situation was described in this way in 1960 by an analyst for the U.S. Bureau of Mines'
Division of Foreign Activities: "The relative volume of Soviet oil now
moving in international trade is small (less than 5 percent of all oil in international trade), but the impact of U.S.S.R.'s petroleum on world oil
markets has been great. Growing Russian oil exports have contributed to
the world oversupply of petroleum, have forced prices down, and have
taken sales from Western oil producers."

The U.S.S.R.'s technique for cracking the cartel's monopoly on the
world's markets was relatively simple: it sold for less. The lower prices
were obviously welcome to countries struggling to get started or to maintain their industrial equilibrium. As Mattei explained in July 1961, "In
the past eleven months, we have spent $100 million for Soviet petroleum.
If we had bought the same quantity of oil from Western companies, it
would have cost $140 million."

Although one might expect that price competition would have been
welcomed in Washington as a sign that the Russians were adopting a
basic principle of capitalism, such was not the reception. Rather, the
Soviet move was seen as sneaky. A Library of Congress study done for
the Senate Internal Security Subcommittee in 1961 (then chaired by
Senator James Eastland of Mississippi) and clearly reflecting the right-
wing ideology of the SISS, spoke of the U.S.S.R.'s "ulterior motives" for
the competition. It also heaped suspicions on those, especially Italy, who
succumbed to the lure of the lower Soviet prices. A portion of the study
outlines the plot:

"These moves confirm the intention of the U.S.S.R. to capture a substantial share both of oil markets in Western Europe and of such new
ones as develop in Africa and elsewhere . . . Already it has penetrated

into the European area originally monopolized by American, British, Dutch, and French oil investment capital . . .

"Generally speaking, the prices for Soviet oil and oil products in the export trade have been adjusted to suit both Soviet political aims and specific market situations and—depending on circumstances—have been pegged well below prices previously accepted as standard in the international market . . .

"In 1957, as reported, the average price of crude oil sold on the international market by the U.S.S.R. was $2.06 a barrel as compared with $2.79 a barrel for Middle East oil and $2.92 for Venezuelan oil. In 1958 the Soviet Union is said to have sold oil in Argentina at an average price of $1.60 a barrel . . . By the Soviet arrangement with Italy in November 1960, crude oil was to be supplied at Black Sea ports at $1 a barrel, which indicated a cost at Italian refineries at about 62.5 percent of the delivered cost of oil from Persian Gulf ports . . ."

The agreement by which Italy consumed about one ninth of the Soviet oil exports at that time and which satisfied about 20 percent of Italy's oil requirements, was especially disturbing to the cartel, the Library of Congress study noted, because:

"In the first place, the terms on which Soviet oil was to be supplied could not possibly be met competitively by the major oil companies. Those operating in Kuwait, for instance, where production is the cheapest in the world, under contract to share oil profits with the Sheikh on a 50-50 percent basis, would have to pay the Kuwait government 69.5 cents, based on prices then posted at Persian Gulf ports, on each barrel of oil shipped. Clearly, they could not supply Kuwaiti oil to Italy at a price approaching that in the Soviet contract [$1 barrel at Black Sea ports]. In the second place, Soviet oil once processed in Italian refineries is deemed to be Italian oil and this—presumably—has a European Common Market status. Additional offerings of Soviet oil to Italy on the same terms for resale abroad suggest a Soviet intent further to invade the markets of other Common Market countries. Thus, with the European oil market already saturated, Middle East oil is being crowded out about to the extent of the acceptance of Soviet oil by West European states.

"In the third place, the dependence of any member of the NATO alliance on Russian oil in a substantial measure inevitably has a significant bearing on its position relative to the security of the Western World. With Italy becoming increasingly bound up in Soviet oil schemes, the question is bound to arise as to its probable behavior in the event of a serious crisis in the cold war."

It was a harsh indictment. Not only was Italy—and of course all other nations that bought the cheaper Soviet oil—accused of depriving the Western cartel of some of the profits it had come to accept as its due, but

Italy (or, rather, Mattei and his ENI) was an antiprofit virus that might spread throughout the entire Common Market; and worst of all, in any conflict between the West and the U.S.S.R., Italy could not be counted on to take the capitalist side. To some U.S. politicians and bureaucratic potentates, then, Italy was seen—or was imagined—to be a NATO link weakened by the saturation of Soviet oil. Could the West allow one man to cause so much trouble?

All of this rested rather lightly on Mattei. He was used to it. His office library contained twenty-three volumes filled with clippings and letters denouncing him sometimes as a Fascist bastard and at other times as a Red bastard; among the letters was one from the American ambassador to Italy, accusing him of developing a "stab in the back" policy. There were also, sprinkled through the Mattei archives, several threats on his life. But he did not take these seriously either. On October 27, 1962, just over a year after the pact with the Soviet Union had been negotiated and after the offer to assist Iraq had been made, and less than four months after the U.S. Senate's patriots had begun to zero in on his "betrayal" of the cartel, Mattei's private plane crashed near Milan and he was killed. Some Italians said there were unexplained things about the crash that looked suspicious, but no mischief was ever proved.

But Mattei had the last laugh, in the afterworld. He had indirectly brought about the creation of a force—the Organization of Petroleum Exporting Countries—that would ultimately strip the major oil companies not of their profits from, but of their control of, the Middle East. He had brought about a movement that would ultimately put them in the same unpleasant role that he had occupied, because of their arrogance, for so many years: the role of supplicant.

His contribution to the organization of OPEC came about like this: From 1959 through 1961, the Soviet oil poured into Italy in such great volumes that Italy could not begin to use it all, so Mattei, after processing it in ENI refineries, dumped it on the European market at prices far below those being charged by the major oil companies. The biggest of the lot, Standard Oil of New Jersey, was especially hurt.

Leonard Mosley, in *Power Play: Oil in the Middle East*, makes the telling point: "In the days of John D. Rockefeller a savage price war would immediately have ensued in which—backed by unlimited supplies of oil —Standard Oil would have flooded the market with cheap gasoline until the enemy ran out of gas and money. But Mattei had access to all the crude oil he needed, and under the circumstances the Soviet Union was not worried about how cheaply it was sold. On the other hand, as a member of Aramco and other combines in the Middle East, Jersey Standard had to maintain the posted-price system and could not cut the price of its crude without reducing its own profits and the revenues of the Middle East oil-producing countries. To some degree this was a dilemma facing all the major companies, but for Standard of New Jersey it was by far the most economically damaging."

Finally Jersey Standard broke under the pressure. Having watched its European markets dwindle critically, it cut the posted price of its Middle Eastern crude—thereby protecting its own profit margin but seriously reducing the incomes of the producing nations. The first cut was 10 percent, in 1959; the second, 7½ percent, in 1960. This action was taken despite pleas of the other major companies, which feared, quite properly, that the producing nations would retaliate. They did. Saudi Arabia, Iran, Venezuela, Iraq, and Kuwait set up OPEC in September 1960. By the end of the decade, a dozen other producing nations had joined and 75 percent of all oil reserves lay within the jurisdiction of OPEC. For the old world of colonial oil production, it was the beginning of the end.

* * *

The development of OPEC as a commanding organization was, however, slow and awkward. During the 1960s, the Seven Sisters continued to lose the exclusive concessions they had extracted from weak rulers between the two world wars. But even after the establishment of OPEC, the Sisters still controlled the pricing of oil, and OPEC was happy that they did, for in those days—with a world glut being the big problem—the main objective was not to raise prices but to keep them from declining, and it would take the ruthless genius of the international companies to hold the line on that. As for the oil companies' opinion of OPEC, they held it in contempt, but grudgingly appreciated it, because organization —even sloppy organization—is the key to price fixing.

But as the 1960s and the glut ended, members of OPEC grew tired of their submissive role. Now they were ready to begin thinking more aggressively of taking the power of pricing away from the majors and controlling it themselves. It could be done only in a sellers' market, and that is exactly what began to develop toward the end of the 1960s.

The first major step toward control over pricing was taken, appropriately, in Libya. "Appropriately" is the right word because Libya was the one important producing country in that part of the world where the majors were not dominant. Libya, where oil was first discovered in 1959, had taken a unique approach to selling its oil. In such places as Saudi Arabia and Iran, the traditional practice had been to give exclusive concessions to one company or to a group of companies, such as Aramco, or the Iranian consortium. Libya, instead, had thrown open its land—block by block—to all bidders. Under this system, independent oil companies began cutting a wide swath; indeed, by 1969 Occidental Petroleum Corporation was the chief concessionaire in Libya and, generally speaking, as the Report of the Senate Subcommittee on Multinational Corporations would put it years later, "Libyan oil was in the hands of independents who had neither the incentive to moderate their output nor the capability of offsetting it with reductions elsewhere."

That is, the independents hadn't the capability of playing off other countries against Libya, or Libya against other countries—as Exxon could do, or Mobil, or Texaco. The independents in Libya were so isolated and vulnerable that they had to show a modest willingness to cooperate with the host country that the big Western oil companies had never been forced to show.

All it took to exploit this situation—and demonstrate to other OPEC nations how to twist the noses of Westerners—was a tough ruler. And just such a ruler surfaced in 1969 in Muammar el-Qaddafi. A 27-year-old army colonel, and like Mossadegh, a religious zealot, Qaddafi in September led a coup that overthrew Libya's old, corrupt King Idris.

Ten years before Qaddafi came to power, Libya was one of the poorest nations in the world ($40 per capita income). Ten years after he came to power, it would be one of the richest ($4,700). The source of this amazing turn of fortune was, of course, oil. Although he was a genius at collecting riches, Qaddafi could not take credit for having opened the door to them. By the time he seized power, Libya was already the world's fourth-largest exporter of petroleum (in 1969 it became the first oil exporter to reap a billion dollars in revenue from this commodity), supplying 3.3 million barrels daily to twenty-two nations. For Europe the appeal of Libyan oil was that it was so handy, and by 1969 Europe was dependent on Libya for 31 percent of its crude; for the United States, Libyan oil appealed because it was so sulfur-free and sweet for the environment.

But, for the international cartel, Libyan oil would soon have all the appeal of poison. Its brilliant exploitation by Qaddafi would prove the turning point, after which the Western powers would swiftly lose their control over OPEC's oil supplies and prices. Qaddafi would be instrumental in a shift of power and attitude that would help change the character of the world.

> "I don't call myself a conservationist to the extent that some enthusiasts do. I wouldn't expect to find the Getty Oil Co. lobbying against the Alaska pipeline."
>
> J. PAUL GETTY

THE ALASKA PIPELINE

Throughout the Nixon administration, oilmen had ready access to top White House assistants, and the biggest oilmen had ready access to Nixon himself. None, it was said, was looked upon with more favor than

Robert Orville Anderson, creator and chairman of Atlantic Richfield (ARCO).

This was indeed fortunate for ARCO; at that moment, it could certainly use a friendly administration in Washington. For one thing, it needed a closed-eyes policy in regard to antitrust activities—the same kind of favoritism that was shown in 1966, when ARCO was created without a particle of opposition from Lyndon Johnson's Justice Department, even though a number of antitrust principles seemed to have been violated in the merger of Atlantic Refining Co., one of the largest distributors in the East, with Richfield Oil Co., one of the largest distributors on the West Coast. The new company, with assets totaling more than $1.4 billion, made it the largest merger up to that time, and to say that it reduced competition was putting it mildly—but the Johnson administration's antitrust lawyers did nothing but huff a bit. Now ARCO was ready to push its luck farther, and once more it needed government cooperation. On March 4, 1969, ARCO announced its merger with Sinclair Oil Company. Again it was the biggest merger in history. ARCO easily broke its previous record, for now it had assets of $2.4 billion and Sinclair was reputedly worth $1.8 billion—a nice, plump, $4.2-billion combination—and the Justice Department did nothing except require that ARCO sell 1,800 of Sinclair's 10,500 service stations (mostly, the 1,800 were in the Midwest and the East) to British Petroleum (BP).[1]

ARCO and its friends also needed swift government action to help them get into production in Alaska. The riches awaiting the companies made impatience very understandable. On July 18, 1968, just two years after the Interior Department opened the area, ARCO and Exxon had announced the discovery of oil near Prudhoe Bay, on Alaska's North Slope, the northern slope of the Brooks mountain range, at the top of the state. In early 1969, just three miles south of the ARCO-Exxon discovery, British Petroleum also hit oil.

(Just how much ingenuity was in these discoveries is very debatable. The U.S. Navy and the U.S. Geological Survey, at a cost of $50 million,

---

1. It would be incorrect to conclude that this "forced" sale was an imposition; in fact it was quite the contrary. The purchaser of the stations, BP, was by that time ARCO's partner in the great Alaskan adventure at Prudhoe Bay. For British Petroleum, the acquisition of the service stations was the fulfillment of a vintage dream. For twelve years it had tried without success to crack the U.S. market. It had been handicapped, for one thing, by British restrictions on taking much money out of the country. But with its oil discovery at Prudhoe Bay, BP was ready to move. By cleverly bartering oil from future production in Alaska, British Petroleum was not only able to swing the purchase of Sinclair service stations from ARCO, but it was also able to buy a controlling share of Standard Oil of Ohio, thus giving British Petroleum nearly 4 percent of the U.S. market and tightening the ties of the international oil giants. The brilliance of BP's move should be savored: It took oil lying under federal lands and belonging to the U.S. citizenry and then hocked it to buy a significant share of the U.S. market. A very neat trick.

had explored all of the North Slope and much of Prudhoe Bay between 1944 and 1953, and, when Eisenhower was sworn in as President, were about to sink the deep wells that would have discovered the big field— the rig was in place, the workmen were waiting for orders to begin. At the insistence of private oil companies, Eisenhower stopped further explorations by the Navy and USGS, but, according to Lieutenant Commander Kirby Brant, a former deputy director of the Office of Naval Petroleum and Oil Shale Reserves, the basic data from those early navy tests were passed on to the oil companies, and through them they were able to pinpoint the most promising portions of the North Slope.)

These were no ordinary discoveries. They were gigantic. First estimates ranged from 5 to 10 billion barrels. Later estimates would balloon, perhaps unrealistically, to 40 billion barrels. At ten billion, it would be equal to more than 25 percent of the total proven U.S. reserves.

The North Slope oil discovery would inspire more controversy than anything that had happened in the industry since the oil import system was imposed, in 1959. ARCO's Anderson had no way, of course, to see the magnitude of the troubles ahead, but he did know that even under the smoothest of circumstances the oil explorers would be confronted with all sorts of red tape and would need a Secretary of the Interior who was, to say the least, sympathetic.

Anderson had his eye on just the right man for the job: Walter J. Hickel, a real estate millionaire who had recently left the governorship of Alaska. In that job, Hickel had shown his willingness to be very cooperative. Following the discovery of oil at Prudhoe Bay, he had rushed the state into building a road nearly four hundred miles long, from Fairbanks to the Arctic Ocean, so that trucks could carry equipment to the boom area. (Up to then, all equipment was flown in.) The highway— named the Walter J. Hickel Highway in honor of the governor—was a budgetary, engineering, and ecological disaster. It was, in the words of a University of Alaska professor, "the biggest environmental screwup in the history of mankind in the arctic." Costs, which originally were estimated at $125,000, eventually climbed to $1 million. With the spring thaw in 1969, the road became an impassable, water-filled ditch. Writer George Marshall accurately described the Hickel Highway as "the first violent change, the first major intrusion of the modern industrial world" into the last great wilderness in North America, all the more shocking because "the great Range [Brooks range] had been split and its unity with past ages destroyed—destroyed without a public decision, destroyed without the knowledge of most Americans."

Anderson persuaded Nixon not to appoint Montana Governor Tim Babcock to head the Department of the Interior—though Nixon was then leaning toward Babcock—and instead appoint Hickel. Hickel could be expected to see things from industry's position. After all, he owned

32,316 shares of Alaska Interstate, a company whose subsidiary was financially tied to Union and Marathon oil companies.

But it was a flawed scheme. Environmentalists' opposition to Hickel's appointment was so bitter and so intense that at his confirmation hearings, he was forced to make promises of good conduct that would, as it turned out, greatly reduce his usefulness to the oil companies. For one thing, he promised not to make any changes in Alaska's landscape to provide the oil companies with highways, airports, and pipelines without first getting permission from the Senate Interior Committee. He promised to do everything right out in the open; and although there were no solid signs that he went back on his word, there were rumors—enough to make environmentalists nervous—that he and other Interior officials were allowing the oil companies to proceed secretly with preliminary work on the right-of-way without benefit of permit or law.

**

Gloriously rich though the Prudhoe Bay discovery was, it came heavily wrapped in frustration. It would not be easy to get to market. The discovery consortium—ARCO, Exxon, and British Petroleum, operating now as the Trans-Alaska Pipeline System (TAPS)—announced, in February 1969, plans to build an 800-mile pipeline from the North Slope to the other side of Alaska, terminating at Valdez, a tanker port. It would be the largest private construction project in the world. The costliest. The most daring. And potentially the most destructive of nature, for it would cross some of the most unspoiled and the tenderest terrain on the North American continent. Because there is relatively little sunlight in the Arctic, plants grow very slowly and very sparsely there. The earth and its vegetation are slow to recover from what in warmer parts of the globe would be considered minor damage. A few rainstorms, a bit of wind, a lush outburst of one spring's worth of grass and weeds would take care of wheel tracks left in, say, the wilderness of California. But, in Alaska, wheel tracks left in the tundra a quarter century ago by earlier oil explorers are still ruts, as ugly as the day they were made. Ecologically, the pipeline would be a vastly dangerous undertaking. TAPS seemed unconcerned. On June 6 it filed an application with Interior to begin building. It asked, and expected, prompt action.

Not to worry, Under Secretary of the Interior Russell E. Train told environmentalists; the Interior Department would, he said, do everything necessary to make sure that the pipeline was ecologically safe and that the vulnerable arctic would be amply protected. And having given that breezy assurance, he announced in August that hearings on the pipeline would be held both in Alaska and Washington to expedite its beginning.

*

For the moment, however, officials, both state and federal, seemed much less interested in protecting the tundra than in collecting money. Before environmental hearings would be held, Interior would accept bids on some new oil leases. The big day was September 10, 1969. By 7 A.M., the oilmen and their bankers were lining up outside the squat concrete building in downtown Anchorage waiting for the doors to open and the bid-reading to begin, at 10:30. Many were sleepy and disheveled. They had been up most of the night calculating the best offer. Secrecy was the key. Some companies had reserved all the hotel rooms adjacent to their official suites so that rival companies couldn't use electronic devices to overhear their bid planning. Some had wrapped their bid sheets in aluminum foil, on the off chance that some rival had an X-ray camera. One group had hired a special train for the previous five days and had shuttled slowly back and forth between Calgary and Edmonton while they threshed out their final plans.

If the oilmen were groggy, Alaskan officials had been that way for days, yearning to get their hands on all those oil royalties, not to mention the estimated $1 billion in construction money that would be floating around (that estimate turned out to be about $8 billion too low). On television the previous night, Governor Keith Miller proclaimed, "We are on the eve of the greatest day our state has ever known. Tomorrow we will reach out to claim our birthright. We will rendezvous with our dreams." By the time the nine hours of bidding was through, 179 four-square-mile leases had been peddled for a total of slightly more than $900 million—by far the most ever collected in one bidding, and about six times the annual operating budget for the state of Alaska.

Out of this auction came five new members of TAPS: Mobil, Phillips, Union, Amerada Hess, and Home Oil of Canada. Later, Home sold out to the others. (Eventually TAPS would incorporate the Alyeska Pipeline Service Company to design, build, and operate the pipeline system. Actually it would have preferred to do business strictly under its old alliance, for it had no formal corporate structure at all and therefore was almost impossible for the government to regulate. Hickel later complained of TAPS that "by the time all the principals could be telephoned in Texas, New York, California, and London, it could take weeks just to get an agreement on what color to paint the toilets in the construction camps." So, to avoid embarrassing Hickel by showing how little regulation Interior was giving, the oil companies entered into the formal Alyeska corporate arrangement.)

*

Swept forward by the euphoria of the big auction and obviously under intense pressure from the oil companies, Interior officials resisted appeals for environmental caution. On October 16, Under Secretary Train told the Senate Interior Committee that TAPS was "reluctant" to wait until the Interior Department decided that the entire pipeline scheme was technologically and environmentally safe. He said he was appearing before the committee to repeat Secretary Hickel's plea for a right-of-way permit on a piece-by-piece construction schedule. He admitted that neither TAPS officials nor Interior's officials had all the answers to the pipeline's environmental problems, but urged that Congress allow the tractors and bulldozers to start rolling at once, rather than wait until a permit could be safely issued for the whole pipeline.

House and Senate members, less cautious than environmentalists, were willing to trust Hickel's promises to keep the oil companies in line, and they voted to lift the land freeze. Ordinarily, that would have been all that was needed to get the pipeline under way. But a new complication was at hand. A few weeks later, just into 1970, President Nixon would sign the National Environmental Policy Act. The NEPA required that no federal project be funded and no use of federal land be made (most of the pipeline would be over land owned by the U.S. taxpayer) until the people involved in the project prepared a full statement of the project's impact on the environment. This impact statement was supposed to weigh the social advantages against the environmental disadvantages. It was supposed to show that no alternative plan could be substituted with better results. It demanded answers that would take a great deal of time to prepare. From the NEPA, environmentalists would draw strength to wage a David-Goliath court battle against the Alaskan pipeline that would last for years.

They would take their fighting inspiration from something that had occurred three thousand miles from Prudhoe Bay (for a full account, see the SANTA BARBARA entry in the Appendix).

The blowout of the well in the Santa Barbara Channel on January 28, 1969, and the leakage that continued for many months—at its worst, putting oil on beaches for more than thirty miles and creating an ocean slick of eight hundred square miles—did not produce the most damaging pollution of beaches that has occurred, and the amount of oil the blowout dumped into the ocean was trivial compared to, say, what happened at the Ixtoc I oil well, in the Bay of Campeche, ten years later. But because the Santa Barbara blowout was the first offshore oil well disaster of the modern Environmental Age, and because the disaster struck at one of America's most beautiful small cities, the name "Santa Barbara" took on a special meaning. It came to symbolize greed's triumph over aesthetics, corporate callousness toward the environment, and the government's eagerness to give economic exploitation a higher value than community happiness. "That mess," one oil foe in the Senate told Newsweek, "did us more good than a million words in Congressional testimony." The Santa Barbara Channel leases had been approved by Interior Secretary

Stewart L. Udall. Out of office, he would say, "If there was one decision I made in all my tenure as Secretary of the Interior that I regret and, if I had the chance, that I would retract, it would be the offshore oil leases in the Pacific." More than a year after the blowout occurred, Frank Ikard, president of the American Petroleum Institute, was still complaining about the setback it had dealt to oil's image. "Some of you may know that St. Barbara is the patron saint of arsenals and powder magazines," he told one audience. "It is an unhappy coincidence that the channel named after her should have been the site of an oil spill with explosive consequences for the petroleum industry. The oil has been completely cleaned off the beaches there, but it is still smearing the industry's reputation."

Environmentalists went on an organizational binge. Locally, in Santa Barbara, the communal voice of outrage was named GOO—Get Oil Out— a group that hadn't existed before the spill. Nationally there were outfits whose potency had nothing to do with their age. The Environmental Defense Fund had been in existence only since 1967 but soon was winning big antipollution battles in court. The Center for Law and Social Policy came into existence in 1969 specifically to fight some of the proposed oil schemes in Alaska. Even some of the old clubs, which for years had seemed little more than drowsy bird watchers, suddenly were caught up in the sue-the-bastards spirit of the era. Thomas L. Kimball, executive director of the National Wildlife Federation, came back from an inspection tour of Alaska full of wrath about "the oil industry, and others, [who] in haste to develop oil resources of the region have created a mess in some areas." Other environmentalists were making similar complaints. They would ultimately join in historic litigation.

They would do it with an argument accurately summarized, and endorsed, by the New York *Times* editorially on November 10, 1969:

"To date there is not the least assurance that oil can be piped over such a distance, across land that can be scarred for a quarter-century by the track of a bulldozer, without causing irremediable destruction. In this tundra a 48-inch pipeline filled with hot oil could produce rapid and disastrous erosion in the underlying permafrost. Taking gravel from the river bottoms to lay a foundation over the tundra for roads, camps and airstrips would destroy spawning grounds, and running the pipe above ground would create a barrier to migrating caribou and other wildlife— all necessary to the ecological balance of the region.

"Beyond these dangers, the risk of leaks in the line, or outright breaks, is extremely grave. Last year there were more than 500 such leaks in the United States, not to mention the devastation off Santa Barbara. The Alaskan line would pose a far greater hazard, being four times as wide as most—a half-million gallons of oil for every mile of pipe—and traversing an area notoriously prone to earthquakes. In the slow-healing permafrost of the Arctic a huge oil slick would last for decades, perhaps for centuries, killing all the wildlife in its way, with unforeseeable damage to the total environment."

"Few U.S. industries sing the praises of free enterprise more loudly than the oil industry. Yet few industries rely so heavily on special governmental favors."

MILTON FRIEDMAN

THE MANDATORY OIL IMPORT CONTROL PROGRAM

This, the longest-running fright campaign of them all, resulted in one of the most elaborate and efficient price-fixing devices ever concocted, one that would last from 1959 until the early 1970s, at which time it died, not because justice had finally caught up with it but because world changes no longer made it useful to the major oil companies.

Until the 1950s, the international giants had the world market nicely under control. Price-fixing was easy as pie. In the United States, they controlled domestic production by controlling the state agencies, such as the Texas Railroad Commission; in the rest of the world it was even easier, because the five largest American oil firms—Exxon, Texaco, Socal, Mobil, and Gulf—together with their two foreign partners, Shell and British Petroleum, controlled nearly all production (I mean, something like 99 percent) outside the Soviet Union. And of course, most of it was centered in the Middle East, where production was incredibly cheap, in some areas costing less than one tenth the cost of raising oil in the United States.

Although the majors sent some of this cheap oil to the United States, they meticulously refrained from swamping the U.S. market with it, for that would simply undercut domestic prices and hurt the majors more than anyone; they were, after all, the biggest owners of domestic oil too. Instead, in the immediate postwar period, they used most of their Middle East oil to expand their European and Japanese markets. (During this period they built most of their refineries in Europe, not in America, a decision that would, in the 1970s, help to create gasoline and heating-oil shortages in the United States.) Everything was working out just wonderfully for them: while maintaining high prices in the United States through state "prorationing" agencies, they could use their foreign supplies to rebuild war-blasted Europe with a filling station on every corner.

But this beautiful world depended entirely on one thing: the majors' continuing their control over the foreign sources. In developing their holdings in the Middle East and expanding their control over that part of the world, they had created a monopolistic edifice that was as delicate as it was large. It was like a gigantic derrick of matchsticks. So long as the major companies had full control of the edifice, of the ground on which it was built, and of the world environment that allowed it to exist—as long as they made all decisions as to how much should be pumped, what price to ask, how much should go into which markets—the derrick stood as solid as concrete.

Unfortunately, even the best schemes eventually begin to come apart. In the bright blue skies of foreign exploitation, a cloud appeared. At first so small as to be hardly noticeable, it soon became enormous and cast a frightful pall over the market. Suddenly the majors were aware that they no longer had the almost total control over foreign production that they had had before World War II.

They had failed to take one thing into consideration: A loophole that applied to them would also have to apply to oil companies of any size doing business overseas. The foreign tax credit, and the cheap oil, began luring many smaller oil explorers to move into foreign fields. In the postwar boom, some very aggressive independent oilmen—fellows such as Getty and the Kecks and the Hunts (fathers and sons)—started making their own deals with the rulers of the oil countries, and doing it very successfully. Moreover, they had no reason to be clubby. The majors had never done anything for them, so why should they team up with the majors to control the supply? They were tough go-getters who didn't play by the comfortable rules the majors had used to maintain supply stability. On the sensitive world oil market, stability can be preserved only by a most careful effort at balancing, and the independents were not careful fellows. They were wild hares, who weren't afraid of price wars and who were eager to dump their newly acquired oil on the U.S. market or any other market and hang the consequences. Though they controlled only a small fraction of the foreign fields, they were pumping so rambunctiously that by 1950 the price of Mideast crude had dropped to two thirds the cost of comparable U.S. crude, and Mideast oil had begun to flow into U.S. refineries at a startlingly faster pace. Crude imports climbed from 272,000 barrels a day in 1947 to over 900,000 barrels a day in 1956.

If that continued, it would result in deliciously cheap oil for American consumers. It would also allow us to save our own oil reserves for future use while burning up abundant imports.

But the happiness of American consumers and the conservation of U.S. resources were not exactly what the major oil companies were in business for. And so, knowing he was always delighted to oblige oilmen, they went to President Eisenhower and asked him to impose import restrictions. All oil price-fixing schemes are launched in the name of either conservation or national security, or both. Since an import quota would mean depleting our resources more swiftly, it could hardly be proposed as conservation, so it was offered to the shrine of national security.

The argument was that if all that cheap foreign oil was allowed unrestricted access to the U.S. market, it would seriously undercut our own producers and drive many out of business, thus making us dependent on unreliable foreign supplies. That would be bad enough in peacetime; it would be unthinkable in wartime. So it was necessary to protect domestic producers from foreign competition as a matter of national security. To hear Eisenhower and his oil friends talk, the purpose of the import restrictions sounded very high-minded and humanely protective. Not a word, of course, was said about the quota system being simply another price-fixing scheme. No, no, it was strictly a matter of national security. We must avoid vulnerability!

As always seems to happen, Allah provided the majors with a Middle East crisis to underscore their argument. In the fall of 1956, Israel launched a preventive war, sending its troops against Egypt across the Sinai Peninsula. British and French armies moved into the Suez Canal zone. And Egypt, understandably feeling that it was under severe provocation from the West, began sinking ships in the Suez Canal, thereby bringing to a halt the daily traffic of about 1.5 million barrels. Meanwhile, saboteurs were busy elsewhere, cutting the Iraq Petroleum Company's pipelines, which were carrying five hundred thousand barrels a day to eastern Mediterranean ports.

Although the convenient crisis was over within a few months, the majors had made their point. Hadn't the breakdown in the Middle East caused critical shortages in Europe? Hadn't factories closed on the Continent? Hadn't Europe been saved from disaster only by the swift diversion of Texas oil to that market? Well, there you are: foreign oil is unreliable, and just because it is cheap is no reason to permit it to be brought into the United States in such quantities as to cripple the domestic industry, which can always be counted on in a crisis.

The majors were joined in this argument by the smaller independent oilmen—not the Kecks and the Hunts and the Gettys, who had overseas oil they wanted to bring in, but the smaller fellows who hadn't the capital to take part in the foreign oil boom. Their fortune was locked in U.S. soil; they were entirely dependent on the home market, and they vehemently opposed the competition of imports. Because of this group, the majors could pretend that they wanted limitations on oil imports simply because they were concerned about the little fellows. "The torrent of foreign oil . . . robs Texas of her oil market," said Ernest O. Thompson, of the Texas Railroad Commission, which at the moment was rationing wells to only fifteen days of production a month.

So in 1957 President Eisenhower, whose ties to oil were very close and whose most trusted adviser in such matters was Treasury Secretary Robert Anderson, a Texas oilman (see Appendix entry on *ANDERSON* to learn more about how this dandy scheme originated), imposed voluntary restrictions, hoping that the industry would police itself. But voluntary controls don't work with oilmen, so on March 11, 1959, he proclaimed the beginning of the Mandatory Oil Import Control Program.

Clearly it was intended to help the biggest companies. Only those with refineries were permitted to import oil; most small oil companies do not have refineries, so they were automatically eliminated.

For the big companies that qualified, the quota program was an enormous windfall. The quota licenses could not be sold, but they could be swapped. A landlocked refiner, such as Standard of Indiana, that could not utilize imported oil directly could still exploit the program by swapping its license to import a $2 barrel of foreign oil to a coastal refiner in return for a $3.15 barrel of domestic oil delivered to its inland refinery. A company was, by being issued an import quota, literally given millions of dollars a year.[1]

But, by the early 1960s, the independents were terribly unhappy. They did not want to do away with import controls; after all, the import restrictions helped maintain prices of about $3 to $3.25 a barrel in this country while world market prices sometimes fell to less than $1.50 a barrel; the independents felt bound by self-interest to an alliance with their natural commercial adversaries, the majors, in fighting any proconsumer effort to do away with the quota system altogether. They were unhappy with the program for other reasons. The larger independents who had gone abroad and found oil (but who didn't have refineries)

---

1. The inequities of the program could be seen by comparing the exclusion of Superior Oil Company with the inclusion of Standard Oil of Indiana.

Although Superior is the largest independent oil company in the United States in terms of the oil reserves it controls, it is not in the refining business. Since the import quotas were handed out strictly to refineries, this left Superior in the lurch. It seemed a harsh reward for taking risks. Superior had spent $83 million exploring Venezuela and discovered one of the great oil reservoirs in that country, but it was allowed to import none of its own oil, because it did not fulfill the import system's basic refinery requirement. Standard, Sun, Gulf, Atlantic, and other larger companies followed Superior into this area of Venezuela and shipped back their oil. But Superior, the discoverer, could not. Finally, bowing to the pressures of the anything-but-free marketplace, Superior sold its Venezuela concessions to Texaco.

Standard of Indiana, on the other hand, had a large refining capacity but, except for a small amount in Canada, it had virtually no foreign production. Indiana Standard was not an exploring company; it had put up very little risk capital overseas. Fair play would seem to have dictated no import quota at all for Indiana Standard. Instead, because of its refining capacity, it became one of the nation's largest importers, and since each barrel of quota it received equaled a flat-out gift of $1.25 to $1.50, it proceeded to use the quota system to subsidize world oil exploration and exploitation on a grand scale. Today it is a major overseas producer.

(Why single out Indiana Standard? Some believe that that company had some questionable influence in setting up the program; see the Appendix entry on *ANDERSON*.)

were unhappy because they couldn't bring some of it in to sell at domestic prices; *both* large and small independents were unhappy that so much foreign oil was slipping around the controls.

The import system did not restrict imports to 12.2 percent of domestic production as it was supposed to do; by the time all the oil that came in through loopholes was toted up, the ceiling was more nearly 20 percent of domestic production—not enough restriction to really give independents strong protection. Indeed, so much foreign oil was slipping in that at times magnificent gluts allowed consumers to be treated to price wars. (In the early 1960s, gasoline briefly sold as low as 13.9 cents a gallon in some Texas towns, and Brownwood, Texas, had a gasoline price war that lasted more than six years.) And besides everything else, both small and large independents were outraged that only refinery owners got to profit from the import tickets.

On that last point, they worked up a plan in 1963 that, if accepted by President Kennedy, would give them a chance at the pie. Their idea was that the import licenses, instead of being given away, be sold to the highest bidders at auction, so that anybody who could afford to bid—not just favored refinery owners—would have a chance at the profits. A second advantage of the plan was that the U.S. Treasury could pocket the auction income. It was a reasonable plan, and *The Oil Daily* of July 22, 1963, reported that Kennedy "coveted" the millions that would come to the Treasury from such a shift.

Independent oilmen got Texas Governor John Connally to promise that he would lobby Kennedy heavily on behalf of the plan when he reached Austin after visiting Dallas on November 22. But of course Kennedy did not get out of Dallas alive.

President Lyndon Johnson kept the quota system going, although he pretended not to have anything to do with the decision. Sensitive about his reputation as an oil politician,[2] Johnson had scarcely taken office when he announced that he was shifting oil policy making out of the

---

2. The public was, understandably, convinced that he was a tool of the oil interests. After all, it had been Lyndon Johnson in 1949, the first year of his Senate career, who led the successful character assassination that blocked Leland Olds's renomination to the Federal Power Commission; Olds's sin, in Johnson's eyes, was that he had prevented price increases in natural gas and thereby saved consumers billions of dollars. It was Johnson in 1954, the first year of his de facto majority leadership, who rammed through the Senate a bill to free the natural gas industry from all federal regulation; when the industry's bribe efforts were uncovered, Eisenhower, to his unhappiness, had to veto the bill. Lyndon's highly profitable friendship with Brown & Root, one of the world's largest oil construction firms, was well known and frequently mentioned in the press. It was also well known that such oilmen as H. L. Hunt and Stanley Adams, president of Phillips Petroleum, had worked very hard to block Kennedy and get the nomination for Johnson in 1960. (In 1964, contributions from members of the American Petroleum Institute to the Democratic presidential campaign would jump 400 percent over what they had been in 1960.)

White House and into the Department of the Interior. Presumably, since he had been one of the half dozen men believed most influential in writing the original oil import quota system and getting it through Congress, this was supposed to make it appear that he was holding oil decisions at arm's length. From now on, he implied, Interior Secretary Stewart Udall would make the hard decisions on the import program. The American Petroleum Institute hailed the transfer of authority as "entirely logical," and it was easy to see why they thought so when Udall, with strong backing from the White House, appointed Elmer L. Hoehn to be oil import administrator. Hoehn had been executive secretary of a Midwestern oil producers' association.

Under Udall and Johnson, reform of the program was out of the question.

But by President Nixon's first year, opposition to the import system had become so intense, not only from liberals but also from free-market conservatives such as Milton Friedman, that something seemed likely to give soon. The free-marketers' feelings were eloquently summarized by Allan T. Demaree in *Fortune:*

"The quota system that chokes off the free flow of oil into the U.S. costs the nation billions and shelters gross inefficiencies in the domestic crude-oil producing industry. Imposed in the name of national security just a decade ago, it has become the object of mounting discontent. It has given government officials the power arbitrarily to parcel out enormous fortunes to individual companies . . . It has caused huge domestic industries, regions of the country, and even nations to pit themselves against one another in an unseemly battle for political favor in Washington. All in all, the quota on oil imports has proved to be one of the most ill-conceived and ill-executed federal regulatory schemes since the abortive flight of the NRA's Blue Eagle.

"Once above the scrutiny of Congress, the oil quota is now being subjected to searing criticism there."

Indeed it was. Hearings before the Senate antitrust subcommittee in 1969 produced evidence that since the program began, the quotas had cost consumers an extra $50 billion, which, to put it in perspective, was equal to 60 percent of the entire federal budget for 1959, the first year the import quota system was in operation.

But, putting aside the plight of consumers, there was also clear evidence that the program was failing singularly in what it allegedly had been set up to accomplish: the strengthening of the domestic oil industry. Just the opposite was occurring.

Statistics compiled by the industry itself clearly showed that the domestic companies were declining in number, in enthusiasm, and in productivity. In the dozen years prior to 1969, the number of wells drilled in the United States had dropped 43 percent. Three thousand of the twelve

...ling to the book.
...ortland, Maine,
...ystem forbade
...anada, where
...ic stuff that
...consump-
...tic injus-
...efineries
...as were
...ed oil
...out a

...57 had gone out of business. The
...re being swallowed wholesale by
...staff reported that since the
...rs had bought all or part of
...es.

...companies to explore for oil in
...usly encouraging them to explore
...rengthening "national security." In
...system went into effect, American oil
...penses of $650 million in this country and
...spending for domestic exploration had in-
...percent) while it had gone up $255 million
...n countries. With the major companies throwing
...nto the development of foreign fields, it was only
...ould build their refineries overseas as well. The result
...be a refinery shortage in this country. Between the start
...rt system and 1969, U.S. refining capacity rose less than 25
...ough demand for oil products increased more than 50 per-
...ng that decade, the majors had built the great bulk of their
...s in Europe and in the Caribbean to exploit the cheap foreign oil
...he import quota system was keeping out of this country.

The administration of the quota system had developed a highly unsavory reputation. The import licenses were worth a half billion dollars a
year, quite enough to prompt larceny. The Department of the Interior
was suspected of collusion when it was caught issuing quota licenses to
nonexistent refineries and to refineries that had gone out of business.

The system had also developed a reputation for wackiness. If the idea
was to develop sources that would be safe during national emergencies,
why put any restrictions on imports from Mexico and Canada, which
were almost as dependable as U.S. supplies? (Senator Russell Long had
argued that the Canadian quotas were justified because there was always
a possibility of war between the United States and Canada, but in those
days Senator Long was having a drinking problem; not many of his colleagues would have considered making such an absurd argument.)

The program had been written to exclude all but overland deliveries
of oil from Mexico. Since there was no pipeline between Mexico and the
United States, and since the long haul by truck from the Mexican fields
was uneconomical, the only feasible way to transport Mexican oil to this
country was by ship. But oil transported by ship could not legally be sold
here. It was a stupid regulation that inspired some ingenious cheating.
The result: El Loophole. Mexican oil was shipped by sea to Brownsville,
Texas, where it was unloaded into trucks; the trucks were driven a few
miles to the Mexican border, then just over the border to Matamoros,
and then immediately back to Port Brownsville to be reloaded onto

tankers and taken to U.S. refineries—all legal and accord

Oil shipped from Africa and the Middle East to P
could not be used by the residents of Maine. The import
it. So it was piped 230 miles across the state to Montreal, Q
it was sold for three cents less per gallon than the domes
Maine was having to ship in from the Gulf Coast for its ow
tion.

The plight of New England was, in fact, one of the more idi
tices of the program. Quotas were assigned to refineries; most
were, for obvious reasons, built near oil fields; so most of the quot
channeled into states where oil was already abundant. No impor
went directly to New England, the only section of the country with
refinery.[3]

***

By the time Nixon moved into the White House, extraordinary congre
sional pressures to break up the import program and adamant oppositio
to these efforts had created an explosive situation that demanded his immediate attention. Shortly after being sworn in, he announced that he
was shifting the Interior Department's policy-making functions back to
the White House and taking personal charge of them. The first item on
his agenda would be the import program. But he needed instructions, a
game plan; and so, for four days in February 1969, he and his economic
advisers met with top oil executives, including Michael Haider, former
chairman of Jersey Standard and outgoing chairman of the American Petroleum Institute, and Frank N. Ikard, president of the API.

3. The obvious question was, Why not build a refinery in New England—which regularly paid some of the highest fuel bills in the nation—so that it could import some of
the cheap foreign oil? This was exactly what Dr. Armand Hammer, chief executive of
Occidental Petroleum Company, proposed. He was an unorthodox fellow, viewed with
suspicion by many members of the oil industry, possibly because he had fresh ideas.
In little more than a decade, Hammer had transformed Occidental from a dying husk
of a company into one of the most efficient in the business (from 7 cents a share in
1956, its stock had climbed to $45). In 1967, Hammer had won concessions from
Libya, buying up some of Mobil's discarded fields and finding oil where the giant firm
had failed. Now he wanted to import this Libyan oil.

Hammer asked Washington to establish a "free trade zone" in Machiasport, Maine,
where he could build a refinery and process three hundred thousand barrels of imported crude a day. (A "free trade zone" is physically in the United States but, for
customs and trade purposes, is considered to be outside the country.) To win the concession, he offered inducements. If he got the trade zone, he said, he would lower
prices on defense fuels, gasoline, and home heating oil by 10 percent and set aside a
certain sum for marine research. Even with a 10 percent cut, he said, he could still
make a fine profit.

That sort of free enterprise was highly objectionable to all the major oil companies
and most of the independents. Almost as one man they rose against the Machiasport
proposition. Some of these honest gentlemen went so far as to accuse Hammer of trying to bribe his way to success.

Haider emerged from the meetings declaring that he and the other oil-men had had a "very good conversation" with the President and that he, Haider, was "feeling more optimistic about the handling of petroleum-industry problems in Washington," because "Nixon has a good grasp of the problems surrounding oil-import controls."

What happened next indicates that Nixon and his oil advisers had agreed on stalling action.

Nixon ordered a high-level review of the import program—something that would consume most of the year. The task force assigned by Nixon to do the study was chaired by Labor Secretary George P. Shultz. Others on the panel were Hickel, Commerce Secretary Maurice H. Stans, Defense Secretary Melvin R. Laird, Secretary of State William Rogers, Treasury Secretary David M. Kennedy, and Brigadier General (retired) George A. Lincoln, head of the Office of Emergency Preparedness.

It looked like a single-minded, Nixonian rubber-stamp lineup. But, amazingly enough, it didn't turn out that way at all; the panel's professional staff and Chairman Shultz kept the operation reasonably honest. When it became apparent that honesty might prevail, startled industry leaders and their friends in Congress tried some heavy-handed influencing. On July 11, Representative Wilbur D. Mills, of Arkansas, chairman of the House Ways and Means Committee, fired off an unusually blunt telegram to Phillip Areeda, executive director of the task force staff, warning him against "tinkering with the matter of oil import quotas," lest it be "injurious" to the national interest.

On November 7, four governors representing the Interstate Oil and Gas Compact Commission—Preston Smith of Texas, Robert B. Docking of Kansas, Stanley K. Hathaway of Wyoming, and Richard B. Ogilvie of Illinois—met with Nixon's oil adviser, Peter Flanigan. They brought telegrams from thirteen other governors supporting the quota system. After the group had its pitch well rehearsed, Flanigan invited members of the President's task force to come in and get lobbied by the governors. When word of the secret get-together leaked, Senator William Proxmire, pointing out that "even a cursory examination of the telegrams from the governors who could not attend the meeting shows they are almost all in identical language," came to the hardly profound conclusion that they had been cranked out by the same PR office and were part of a "planned campaign of pressure by the oil industry through the Interstate Oil Compact Commission."[4]

Whether because of pressure from the oil industry generally or because

---

4. The commission had been established by Congress with one, and only one, statutory responsibility: to conserve oil and gas within the United States. Of course, restricting foreign imports, as these fellows were urging, did just the opposite, which is why the quota system was sometimes called DAFT: the "drain America first treatment."

of loyalty to the source of his family's great wealth, New York Governor Nelson Rockefeller was one of the thirteen to send telegrams supporting the quota system, which put him rather at odds with New York City Mayor John Lindsay, who believed that the restrictions against bringing in cheap foreign oil were costing New York City residents between $100 million and $250 million a year.

But maverick influences were also at work. Several important federal agencies submitted written opinions to the task force that effectively torpedoed the whole concept—national security—by which the quotas had been peddled. One of the confidential opinions came from Interior Department staff experts—acting, needless to say, independently of Interior Secretary Hickel. In their opinion, the quotas were costing American consumers from $7 billion to $8 billion a year in higher gasoline and heating-oil prices. If the United States was sincerely worried about maintaining an oil supply for emergencies, the Interior rebels wrote, it could store an emergency supply much cheaper than the cost of the import restrictions program. The task force refused to release the Interior study, but congressional sources leaked it to the press.

Next came the damning—and, considering the source, startlingly candid—opinion of Richard McLaren, assistant attorney general in charge of the Justice Department's Antitrust Division, who told the task force that the quotas cheated consumers, damaged the economy, repressed competition, and encouraged inefficiencies in the domestic oil industry. His opinion was sent *without* the approval of his boss, Attorney General John Mitchell. Oil lobbyists demanded that Mitchell act at once to counteract the testimony of his subordinate. At one of the panel's last meetings, Mitchell made a surprise appearance to plead, "Don't put the President in a box." He did not explain what he meant, but the consensus of those present was that he was urging them not to support an import policy that would either force Nixon to repudiate their advice or to offend his supporters in the oil industry.

Oil lobbyists were very concerned, and with good reason. The task force was becoming a runaway grand jury, and long before it came out with its final report, there were rumors of stormy sessions at which the two encrusted Nixonians on the panel—Hickel and Stans—futilely attempted to force their colleagues to join them in recommending that the quota be preserved.

But they failed; by a 5–2 vote, in December, the panel advised President Nixon to scrap the existing import system in favor of a tariff.

If the recommendations were followed, it was expected that within three years refineries would be paying about the same for domestic oil as for foreign oil—a half-billion-dollar-a-year saving, some of which, with a little luck, might be passed on to the consumer. Under the proposed tariff system, foreign oil could be imported by anybody, not just by the favored major refineries, and consequently, as the panel's report pointed out, "the ever-present risks of corruption" would be considerably lessened.

All of which was not only factual but made good sense. However, good sense had never had much impact on the Mandatory Oil Import Control Program, and it wouldn't this time either. With the help of Nixon, it would continue to live until another price-fixing apparatus—a vitalized OPEC—was ready to take its place.

Q. Are oil companies making excess profits?
A. No.
Q. Then, you believe profits being made by the oil companies are justified?
A. I didn't say that . . .

Chicago *Tribune* interview
with John E. Swearingen,
of Standard Oil of Indiana

THE SURRENDER OF THE FEDERAL POWER COMMISSION

No energy battle of the 1970s would be more intense than the one over the pricing of natural gas; it would be a battle waged with the usual scare tactics, built on contrived shortages and highly controversial claims of potential shortages. At times, the oil/gas industry got downright vicious with its customers. This was simply the last throes of an old struggle.

Most regulatory commissioners come out of relative obscurity, serve in Washington in virtual anonymity, and when their terms are up they usually vanish again (which is sometimes their one propublic action). Yet the decisions they make during their bureaucratic interim are sometimes of enormous importance in setting the mood and affecting the prosperity of the nation. Certainly this was true of the men who served (no women ever did) on the Federal Power Commission.

Since 1938, the Federal Power Commission had been statutorily empowered to supervise the sale and distribution of interstate natural gas. (For a longer history of this always controversial and fascinating agency, please see the Appendix entry on *REGULATION—NATURAL GAS*.) The local gas company, with the approval of the state utility commission, had the last word on what price consumers paid for their gas. But that price was built on other, more obscure prices. Back at the starting point, when the gas was brought out of the ground, it was supposed to be the FPC that ruled how much the producer could charge the interstate pipeline company (intrastate gas wasn't controlled by the FPC), and then it was the FPC that said how much the pipeline could charge the local distributor.

For years, the oil/gas industry had been trying to persuade Congress to free natural gas from price regulation. Failing in that, it had tried to get Presidents to appoint proindustry commissioners. Under Eisenhower, the FPC was a lopsided 4 to 1 in favor of industry, and the one, Leland Olds, was finally driven off the Commission by Senator Lyndon Johnson's infamous character assassination. Under John Kennedy, the Commission became just about as lopsidedly proconsumer and (because of Johnson's dread of seeming an oil-biased President) it remained so, usually by a count of 3 to 2, until the coming of Nixon. Then the FPC became, and would remain, solidly proindustry.

Among the campaign promises Richard Nixon made in 1968 was one to reverse what he called the "heavy-handed bureaucratic regulatory schemes." The Federal Power Commission was central to that promise. Seven months after his inauguration, Nixon plucked John Nassikas out of New Hampshire and made him chairman of the FPC. If Nixon hoped that Nassikas would make the Commission a friendlier place for the natural gas industry, his hopes were fulfilled. Nassikas worked to that end with such enthusiasm and efficiency that the FPC sometimes seemed almost an adjunct of the industry. Its traditional regulatory apparatus was demolished. Never before had gas producers enjoyed such riches, with the help and blessing of the regulatory agency that was supposed to "control" them.

What was behind the Nassikas nomination? Some Senate staffers, claiming to have inside information, say that, prior to his nomination, Nassikas was called to the White House and told that he wouldn't get the job unless he promised to raise gas prices. Other Capitol Hill gossips say that Nassikas spent one long, long evening with leading gas industry executives so that they could pick over and shred his philosophy to make sure that he was the right man for Nixon to appoint.

Whether or not the stories were accurate, the way they were usually told—to imply that Nassikas had to bend his will to others—did the man a disservice. Nobody had to lean on Nassikas. Senator Philip Hart, chairman of the Senate Subcommittee on Energy, which watched the FPC, put the Nassikas philosophy in the right perspective: "Nassikas would resent being called the mouthpiece of industry, just as I would resent being called the spokesman for the United Auto Workers. I'm sure he is not taking the positions he takes just because industry wants him to. I'm sure he really believes those things."

No doubt Hart was correct. Nassikas was sincere, and a quick review of Nassikas' background will show that Nixon knew he could depend on that sincerity.

Nassikas was a well-known corporation lawyer in New Hampshire, but that didn't take much doing, for at that time there were fewer than four hundred practicing members of the bar in New Hampshire. Although locally Nassikas was known as a good Republican organizer and fund raiser, nationally he had never gotten his feet even slightly wet for the party. But there were other basic qualities about Nassikas that the White House talent scouts recognized, qualities that to understand requires going back to the immigration to America in 1902 of Nicholas Nassikas, young Macedonian Greek on the make.

He made good. First as an importer of olive oil; then, as a grocer and manufacturer of feta cheese during World War I (when German subs ended the importation of such items), he parlayed his savings into a classic milk-butter-creamery-operation in the city of Manchester, New Hampshire. And from that he moved on to an ice-cream wholesale business called NICCO (Nassikas' Ice Cream Company), which he sold for a tidy sum in 1932 to H. P. Hood and Sons, the largest dairy distributors in New England.

As soon as he started hitting it financially, back to Greece he went and married Constantina Gagalis, who lived in a village ninety kilometers from his own home; and when he returned with her, he returned also with his two brothers, who went to work for him; as for the home folks who couldn't come, he sent money to Greece to support an assortment of two dozen cousins and aunts and nephews for the next fifty years.

John Nassikas was born in 1917. By this time, his immigrant father was already wealthy, and the son grew up pampered not only by his parents but by two older sisters. Although the depression began settling into New England as early as the mid-1920s with the movement of the textile mills to the South, the Nassikas family never felt the pinch. When it came time for college, in 1934, with unemployment in the nation at its highest, off John went to the fraternity life at Dartmouth. He did work a bit—lighting fires at what were called "eating clubs"—but only for extra pocket money.

For two years after he graduated from Harvard Law School, in 1948, Nassikas practiced privately, and then he accepted a job on the state attorney general's staff. During this period, Nassikas got a taste of consumer advocacy. He represented the state in successfully opposing several efforts by railroads to discontinue passenger service. He also helped prepare the case that blocked a major rate advance by the New England Telephone and Telegraph Company. And again, in 1953, after he had left the attorney general's office, he was hired by the state as a special attorney to oppose the electric rate increase sought by Public Service Company of New Hampshire.

And that was pretty well the end of the consumer side of his career.

After that, Nassikas became best known as a lawyer for insurance, banking, and utility companies. Some of the biggest in New England retained his firm. Now his successes went in the other direction. In the early 1960s, he was hired by the Boston and Maine Corporation to seek discontinuance of passenger service in New Hampshire, Maine, and Vermont. He succeeded in knocking off lines he had previously fought to preserve. Later he was to concede that he could "understand why some observers call lawyers two-faced. Take me: I started off defending consumer interests [a reference to his attorney-general service] against utilities with vigor and success. Then the utilities came to me and I defended them; many's the passenger run I helped eliminate. But my view is that a good lawyer is a man who can defend either side with equal vigor and effectiveness."

Nassikas emerged from the boondocks in 1968. Just why he accepted temporary employment as minority counsel on the Senate Commerce Committee isn't quite clear. He says he did it as a personal favor to Senator Norris Cotton of New Hampshire, an old friend; but that's a rinky-dink job even for a lawyer who is big only by New Hampshire standards. Anyway, he came to Washington and he served on the staff for six months, which was hardly enough time to make much impression. One Democrat who observed him closely during this period types him as "a fairly decent guy—he wasn't venal, he wasn't a whore—but he seemed to have a hard time keeping his eyes on the central issue. He kept getting tangled up in, and obsessed with, minor issues."

But Republican businessmen who knew him had a different appraisal. Nassikas already, in a regional way, had a good reputation with industry. While working on the Commerce staff, he made additional friends. He was no longer the 128-pound fellow who had participated in every sport but basketball at Dartmouth (five foot seven was a bit short for that). Now he was fifty pounds heavier, and a vest and gold chain covered his corporate paunch, but he was still good at tennis and golf. Many of his off-hours in Washington were spent on the courts and links with energy-industry officials and industry lobbyists. They liked him; he talked their language.

It was the language of Horatio Alger capitalism, inherited from papa. "The independence, the self-reliance, the initiative, the resourcefulness, the nondependence on government, the concept of working your own way with your own talents as did my father and my father-in-law and others," says Nassikas, "all of these things I considered virtues and they are part of my belief in the free enterprise system, in the sense that if somebody in this country wishes to get ahead financially or otherwise the opportunity is there."

If you want to compete with El Paso Natural Gas Company, go build your own $100,000,000 pipeline—in this country, anything is possible. He believed it. To the second-generation American who has gotten to the top of the melting pot, the escaping gases can be hallucinatory.

He loved the corporate world. He loved to roll phrases like "liberalized appreciation and accelerated amortization" around on his tongue. He loved the pomp and weight (literal) of corporate law, a predilection that revealed itself at Capitol Hill hearings, where Nassikas was apt to show up with a retinue of a dozen advisers and carrying ten pounds of statements and statistical graphs which he entered into the record and thereafter referred to—to the confusion and irritation of some congressmen—as "Appendix J" or "Appendix K," as if they should know what he was talking about.

**

John Nassikas was not all-powerful at the FPC, of course. What occurred during his term was done with the aid of like-minded colleagues, some brought to the FPC staff by Nassikas and some sent to the Commission by Nixon. Added to the staff, for example, were men whose previous careers promised sympathy for industry, men such as T. A. Phillips, former vice-president of the Arizona Public Service Company, an electric utility, who became chief of the FPC's Bureau of Power; Thomas J. Joyce, chief of the Bureau of Natural Gas from 1969 until September 1973, had been a vice-president of the Institute of Gas Technology, in Chicago, in which position he had directed economic and market research studies for gas utilities, pipeline companies, gas producers, and equipment suppliers. Kenneth Lukas, whom Nassikas named as his own assistant, had previously been president and treasurer of the Manchester (New Hampshire) Gas Company, a client of Nassikas' old law firm, and before that had been a vice-president of gas companies in Minneapolis and Montreal.

One of the most important members of the Nassikas team was Gordon Gooch, who emerged from seven years at Baker, Botts, Andrews & Shepherd, a Houston law firm, to become the FPC's chief attorney, a most potent position in shaping rate cases. According to the comptroller general's study of the FPC during the Nassikas years, "Before FPC employment, Mr. Gooch also received dividend income from a trust fund comprising stocks, including those of many companies under FPC jurisdiction. Mr. Gooch's financial statement, filed when initially employed [by the FPC], showed that he no longer owned these securities." Gooch participated in the old revolving-door routine. When he quit the FPC, in 1972, he went back to Baker, Botts (after first helping in Nixon's reelection campaign).

Baker, Botts is not, as a matter of fact, *just* a Houston law firm. It is one of the three most powerful law firms in that oil town and, although it has crack lawyers for every field, it is especially hot as an oil and gas law firm. One of the senior partners of Baker, Botts was at that time also gen-

eral counsel for Pennzoil United—a multibillion dollar "natural resources" conglomerate that owned, among other things, United Gas Pipe
Line, reputedly the highest-volume pipeline in the country. It, of course,
was regulated by the FPC.

According to a staff report made a couple of years later by the House
Banking and Currency Committee, Pennzoil United figured in some of
the heavy campaign money sent in suitcases via Mexico to the Committee to Re-elect the President. Apparently Pennzoil was simply showing
its gratitude. In its 1970 annual report it observed: "Recent developments are encouraging. The past two years brought more serious concern
[for industry's position], especially by the Federal Power Commission,
than the entire decade before."

Baker, Botts was the way station for another of the men Nixon sent to
the FPC to bolster the Nassikas philosophy. Rush Moody, Jr., who graduated from the University of Texas Law School in 1956, stopped off at
Baker, Botts before going on in 1960 to join and in 1963 to become a
partner in the Midland, Texas, firm of Stubman, McRae, Sealy, Laughlin
and Browder—a firm that draws much of its business from petroleum. It
handled some of the biggest rate cases before the FPC.

Senator Frank Moss (Democrat, Utah) claimed that Pennzoil's president had first asked one of the firm's senior partners, Tom Sealy, an important power broker in Texas politics, if he wanted to go on the FPC
but that when Sealy heard about the $38,000 salary he laughed and
suggested maybe it would be better to get somebody who was just as
friendly to the industry but could stand that kind of income. Somebody
like Moody.

Moody's nomination naturally caused some concern among consumer
groups, but the young lawyer promised to sell his modest oil and gas
stock—Coquina Oil Company, New Zealand Petroleum Company, Pennzoil Offshore Gas Operators Inc., and Windecker Research Inc.—and sell
his Texas oil and gas royalty arrangements, and to step aside when his
old law firm brought a case to the FPC. (Oh, yes, there was one other
block of stock—five hundred shares of Lone Star Gas Co.—which he
neglected to mention in his statement of holdings as submitted to the
Commerce Committee. Moody said it was just an oversight. He sold the
stock to Charles L. Tigh, a partner in his law firm.) Such measures of
purification, however, still left some uneasy. Senator Thomas McIntyre of
New Hampshire, for example, said at the time that it did seem to him
"highly illogical" to expect the young man "to reorient the direction of
his allegiance overnight, to become, in effect, a dispassionate umpire instead of an impassioned player."

Over the next several years, Moody would be criticized for actions that
some thought were of questionable propriety. In 1973, for example, when
he wrote the FPC's majority ruling giving a 73 percent increase in the

price of new natural gas at the wellhead, Representative George E. Brown, Jr. (Democrat, California) pointed out that one of the three producers winning the precedent-setting increase was Texaco, which was a client of Moody's former law firm, in Midland. Brown felt that Moody should have disqualified himself. Moody never tried to hide his feelings that the gas industry should not be subjected to price regulations, and when he quit, in 1975, he angrily accused Congress of "deceiving the American people into the belief that . . . price regulation serves the public interest." He had done all he could to wipe out such regulation, and as Representative John Moss (Democrat, California) pointed out, during Moody's nearly four years on the FPC, the price of natural gas had been raised by nearly 200 percent.

Another recruited to the Commission by Nixon was Pinkney Walker, a Texan who had been employed by the University of Missouri as an economics professor and business-school dean. Consumer groups were also worried about him, because at various times he had served as a consultant for Southwestern Bell Telephone Co., Mississippi River Transmission Corp., and Missouri Power and Light, and had participated for a fee in programs set up by the Panhandle Eastern Gas Pipe Line Co., the Eastern Gas Line Co., American Gas Assn., and the Bendix Corp. In every consultant case, he espoused higher profits for the companies and higher prices for the consumer. He owned $127,000 in bank stock, had helped organize two banks, and was on the boards of directors of three banks and an insurance company. All this he gave up and promised to serve his country fairly and impartially. As soon as he joined the Commission, he began saying that natural gas should be deregulated.

A brief holdover from the Johnson era was Republican Carl E. Bagge, whose attitude toward controlling natural gas prices was made rather clear when, even while serving as a supposedly impartial member of the FPC, he assisted Senator John Tower of Texas in writing legislation to deregulate the entire natural gas industry. In 1970, Bagge would quit the FPC to become head of the National Coal Association, which of course was dominated by the oil companies that had recently bought so heavily into that industry.

Another interesting holdover from the Johnson period was Commissioner Albert Bushong Brooke, Jr., who was named to the FPC in 1968 and reappointed by Nixon in 1969. He was sponsored by Illinois Senator Everett Dirksen—whose profitable ties with the oil and gas industry constitute one of the more sordid chapters in senatorial ethics—and by former Kentucky Senator Thruston Morton. For ten years, Brooke was a staff assistant to Morton, before Morton left the Senate and became a director of Texas Gas Transmission, one of the major pipeline companies regulated by the FPC. When, on the eve of Brooke's confirmation hearing before the Commerce Committee, this was mentioned by the Washington *Daily News,* the seeming conflict of interest was smoothed over by Senator Norris Cotton, who brought to the committee a message from Morton: "He wished the statement made that his connection with Texas Gas Transmission is purely because of the fact that they own the principal bargeline on the Ohio River and, as he phrased it, 'My interest in the Ohio River is one of my three main interests in life—fast horses, tobacco, and the Ohio River confluence.' . . . Furthermore, he has not and would not dream of exercising any influence on his former administrative assistant, Commissioner Brooke, in connection with any case, and certainly not one affecting the Texas Gas Transmission Co."

**

Within seventy-two hours after taking office, Nassikas was publicly stating that the price of gas should be raised. Some wondered how he could come to such a quick conclusion about such a complex subject. The criticism became so sharp, and so snide, that Nassikas' mentor, Senator Cotton, struck back in an unusual show of anger, accusing the last Democratic chairman of the FPC, Lee White, of "coaching and inspiring" the critics.

"Let's have things right out on the table," said Cotton. "I have had people creeping up on my blind side, and I know where they came from . . . saying now is it true what I hear that this chairman [Nassikas] is an economic Tory? They say he is going to be all for utilities and all for the gas companies and all for these corporations."

Cotton said that was such a stupid idea "it makes me laugh," for "I regard him as one of those liberal Republicans." No, not merely a liberal Republican but "a Rockefeller liberal Republican. I thought I was pretty lucky to get him confirmed before President Nixon found that out. So I don't regard him as a champion of entrenched power on the part of private corporations."

The proindustry judgments persisted, however, and not only among liberals. Within two months after he took over, *The Wall Street Journal* (September 25, 1969) was commenting on his "friendliness toward industry"; and in its November 1, 1969, issue, *Forbes* magazine, which is not noted for consumer bias, was moved to paeans: "Too good to last? It's hard to see how the troubled natural gas industry could have a regulator more to its taste than the new chairman of the Federal Power Commission . . . [he] sometimes sounds more like a natural gas executive expounding about how the FPC should regulate his industry than a man burdened with the actual responsibility of regulation."

It was a prescient appraisal, but subsequently Nassikas did much more than "sound" like an ally. Aside from presiding over some staggering rate increases, he helped maneuver through the FPC a dazzling array of other proindustry rulings: forgiving nearly $400 million in overcharges;

granting (for the first time in history) price increases for "old" gas—gas that is already flowing and whose production costs have already been written into the price contract—which is about the same as if General Motors were allowed to go back and raise the price of a car after the consumer had been paying on it for a year.

And most significant of all, for the first time, the FPC would give rate increases not on the basis of the cost of producing gas, not on the basis of a fair profit, *but as a matter of incentive.* Traditionally—and legally—the FPC had set prices according to what it felt would be a reasonable return on investment, and it had been generous in its interpretation of "reasonable." The frightening problem arising from the development of a natural resource by private enterprise is that it is always in danger of being held for ransom: the developer will not release the resource without a payoff that meets his, however greedy, demands. When dealing in a necessary fuel, the potential for holding the resource hostage is especially great. Only government regulation of prices can eradicate the threat. Which is exactly why the FPC had been set up and been given authority over natural gas prices to begin with. The Nassikas FPC did not want to carry out this part of its mandate, but since it could not legally stop setting prices, it thought up the gimmick of "incentive pricing," which, in effect, allowed industry to set its own prices. "Incentive prices" are prices that the industry says will encourage it to do its job right—and since incentives are strictly a psychological matter, only the industry could say what the right price was. The move to incentive pricing of course meant the end of consumer protection.

*

The FPC's excuse for incentive pricing was that the industry had suddenly, and surprisingly, begun reporting that the natural gas supply was getting short. Consumer groups greeted this excuse with anger and ridicule. What proof did the FPC have that there was a "shortage"? None at all. It had only the industry's word for it. Testifying before a Senate Interior subcommittee, Edward Berlin, counsel for the Consumer Federation of America, demanded: "How do we know that there is a shortage? On what is all of this shortage hysteria based? It is based presumably on the considered judgments of the two agencies of government to which we all must look for guidance in this most complex area: the Federal Power Commission and the Department of the Interior. But have they made studies? No. Have they undertaken any hard probing? No. They have simply announced that there is a shortage. They know that there is a shortage because, they candidly tell us, the industry that is trying so hard to squeeze the consumer for higher prices through scare tactics and threats had told them that there is a shortage.

"Just look at the Commission's so-called staff report . . . 'For purposes of this report we have accepted at face value all industry-furnished supply data.'

"This is what you are being asked to accept on face value, to swallow hook, line and sinker. This compilation of propaganda designed by two staff people, not based on any record, not subject to cross-examination, but nonetheless the welcome recipient of the Commission's impressive cloak of authority.

"The story is the same with the Interior Department. It bases its decision to cry wolf *not* on data collected as the agency responsible for public resources, but . . . because an emergency advisory committee composed of 30 top-level officials of the gas industry met on September 29 and quickly concluded that the long-term supply situation is bleak.

"I do not profess to be an expert on gas supply, but I do know enough to be absolutely amazed that the FPC is so content to embrace so warmly a report written in inflammatory language and reading more like a public relations release than a scientific appraisal, a report whose conclusions are on no firmer foundation than a house of cards. And I might add the deck seems quite heavily stacked . . ."

Consumer organizations had contempt not only for the FPC's willingness to accept the industry's unverified claim of a shortage, they had even more contempt and ridicule for what they viewed as the industry's clumsy and transparent conspiracy to juggle statistics in such a way as to create the appearance of a shortage.

The best evidence of the conspiracy, they felt, was in the timing of the "shortage." Since 1954, the natural gas industry had been trying to get the federal courts to agree that the FPC was not legally empowered to set the price of natural gas at the wellhead; but its argument seemed to be based less on law than on fear. It had told the U.S. Supreme Court, in effect: the gas reserves are falling at a perilous rate, but if you remove the FPC shackles and let us work freely at whatever profit the market will bear, we will find all the gas this nation needs.

However, the Court didn't buy that argument. After looking over the data supplied by industry, the justices had decided just the year before, in 1968, that they didn't see any sharp decline in reserves and certainly didn't see any emergency, and that the FPC was definitely empowered to set wellhead prices not for "incentives" but according to a "just and reasonable" criterion (*Permian Basin Area Rate Cases,* 390 U.S. 747).

Furious with this ruling, the industry immediately began developing doomsday statistics. In 1969 the American Gas Association (AGA), keeper of industry's statistics, reported a significant drop in reserves, a drop so sharp as to make even a Supreme Court justice sit up and take notice. Indeed, industry leaders became so excessive in their desire to "show" the Supreme Court that they even went back to 1968 and *deducted* some of the reserves that they had previously recorded.

There was something indeed fishy about all this frenzied reworking of the books. Queried about it by the FPC, the chairman of the AGA's Natural Gas Reserves Committee responded with a straight face, "We do not know what factors account for the decline."

The coincidence of the Court's ruling and the industry's sudden poverty of reserves was difficult for many observers to accept as legitimate. Among the more eloquent doubters of the AGA's new statistics was Charles F. Wheatley, Jr., general manager of the American Public Gas Association (APGA), which is run by municipal gas distributors; at the other end of the commercial spectrum from the AGA, the APGA is as nearly consumer-oriented as any part of the energy industry is likely to be. Wheatley noted with lush sarcasm that "the timing of the present asserted natural gas shortage is quite interesting," because the industry's chief lobbyist for a rate increase "has stated that he did not realize until late in 1968 or into 1969 that there was any real shortage." Wasn't it odd that the "shortage" should sneak up so quickly on the very gas producers who kept the books? Or was it strange? Could it be that the suddenness of the onslaught of shortage had something to do, in a very calculated way, with the Supreme Court's decision in 1968? Wheatley was decidedly of that opinion.

Testifying before a House committee, he pointed out the most glaring evidence that the AGA's claimed "declining reserves" was a hoax: "Now, the startling thing about this precipitous drop [in reserves] is that it bears no relation to the drilling effort. In 1969 there was more successful gas well footage drilled in south Louisiana [the most bountiful of the gas fields] than in any year since 1962, and the next-highest year in the period was 1968. For the seven southwest states there was more successful exploratory gas footage drilled in 1969 than in any year subsequent to 1960."

To Wheatley, the reworked statistics were made more suspicious by the remembrance of something that had happened fifteen years earlier: although 1954 had been a banner year for drilling, "a similar shortage claim was made in 1955 when the industry sought passage of legislation to exempt producers from FPC regulation."

There were just too many suspicious things about the American Gas Association's statistics. How could Nassikas accept them with such naïve eagerness? It was a question that consumer organizations would ask, with increasing frustration, in the years immediately ahead.

"Let's talk frankly about energy."
    CLIFTON C. GARVIN, JR. *chairman, Exxon Corp.*

PROPAGANDA

To a significant degree, the energy war would be fought throughout the
1970s with the guns of propaganda. There would be continued use of the
traditional fright campaigns; though crude, they had never failed in their
purpose. And there would also be a continued dissemination of, to use
the kindest words, erroneous and misleading information. As examples of
the latter, consider two noteworthy predictions made in 1969. Mobil
officials said the nation's domestic demand would reach 17.7 million barrels daily in 1980. As it turned out, they were off by seven years: the nation passed 17 million barrels daily consumption in 1973. Also in 1969,
testifying before the Senate Antitrust Subcommittee, M. A. Wright, then
chairman of Exxon, predicted that even as late as 1985 the United States
would be able to meet about 82 percent of its oil demand from its own
supplies. By the end of the decade, we were importing nearly 50 percent
of our oil from abroad.

Now, of course it could be that these oil companies were simply victims of miscalculations; but, on the other hand, it could be that they
were coaxing the nation along with falsely optimistic expectations so that
the shortages that they knew lay ahead (that is, we can assume this if we
are willing to believe a Mobil ad in the New York *Times* of January 18,
1973, that begins: "Oil companies knew the shortage was coming.")
would hit us more traumatically, reduce us to panic, and make us more
willing to accept the kind of federal policy changes that the oil companies demanded.

And if the oil companies did know shortages lay ahead, as Mobil
claimed, was this because they also knew they were going to help create
them? Or was it simply because they sat on top of all the data needed to
make an intelligent prediction? If there wasn't conspiracy, there certainly
was harmful secrecy. Indeed, the main reason the industry was so successful at manipulating our anxieties was this: It controlled the books. It
controlled the statistics.

No other industry of comparable importance gets to operate with such
secrecy. If the government wants to know how many cars GM has in inventory, the government need only send an agent around to GM's storage lots and start counting. But if the government wants to know how
much oil and gas Exxon—and Gulf and Texaco and all the others—are sitting on, it must beg for the statistics. It *needn't* be that way, of course,
but it has always been that way. And whether or not the statistics it

finally receives from industry (*if* it receives any) are accurate is anybody's guess. When it comes to oil and gas, the government is blind; the industry, with a great show of generosity, supplies it with a cane and occasionally shouts a few vague directions, but the government, tapping and stumbling along, never really knows where it is going.

The U.S. Geological Survey from time to time issues an estimate of present and future oil and gas reserves. But the U.S. Geological Survey has always depended on the industry for its basic data. With a flourish of expertise, the Department of Energy issues all sorts of data about production and shipments and exploration and reserves. But the Department of Energy is a pretender; it, too, depends almost wholly on industry sources for information about what's going on. Congress is in the same bind.

The only experts in how much oil and gas exist in the world, and where, are those who actually sink holes to find out. The U.S. Geological Survey doesn't do this. Neither do Department of Energy bureaucrats or members of Congress. Obviously, those in the oil and gas business do drill wells and they have a great deal of data. But they prefer to keep it secret, and they do keep most of it secret. Rawleigh Warner, Jr., chairman of the Mobil Corporation, was quite correct when he wrote to the editors of the New York *Times* that this is "a time when facts, and not villains, are badly needed." But the reason the public, and some members of Congress, were so understandably willing to make villains of the oil companies in the 1970s was because the oil companies so blatantly made every effort to suppress facts. And they were successful.

In 1974, Representative John Dingell of Michigan complained that energy policy was being made in "a total vacuum" of reliable data and that it was impossible to determine whether the oil shortage was "fact or fiction," because federal officials who should have been trying to collect reliable data had "completely delegated their responsibility to the oil industry."

In 1977, when the White House was trying to move Congress to vote on the natural gas bill, Senator John Durkin of New Hampshire said the information he was getting from industry and the bureaucracy left him totally baffled as to whether we "are running out of natural gas, or swimming in it . . . We sit here today like map makers of centuries ago, attempting to chart unseen lands by relying on secondhand information."

He had cause to complain. One official at the Energy Research and Development Administration had just finished a study showing that there would be plenty of affordable natural gas for at least the next forty years. But since this conflicted with the gloomy forecast currently pushed by industry, his superiors killed his study and replaced it with one more nearly attuned to the industry's viewpoint.

The runaround, and the complaints about it, were constant. Representative Bob Eckhardt of Texas, then chairman of the House Commerce Subcommittee on Investigations, complained in 1979, "The Department of Energy relies solely on information it pumps from the companies, and that's one hell of a hard pumping job. The information DOE gets is always at least two or three months old. Congress goddamn well isn't going to make sensible decisions concerning problems it's facing right now on information that old. I've been pressing hard to get monthly crude production figures out of DOE and they've been trying to get the figures from industry. That should be simple to get, but here it is August and they've just now managed to get March's figures for me. And the preliminary information the companies hand out is way off. Their preliminary figures may be as much as 10 percent at variance with the facts. You can't work intelligently with stuff like that. Even an error of 5 percent makes a hell of difference."

Deep in the twisted bowels of the Department of Energy, at a level Dante would not have bothered listing, is the Energy Information Administration; its Financial Reporting System carries a mandate from Congress to collect from the oil companies their record of profits, investments, cost of exploration and production, and so forth. But when the Energy Information Administration goes to the industry and asks for sensitive details that would be really useful, the oilmen take the bureaucrats to court and fight for their secrecy. It's a tough way to get the full picture.

The upshot of all this was that when Congress was confronted with such questions as whether or not to deregulate natural gas or whether to permit the President to decontrol the price of oil, it had to base its judgment on only such information as the target industry would release.

Because they are using statistics that are grotesquely unreliable and subject to the economic whimsy of the oil industry, government officials have racked up an almost perfect record of inaccurate predictions. In 1970 the President's cabinet group studying oil imports concluded that if the import quota system was phased out rapidly, the U.S. and Canadian oil industry (it was fair to think of them as a unit, since about 75 percent of Canada's oil was controlled by U.S. companies) would be so productive that in 1980 it would be able to supply 92 percent of those two nations' needs without rationing and more than 100 percent of their needs with rationing—*even if they were cut off from all, yes all, Middle Eastern and Latin American imports*. That was the prevailing wisdom in Washington as the decade opened, and it was a wisdom developed from the industry's own statistics. But, at the end of the decade that forecast was supposed to cover, the oil industrialists said they were helpless to meet America's demands without importing at least a third of its oil from abroad. The two positions simply could not be reconciled. Obviously, there had been such a manipulation of the market in the intervening years that neither the statistics of 1970 nor the statistics of 1980 had any usefulness at all.

***

Oilmen would continue to keep the government scared and ignorant through the 1970s, but they also took a new tack: heavy dependence on the real Madison Avenue stuff. As the 1960s came to a close, they began cranking up slick, heavyweight propaganda campaigns on specific economic issues—the kind of effort that, in 1969, saw them spend half a million dollars on advertisements defending the import quota system; but one-shot efforts such as that were clearly not enough. Although accustomed to being distrusted by a large part of the American people, the oil companies were nevertheless shocked by the intensity of the resentment they began to feel in 1969, and from that shock came the realization that they desperately needed a much costlier, broader, and more enduring propaganda drive than they had ever attempted before—a drive to sell, sell, sell themselves as the noble defenders of the American way of life, and they must do it with more ingenuity than they had shown in peddling their gasoline in the past. This time, premiums of tableware and balloons would not be enough. Interior Secretary Hickel told Louisiana oilmen on October 16 that they had been "so engrossed in selling your products to the people you have neglected to sell your industry to the people." M. T. Halbouty, one of Houston's best-known oil engineers and a former president of the American Association of Petroleum Geologists, gave a rousing speech in the fall of 1969 that was reprinted and widely distributed among oilmen. Halbouty warned that "Frankly, all of us took it for granted that our little red house would never be blown down by those howling wolves. So we find ourselves behind the eight ball . . . We see serious attacks being made on [tax loopholes and] other incentives. The mandatory import program is in trouble . . . The shortcoming in our own case has been a lack of communication with the people who really count in this country—the people who vote." American Petroleum Institute president Ikard predicted "a pretty substantial change" in the industry's image-building crusade.

The change was indeed very substantial. The year 1970 saw the real beginnings of Big Oil's new, giant advertising budgets—new in the sense that their millions began going more and more to brighten their image, rather than push a product. They presented themselves as corporations made up of thoughtful, humane, nature-loving, patriotic neighbors. Their money now began flooding into the support of public television programs (it finally reached the point that the Public Broadcasting System was cynically referred to as "petroleum broadcasting system"), of educational and highbrow programs on the major networks, of "idea" advertising in newspapers and magazines—advertising dealing with social and political issues, rather than clean rest rooms and no-knock gasoline. Before long, magazine pages would be blossoming with Texaco ads bubbling over with the good tidings: fish just *love* to swim around offshore oil rigs. Continental Oil Company would begin using quotes from Thomas Jefferson and Patrick Henry to promote the free-enterprise system.

Ruddick C. Lawrence, vice-president of Continental Oil Co., and former chairman of the API's Public Relations Advisory Committee, looking back from the propaganda peak of 1974 in an interview with Robert J. Samuelson, recalled, "The petroleum industry, by its very nature, has a lot of secrets that have to be kept close . . . You can't be as open as the dry goods business. But, as of 1970, we had an aggressive program to open up, to respond more openly and aggressively to press questions and to go out and meet the press . . . There are people in the industry—who came up through the production or exploration side—who had the tradition of being closed-mouth. They realize that this is a different world." Which was an accurate portrayal only by comparison. They were still *far* from openmouthed; but they were quickly learning the advantages of being so in a highly selective way. (And as will be seen during some of the most conflict-ridden years of the 1970s, even the more sophisticated oil companies were still subject to panicky lockjaw.)

Of all the oil companies turned propaganda machines, none was so imaginative as Mobil. Ultimately, Mobil would be spending about $20 million a year on propaganda and public relations of various sorts, which was no great shakes for a corporation with annual *net* profits of more than $2 billion, and it certainly did not make Mobil a more generous self-imagizer than, say, Exxon.

What made Mobil different was that it was so bold in its pitch and candid about what it was up to. Rawleigh Warner, Jr., was elected chairman and chief executive officer of Mobil in 1969. Warner, a liberal Republican of Princeton pedigree, was unusually flexible for a corporation boss. He sensed that it was a waste of time to go on buttering up just to grumpy conservatives, for, after all, they were already safely in pocket. He decided instead to beguile the Left and the Center with earnest little pep talks and lollipop entertainment. And so it came to pass that Mobil started spending millions for PBS's soap operas—the equivalent of an occupying army's distribution of candy and cigarets. Herman J. Schmidt, a top Mobil official, explained: "A reader sees a Mobil message, and associates it with Big Oil. So he may be wary. But he also associates it with the company that brings him *Upstairs, Downstairs*, so maybe he's a little more open-minded and a little more receptive." Another Mobil public relations official, Raymond D'Argenis, was even more forthright. "These programs," he said, "build enough acceptance to allow us to get tough on substantive issues."

For his toughest guy on substantive issues, Warner chose a young

Mobil labor relations lawyer named Herb Schmertz and elevated him to vice-president in charge of public relations. Warner thought Schmertz would be especially potent because although he was a thoroughgoing economic conservative, he knew how to run with the liberals and talk their line. His credentials were just the sort to give him safe-conduct into what Mobil once would have called enemy territory. He had helped in John F. Kennedy's 1960 presidential campaign, and he had taken time off from Mobil to work as an advance man for Robert Kennedy's 1968 campaign (Schmertz would take a leave from Mobil again in 1979 to set up Senator Edward Kennedy's presidential TV staff; Edward Kennedy had been, at least on the record, one of the most adamant opponents of all pro-oil legislation in recent years).

Schmertz was also invaluable as a propagandist, because, unlike most oilmen, he not only could see the industry's defects but would publicly and disarmingly admit a few of them. In the mid-1970s, I asked him why the oil crowd had been so late in modernizing its propaganda techniques. "It's very simple," he said. "For many years this industry relied on a small number of legislators to look out for the oil industry in the Congress of the United States. And you know who they were as well as I: Lyndon Johnson, Bob Kerr, Sam Rayburn, et cetera. Over the past several years the composition of the United States Congress has changed substantially. Senators and congressmen whose constituencies were not interested in the oil problem have gained a great deal of seniority and a great deal of control over the Senate and the House. At the same time, those legislators who came from areas that had oil constituencies died. This industry never figured that people die. Which may or may not tell you something about the industry." So, having failed to pay attention to what was going on, Schmertz continued, "this industry found itself with a very hostile group of legislators" and also confronted by "an enormous amount of public hostility" because of "the kind of business we're in, which makes us a marvelous sort of prototype for what a culprit should look like—we deal with very strange people around the world (I'm serious), we move a large amount of a very dirty product, hundreds of millions of barrels of it, and we move it by night (as well as by day), in ships that are alleged to be about to blow up at any moment, and we deal in a variety of currencies in numbers that boggle even our minds—so you put it all together and, let's face it . . . it's either us or the cop on the beat. And that's about the size of it. And in the process we've become paranoid."

It was quite captivating semicandor.

Schmertz is credited with shaping Mobil's plan to invade the editorial and op-ed pages of America's leading newspapers to launch a unique dialogue with opinion shapers. Planning the editorial blitz began in 1969, after environmentalists and tax reformers had had an especially good run at arousing some parts of the public and Congress to consider ways of making Big Oil behave. Just buying any old ad space wouldn't do the job Mobil had in mind. It didn't want its propaganda buried among commercial ads for nylon stockings and look-alike automobiles. It wanted its advertisements framed and set apart and treated with journalistic reverence, and it wanted this to happen in the most prestigious newspapers. Before he was through, Schmertz, or rather Mobil, virtually owned the lower-right-hand corner of the New York *Times*'s op-ed page. When an oil issue heated up in Congress, Mobil regularly bought idea ads in one hundred newspapers, and the group always included the Boston *Globe*, *The Wall Street Journal*, the Washington *Post*, the Chicago *Tribune*, and the Los Angeles *Times*. But it was the New York *Times* op-ed franchise that Mobil relished the most—right in there with the heavy thinkers, consuming more space, per appearance, than James Reston or Tom Wicker or William Safire.

The petroleum corporation as packaged thinker was being born.

Mobil's effort to present itself as the "intellectual" oil company aroused some resentment among other majors and drew some jabs from the press. *Fortune* magazine observed: "The virtue Mobil perceives in being regarded as 'different' is that it can more readily sell its case to the traditional critics of the oil industry. When it gets down to fundamentals, however, Mobil has no message substantially different from that of the rest of the oil industry, or indeed from that of large corporate enterprise in general."

Nevertheless, for all its pretentiousness and frequent deceit, Mobil displayed a brashness that even its critics had to grudgingly admire. It had the money to talk back, and it did so. In July 1973, for example, when numerous members of Congress were accusing Mobil (and other companies) of manipulating gasoline supplies to create shortages and higher prices, Mobil bought ads in the newspapers circulating in the congressional districts of all of its critics. The cost was more than $200,000.

It was in this preeminent role of soapbox crusader, of a corporation willing to put its mouth where its money was, that helped spark a revolution of sorts. Quicker than any other member of the industry, Mobil caught on that the First Amendment belongs to oil people too; and when that lesson finally penetrated the minds of all its peers, the age of oil propaganda, paid for by every major and many minor companies, was under way with a flood.

"Why should we go on taking the rap?"
THORNTON BRADSHAW, *president, Atlantic Richfield*

THE GREAT PUBLIC RELATIONS GESTURE

Solid proof that the oil industry ended the 1960s with a much more sophisticated concept of public relations could be seen in its handling of the 27½ percent oil depletion allowance—the notorious tax gimmick that developed, with later modifications, from the fright campaign of 1918 (see the Appendix entry on *EARLY FRIGHT CAMPAIGNS*).

Over the years, no corporate favoritism had infuriated onlookers nearly so much as that figure. It was a hated symbol, capable of raising the hackles of millions of Americans of all ideologies. Speaking for them in the 1969 debates over this issue was Senator Edward Kennedy: "In many respects, the 27½ percent depletion allowance for oil and gas is the single most flagrant loophole in our entire tax system. Indeed, I believe that one of the most significant achievements of the taxpayers' revolution this year has been its extraordinary success in focusing the spotlight of public opinion on this special tax preference that is available to the oil and gas industries. For the first time in many years, there is a real likelihood that the cause of reform will prevail, and that this notorious tax loophole will be closed."

That was a singularly distorted claim of strength. In fact, the insignificant change that would be made in the tax came not as the result of a taxpayers' revolution so much as it did from a high-level decision among oilmen to *let* the reform take place. Knowing that much more important issues would press down on them in the 1970s, the major oil companies decided, in the fashion of the legendary Russian escape (throwing a baby to the pursuing wolves so that the sleigh load of adults could buy time), that it would be expedient to sacrifice a small piece of one juicy tax item to appease momentarily "those howling wolves" whom Houston oilman M. T. Halbouty had identified. What would distract them the easiest? Why, a morsel of the 27½ percent, of course.

*

Looking back on it now, the liberals' passionate battle against the percentage depletion allowance seems somewhat overblown in importance even if it was thoroughly justified. Compared to such things as the "prorationing" system and the oil import quota and the horizontal monopoly of energy sources and the vertical monopoly of oil-industry functions, the depletion allowance was probably one of the lesser evils (probably even a lesser evil than other tax loopholes, such as the oil industry's foreign tax credit and the esoteric "expensing of intangibles," which most people outside the oil industry had never heard of).

But evil—if unjustness is evil—it certainly was. Congress has passed few pieces of special-interest legislation that made less sense, but it was so solidly in place that nothing seemed capable of shaking it. Opponents fought it with logic and sarcasm. Senator Richard Neuberger of Oregon, for example, proposed that if oil companies got special treatment for selling off their oil, then people over the age of forty-five should get special tax deductions too, because "a locomotive engineer's eyes, a schoolteacher's frayed nerves, a day laborer's legs, an author's brain . . . wear out, also . . . We should have a depletion allowance for people."

Accepting such bitter humor in the spirit of a true martyr, the oil industry argued that critics simply didn't realize that the depletion allowance was a necessary incentive to keep our nation strong and independent, that without the incentive of this tax break, oilmen could not afford to take the heavy risk of looking for more oil. That was the key word, *risk*, and nobody used it so frequently as executives of the major oil companies, who enjoyed pretending that they were of the old wildcatting breed—a breed that had produced such stubborn gamblers as D. H. "Dry Hole" Byrd, who drilled fifty-six dry holes in a row, and Michael L. Benedum, who spent seven years drilling nothing but dry holes before making the marvelous Yates Field discovery, in Pecos County, Texas.

One might have gotten the impression that Bob Dorsey, president of Gulf, was that kind of wildcatter, for he argued that "About one time in ten, those investing in wildcat drilling will find oil, but only about one in fifty has a favorable return on that kind of investment. Yet such investments have been made possible because of . . . percentage depletion."

In fact, the Dorseys of the oil world are a different breed. They let the independent oilmen take most of the risks, and then follow with sure-thing drilling. In his 1969 review of the depletion allowance, Ronnie Dugger showed how misleading it was for the majors to use Dorsey's argument: "The often used one-in-ten . . . figure, however, applies to new-field wildcat wells, which make up only a seventh of the wells drilled. The success ratio is higher for every other type of well . . . Three out of four of the development wells, which drain proven fields, are successful. The majors drill mostly development wells . . . It is the independents who do most of the exploratory drilling, 85 percent of it . . . Yet the depletion allowance goes in overwhelming bulk to the majors, not the independents, and it rewards not discoveries, but pumping oil out of the ground. For a dry hole, you get nothing."

Efforts to eliminate or reduce the depletion allowance had met regular defeats in Congress. In 1950, President Truman said no tax loophole was "so inequitable" and he cited the shocking example of one oilman who built a tax-free income of almost $5 million. Truman said he favored cutting the benefit to 15 percent, but liberals in Congress said he gave them little support in their effort to cut it. President Eisenhower made no effort at all to change the depletion allowance. Amendments offered, variously, by Senators Douglas, Williams (Delaware), Proxmire, and Humphrey to reduce the allowance to 21 percent or 15 percent, or to give the allowance only to oilmen with incomes below a certain level (the particulars of their bills changed from time to time) were defeated in 1951, 1954, 1958, 1962, 1964, and 1967. The most votes they could muster, prior to 1969, was thirty-five, in 1964.

The typical delaying tactic was to do another "study" of the problem. A hostile reporter once asked Douglas Dillon, who had close ties to oil before joining Kennedy's Cabinet as Treasury Secretary, what his attitude was toward the oil depletion allowance. He is reported to have replied, "We have studied that matter at some length. We probably have not studied it enough. I do not know how to study it enough."

And so things rocked along until 1969, when critics of the program once again became unusually rude. In a letter to House Ways and Means Committee Chairman Wilbur Mills on July 10 (and simultaneously released to the press), Congressman Bertram Podell (New York)—after pointing out that Gulf Oil had paid only .81 percent in federal taxes on nearly a billion dollars income the previous year; Mobil paid 3.3 percent; Atlantic Richfield paid 1.2 percent, et cetera—hailed the industry's "passionate devotion to old-fashioned virtues, such as greed," declared that the "oil industry makes the Mafia look like a pushcart operation," and that "through our various tax loopholes, professional tax evaders like the oil industry churn like panzers over foot soldiers."

Congressman Charles Vanik (Ohio), a House Ways and Means watchdog, pointed out that the percentage depletion allowance had cost taxpayers $140 billion in lost taxes since its beginnings.

Increasingly there was criticism of the program's rationale: incentive to find more oil to make America stronger. A study financed by the U.S. Treasury and conducted by the Consad Research Corp., of Pittsburgh, a private think tank specializing in economic issues, showed that it was costing the taxpayers $11 in lost taxes to get $1 in new oil reserves. (When Consad's study was sent to the Treasury, oil bureaucrats first tried to bury it and then tried to discount it as a botched job.)

Obviously, the depletion allowance in its most easily identified form—27½ percent—had become a gold-plated albatross; and so it came to pass that many executives of the majors were willing at last to give up part of it, perhaps a few feathers, as an easy price to pay for better public relations.[1]

As early as May 1969, Ways and Means Chairman Mills was saying publicly what his chums in oil were saying privately, that 27½ was "symbolic" and that the industry would be doing itself a favor if it allowed the percentage to be trimmed slightly.

Big Oil's tactics became clearer when a motion to cut the depletion allowance from 27½ percent to 20 percent was made by none other than Congressman Hale Boggs of Louisiana. With only a token show of resistance, oil's legislators permitted it to slide right on through.

This was the first step in preparation for the "sting." But there was one slight stumble before the con men got their signals worked out perfectly. Nixon had repeatedly stated during the 1968 campaign that he favored retaining the 27½ percent allowance. Now he would have to modify that position. On August 28, Senator John Tower, the Texas Republican, and Congressman George Bush of Texas, whose family had helped create Zapata Oil Co., flew to San Clemente to consult with Nixon on the changes that would satisfy the industry.

A few hours later, Treasury Secretary David M. Kennedy joined them in San Clemente to get Nixon's instructions on what he was to say when he appeared before the Senate Finance Committee on September 4. Either Nixon or Kennedy got his instructions mixed up. Kennedy testified that while Nixon would prefer to keep the 27½ percent, he would accept 20 percent. No, no, no—*that* wasn't what Tower and Bush had told Nixon to say. He was supposed to say that he would accept *whatever Congress passed*. Sure, the House favored a cut to 20 percent. (It would pass the bill on October 7 by a vote of 394 to 30—with Congressman Bush voting for the cut.) But the industry didn't really want it to go that low, and

---

1. Albatross is the word Thornton Bradshaw, president of Atlantic Richfield, fourth-largest producer of domestic oil, would use four years later. ARCO, in December 1973, became the first oil producer to come out in favor of *totally* eliminating the tax write-off. Bradshaw called it "an albatross around our necks." It was useful once, he said, but no longer useful enough to compensate for "taking the rap." He said, "The problem, now . . . is that the oil industry has a poor public image partly because of pollution and partly because of profits. The public thinks all oil companies make much too much money . . . We have got to get some credibility with the public, or else the public might decide it doesn't need the private oil industry anymore." Eliminating the oil depletion allowance, Bradshaw said, would be one way of restoring credibility. Naturally, Robert O. Anderson, ARCO's board chairman, agreed in every way: "The oil depletion allowance once had validity and good purpose, but unfortunately it has become an absolute battlefield for the industry."

Which isn't to say that ARCO's sentiments were universally shared by its heavy-weight peers; ARCO always did have more sensitivity for public relations than some of the companies that were given too much credit for being PR-oriented simply because they spent big bucks on public television.

Senator Russell Long, himself an oil producer,[2] certainly had no intention of going that low, as he made abundantly clear when he permitted his Finance Committee, on October 24, to pass a bill cutting the allowance only to 23 percent. So, to prepare the way for a Longish compromise, Nixon was supposed to step back and say simply that he would accept whatever came to his desk. Well, no great harm had been done. The slip was correctable. Nixon's deputy counsel Harry S. Dent promptly wrote a letter to a Midland, Texas, county judge (with the letter leaked to the press) saying that Treasury Secretary Kennedy was in error about favoring 20 percent and that "the President will abide by the judgment of Congress."

Long's 23 percent position was feared by true reformers because, as one of them, Martin Lobel, Senator Proxmire's legislative assistant, pointed out, "If the committee cuts back the depletion allowance by a modest amount—say to 23 percent—it may present a low enough profile that Senate liberals will have a more difficult time cutting it further."

This was exactly what the majors and Long had in mind. The conference committee cut the allowance to 22 percent—only one point below Long's figure—and in lopsided votes both houses, with the tacit blessing of the majors, accepted the legislation.

After the dust had settled and unwitting liberals had finished their victory celebration, it was noted that in fact the reform would make little difference, for the *effective* depletion allowance (because of smaller profit margins for the independents) had been running at about 23 percent all along, not 27½ percent. If Congress had accepted the House's 20 percent, the additional taxes on the entire oil industry (according to American Petroleum Institute figuring) would have come to only $550 million a year—a mere trifle. At 23 percent, the additional taxes were hardly worth talking about: $175 million a year.

The important result was that the symbol was gone, and the pressure was gone with it, at least for a while. The majors were pretty smug about their victory. Emilio G. Collado, Exxon's executive vice-president, estimated that the loss of 5½ percentage points of "incentive" would have no effect whatsoever on oil production for at least the next five years, if ever. And Exxon's Michael Haider added, "Of course we can live with the new taxes. We obviously aren't going out of business."

---

2. Senator Long inherited the bulk of his oil holdings from his father, Huey, the populist governor and senator who was assassinated in 1935. The family company originally carried the colorful name Win or Lose Corporation. Long always won. In 1969, reporter Patrick Riordan estimated that Long's income from his petroleum-based portfolio came to more than $420,000. That's just a good, educated guess, since the Louisiana Mineral Board refused to divulge information about state leases that the law required it to divulge. Naturally, Mr. Long favored the depletion allowance, but, as was his fashion, he claimed there was nothing selfish about his actions. He said he just wanted "to protect Grandma Jones's little $20 dividend."

SHOWTIME
THE '70S

"The problem of industry credibility has been so severe that many people believe that our mistakes are intentional . . ."

CHARLES DIBONA, *president, American Petroleum Institute*

This was the year that the terrible-tempered Colonel Qaddafi showed his brethren in OPEC that the supposedly unbeatable oil companies could indeed be beaten until they whimpered.

This was also the year that these same oil companies subjected the United States to what might be called, for the sake of a pun, a traumatic "dry run" of multiple shortages—in fuel oil, in natural gas, in coal. After going through months of painful suspense, thinking that the upcoming winter would see some utility plants, factories, and buildings without the energy needed to turn machines and heat offices, the nation came out of the year unscathed. The threat had vanished in a great puff of profits for the oil companies.

To what extent had the threat of shortages been real, and to what extent was the threat merely the stuff of propaganda, inflated by fear far beyond its true dimensions, part of a conspiracy aimed at winning more political strength and more money? These were not questions raised by hairy environmentalists and shrill consumer organizations, but by some very staid and proper establishmentarians. From one such person, ensconced in the very bosom of the Nixon Cabinet, that uniquely candid gentleman George P. Shultz (first Nixon's Labor Secretary, then head of the Office of Management and Budget, then Secretary of the Treasury, and, as we have already seen, chairman of the Cabinet Task Force on Oil Imports), came the admission in 1970 that "there is a danger" that "either [due] to overreaction" to some government program or for a "deliberate purpose . . . exploration might be artificially reduced" by the oil industry. He said he believed "the industry is capable of behaving irrationally for short periods, and even of contriving an apparent disaster by . . . dramatically revising its reserve conditions downward, and closing up intramarginal properties perpetually, and so on." And he went on to say that the government was really powerless, as things were then set up, to protect itself from the industry's fake shortages. "We have no assured means of preventing overreaction or downward manipulation, nor is it clear how the administration would distinguish between a fake disaster and a real one."

Industry spokesmen were terribly offended at the suggestion the shortages might be faked and manufactured. But, at the same time, they were quite frank to admit that the "shortages" were *not* natural, but man-made. However, they claimed that the men who made the shortages were not in the oil industry but were politicians and bureaucrats who had cooked up and stubbornly insisted on administering the wrong programs, programs that prevented the industry from charging anything it wanted to charge and drilling for oil anywhere it wanted to drill. The oil and gas fellows were charmingly open about it, and so ingenuous as not to realize that it sounded a great deal like blackmail when they said that if the public wanted more fuel, if it wanted to avoid the threat of shortages, then the public should persuade Washington to give the oilmen carte blanche. They were fed up with price controls on natural gas, with the federal government's caution in leasing offshore lands, and with the new environmental laws that were slowing the construction of nuclear utilities and blocking the use of sulfur-heavy coal and retarding the search for oil in such ecologically sensitive areas as Alaska.

In a little speech to a group of Capitol Hill friends in September 1970, API president Frank Ikard admitted that the industry's claim of an energy shortage would be difficult for the public to swallow. "The 'energy crisis' is much in the news these days, and its existence must be both a surprise and a puzzle to many Americans. They have been told that their nation has almost inconceivably large deposits of coal in the ground. They have read reports of huge potential reserves of oil and natural gas remaining to be discovered. They have heard many glowing predictions about the future of nuclear energy in power generation. To the public the energy crisis must seem a strange and paradoxical instance of scarcity in the midst of abundance. However, the energy crisis certainly does exist. It has been brought about by a complex combination of factors and forces," which he listed as too much federal interference, too much concern for the environment, and too little profit. Turn the industry loose, "give it a fair profit, that's all we ask," he said, and the shortages would evaporate quickly.

"To get that fair chance," he went on, "we will have to get the facts about our industry . . . before the public of the consuming states . . . We are trying to get the facts spread out in such a way that no one can ignore them or evade them."[1] By that, he said, he meant the "entire pe-

---

1. One of the most plaintive echoes of this theme was made the next year by G. J. Tankersley, chairman of the American Gas Association and president of the East Ohio Gas Company: "With the story we have to tell, it is nothing less than a tragedy that we are not better heard, understood, and recognized as the vital consumer and environmental improvement force that we, in fact, are." Just exactly what was the story the AGA had to tell? Tankersley explained: "Consumers must understand that natural gas . . . is in fact a premium fuel whose price has been artificially kept below that of other fuels. *This is the crisis.*" (Emphasis added)

troleum industry" is "mapping its plans" to continue the propaganda drive that had been launched in '69. Although this included lush advertisements expounding the industry's love of nature and its lavish effort to control its own pollution, much of the drive was aimed at whipping up an awareness of what Herb Schmertz, Mobil's propaganda chief, called the public's "lack of understanding" of the "energy crisis." Correcting this deficiency was achieved via one of the industry's familiar fright campaigns.

This campaign is easily traced in the Readers' Guide to Periodical Literature. From March 1968 to February 1969 (this twelve-month period is used merely as a sample, but in fact one may go back for several years with the same results), the Readers' Guide listed not one magazine article on the topic of energy shortage. Then, suddenly, articles on the prospect of "crisis" exploded in print, especially in magazines that can be counted on to give industry a helping hand: *Business Week, Nation's Business, U.S. News & World Report, Fortune,* and *Forbes.* In the *next* twelve months, the industry's publicists really got the press's range, with no less than twenty-five articles in the magazines indexed by the Readers' Guide (to say nothing of the dozens of articles in publications not indexed there). Now America was subjected to headlines such as "LOOMING CRISIS IN NATURAL GAS," "SCROUNGING FOR FUEL," "IS THE CUPBOARD BARE?" et cetera. Usually the articles were replete with messages aimed at persuading the public that controls should be relaxed and prices increased. Typical was "U.S. Moves Toward a Fuel Crisis," in the August 24, 1970, *U.S. News & World Report,* in which Charles Primoff, chief of the fuels and energy division of the White House Office of Emergency Preparedness, was quoted as blaming the new clean air laws ("Environment is a principal reason for this sudden plunge into fuel scarcity") and John D. Emerson, of the energy-economics division of the Chase Manhattan Bank, proclaimed, "The days of artificially low energy costs are drawing to a close."

The expertise of the new public relations crowd would reach a peak of aggressiveness, if not sophistication, at Continental Oil Company. Selecting fifty members of The Society of Magazine Writers, Conoco's head publicist sent out a large packet of "sample" articles and "suggested topics" and a letter in which he offered to help the magazine writers do industry-oriented articles. The letter promised: "We'll even do typing, editing and proofing for you, if you like! And in certain instances we'll arrange transportation" on Conoco planes that happened to be going in the right direction. Some of the material from Conoco had to do with the "energy crisis."

But magazine writers weren't the only target, nor even the most important. Now too, the industry's publicists began to find a very sympathetic ear at such potent newspapers as the New York *Times,* the Washington *Post,* and the Los Angeles *Times.*

One of the interesting articles of the period appeared in the Sunday, July 26, 1970, New York *Times* financial section under an eight-column picture of an oil tanker and the headline "U.S. Oil Industry Regrets It Was Right." The gist of the piece, written by William D. Smith, was that if the oil industry had a face, it would be "wearing a bittersweet smile . . . because some of its serious forecasts and urgent warnings have proved correct." The "warnings" had to do with claimed shortages and with the insecurity of foreign imports. Smith's piece pleased oil-oriented senators so much that they inserted it into the Congressional Record not once but *four* times. However, a writer for *The Washington Monthly,* Richard Karp, judged the piece to be "consistently misleading, flatly false in some places, and little different on the whole from oil industry journals." After ticking off what he considered to be glaring errors, Karp asked: "How does it happen that a member of the public press serves the oil industry so well? In an interview with Karp, Smith explained it this way: 'I know that some of my data may have been a little imprecise. I had to slap the article together in an afternoon. I was working on a short piece about natural gas when my editor told me he needed a lead story with a big picture for the next day. I don't remember where I got some of the facts, but if you think someone planted them on me, I doubt it.' When asked if he had interviewed any people who might be considered oil critics, Smith replied, 'No, antioil people don't come up here badgering us to get their points of view across; the industry does. My job is to report about the industry; other reporters down in Washington get the government's story. I interview the president of Standard Oil of New Jersey; he gives me the party line and it is my job to quote him.' "

***

As soon as the Oil Import Task Force's recommendations to scuttle the import program began to leak out, in December 1969, the industry had gone to work vigorously to prevent Nixon's adopting the recommendations—if, though doubtful, this was even a remote possibility. By January, the pressures were blatant and undisguised. On January 8, on a letterhead giving his own name and the street address of his oil company's New York City offices, Kerryn King, vice-president of Texaco for public relations, mailed a "Dear Friend" solicitation for money to help "financially deserving candidates" for governorships and for the House and Senate. His pitch in the letter was that "it is almost incredible that many congressmen are willing to sacrifice the national security of this country to the siren song of low-cost foreign oil." How many other oil executives were twisting pocketbooks for the 1970 campaigns was a matter of speculation. But it was well known that the industry was primarily depending on repayment for past favors, especially those done to Nixon. An industry source told Murray Seeger, of the Los Angeles *Times,* "It is no secret that the oil industry supplied much of the Nixon campaign financing. This has been brought to the attention of the Administration." Seeger reported that if Nixon showed any wavering, "two congressional committees headed by friends of the oil industry are preparing to step into the dispute as soon as a presidential task force makes its report on the 10-year-old quota system. The committees, it was learned, will accuse the task force of being biased against the industry, of neglecting the future needs for natural gas and of weakening American security as represented by a strong domestic oil industry. By stepping into the controversy quickly, the committees will allow the White House to delay taking any action on the task force report . . ."

This strategy was not needed. Nixon had his own plans for stalling. On February 20, the White House released the 400-page report. In it, the task force proposed everything that the oil crowd had feared: that the quota system be phased out, and the amount of foreign oil used by U.S. refiners be limited only by the importer's willingness to pay proposed tariffs.

It urged that a tariff of $1.45 a barrel be placed on the least-secure oil from the Middle East, that a $1.25 tariff be placed on Venezuelan oil, and that Canadian and Mexican oil be allowed to enter the country tariff-free. The tariff would, the task force majority predicted, result in a decline of 30 cents in the price of domestic crude, bringing it down to $3.00 a barrel, short-term, and ultimately would drop domestic oil to $2.00, the world price, thus saving consumers many billions.

To be sure, the seven-member panel did not make its suggestions with one voice. Two members—Interior Secretary Walter Hickel and Commerce Secretary Maurice Stans—opposed virtually every point in the report. And even among the five majority members, all was not harmony; Secretary of State William Rogers and Secretary of Defense Melvin Laird wanted to delay making the changes until our economic allies had been consulted, as a matter of protocol; and Treasury Secretary David Kennedy and Office of Economic Priorities (OEP) director George Lincoln, though they signed the report without reluctance, would have preferred a minor alteration here and there in the proposals. In fact, only the task force chairman, Shultz, advocated swift and unequivocal implementation of the changes. Nevertheless, though there was some waffling in the traditional task force fashion, the count was still a solid 5 to 2 and, equally impressive, the majority included the men who spoke most influentially on national security matters, the Secretaries of State and Defense. How could the import quotas possibly be continued on national security grounds? Wasn't that question now settled once and for all? Not for President Nixon it wasn't; 5 to 2 or no 5 to 2, Nixon sided with the minority—and that was the end of that.

Simultaneously with the release of the task force report, he announced that he would postpone indefinitely any "major" change in the quota system. From all the task force recommendations, Nixon chose to adopt only the blandest one: that he create a new Oil Policy Committee within the Administration. He liked that idea very much, for it would give him a chance to delay further decisions until the Oil Policy Committee studied and studied and studied and restudied the problem that the task force had just spent most of 1969 studying, while listening to testimonies that filled ten thousand pages.

The new Oil Policy Committee, Nixon announced, would be composed of Secretary of State Rogers, Secretary of Defense Laird, Treasury Secretary Kennedy, Interior Secretary Hickel, Commerce Secretary Stans, Attorney General Mitchell, Council of Economic Advisers Chairman Paul W. McCracken, and OEP director Lincoln. Lincoln would be chairman.

There was a clear message in that lineup. The old task force was all present—except for its chairman, Shultz, who had been the stubbornest and most eloquent advocate of its report and who had wanted to drive oil prices down faster and twice as far as other members. He was gone.

In his place was Attorney General Mitchell. The new committee was expected to pay more attention to Mitchell's earlier request that Nixon not be "boxed in."

Industry had won once more, and knew it. L. R. Forker, president of Quaker State Oil Refining Corporation, said, "It sure is good news. My guess is she [the task force recommendations] is sure dead for a year." He was sure right.

* * *

But Nixon's action also had an accidentally beneficial side. Some of the experts who had talked to the task force privately felt insulted that their advice had been brushed aside so offhandedly by the President; now some of these experts were willing to step forward and say publicly what they had previously said behind closed doors, and what they said did not exactly burnish the oil industry's reputation.

The hoary national security argument, for example, was shredded by the most authoritative voices in the Pentagon.

Most impressive of all was Barry J. Shillito, assistant secretary of defense for installations and logistics. He testified on March 9, 1970, before the House Subcommittee on Mines and Mining, chaired by Congressman Ed Edmondson of Oklahoma. It was, to say the least, a hostile environment—hostile, that is, to any proponent of an end to the quotas. But Shillito held firm (as did the two Pentagon officials accompanying him, Paul Riley, deputy assistant secretary of defense for supply and services, and Richard T. Mathews, special assistant for petroleum).

Shillito opened by laying a groundwork of the obvious: Oil was considered "a strategic material and one of the few items that is absolutely essential and foremost in the minds of military commanders. Along with weapons and ammunition, petroleum receives maximum attention." Moreover, it is an essential war material with its special problems. "Petroleum cannot be stockpiled like hardware—the quantities required are too great." Or at least it cannot be stockpiled in any comforting quantities.

The Pentagon's dependence on oil was written in the budget. Since 1949 the military's consumption had more than tripled (from 330,000 barrels a day to 1.2 million barrels a day). Military equipment was becoming more gluttonous. The supersonic fighter planes of 1970 burned two or three times more fuel than the jet fighters of the Korean war. The mechanization of the Army's land equipment, too, was calling for more oil. "The Department of Defense oil bill for fiscal year 1969 was over $1.9 billion. We are the world's largest single oil purchaser. Success or failure in any conflict hinges on oil."

So if any agency of government had good cause to show excessive caution about importing oil that might jeopardize U.S. oil production, it was the Pentagon. Yet the men who seemed from time to time so willing to detect missile gaps and megatonnage gaps and silo gaps and submarine gaps and radar gaps were refusing by 1970, to the great consternation of the oil industry, to go along further with the pretense of a potential fuel gap. Something in their warrior hearts apparently rebelled at the thought of being exploited as part of this particular commercial ploy. They may have tolerated the use of quasi-military arguments to establish the import restrictions originally, but from now on the oil merchants would have to carry that argument on their own, for the Pentagon position as stated by Shillito was that "the [oil import] quota system, actually as it developed, as it operates, really bears no reasonable relationship to national security."

One by one, Shillito demolished the various "crisis" potentials:

Even if *all* foreign sources of oil were cut off, he said, "the military needs of the nation in an emergency are such a small fraction of total domestic consumption that oil supply for the Armed Forces is very unlikely to be placed in jeopardy. For example, although our military demand increased almost 30 percent during the Vietnam buildup (1965–68), the percentage of military to total U.S. demand during the same period increased only 0.8 percent, that is, from 7.3 to 8.1 percent."

There was a time when the buildup of a war wrought havoc to the oil supply. World War II was the perfect example. At the beginning of that conflict, he said, military demand was around forty thousand barrels a day, or only 1.1 percent of U.S. production; but when we really got the tanks and planes in motion, the military consumption rose to 1.6 million barrels a day, or 33 percent of U.S. production. A mere conventional war would never again disturb us in that fashion, however, for the simple if unpleasant reason that we had never got *off* a war footing in our petroleum use. Even in peacetime our military forces were using oil in quantities such as they would in a conventional war. Shifting from the pretended to the actual would bring no jolt.

Nuclear war? Oh, yes indeed, if there were an atomic war, the fuel supply would be disrupted, as life itself would be disrupted. Shillito admitted that, but, with wonderful wryness, added: "If a large-scale nuclear exchange did occur, the continuity of oil supply would not likely be a matter of major significance." With no machinery left to operate, little oil would be needed. "It is considered probable that production of crude oil would be in excess of actual consumption in a shattered economy in the aftermath of a nuclear exchange."

As for a general nonnuclear war between America and another superpower, with submarine and air power interrupting tanker shipments for months, that posed no great threat. Looking as far into the future as the needs of 1980 and predicating their estimates on the very worst conditions (*absolutely no oil importable from the Middle East or Latin America for up to one year*), Pentagon analysts believed that "only about 8 percent of the United States and Canadian demand" would be left "unmet, a deficit well within rationing potential."[2]

Much more likely than either a nuclear or a nonnuclear war as a cause for interrupting the foreign oil supply was a *politically* inspired interruption, said Shillito—with the sheikhs of Saudi Arabia turning sullen, or the Shah of Iran going sour, etc.—the kind of oil insecurity that had already been experienced several times, as when the Arabs closed the Suez Canal in 1965 and 1967 and when they refused temporarily to allow U.S. companies to pump their oil because our foreign policy favored Israel.

It would undoubtedly happen again. But if it did, Shillito implied, so what? What if the Middle East threw an enormous, economically suicidal tantrum and closed down all its wells? Europe would suffer, and so would Japan. But the Western Hemisphere would roll merrily along; and even if Venezuela had to ship all its oil to stricken Europe and Japan, leaving the United States and Canada to fend for themselves, we would not even notice anything was amiss.

Shillito pointed out that the United States was then getting only 3 per-

---

2. This prediction by the Pentagon, said Shillito, was based on the assumption that the oil import program would be phased out gently enough to permit domestic producers to adjust. If the import system were lopped off so suddenly as to send the domestic market into a tailspin, then, he said, domestic production might be hurt enough that in the above hypothetical situation the unmet demand in the United States and Canada would be 21 percent, not 8 percent.

cent of its oil from the Mideast—none of which was actually necessary; it was a margin that could be easily made up with a little extra pumping in Texas.[3] With the United States and Canada capable of producing 92 percent of the oil they needed, life without a drop of Middle Eastern oil could go on quite nicely with only a tiny bit of civilian rationing.

In the face of such optimism on the part of the Pentagon, it was difficult to continue the national-security pretense.

But inasmuch as national security was, as both sides agreed, the *only* legal basis for the establishment and perpetuation of the import system, the pretense had to be continued, one way or another, and it was plain that what was needed immediately was some kind of overseas crisis to underscore once again the unreliability of Middle Eastern oil. Looking back on the oil debate over the years, it is quite remarkable how many times a "crisis"—an "interruption" or "shortage"—popped up in the Middle East just when it was needed to bolster the oil companies' arguments.

Once again, the Middle East would not let them down.

*

But first President Nixon took a step that seemed very queer indeed but which, if a shortage was needed to frighten the public, was in fact a logical precursor to the Middle Eastern action. In April, he imposed—for the first time in history—an oil import restriction on the flow of Canadian oil into this country. Why would he want to do that? If national security was the paramount consideration, it was plain that Canadian oil, being as secure as our own oil, should be welcomed and production in Canada should be encouraged, not discouraged with border restrictions. The previous year, Canadian Government officials had gone to Washington with a brilliant proposal. They had suggested that their country and our country look upon the energy supplies of both countries as unified. They proposed that the United States and Canada pursue not nationalistic energy policies but a continental energy policy. Canada's government asked for unrestricted access to U.S. markets as the best way to encourage the development of Canada's vast oil and gas resources. In short, they asked that Washington accept the view (as the New York *Times* put it on May 17, 1969, with editorial approval) "that Canadian oil reserves are as much a part of the United States strategic resources as Texas and Louisiana." (Four years later, U.S. officials would be begging Canada to revive this idea, but by then Canada would have retreated into a nationalistic development of their resources, recognizing that the United States, like the Middle East, was too politically unreliable to count on.)

---

3. Of course Shillito could not have foreseen—nobody in our government foresaw—the enormous leap in dependence on foreign oil, and especially Middle Eastern oil, that was to take place in the next four or five years—a plunge into dependency that remains something of a mystery.

Not only was the Canadian proposal rejected, but Canada's oil shipments to the United States were placed under the quota system.[4]

This, of course, made the United States all the more dependent on Middle Eastern oil and helped set the stage for a "shortage," which followed within a few weeks.

❖

On May 3, a bulldozer cut through the Trans Arabian pipeline— whether by accident or design has never been determined—and put the pipeline out of service. Normally the line moved 475,000 barrels of crude oil a day from Saudi Arabia across Syria to the eastern Mediterranean. It could have been repaired within a few hours, but for some reason the Syrian Government refused for months to permit pipeline company personnel to come into the country to make repairs; pressure by our government on Syria to change its mind seemed strangely absent.

Shortly thereafter, the new government of Libya, the government headed by the slightly berserk revolutionary Qaddafi, ordered production cutbacks, which eventually reached some 780,000 barrels a day (about 15 percent of Libya's output).

Together, these reductions meant that about 1.2 million barrels of oil, which normally would have moved the relatively short distance across the Mediterranean to European ports, was no longer moving; it was instead being replaced with an equal amount of Persian Gulf oil that (because the Suez was closed) had to be shipped around the Cape of Good Hope, a trip that takes six to eight times as long as the Mediterranean crossing. As a result, the demand on the world tanker pool was increased by about 7 percent and, since there was at that time little spare shipping capacity, the increased demand was translated into tanker shortages and soaring prices for individual ship charters. *Some* of the oil that had cost only $1 a barrel to ship from the Persian Gulf in May was costing $3 to haul by September.

In the import debate, this was, for the oil companies, a fortuitous development. Although nothing had happened to change the cheapness of Middle East oil at the source (it was still being pumped for virtually nothing: 5 to 15 cents a barrel), the increase in spot tanker charges could be whooped up and exclaimed over by the companies as a way to suggest—quite falsely—that it was much more costly to bring in Middle East oil than to buy domestically, and therefore it was uneconomical for the United States to increase imports. For instance, oil's faithful troubadour Senator Clifford Hansen of Wyoming said that the cheap Middle

---

4. The task force had based all its assumptions on an integrated U.S.-Canadian oil system. As Secretary Shultz said, "We consider the two countries together because of the existence of an integrated transportation network and the likelihood that we would consult closely together during a future crisis as we have in the past."

East oil "is now costing about 74 cents a barrel more delivered to East Coast ports than the delivered price of U.S. crude oil." He was telling the truth as far as he went, but he only went about 10 percent as far as he should have gone to give an accurate picture, for actually only about 10 percent of Mideast oil was being brought in on the expensive spot-charter tankers (90 percent of the world's tankers were owned outright by or were on long-term lease contracts to the major oil companies, and transportation on these vessels hadn't changed in cost).

Using the same false argument of tanker rates, API president Ikard went out of his way to stick it to his most vocal opponents in New England. "Protests against the present oil import quota system have come mainly from the East Coast and especially from the New England States. But think what a financial bind these states would be in today if they were completely dependent on what is currently that high cost foreign oil. It seems to me that this situation should encourage some second thoughts among those who want to do away with, or radically curtail, the oil import control system. For now we have proof that the low cost of foreign oil is no more dependable than the supply itself."

The reason oil industry spokesmen had to concentrate their propaganda on the northeastern states was that this was the only region suffering from the interruption of supplies. In fact, it was the only region that was at that time truly vulnerable. Later in the decade, any significant cutback in foreign imports would hurt the entire country. But in 1970 the United States drew only 3 percent of its crude oil from the Middle East and North Africa, and the unpleasantries then being experienced in Libya and Syria crimped only 1 percent of our national needs. The northeastern states, however, were a different matter indeed.

But, for industry's spokesmen to constantly refer to the plight of East Coast users as proof of "what happens when you become dependent on foreign suppliers" was rather hypocritical, inasmuch as the oil companies themselves had forced the East Coast, and especially New England, into this dependency. Like drug pushers, the oil companies had hooked eastern consumers on foreign residual oil and then, to force prices up, had cut down on the supply.

The story of how the East Coast became hooked in this way tells a lot about the complexities from which our national troubles grew. As mentioned earlier, oil companies operating in the Middle East and North Africa increased production so much after World War II that there was a serious problem of what to do with it all. The majors didn't want to glut the United States with it, thereby undercutting prices in their most profitable market, so they persuaded Eisenhower to set a quota on oil imports to keep it out of the United States, and at the same time they turned to developing the European market, which was trying to build its way out of the war's rubble. To handle the flood of cheap Middle East-

ern and African oil, most of the majors' postwar refineries were built *not*
in the United States but in Europe. For many years, this did not put us
at a disadvantage.

But then—because of one of the lowliest products of the refinery process: residual fuel oil—the decision to build in Europe began to hurt. For
this reason: until about 1965, demand for residual oil on the East Coast
had increased only about 1 percent a year—far below the normal growth
rate for petroleum products as a whole. But then, turning custom on its
head, demand began to shoot up. Cities and states, swept along in the
new environmental reform movement, began passing strict laws against
the use of fuels with high sulfur content. Responding to these air purity
regulations, many large users of coal—particularly the utilities—began
looking for cleaner, alternative fuels. Many shifted to better-quality residual fuel oil.

But they couldn't get enough from U.S. refineries. Our neglected
refineries weren't up to the job. Because of the shift to Europe, their capacity hadn't expanded with the market; and in the second place, U.S.
refiners, at a serious economic disadvantage when competing with cheap
foreign residual imports, had cut back on their residual output by increasing their more profitable gasoline output.

(By subjecting crude oil to high temperatures, various products are
produced—"refined." Gasoline is one of them. Residual oil is, as the name
implies, the part of the crude that is left when all the other products are
removed. There's no way to get more gasoline out of a barrel of crude
than nature put in. However, the residual oil can be subjected to a
highly complicated process called "cracking"—the molecules are broken
up—by which further gasoline can be squeezed from it.)

So, unable to get their fix from domestic refineries, the northeastern
states demanded that the import quota be relaxed to let them get it from
foreign sources. The majors who owned those European sources were
only too happy to support *this* demand, and the government complied; in
1966 the quotas on residual imports to the East Coast were, for all practical purposes, abolished. From that time on, the East Coast's purchase of
residual shot up at an unprecedented rate. In 1969, consumption of East
Coast residual jumped 11 percent over 1968, and the first half of 1970
saw another jump of 20 percent. At East Coast utilities, the increase was
even more dramatic: up 63 percent between 1967 and 1969, and up another 44 percent in the first three months of 1970.

Which is why Wilson M. Laird, director of the Interior Department's
Office of Oil and Gas, sounded so nervous in 1970. Looking broadly at
the needs of the United States, there was nothing to worry about. But if
the focus was narrowed to the East Coast and to residual oil alone, one
could see a picture of frightening, almost total, dependency: the 440,000
barrels of residual fuel oil landed at East Coast ports in 1969 was 40 per-

cent of the nation's *entire* petroleum imports that year. *Half* the energy used by commercial and industrial establishments on the East Coast in 1970 was residual fuel oil and 94 percent of that came from overseas, either as foreign crude processed in this country or (10 percent) as already processed residual, direct from Western European refineries.

And now, because of the trouble in the Middle East and the tanker shortage, it appeared likely that this flow from abroad might be cut back sharply. Exploiting this threat, the oil companies, by July, were charging twice as much for fuel oil as they had charged a year earlier and, to top it off, they were talking about putting their customers on reduced rations. (Before the year was over, they would be charging *three* times more for fuel oil than in 1969.)

The outlook for the winter was bleak. In Boston, one of a number of Massachusetts cities plagued by a serious shortage of fuel oil, Mayor Kevin H. White reported in late September that orders for 240,000 barrels to heat Boston municipal buildings could not be filled. The town of Braintree, Massachusetts, asked for bids on fuel oil to run its generating plant for another twelve months. No bids were received. These frightened city officials considered themselves lucky when, finally, they were allowed to buy fuel at 275 percent of the price of the previous year.

❋

Elsewhere in the nation, other major fuels also were disappearing from the shelf. Natural gas was featured in an incredible vanishing act. In August, Federal Power Commission chairman John Nassikas said that the demand for natural gas in the upcoming winter would exceed the supply by three billion cubic feet per day. Big gas companies in such cities as Chicago and Baltimore started rationing their largest industrial customers. East Ohio Gas, over a 10-month period, turned down orders by steel, chemical, and rubber companies for an additional 27 billion cubic feet of gas. Panhandle Eastern Pipeline Company warned its distributors in the Great Lakes region that they were asking "for volumes of natural gas far in excess of our present ability to supply."

Hardships from the predicted fuel oil and natural gas shortages promised to be so extensive that proposals were revived to make the federal government an oil operator.[5] In a letter to Defense Secretary Melvin Laird dated October 30, Senator Edward Kennedy of Massachusetts asked him to "determine what the limits of the federal government's power would be to assume operational responsibility over petroleum refining and distribution facilities to meet defense or defense-related civilian needs for oil products if the crisis deepens." Charles R. Ross, a for-

---

5. For other proposals along this line over the years, see Appendix entry on *FEDERAL OIL AND GAS CORPORATION.*

mer member of the FPC, sounded more permanently socialistic. In a report to the President's Office of Science and Technology, Ross proposed the creation of a government company to drill on federal lands offshore and onshore. He was the second FPC alumnus to talk that way. Only the year before, Lee White, on stepping down as chairman of the FPC, had proposed setting up a federal oil company.[6]

Coal was also suddenly in short supply. By September, the Tennessee Valley Authority, the world's biggest buyer of coal, was down to a 10-day supply instead of its usual 60-day supply (at two of its plants, supplies were down to 4-day quantities), and the price of the skimpy amount they did manage to get was 56 percent higher than in 1969. Similar complaints about coal shortages, much higher prices, and resulting increases in customer rates (TVA's rate went up 23 percent in 1970) were heard from utilities all over the East and in parts of the Midwest.

*

The shortages and resulting price increases aroused enormous skepticism as to their cause. Senator Phil Hart, chairman of the Senate Judiciary Committee's Antitrust and Monopoly Subcommittee, ridiculed the industry's argument that lack of tanker space was a logical explanation for the increases in consumer prices of $1.25 billion a year (including home heating oil, diesel oil, kerosene, jet fuel, and heavy fuel oil). "Despite the need to charter some spot tankers to make the run around Africa to compensate for the loss of available Mediterranean oil, still the average cost of Middle Eastern crude oil delivered to the U.S. seaport refineries is probably well below $2.50 a barrel—in contrast to the $4.20 and $4.25 per barrel East Coast refineries are paying for oil from the U.S. Gulf Coast," he said. "The supply, price, and transportation cost of foreign oil provides no justification for the increase in domestic crude prices."

Others condemned as fraudulent the industry's explanation that the residual shortage was even indirectly caused by the cutback in Libyan production and the pipeline rupture in Saudi Arabia. Congressman Silvio Conte, member of a House subcommittee investigating the shortage, began to suspect a hoax. His reasoning: The oil industry had begun complaining about a "shortage" and had started pushing up its prices in April 1970, but, said Conte, "the pipeline didn't break until May 3, 1970,

---

6. White's explanation: "You and I, the citizens of the United States, own an awful lot of gas reserves. We own some onshore—the shale lands and the public lands of the west—but the greatest and most prolific we own is the federal offshore areas. And it occurred to me that it is very difficult for an industry like the gas industry that is motivated by profit to respond to national needs. It occurred to me that maybe it would be useful to have an instrumentality that was not basically profit oriented, but that was energy or people or resource oriented, so that we would at least have the darn stuff available."

and the Libyan cutback occurred sometime thereafter." Furthermore, the pipeline was shut down for other reasons one hundred days during 1969, yet there was no claim of a shortage or any increase in prices that year.

Putting it all together, Conte concluded, "The price had gone up by such a huge amount—in some cases as much as 130 percent on the East Coast—because, I felt, there was a conspiracy among the domestic oil companies, the producers, in making this oil scarce, so that the price could be increased. Let me put it this way. It is either a conspiracy or a gross miscalculation by the oil companies. And I can't believe that the oil companies would miscalculate the situation, because they certainly have the finest backup force of any industry in the world, and they very, very seldom make a miscalculation."

"Conspiracy" would be a word heard many times during this decade. Some knowledgeable observers who didn't use the word obviously had it in mind.

When Alex Radin, general manager of the American Public Power Association, said many observers had the "strong suspicion that the production of gas was being artificially withheld to drive up prices," he wasn't talking about radicals but about such journalists as those who worked on *Business Week* magazine and the New York *Times*. On August 1, 1970, *Business Week* stated: "The major oil companies, which control most of the natural gas supplies in the U.S., have made it clear that they are not interested in increasing gas production until it becomes more profitable than other investments they can make. But that could mean a 60 percent increase in the present ceiling prices that producers can charge for natural gas." And the New York *Times* on October 2 added its opinion that "the major oil companies, which own the lion's share of gas leases, are not averse to an artificially induced gas shortage which would heighten the pressure for a hefty increase in gas prices."

By "artificially induced," the *Times* meant the sort of thing that had been reported by Dr. Bruce Netschert, an economist with National Economic Research Associates, Inc. He said that five hundred gas wells in the outer continental shelf, off Louisiana, had been capped. Senator Hart went farther; he reported that the Louisiana Conservation Department "has found 1,100 gas wells shut in, mostly waiting for higher wellhead prices." He added that "there have been numerous allegations that the producers are collectively withholding information on new discoveries and are awaiting a proposed price increase in order to obtain the higher rate before reporting or developing these new finds."

Pointing out that the rate increases proposed by the FPC to pacify the gas producers would raise consumer costs by 50 to 100 percent, Hart asked the FPC to hold off until the Federal Trade Commission had completed a survey of natural gas reserves to determine whether such a generous "incentive" was needed. Hart's proposal offered little hope; in the first place, the FTC hadn't even begun the survey, and in the second place, the FPC felt under no obligation to time its actions to suit the investigatory pace of another federal agency. But, apparently fearing that the proposal might catch on, Gordon Gooch, FPC general counsel, called Wilmer Tinley, acting general counsel of the FTC, in early September and told him the FPC didn't want the FTC messing around in the gas business.

Some experts, such as Dave Freeman, doubted that many wells had been capped but wondered if maybe the industry wasn't engaging in "a more subtle pressure. Is the industry engaged in a sit-down strike? Are they just not drilling where they know that there is gas because they plan to drill two years from now, or four years, when they think they can earn more from it? Obviously this is happening to a certain extent."

Whether the wells were shut in and whether the industry wasn't really trying to find gas where it knew gas existed were questions that would remain controversial for several years. But there was full agreement from those on both sides that if gas prices were raised sufficiently high, the "shortage" would evaporate. Every trade magazine acknowledged that. So did industry spokesmen. On October 22, 1970, the American Gas Association bought a full-page ad in *The Wall Street Journal* (the same ad appeared in many other large newspapers) to bring the public up to date: "Recent reports of natural gas shortages in various parts of the country have apparently led to speculation that we are running out of natural gas. Now this is simply not true.

"What's happening is this: In certain areas, the demand for additional natural gas has outrun the *present* ability to supply . . . This does *not* mean the country is running out of gas. (In fact, geologists estimate that proved and potential supplies are over 70 times our present annual consumption rate.)

"It does mean both the industry and regulatory authorities must work together to stimulate exploration, to reverse the present imbalance between supply and demand."

And how was this to be accomplished? "It means regulatory authorities must ensure a realistic approach to field prices . . ." By realistic, the AGA meant much higher prices.

The seeming eagerness of the FPC to go along with the idea convinced many observers, in the words of Stephen M. Aug, of the Washington *Star*, that "the FPC is not properly regulating the gas industry—but in fact has become a captive of it." Some consumer groups specifically asked Nassikas and Commissioner Carl Bagge to disqualify themselves from future rate decisions on the grounds that they had prejudged the issue. Both refused to step aside.

***

As for the coal shortage and the rigging of coal prices, these also seemed to be related to what the oil companies were up to. Coal prices were remarkably stable during the 1960–65 period but began edging up after the mid-sixties. Something else happened in the mid-sixties: oil companies began buying up the biggest coal companies and also buying and leasing millions of acres of coal-rich lands. In 1960, eight of the ten largest coal companies were independently owned. By 1970, eight of the ten had been bought by oil companies and other large noncoal corporations (such as General Dynamics and Kennecott Copper). The major oil acquisitions were these: Gulf Oil bought Pittsburgh and Midway Coal in late 1963; Continental Oil bought Consolidation Coal, then the nation's largest coal producer, on September 15, 1966; Occidental Petroleum bought Island Creek, the No. 3 producer, on January 29, 1968, and the Maust Properties on August 8, 1969; Standard Oil of Ohio bought Old Ben Coal, the tenth-largest, and Enos Coal, in August 1968. In response to a Federal Trade Commission subpoena for data, five oil companies— Atlantic Richfield, Continental Oil, Gulf Oil, Exxon, and Sinclair Oil—admitted holdings amounting to more than ten million tons of recoverable coal and 2,491,000 acres of coal lands. In 1960, only one of the companies had had any holdings, and these amounted to only 7.8 million tons of recoverable coal reserves and 4,524 acres of coal lands. Ashland Oil was also beginning to buy coal lands in 1970.

Did a conspiracy theory fit the picture? Senator Albert Gore of Tennessee seemed to think so, and many agreed with him. "The big oil companies are making a determined effort to gain control of all energy sources," he told the Senate Subcommittee on Materials, Mining and Fuels.[7] "In fact, they already, with help from the Nixon Administration, manage effective control of both coal and oil . . . The only remaining hope for competition rests with nuclear fuel. And whose tracks do we find in the nuclear field? . . . Oil companies now control 45 percent of known uranium reserves. Oil companies control uranium milling. Oil companies own four out of five plants for reprocessing used nuclear fuel elements."

Because they held dominance in all energy fields, Gore argued, they were now creating artificial shortages to drive up prices, and what was happening in coal proved it. The new owners of coal were shipping increased amounts overseas to create shortages, he said, and they were reluctant to sell at home even what was available. "Exports are now running at a sharply increased rate and now amount to about 10 percent of total domestic production . . . Coal companies, under their new owner-

---

7. See following page, Diversification Chart, submitted by John Nassikas to Subcommittee on Special Small Business Problems, Select Committee on Small Business, House of Representatives, July 22, 1971.

DIVERSIFICATION IN THE ENERGY INDUSTRIES BY THE TWENTY-FIVE LARGEST PETROLEUM COMPANIES, RANKED BY ASSETS, AS OF EARLY 1970

Petroleum Company	1969 Assets ($ Thousand)	Rank in Assets	Energy Industry				
(1)	(2)	(3)	Gas (4)	Oil Shale (5)	Coal (6)	Uranium (7)	Tar Sands (8)
Standard Oil (N.J.)	17,537,951	1	X	X	X	X	X
Texaco	9,281,573	2	X	X	X	X	
Gulf	8,104,824	3	X	X	X	X	X
Mobil	7,162,994	4	X	X		X	
Standard Oil of California	6,145,875	5	X	X			
Standard Oil (Indiana)	5,150,677	6	X	X		X	X
Shell	4,356,222	7	X	X	X	X	X
Atlantic Richfield	4,235,425	8	X	X	X	X	
Phillips Petroleum	3,102,280	9	X	X		X	
Continental Oil	2,896,616	10	X	X	X	X	
Sun Oil	2,528,211	11	X	X	X	X	X
Union Oil of California	2,476,414	12	X	X		X	
Occidental[1]	2,213,506	13	X	X	X	X	
Cities Service	2,065,600	14	X	X		X	X
Getty[2]	1,859,024	15	X	X		X	
Standard Oil (Ohio)[3]	1,553,591	16	X		X		
Pennzoil United, Inc.	1,356,832	17	X			X	
Signal	1,258,611 [4]	18	X	X	X	X	X
Marathon	1,221,288 [5]	19	X				
Amerada-Hess	982,157	20	X			X	
Ashland	846,412	21	X	X	X	X	
Kerr-McGee	667,940	22	X	X	X	X	
Superior Oil	494,025	23	X				
Coastal States Gas Producing	490,190 [4]	24	X				
Murphy Oil	343,914	25		X			X

[1] Includes Hooker Chemical Co.; [2] Includes Skelly and Tidewater; [3] Includes British Petroleum assets; [4] As of June 30, 1969;
[5] As of September 30, 1969.

Source: Col. (2): *Moody's Industrial Manual*, June 1969 and 1969 Annual Reports.

ship and new management policies, simply refuse to bid when asked to do so. A recent experience by TVA had been duplicated, I understand, in other parts of the country. TVA, which gets 60 percent of its supply from non-coal companies, asked for bids for delivery of 140,000 tons of coal per week for one of its new steam plants. It received only one bid, and that for only twenty thousand tons. And the price was very high."[8]

Anticompetitive mergers are unlawful under the Clayton Antitrust Act. Appeals to the Justice Department from Gore and Representative Richard L. Ottinger of New York and the American Public Power Association and others to take legal action against the petroleum companies to break up what they considered an energy monopoly came to nothing.[9]

Robert E. Mead, president of the Independent Petroleum Association, said, "it is encouraging that those responsible for oil policy [in government] are refusing to be stampeded by these panic suggestions" and have instead "chosen properly to place [their] reliance" on oil industry's leaders, "who have a strong sense of public responsibility."

*　*　*

And what was the President's Oil Policy Committee doing all this while? Was it busily trying to determine whether import ceilings should be raised? Whether the quota system should be thrown out altogether? Whether it should be replaced by, say, a tariff system, as the task force had proposed?

It wasn't doing any of these things. As a matter of fact, even before the outcry over possible winter shortages had reached full voice, the Oil Policy Committee had unobtrusively given up the import study altogether. On Monday, August 18, the White House released a letter from George Lincoln, chairman of the Oil Policy Committee, stating that the committee had decided unanimously that the quota system should be continued. Nixon immediately said there would be no further consideration of a relaxation of import ceilings.

The following day, Lincoln called a press conference to explain the strange turn of events. He said that at a meeting the previous Thursday,

---

8. One of the melancholy features of the energy battles was the frequent desertion of proconsumer advocates when money beckoned from the other side. After Gore was defeated for reelection to the Senate in 1970, the populist fire disappeared and he became chairman of the board of Island Creek Coal Company, owned by Occidental.

9. The Federal Trade Commission—seven months after being asked by Senator Hart and Congressman Joe Evins of Tennessee, chairman of the House Small Business Committee, to make the investigation—agreed to begin studies lasting up to two years to determine the degree of monopoly in the energy industry. The study would supposedly determine whether the producers of the various types of energy—oil, natural gas, electricity, and coal—actually compete. Not much faith was placed in this study's having an impact, however, for the FTC was famous for failing to follow through on its promises.

attended by all members of the Oil Policy Committee, the decision had been reached. Also at that meeting was Peter Flanigan,[10] the White House's oilman, but Lincoln denied that Flanigan had dictated the letter Lincoln released on Monday to the press.

Four of the eight members of the Oil Policy Committee had been on the task force that recommended ending the quota system. Reporters asked Lincoln what had made these four change their minds. Had they come up with persuasive data that hadn't been available to them during the nine months they were on the task force? Why had Lincoln himself flip-flopped? Lincoln hedged, protesting that "I don't want to be too specific," but he did acknowledge that not only was no new information available but that the Committee had made its decision without even any formal discussion or working papers. He told reporters that he and the other members of the Oil Policy Committee had discussed the issue only "now and then, casually."

Spokesmen for the oil industry praised Nixon's statesmanship, but northeastern politicians were livid. Senator Edmund S. Muskie denounced the decision as "blatant and cynical favoritism for a special interest group," and Senator Kennedy announced that his Subcommittee on Administrative Practice and Procedure would hold yet another hearing in what seemed to be an endless Capitol Hill series of investigations on the import programs.

***

As his first official act of the decade, President Nixon signed the National Environmental Policy Act (NEPA), on January 1. The centerpiece of the new law was the requirement that all federal agencies would be required to file with the new Council on Environmental Quality a statement (as Nixon described it) "setting out in detail the environmental implications of all proposals for legislation and for other major activities with a significant environmental impact. With the help of this provision, I intend to ensure that environmental considerations are taken into account at the earliest possible stage of the decision-making process."

No law would inflict a bigger headache on the companies constituting the Trans-Alaska Pipeline System. Early in 1970, certain that they had the deal sewed up and that the government would come through with its permits within a matter of weeks, TAPS began putting out construction

---

10. Flanigan's name was always popping up—and would continue to pop up—whenever there were reports that somebody at the White House had squelched advice to kill the import program. On March 15, 1971, the Justice Department's Antitrust Division distributed a memo to seven top administration officials saying that import restrictions on petroleum products had nothing to do with strengthening national security. Two days later, Flanigan recalled the memorandum, and its existence did not become known publicly for another nine months.

bids, and the first materials and equipment began moving up winter trails north to the Yukon River.

That equipment would not be used for many a midnight sun.

Within a few days after Nixon had signed NEPA, there were rumblings of lawsuits in preparation. The probable basis for some of the lawsuits became evident when the Department of the Interior published a scientist's warning that the burial of a pipeline carrying 140-degree oil could create serious problems by thawing frozen ground along its route and causing the pipeline to buckle and rupture. But the report said the problems could be solved by proper design.

Secretary Hickel preferred to see the bright side of the report. On January 14 he disclosed that he had met with executives from TAPS and had reassured them that such criticism would not interfere and that the pipeline they were proposing "will indeed be built." Within twenty-four hours after the scientist's report was issued, Hickel had reached "full understanding" with the oilmen on "the nature of the unique problems involved with placing a hot oil pipeline in Permafrost." He expressed his conviction "that a resolution of the remaining technical problems would be reached in the near future."[11] Pressure to build the pipeline also was coming from the Department of Commerce, where Secretary Stans was busy overruling environmental scientists in his department. (As part of their hurry-up planning, the oil companies bought $100 million worth of pipe from Japan and laid it out along several portions of the chosen route—a bit of presumption that would cost them $5 million a month just to fight the rust.)

In March and April a variety of environmental organizations (including The Wilderness Society, Friends of the Earth, and the Environmental Defense Fund) that felt the proposed pipeline would damage Alaska's wilderness filed lawsuits charging that the TAPS owners and the Department of the Interior had not met the environmental impact reporting requirements of the National Environmental Policy Act. They also charged that TAPS was asking the government to give them wider right-of-way than the law allowed. At the same time but in separate lawsuits, Alaskan "natives" filed suits against TAPS, the federal government, and the state of Alaska, charging that the project was being routed over lands that the natives had centuries-old ancestral claims to.

TAPS was frozen in its tracks. Hickel's reassurances to the contrary notwithstanding, a "full understanding" arrived at in secret conference

---

11. Hickel was whistling Dixie, and he knew it. Later he would admit in his book *Who Owns America?* that when the oil companies came to the Interior Department for their construction permits, they had made no environmental safety plans at all and didn't care to make any. In the early days, Hickel was a hustler for them; later, as will be seen, he got tired of that role—and that was his downfall.

with the oilmen would not be enough. Indeed, under the bright and shiny new NEPA, Hickel's bureaucrats would have to do a lot of explaining before a pipeline construction permit could even be considered, much less issued.

Would the Prudhoe Bay companies pollute the land as hideously as had the oil explorers at Naval Petroleum Reserve No. 4, just to the east of Prudhoe Bay?—a pollution still marked a quarter century later by disintegrating Quonset dormitories, squalid recreation shacks, rusting bulldozers, broken mobile cranes, and hundreds of rusting oil drums: a vast garbage dump, laced together by miles of ruts through the tundra that will never heal. As a final insult, the federal workers who plundered this field had even left dirty plates sitting on their mess-hall tables. There was no reason to think Prudhoe Bay oilmen would act any differently, for, as one confessed to New York *Times* writer Steven Roberts, "We like to think we're socially responsible, but in the long run our aim is to make money." Would there be endless leaks from the pipe? Would the 41-ship tanker fleet planned by the Alyeska consortium spill so much oil into the waters between the port of Valdez and Puget Sound as to ruin the annual $58 million fishing industry?

Under the National Environmental Policy Act, the Interior Department was required to answer such questions. In April 1970, responding to the environmentalists' lawsuits, U.S. District Court Judge George L. Hart, Jr., issued an injunction stopping construction of the pipeline until Interior came up with some answers.

Ironically, this turn of events was apparently not displeasing to one of Trans-Alaska Pipeline System's charter members. ARCO and British Petroleum were both short of crude; its shallow reserves were what sent ARCO searching the northern wilds in the first place. Now it wanted to get the oil out fast, *needed* to get it out fast. And the same was true of British Petroleum, saddled with its new Sinclair and Standard Oil of Ohio commitments. But Exxon, on the other hand, was in no hurry. It, like all the Seven Sisters of oil, feared disrupting the sensitive world balance of oil. Glut was the nastiest word in the majors' vocabulary. Standard Oil of California was especially concerned that the Alaskan oil, feeding down to the West Coast, would disrupt its market. *Business Week* (February 1969) was not being unrealistically gloomy when it said that "the West Coast market [can't] absorb all the oil that even a comparatively moderate Alaskan field can produce. And that's what leads to the big marketing problems that oil analysts foresee. The first of these problems is whether the present structure of crude prices can withstand the onslaught of cheap Arctic crude." The United States didn't know what to do with its already developed fields. State "prorationing" boards in Louisiana and Texas were holding wells to less than 50 percent capacity during 1969.

So Exxon's languid approach to developing the Prudhoe Bay fields was heartily approved, if not in fact insisted on, by most of the other majors with interests in the Middle East. As an internal memorandum written by Standard Oil of California officials in late 1968 pointed out, it would be much wiser to cut production in Libya, Nigeria, Indonesia, and Latin America so that "politically palatable" production increases could be made in Saudi Arabia and Iran without hopelessly inundating the market.

Holding off production in Alaska would be another handy way of avoiding more glut.

In *The Alaska Pipeline,* Mary Clay Berry writes that, during the early days, "One of the striking things about TAPS had been its inefficiency. Sometimes the major companies in the venture seemed to be operating at cross purposes. In fact, they may have been. BP had every reason to want the pipeline built as quickly as possible . . . On the other hand, Humble Oil seemed to be dragging its feet. It is possible that Humble and its parent, then Standard of New Jersey (now the Exxon Corporation), did not welcome the kind of domestic competition the BP-Sohio combination would provide. At any rate, Interior Department officials who had to deal with TAPS and the parent companies regularly during this period generally agree that Humble was the least cooperative of the companies involved."

In his book *The Seven Sisters,* Anthony Sampson takes the plot a step farther. He reports that BP suspected that Exxon was deliberately holding up the show. BP's chairman, Eric Drake, admitted to Sampson that at one point he was so convinced they were being snookered that he threatened Ken Jamieson, the chief executive of Exxon, with an antitrust lawsuit.

All of which raises a fascinating point of conjecture. Were the conservationists whose lawsuits blocked construction of the pipeline themselves unwitting agents of Exxon? Writes Sampson:

> The conservationists were strikingly successful, to the growing worry of BP and ARCO, who were waiting thirstily for the oil. But Exxon still appeared unconcerned and the suspicion arose in the minds of several BP men: might Exxon be secretly backing the conservationists, as an excuse to delay the production of the oil? The protests of the ecologists set back the transporting of Alaskan oil by four years and the Alaskan alternative was too late to save the West from its dependence on OPEC when the crunch came. It was not until the energy crisis had broken on America that the objections [of the environmentalists] were rapidly overruled.

Sampson is in error on one point. The environmental court battle did not hold up the pipeline for four years. It delayed the flow of Alaskan oil by nearly six years.

***

Throughout 1970 something odd seemed to be happening to Secretary Hickel. He almost appeared to be turning into a crusading environmentalist. Perhaps the ugly experience of Santa Barbara had turned him around. Perhaps he was fed up with environmentalists accusing him of being a patsy for the oil companies. Whatever the reason, Hickel was getting tough, or at least tough by traditional Interior Department standards.

His move toward reform began shortly after he waded into the Santa Barbara goo. On February 17, 1969, he changed regulations so as to put prima facie responsibility for an oil spill on the oil companies. As of that date, federal law said that the oil companies had to pay for cleaning up their own messes. Three months later he stiffened this by imposing unlimited liability on polluters. Not that that was much of a threat. But it was a beginning. Then Hickel found out that the offshore oil companies were disregarding, in wholesale fashion, one crucial antipollution regulation.

Since the Outer Continental Shelf Lands Act of 1953, the federal government had required that offshore oil wells be equipped with "storm chokes," a device that cuts off the flow of oil in case of a fire. It increases the safety factor; it also prevents pollution. But, for eighteen years, the oil crowd generally ignored the law. Furthermore, the Interior Department knew the law was being violated, but it did nothing about it although the law provided fines of up to $2,000 a day. The reason the companies preferred to violate the law was that the storm chokes sometimes slowed down the rate of production. It was strictly a money over safety judgment. They had always gotten by with it, and they thought they always would.

But Hickel decided it was time for them to cooperate. He wanted to help the oil industry. He had done all he could to relieve public apprehension so that he could open up more offshore fields to exploration without arousing hysterical opposition. To this end, he had promised that his field inspectors would apply the old safety regulations much more religiously. But it was impossible to carry out his promised new era of safety without industry cooperation; after all, Interior had only seventeen of its thirty-four inspectors employed to police the more than seven thousand wells in the Gulf of Mexico. Considering the ghastly public relations that had resulted from Santa Barbara, Hickel had every reason to assume that the oil industry would police itself at least until the heat was off. But no; the companies couldn't break their old habits of lawlessness.

He discovered this after he had sent out letters telling the companies to shape up. One of these letters, dated February 5, 1970, went to Chevron Oil (Standard of California). The letter (actually it wasn't directly from Hickel but from the Interior Department's regional oil and gas supervisor, but he was acting on Hickel's orders) observed that "there appears to be a certain hesitancy among some company field personnel to rely on such [safety] equipment."

That mild rebuke did not stir Chevron to action. Five days later, on February 10, a fire swept Chevron's drilling Platform Charlie, thirty miles into the Gulf from New Orleans. There were twelve wells controlled from the platform. The fire lasted for nearly a month before the explosion of four hundred pounds of dynamite snuffed it out. But eight of the twelve wells continued to pour into the Gulf waters. It took seven weeks to cap them. Meanwhile they had produced the biggest oil spill in history—at least twice as much as the Santa Barbara spill. Only luck prevented severe damage. Normally the spring winds blow north. If they had done so in 1970, they would have deposited tons of oil into the estuaries of the Mississippi River Delta and destroyed thousands of acres of oyster beds and shrimp grounds. But, in 1970, the spring winds blew south.

If Chevron had installed the equipment as instructed, the accident would never have happened. But Chevron deliberately flouted the warning and by doing so made a mess of Hickel's safety promises. This left the Secretary with a very narrow choice: he could let Chevron off and lose face entirely with environmentalists, or he could get tough.

He got tough. On March 25, Hickel asked the Justice Department to prosecute Chevron Oil Company for "knowingly and willfully violating Interior regulations in 347 instances." He also asked Justice to convene a grand jury in New Orleans to investigate the "many serious violations" of the fifty other companies operating in the Gulf. Hickel said he assumed "other lessees have similarly failed to comply with the regulations." And he temporarily suspended all pumping in those waters.

Never before in the eighteen-year life of the Outer Continental Shelf Lands Act had any company been taken to court for violating the Act's antipollution provisions, and it made the oil companies and their political friends damned mad. Louisiana Attorney General Jack P. F. Gremillion said that it wasn't the lack of storm chokes that caused the spill but "an act of God." Louisiana Governor John J. McKeithen volunteered to tell the federal grand jurors what a swell job Chevron did in cleaning up its mess. Louisiana Congressman Hale Boggs demanded that Hickel act in "a calm and businesslike fashion" that would allow the oilmen to go about their business as usual, and said it was ridiculous to suggest that a little old spill like that was anything to get concerned about. "In 1942 and 1943, the Gulf of Mexico was a happy-hunting-ground for German submarines, and the area just offshore of the mouth of the Mississippi River was designated by the Navy as 'torpedo junction.' A total of 92 cargo vessels were sunk in the gulf during this period. Many, if not a majority, of these were oil tankers . . . The total oil spillage from the Chevron accident was approximately one third the amount of oil that was discharged into the Gulf by a single 10,000-ton torpedoed tanker. It is easy to see, therefore, that the total amount of oil released in gulf waters during World War II was of astronomical proportions as compared with the Chevron blowout." The oysters survived then, and they would now, said Boggs. And besides, he grumbled, the suspension of pumping was creating "a devastating economic crisis" in Louisiana. The Department of the Interior was guilty of outrageous overreaction. "These actions, taken in the name of environmental control, have consisted of a suspension of offshore lease sales, the shutting in of entire fields, and the overly harsh enforcement of new, stringent regulations and orders that are seriously curtailing [the oil companies'] routine day-by-day operations."

Instead of backing down, Hickel got tougher. Unconvinced that the oil operators of Louisiana were being forced onto food stamps, Hickel on July 24 issued even more-stringent regulations that would make almost any spill, however minor, a breach of the law. Issued under the Water Quality Improvement Act of 1970, the new regulations defined a spill as any oil discharge that causes "a visible film, sheen or discoloration of the surface of the water." Anybody responsible for a spill who failed to make an immediate, detailed report to the Coast Guard would be liable to criminal penalties ranging up to a year in jail and a fine of up to $10,000 per spill. Furthermore, Hickel demanded that Congress double the size of his wretchedly thin army of inspectors to supervise the law.

Industry was sure that Hickel had gone mad. Pressures mounted. On November 25, Hickel was summoned to the White House, spent twenty-five minutes with President Nixon, and walked out to tell the press that he had just been fired, effective immediately.[12]

Ultimately, Chevron paid $1 million in fines after pleading no contest to 500 violations. As the investigation expanded, Humble Oil (Exxon) pleaded no contest to 150 safety-valve violations at 33 offshore wells and was fined $300,000; Union Oil pleaded no contest to twelve counts involving eight wells and was fined $24,000; and Continental pleaded no contest on 121 counts involving 40 wells and was fined $242,000. The prosecution's momentum had been too advanced before Hickel's departure to be stopped by the Nixon administration, but its officials hurried to indicate that they still wanted to be friends. They praised the oil companies' "cooperation" and emphasized that the offenses in the indictments

12. According to sources close to Hickel, the Interior Secretary felt that Nixon had used him in a good-cop/bad-cop routine. Nixon, they said, felt obliged to oil interests because of their hefty campaign contributions but didn't want them to think they had total power of manipulation over him. So he let Hickel crack down as long as he could without showing ingratitude to his political patrons.

were for past actions and that all the companies were now complying with the safety and pollution laws.

Even as they spoke, on December 2, a fire was raging on a Shell Oil drilling platform with 22 wells, ten miles into the Gulf.

***

The hysteria induced by threats of shortage began to subside as the year drew to a close, and by the first of November the Administration's top energy spokesman was beginning to release the pressure. "We believe," said Paul W. McCracken, chairman of both the Council of Economic Advisers and the Committee on the National Energy Situation, "that a near-term balance between domestic needs and supplies generally has been achieved." In plain language, this meant, as the New York *Times* reported a couple of weeks later on the front page, that "the major fuel crisis feared for this winter has apparently been averted." Lieutenant Colonel Anthony Smith, of the Office of Special Assistance for Oil and Energy, in the Office of Emergency Preparedness, also chirruped optimism: "We don't anticipate any generalized fuel shortage. No homes will be without heat, no utilities without power, except in a few isolated communities."

The nation had been rescued not by magic but by money—consumers' money. The fright campaigns' success could be read at the cash register. As the year ended, the price of coal had risen more than 50 percent over the price of a year earlier (TVA's coal prices had been doubled), and the cost of residual oil was up by 60 percent. Furthermore, observers both in and out of the industry acknowledged that the increases were not only permanent but would serve as merely the bottom rung on an endless ladder.

***

Overseas, meanwhile, revolutionary changes were being forced upon the major oil companies by the new government in Libya under Colonel Qaddafi. Because of his success in outbluffing and outwitting the oil companies, the Organization of Petroleum Exporting Countries (OPEC) would come to life at last and would follow Qaddafi's fanatical lead. After 1970, the major oil companies would lose the power that for decades had allowed them to dictate production in the Middle East and to set world oil prices at whim. The old oil cartel—once seeming so permanently indomitable—was about to become the partner or lackey (depending on one's interpretation) of the feudal desert governments that it had for so long despised. To be sure, no lackey had ever before been so well paid. The shift in power from the cartel to the countries would bring enormous riches to both sides; some observers, indeed, felt that the companies had conspired to bring about the shift in power, and their own subservience, for the sake of these riches. Whatever the truth of that theory—and it credits the oil companies with far more imagination and craftiness than they had ever before demonstrated—the fact is that as of 1970 they were launched on a precipitous loss of influence on the production and pricing of Middle Eastern, African, and Venezuelan oil.

No sooner had Colonel Qaddafi overthrown King Idris and seized the Libyan Government than he began demanding more-favorable terms from the oil companies. At that time, the accepted arrangement in most oil-producing countries was a fifty-fifty split of the posted price. The "posted price" was an arbitrary fixed figure. It had nothing to do with production costs or with how much the companies sold their oil for. Usually, because of oversupply, the companies were forced to take it to market at something below the posted price, which meant that actually the host countries were getting better than a fifty-fifty cut. But Libya was not grateful; it wanted much more. And for several very good reasons. For one thing, its fields could not be more convenient for the European market—just across the Mediterranean. The companies had hardly any transportation expenses at all in delivering oil to Europe from Libya. Furthermore, Libyan oil was in one respect more secure for the European market, for it was unaffected by the closing of the Suez Canal. And finally, Libyan oil was high-quality—meaning, it had low sulfur content, which made it very attractive for environmental reasons. Industries that used Libyan oil didn't get nearly as many complaints about fouling the air.

As was their custom, the major companies dealing with Libya had cheated. James E. Akins explained that "They were telling the Libyans . . . that the low-sulfur quality of their oil gave them something on the order of a 10-cent price differential" upward, while they were telling the Venezuelans "that their oil, because of the high-sulfur content, was worth some 50 to 70 cents less than Libyan oil." No company was such a flagrant trickster in this way as Exxon, the biggest producer in Libya and by far the biggest in Venezuela (through its Creole Oil Company, which controlled half of Venezuela's production).

Cheating Libya on its royalties had been standard practice for many years. The independent oil companies had indulged in it even more flagrantly than had the majors. But, in one of the few instances when poetic justice prevailed over greed, this cheating had ultimately caused the thieves to have a terrible falling out, and that falling out had had a domino effect on the industry from the mid-1960s onward. This charming morality tale begins with Libya's oil beginnings.

❖

At the time the Libyan fields opened, in the 1950s, its government officials were as naïve as they were ignorant: they knew nothing about setting up the legal framework for granting oil concessions, and they made the mistake of asking U.S. oilmen for advice. By the time the oilmen got through giving their advice, the Libyan Petroleum Law of 1955 was riddled with sly provisions that benefited them. For one thing, it allowed the companies to pay royalties on the *market* price of oil, which, as mentioned earlier, was almost always lower than the fixed, *posted* price that determined royalties in virtually all other producing countries; that alone would cost Libya many millions of dollars before the loophole was closed, in 1965.

The reason this loophole played such an important part in the history of oil, however, was not that Libya was cheated but that it caused a critical disunity within the industry. And the reason it could cause disunity was that the Libyan Petroleum Law contained other provisions that opened wide the door to independent producers. In effect, the law gave them a special invitation to come and try their hands at finding oil. Libya's King Idris insisted on this. He had witnessed how, in countries controlled by the majors, exploration was often carried out in a very lackadaisical manner, with no rush to production. King Idris wanted Libya's fields developed swiftly, and he knew the independents would oblige.

Sloppy tax laws and overly ambitious independents—ah, there was a formula guaranteed to cause trouble: bitter quarrels between the majors and the independents over whether the Libyan treasury should be pillaged boldly or subtly, even bitterer quarrels over how the loot should be used. It was this dissension that ultimately cost the industry its control over Libya, which in turn allowed Libya to go on to become the devastatingly rebellious element in OPEC.

Unity of action was, and had always been, the key to the majors' power. So long as they ran the show, there was awesome singleness of purpose—in fixing production levels, in allotting markets, in fixing prices. It was the kind of unity and stability that can be achieved only when few are involved. The Seven Sisters knew this and would actually have preferred it if their number had been only five or three. They dreaded newcomers. But after World War II, they could not stop the wave of independent intruders who came abroad like Florida land hustlers, cutting sharp deals, offering wild inducements for contracts, finding oil where it was thought no oil could be found, selling oil at cut rates. When the Libyan fields opened, they came scrambling in to share the boom, and share it they did, winding up with half the leases. The royalty provision of the Libyan Petroleum Act was made to order for them, for in effect it could be used to subsidize a price war—something that was anathema to the stability-loving majors but which the independents immediately began using it for.

Cutting prices was no problem (so long as the royalties, as Libya's did, dropped with the prices). After all, it cost only a few pennies to produce a barrel of oil in the Middle East or Libya. The majors had been selling this oil for $1.80 and up. Obviously the independents could sell at, say,

$1.50 a barrel and still do just fine. Which is exactly what they did. Prohibited by the import quota system from bringing their foreign production to the United States, the independents took their cut-rate oil to the Japanese and especially to the nearby European markets. The effect on price stability, said Alan M. Robertson, executive vice-president of British Petroleum, was "disastrous."

The majors, which were determined to restore stability and were perfectly willing to pay higher royalties to get it, took an extreme and, as it turned out, self-destructive step: they quietly encouraged Libyan officials to join OPEC, all of whose members were paid royalties based on posted prices. It wasn't that the majors approved of or believed in OPEC. Indeed, for most of the 1960s the majors considered OPEC laughable, a hollow organization, hardly worth their notice. They were urging Libya to join the outfit simply as a ploy, not to help Libya but to hurt the independents. They wanted to bring Libya under the same contractual arrangements that the majors had with OPEC producers, so that the independents could not exploit market-price royalties for their cut-rate tactics.

In 1963 Libya heeded the majors' advice and did join OPEC. And of course it also began to insist that the independents pay taxes at the usual OPEC level.

But the majors had outfoxed themselves. They did not destroy their independent competitors. But they did cut the independents' profits, and turned them into enemies. This, the industry's emotional split—the majors' suspicions of the independents, the independents' envy and bitterness toward the majors—would in 1970–71 preclude any chance for the Western oil companies to achieve the kind of unity needed for the battles ahead.

*

Colonel Qaddafi observed all this. And when he took power he lost no time exploiting the industry schism, playing one side against the other.

On January 29, 1970, he told the oil companies that from then on they would have to pay 40 cents a barrel more. The big companies, led by Exxon, refused to increase payments more than 5 cents. It was an insulting counteroffer, but the majors feared no reprisal. After all, most of their oil came from the Middle East and, judging from past experience, if Libya shut down its fields they would simply increase Middle East production to compensate. They would not suffer, or so they thought.

But the independents were in no position to treat Qaddafi's demands so rudely. They needed Libyan oil. This was particularly true of Dr. Hammer's Occidental Petroleum, for Libya was virtually its only source. Qaddafi was aware of Occidental's vulnerability. So when Exxon and its giant allies rebuffed Qaddafi, he did not try to retaliate directly. Instead, he put the screws to Occidental, ordering its production cut from 680,000 to 500,000 barrels a day through May and June. By July Hammer was desperate. He appealed personally to Exxon's chief executive, Ken Jamieson, begging him to make enough crude available to Occidental, at cost, that it could withstand Qaddafi's pressures. With its usual shortsightedness, Exxon refused. Very likely, if they had helped Occidental, Qaddafi's divide-and-destroy tactics would not have worked. If the majors and independents had stuck together in resisting Libya's demands, it is quite possible that OPEC would never have become such a power; at least its coming to power might have been put off for several years.

Hammer, seeing no way out, capitulated. He agreed to pay 30 cents a barrel more at once and to raise the payments to 40 cents over a five-year period. Equally important, he agreed to raise Libya's share of profits from 50 percent to 58 percent.

With the fall of Hammer, others quickly followed. Before the month was out, Qaddafi had won similar concessions from three other independents—Continental, Marathon, and Amerada-Hess—operating as a consortium under the name Oasis. A fourth member of the consortium, Shell, refused to sign. Qaddafi cut off Shell's share of Oasis' production quota; but even though Shell needed Libyan oil it was prepared to tough it out if other majors would join the resistance. Not all were willing to hold out, however. They had been thrown into confusion by that damnable Syrian bulldozer driver who had severed the Tapline: the pipeline from Saudi Arabia to the Mediterranean. The majors' old method of juggling oil between Middle East and Libya—taking more oil from one area when the other began acting up—was shattered. With the Tapline down, the companies would ordinarily have simply increased production in Libya to make up the difference. But even before the pipeline vandalism, Qaddafi had ordered a reduction in production, and after the pipeline interruption he ordered another. There was no handy substitute for Libyan oil. Of course the majors could ship more Middle East oil around the Cape of Good Hope to European refineries (Europe was the sensitive market;[13] the United States still was not receiving enough Middle East or African oil to be hurt by such interruptions). But that was a long and costly trip, and meanwhile the governments of Europe, wanting no part of an oil shortage, were putting pressure on the companies to settle their quarrel with Qaddafi. Some of this pressure was being exerted, indirectly, through our State Department.

When the oil companies first thought about a united front to withstand Qaddafi's demands, they went, as had been their custom for many years

---

13. That is, the most sensitive market among our Western allies. But there was one even more sensitive market, in the Far East: Japan. Its precarious situation was described by Washington *Post* reporter Selig S. Harrison in memorably graphic detail: "More than 90 percent of Japanese oil comes from the Persian Gulf in a round-the-clock procession of 280 tankers all but nudging each other less than 50 miles apart."

in times of trouble, to John J. McCloy. Among the attorneys of the world, he was the industry's top adviser. McCloy, accompanied by some of the most important oil executives, went to Washington to recruit the support of the State Department. Instead of getting it, he found Secretary of State Rogers, Under Secretary Alexis Johnson, and the department's oil expert, Jim Akins, in a strangely vacillating mood. Indeed, Akins took the position that Libya's demands were reasonable and probably should be accepted without a fuss. Reputedly shaken by this reception, McCloy and his clients went their separate ways without having agreed on a strategy, and as economic pressures continued to build, the effort at unity faltered. Within a month, all other independents followed Occidental's surrender. Then the ranks of the majors cracked. The first to capitulate were Standard of California and Texaco, on essentially the same terms that Occidental had accepted, and the other majors weren't far behind. Qaddafi had outbluffed and outsmarted them all, and as Carl Solberg correctly judged, "to the youthful strong man of Libya went by far the greatest victory ever won by an oil-producing country."

The rout did not end there. Other members of OPEC immediately demanded and got the same terms. Apparently ashamed to see how one nation, armed only with fanaticism, had gained more ascendency in a few months than they had achieved as an organization in a decade, OPEC at its December meeting in Caracas gave warning that further increases in the posted price and in the tax rate could be expected in the near future. For the oil companies, the situation was clearly getting out of hand. They should have shown more resistance to Libya. But, having failed in that, they should have fallen back only far enough to regroup for last-ditch resistance. Or at least that was the thinking of some of the oil executives. Occidental's Hammer, remorseful that his capitulation had started the terrible chain of defeats, proposed that when the next round of demands came, the majors should provide a "safety net" source of oil for the independents (much the same proposal he had made, futilely, to Exxon's Jamieson), so that they could resist the producing countries' demands. He was in effect proposing that the majors bring the independents into their camp—on an emergency basis—as equals, to share and share alike in supplies when the showdown came. And come it surely would. OPEC's Caracas meeting had hardly ended before Libya was demanding another 50 cents a barrel. Clearly, unless it was shot down, the frog would keep on leaping. But how to do it? Threaten the producing countries? With what? For the moment, the producing nations had seized the initiative when it came to threats. Three days before Christmas, Dr. Jamshid Amouzegar, Iran's Cornell-educated Minister of Finance, dropped by the plush London office of the Western oil consortium that operated in Iran to say, in kind but firm tones, that if the oil companies had any notion of refusing OPEC's next round of massive tax increases, the countries just might shut off their oil. Totally.

1971

Stunned, angry, and fearful, the oil companies now launched an almost hysterical (or so it seemed) effort to slow OPEC before it reached an unstoppable momentum. Sir David Barran, of Shell, who had shown the most steel in the earlier encounter with Qaddafi, wrote to his colleagues outlining a new scheme: Refuse to deal with the oil producing nations singly. Deal with them only as group to group. No company acting alone, and no negotiations with an individual nation.

His strategy was sound insofar as it would create unity among the oil companies. But would it not also create unity among producing nations? Would it not legitimatize OPEC—the very thing that the companies had been trying, so far successfully, to avoid?

Still, the other companies thought the plan worth talking about, so, at Sir David's suggestion, they met—executives from twenty-three companies—in the offices of the master strategist, John McCloy, on January 11, 1971. If a plan was to be laid, it would have to be done promptly, for OPEC was scheduled to meet again in Tehran in a few days to create new demands.

Also at the meeting in McCloy's office were representatives from the Department of Justice and the State Department. For their unity of action, the oil companies needed the assurance of the Justice Department that they would not be prosecuted for an antitrust conspiracy. Attorney General John Mitchell and Richard W. McLaren, assistant attorney general for antitrust, gave their assurance on that point: the oil companies could act as one with impunity.

And so they did, writing a letter—signed by all twenty-three companies —to OPEC with the seemingly adamant statement that "we cannot further negotiate the development of claims by member countries of OPEC on any other basis than one which reaches a settlement simultaneously with all producing governments."

At the same time, privately, the companies agreed to establish the kind of "safety net" that Hammer had proposed. If one company was singled out for a cutback (as had happened to Occidental in Libya), all the other companies would chip in oil to make up for it. But this appearance of stouthearted camaraderie was illusory.

OPEC showed unusual resistance. The Middle Eastern producers refused to lump their bargaining rights with Libya's. They insisted that, for the moment at least, the needs of the two producing areas were not the same and could not be treated the same. The Middle Eastern nations renewed the threat made by Iranian Finance Minister Amouzegar in December: If the companies did not retract the letter—"the poisoned letter," OPEC called it—they just might shut down all their fields. The Shah of Iran was the most outspokenly hostile, warning the companies that "the conditions of the year 1951 do not exist anymore" (meaning that they were no longer dealing with a Mossadegh, Iran's Premier who had proved no match for the CIA).

In the midst of this turmoil, President Nixon dispatched Under Secretary of State John N. Irwin II on a visit to Iran, Kuwait, and Saudi Arabia to analyze the situation. It was a strange business. For one thing, Irwin had been given only one day's notice that he was to make the trip. He had no time to prepare, no time to learn all the complicated details of the quarrel he was about to be dumped into. And as he later admitted to congressional investigators, he probably wasn't the right person for the job anyway, having no "real background" in the mysteries of oil.

He did not present the hard line that the State Department had promised. He seemed to have no stomach for the fight at all. At every stopover, he informed OPEC members that the United States did not want to disrupt production and would certainly not become involved in the negotiations on the side of the companies. When he reached Iran and was subjected to the anticolonialism tirades of the Shah, Irwin reportedly was struck dumb. And when he was gone, Amouzegar confided to newsmen, "I don't know what Mr. Irwin's visit was for."

At the conclusion of his trip, Irwin recommended that his State Department bosses leave the companies to fight alone, and his recommendation was accepted. But, for the oil companies, it hardly mattered; the harm had already been done. Irwin's floundering visit was the last of several influences that prompted U.S. officials to reverse themselves and to approve splitting up the oil negotiations in exactly the way that OPEC wanted. Ironically, the reversal—betrayal, some said—was done in the name of national security, the very excuse that in other decades had been used by the government to permit the companies to bully and exploit the producing nations. National security, it seemed, could cut both ways.

Perhaps unnerved by the loss of government support, the companies did a rotten negotiating job in Tehran. Rout was in the air. On February 14, St. Valentine's Day—the second St. Valentine's Day massacre—the companies signed a five-year agreement that increased their tax payments to the Persian Gulf producers by more than $3 billion a year, and promised steady increases that would double income by 1975. It was the costliest agreement the companies had ever made with producing countries. Little wonder that, after its signing, Iran's Amouzegar, leader of the producer countries' negotiating team, told newsmen, "I was so happy I had tears in my eyes." And, of course, that was not the end of it. Six weeks after the Tehran agreement had been signed, Libya took its concessionaires to the signing table in Tripoli to let them repeat their act of generosity. The contracts reached at Tehran and Tripoli were supposed to last five years, bringing, or so the companies said, a return of price "stability" to that part of the world. But the companies had shown they could be whipped with regularity, and the producing nations, after undergoing so many years of subservience, greatly enjoyed their new power. Using it was an indulgence they would not resist for long.

***

The above description of events is how it looked from a great distance; it is not offered as fact but as conjecture based on the few visible and verifiable details of events as they transpired. And perhaps things *were* exactly as they seemed; perhaps it was simply the defeat of the cartel by the producing nations, at long last. If so, it is only fair to rejoice at least mildly on behalf of OPEC members, for they had for years watched their natural resources shipped off to make others wealthy, without much recompense for themselves. As Finance Minister Amouzegar pointed out, in January 1971, before the Tehran agreement, "We receive only one dollar out of $14 paid by the consumers. That is only 7 or 8 percent of what the consumer pays for oil."

On the other hand, perhaps the seeming defeat of the cartel was not that at all. There was something fishy about this episode. In *The Control of Oil*, John M. Blair writes of it, "The only conclusion to be drawn is that the abortive effort toward a 'joint approach' was either an incomprehensible blunder or an elaborate charade, deliberately designed to divert attention away from policy decisions that had already been made at higher levels." Charade is a good description of the possibility that the strengthening of OPEC was done on purpose by the oil companies to raise their own profits—enormously—while laying the blame on Iranians and Arabs. The evidence for this conspiracy is ample.

In the late 1960s, it was conceded by everyone in and out of the industry that the big problem for the companies was trying to figure out a way to keep prices propped up in the face of an oil surplus. As late as 1969, it was fear of an oil surplus that the majors talked about privately. An internal study by Standard Oil of California, owner of 30 percent of Aramco,[1] predicted a "large potential surplus" at least through 1973 and,

---

1. The Arabian American Oil Company, whose owners, in addition to Socal, are Texaco, Exxon and Mobil.

if Alaskan oil was coming out by then, a much larger surplus by 1978. Obviously, any manageable disruption of oil output along the way would be gratefully received.

Among the principal causes of the problem were those rambunctiously aggressive independent oilmen. Surveying in February 1965 what he accurately called "The Boiling World of Oil," Gilbert Burck had written in *Fortune* magazine:

"About 90 percent of the business, ten years ago, was done by the 'Big Seven'—Standard of New Jersey, Royal Dutch/Shell, Gulf, Texaco, British Petroleum, Socony Mobil, and Standard of California; today, owing to the influx of dozens of newcomers, the Big Seven probably account for less than 70 percent of the industry. Almost everywhere in the free world, from the Arctic's icy mountains to Africa's golden sands, established companies and newcomers have been looking for—and finding —lots of oil. To latch on to the handsome profits in crude they had to sell the crude, and to sell the crude they had to cut prices. For the past eight years, accordingly, prices have been declining more or less steadily, *and they probably will not be leveling off, to say nothing of rising, for some time.*" (Emphasis added)

Pause for a moment to consider who is writing this, and where. It is safe to assume that *Fortune* had no animosity toward the oil industry, no reason to picture the situation other than as the oil industry itself saw things. It is plain that Burck had traveled far and interviewed widely, and that his conclusions were undoubtedly an objective compilation of views expressed by oilmen in their most candid moments. It seems reasonable to assume that what a reporter like Burck wrote for a magazine like *Fortune* would be the gospel according to Big Oil. That benchmark quality of this particular article makes it worth quoting from at some length.

Burck came away from his interviews concluding that even without the recent lush discoveries in the North Sea "the world has enough proved reserves of cheap oil to last a long time. How long is a matter of opinion, but manifestly, so long as the market is not controlled or rigged, an oil scarcity is too remote to force prices up, while supply is so abundant and cheap that the downward pressure is still on. Prices have come down a lot since 1957 or 1958, when the real cutting began. Middle East crude is still posted at its 1960 levels. But oil listed at, say, $1.80 a barrel is being sold for as low as $1.35, taking into account concessions like freight discounts . . .

"Today . . . there is enough assured oil to last almost indefinitely, or at least long enough so that no man can worry about it intelligently. Yet the search for more oil goes on almost frantically. It goes on not merely because companies want several sources of supply, but mainly because prices are high enough to make the search worthwhile, and it will go on so long as prices do not fall enough to discourage it. Here then is the box in which the oil industry and its hosts find themselves: If prices are artificially maintained, the glut will grow and the pressure on prices will grow with it. If enough oil is found in enough places, no power on earth can maintain prices."

One oil authority, Morris Adelman, an economist at the Massachusetts Institute of Technology, was quoted by Burck as predicting that Middle Eastern oil selling for as low as $1 a barrel was a fifty-fifty possibility within five years if production continued at the 1965 level. A dollar a barrel! With the companies paying 50% taxes on the posted price of $1.80 a barrel, there was no way they could continue to do business if they sold a barrel for a dollar. Clearly, from the companies' point of view, something would have to be worked out so that exploration and production could continue apace *and* prices could be raised at the same time, even in periods of glut—in short, some artificial stabilizing machinery would have to be used to reverse the normal market forces. That artificial machinery was at hand: OPEC. Burck informed his *Fortune* audience that "some speculate that OPEC may yet 'force' them [the companies] into an unholy alliance that will try very hard to hold the rest of the world up for ransom." He concluded that only some conspiracy of that sort could prevent oil prices from continuing at a low level that would make consumers very, very happy. "Barring a great international cartel that will tie up the world of oil as no international organization has ever tied up anything before, everyone in the oil business faces a long series of adjustments . . . Consumers everywhere, industrial and civilian, should rejoice."

That report of plentiful oil, dropping prices, a consumer market, etc., was written, bear in mind, *in 1965—only four years before Colonel Qaddafi subdued the oil cabal with astounding ease and only five years before OPEC seized the pricing apparatus from the majors without a fight*. Such a turnaround is difficult to accept as anything but part of the major oil companies' plan.

*

There is other evidence pointing to the same conclusion. Cynics are justified in asking, for example, why the companies capitulated without even the vestige of real resistance and why the United States Government encouraged them to surrender. The excuse given was that neither the companies nor our government wanted to subject the industrial countries of Western Europe to an interruption in their oil supply. (Neither the companies nor our politicians could pretend that the closing of the pumps, as OPEC threatened, would matter much to us, since we were getting only about 3 percent of our oil from that part of the world.) But was Europe actually in much immediate danger? Europe's dependency on Persian Gulf oil was probably exaggerated by the companies. About half Europe's energy was supplied by coal. Oil accounted for the other half. But how much of that oil came from the Persian Gulf? It wasn't clear. The companies claimed that Europe was dependent on the Middle East for 75 to 80 percent of its oil, and these were the figures usually quoted by reporters. But the Associated Press, which kept an especially accurate watch, reported in February that Western Europe received "just under half its oil needs" from the Middle East. Another who set a much lower figure than most reporters was Selig Harrison, of the Washington *Post's* foreign news service. In February he reported that Europe "has reduced its dependency on the area to 58 percent." But even assuming the higher percentage—75 to 80—was accurate, it should be remembered that this was 75 to 80 percent of the 50 percent of Europe's energy needs *filled by oil*. So Western Europe looked to the Middle East for 37 to 40 percent of its energy, an impressive amount indeed, but hardly enough to force an immediate price capitulation, at least not if the majors and the U.S. Government really wanted to put up a fight. Even on its own, Europe was far from helpless. The Associated Press reported in February that if the Persian Gulf countries should shut down their wells to extort higher prices, "Western Europe's major countries have reserve stocks to last them two to six months. Austria, Belgium, Spain and Switzerland are in the best shape, with six months' supply. France has enough for four months, Britain for three, and West Germany for 2½ months."

Moreover, this does not take into consideration the help that could have been given the European nations by the United States. Only forty-five months earlier, in June 1967, after the outbreak of another round of Arab-Jew warfare and the closing of the Suez Canal and the shutdown of Libyan wells, the United States had stepped up production enough to take care of the disruption in Europe's oil supply. Western Europe in 1967 was not then much less dependent on Persian Gulf and North African oil than in 1971, and yet U.S. oil suppliers had easily made up the difference. The New York *Times* could report on August 20, 1967, "Production [in the United States], refining and shipping are at record levels. Yet the industry is not really straining. Only breathing hard. No major emergency measures have been put into effect, but oil is available here and we are helping to meet the needs of Europe. The industry took the emergency with the calm assurance of a professional that knows he can handle almost anything." Indeed, during those 1967 troubles, the oil industry intentionally kept production in this country far below full capacity because it remembered that during the 1957 Middle Eastern crisis—and the first closing of the Suez Canal—production was stepped up so much that price-cutting battles broke out, slashing overseas profits in half, dropping gasoline prices to a 12-year low by 1964, and helping hold down prices for nearly a decade. "We all remember what happened last time," Herman J. Schmidt, executive vice-president of Mobil, said. "Certainly we won't fall into a new oil glut unthinkingly." Nevertheless, so great was the industry's capacity that even after taking all precautions, overproduction became the chief danger. *The Wall Street Journal* reported on August 24, 1967, "Less than five months after the Arab-Israeli war in June touched off a world oil-supply crisis, oil men worry that a new global petroleum glut may be in the making . . . U.S. oil production has run above any pre-1967 level for fifteen straight weeks, to make domestic oil available to Europe and to replace oil diverted to Europe by Venezuela, a traditional supplier of the U.S. market. But already regulatory authorities [chiefly the Texas Railroad Commission] are cutting permitted output as the supply pinch eases. Production from Texas and Louisiana wells has been cut by nearly 500,000 barrels a day from the peak, canceling about half the increase in their output during the crisis." The flood of surplus oil was coming from nations that had stepped up production to fill the supply gap and now were reluctant to surrender their larger share of the world oil market. Furthermore, the 1967 crisis "spurred development of new oil fields in lands such as Australia that hope to become significant oil producers—without causing any cutbacks in development of new fields in the Mideast." Other new fields were coming into production in Alaska, Canada, West Africa, the Amazon Basin, and Indonesia.

It is unlikely that the world's oversaturation of 1967 could have changed to a real shortage or even potential shortage by early 1971 —without a radical jiggering of the pumps by the oil companies. It is also unlikely that a Middle East shutdown in 1971 could not have been met almost as easily as in 1967. And yet the negotiations with OPEC in 1971 were conducted as though the victorious experience of 1967 had never occurred and the Western industrial world would be helpless in the face of a shutdown by OPEC.

*

The usual history of this period assigns much of the blame for the oil companies' defeat to the bungling and cowardliness of federal officials in failing to give the oil companies the support that had been promised. Stephen Nordlinger, for example, wrote in *The Nation* ("The 'National Security' Cartel, 1974") that "the heaviest blame for what transpired at Teheran must fall on the U.S. government, which for more than twenty years had encouraged the companies to enter the waiting trap and then out of ignorance and fear undermined their bargaining position at the fateful negotiations." This is a conclusion, however, that contradicts history and experience. There had rarely been an instance in all of its dealings with the multinational oil companies that the United

States Government went against their wishes. In all matters relating to the oil companies' dealings with other nations, our foreign policy was almost without exception shaped by their corporate policies. There is no reason to suppose that on this occasion our government varied from that rule. Nixon, the industry's great friend, was in the White House. The State Department, as always, was loaded with friends of the major oil companies. The key Administration official in shaping Tehran strategy was Nixon's aide Peter M. Flanigan, whose connections with the industry have already been noted. It is unthinkable that Flanigan would have done anything that did not have industry's approval.

Clear evidence that the government was once again following oil company dictates could be seen in the Justice Department's suspension of antitrust laws so that the oil companies could act as one. Authority to act with impunity from antitrust had not been given since the Suez crisis, in 1956. Antitrust chief McLaren was a strict fellow, a relatively aggressive prosecutor of antitrust violations. He was reluctant to approve immunity, but he was persuaded to do so on the grounds that it would give the companies the necessary strength to fight. With that in mind, McLaren said go ahead, but he emphasized that the immunity applied *only* to the original letter to OPEC from the twenty-three oil companies, in which they demanded that negotiations be conducted with OPEC as a whole, not with individual countries. In short, McLaren said the companies could act as one so long as they were *fighting* OPEC. But, as it turned out, they used the immunity to act in concert to *surrender*—to join OPEC, as Burck had put it in his prescient article, in "an unholy alliance that will try very hard to hold the rest of the world up for ransom."

*

There was certainly no sign that the oil companies were unhappy with the result of Tehran. Lord Strathalmond, a managing director of the British Petroleum Company and a cochairman of the five-man company negotiating team, boasted that the agreement "insures stability and security for the oil industry in the Persian Gulf for five years," and consequently, he said he and his colleagues were "satisfied." Earlier, as the companies' resistance began to crumble during the negotiations, George Piercy, a vice-president of Standard Oil of New Jersey, said, "We can smile."

And why not? OPEC, spurred by Colonel Qaddafi, had achieved for the international oil companies what they had been unable to achieve on their own: not merely a halt to the decade-long decline of prices but a sharp increase, with promises of more ahead, without limit—and without any reference to supply. Lost to the attention of the consuming public was the fact that while OPEC stood to gain billions under the new arrangements, so did the oil companies. And it was coming to them just in the nick of time, for the companies were fast approaching the outer limits of traditional borrowing capacity, while they were faced with the need for enormous capital to continue hunting for oil around the world. Chase Manhattan Bank in late 1971 estimated that the companies needed "well in excess of $500 billion" by 1980 for the hunt and now they wouldn't have to lean on their banking friends at Chase and elsewhere to get it. They could squeeze the needed billions out of the consumers. OPEC had seen to that.

Little by little over the next half-dozen years the public would catch glimpses of the truth: that OPEC and the oil companies, despite their heated rhetoric and power struggles, were allies in profiteering.[2]

*

Beleaguered consumers should also consider the possibility that the Nixon administration (and the Ford and Carter administrations) encouraged the strengthening of OPEC and the acquiescence to its price demands not only to help the oil companies but to bolster U.S. defense and trade positions. One of the commonest rumors, supported to some extent by State Department documents leaked to the press and sup-

---

2. One revealing glimpse would be had in 1976, when officials of the Federal Energy Administration finally admitted that OPEC's price increases had rescued the Alaska consortium from a very unpleasant situation. Summarizing the data just released by FEA officials, Wallace Turner wrote in the New York *Times*, "The massive price raises in late 1973 by the Organization of Petroleum Exporting Countries provided an economic justification for the project, which until then had appeared questionable. In 1968, when the first wells in the North Slope's rich Prudhoe Bay field were brought in, Saudi Arabian oil was being delivered to refineries in the San Francisco area for $2.50 a barrel. Prudhoe Bay oil could not compete at that price." That revelation would help explain why neither the Alyeska members nor their friends in the federal government had fought the environmentalists' lawsuits with much enthusiasm until 1973. If the oil had been brought out before OPEC's embargo took the lid off prices, the companies would have lost their shirts.

Eventually it became rather commonplace for oil executives to admit they appreciated OPEC's price escalations. In an interview with a Washington *Star* reporter, James Lee, president of Gulf Oil Co.-Eastern Hemisphere, London, pointed out that if it hadn't been for the Tehran agreement, the oil peddlers wouldn't be making nearly as much money. The reporter asked, "Aren't you saying in effect that OPEC is a good thing?" Lee said sure, that's what he was saying and had said publicly before, "that they perhaps may have done us a favor by forcing the price of oil as they did . . ." And Carmichael C. Pocock, chairman of Royal Dutch Shell, would also later admit that "our role in the OPEC countries is now much happier," as the result of OPEC's intervention in pricing. John G. Phillips, chairman of Louisiana Land and Exploration Company, one of the largest of the independents, told the New York *Times* in 1974 that he appreciated what OPEC was doing for his company's overseas business. "We always were sure we could find oil overseas, but we were doubtful that we could make money. Now, however, OPEC has made it possible for us to make money overseas by pushing up prices."

But candor of that high quality would not be commonplace for another several years. In 1971, most oilmen felt it to be a much wiser public relations policy to pretend they were angry and dismayed by OPEC's actions.

ported also by reasonable deductions drawn from happenings, was that Henry Kissinger and President Nixon chose the Shah of Iran as their instrument for dominating the Persian Gulf militarily, using oil prices to strengthen him. In 1971, British forces withdrew from the Persian Gulf, leaving a power vacuum. The Kissinger-Nixon plan for filling that vacuum depended to a large extent on the Shah, and on allowing him to buy U.S. arms to his heart's content. Nothing could have suited the Shah better; it appealed to his dreams of a "new Persian empire." So he bought with gusto. Whereas in 1971 Iranian arms purchased from the United States totaled only about $500 million, over the next five years the Shah would buy $18 billion worth of American arms, and place back orders for billions more—such an orgy of militarizing that even the militaristic U.S. Senate would begin to murmur that sales to the Shah were out of control.

To obtain the money needed for his military ambitions, the Shah kept raising the price of his oil. Did Kissinger encourage him to do so? There were persistent rumors inside and outside government that this was the case. Some said the terms by which the new alliance was sealed—terms including virtual carte-blanche oil price increases—were actually put in writing; others in the international bureaucracy claimed that the deal was simply an implicit one, an "understanding" between Kissinger (and Nixon) and the Shah. In any event, though the Shah, even more than Qaddafi, broke contracts and raised prices in an unconscionably bullying fashion, no administration—neither Nixon's nor Ford's nor Carter's—ever condemned his actions as they did the colonel of Libya. Indeed, they did not even scold the Shah. Eventually, after this had been going on for several years, liberals in the Senate would wake up to the obvious and timidly question the propriety of U.S. policy. Senator Gary Hart, the Colorado Democrat, would ask, for example: "What is the relationship between the price of oil and the level of military sales in the Persian Gulf? Certainly Iran has been our primary customer and has also been in the forefront of those OPEC nations pushing for higher oil prices. Are we unwittingly fueling pressures for higher oil prices by the large volume of military sales?" The answer was, No, the United States was doing it quite wittingly.

Aside from the U.S. Government's scheme to let higher oil prices subsidize the military expansion of its chosen Mideast allies (Saudi Arabia as well as Iran), there was also evidence that the United States encouraged the price escalation as a way to hurt its Japanese and European trade competitors, who depended much more heavily on the newly expensive foreign oil than did the United States. As the Washington *Post* would editorialize in 1972, "At the moment, the United States may be in a position to weep crocodile tears as the price of oil paid by its industrial competitors in Europe and Japan rises. But inevitably the advantages which American oil interests have enjoyed in the producing countries are going to be trimmed . . ." And so they were. But they were not trimmed enough to wipe out our advantage. Five years later, with the U.S. trade position and the dollar much improved, skeptical Europeans were not shy about theorizing that the United States and OPEC had been in cahoots all along.

In any event, the sincerity with which the international oil companies and the U.S. Government deplored what happened in 1971 can be measured by what they did, or did not do, to prepare for future confrontations with OPEC. Many oil analysts who believed that the Tehran and Tripoli agreements would fall apart, or could be countered, if the major industrial nations acted quickly and decisively to prepare a defensive mechanism, urged that the consuming nations build bigger oil stockpiles, set up rationing systems, and diversify their sources among emerging oil nations of importance, so that they could be played off against the old-line OPEC nations. The United States Government took none of these, or any other, strategic actions in preparation for what the public was led to believe was an ongoing war with the Middle Eastern producing nations.

***

At home, a piling up of events pointed to rough times ahead for consumers. A roster of the Interior Department's Office of Oil and Gas, submitted to a congressional committee in 1971, showed that almost every employee had worked for a major oil company at one time or another. John Connally of Texas joined Nixon's Cabinet as Treasury Secretary and immediately became the President's chief oil adviser. The year saw oil and gas prices rise sharply and environmental and antitrust regulations decommissioned either by fiat or disuse.

In September, the Cost of Living Council found that 144 oil companies had violated the President's wage-price freeze. The Justice Department took no action. Senator William Proxmire, chairman of the Joint Economic Committee, charged that a "high administration official" had tipped off the industry to the coming of the wage-price freeze before it took effect on August 15 so that the industry could legitimately hurry up gasoline price increases before that deadline; as a result, gasoline prices were a leading factor in the sharp consumer price index advance.

In July, the Justice Department came to settlement of a six-year-old quarrel with seven major oil firms—American Oil Company (Amoco), Atlantic Richfield, Cities Service, Gulf Oil, Humble Oil, Sinclair Refining Co., and Mobil—whereby Justice agreed to drop antitrust charges in return for a small fine. The seven companies had been accused of price fixing and of conspiring to monopolize the sale of gasoline in New Jersey, Pennsylvania, and Delaware between 1955 and 1965. In a typical year, 1960, the seven firms sold more than 3.6 billion gallons of gasoline in the three states with a retail value of more than $720 million. Total fines of only $550,000 were imposed.

*

Even companies that chose to operate legally were suspected of phony advertising. In hearings before the Senate Antitrust Subcommittee, Chairman Philip Hart said that although the industry's multimillion-dollar ad campaign "constantly tells us . . . each brand of gasoline is unique," an investigation by his staff had found that "basically there is no functional difference in gasolines. Moreover, the oil companies exchange gasoline among themselves." He got support from several witnesses who should have known what they were talking about. One was Major General Charles C. Case, who directed the Defense Department's purchases of 300 million gallons of gasoline a year. He said that so far as he could discover, there was no significant difference among the brands. Any brand would do for the military, he said, and for his own autos "I usually go to the most convenient station which has a brand for which I have a credit card." Dr. John Krynitsky, chief of technical services at the Defense Department's Fuel Supply Center, said he knew of no differences in gasoline and that personally he shopped only at cut-rate filling stations. Of course, industry supplied a witness who felt obliged to keep up the pretense. Alton W. Whitehouse, Jr., president of Standard Oil of Ohio, told the subcommittee that his company's gasoline was considerably different from other companies' in "smoothness of start," etc., but he admitted, under questioning, that sometimes there were "emergency" situations in which his company sold a competitor's gasoline—without telling the customers, naturally.

*

Three years earlier, in 1968, Congress had responded to Ralph Nader's cry of alarm by enacting a law to regulate gas pipeline safety. But testimony in 1971 indicated that the law was as hollow as the pipes themselves. "There is no real enforcement of safety standards for interstate gas pipelines," warned Joseph C. Swidler, former FPC chairman who had moved on to become head of the New York State Public Service Commission. Joseph C. Caldwell, acting director of the Department of Transportation's Office of Pipeline Safety (OPS), admitted that "obviously, with the staff we have, very little monitoring goes on." The OPS had a staff of eight engineers to inspect 1.4 million miles of interstate natural gas pipeline. Swidler pointed out that actually the 1968 federal law had weakened safety enforcement and "the cynical would say it was all planned that way." He pointed out that before the federal law was enacted, New York and some other northeastern states required interstate transmission lines to odorize the natural gas in transit so that leaks could be more easily detected. The OPS decided that odorization wasn't necessary for the high-pressure interstate lines and did away with the requirement, and its ruling took precedence over state requirements. OPS chief Caldwell explained that he had done away with the odorization requirement to save the companies that expense. Meanwhile, deaths from pipeline explosions increased; forty were killed in 1970.[3]

*

The FTC interrupted its investigation of oil company acquisition of coal companies and coal reserves to announce on July 13 that it might lodge antitrust action against some of the mergers even before all the evidence was in. The announcement followed by only a few weeks the release of a private study (*Coal: The Captive Giant*, by Laurence D. Beck and Stuart L. Rawlings) that pointed out that the Justice Department and the FTC had run up an "incredible" record of doing "absolutely nothing" to prevent the mergers. The study pointed out that although seven of the fifteen largest coal producers (accounting for 28 percent of coal production) had been bought by oil companies—an increase in five years of 400 percent in oil's invasion of coal—neither Justice nor the FTC had challenged the concentration despite "numerous anticompetitive possibilities." An investigation by a House Small Business subcommittee came to similar conclusions. Its statistics, even more impressive than Beck and Rawlings', supported charges that "four of the largest oil companies accounted for about 23 percent of domestic coal production." These accusations, which by now (in one form or another) had become commonplace, were accompanied by some fresh data from the Bureau of Labor Statistics that showed the coal companies had raised prices per ton by 83 percent in the previous four years. The FTC, congressional investigators, and Beck and Rawlings all agreed that the Continental Oil–Consolidation Coal merger, in 1966, was the most important—and damaging—of the mergers and had probably triggered the wave that followed. C. Howard Hardesty, Jr., a senior vice-president of Continental Oil, and Frank Ikard, president of the American Petroleum Institute, both argued that the sharp price increases in coal were not the result of the oil-coal mergers or to any industry collusion. "We're not scared of a grand jury investigation," said Hardesty, challenging the critics to "put up or shut up" about a conspiracy.

---

3. In 1972, things would get even worse, as the OPS was given responsibility for the safety of the 220,000 miles of oil pipelines as well. There were several hundred oil pipeline accidents every year (nobody knew how many for sure, but it was thought no more than 10 percent were reported to the OPS), with several hundred thousand barrels of oil lost through spills. To supervise oil pipeline safety the OPS employed one (1) engineer.

***

A dramatic demonstration of the oil industry's ability to avoid antitrust policing came on October 21, when the Senate Commerce Committee opened a two-day hearing on a bill that would have permitted El Paso Natural Gas Company to hang on to an illegal monopoly. The amazing thing about this legislative move was that it dealt with a situation that supposedly had been settled by the United States Supreme Court seven years earlier, in 1964, when the Court ruled against El Paso, a ruling that it repeated in 1967 and again in 1969—and yet here was El Paso not only still in possession of illegal property but seemingly about to win a congressional exemption from antitrust laws. El Paso had successfully prolonged the case beyond any other in the history of the antitrust laws.

The litigation had actually begun fourteen years earlier. The background was this:

In 1954, Pacific Northwest Pipeline Co., a new company, built a pipeline from New Mexico gas fields to the Northwest. Then Pacific Northwest found that, due to other gas sources it could tap in Canada, it had a surplus; so it decided to look for a new market in California. This coincided splendidly with what California officials had in mind. In 1956, Attorney General Edmund G. Brown instructed his deputy attorney general, William Bennett, to try to get a competing pipeline to come into California "so that we would not be solely dependent on El Paso Natural Gas Company, to which at that time we were paying in excess of $400 million for out-of-state natural gas," as Bennett recalls. So Bennett went to Ray Fish, president of Pacific Northwest, and "in short an understanding was had that he would come to California to supply gas to our state."

This arrangement, to put it mildly, alarmed El Paso Natural Gas Company, which was the only non-California supplier of gas to the endlessly growing California market. El Paso, being a much richer and more powerful company, attacked in the customary style: it offered a stock exchange to Pacific Northwest shareholders so far in excess of book value and so far in excess of market value that it wound up with just about all of Pacific Northwest's stock. In August 1957, El Paso asked the Federal Power Commission to approve the merger.

California Attorney General Brown was so infuriated by this move that he ordered Bennett to launch a full-scale fight. Bennett went to U.S. Attorney General Herbert Brownell and to the Securities and Exchange Commission. Both joined California in warning El Paso that they were violating federal antitrust laws. (Most Western states, however, backed El Paso.[4] Attorney General Will Wilson of Texas said he thought the

---

4. It's safe to say that they did not do so out of logic but out of fear or self-interest. This, for example, was certainly the case in Oregon. Howard Morgan, who was Utility

merger was a good idea; so did the attorney general of New Mexico, and
when he later went into private practice he got El Paso for one of his clients. Only California, among western states, opposed the merger.)

Within six months after the stock swap, Brownell sued El Paso under
Section 7 of the Clayton Act, charging that the purchase of Pacific
Northwest stock had destroyed competition. As indeed it had. With the
death of Pacific Northwest, El Paso held a monopoly not only as the sole
out-of-state supplier to California but to Oregon and Washington as well.
But, despite the suit, El Paso went right on blithely with its merger
plans, assisted by the Federal Power Commission, which in 1959 gave its
blessing to the transaction, and assisted also by a federal district court
that sometimes actually seemed to be in the employ of the company. But
the U.S. Supreme Court was made of sterner stuff. In April 1962 it struck
down the FPC's approval, saying that the FPC had no jurisdiction over
mergers and should stick to its proper business. That ruling, however,

Commissioner of Oregon at the time (Oregon had the nation's only one-man state
regulatory commission), tells how Paul Kayser, then president of El Paso, visited his
office in January 1957, accompanied by attorneys general and deputies of several
southwestern states traversed by El Paso's main system. Kayser was there to give Morgan a very handsome pitch: if Oregon would support El Paso's acquisition of Pacific
Northwest, or at least stay neutral in the fight, he would see to it that there would be
no pipeline rate increase in Oregon for several years. "This," says Morgan, "was one
of those skillful proposals so appealing to the pragmatist in each of us, especially
when it calls for nothing more than inaction on one's own part and offers a chance to
avoid real difficulty or expense in one's own jurisdiction while ignoring what is happening in someone else's bailiwick." With "considerable misgivings, offset to some extent by the usual rationalizations and the usual encouragements of the local gas distribution company," Morgan accepted the proposal. Kayser kept his word and
maintained the price moratorium not only in Oregon but in the whole northwest region. "It appeared that a good result had been achieved, even though the means
selected were somewhat dubious at best," Morgan recounts. "What I was totally
unprepared for, however, was the appalling effect of the continued merger on the gas
consumers of Southern California, and this I was to begin learning about shortly after
I was appointed to the Federal Power Commission by President Kennedy in early
1961. Far from being satisfied to extract merely enough extra revenue from its captive
Southern California customers to balance deficient earnings of its Pacific Northwest
line—a comparatively paltry sum of a few million dollars—El Paso, freed of competition, had proceeded with unexampled rapacity. As a member of FPC, I was shortly
obliged to sit in judgment on refund proceedings brought against El Paso by the State
of California that staggered the imagination. The FPC staff calculated with flawless
arithmetic that El Paso's excess and illegal profits during the comparatively brief period covered by the complaint were on the order of $220,000,000 and demonstrated
conclusively that El Paso's California customers were legally entitled to that amount
as a refund. We [the FPC] actually ordered El Paso to repay more than $155,000,000
in cash—the largest refund in the history of utility regulation—being restrained from
ordering the larger amount only by fear of demoralizing the financial community and
thereby crippling El Paso's ability to keep pace with the demands of its expanding
market. El Paso was aware that our award was a compromise and did not appeal. If
this seems to suggest that because of the absence of competition El Paso could and
did, even after such an enormous refund, pocket another $65,000,000 of illegal profits
from the California market, that is exactly what I mean to suggest."

did not touch on the antitrust question, which would come before the Supreme Court as the result of a ruling by the U.S. district court in Utah later that year. The district court ruled that the merger did not hurt competition and thereby did not violate the Clayton Act's antitrust provisions. The Supreme Court (in an 8 to 0 vote) could hardly restrain its contempt for the district judge. Pacific Northwest, it said in its opinion, was a "prospering" company when El Paso raided and overpowered it. "If El Paso can absorb Pacific Northwest without violating section 7 of the Clayton Act, that section has no meaning in the natural gas field." (The Clayton Act prohibits mergers in which "the effect of such acquisition may be substantially to lessen competition, or to tend to create a monopoly.") It ordered El Paso to divest itself of its Pacific Northwest stock "without delay."

But El Paso had no intention of doing so. Time and again it worked out divestiture deals creating what the Supreme Court looked upon as dummy companies that would still be under the corporate thumb of El Paso. The Justice Department almost routinely approved El Paso's schemes, and the district judges did too, but the Supreme Court just as routinely knocked them down, on one occasion accusing the Justice Department of having "knuckled under" and on another occasion telling the lower court to give the case to a new judge. In 1967 and 1969, the Supreme Court renewed its divestiture order. But El Paso continued to stall and continued to recruit allies by various means.

So here it was 1971 and yet another divestiture scheme was being worked out under the eye of the federal district court in Utah. It had been indeed an amazing display of staying power. Senator Fred Harris, the Oklahoma populist, observed that the pipeline company had shown other utilities "that they can violate the law with impunity." It certainly seemed so. Having avoided obedience to the Supreme Court's order for nine years, the company now seemed very likely to get congressional assistance to avoid the law altogether.

When El Paso came to Congress, those sensitive politicians took notice, for it was a formidable petitioner. It operated 11,400 miles of gas transmission lines, supplied gas to 109 utilities and municipalities in the West, and held leases on 1.6 million acres of oil- and gas-producing land. In short, many areas of the West were held hostage to El Paso's service. If it cut back on its gas supply to private industries and municipalities, there would be great economic discomfort. Western politicians were well aware of this, and they were only too eager to leap to El Paso's assistance. So, in this instance, the bill to free El Paso from the Court's divestiture order was sponsored by eleven western Senators, Democrats and Republicans, and the chief sponsor was none other than Warren G. Magnuson of Washington State, chairman of the Senate Commerce Committee. After Magnuson had been around the Senate long enough to achieve potent seniority, he had learned to wheel and deal with the captains of industry. In that era, he had developed a troublesome image of being too close and too responsive to many of the vested corporate interests. The folks back home in Washington took notice and their enthusiasm for him began to cool. In the 1962 election, Magnuson came within a hair of being defeated by a political unknown. Thereupon, determined to change his image, he hired a bevy of bright young aides who helped him develop the reputation of being proconsumer. He became highly popular with the Washington electorate once more. He did not want to lose that popularity. After all, Richard McLaren, the Justice Department's antitrust boss, had publicly damned El Paso as being very anticonsumer and had pointed out that "since 1968, El Paso has increased its rates by a total of $151,262,810, while at the same time failing to accumulate significant additional reserves." McLaren heartily opposed any legislation to rescue El Paso. So when Magnuson was asked by El Paso partisans to introduce the legislation to nullify the Supreme Court's divestiture order, he was extremely wary. He refused to touch it unless every governor in the affected states formally urged him to do so. El Paso, always generous with its favors and threats, easily rounded up public endorsements from governors Dan Evans of Washington, Tom McCall of Oregon, Ronald Reagan of California, all Republicans, and Cecil Andrus of Idaho, a liberal Democrat.

El Paso had many powerful supporters in the East as well, most of this support resulting from bountiful financial arrangements. Among the several law firms in its employ was the one from which President Nixon himself had emerged. It also bought the legal services of law firms in which such Democratic powerhouses as Clark Clifford and Joseph Califano were partners. The list of purchased allies was long indeed, as might be expected, considering that El Paso had spent $12.6 million for lawyers and lobbyists over the previous fourteen years and was, in 1971, spending $893,862 for help in its legislative fight to whip the Court. With that kind of money floating around, it wasn't surprising to find El Paso with some unexpected friends. Such as Edmund G. (Pat) Brown—yes, the same Pat Brown who, as attorney general, had launched the fight against El Paso in California in 1956, but now, having put on the coat of a private lawyer, was popping up in Washington to say nice things about the corporation.

Naturally El Paso was eager to leave the impression that those who supported its bill would be well rewarded. For instance, it announced on October 20 that if it remained financially healthy enough to do so (that is, if it wasn't forced to divest itself of any of its pipelines), it planned to build six ships, each costing more than $70 million. Moreover, it promised to build them in American shipyards, which were suffering a depression. This would create as many as forty thousand jobs. And it promised to man the ships with American crews (something that most companies try to avoid because U.S. seamen demand much higher wages than others). Seafaring unions, notoriously willing to buy politicians, immediately began putting the pressure on Capitol Hill.

In short, it looked as though El Paso's antitrust exemption bill was almost certain to pass without a great deal of opposition, or even attention. But on the very first day of the Magnuson hearings, things began to go wrong for El Paso. It was as though the giant pipeline was another *Titanic*, floating high and cocky, only to run onto a waiting iceberg. The tip of the iceberg, so to speak, was the very rude and forthright William B. Bennett—the same Bennett who had launched the fight for California in 1956. He had taken his assignment so seriously that after he left public employment, he kept right on fighting El Paso's monopoly. When he heard about the Magnuson bill, he wired the chairman for permission to testify and advised him: "I wish to tell you about areas of investigation of activities of El Paso. You should investigate lobbying activities of El Paso, past, present and future, promised political contributions to public officials. I know you will not hesitate to investigate such matters as political contributions, even including any to yourself from El Paso which are possibly unknown to you. It is possible that your high office is being used without your knowledge as to outrageous lobbying and pressure tactics indulged in by El Paso." He also suggested that they investigate the reason Governor Reagan, who once opposed El Paso's monopoly, now supported it.

Bennett was given time to appear before the committee to repeat his insinuations. At one point he asked for a "disavowal from you in this room [the Senators on the committee] that you have not ever taken any political contributions . . . directly or indirectly" from El Paso.

Chairman Magnuson was furious. His face grew red. He began to shout: "If you want the answer, the answer is *no!* I think you ought to be ashamed of yourself to be doing this without some background or some facts."

Bennett, unaffected by the bluster, replied, "I'm not ashamed, Senator . . . but I'm pleased to hear your answer."

Magnuson continued shouting at Bennett: "If we weren't all in the Senate, we'd get together and sue you for libel."

Bennett went right on slugging, dragging out accusations and dramatic anecdotes to illustrate what he considered to be El Paso's transgressions and abuses. He told what had happened to him after he had left the California Attorney General's Office and had become a member of the California Public Utilities Commission and his old boss, Pat Brown, had become governor: "I was about to appeal what is known as the third El Paso case. I was called by Mr. Gregory Harrison, the attorney for the El Paso Natural Gas Company, who asked me if I am about to appeal the case and I said, 'I am thinking about it. Why?'—and this is all from notes that I have in my files—'Because if you do,' he said, 'we will have you removed from the case.' Now, that was a novel thing and perhaps shocking in a way. I was a public official and here was an attorney from El Paso saying he would have me removed from the case. I filed the appeal promptly. Thirty minutes later I received a telegram from Governor Brown removing me from the case."

He told of how other western state officials had been subjected to unseemly pressures from El Paso over the years. Magnuson was impatient with this litany. "I don't know what El Paso did in the past," he said, "and I don't care." Others on the committee seemed equally uncaring. But Bennett's testimony had clearly made them nervous. The atmosphere was changing, and it changed further—dramatically—with the testimony of another witness, Beverly C. Moore, Jr., representing one of Ralph Nader's outfits, the Corporate Accountability Group. He charged that Pat Brown and other California officials who had once been against the merger were now for it because they had been swamped in "El Paso's economic power—unchallenged, unchecked, unrelenting, highly disciplined, mobilized and advancing upon the members of the United States Congress" as well as upon most important public officials in the western states.

Getting down to specifics, he said he knew of a bank "where it is said that an official was approached by a representative of El Paso who offered to deposit $100,000 in that bank, interest free, a windfall to the bank, of course, if that official would come out in favor of this bill."

It was the most serious accusation the committee had heard. What sort of shenanigans was El Paso up to? Could Moore substantiate his accusations? Scott Cuming, vice-president and general counsel of El Paso Natural Gas, said that Moore's charge was "an absolute, unmitigated lie," and the reason he knew it was a lie was that he knew all the top-rank people at El Paso and "they are fine, fine people."

But, two days later, Moore's story was supported by the appearance of the very banker to whom the offer allegedly had been made, John H. Klas, vice-president of the Continental Bank and Trust Co. of Salt Lake City and chairman of the Utah Democratic State Central Committee. Klas said that he had been approached by an El Paso lawyer, Daniel L. Berman, with the $100,000 offer on the assumption that this would "dampen" his long-standing opposition to the merger legislation. Berman then took the stand to brand the accusation "an absolute lie."

There was no way to tell which of the men was lying, but the whole episode was enough to chill Magnuson. For practical political purposes, he shelved the bill, explaining to a Washington reporter that he had a bellyful of all the gas companies. "None of them are lily pure," he complained. "You've got to watch them all the time."

***

Suspicions about the international oil companies' role in creating U.S. policy in the Vietnam War surfaced in the spring. The issue arose after the Saigon government announced, in December 1970, that in February it would offer its continental shelf for oil exploration bids. When members of the antiwar movement in the United States heard about this, many of them concluded that the American troops were being kept in Vietnam to fight a war for oil. A group known as Another Mother for Peace sent the Senate Foreign Relations Committee about ten thousand letters demanding an investigation and public hearings. But, in varying ways and degrees, the suspicions were held not only by "peaceniks" but by more orthodox critics, such as Michael Tanzer, an international management consultant and oil expert, who expressed his belief that U.S. oil companies were eager to block non-American competitors from getting into the large oil reserves in that area, because it would give them an advantage in supplying the nearby Japanese market, one of the biggest in the world.

Suspicions became so rampant that Saigon canceled the February bidding, and the State Department on March 12 tried to soothe tempers with the proclamation: "There is, of course, no relation between the rate of our troop withdrawals and offshore drilling rights . . . There is likewise no basis for the allegation that we are in Vietnam because of large American investments there."

Oddly enough, on April 2, Washington *Post* economic reporter Bernard D. Nossiter, often a critic of big oil, wrote an article ("Deflation of a Phony Boom: No Gushers in Vietnam Waters") for his paper's op-ed page in which he helped take the heat off the industry by belittling the notion that oil interests had anything to do with shaping Vietnam policy. He said the whole thing was overblown by "economic determinists who have never been happy with ideological or bureaucratic explanations of the war." He pointed out that "not a drop of oil has yet been found in or offshore Vietnam." He brought in one of the heroes of the antiwar and consumer movements, Senator Hart, for this vacillating confirmation of his viewpoint: "There may be an element of metaphorical truth to saying we are fighting in Vietnam to protect our oil interests. Clearly, the air war in Vietnam generates almost as much demand for petroleum products as the interstate highway system. America's largest oil companies are also among her largest defense contractors. War, the threat of war and the threat of Communist-inspired political instability have traditionally provided the arguments for granting oil highly profitable special privileges such as the import quota system. But none of these points make oil the real reason for our continued involvement in Vietnam."

Maybe not, but Nossiter's "deflation of a phony boom," as the headline put it, was premature at best, and somewhat misleading. A boom did indeed exist in that part of the world. *Fortune* magazine called the boom "reminiscent of the Alaska-Yukon gold rush." Writing in the September 22, 1970, *Wall Street Journal*, William D. Hartley reported from Singapore that "Southeast Asia is gripped in the excitement of oil fever and just about every international company with position in the petroleum business has rushed to Singapore, which most use as headquarters, to get in on the action. The tempo is increasing. Preliminary seismic work is mostly finished and exploration drilling rigs are moving in . . . Chase Manhattan Bank estimates that $6 billion will be spent in the Asian area on exploration and production between now and 1980, if oil is found. The oil men are working in one of the biggest areas they yet have tackled. It is probably the largest continuous continental shelf in the world, and one of the last major ones to be explored . . . Anywhere from 600,000 to 900,000 square miles of shelf—geologists still are a bit unsure of the extent—are open for exploration. In the biggest area, the South China Sea from South Vietnam across to Borneo, the waters aren't deeper than 600 feet . . . One persistent rumor is that Jersey Standard has struck oil in its 28,000-square-mile concession off the east coast of Malaysia. *Jersey Standard won't talk about it and other oil executives speculate that one reason, if the report is true, is that the company's block abuts the last area of the South China Sea still not handed out as concessions. The area is South Vietnam's continental waters. The Vietnamese have divided the area into 18 blocks, which are expected to be parceled out soon, probably mostly to Americans.*" (Emphasis added)

Two years later, in May 1973, Washington *Post* reporter Thomas Lippman reported from Saigon that representatives from twenty-four major international oil companies had slipped quietly into town to complete purchase agreements for South Vietnam's coastal waters. In July, eight oil concessions encompassing twenty thousand square miles were auctioned. Among the successful bidders were Exxon, Shell, and Mobil. On December 10, the *Post* reported "accelerated" exploration. In June 1974, with the war still going on, Shell and Mobil signed for more leases and this time they were joined by Skelly, Marathon, Sun, Union, Texaco, Amerada Hess, Cigo of Canada, and one Japanese and two Australian companies. Four months later, a story by James Markham in the New York *Times*, "Another Oil and Gas Discovery Is Reported Off South Vietnam," told of a Shell subsidiary's second successful wildcat well, with a test oil flow of commercial rate and a "respectable" gas flow rate. The Washington *Post* reported that "company and government officials alike were ecstatic over the results."

With a North Vietnam–Viet Cong victory certain, United Press International reported on April 22, 1975, that "Western oil companies looking for oil off the South Vietnamese coast secretly have contacted Hanoi and the Viet Cong to inquire about drilling rights, according to industry sources." UPI quoted one industry spokesman as saying the companies "are prepared to work under any government so long as they are guaranteed a return on their investment." As the military situation deteriorated, the companies had been forced to plug their offshore wells and mark them with electronic beepers, but they hoped to come back soon. UPI quoted one American source as evaluating the offshore prospects as "stunning." The Associated Press on April 21 reported that "new strikes were announced in Southeast and East Asia practically every month last year" and quoted a petroleum engineer as saying, "There's oil all over the place." Three days later, Thomas O'Toole, of the Washington *Post*, reported that the companies were sorrowfully pulling out of the South Vietnam offshore area, leaving "an investment of as much as $100 million paid in bonuses." Corbett Allen, vice-president of Global Marine Co., which had been operating a drilling rig for Mobil Oil Corp. in that area, told O'Toole, "It's a shame. That whole part of the world looked like it was going to be the world's next oil province."

Thus, from the prospect of 1975 one would have been able to look back with a lucidly cynical eye and see that Nossiter's "deflation of a phony boom" was about as erroneous as it could be and that the notion surfacing in 1971 that oil helped shape foreign policy and military policy in Southeast Asia apparently wasn't so farfetched, after all.

* * *

This was the year the Federal Power Commission began to give away the store in earnest. No more fooling around. Now Chairman John Nassikas and his men were clearly intent on presenting the natural gas industry with nothing less than a bonanza.

The background for the FPC's action was this: Three years earlier, in 1968, the Johnson-era FPC had set rates for the southern Louisiana area, the nation's richest fields, where nearly half our entire supply came from. The rate was generous, allowing a 12 percent return *after all costs:* the cost of leasing, of exploration, of development, even the cost of dry holes. Everything was allowed to be factored in before the FPC added 12 percent on top, and in those days 12 percent return was very good indeed. But, at the same time, the FPC ordered producers to pay $376 million to pipeline companies for overcharging.[5]

That really ticked the companies off. They hated being limited to a 12 percent net profit, and they hated the congressional mandate that required the FPC to make consumer protection its primary goal. They wanted to be free of such restrictions—free of regulatory moralisms that

---

5. Not that the pipeline companies (many of which were owned by producers) were hurt; they had simply passed the overcharges along to local utility companies, which in turn had passed the overcharges to consumers.

bothered with the concept of "over" charging. So the companies at that point launched their first natural-gas fright campaign as a way of getting people to stop thinking about whether they were paying too much and to start worrying about whether they could get gas at *any* price.

Having softened up the public and many politicians and, they hoped, the courts with the talk of dwindling supplies, the natural gas producers appealed the 1968 southern Louisiana rate decision to the federal courts. They argued that the FPC should have considered not merely what was a "fair and just" price in relation to consumer needs but should also have considered (1) the intrinsic value of a vanishing commodity and (2) the need to give producers more incentive to go out and search for gas. In March 1970, the Fifth Circuit Court of Appeals ruled that the FPC's 1968 rates were okay. But, at the same time, it said that the FPC could reopen the southern Louisiana proceedings in order to take into account the question of an alleged natural-gas shortage. While noting "the frequency with which this argument [shortage] has been effectively categorized as a 'cry of wolf,'" the court said it was concerned over "the *possibility*" of a shortage and therefore it would allow the FPC to take supply into consideration in setting prices.

Consumer groups immediately challenged the decision, arguing that the FPC was not legally empowered to make assumptions as to the alleged shortage or to make rate increases to encourage exploration; they argued that the FPC was established by Congress strictly to protect the public's pocketbook, not to baby the producers, that it was supposed to create its price structure on the policy of cost plus a fair profit. No more, no less. But, in December 1970, the Supreme Court, now headed by Chief Justice Warren Burger, refused to hear the case, and the appellate court's decision stood.

Now nothing could stop the FPC's move to a pricing standard that would lift the price in direct relation to the industry's claimed drop in supply. This meant that, in effect, the oil companies would set their own price for natural gas; for inasmuch as the only proof of production and supply was the figures in the companies' books, and inasmuch as the companies refused to allow the FPC to look at their books, it meant that in a very real sense the industry established its own prices by forcing the FPC to act in ignorance.

By mid-1971, with the explanation that it was "appropriate and in the public interest to enhance the cash flow for gas producers . . . for the special purpose of stimulating further exploration and development,"[6]

---

6. If Nassikas was so worried about the gas shortage, why didn't he get the FPC to stipulate that the producers would have to spend some of their new profits for hunting gas? He had no answer to that except to say he "thought" industry would act properly. Industry spokesmen waffled on this point. When Carl G. Herrington, vice-

the FPC allowed what to the public probably sounded like trivial increases—just a "few pennies" more per thousand cubic feet above the 1968 rates. But in effect the new rates would increase gas bills as much as one third in some parts of the nation. One simple way to measure the stake was offered by Joseph Swidler, former FPC chairman, who was opposing most of the new increases. Swidler put it this way: "There are probably some 1,500 trillion cubic feet of gas in our underground resources. Each cent increase on the price per thousand cubic feet thus represents $15 *billion* more that the consuming public must pay."

The queer thing about the fright campaign, which of course would continue into the indefinite future, was that while the industry was always talking about terrible shortages and sometimes closed the spigot on enough industries to promote scare headlines, actually everybody agreed that there was no real physical shortage. If one took the long-range view and allowed for normal growth, there was, according to the FPC's own staff experts, enough reachable natural gas to last between forty-five and sixty-five years. That was a conservative estimate. For the immediate future, the supply was also ample—maybe requiring a tiny bit of juggling to meet all needs, but still ample. The FTC's Bureau of Natural Gas estimated that, in 1971, 96.6 percent of natural-gas consumers would get all the gas they needed. And if even a small fraction of the industrial consumers of natural gas switched to coal or fuel oil, which most were equipped to do and which they probably should have done long before, rather than burn the more precious gas, then everyone could be easily taken care of. Indeed, the big gas users were those needing it least: the power companies and factories that together burned 71 percent of the natural gas sold in the United States. And they paid much less for the

---

president of Humble Oil Company, went before Iowa Congressman Neal Smith's energy investigating subcommittee, he was asked if he would assure the public that in return for the $4.7 billion generated by proposed new gas rates, industry would come up with additional supplies. Herrington ducked and sidestepped. "Well," said he, "I think, sir, that . . . it is certainly reasonable to expect some results from it. But I do not think anybody can actually predict the results of exploration work." In other words, no promises. No promises on production, but none on additional exploration, either. Was that fair to the public?

Former FPC chairman Lee White didn't think so. "If you assume today that there is a shortage and you ask the Federal Power Commission what do you think ought to be done about the shortage, some commissioner will say, 'I've got it, let's raise the rates and increase the incentive.' And you say to the producer, 'I'm a consumer and I'm willing to pay more if I can get more gas. If the price goes up a nickel, how much more gas am I going to get?' And the producer will say, 'Jeez, I wish I could tell you, but I can't. All I can say is that if I get more money, chances are we'll be willing to spend more looking for gas.' That's not good enough. It really isn't . . . *There has not been one member of the petroleum industry so far as I know* who has said publicly, 'Gentlemen, if you increase the rates so much, then we pledge to devote X millions to finding this gas and sticking it into the interstate pipelines.' They don't say it because they don't have to."

gas they used to cook a steel ingot than the housewife paid to cook a pot roast. For years, they had been the pampered customers, even though they were the least-efficient users of the fuel. Force a few of them to move to other fuels, and everything would be swell. (The FPC had the power to allocate natural gas between industrial and home users. In 1972, the U.S. Supreme Court would uphold this power.)

In clubs and boardrooms and among their business peers, industry spokesmen not only readily acknowledged that there was no shortage but actually joked about the way people were so spooked. In a speech to the Financial Analysts Federation convention in Cleveland in 1971, Leonard W. Fish, a vice-president of the American Gas Association, was bubbly. He said natural-gas stocks were taking on a "new sparkle." Shortages? Ah, he advised the financial analysts not to get the wrong ideas from all the shortage propaganda. "To begin with," he said, "it is important to establish what we mean when we talk about a gas shortage. The word shortage really applies only to our ability to supply *new* customers. Most companies have ample supplies for existing customers and many have supplies for a continued modest growth because of long-term contracts entered into some years ago . . .

"At present, we have a 13-year supply of gas 'in the bank,' as it were, and we believe there is over four times as much gas yet to be discovered in the U.S. . . .

"Many financial analysts are worried about the gas industry because we have more customers with more money than we can take care of. How would *you* like problems like those?"

In fact, the industry wasn't admitting the nonexistence of a shortage in private only; it was also saying so publicly. The American Gas Association took out ads in national publications to assure people that as long as they were willing to pay the right price, there would be gas. A cash register was the only tool the AGA needed to drill for more gas. The pitch was clarion clear in this *Life* magazine ad: "There's no worry that your home will run short of gas. In some areas, the amount of additional [note that word] natural gas to large-scale industrial users is limited. But wherever there is any problem, gas companies are giving top priority to their residential customers. We've been serving you for a hundred years—and we don't intend to stop now." However, said the AGA, there would be one little burden the gas patron would be asked to bear: "It will take higher prices to keep the gas coming."

How much higher? *Business Week* had flatly predicted that the industry's goal was a 60 percent increase. Other outsiders estimated 100 percent. But more-realistic observers knew that the industry was in fact playing for much higher stakes: total decontrol and a several-hundred-percent price increase. John G. McLean, president of Continental Oil Company, speaking to the Harvard Business School Alumni Club in

Houston on December 17, said that the number-one goal was decontrol of gas prices, after which, he predicted, "they would probably rise to about $1" per thousand cubic feet. At the time he spoke, that would have been a jump of 400 percent.[7]

*

Throughout this debate over natural-gas reserves—over the reality or myth of shortages—one stubborn question kept intruding: Why was the United States Government so helplessly ignorant? Why was it so dependent on the industry itself for data about reserves?

Dave Freeman felt that the problem, far from being insoluble, would be fairly simple to solve. "My own feelings," he said, in an interview with the New York Times, "are that we don't need any new laws [to permit the FPC to get data about reserves, etc.]. The federal government owns most of the land on which the oil and gas is drilled. The Department of Interior, which has the responsibility for managing our federal land, has all the authority it needs in leasing the land to require as a condition of the lease that the lessee supply all the detailed data about what oil and gas is there."

But this had never been seriously contemplated. Instead, the accepted ritual was for the industry to give the FPC a pasteurized version of its data. This was done through the industry's trade association, the American Gas Association. Each of the natural-gas regions had its own AGA subcommittee, and these subcommittees pretended to be, as one AGA member put it, "independent geologists performing a public service for the good of the country." But in fact these independent, public-spirited fellows were all on the payroll of the major gas-producing companies: Exxon, Mobil, Standard of California, Shell, Gulf, etc. Only nine major producers in the southern Louisiana area had total control over the gathering of reserve data for that crucial region.

Each company had the usual suspicions of competitors and closely guarded all of its production data. Consequently, the information supplied to the FPC was not likely to be fulsomely candid; after all, how could the companies be sure the data wouldn't fall into the hands of their competitors? They just naturally hedged, fudged, and cheated on the information they gave. Among other things, as will be explained later on, they had strange and illogical—if not downright dishonest—ways of rating what were reserves and what weren't; it had everything to do with money and very little to do with the product itself.

The FPC was left very much in the dark. Chairman Nassikas said he was confident industry figures were "reasonably reliable," but that was

---

7. When phased decontrol began, in 1980, prices soon shot up 1,400 percent above what they had been in 1971.

only his personal hunch. He had no way of knowing. Nobody in the United States Government knew if the industry was lying or not lying. And most discouragingly, few in the bureaucracy seemed to care.

Only occasionally did members of the FPC complain about the secretiveness of the industry, and then they complained only among their industrial associates. One of these rare outbursts came in the summer of '71, when FPC Commissioner Lawrence J. O'Connor, Jr., told a convention of the American Association of Petroleum Landmen in Oklahoma City that producers had regularly refused to give the FPC information about their intrastate sales or about their income. Furthermore, he pointed out, "the gas-producing industry has notoriously given little information in its stockholders' reports with respect to reserves—its most valued asset," and in fact the producers' bookkeeping practices were not only so secret but so shoddy that "regulators and producers themselves have often been at a loss as to what it really cost to find and produce natural gas."

Nevertheless, even though members of the FPC were aware that producers' bookkeeping was often sloppy, even though they were aware that the information they received from producers was not precise but generalized and had to be taken on the flimsiest of faith, they had traditionally done just that. Prior to 1969, there hadn't been much reason to be concerned about it, because natural-gas prices were holding steady, or sometimes falling; but now, with industry demanding sharp price increases based on the claim of plummeting gas reserves, it behooved the FPC to demand total candor.

The commissioners could hardly claim innocence. There was a growing mound of evidence—a mound swiftly becoming a small mountain—that industry data were unreliable. Some of the most persuasive evidence was coming from the FPC's own staff (which often was at odds with the bosses). Just the previous year, on February 2, 1970, Haskell Wald, the FPC's chief economist, in a confidential memorandum to Chairman Nassikas complained of American Gas Association "statistics which we have no way of corroborating"; of reserves data sent to the FPC that "can hardly be said to match" data published elsewhere by the AGA, data that contained such "large divergences" that "on the surface" at least made them "suspect." On February 19, 1970, Wald had sent a fuller memorandum to Gordon Gooch, the FPC's general counsel, in which he spelled out at length the reasons the Office of Economics was "concerned over the apparent lack of adequate checks on the statistical reporting operations." He called attention to the AGA's "large reporting error in the reserves data for 1967"—it had overestimated the decline in reserves by 1.3 billion Mcf [thousand cubic feet]—and then, instead of correcting the error by issuing an errata sheet (standard procedure) had instead "adjusted for the error by reporting it as a negative revision in 1968."

Wald complained that it was difficult to keep up with such juggling. Among numerous other strange techniques used by the AGA to disguise true reserves supply was what Wald called "the problem of 'expendable holes' in the offshore area." He commented: "We understand that these wells are plugged even though commercial production is possible and that they are not counted as successful wells."[8]

Wald had also pointed out other puzzling—if not downright dishonest —aspects of the AGA's way of estimating reserves. It claimed that "existing economic and operating conditions" determined which should be classified as "recoverable." And yet price changes never seemed to make any difference. Surely, he wrote, "each rise in field prices should bring an upward adjustment in the AGA estimate of recoverable reserves." When fields that were once considered "uneconomic" become potentially profitable because of changing prices, shouldn't they be added to the reserves? Wald thought so. But the AGA wasn't making these adjustments, and so, said Wald, "we cannot make any sense" out of the AGA's estimates.

The gas producers were trying to have it both ways: They were arguing that if the FPC allowed prices to rise, they would string pipe to more remote wells and bring in wells at greater depths where there was known to be plenty of gas but recoverable only in costlier ways; but then when the prices were increased, the producers did not add these remote

---

8. Four years later, an official from Continental Oil testified before the Federal Trade Commission that if the company had not set up production machinery, it meant that it did not consider a well of commercial value and therefore it would not be counted in its reserves—*even though a test well had shown there was gas at that location.* In other words, reserves were considered as reserves only if they were "commercial," and they were judged to be "commercial" only if the company had set up machinery to go into production. Swingle, of Shell Oil, said the same thing: "If a company can't afford to put a platform in, you have no reserve. It is not producible." (*Shell* couldn't *afford?*) So the companies were giving their own unique interpretation to the word "reserves," and that interpretation was entirely mercenary. Even if by a geologist's criterion there were substantial amounts of proved reserves on a lease, the producers could claim that the necessary equipment for production wasn't currently available, or that they lacked the necessary capital to develop the lease, when in fact they were simply waiting—as many had been doing for several years—until natural-gas prices were raised to a price that was appealing. Meanwhile, that particular gas was, to the companies, not considered "reserves."

Under the Outer Continental Shelf Lands Act, a company that leased offshore land had five years to start the production and sale of oil and gas; if it failed to do so by that time, the lease was canceled. However, exceptions were made—often. If the company met two conditions—if (1) the company drilled a well within the five years that showed oil and gas of paying quantities and if (2) the company gave a "good" reason for not producing the stuff—the lease could be extended on a one-year basis forever. A full 20 *percent* of the leases held offshore southern Louisiana in 1975 but not in production were beyond their five-year original lease, meaning the companies had proved there was payable gas out there. No doubt the same was true in 1970, when Wald made his comments.

and deeper wells to their estimate of recoverable reserves. So no matter how high the price went, the AGA and its producer members continued to paint an unrelieved crisis.

In November 1970, Wald had again warned the commissioners that the industry was badly misleading them; he reported that staff estimates for gas fields off the Louisiana coast were *42 percent higher* than AGA estimates.

These warnings got little response from Nassikas and the other commissioners. So now, in 1971, some members of the FPC staff began to leak their findings to the press. These leaks prompted at least rhetorical action in Congress. Senator Hart, as usual, kept his antitrust subcommittee plugging away at the issue. He had already asked the FPC to investigate the AGA reports, and this had begun. Representative Neal Smith launched an investigation in his small-business subcommittee to see if the FPC was improperly relying on industry data. And Senator Magnuson introduced legislation to require the FPC to independently determine natural-gas reserves in the United States. "Industry cannot have it both ways," declared Magnuson. "There are those who believe the gas shortage has been deliberately exaggerated as a scare tactic by industry to panic the Federal Power Commission into indiscriminate rate increases. If the industry is to set these fears to rest, then it must give up its obsession with secrecy and make available the facts upon which it bases its claim."

To quiet the critics, Nassikas took action—of a sort. The FPC set up a National Gas Survey Executive Advisory Committee and a Technical Advisory Committee for the purpose of overseeing an "independent" survey of gas reserves. The appointees were largely made up of industry moguls: executives from Phillips, Texaco, Exxon, Shell, Consolidated Natural Gas Company, Amoco, Tenneco, et cetera. Some obviously knew their way around politically; eleven on the Executive Advisory Committee had contributed from $500 to $45,000 (most contributed $1,000) to the Republican party in 1968. The committee had a very clubby air. After looking over the list of committee members, John Rayburn, counsel for the House Subcommittee on Special Small Business Problems, asked Nassikas if he didn't think the consumer should be more prominently represented. Nassikas was cool to the idea. He said he'd have to know whom Rayburn had in mind before he would agree. Anyway, Nassikas added, "the Federal Power Commission is representing the consumer predominantly." Asked if the public would get to know what the surveyors discovered (the survey was not expected to be finished before 1973), Nassikas said absolutely not. Those, he said, were trade secrets. But once again he insisted that the FPC "is representing the public" and, just as the FPC has faith in industry data, "the public must have some faith in what we do." It was asking a lot.

Senator Lee Metcalf of Montana introduced legislation in 1971 to require public representation on government advisory committees. The National Petroleum Council joined the White House in opposing the bill. It died.

"Quite frankly, the oil industry has developed the reputation over the years of being a robber, cheating and despoiling the environment."

FRANK IKARD

Now the oil-producing nations began to turn the last screw. Some called it nationalization, some called it participation. It meant the same thing, differing only in the speed with which the OPEC countries took over ownership. It was a classic case of the good-cop bad-cop routine: the belligerent left-wingers such as Algeria and Libya and Iraq preferring immediate nationalization, while Saudi Arabia and its Persian Gulf satellites were willing to move more gradually. So the latter were seen as our "friends." Even at this early stage, Sheikh Ahmed Zaki Yamani,[1] Saudi Arabia's Oil Minister, was establishing himself as the wizard of ooze, the low-keyed, polished, ever-reasonable hit man for OPEC. While Qaddafi ranted and the Shah of Iran made threats, Yamani was always conciliatory—on the surface. A Standard Oil executive said of Yamani, "He speaks very softly, is eminently reasonable, never issues ultimatums, and is without a doubt the toughest man I have ever faced across a negotiating table." Another oil executive, recalling Yamani's predecessor, the volatile Abdullah Tariki, said, "Give me the rantings and ravings of Tariki any day. Yamani drives you to the wall with sweet reasonableness." In the years ahead, that would be his hallmark: deadly sweet reasonableness. Each time the Western oil companies would begin negotiating with OPEC over price increases, Yamani would state publicly that he was going to do his utmost to keep the price down but that other members of OPEC were adamant on sharp increases, so the job would be difficult, but— He would shrug as if to say it was in the hands of

---

1. Yamani was born in Mecca in 1930. His father was the Chief Justice of Saudi Arabia, and his grandfather was the Grand Mufti, the chief legal officer under the Ottoman Turks in Arabia. After receiving his undergraduate degree in French and Arabic law at the University of Cairo, he studied common law and business law in New York and Boston. He met his wife-to-be, an Iraqi, while in America and became westernized at least to the extent of becoming fond of classical music. (He says he did not take up golf because "it is very hard to find good greens in Saudi Arabia.") In 1959 Faisal, then Prime Minister and crown prince, picked Yamani to be Minister of State Without Portfolio. At twenty-nine, he was the youngest Saudi ever to hold a cabinet post. Some members of the royal family were unhappy that Faisal selected a commoner for such a high post, but instead of being swayed by their unhappiness, Faisal, after becoming King, named him Oil Minister. It was a profitable appointment.

Allah. Then there would ensue a period of several days in which the brasher members of OPEC made their extravagant demands and Yamani would coolly insist on something less, and the outcome of the negotiations would be a new set of prices slightly toward the Yamani end. And then Western editorial writers would express gratitude for Yamani's help in preventing the industrial world's being gouged even more painfully. Seldom has a brigand received so much gratitude from his victims.

It was typical of Yamani that he should come up with the phrase "participation," which sounds so congenial, as an alternative to "nationalization," which sounds so bellicose. Perhaps for guidance as to what *not* to do, he looked to Qaddafi, whose grating threats of nationalization got on everyone's nerves and whose relationship with the international oil giants was obviously destined to be short-lived. Or perhaps Yamani's lesson was drawn from the disastrous experience of Mossadegh, who, in the 1950s, nationalized Iran's oil industry. Not only had Mossadegh acted with rude abruptness, he had used harsh, uppity language, and the major oil companies' executives, who, like all colonialists, believed as firmly in caste as in cash, responded with equal harshness. They closed their markets to him, and thus Iran's oil business momentarily died. Yamani preferred not to run such risks; he would ease into nationalization via participation. The companies would be required to give up a little, then a lot, then everything. He outlined his idea for the first time in a lecture at the Arab University of Beirut in June 1968. Old-style, wham-bam-takeover nationalization, he argued, "killed the goose that lays the golden eggs." He liked that fabular allusion, and in the years ahead he would constantly talk of "squeezing the goose without killing it."

Having discovered at Tehran and Tripoli that the goose was too fat to fight back, Yamani and his colleagues were now ready to intensify the squeeze. In January, OPEC summoned the world's biggest oil companies to Geneva "to negotiate on participation in existing concessions." Thus ended, after less than a year, the peace and stability that the companies thought they had obtained with the Tehran and Tripoli agreements—agreements that they had purchased by adding an additional cost to consumers of something between $10 billion and $31 billion (depending on whose estimates you took) in higher oil prices over the next five years. Still operating under the antitrust immunity granted by the Nixon administration,[2] the U.S. giants joined with their European peers in a flabby

---

2. In granting antitrust immunity, the U.S. Government was in effect telling the companies that they were empowered to negotiate on behalf of the United States. Showing their usual shortsightedness, government officials apparently believed that since at that time the United States was receiving only 3 percent of its crude from the Middle East, the negotiations were not important. However, an entirely different attitude was shown the same year when Venezuela began talking about nationalizing the oil industry; at that, the U.S. Government became alarmed—for Venezuela was, and for years

front of opposition to— to what? Not to the participation demands, but to the price OPEC "participants" were willing to pay for the new arrangement. Once again the giants folded without a struggle. The only essential differences that arose between them and their host countries was over compensation. The companies demanded that they be paid the market value of their assets plus payment for loss of profits until their concessions expired. The countries offered to pay the much lower book value; which is to say, they led the companies into a trap of their own making.

For tax purposes, the companies had always grotesquely understated the book value of their investments in the Middle East. For example, in 1972 the majors said the book value of all investment in the Middle East was about $1.5 billion—a ridiculously small fraction of the value of the oil they controlled. But that's what the companies claimed, and that's what the United States Department of Commerce (under instructions from the companies) printed in its official accounts. So the OPEC countries could say—when they were able to control their laughter—all right, we are willing to pay you in full, based on *your own book value* claims.

On the other hand, said OPEC officials, the companies actually deserved no compensation at all, for they had recovered their investments many, many times over. To prove that point, Dr. Nadim Pachachi, secretary-general of OPEC, pointed out that the Western-owned Iraq Petroleum Company had *annual* returns on investment of 56.6 percent between 1952 and 1963, that the Arabian-American Oil Company had 61 percent returns on investment annually from 1956 to 1960; the Iran Consortium, 69 percent returns from 1959 to 1964; and that the average annual rate of return on investments in the Middle East from 1948 to 1960 was 67 percent. Furthermore, he said, things seemed to be getting even more profitable. Citing the Department of Commerce's own figures for 1970, the rate of return for U.S. oil company investments was 79.2 percent.

The outcome was never in doubt. Although there was a moderate amount of face-saving bluster on the part of the companies, and some needless ultimatums issued by the host countries, the transfer of partial ownership was accomplished, with little real animosity, in early October. The OPEC signers would receive 20 percent of all concessions immediately and a controlling, 51 percent interest by 1983.[3] Actually, not all the majors were upset by this development. I. G. Davis, executive vice-

---

had been, our most ample and dependable supplier; at the time, it was sending us nearly four times more than we got from the Middle East—and immediately made it known that it considered the situation much too critical to leave to the companies; it demanded government-to-government negotiations.

3. The contract was clearly an imperfect marriage. By the time it was signed, Iraq, Libya, and Algeria had already taken steps of various lengths toward nationalization. Venezuela was talking earnestly about doing the same.

president of Gulf, which was a 50 percent partner with British Petroleum
in the Kuwait Oil Co., said, ". . . participation is not a nasty word."
Some companies saw participation as a clever device for getting OPEC
more intimately involved in the oil cartel's old scheme for holding up
prices by holding down supply. Now that they owned part of the goose,
wouldn't they be all the more interested in fattening it? To be sure,
OPEC did not seem to be the most stable partner, but there would be
time enough to worry about that later on; after all, wouldn't the companies be in control of the Middle East fields for at least another decade?
Even in the face of OPEC's clear willingness to tear up contracts at
whim, many of the major oil companies actually thought that now at
least they had a ten-year breathing space.

*

In their self-conscious willingness to get along with their new partners,
the majors began to scold the U.S. Government for being too pro-Israel
in its foreign policy. The companies might have propagandized voluntarily anyway, but they also were under pressure to do so. In the summer
of 1972, Saudi Arabia's King Faisal called executives of Aramco together
for a secret meeting at his summer palace at Taif and informed them
that he expected them to give the Arab cause vigorous public support.
They did as bidden, demanding—both in commercial broadcasts and in
congressional testimony—that the United States make a "sober reapprai-
sal" of its traditional pro-Israel position. They also urged their stockholders to do the same. The oil companies' pro-Arab stance was so solid
and sincere that Al Fatah, the Palestinians' biggest commando group,
banned attacks on Aramco property. "In effect," one Aramco executive
told *Newsweek,* "we carry the enemy flag in the Mideast."

***

Endlessly creative in its desire to help the oil industry (remember: of the
fifteen top gas producers, fourteen were oil companies), the Federal
Power Commission on April 6 came up with a new gimmick called the
"optional pricing procedure" for natural gas, which allowed producers to
get together with their pipeline customers and work out a higher rate
than had previously been permitted by the FPC. Then the producers
would bring this negotiated contract to the FPC for approval, which was
almost automatic. In short, it was simply another way of allowing the industry to set its own prices while the FPC fulfilled its chosen role of
rubber stamp. The old rate ceilings based on cost of service were virtually destroyed. *Business Week* reported that some experts thought the
new policy would cost customers as much as $500 billion.

As expected, the move aroused immediate and forthright denunciation
from liberal politicians, such as Senator Philip Hart, and from consumer
groups. Former FPC chairman Lee C. White described his successor's

action as "to put it mildly . . . outrageous. It is probably illegal, unlikely to work as intended, a startling usurpation of authority by a federal agency." He predicted that the FPC's action "will inevitably result in higher prices . . . without any assurance of new supplies being discovered." He pointed out that the FPC had raised price rates eight times in the past three years and yet new gas reserves were being discovered at a decreasing rate. Senator Hart agreed that the money seemed to be buying no security for consumers. "We find no evidence," he said, "of any substantial increase in private investments in exploration and development during this period of increasing rates by the FPC."

So heated was the opposition that the FPC went under cover. It handed down its first decision under the policy (approving a 5-cent—or 25-percent—increase) without issuing a press release, as would have been customary. The FPC's press official said the secrecy was ordered from above.

A few weeks later, Texaco, Belco Petroleum, and Tenneco came to the FPC for approval of contracts that would have allowed them to nearly double the prices they were charging for gas from offshore Louisiana wells. Some of the public utility commissions representing states hardest hit by the natural-gas price increases headed them off with some tough and practical questions. Since the FPC had been excusing the rate increases as "incentives" to look for more gas, the New York State Public Service Commission, for example, asked Texaco whether it would be willing to make approval of the contracts conditional on their promising to plow the additional revenue back into exploration wells. No way, said Kirk W. Weinert, Texaco's lawyer. Texaco wasn't making any such promises.

***

While the natural gas producers received the most headlined attention, the pipelines were coming in for their share, too. Most of it was unflattering. On April 17, the Supreme Court reaffirmed, for the third time, its 1964 order that El Paso Natural Gas Company divest itself of its Pacific Northwest pipeline property. And yet El Paso continued to press for congressional legislation giving it immunity. Its effort in the Senate was beginning to falter, but its lobbyists continued to work feverishly on the House Interstate and Foreign Commerce Committee, arguing that if dissolution of the merger was forced upon El Paso, this would endanger El Paso's gas supplies for its 35 million customers, especially those in California. El Paso claimed that its gas reserves had declined to a "crisis" point. However, the company was having trouble maintaining its credibility, because in January, Howard Morgan, a former vice-chairman of the Federal Power Commission, had broken a long silence to challenge the honesty of El Paso's claims. His attack, in a letter sent to each member of the Senate Commerce Committee, was devastating.

Morgan pointed out that on seven occasions between 1958 and 1970, El Paso had appeared before the FPC to get approval for increasing the size of its California market. On each of those seven occasions, El Paso had had to swear, and prove, that it had enough gas reserves to take care of the additional customers for many years. On its last appearance before the FPC, March 13, 1970, for example, it had made a commitment *for 33 years* and had proved itself capable of meeting its promise before receiving an FPC certification.

"These FPC certification procedures," wrote Morgan with heavy sarcasm, "are not designed merely to give the highly professional staff of the FPC something to keep them busy. Nor are they designed to allow pipeline corporations to play semantic games with the public or its protective agencies. The proceedings are designed to assure the public—the whole public—that it will be safe in allowing its homes, industries, hospitals, schools and all other vital activities to become dependent on continued supply by the pipeline over the long life of the new or expanded supply contracts."

He pointed out that on July 29, 1970, El Paso also gave *sworn* assurances to the Securities and Exchange Commission, supported by a report from a well-established Houston engineering firm, that (this is a quote from El Paso's own report) "El Paso should be able to obtain, in competition with others, sufficient gas to supply the markets served by each of its pipeline systems for a period beyond 25 years."

And yet, Morgan continued, "In October 1970, less than 90 days later, El Paso was offering testimony, also under oath, in divestiture proceedings in Federal Court in Denver to the effect that their reserves would barely cover delivery commitments for 3 years and perhaps less." This was part of El Paso's "current campaign of terrifying its various market communities" and trying "to panic practically everyone in the Pacific Northwest and Southwest" into supporting the legislation that would immunize it from the Supreme Court's divestiture order.[4]

---

4. El Paso's legislative efforts failed. In 1974 a new company—Northwest Energy Company—would be formed as part of the court-ordered divestiture. Was this a defeat of bigness? Only momentarily. In the oil business, small companies can't wait to get big and adopt the viewpoint and ethics of bigness. Over the next eight years, Northwest Energy would become very big indeed, doubling its size by buying Cities Service's pipeline unit for $530 million and thereby itself becoming one of the nation's biggest pipeline operations, both in area covered and in reserves (second only to El Paso).

Were consumers helped by El Paso's divestiture? It's doubtful that they thought so. As things turned out, Northwest usually charged some of the highest rates in the country.

Considered an underdog during the marathon court fight, John G. McMillian, chair-

* * *

At the same time that El Paso was catching it from one direction, Colonial Pipeline Co., of Atlanta, the nation's largest oil and oil products pipeline, was catching hell from another direction. It was being hounded by a House Small Business subcommittee because of its soaring profits. Colonial had after-tax profits of $27 million on a gross of $109 million in 1971. Representative Silvio O. Conte of Massachusetts said that the $27 million paid to Colonial's owners, ten major oil companies,[5] constituted "one of the most lucrative dividends of any company in the world." Conte, a Republican, got hefty support from Beverly C. Moore, Jr., of Ralph Nader's Corporate Accountability Research Group, who set out to show that Colonial's "sustained monopoly profits are unrivaled in the American economy except perhaps in some segments of the television broadcasting industry." Moore's reasoning: Colonial's owners invested 10 percent of the initial capital outlay of $378 million; figured on that "relevant" investment, Colonial earned 95 percent before taxes in 1970 and more than 100 percent in 1971; 70 percent *after* taxes in 1970, and 72 percent in 1971.

(Colonial should have hired the FPC to defend it. The FPC could usually find some friendly excuse for permitting luscious gas pipeline profits. When the *National Journal* asked FPC chairman John Nassikas how the nation's leading gas pipeline companies managed to chalk up a 31-percent increase in net profits from fiscal 1971 to fiscal 1972, Nassikas couldn't answer. He called in his accounting experts, and they couldn't answer either. The next day, Nassikas telephoned the *National Journal* with a cheery explanation: ". . . there's no problem . . . It's a question of the mystique of accounting.")

The hearing on Colonial's profits threw new light on the oil industry's legendary ability to avoid antitrust prosecution. The enlightenment came in the testimony of Hoyt S. Haddock, executive director of the AFL-

---

man of Northwest, had mastiff ambitions. In 1977 he would help put together a plan by which a consortium would build a natural gas pipeline across Canada to Prudhoe Bay. First cost estimate: $10 billion. But, by 1981, the anticipated costs would soar to more than $40 billion. This would make it history's biggest construction gamble. Neither the majors at Prudhoe Bay—Exxon, etc.—nor the banks wanted to risk that much. So McMillian hired Robert Strauss, former chairman of the Democratic National Committee; the law firm of Charles Manatt, then DNC chairman; former Vice-President Walter Mondale, and a few other luminaries of slightly less wattage. They led his "good will" team into the corridors of Congress; and Congress, always sympathetic to a swell guy whose generosity crosses party lines, passed legislation that would have forced consumers to start paying for the pipeline long before it was completed. Indeed, they might help pay for it even if they never received a speck of natural gas from it. What a deal! El Paso had never had *that* much brass.
5. The owners of Colonial and the percentage of their ownership: Gulf, 16.78 percent; Standard Oil of Indiana, 14.32; Texaco, 14.27; Cities Service, 13.98; Mobil, 11.49; BP, 8.96; Continental, 7.55; Phillips, 7.10; Union, 3.97; Atlantic Richfield, 1.58.

CIO's Maritime Committee, who told this tale: When the ten majors teamed up in 1962 and announced that they were going to build a 1,600-mile pipeline between Houston and the New York metropolitan area, seamen's unions got very upset. The pipeline would carry 1,152,000 barrels a day between the two areas. That would put the equivalent of seventy 50,000-deadweight-ton tankers with the same oil-bearing capacity out of business—meaning the loss of several hundred seamen's jobs. Haddock went to Attorney General Robert Kennedy and asked if he didn't think that ten oil companies ganging up like that to destroy competition was in violation of antitrust laws. Kennedy agreed, and in March 1963, the Justice Department's Antitrust Division launched an investigation. But it bogged down when Colonial resisted demands for certain records. Anyway, Colonial argued that it should be immune from antitrust investigations, because the pipeline was good for national defense, eliminating the need for tankers, which would be vulnerable to submarines.

When union officials complained to Kennedy about the lack of action, Kennedy (according to Haddock's testimony) acknowledged that the pipeline "was in violation of the antitrust laws but that nothing could be done about it." Haddock said his "impression" from Kennedy's remarks and conduct on that occasion indicated "he just thought that there was too much economic strength in these big companies for the federal government to do anything about it." Haddock said that he took his complaint also to Attorney General Nicholas de B. Katzenbach, in 1965, and "this is basically what we were told again." It was plain that the ten-company pipeline had beaten the government, for in 1971—nine years after the investigation was first launched—officials in the Antitrust Division claimed they were still "deeply concerned with the implications for competition" in the case but that they had no idea when the investigation would end, if ever.[6]

*   *   *

When the Department of the Interior put up 366,000 acres off Louisiana for leasing to the oil companies in December 1971, three environmental organizations (Natural Resources Defense Council, Friends of the Earth, and the Sierra Club) blocked the move with a court injunction, successfully arguing that the federal government had not provided an adequate

---

6. Four years later, an Ashland Oil, Inc., internal memorandum was released by the Justice Department—under pressure from consumer groups—that claimed a company such as Colonial, which it mentioned by name, by controlling pipeline supplies to the East Coast held a monopoly and a stranglehold on consumer prices. Ashland's accusations were not made public until December 11, 1976. However, the Justice Department somehow had been unable to come to this rather obvious conclusion after sixteen years of investigation and, earlier in 1976, had closed its Colonial investigation without taking any action.

environmental impact statement as required by the National Environmental Policy Act of 1969.

The question of offshore drilling was becoming stickier because of public awareness of the sharp increase in oil pollution. Popularizing the ecological problem was now routinely done by all national magazines and newspapers. *Newsweek,* for example, reported after an international antipollution convention in London: "The main danger to marine life and human health comes from wastes that are exceptionally long-lasting or highly toxic. The worst offender in terms of quantity in this category is oil. Each gallon spilled in the ocean depletes the oxygen in 400,000 gallons of sea water, thus decimating all fish life in the area." No insignificant matter, considering that, at the time, the annual oil pollution in the world's oceans was 100,000,000 (one hundred million) *tons.*

The Coast Guard admitted that the number of oil spills into U.S. waters had doubled between 1970 and 1971, although the volume was down (except for tanker spills; they had almost doubled). But the Coast Guard didn't seem terribly concerned; of the 8,496 oil spills during 1971, the Coast Guard referred only 372 cases to U.S. attorneys for prosecution and assessed civil penalties in only 145 cases.

Fearful that the federal government would allow runaway drilling that would result in massive spills—hurting fisheries and coastal tourist industries—the governors of fourteen East Coast states, from Maine to Florida, met with new Interior Secretary, Rogers C. B. Morton, on January 11 to demand that they be consulted before the feds allowed offshore oil drilling in the Atlantic. It was an offshoot of an old argument: Who should control the outer continental shelf—those offshore lands beyond the three-mile limit—the states or the federal government? That question wasn't resolved, but Morton did promise to talk with the governors before issuing permits. He didn't sound very warm to the idea. "We must achieve," he said, "a balance between environmental protection and energy resource development." But his promise to set up a "meaningful communications system" with the states came easy, because, Morton said, "at the earliest, even if the legal and environmental hurdles were crossed, it would be seven to ten years before we could get significant production from the Atlantic outer continental shelf if, indeed, oil exists there. We do not know if it does."

He was not being entirely candid. Everyone in the oil industry was aware that Mobil had hit sizable oil and gas deposits at Sable Island, a sandbar in the Atlantic off Nova Scotia, in 1971. As usual, nobody was saying anything about the size of the field, but the *Oil and Gas Journal* had said at the time, ". . . the Sable Island discovery off Nova Scotia has excited the oil world almost as keenly as did the North Sea."

If there was still some mystery about the new Atlantic fields, there was no question about the size of the offshore Louisiana fields. They were lush. And the industry could hardly wait to get drills into every acre. The environmentalists were the big hang-up. Having lost to them, temporarily, in court, the oil companies set out to flank them with a massive propaganda campaign that would promote both Gulf and Atlantic drilling. The American Petroleum Institute in July screened for Washington newsmen a 27-minute color movie, *The Steel Reefs*, which showed fish frolicking around the drilling platforms in the Gulf of Mexico. API also sent out one hundred fifty prints of the film (free) to television stations, especially on the East Coast, and to private organizations. API also sent out four hundred fifty copies (mostly to news organizations) of a 42-page booklet entitled "One Answer to the Energy Crisis"—the one answer being production of offshore oil.

*

All of that was the standard stuff. But, earlier, API had sent out a propaganda missive that stirred considerable controversy. A June 26 release from API was headed *Fish Catch Increases in Gulf of Mexico But Decreases in Atlantic Waters.* The first paragraph informed readers that "A top petroleum geologist today noted that catches of fish in the Gulf of Mexico—where there are numerous drilling rigs—have increased dramatically in recent years but have declined in waters along the U.S. East Coast where there are no rigs."

And who was the "top petroleum geologist"? None other than Dr. Wilson Laird, director of the API's Committee on Exploration.[7] Laird argued that the submerged portions of the petroleum rigs in the Gulf of Mexico acted as artificial reefs, which attracted various kinds of small marine organisms, which in turn attracted fish looking for a meal. "Sports fishermen are drawn to these rigs like iron filings to a magnet," Dr. Laird said. "They have learned that casting and trolling around a rig structure is the closest to heaven a fisherman can get while still alive." He said that the commercial fish catch in the Gulf had increased more than threefold between 1950 and 1971, while the commercial fish catch in New England and Atlantic waters had dropped by more than half during the same period.

A nice story. But was it misleading? What Dr. Laird forgot to mention was that his figures were accurate if you counted only the catch of United States fishermen. If you took into account the catch of foreign ships in New England and Atlantic waters, then the overall catch in the previous twenty-one years had "increased immensely," according to Milan Kra-

---

7. Laird was another who had gone through the swinging doors linking government and industry. Until recently he had been head of the Interior Department's Office of Oil and Gas.

vanja, foreign affairs officer of the National Marine Fisheries Service. Indeed, counting the foreign catch, the total in 1971 was *four times* larger than the figure used by Dr. Laird in his press release.

The API's tone vacillated between querulousness and unction. On the one hand, it was constantly sending out press releases headlined "API Spokesman Warns of 'Overkill' in Environmental Regulations" (March 7), "Enforcement of Environment Law Said to Delay Search for Energy" (April 11), and the like. On the other hand, the API was publishing and distributing booklets on how to clean oiled birds (*Operation Rescue*) and issuing press releases that claimed, "Oil Companies Spend Millions Daily in Drive to Protect the Environment." (November 13) One of its boasts was that the industry was cooking up a "sonic scarecrow" that would frighten birds away from oil spills. (August 17)

Individual oil companies were also swarming over the public with the new, Mr. Clean appeal. Generally, they were much more subtle and smooth than the API. Exxon bought an eight-page insert in *The New Yorker* to blend the argument of need with assurances of care.[8] "The New Adventurers," it was called, with the three-question subtitle: "Why do they search for oil and gas offshore? What are the risks they take? Do they pollute our coastal waters?" The accompanying illustrations included pictures of scuba divers cavorting with fish under a drilling rig, but they did not include any pictures of oil slicks. To read the text of this eight-page insertion, one might have reasonably concluded that anybody who worried about the risks of offshore drilling was as old-fashioned as people who disputed Darwin. "Many people probably think of offshore drilling as a fairly recent development—especially since the 1969 blowout in the Santa Barbara Channel focused public attention so dramatically on the environmental aspects of these operations. Actually, producing oil from coastal waters dates way back to 1894. It began from piers built in that same Santa Barbara Channel. But it wasn't until 1947 that the first true offshore platform was built in fifty feet of water off the Louisiana coast. Since then, some 20,000 wells have been drilled off the coasts of 70 countries, and one sixth of the world's oil is now being produced from offshore fields." No need to worry—it's an old, tried-and-true routine.

On the very last page, Exxon decided, with goggle-eyed innocence,

---

8. Of course, this was only one of many print advertisements on this issue purchased by Exxon, and print advertising was only one approach. Exxon also distributed a color film entitled *The Challenge of Santa Barbara*. Scarcely alluded to in any of this advertising was the fact that Exxon probably stood to lose more than any other company from the drilling stalemate. Exxon was the major leaseholder in the Santa Ynez field, a large oil and gas province in the Santa Barbara Channel, which was believed to contain up to 2 billion barrels of oil and 1 trillion cubic feet of gas, according to Geological Survey estimates.

that, well, maybe drilling at sea might be a little bit dangerous; but it hurried on to assure its readers: "The tragic Santa Barbara blowout wasn't at one of our wells. But that's beside the point; we do drill there. That blowout caused the death of about four thousand birds, and a terrible, but temporary, blight to a beautiful shoreline. The entire oil industry is paying for this accident—in millions of dollars' worth of drilling delays, and a lot more in reputation.

"Our industry's excellent safety record has been marred severely by that one event.

"We aren't trying to make excuses for what occurred, but some of the aftereffects seem to have been exaggerated."

And so on: very cool, reasonable, willing to give a point to make a point. It was typical of the new era of mellow, we're-in-this-crisis-together-and-just-doing-the-best-we-can-for-you-folks advertising. For the year, only one other advertisement oozed quite so unctuously as Exxon's, and this rival overdid it. Texaco's ad was illustrated with a photograph of a veritable Peaceable Kingdom: a panther, a duck, two goats, two rabbits, three sheep, one wolf, a deer, a turkey, a donkey, a black bear, a bison, and a little girl holding a baby duck. Ah, it was sweet, and the text was almost biblical: *"Texaco announces some good news for all living things on this earth.* If man continues to let pollution go unchecked, all of us, even creatures in the most faraway forests, will one day feel its effects. So, for all living things on this earth, Texaco would like to announce some good news concerning our environment." After that buildup, the good news was something of a letdown. Texaco, it seems, was going to create a new department of environmental protection "made up of Texaco people who are dedicated to finding ways to protect the earth, the air, and the water . . . while Texaco provides the petroleum energy people need." The ducks and sheep could sleep better at night knowing, et cetera.

* * *

The selling of the energy crisis was becoming a very big business. According to the calculations of Knight Newspapers reporters, just four big oil companies—Exxon, Shell, Texaco, and Gulf—spent nearly $22 million in 1972 to try to convince Americans that the energy crisis wasn't phony (this was in addition to the estimated $115 million they spent on product advertising). Millions more were being spent by such companies as Mobil, Phillips, Standard of Indiana, et cetera, to make the same pitch: absolving the oil companies from blame while laying it on environmentalists, consumer groups, and similar do-gooders. Of course, the industry's chief lobbying organization, the American Petroleum Institute, was doing its share: $3 million worth of propaganda in 1972. "No public issue since the end of World War II," said the New York *Times*, looking over the year's puffery, "has generated as much corporate advertising."

Television was blanketed with an ad declaring, "A nation that runs on oil cannot afford to run short." As the message flashed on the screen, there was background sound of a thumping human heart. The API estimated that the message reached 95 percent of all American homes with television sets. "We watch this advertising with growing horror," said George Alderson, legislative director of the Friends of the Earth Foundation, "with the way they're trying to mislead the American public into a crisis attitude."

The horror felt by consumer groups was not only in the message but in the size of industry's PR budget, which they could not hope to match. As propagandists, the consumer groups simply had little financial clout. Largely, they had to beg space. Media Access Project, a public interest law firm, tried to persuade radio and TV stations to give time to groups who believed the energy crisis was a hoax—or, as the Project's director put it, groups who believed that maybe the oil companies weren't "outright liars but that there is another view to be heard." It had minimum luck.

The oil crowd had so much money that they could specialize. Not only did the API have its multimillion-dollar program for the general public, it also was cooking up a special $2.5 million program, which might not be ready until 1973, to be aimed particularly at community and business leaders and opinion molders in the press. This propaganda drive would be carried out not only in such upper-middle-class magazines as *Harper's, The Atlantic, The New Yorker,* and *National Geographic,* but also through trade publications such as *Editor & Publisher* and *Broadcasting.* The American Gas Association had a $6-million public relations budget. And in addition, individual oil corporations were chipping in generously. In November and December, Continental Oil Company made a major corporate commitment, flooding the nation with an ad, headed "Energy & America," featuring excerpts from a speech by John G. McLean, Conoco's president. More than seventy thousand copies of the full text of the speech—which was offered in the ad—were ordered. Conoco's PR chief called response "in every sense a blockbuster" and offered as proof the fact that "Cronkite displayed the ad on his news show."

It was the propaganda of doom, and it was quite candidly aimed at higher profits. None of the doomsayers had such a large repertoire as API's president, Ikard. Speaking to the Ohio Oil & Gas Association in March, he announced that for "the first time in our history" this country could not meet its own oil needs if foreign oil supplies were suddenly cut off. "Never before have we been in a bind like this," he said, "and it's going to get worse." In June, the Columbia Gas System, the nation's largest integrated gas system, began buying full-page ads in the New York *Times* with headlines like:

THE
ENERGY CRISIS
IS THREATENING
YOUR WAY
OF LIFE!

and

THE GAS
SHORTAGE:
WHAT YOU CAN DO ABOUT IT!

The black-bordered ads contained information and advice of unrelieved bleakness. The threat: "The situation is getting worse every day, and unless the public recognizes the problem and urges government to cooperate with industry for an early solution, disaster could strike as early as the winter of 1973–74. Industries could shut down because of lack of energy, resulting in great unemployment. Homes and commercial establishments could be without enough energy for their daily needs." The solution: "The prices of all forms of energy must increase sharply if the nation is to have the supplies it needs." John W. Partridge, chairman of Columbia, said he thought that if gas prices were permitted to double, that "would provide ample incentive for producers to get interested and do a lot of exploration." At the price gas was then selling for, doubling would have put another $260 billion into the pocket of industry, based on the minimum reserves estimates, and one-half trillion dollars if based on the maximum estimates of that day.

As the year rolled on, the alleged doom grew thicker. On August 1, Assistant Interior Secretary Hollis M. Dole (who, eight months later, went to work for Atlantic Richfield as boss of ARCO's shale operation) told a House Public Works subcommittee: "This is quite extraordinary. There are unmistakable signs that even gasoline—which most people take for granted just as much as the air they breathe—may become in tight supply in certain sections of the country by late summer of this year." On November 30, the Federal Power Commission warned that the 1972–73 shortage of natural gas would be twice as great as the previous winter's.

***

Not wanting their doomsayers to appear ridiculous, the major oil companies made their predictions come true in 1972 by creating an honest-to-goodness shortage, and a serious one at that—the first peacetime energy shortage of threatening proportions in our history. And it achieved some of the things that the international oil companies had been so rambunctiously aiming at: prices were launched on an endless upward spiral; after 1973, anything resembling "independence" among independent oil producers, independent refiners, and independent retailers—even the semblance of competition from the underdogs—was gone; consumers were reduced to such a state of bewildered panic that they were much less willing to oppose the profits of those who had the power to give or withhold the luxuries of a warm house and a full gas tank; and an even stronger cartel arrangement was created between OPEC and the majors to guarantee an extension of all the above developments.

The underlying historical cause of the shortage was, of course, the ubiquitous oil import restrictions that had been in effect for fourteen years. If these had been lifted when Nixon's own cabinet task force urged him to do so, in 1970, there would have been no supply problem in 1972. Indeed, the influx of foreign oil that would have resulted from a lifting of the quotas would have made it virtually impossible for the majors even to simulate a shortage. But with the import restrictions in effect, the oilmen—and their allies in the government—easily managed to manipulate the nation into a shortage (and resulting national trauma). It was done behind a smokescreen: by issuing false information, exuding optimism where no optimism was justified, leading the citizenry to suppose that the nation would make it through the year with a comfortable supply when, in fact, the majors were taking steps—some secret, some not so secret—to guarantee that an adequate supply was impossible. Government officials who should have known that the industry was issuing misleading data did nothing to head off the crisis. Indeed, throughout most of the year, some of the top officials at the Department of the Interior and especially at the Office of Emergency Preparedness (OEP) were so extraordinarily neglectful in protecting the public that they might as well have been working for the oil industry. The actions of General George A. Lincoln (U.S. Army, retired), head of the OEP, are especially worth noting.

*

In retrospect, the shortage was so blatantly contrived as to make the word conspiracy seem justified. If it was a conspiracy, did some federal officials, including President Nixon, play a part in it? There can be little doubt of that. The only question is, Did they play their part knowingly or out of stupidity and gullibility, accepting the oil industry's advice and doing its bidding without question? For example, in the spring of 1972 Canada virtually begged the United States to take more Canadian oil; our own domestic supplies were dropping and a more bountiful tie with Canada's dependable fields was exactly what we needed, but under pressure from the major oil companies, who wanted to keep supplies tight, our government rejected the proposal out of hand. In the fall of 1972,

Saudi Arabia proposed that a "special relationship" be established between that country and our own that would have assured the United States an ample supply; again, the U.S. Government rejected the proposal. (Within a year, the proposals would be withdrawn by Canada and Arabia, and in fact, both countries would begin reducing their supplies to this country.)

Rejecting these offerings from foreign sources might—just might—have made sense if the available oil in this country were plentiful—and that doesn't mean the United States' *potential* oil supply, but the supply that had already been found and was ready for, or already under, production. But, for some time, there had been indications that perhaps this ready supply was not nearly so bountiful as the public had been told. As early as February 1970, the Texas Independent Producers and Royalty Owners association (TIPRO), the most important trade organization in the nation's most prolific oil state, was asserting that the United States no longer had a surplus production capacity and was urging the major oil companies to admit that the surplus capacity had been exhausted. TIPRO warned that although at that time the Texas Railroad Commission, which set daily "allowables" according to market demand, was *supposedly* holding production from Texas wells far below their maximum potential, in *reality* the wells were producing very close to—or at—full capacity already.

Now, two years later, the Texas Railroad Commission agreed with this assessment: Texas fields had nothing to spare. On March 19, Byron Tunnell, chairman of the Commission, announced, "We feel this to be an historic occasion. Damned historic, and a sad one. Texas oil fields have been like a reliable old warrior that could rise to the task when needed. That old warrior can't rise anymore." That was by way of announcing that for the first time in twenty-four years Texas wells would be allowed to run at 100 percent capacity. The last time was in 1948, to replenish the inventories drained by the demands of World War II. This time they would be running at 100 percent to try to keep up with national consumer needs—and the implication was, they might not be able to cut it. In early 1972, industry journals were reporting that crude production in both Texas and Louisiana was declining. The Interior Department in April officially took the position that the United States' spare productive capacity had dropped to zero. Was all of this true?

If true, this was terrible news for refineries, because the spare capacity of Texas and Louisiana, the two largest oil-producing states, had always acted as the "balancing wheel" of crude supplies: it was always there to be turned up or down as the refineries needed. If the Texas and Louisiana pumps could no longer be turned up, the flexibility of supply was gone, and it could be restored only by increasing the level of oil imports sufficiently to maintain at least a small surplus in Texas and Louisiana. Since Nixon controlled imports, it was up to him.

But not everyone in the oil business agreed on the tightness of supplies. There were clashing opinions, obviously based on differing economic interests or on a wish to deceive. Minutes of the Texas Railroad Commission for March 16, 1972 (not released until the next year, and then only under congressional subpoena), made this point: "Some executives felt that domestic production is already at a peak, but others thought additional 200,000 b/d [barrels a day] might be squeezed out of present reservoirs." Humble Oil Company (Exxon) argued that TIPRO was getting a bit hysterical. On March 23, 1972, Don Smiley, of Humble, told the federal Office of Emergency Preparedness that supplies were adequate and that "there was no need for additional imports in 1972, so far as Humble was concerned." Indeed, Smiley produced documents purporting to prove that the company had crude oil to sell but had had "no takers in recent weeks." Elmer F. Bennett, assistant director of OEP, on March 23 filed a memorandum that "Humble at present is of the opinion that the shortfall in Texas production is a reflection of market conditions and not truly a reflection of the decline in production capacity, if any."

Which side should be believed? Perhaps neither. There were widespread rumors that many productive wells had been capped in Texas and Louisiana, waiting for higher prices (the same technique used for prying higher prices for natural gas). There were also strong rumors—easy to believe—that the larger companies were deliberately slowing production while at the same time overstating supplies in order to produce a supply squeeze that would force prices up. In short, chaos reigned; and since the industry, as always, held all the data and government officials held none independently, there was no way to know for sure who was telling the truth.

In such a situation, one might have fairly expected the government to come down on the side of safety: to react in such a way as to protect consumers even if that meant overreacting, assuming the worst about domestic supplies and raising imports even more than needed to meet demands. This was the attitude of the OEP's staff. Elmer Bennett, in a handwritten memo to his boss, General Lincoln, on March 21, counseled: "Any reserve capacity is small at best. Consequently, I think we are faced with increasing imports even if the majors (or others) are withholding some oil from the market. We should be able to defend our action either way; i.e., if there is some capacity available, or if there is not." Phillip L. Essley, Jr., the most experienced oil economist on General Lincoln's staff, wrote a memo on March 30 arguing that domestic crude producers might indeed be reaching peak production, that perpetuating a tight crude-oil market by holding down imports would give the largest oil companies greater power and higher profits and work to the disadvantage of "crude-deficient" independent refiners.[9]

His prophecy was fulfilled.

The crude-oil shortage of independent refiners—outfits such as Ashland, Champlin Petroleum, and Crown Central Petroleum—was so critical as to make especially persuasive the argument that this was no time for restraint. Better to err on the side of an import oversupply, if it came to that. Independent refiners got about half their crude from major oil companies, about 20 percent from independent producers, and the rest from foreign sources. When supplies got tight, the majors kept the crude for their own refineries and stopped selling to the independents, whose only salvation lay in increased imports. On March 21, William Truppner, assistant director for resource analysis for the OEP, notified General Lincoln that whether the shortage was contrived or real was beside the point; the point was, independent refiners were having "extreme difficulty obtaining supplies and could face severe financial hardship unless the tight supply situation is relieved."

All these warnings were passed on to Nixon. But he acted with a strange sluggishness, and when he finally did act it was with indecisiveness. On May 11 he increased the level of imports east of the Rocky Mountains by another 15 percent (the fourth time he had raised import quotas since 1970, when his cabinet staff investigators started urging him to do away with import quotas altogether), but this was not nearly enough. It did not come close to restoring the surplus "balancing wheel" capability of Texas and Louisiana.

At the same time, Nixon's tinkering with the economy had encouraged another refinery screw-up. In August of the previous year, Nixon had launched Phase II of his wage- and price-control program. He froze gasoline prices at their peak and heating-oil prices at their lowest seasonal level. It was obvious to everyone in and out of government that unless the price imbalance was corrected, the oil companies would instruct their refineries to concentrate on the production of gasoline and to hell with heating oil.[10] The only incentive to do otherwise would be pity for peo-

---

9. When Essley's memorandum, along with sworn statements from six former federal officials who had been involved in pre-crisis energy planning, came to light in an investigation headed by Senator Henry Jackson, General Lincoln said he did "not recollect ever seeing Mr. Essley's paper." The various documents and statements put Lincoln in such a bad light that at one point he interrupted his testimony to burst out, "I think this reflects on my integrity—I am called a damn fool . . . I have searched my mind for things that might have been done better, and certainly with 20-20 hindsight we ought to be able to find some, but certainly we were neither knaves or fools." He had a right to his opinion.

10. One of the curious things about the high price of gasoline on August 15, 1971, when Nixon's price freeze went into effect, was that it was so extraordinarily high. Since oil companies make their biggest profits from gasoline (it used to be that they

ple living in the colder regions of the country, and pity had never been known to guide the hand of the oil industry.

Aside from the misdirection of production, there were ominous signals of low total production. In the first four months of the year, refineries ran at 84.2 percent of capacity, which was lower than for any comparable month in 1970 or 1971. The rate meant it would be extremely difficult to build up distillate stocks (home heating oil, diesel fuel, etc.).

Independent refineries running short of crude, major refineries slowing down production and tilting their output to gasoline profits—these solid warnings that there could be a heating oil shortage the next winter, warnings that came as early as the spring of 1972, were completely disregarded, or willfully played down, by the Nixon administration.

In April, thirty-four Senate and House members asked the Office of Emergency Planning to tell them that the rumors they were hearing about cold times ahead weren't true. General Lincoln, who could speak with the authority not only of OEP director but also chairman of Nixon's Oil Policy Committee, told them not to worry, there would be no hardships in the winter of 1972–73. He said that a survey, completed on April 24, "showed conclusively that there had been no shortage, there is no current shortage and none is foreseen in the coming winter. Domestic producers indicated that supply is adequate and that additional oil can be produced and delivered to New England if necessary." On April 26, Lincoln gave further assurances to the New England Governors' Conference: "My office has checked with the major suppliers on the availability of No. 2 heating oil for the coming year and have assurances that, if anything, the industry capacity to produce No. 2 has been under-used, and that the industry can supply the heating oil needed for the coming season."

---

made their biggest profits on crude oil, but beginning in 1971 that situation changed), naturally they would have been especially eager to escalate those prices before they were frozen in place. Nobody was supposed to know when the freeze was coming. And yet the companies had "accidentally" raised prices just in time. How were they so lucky? There were very, very strong rumors that surfaced later—and were investigated by a federal grand jury, to no effect—that a "high-ranking federal official" tipped the oilmen off to the imminence of the 1971 freeze in time for the companies to juice the prices upward. The record shows that the sharp escalation came about when the majors and the biggest independent refiners withdrew what were called "temporary competitive allowances" (TCAs) from service stations. TCAs were emergency discounts on wholesale gas that enabled a dealer to hold prices down at the pump, especially for price wars. When they were withdrawn, prices automatically went up. In this instance, the removal of the TCAs sent the national average from less than 34 cents a gallon to more than 37 cents. In some markets, prices shot up more than 6 cents a gallon in just a few days. Every penny increase meant a billion dollars a year to the oil companies. Naturally, the oilmen denied any conspiracy. A Texaco spokesman called the increases "a natural firming up of prices."

These assurances proved to be so much air. By midsummer, Lincoln must have been aware that trouble very likely lay ahead. Detailed reports from his own staff predicted a shortage of crude oil and refined products in the coming winter. But he ignored his staff and turned to the oil industry for advice. What he got were vague promises of questionable cooperation—indeed, the promises often sounded like threats. Although outfits like Exxon continued to promise that they would "do their best" to provide the needed heating oil, they were also dropping heavy hints— this was in late July, with the heating season only two months away—that the price was definitely not right and that if the price wasn't raised, they just might not be able to run their refineries at the required capacity. Continental Oil Company, for example, wrote the OEP on July 26 that "the industry still has adequate capacity to supply heating oil demands for the coming winter" but "because of existing price controls, the industry will have difficulty in making the necessary refinery yield adjustments to supply those demands." Internal OEP memoranda indicate that Lincoln's staff viewed this as blackmail—"another step in the threat/pressure campaign for price control relief—and nothing more in my opinion," as one OEP staff member put it. Blackmail or not, the oil crowd obviously intended to hang tough.

Indeed, they were already carrying out their threats. Even as fuel-oil inventories dropped 10 million barrels below the previous year, the major oil companies took steps to see that they would drop lower. They did it very cleverly, by using a long-established system of manipulating the Texas Railroad Commission. The Commission set its allowable production of Texas wells according to the projected national market for crude oil and gasoline and distillate fuel. Since the major oil companies controlled most of the refineries, they were of course the principal purchasers of Texas oil. Therefore, their projections of needs controlled Texas pumping. In late August, eight majors—Exxon, Texaco, Mobil, Shell, Atlantic Richfield, Gulf, Standard of Ohio, and Amoco, whose purchase orders and own production controlled a decisive part of Texas production—told the Commission that they would need *less* crude oil in 1972 than they had in 1971. As for distillate fuel, they informed the Commission that they did not need as much of that either and were therefore *cutting their inventories by 10 percent.* This brazen deception was performed in the face of clear evidence that oil demands would rise, not fall, in comparison to 1971. Among many who had come to this obvious conclusion was the Industry Research Foundation, which told both the Department of the Interior and the OEP that its analysis showed market demand jumping not by its usual 2-percent increase but by 8 percent in the last quarter of the year.

Industry's deception was echoed by top government officials, such as General Lincoln, who, on September 20, told a Senate Banking subcommittee, "We don't see shortage in fuel oil. And we don't see shortage in other products either . . . I have been assured by several major suppliers that there should be an adequate supply of No. 2 [home heating] oil during the coming winter . . . The industry has the necessary feedstocks [raw material] to insure an adequate supply." And why did he think that they would be guided by the public's interest to transform the crude into heating oil? Quite simple: he had "very considerable faith in the industry meeting the challenge." Another who had faith in the oil industry was Stephen Wakefield, deputy assistant secretary for energy programs at Interior,[11] who told the senators, ". . . we do not see any potential for overall shortages of No. 2 fuel oil on a national or on a regional basis." He said a department study showed that the oil industry would produce enough heating oil to take care of even an "abnormally cold" winter, one likely to occur only once in five years.

How could they possibly draw such a conclusion? The declining supply of natural gas—which Nassikas had warned the OEP was sure to occur in the winter of 1972–73—would surely mean a greater drain on heating oil.[12] The new environmental laws would also cut sharply into the heating-oil supply, for utility companies were diverting huge volumes of home heating oil from its normal market to blend with the lower-grade fuel oils to make an acceptably low-polluting fuel for their steam boilers. The 1972 level of home heating-oil use by electric utilities was almost *double* that of 1971 and nearly *triple* that of 1970.[13]

And what made Lincoln and Wakefield think there would be enough *crude* oil? Already the independent refineries, which were so dependent on supplies from the majors, were reporting stiff cutbacks and pleading for emergency rations from foreign imports. Even some of the biggest refineries were making dire projections. Standard Oil of Indiana, whose empire was more tuned to refining than producing, wired the OEP on September 1 that it foresaw the industry as a whole suffering a shortage of about 600,000 barrels of crude oil a day for the rest of the year.

Clearly, instead of airy optimism, federal action was called for, and fast. But Nixon waited another critical 17 days before announcing that he was going to permit all importers east of the Rockies to draw on their

---

11. On leaving government service, Wakefield joined Baker, Botts, one of the largest law firms headquartered in Houston, the corporate oil capital of Texas.

12. The gas shortage and an unusual cold snap helped send the demand for heating oil up a staggering 15 percent the last three months of the year.

13. To put this in perspective, the electric utilities on a daily basis were gobbling up the lighter heating oil at a rate equal to 80 percent of the distillates burned by all of America's railroads. Or consider: the 4 billion gallons of home heating oil used by Consolidated Edison in New York in 1972 was enough to heat over a quarter of a million homes for an entire year.

1973 calendar year import allocations by up to 10 percent. He also permitted a few other minor increases, such as in the Canadian imports. All told, the new authorizations totaled 155,650 barrels a day, but, of that amount, 113,200 barrels a day could be imported only if the oil companies borrowed on their projected 1973 quota. *Absolute* import quota increases came to about 42,000 barrels a day for the rest of the year; this was a trifling amount, a frivolous amount, so little as to be a bad joke.

Most of the major oil companies were delighted with the President's action, for it gave them the power to keep the supply painfully tight, to increase imports or not as they pleased, to borrow or not borrow against their 1973 quotas. An official from Exxon dropped around on September 25 to tell General Lincoln that (in Lincoln's words) he "was certainly glad to see the way we handled additional allocations for 1972." It soon became clear that when Exxon spoke of "additional allocations" it meant in reality no additional allocations whatsoever. Exxon borrowed zero of its 1973 quota. When congressional investigators later asked why they hadn't, Exxon officials pretended to have been helpless, saying that there was a worldwide shortage of crude that prevented their bringing in more. Here was a strange excuse: the world's largest oil company, a major shareholder in the world's largest oil pool, in Saudi Arabia, claiming to have been unable to find any oil overseas to bring into this country —although small refineries that owned no foreign oil somehow managed to find some overseas supplies and borrowed against their future quotas to bring them in.

Exxon was not the only importer to draw *none* of the permitted increase. Among others were Shell, Gulf, Phillips, Union Oil of California, Amerada Hess, and Tenneco. Among those who drew some advance, but far less than they were allotted, were Atlantic Richfield (it did not use two thirds of its increased allocation), Sun Oil Co. (ditto), Standard Oil of Ohio (it used a little more than half its increased allocation), Standard Oil of California (it left about five sixths of its allocation untapped).

Industry-wide, only 35 percent of the advance allocations were utilized.

Since the majors clearly had no desire to meet the nation's needs by importing more crude, it came as no surprise to discover that they were reducing their refinery operations, too. After all, crude supply and refinery production go together. In October, East Coast refinery operations averaged only 82 percent of capacity. November saw operations still woefully down: at 84 percent. By October, fuel-oil inventories were twenty-eight days below autumn levels for 1970 and 1971. Now, at last, General Lincoln was beginning to get concerned—although he did not publicly let on. His frothy forecasts in September had been based, as he told congressional investigators at that time, on the assumption that industry would operate its refineries at 92 percent capacity for the rest of

the year. Now it was clear that industry had no such intentions. (In a retrospective of 1972, Treasury Department analysts would discover that
the industry had *decreased* its refining capacity by eleven thousand barrels a day even though demand was growing by more than 1 million barrels a day.)

The *Oil and Gas Journal* was publicly more candid than the government's own officials. In its October 9 issue, it offered a forecast that was
swaddled with so much caution as to offer only the chilliest hope. *If*
refinery runs were high, the *Journal* said, and *if* the winter was not extra
cold and *if* a stock buildup occurred—*if all* these blessings were heaped
on the country—*then and only then* could the nation hope to make it
through the winter with enough fuel oil.

By November, with the country headed certainly for a serious heating-
oil shortage, the majors stopped pretending that they would try to help.
Cities Service, for example, told OEP officials that, sure, the company
could switch from gasoline production to heating-oil production at its
refineries if it wanted to, but it didn't want to, because the company had
a market for all the higher-profit gasoline it could produce.[14] Exxon was
equally arrogant; at a November 3 meeting with OEP officials, Exxon
spokesmen acknowledged that the oil industry would have to run at 93.9
percent of capacity the rest of the year to produce enough heating oil,
but "economic incentive to operate at these levels does not exist." And so
it went, with Shell, Mobil, Texaco, Sun, and the other big outfits offering
a variety of excuses for not producing.

Industry's shameful performance was even embarrassing to its voice,
the *Oil and Gas Journal*, which, on Christmas Day 1972, carried an editorial warning that the oil industry had better run its refineries full throttle
to make enough fuel oil to meet the nation's needs—even if the industry
lost money doing it. Any "foot-dragging" by oil companies at this time of
shortage could be "disastrous to the industry's public image," the *Journal*
added, nicely ignoring the fact that the industry had been dragging both
feet all year. "The industry must supply the public. It'll be damned if it
fails," the *Journal* said, and then tried to persuade their patrons that even
if they were not moved by the spirit of public service, they should be
moved by selfish craftiness to realize that if they fashioned a "generous
policy" at that moment of national need, the American people would be
more understanding toward the oilmen in their battle with the environ-

---

14. This was certainly true. Emission-control devices required by new environmental
laws were lowering the efficiency of new cars and creating an additional daily demand
for three hundred thousand barrels of gasoline. A full 83 percent of the cars on the
road were still 8-cylinder gas-guzzlers. More than ever, the public was ordering
gasoline-consuming power options on their new cars: 69 percent ordered air conditioning, 90 percent ordered automatic transmissions. Forty percent of the oil consumed in
the United States was consumed as gasoline.

mentalists and less offended when the industry socked the public with higher prices.

There was no indication that, as persuasion, the editorial was very successful.

***

The effort by consumer protection agencies to make natural gas producers disclose the true size of the nation's gas reserves continued, but as usual the producers stalled very successfully. The previous November, the Federal Trade Commission had issued eleven subpoenas to the biggest producers in the southern Louisiana fields, demanding reserves and production data. The companies asked the courts to quash the subpoenas because the FTC was asking for information that was "too sensitive" to give to the government, even though many of their leases were on federal public lands.

While the courts mulled over that quarrel, Alan S. Ward, director of the FTC's Bureau of Competition, went to the Senate Commerce Committee with data that implied that the gas producers were not being candid. Ward drew his material from the American Association of Petroleum Geologists. The AAPG had previously pointed out that the task of measuring reserves in offshore Louisiana was distorted "by the practice of some operators to plug wildcat wells even though commercial accumulations may have been found." This merely corroborated views previously expressed by Louisiana's own officials. But this time the AAPG, said Ward, had even more important evidence of deception: this time, it had data that threw new light on the debate over whether the American Gas Association was lying when it said that, since 1968, producers had been finding less gas than the nation was using. Whereas the AGA reported only 1.4 trillion cubic feet of new natural gas discovered in 1968, the AAPG reported new field discoveries of 6 trillion cubic feet. The same startling discrepancy was true for the next two years as well: the AGA reporting 1.76 trillion for 1969, the geologists reporting 4.5 trillion; the AGA reporting 1.77 trillion in 1970, the geologists reporting 5.2 trillion. He reminded the senators that the geologists' figures "are regarded as normally conservative and have often required upward adjustments."

***

On March 20 the Interior Department released an impact statement for the proposed Alyeska pipeline, as required under the National Environmental Policy Act of 1969. A year earlier, on January 14, 1971, it had issued its first environmental impact statement on the pipeline, but that had been so cursory, so lightweight, so feeble, and had been done in such an obvious rush to help the oil companies get their product to market, that it was greeted with hoots and jeers from the press, as well as from many scientists, conservationists, and members of Congress. That earlier statement ran to two hundred pages. Under pressure of criticism it was withdrawn, and Interior settled down to a different form of attack: overkill. The new statement ran to thirty-five hundred pages—nine volumes, weighing twenty-five pounds.

Under the best of conditions, the ponderous study could not have been properly appraised in less than three months. But Interior Secretary Rogers C. B. Morton made certain that conditions for appraising it would be poor indeed. For one thing, in issuing the impact statement, he announced that he would hold no public hearings on it prior to making his final decision. He said he feared that the hearings would turn into a "circus." (This was in direct conflict with the Council on Environmental Quality guidelines, which held that on major environmental matters "the heads of the federal agencies shall . . . include whenever appropriate, provision for public hearings, and shall provide the public with relevant information . . .") The Interior Department also made it pretty hard for the general public to even read the impact statement. The Department made only seven copies available, and those seven were all held in Washington, D.C. As Congressman Les Aspin of Wisconsin pointed out on April 28, "There is not one impact statement publicly available in New York, Chicago, Milwaukee or Detroit. In fact, there is not one copy available in the 3,000 miles between Washington, D.C., and San Francisco." Furthermore, "even if you are willing and rich enough to be able to afford the $42.50 price tag" on the study, said Aspin, the Department might not let you have a copy for weeks. He said that on March 24, lawyers representing three environmental groups suing to prevent construction of the Alaska pipeline tried to get copies but were told it was out of print and would not be available for another two weeks. Three weeks later, on April 14, they were told that their order was still not ready. They finally got copies of the statement on April 21. "If there were a conscious conspiracy to prevent public scrutiny of the impact statement," said Aspin, "it couldn't be accomplished much more effectively than this."

These contrived delays were no trifling matter, seeing as how Secretary Morton had given only forty-five days for public comments and rebuttals to be submitted for his consideration.

For anyone coming cold to the debate, forty-five days would have been much too brief a time in which to prepare responses. But The Wilderness Society, Friends of the Earth, and the Environmental Defense Fund—which had kept right on top of the situation all along—fooled Morton. Despite the absurdly skimpy time allotted, these groups managed to pull together a stiff argument running to thirteen hundred pages to show that the trans-Alaska pipeline was a bum idea that would imperil fish, birds, animals, human beings, and tundra.

Experts whose opinions could be ignored only by willingly ignorant bureaucrats had trooped forward to assist The Wilderness Society et al. Dr. Harry Brandt, chairman of the Department of Mechanical Engineering at the University of California at Davis, pointed out that the quality of steel in Alyeska's pipes was *not*—as the pipeline company claimed—"exceptional quality" but was in fact "a common low-alloy mild steel without any unusual properties." Furthermore, wrote Dr. Brandt, "Contrary to claims in the impact statement, the pipeline has not been designed in accordance with the highest engineering standards . . . Not only has Alyeska proposed, and the Interior Department accepted, a standard unrelated to the unusual conditions found in Alaska, but in conflict with the clear intent of that standard, Alyeska plans to operate the pipeline at stresses near or above the yield strength of the material." Dr. Robert E. Henshaw, assistant professor of biology at Pennsylvania State University, predicted that the pipeline would result in the "likely doom for at least one of the two large caribou herds of the North Slope." All together, there were seventy-five experts who raised such objections in the rebuttal document.

Persuasive as the 1,300-page response of the nature-loving organizations may have been, it actually was not nearly so damaging to the cause of the Alyeska pipeline proposal as was Interior's own study. It was not surprising that Morton and the pipeline company tried to keep the public from reading the government's 3,500-page impact statement. It was devastating in its candor. Everywhere in those volumes were chilling admissions of great danger. Paraphrased, some of the high points of Interior's study went like this (direct quotes are from the documents themselves):

Every year, Alaska has more than a thousand earthquakes; most of these are slight, but the pipeline would cross three faults where two dozen significant earthquakes have been recorded in this century. "Any point along the southern two thirds of the proposed pipeline route could be subjected to an earthquake of magnitude greater than 7.0 on the Richter scale . . ." and in some areas earthquakes of up to 8.5 magnitude should be anticipated. (The Alaskan earthquake of 1964, which cost $500 million in damage and caused a tidal wave that wiped out the old Alaskan town of Valdez, had a magnitude of 8.5. The energy released by that earthquake was twice as great as the San Francisco quake of 1906.)

Aside from the quakes, much of the ground along the pipeline route is highly unstable. Landslides could be commonplace, and they would cause pipeline leaks and ruptures. "In the event of a pipeline rupture, 14,000 barrels of oil could leak out during the time required for pump station shutdown and valve closure. After shutdown and valve closure, up to an additional 50,000 barrels of oil could drain from the pipeline at some localities." With smaller leaks, as much as 750 barrels of oil could be lost every day without being detected.

Since the pipeline would cross 350 streams, there would be major water pollution. As for land pollution, Atlantic Richfield admitted that a spill of 25,000 barrels—a moderate spill by Alyeska standards—would cover 6.6 acres in winter, in level country (ARCO gave no estimate for hilly country in the summertime, when oil would run farther and faster). "There are no methods to remove oil from terrestrial surfaces without some destruction of vegetation." Some of the plant life along the pipeline route is found in no other part of the world. It could be wiped out.

Between Deadhorse and the Yukon River, a road 361 miles long would be built parallel to the pipeline; it would be laid on a base of gravel between 3 and 5 feet thick—requiring the excavation of about 21 million cubic yards of gravel, much of which would be scraped out of riverbeds, with great harm to fish life. The entire pipeline project would require quarrying about 67.5 million cubic yards of material, and this wasn't counting the 16 million cubic yards needed for developing the oil field itself. Where this stuff was dug, massive running sores—not scars—would be left in the tundra.

The Prudhoe Bay oil field was expected eventually to cover about 880 square miles, and while that was only 0.15 percent of Alaska's total land surface, it was quite enough—coupled with the pipeline and roadways feeding into it—to leave indelible evidence of man's presence: gouged, smeared, torn, and built across so much of the terrain that "north of the Yukon River the proposed project would irreversibly and irretrievably affect wilderness values." From the road north would sprout other roads, and from them still others, until Coke bottles and Schlitz cans covered the track of the caribou and man's spoor "irretrievably and irreversibly bisects a vast wilderness area."

This (in part—there was much, much more of the same) was the tragic future, possible and probable, described by the government's own experts. If Secretary Morton could ignore their dire predictions, and he proved perfectly capable of doing just that, then he could hardly be expected to heed the arguments of outside environmentalists. And he didn't. At 3 P.M. on Thursday, May 11, while Interior Department workers filled the lobby waiting for him to come down and kick off the annual campaign to buy savings bonds, they were informed he was too occupied at "another meeting upstairs." At that upstairs meeting, Morton was announcing the most important environmental decision of the Nixon administration: approval of a permit for the construction of the trans-Alaska pipeline, if the courts would permit it.

Except for Morton's haste in making it, there was nothing surprising about the decision.[15] But many had expected Morton and the Nixon ad-

---

15. Eight days after Morton had released his environmental impact statement, back in March, Donald S. Macdonald, Canada's Minister of Energy, Mines and Resources,

ministration to be a bit smoother about it; many expected them to wait a few months before announcing their decision, to present a more convincing act of "weighing both sides." After all, it was a presidential election year. But Morton wasted no time on pretense. The thirteen-hundred-page challenge written by lawyers for the three environmentalist organizations had been presented to the Department of Interior on May 4. On May 8 this material, much of it highly technical, had been distributed to Interior "reviewers" with orders to have their reviews in Morton's hands within forty-eight hours. This was done. Twenty-four hours after that—a total of four and one-half working days after the challengers had handed in their comments—Morton brushed them all aside and made his decision. He did not try to rebutt the rebuttal; he simply ignored it. "Obviously," said Stewart M. Brandborg, executive director of The Wilderness Society, in what was a remarkable understatement, "the invitation for comments was a mere charade."

*

Morton's decision returned the pipeline issue to the federal courts, where, since April 1970, Interior had been stymied by the preliminary injunction issued by U.S. District Court Judge George L. Hart, Jr., barring any right-of-way grant without court approval. At that time, Judge Hart had found the Interior Department in violation of both the National Environmental Policy Act of 1969 (NEPA) and the Mineral Leasing Act of 1920.

As mentioned earlier, NEPA's two principal requirements were these: (1) Before Interior could take any action that would "significantly affect the quality of the human environment," it had to make a public report on the environmental impact of the proposed action and show that the ecological drawbacks to the plan were more than offset by its social benefits, and (2) it had to determine that there was no alternative action that would pose *less* of an environmental threat.

Had Interior now satisfied those requirements? Quite the contrary. C. Robert Zelnick was justified in his Washington *Post* observation that the Interior Department's impact statement "conceded every significant ecological objection ever voiced against" the trans-Alaska pipeline, and the New York *Times* was similarly justified in its sarcastic editorial remark that "probably the most documented case, as far as the environment is

---

had met with Morton to express Canada's desire "for the construction of a Mackenzie Valley pipeline" instead of the trans-Alaska pipeline. Macdonald left the meeting to tell reporters that it was his "impression" that Morton had already made up his mind. Also in March, when Morton testified at a Senate hearing on the effects of the National Environmental Policy Act on actions by his department, he hinted strongly that the pipeline permit would be approved. Speaking of the pipeline permit as though it were in the bag, Morton on that occasion said he doubted that "any work of man" had ever been given such protracted environmental consideration.

concerned, ever made against the trans-Alaska oil pipeline is contained in the Interior Department's own" impact statement. Of course, if taking the oil across Alaska was the only way to get it out, and if the oil was desperately needed, then Interior would have had a strong argument for placing the welfare of chilly citizens in the Lower 48 over the welfare of Alaskan moose and lichens. But in fact there was a preferable alternate route: down through the Mackenzie River Valley, in Canada, to Edmonton and then on to the middle-western and eastern U.S. states—a route that was not only available but had been vigorously lobbied for by many politicians, environmental organizations, and just plain energy-consuming citizens on both sides of the border.

The loudest, and sometimes almost threatening, advocates of the trans-Canada route were middle-western and eastern members of Congress (of both parties), who were under tremendous pressure from constituents who had been getting shorted in the distribution of petroleum products. The people of those two regions lusted at the very thought of a trans-Canada pipeline pointed in their direction. Any time the oil companies crimped back on fuel oil and gasoline, the Midwest felt it the worst and the East Coast felt it next-worst.

With the truly needy consumers living in those regions, why in the world were the oilmen planning to take their commodity to the oil-rich Pacific Coast states? That market made no sense. As Alaskan newsman Zelnick wrote at the time, "Simply stated, a careful reading of Interior's economic analysis provides no clue as to why Alaskan crude should go to the West Coast in the first place, certainly none justifying an iota of increased environmental risk. The West Coast is second only to the Southwest in the production of petroleum. It will not need any Alaskan crude for the next few years, will not be able to absorb 2 million barrels a day from the North Slope until well into the 1980s, and, if as expected, Alaskan production increases to 5 million barrels a day, the West Coast will not be able to absorb the surplus during the life of the pipeline."

There would have been no trouble getting cooperation from Canada. Its officials much preferred the trans-Canada route. First of all—though this route was longer and would also pose environmental problems—it was much more comforting for them to contemplate than was the specter of a tanker fleet spilling oil along their West Coast beaches. Secondly, if the pipeline was built across Canada, it could also be used to ship Canadian oil.

The government of Canada was at that moment spending $43 million to study the environmental implications of overland pipeline construction through Canada, and the studies were supposed to be completed within the year. But Morton didn't even bother to ask to look at the data. If the United States cared to wait until those studies were completed before making its decision, said Energy Minister Macdonald, Canada would be willing to supply additional quantities of oil to the United States during the wait. U.S. officials ignored the offer.

The Alyeska Pipeline consortium refused to even consider switching their trans-Alaska oil pipeline plans, and Secretary Morton, as their point man, was equally adamant against considering the Canadian route, even though his own staff concluded that the Canadian route was ecologically superior (this conclusion was omitted from Interior's impact statement) and even though Interior's economists admitted that if the Canadian route was chosen instead, the oil companies would come out with as much profit as via trans-Alaska.

One of Morton's truly bizarre arguments against the Canadian route was that it was necessary for our "national security" to keep the oil totally in U.S. hands all the way to market—the implication being that Canada, our closest ally, could not be trusted in an emergency. Morton's argument disregarded two obvious points: (1) In a war, the trans-Alaska oil would make the second lap of its journey on tankers and would have to dodge submarines, whereas the trans-Canada oil would be routed so deeply through the boondocks all the way to market that saboteurs would get frostbite trying to even find it. Interestingly enough, when the Justice Department in the early 1960s decided to immunize ten oil companies from antitrust laws so that they could join forces to build the Colonial Pipeline, from the Gulf of Mexico to New England, the excuse given was that the pipeline would be more secure than tanker traffic and therefore would strengthen our national security. That was to please the oil companies. Now, to please the oil companies once again, the government reversed itself and decided that tankers were safer than a pipeline. (2) Far from being an unreliable source of oil (such as the Middle East), Canada had been a generous and pliable ally who usually tried to sell us more oil than our refineries wanted to buy. In any event, the Department of Defense, apparently embarrassed by Morton's foolishness, pointedly refused to endorse the national security argument for the trans-Alaska route.

*

Unfortunately, the general public was not really paying much attention to the trans-Alaska versus trans-Canada debate. Although the outcome would have a significant effect on their heating and gasoline bills, the American people were not yet stirred up over energy issues. The painful shortages and even more painful price increases had not yet cascaded upon them. If the public *had* been paying attention, it would have noticed all sorts of lunacy. The national security argument was one part of that lunacy, but another part had to do with the two faces of Interior and the oilmen in regard to the Canadian route. On the one hand, the oil companies kept saying that the Canadian route just wouldn't work, that it was a lousy idea, that it would take too long to build, that it wouldn't be profitable, etc. That was in regard to an *oil* pipeline. But, on the other hand, when talking among themselves in such places as the *Oil and Gas Journal*, they were saying that the *only* sensible and profitable way to bring *natural gas* out of Alaska was across Canada. Interior's top experts privately acknowledged that a natural gas pipeline across Alaska was only a "remote possibility" and that the natural geographical conduit was down through Canada's Mackenzie River Valley. Indeed, Secretary Morton had already, without fanfare, set aside a 300-mile corridor in Alaska for the eventual linking up with a trans-Canada gas pipeline. Interior's environmental impact statement also conceded repeatedly that the natural gas produced in Alaska would have to be transported overland through Canada. The reason the oilmen and their bureaucratic allies came to that conclusion was obvious enough: the Canadian route would be much more efficient and profitable. If they took the natural gas across Alaska to the Pacific, they would have to build not only enormously expensive plants for liquefying the gas, they would also have to build a staggeringly expensive fleet of tankers to carry the liquefied natural gas.

So if the natural gas being discovered with oil at Prudhoe Bay would ultimately be brought out across Canada, why wait until the trans-Alaska *oil* line was finished and then build the gas line separately? Why not bring it out from the very start, across Canada, building an oil pipeline right beside a natural gas one? From the consumer's standpoint, there was no good argument against the Canadian route. But there were many bad reasons the Alaska line would prevail. The main reason was that it would allow the companies to keep the Alaskan oil on the West Coast of the United States and away from the hungry markets of the Middle West and East, and thereby would allow them to continue to exert the merciless pressures for higher prices in those areas. The Canadian pipeline would have made the source-to-market routing inflexible, whereas the trans-Alaska pipeline, by feeding into a tanker fleet, would give the oil companies a way to play with their commodity on the national and world markets—making it appear and disappear as needed to whipsaw prices upward. Another reason the oil companies didn't want to change their plans was that they had already laid out their pipe along the Alaskan route and were just waiting for clearance to put it together; it would have been a tough and costly job to gather it up and take it to Canada.

Clearly, the Interior Department's environmental impact statement had fallen far short of meeting NEPA's requirements. But what about the other law on which Judge Hart had based his injunction: the Mineral Leasing Act of 1920? Had the Department of the Interior or Alyeska done something to clear up that problem? Not at all. The Mineral Leasing Act permitted the government to grant rights-of-way for pipeline construction on federal lands only if the grants did not exceed twenty-five feet on each side of pipeline. Counting the diameter of the pipe (four feet), Alyeska could be granted a 54-foot right-of-way. But the oilmen claimed that this was an impossibly narrow corridor to work along, and they were right. Some of their equipment was truly mammoth. Besides, they wanted to build access roads and pumping stations beside the pipe. They claimed they needed four times the allowed width. Short of changing the law, they were stymied. But the law in 1972 was still the same as it had been in 1920.

So—Secretary Morton's willingness to plunge ahead notwithstanding—what would Judge Hart do? Could he possibly ignore the negative candor of the impact statement? Could he, with an even more dazzling bit of footwork, try to sidestep the Leasing Act, of which he had taken such clear-eyed notice in 1970?

Indeed he could, and did. On August 15, Judge Hart ruled in favor of Interior and the pipeline consortium. He lifted the injunction. He was satisfied, he said, that Interior had done all that was needed. And even if it hadn't, he was tired ("dead tired" was the phrase he used in an interview) of the debate and wanted to pass the buck to the appellate system. "It can be confidently anticipated," he said, "that the final decision in this matter rests with the Supreme Court of the United States."[16]

* * *

This was the year of the great reaping. Nearly $6 million was traceable from oil coffers to the Nixon campaign treasury. Doubtless, several millions more were given before laws relating to political contributions were tightened. One of the most generous was Richard Mellon Scaife, a principal stockholder of Gulf Oil, who presented Nixon with a nice round one million dollars. For others, it was not so much the size of the gift as the spirit behind it. Although J. Paul Getty had refused to ransom his kidnaped grandson (with the result that his grandson's ear was cut off), he somehow found $197,000 to help reelect his President. It would be several years before the full extent of Oil's generosity in 1972 could be

---

16. Apparently the thing that had exhausted Judge Hart was the thought that his injunction was costing the oil companies a considerable amount of money. Discussing the case later with reporters, he said the delay had already cost a billion dollars—about $2 million a day, by his reckoning—and that he just couldn't go on bearing that responsibility. It was a typical response for Judge Hart. He had always had a soft spot for the establishment, and an even softer spot for the moneyed establishment. Hart had risen to the federal bench from the ranks of political hacks. He had been Republican chairman for the District of Columbia before President Eisenhower elevated him to the federal judiciary, in 1958. After that, his rulings were notoriously kind toward those who make the Washington world go around.

tallied up. Some of the illegal gifts, the shady gifts, would be uncovered only with effort, and in bits and pieces.

When some of the gifts were revealed, it appeared that there just might have been some quids for the quos. Executives of Amerada Hess gave $268,000 to Nixon's campaign; not long thereafter, Amerada Hess's Virgin Islands refinery got an increase in import allocations worth about $6 million. Ashland Oil gave $100,000, illegally; Ashland got government help in making an Iranian deal that could have been worth billions. Armand Hammer gave $46,000, and his Occidental Petroleum got crucial government help in swinging a Russian liquefied natural gas deal. Of course, there was always the strong possibility, considering the Nixon administration's natural affection for oilmen, that such help would have been forthcoming without the contributions. But it was also clear that for several years the Nixon gang had been carefully cultivating the oilmen. Nowhere was this plainer than in its handling of the trans-Alaska pipeline problem.

From the very beginning, the partnership involved in the Trans-Alaska Pipeline System and its successor, Alyeska, looked a lot like the sort of concentrated power that violated antitrust laws. After all, only three companies—Exxon, ARCO, and BP—owned 80 percent of TAPS. The Justice Department began a routine investigation of the pipeline in 1969, and by February 1970 the Department's antitrust lawyers had uncovered enough to warn Interior Secretary Hickel that it looked as though TAPS had real problems. That warning fell into a hole. In 1971, the Justice Department Antitrust Division took a tougher line, issuing a series of administrative subpoenas on the Alyeska oil companies to divulge certain information. But, in August 1971, Attorney General John Mitchell ordered his lawyers to cease the investigation immediately, explaining, "In view of what is going on, this is not the time." What was going on was the accumulation of the greatest political slush fund in history.

"I think it's fun. It's patriotic. People are saying, 'We won't let those blankety-blank Saudi Arabians blackmail us.'"

JOHN C. SAWHILL, *Deputy Administrator*
Federal Energy Office

"If anyone still needs evidence that this country's jerry-built system for supply and distribution of fuels and energy has collapsed, look around," the New York *Times* editorialized as the third week of January opened in bleakness and some fear. "From the Rocky Mountains to the Atlantic, schools and factories are threatened daily with midwinter closedowns for lack of heating oil. As emergency stocks become available, trucking lines find themselves so short of diesel fuel that they may not be able to deliver what there is. Were it not for a fortuitous few days of unseasonable warmth, the Northeast would be an icy disaster area."

It was true. Scheduled nonstop transcontinental flights took off from New York with such light fuel tanks that they had to make intermediate stops to refuel. Exxon, Texaco, and Shell were all short of jet fuel in the New York region. Two oil companies cut diesel deliveries in the East by 25 percent in January. But the Northeast was getting off lightly indeed, compared to the central states. There, winter storms triggered one of the worst fuel shortages to strike any region of the country in twenty years. With natural gas, propane, and heating-oil supplies low and getting lower from Colorado to Ohio, many factories, schools, churches, and civic buildings were temporarily shut down. Briefly, Denver closed all its secondary schools and was able to keep open only five elementary schools. Wichita put its high schools on a three-day week. Officials at Denver's airport said they were relying on body heat to keep commuters warm. Millions of bushels of grain were threatened with spoilage, because there was no fuel for drying it out. Grain shipments were stranded on barges in the Mississippi and Ohio rivers. Federal and state officials went to Canada to beg (and receive) extra oil rations to prevent homes from running out of fuel in Minnesota, Michigan, and Maine. The Red Cross mobilized workers in Minnesota to care for people evacuated from their cold homes. That was in January. By February, things were so bad that Minnesota Governor Wendell Anderson asked Nixon to declare the state a disaster area, because the heating-oil shortage threatened to close five hundred forty factories and eighteen thousand stores.

The Middle Atlantic states did not escape entirely. Texaco, the nation's

largest marketer of oil products, announced in late January it was temporarily cutting off or sharply reducing deliveries of heating oil in New Jersey, Maryland, Delaware, and Pennsylvania. Maryland eased the state
air pollution standards for large factories to conserve heating oil. Virginia, short on kerosene for space heaters, asked the federal government
to divert navy supplies in the Norfolk area to civilian use.[1]

Even in the South and Southwest, which generally came through the
winter unscathed, there were some ironic spot shortages. The University
of Texas, although endowed with hundreds of thousands of oil-rich acres,
was forced to cut off heat to student dormitories in Austin and delay by a
week the start of its second semester. Louisiana, the second-largest natural gas producing state in the country, had to ration natural gas to industries; its sugarcane crop was threatened because of mill cutbacks due to
energy shortage.

In February, Canada—which had been rebuffed the previous year in
its efforts to establish a joint energy policy with the United States—
notified Washington that in the future it would set a ceiling on energy
exports to the United States in order to hold enough fuel reserves for its
own people.

The chilly helplessness that gripped half the nation left the Nixon administration and the oil industry singularly unmoved. On January 11,
Nixon ended mandatory price controls on petroleum products and told
the companies to operate under "voluntary" price controls. They immediately raised home heating-oil prices 8 percent.

Not that that made the product any easier to obtain in some areas. It
almost seemed there was a conspiracy to keep oil, at any price, out of the
Midwest. Amerada Hess Corp. had been favored with permission to import an extra 6 million barrels of heating oil to ease the nation's shortage.
But the company preferred to sell in the East, rather than in the harder-
pressed Midwest, and Nixon's Office of Emergency Preparedness refused
to intervene to persuade the company to spread its wares around. James
Erchul, head of Minnesota's Office of Civil Defense, begged for a share
but was rejected. "This," said the defeated Erchul, "is a cruel, hard and
difficult competitive system we have." Indeed, the cruelty and stupidity
of the allocation system provoked so many cries of rage from its victims
that Nixon, to quieten them, declared on January 17 that for the next
three and a half months all import ceilings would be lifted from heating
oil; furthermore, the 1973 quotas for other oil imports would be increased to their highest level in fourteen years, he said, to permit the im-

1. For the most part, the Pentagon was much less interested in Americans' comfort
than they were in the comfort of military allies. Despite the fuel crunch at home, the
Pentagon went right on sending oil to the governments of South Vietnam, Cambodia,
and Thailand.

portation of nearly a million barrels more of foreign crude into East Coast ports, and this in turn would free Gulf Coast oil for the fuel-starved Midwest.

Hurrah? Well, not quite. The biggest companies were in no rush to start bringing in the new allowables. They were making too much money out of scarcity.

On February 28, six weeks after the ceilings were lifted, Senator Edmund Muskie complained that "there has been no concrete evidence offered by the major oil companies that they have increased supplies as a result of the President's relaxation of controls." He said officials back home in Maine had asked the oil companies for specific information as to how much and when oil imports would increase, but had received only vague and incomplete answers.

By March, two things were evident. First, the oil companies were rolling in dough as the result of recent price increases. Prices had, in fact, pushed up so sharply less than two months after Nixon lifted mandatory controls that he had to clamp them on again. Even so, profits soared. First-quarter profits for most of the big companies were up 25 to 50 percent, and some were much higher. Second, industry had made such a mess of refinery priorities in 1972 that the mess would continue through 1973. The year had hardly gotten underway when government and industry officials were predicting a gasoline scarcity come summer, and the robins were just starting to come North again when the experts were ready to predict another heating-oil shortage during the next winter. To create the shortages would take some doing, however, for as the New York *Times* noted, "The warnings are surprising some people, because the stocks on hand seem to be larger than they were at this time last year."

The origin of the coming gasoline problem was plain enough: having cut back heating-oil production so much as to endanger normal life and commerce, the oil companies had to scramble (beginning in early 1973) to prevent the situation from getting completely out of control. Refining of heating oil was raised sharply. Cities Service, for example, claimed that as of February it was forcing its equipment to operate at 103 percent capacity.

But, having turned perversely late to the production of heating oil, the refineries were left with scarcely enough capacity or time to produce the gasoline that would be needed for the peak motoring seasons of spring and summer.

In early February, oil industry officials began warning that within a few months long gas lines would appear. A. M. Card, a senior vice-president of Texaco, told the Cost of Living Council that "already signs are developing that there will be a severe shortage of gasoline." Terence B. Redmond, a vice-president of Amoco, Standard of Indiana's refining and distributing branch, told the Council that his company was refining heating oil "as hard as we can. Normally we could be moving back to gasoline at this time. We haven't done this yet." So he saw a "tough" gasoline situation, come summer.

That hardly showed great foresight. A tough summer was obviously the companies' goal, and they had the power to reach it. After the very brief flurry of refinery activity at the first of the year, they cut back sharply once again. By early April, refineries in the United States were running at only 88.7 percent of capacity—the lowest since the previous December. Refineries on the Texas and Louisiana coast, on which the nation depended for more than a third of its gasoline, were operating far below the previous year's level, even though consumer demand was much higher than in 1972. Many refineries were closed down entirely for "repairs."

Overtaken and overwhelmed by the Watergate scandals, President Nixon showed little interest in the energy mess. Weeks went by without any guidance from the White House. When his long-awaited energy message was finally issued, on April 18, it was a dry hole. Perhaps the do-nothing quality of the message could be attributed, at least in part, to the fact that, five days before the message was delivered, fifty-five corporate energy executives had had a friendly discussion with eleven top government energy officials—including George Shultz, William Simon, and Charles DiBona—in the Bahamas. The press was not invited. Mark Green, a sparkplug with the Nader organization who had been watching the meeting from a distance because he was not allowed to get closer, reported: "One conference organizer explained the situation to me in a logic Casey Stengel would appreciate. 'We want an open discussion,' he said, 'but if we opened it to the outside people it wouldn't be open.'"

Members of Congress who were obliged to come up with energy answers greeted Nixon's message with irritation and insulting adjectives: "inadequate," "timid," "asinine," "halfhearted." One congressman remarked, ". . . it would have been a great message six years ago. When compared with the urgency of the energy crunch, it seems somehow inane and embarrassing."

Sagging under cliché solutions, the message had obviously been shaped to please industry. Nixon proposed that natural gas prices be deregulated at once, that federal lands be opened for three times more oil-industry exploitation than ever before, that the Clean Air Act be weakened to allow the use of more high-sulfur coal. At the same time, he brushed aside both the idea of conservation,[2] which could have had swift

---

2. Although there were no official figures on the amount of energy wasted each day, expert estimates ranged from 20 to 40 percent. Cars were especially wasteful. One fourth of U.S. energy was consumed in transportation, but auto engines were so

impact on energy consumption, and the idea of major research-and-development programs, which could assure long-term security.

The only historic step taken by Nixon was to end the 14-year-old quota system on oil imports, but this much-fought-over program had been peeled away in recent months by so many upward adjustments of the ceiling, and the rumors of its imminent demise had circulated for so long around Washington, that this action hardly had a dramatic impact. Indeed, with new energy shortages—contrived and otherwise—popping up every month, and with some of his own advisers nervously demanding that Nixon wash his hands of the quota system, it was only surprising that he had managed to hold out so long. The duration of the holdout, in the face of repeated emergencies, testified to the heavy influence of the majors, as did the timing of the import system's demise. After all, now foreign oil cost as much as domestic, and sometimes more. Libyan crude landed at Baton Rouge, Louisiana, in April cost $4.36 a barrel, compared to a maximum price of offshore U.S. oil of $4.07. Consequently, imported foreign oil would now only drive the price of domestic oil higher. Nixon had waited long enough to make sure that U.S. consumers would not benefit from the end of the import quota program.

Considering the timing of, and the strategy behind, this step, it was only too appropriate that Nixon had assigned the writing of the first draft of the speech to one who had been outspokenly in favor of higher OPEC prices: James E Akins, who had come to the White House staff after four years as head of the State Department's Office of Fuels and Energy. He was the chap who, after Libya had triggered the everlasting upward spiral of prices, had told Congress that the Middle Eastern—and all other—oil price increases were normal and reasonable. Many considered Akins to be proindustry, and his record did show him to have helped the oilmen at several crucial moments. For example, he was on hand in 1971 when Big Oil's ambassador John McCloy worked out the antitrust exemption. Many considered Akins to be pro-Arab, and they had good reasons to think so. Almost simultaneous with Nixon's energy speech came the appearance of Akins' article "The Oil Crisis: This Time the Wolf Is Here," in the quasi-official quarterly *Foreign Affairs* (April 1973). In this article, he argued that if the Arabs did use an oil boycott as

inefficient that they used only about 20 percent of the energy potential in gasoline, the rest being thrown off in heat and exhaust. The Office of Emergency Planning said that more than half of all auto trips were less than five miles—to the drugstore to buy a pack of cigarettes, etc.—and that on longer trips the average 6-seat car carried only 1.4 persons. Some people proposed that big cars with the poorest gas-mileage performance be subjected to an extra tax. Detroit didn't like that idea at all, and neither did Nixon. Nor did Nixon cotton to any of the ideas for rationing gasoline or allocating the supposedly scarce energies for their most efficient use (using natural gas for homes, not for industry, for example).

a political weapon, there were only three ways the United States could respond: "We could try to break the boycott through military means, i.e. war; we could accede to the wishes of the oil suppliers; or we could accept what would surely be severe damage to our economy, possibly amounting to collapse." In reality, he was suggesting only two courses of action: (1) give in to OPEC's demands, (2) go to war. And since the United States was not exactly in the habit of going to war for the luxury of topping its gas tank, Akins was obviously of the opinion that there was only one thing to do: give in. Coming from an adviser to the President, the Arabs must have seen this as encouragement to launch their embargo. Eliot Marshall would later comment in *The New Republic* (August 16 and 23, 1975), "This article could not have come at a time more propitious for OPEC. Tension was mounting over the conflict between American business and political interests in the Middle East. The unanswered question was, what would America do if threatened with the oil weapon? . . . Akins' answer to the big question was clear: an embargo will work and the U.S. won't resist . . . By publishing notice that the U.S. wouldn't react violently, Akins removed the last argument the [Arab] moderates might have used to forestall an embargo."

Within a few months after writing Nixon's speech, he was named ambassador to Saudi Arabia. The years ahead would find Akins unswerving in his philosophy. When the United States sent strongly worded warnings to OPEC countries in July 1974 about not pushing prices too high, Akins—according to top sources—declined to carry the message to King Faisal. At the same time that Treasury Secretary Simon was trying to jawbone OPEC into lowering prices, Akins blithely predicted that OPEC prices would keep right on soaring and that they would get by with it. In 1975, when Defense Secretary James Schlesinger and Henry Kissinger warned OPEC that another Arab embargo might provoke us to military action, Akins reportedly appeared on Saudi national TV to say that people who talk about intervention have "sick minds."

* * *

And so the nation floundered on. A new and frightening development was the disappearance of thousands of independent gasoline dealers. They were being killed by the majors. In June, the Society of Independent Gasoline Marketers of America, whose members bought fuel from major oil companies and sold it at cut rates, reported that, since the previous fall, 1,452 of its 25,000 members had been forced to close permanently. The technique used to wipe them out was quite simple: the majors either stopped selling gasoline to the independent filling stations, or they cut down drastically on the crude they supplied to independent refiners, who sold much of their gasoline to the private-brand and unbranded retailers. Or they did both. The starvation of the independent refiners was measured in 1973 by the fact that while refineries owned by the majors were, at management's choice, running at less than 90 percent capacity, those owned by independent companies were able to operate at only 50 percent—a few were down to 20 percent of capacity—because they didn't have enough crude.

Why had the majors decided to destroy the independents? Because the majors no longer needed them. It hadn't always been that way. For most of the postwar era, the majors had been plagued more with crude-oil surpluses than with crude shortages. The greatest tax advantages and profits were in the production of crude, especially in the Middle East. Before Colonel Qaddafi led OPEC into rebellion, in late 1970, the international oil companies operating in that part of the world figured the per barrel profit on Saudi Arabian oil (which cost 4.6 cents to pump and load aboard a tanker) at about 53 cents; Iranian-oil (which cost about 12 cents a barrel to pump and load) profits were about 45 cents. Those were golden days for producers; and because their greatest treasure lay at the wellhead, the international giants looked upon their refining and marketing operations only as a way to get rid of the crude that was so profitable. They hardly cared if refining and marketing made money.

Consumers were urged to gorge on gasoline. The major companies made their service stations as alluring as possible, cheerful little plantations on the highway and clubby places at the city corner, tempting the motorist to stop and fill up with cheap *power*. They even offered service, friendliness, reliability. It was central to their advertising. They were so rash as to promise clean rest rooms. They acted as though it was their greatest delight to process credit cards. They offered trading stamps and free drinking glasses as premiums. The typical service station franchised by a major company had attendants to spare, all seemingly eager to check the air in tires, to wash windshields, to empty ashtrays, to dispense free road maps. They sold gasoline, but they threw in even more hospitality and goodwill and the feeling that they really did want you to come back. They had to get rid of that gas; they had to, because those wonderfully profitable wells were churning around the clock, and to keep them churning, you and I had to keep using, using, using.

Needing every outlet to unload their crude, the majors also encouraged independent dealers to build stations and to buy their slopover refinery products. For many years, the relationship worked very well for both parties. By offering cheaper gas without service, by utilizing cheaper facilities, higher volume, mass-marketing innovations, and the added advantage of not having to pay the two-cent-a-gallon franchising fee paid by the major-brand dealers, the independents were able to expand their market until, by 1972, they accounted for 7 percent of the nation's retail outlets and 30 percent of retail sales.

But, by the end of 1972, the system had begun to change radically.

The majors were losing control of Middle East and African supplies. Already OPEC, on its own, was trimming production. The companies were also losing control of overseas pricing. OPEC was now obviously determined to push prices through the ceiling; the companies would reap their share of the profits, but no longer at the old, intoxicating cost-to-profit ratios, which ran as high as 1:10. From now on, company profits would not come from unloading on the consuming world an ocean of cheap oil—it would depend on helping OPEC maintain a tight balance of very high-priced crude and on reasserting and exploiting the companies' dominance in downstream activities: refining and retail marketing. An editorial in the *Oil and Gas Journal* noted on January 1, 1973, that the Mideast revolution had established conditions that "call for a new set of priorities creating stable profit centers in refining and marketing. The time has long gone when a company can underwrite refining-marketing losses with production profits."

So by 1973 the majors no longer needed the independents as they once had: in the face of a more tightly controlled crude supply, they no longer needed the independent refiners to catch their slop-over surplus and, in the face of their own refinery restrictions (between 1970 and 1973, no new refineries had been built in the United States and none were under construction), no longer needed the discount and unbranded filling stations as outlets for their surplus gasoline. In fact, the existence of both independent groups was now looked upon as a costly nuisance.

The majors set out to get rid of the independent dealers by stealing their tactics. The fancy big stations that manned many pumps and sold tires and batteries and did auto repairs began to disappear. The big-name brands began switching over from full service to partial service to no service: the rest rooms got filthier, the free maps disappeared, and so did the Green Stamps and free kitchen glasses. You wanted gasoline? That's what they offered. And with the shedding of service and frills, they could afford to meet the discount stations' prices.

And then, finally, they simply stopped supplying gasoline to many of their old unbranded customers. If it seemed a ruthless step, the majors were willing to weather the bad public relations that resulted. Lee White, former chairman of the FPC, testified to a Senate committee in May 1973 that a top executive with one of the majors had told him: "'These companies that you are talking about are part of the private enterprise system. We are sellers, and in a seller's market, and we have no obligation to the public in any form of the legal sense. Certainly, insofar as our having to supply independent refiners and marketers, there is nothing that I have seen anywhere that says it is incumbent upon us to keep our competition in business.'" A director of Shell said, "The independents make their money from surpluses. To save them is like lending a bed to your wife's lover."

By early March, the Society of Independent Gasoline Marketers of America, which had about two hundred private-brand members, reported that all its members were running short.

Martin Oil Co., the biggest of the little oil companies in the Midwest (two hundred stations), had knocked on the door of fifty-three oil-refining companies during the winter and had been able to buy less than one third the gasoline it would need in 1973.

Urich Oil Company, the company that invented the self-service gas station, after World War II, had had to put up with spot shortages all winter, and now, in March, its major gasoline supplier was about to end its contract. Hugh Lacy, vice-president of Urich (which owned one hundred stations and wholesaled gasoline to three hundred others), declared, "This whole damned industry [the independent dealers] is going down the drain" as the result of a "two-pronged war" waged by the majors. One prong was a cutoff of supplies; the other was the creation of a slightly disguised competition at the independents' price level. Even as the major oil companies were closing their unprofitable brand-name stations all over the United States, they were opening many new "discount" stations with strange-sounding names. Exxon, for example, began marketing gasoline at "Alert" stations, Mobil came out disguised as "Sello," and Phillips masqueraded as "Blue Goose," Gulf as "Economy" and "Bulko," Shell as "Ride."

At the end of March, Mobil and Texaco announced that they would limit distributors to the same amount they had received in 1972 (guaranteeing at least a 10 percent shortage) and Cities Service and Sun Oil Company said they couldn't do more than 90 percent of 1972. Over the next three months, most of the other majors announced curtailment plans of one sort or the other for their own stations; they imposed much harsher reductions in sales to the private-branders or cut them off entirely. British Petroleum, for example, which had been selling gasoline to the Greenbelt Consumer Services chain for ten years, suddenly announced that the contract would end as of July. Some of the private branders who managed to stay alive did so by buying black-market gasoline, at exorbitant prices.

In May, Senator Adlai Stevenson chaired a Senate investigation based on the thesis that, as he put it, "circumstantial evidence supports the conclusion that the major oil companies are using the fuel shortage they helped create to drive out their competition." He felt the federal bureaucracy was contributing to the debacle by leading the independents up blind alleys when they tried to escape from the majors. He said that in Illinois alone (his home state) there were scores of "independents and customers of independents, particularly farmers and municipalities, whose supply has been cut off or severely cut back" and who had been pleading with Washington for emergency supplies. "Once they know where to call," he recounted, "many spend days hearing a busy signal at the other end of the telephone line before they even make contact with someone in the Office of Oil and Gas. Of those who do make contact, many are told that they will be called back and are never called again. In several cases with which I am familiar, constituents first called Chicago and were told to call Washington. When Washington never called back, they called Washington again and were told that the rules had been changed and that they should now call Chicago again. When they called Chicago last week, some three weeks after their first call, they were told nothing could be done for them . . . Of the 108 cases which have been filed with my office, I am aware of only three in which positive action has been taken, all requiring my personal intervention. Even this relief is only partial. The 17,000 farmers supplied by two of these constituents and the hospitals supplied by the other are assured of adequate supplies only through next month."

He wasn't exaggerating the trouble. Already some farmers in the Plains states had run out of diesel fuel for the pumps that send water into the alfalfa and corn fields. In Colorado and Kansas, some harvest crews refused to bring their machinery into an area unless the farmers could guarantee fuel. City governments were running into a price wall. Los Angeles expected to pay $3 million for gasoline for its vehicles; it had paid $2 million the year before. Detroit was paying 47 percent more, Cincinnati 45 percent more, for gasoline and having a hard time stocking up even at those inflated rates. Memorial Day weekend travelers found many gas stations closed or limiting their sales per customer. The gasoline shortages were not critical, but they were beginning to make people nervous. And summer had just begun.

The problem was not just a matter of how much total energy was available nationally, but of how the energy was allocated. With just a little restraint and wisdom on the part of consumers, there would have been enough energy to go around—*if* the major oil companies didn't try to play tricks with it, hiding some here, diverting some there, selling some where it wasn't needed. There was evidence all around, however, that the majors weren't playing square. In a wide-ranging investigation of the fraudulent qualities of the 1973 shortage, two Philadelphia *Inquirer* reporters found that on May 15 Standard Oil of Indiana (Amoco) had placed a full-page advertisement in *The Financial Times*, of London, soliciting new industrial customers, promising "secure" and inexpensive gasoline; five days later, Amoco was placing a two-page advertisement in the Washington *Star-News* explaining that its American customers would "have to get by with a little less for a while, so there'll be enough to go around."

Indeed, the United States was the only major industrial country undergoing energy shortages at the time. Elsewhere in the world, the oil companies were marketing with their usual bounty.

The shell-game atmosphere was further heightened when, in the midst of a claimed shortage, some U.S. distributors were caught shipping oil produced in this country to Europe to reap the higher profits there. The trade publication *Oil Buyers Guide* disclosed that low-sulfur oil was bought on the Gulf Coast for 21 cents a gallon, shipped to Rotterdam for 3.5 cents a gallon, and then resold for 34 cents a gallon.

There were no price controls for petroleum products in other countries, so there was nothing to prevent U.S. exporters from doubling or tripling the profits they would have gotten for the same oil if sold here; which is why, between January and October, exports of U.S. distillates reached 1.5 billion barrels. Indeed, by autumn, U.S. exports of oil and gasoline hit a rate of more than 1.7 million barrels a month—five times the normal export traffic. The racket worked in both directions. Although domestic oil and refined products were subjected to an on-again-off-again price control program, there were no price controls on oil products refined abroad and brought into this country; the situation was ripe for exploitation, and the Interior Department "suspected"—and when that department suspected wrongdoing by oil companies it was almost certainly a fait accompli—that products from U.S. refineries were being shipped halfway across the Atlantic to "Europeanize" the cargoes, and then the ships sailed back to the United States with their control-free wares. Interior officials said they were trying to crack down on the traffic, but there was no sign of enthusiastic policing.

The intentions of the industry were also brought into question when reporters discovered that crude-oil inventories from Indiana to Oklahoma had risen by 7.3 million barrels in May, although field production had not increased. If the story told by these figures was accurate, then obviously the oil was being stockpiled—held off the market—while refineries operated at less than full capacity. If the stockpiled crude had been promptly processed, it would have increased gasoline production by 120,000 barrels a day, and the fact that it wasn't being refined was, said Representative Les Aspin of Wisconsin, "just one more piece of evidence that this summer's gasoline shortage is probably being created by the big oil companies."

Sometimes the industry's own figures showed that the shortage was at least partly the result of willful lack of production. The American Petroleum Institute reported that, at the start of 1973, U.S. wells were capable of producing 10,301,000 barrels of crude. But in December 1973, when the "shortage" was supposedly most intense, U.S. wells were producing only 8,625,000 barrels of crude—16.2 percent less than their maximum capacity.

Not only did crude statistics indicate an industry conspiracy, so did statistics for petroleum products. Government investigators discovered that inventory levels of gasoline during the summer were downright comfortable, the largest in history—at the same time that cars were beginning to line up at gas-short service stations. When a *National Journal* reporter asked an official at the Interior Department's Office of Oil and Gas about that, the bureaucrat replied, "I've always viewed this as an economic shortage, not a physical shortage. I suppose they [the major companies] feel they are doing a patriotic duty by contriving this shortage at a time when they can cope with it, instead of in three or four years."

The comfortable inventory levels of gasoline were one reason top law-enforcement officers from six states (Connecticut, North Carolina, Michigan, Massachusetts, New York, and Florida) showed up at a hearing before the Senate Antitrust Subcommittee to charge that the gasoline and fuel-oil shortages were the result of a conspiracy.

Noting that as of June 1, gasoline reserves in the United States totaled a whopping 202.5 million barrels, New York State's Assistant Attorney General Charles A. La Torella, Jr., asked, "What shortage?" Pointing out that in 1972, when no "crisis" occurred, the gasoline reserves were 1.6 million to 9.6 million barrels less, La Torella repeated his question: "What shortage?"

Other state lawyers overflowed with similar skepticism and bitterness. Connecticut Attorney General Robert K. Killian: "Big oil is bigger than the United States Government." North Carolina Attorney General Robert Morgan: "The shortage is a result of the combined collaboration of international oil companies with foreign governments." Michigan Attorney General Frank Kelley said the only regulation was not of the oil industry but of oil consumers: "clandestine regulation by a few oil companies . . . not accountable to the people." Massachusetts Attorney General Robert H. Quinn accused the majors of "seizing on the present crisis as a means of squeezing the little guy out of the market. The majors are taking over the choice locations, putting up 20-pump stations with 24-hour service and are replacing the small dealers." Daniel S. Dearing, of Florida's Department of Legal Affairs, said, "There is no energy crisis. There is a competition crisis. We are convinced there is major collusion." Their proposed remedies ranged from an investigation of international scope, to antitrust lawsuits, to smashing the majors in such a way that those who produce oil could no longer exploit the public at the retail pump.

Several states decided to do more than grumble. They filed antitrust suits aimed at breaking up the oil industry. But nobody took these suits very seriously. If the U.S. Government couldn't whip the oil industry,

what made the individual states think they would have better luck? Ultimately these state suits faded out.

*　*　*

More impressive was the antitrust suit filed by the Federal Trade Commission on June 17, charging the eight largest oil companies—Exxon,
Texaco, Gulf, Mobil, Standard of California, Standard of Indiana, Shell,
and Atlantic Richfield—with all sorts of sins: unlawfully monopolizing
refining, driving independent oilmen out of business through collusion,
aggravating gasoline shortages in order to reap excessive profits. The key
charge was that they had tried to monopolize the refining industry for at
least twenty-three years. Together, these eight companies, representing
assets of $76 billion, controlled 51 percent of domestic crude production,
owned 58 percent of refinery capacity and 64 percent of proved domestic
reserves, and accounted for 55 percent of all retail gasoline sales.

Eight companies was a big enough bite—and too big, as it turned out—
but logically the FTC need not have stopped there. Why not take on all
eighteen majors? Their domination was not only impressive but downright awesome: 83 percent of refining capacity, 67 percent of all crude
produced in the United States, 75 percent of retail gasoline sales, virtually all of the 209,000 miles of oil pipeline. The FTC might as well have
taken on the whole gang, for all the good it did.

Senator Philip Hart, who had, three years previously, asked the FTC
to undertake the investigation that led to the complaint, welcomed the
action but was presciently gloomy: "The day many predicted would
never come is here . . . I feel like we've won the Irish Sweepstakes. But
the sad part is that we won't get a verdict—and relief—for eight to 10
years. FTC has to prove not just monopoly power, but anticompetitive
behavior. This will mean a search of millions of documents to confuse
everyone."

It was a solid prediction. The suit would still be bogged down eight
years later, not yet reaching court, much less settlement. From the beginning, FTC investigators knew they were in for some very tough jungle
fighting. Not only were the accused oil companies refusing to give the
FTC investigators the data they were requesting, and not only was the
Justice Department unwilling to give its investigation much help (Justice
had waited a year and a half before promising to enforce subpoenas for
the needed data), but the White House itself was sniping from behind.
William E. Simon, chairman of the President's Oil Policy Committee and
deputy secretary of the treasury, wrote Lewis Engman, chairman of the
FTC, to complain that the lawsuit's effort to split up the majors' well-to-
nozzle control of the industry "gives me a great deal of concern because
of its implications for domestic energy supply in the next few years."
Simon argued that the oil industry was highly competitive and that the

independent refiners and marketers weren't of much use to the nation any more anyhow. He suggested that he and Engman sit down together so that he could straighten Engman out before the FTC made its final recommendations. Since FTC commissioners act in a quasi-judicial capacity, they are prohibited, just as judges are, from discussing pending cases; Simon's suggestion was obviously a highly improper one. When he was hauled before the Senate Antitrust Subcommittee to explain his actions, he admitted weakly that "antitrust policy is a little bit out of my line."

But that did not prevent his continuing to intrude in other ways. On August 27, he released a study of his own (Staff Analysis of the Energy Adviser, Treasury Department . . . *Investigation of the Petroleum Industry*), in which he tried to peddle some inaccurate information to prove that the FTC was wrong when it said that the majors had built no new refineries on the East Coast since 1950. Several of the refineries listed by Simon actually turned out asphalt, not gasoline or heating oil, and had nothing whatsoever to do with the shortages. Simon said that the FTC counsel was "absolutely insane" to suggest that the eight companies under investigation had influenced his report.

* * *

Both houses of Congress prodded Nixon to set up a mandatory allocation program, to make sure that the oil was fairly distributed among the various regions of the country and to make sure that it was fairly distributed between majors and independents. "We've got to have a mandatory allocation program," said Senator Henry Jackson, the Senate's most important spokesman on energy, "or we won't have any independents." But the Administration kept putting it off.[3]

Failure to allocate, said Senator Hubert Humphrey, from hard-pressed Minnesota, was resulting in some midwestern refineries "operating at 20 percent of their capacity. Some of them get no crude oil at all. It is not sufficient merely to remove import quotas. We have to have a movement of the crude oil that comes into this country on an equitable basis to all sections of the country. Presently, when it comes to the eastern seaboard or the western seaboard, or to the Gulf states it has difficulty finding its way to our part of the country. The pipeline does not seem to reach that

---

3. If the Administration seemed intent on doing what industry wanted, rather than what the public needed, perhaps that's because in fact this was its intent. At a private meeting in the White House with oil executives on August 16, Interior Secretary Rogers Morton assured them that the Office of Oil and Gas, which had been set up to establish the nation's energy policy and which would later become the Federal Energy Administration, was not the watchdog that the public had been led to think. In fact, the OOG, said Morton, "is an institution which is designed to be *your* institution and to help *you* in any way it can . . . Our mission is to *serve* you, not to *regulate* you. We try to avoid it . . . I pledge to you that the department is at your service."

far and if it does, what comes out of the pipeline is less than adequate for our needs."

He was right: the Midwest was constantly being picked on, abused, cheated, shortchanged. Although the northeastern states were totally without refineries, they had more political clout than the midwestern states and, though often subjected to price squeezes and phony short-ages, could generally rely on refined imports to see them through. The midwestern states were, during this period of mischievous supply jug-gling, much more vulnerable to oil-company plots. When the majors wanted to elicit extreme pain to dramatize "shortages," they concen-trated on the upper Midwest. Senator Frank E. Moss of Utah, for exam-ple, disclosed in 1973 that an investigation by his Subcommittee on Inte-grated Oil Operations had found that about 11 million barrels of home heating oil were stored on the East Coast during the hard winter of 1972–73 while residents in the upper Plains states went without. Moss's investigators had found "much activity, unusual and suspect, on the part of the oil companies that made whatever scarcity there was far worse than it need have been and much more severe in some areas of the coun-try than others. We have uncovered strong evidence of mass withholding of winter fuels, diversions of supply from one area of the country to an-other, and inexcusable failures to produce." The crippling shortage in the upper Midwest, he said, could be traced to some very suspicious conduct on the part of the Colonial Pipeline, which, owned by ten major oil companies and handling more than half the total refined products in the United States, obviously had the power to juggle the market.

Among the several futile efforts made to reclaim the power of alloca-tion from the oil companies was a bill introduced by Congressman Don-ald Fraser of Minnesota, an amendment to the Interstate Commerce Act to make it unlawful for an oil pipeline company to ship its own oil or that of an affiliated company. It was an amendment modeled on the rail-road commodities clause of the Interstate Commerce Act, which pro-hibits railroads from dealing in the commodities they carry—a clause enacted in 1906 to break up the railroads' monopoly over the coalfields of eastern Pennsylvania and West Virginia. Wasn't it plain that something similar should be done to loosen the oil companies' tight control over production, distribution, and marketing of oil? After all, said Fraser, "Of all the major industries, only this one has its own transportation system devoted exclusively to hauling its bulk commodities. Within the oil in-dustry, the pipeline system is now wholly controlled by the large inte-grated companies, who are free, within broad limits, to deny access to the system to lesser competitors or permit access only on payment of penalty costs. It is as if General Motors owned the Interstate Highway System and charged a special toll for all cars that it did not manufacture itself." But Fraser was aware that, for three generations, reformers had been trying to get the government to crack down on the pipeline monopoly, without success, and he indicated his effort would probably meet the same fate. It did.[4]

***

The gasoline, natural gas, and fuel oil shortages were driving some politicians, editorial writers, scholars, and energy experts to make extremely nasty remarks about the oil industry's ethics. The overall situation was aptly described by *The Wall Street Journal* (although it did not agree with the description): "In contemplating the recent shortages of gasoline and natural gas, many Americans seemed convinced that something funny was going on, that perhaps as Adam Smith observed two centuries ago: 'People of the same trade seldom meet together, even for merriment and diversion, but the conversation ends in a conspiracy against the public or in some contrivance to raise prices.'"

David Freeman, certainly no firebrand—until recently he had been energy adviser at the White House and would later head up a Ford Foundation study of U.S. energy—told a Consumer Federation of America conference: "The 'energy crisis' could well serve as a smoke-screen for a massive exercise in picking the pocket of the American consumer to the tune of billions of dollars a year." Robert Moretti, speaker of the California Assembly, called the gasoline shortage "the greatest pure hustle in American business history." Senator Muskie said of the shortages: "Either the federal officials responsible for oil policy in this country displayed an unbelievable level of incompetency, or the petroleum industry itself misrepresented the facts. I personally believe that a combination of both factors was at work."

Senator Jackson wrote FTC Chairman Engman to say it was damn well time the FTC showed more interest in the widespread conviction that the fuel shortage is "a *deliberate, conscious contrivance* [his emphasis] of the major integrated petroleum companies to destroy the independent refiners and marketers, to capture new markets, to increase gasoline prices, and to obtain the repeal of environmental protection legislation. Allegations and some circumstantial evidence of this sort are coming increasingly from oil independents, consumer organizations, students of the industry, Members of Congress, and from the chief legal officers of local and state governments."

4. The Fraser-Moss bill even got some surprise support from an official of the Justice Department. Testifying on the bill, Keith I. Clearwaters, deputy assistant attorney general for antitrust, said there were many "sound reasons" for freeing the pipelines from control by companies that owned oil, but he warned that building the case would be difficult, because the people with the information that would help were also the very people whose business depended "upon the good will of the major oil companies," and therefore they would be afraid to testify. He was so right.

Another whopping natural gas price increase inspired Congressman David Obey of Wisconsin, ordinarily a very moderate fellow, to suggest nationalizing the industry: "When the companies imply—as they have—that they will not be doing more exploration and development for additional gas reserves, unless the prices they get are substantially increased, then it's time for the government to say: 'To hell with you, we will do the job ourselves.'"

And always there were those who reminded the public that the oil companies had historically played on "crises" for profits. Attempting to swing support for his pipeline divestiture bill, Congressman Fraser told his colleagues: "This is not the first time a crisis in the oil industry has been used to justify emergency solutions leading to higher prices and decreased competition. Since World War II, there have been several such crises, notably: the heating oil shortages on the east coast in 1948 and 1952, which were resolved by having voluntary cartels deliver oil at substantially higher prices; the Iranian crises of the early 1950's, which were handled in the same way, through cartel arrangements and higher prices; and the Suez crisis of 1956–57, which was treated in a similar fashion. Although the urgency of the 1957 Suez situation subsided through these means, a crisis atmosphere continued on into the OPEC negotiations of 1970–71, to be resolved again by a cartel arrangement and higher prices. And finally, today, we have the Environment-Alaskan Pipeline-OPEC crisis. As in the past, we are given no alternative but to establish an 'allocation program' to mitigate shortages—of course, at higher prices with less competition.

"Somewhere in this process we ought to pause to take a long look at a business system which so regularly produces emergencies resulting in protective government intervention and higher prices, and which at the same time continues to show higher profits and faster growth than the rest of the economy."

The public's bitterness rolled toward the industry in a great flood, which the oilmen had little luck in holding back. As would occur time and again throughout the decade's propaganda war, Mobil spoke loudest, but this time its arguments were remarkably feeble. Rawleigh Warner, Jr., chairman of both Mobil and the American Petroleum Institute, called the conspiracy charge "nonsense," but the only thing Mobil could think up as a counterargument was to say that "conspiracy requires secrecy . . . We operate in a fishbowl." Which was hardly true; whether or not the general public knew it, every member of Congress and every bureaucrat in Washington was well aware that it was virtually impossible to pry loose from the oil industry such data as would be needed to know what was going on. At that very moment, the Justice Department was suing a group of majors for more data on reserves.

Mobil had reached a peak of chutzpah, probably never to be attained again, on February 25, when it spread full-page ads in newspapers across

the country with the head "Is Anybody Listening?" Totally ignoring the
fact that major oil companies had been building their refineries in
Europe and in the Caribbean, and refusing to build them in the United
States, for many years before there was anything remotely resembling an
environmental movement, Mobil declared: "Oil companies said that unless new refineries were built in this country, a severe winter could produce critical heating oil shortages. Not a single refinery is under construction in the U.S. at this time. Lawsuits and regulations stemming
from exaggerated environmental fears have blocked the construction of
new refineries."

Mobil was nothing if not persistent. The conspiracy charges especially
rankled its officials, and they decided to go nationwide again on July 9,
in full-page advertisements—under the heading "An Open Letter On the
Gasoline Shortage to Senator John Doe and Representative Richard
Roe." The ads were placed in newspapers in every congressional district,
at a cost of more than $200,000. The ad counterattack was timed to as-
suage tourists angered by the uncertainty of supply and rising prices of
gas. Naturally, it portrayed just about everyone as being responsible *but*
the oil companies. Blame the politicians for not letting the oil companies
drill offshore as much as they wanted to, Mobil argued. Blame the politicians and the courts and the environmentalists for blocking Alaskan oil,
said Mobil—*"Oil companies had no control over this."* Blame the politicians for the oil import program that kept oil supplies so low that new
refineries were discouraged from being built—*"Oil companies had no
control over this."* Blame "ill-advised government regulatory policies" for
discouraging natural gas production—*"Oil companies had no control
over this."* (And so on.) To hear Mobil tell it, such innocence had never
been seen before as could be found among oil industrialists. They were,
it seemed, not perpetrators of a fraud, but mere victims of hardhearted
environmentalists and stupid politicians.

If the advertisement made new friends in Congress for Mobil, it wasn't
evident. The Congressional Record suddenly blossomed with speeches
by congressmen made irate by Mobil's efforts to dump on them. One of
the mad members was Congressman Michael Harrington of Massachusetts, who derided Mobil's pretense of wanting to discuss the energy
problem. He told how Mobil had refused to send anyone to an open
meeting, then had refused to meet with him privately. So he had sent
nine oil companies, including Mobil, a list of questions on the supply and
price situation. "The president of Mobil's North American division, Richard Tucker, wrote me back saying that 'I will not discuss or attempt to
justify individual business decisions made by Mobil.' Mobil was the only
company that refused to answer my questions."

Nor was Mobil making friends in the bureaucracy. Its newspaper advertisements blaming automobile antipollution devices for the gasoline
shortage ("The $66 Billion Mistake" was the way its ad put it) so an-

noyed Russell Train, chairman of the Council on Environmental Quality, that he publicly condemned the spate of advertising for "obscuring the facts and confusing the issues." He pointed out that the Environmental Protection Agency, after studying two thousand 1973-model cars, found that fuel economy loss (in miles per gallon) due to pollution-control systems was less than 8 percent and that "by comparison, the fuel economy loss due to air conditioning averages about 9 percent, and can run as high as 20 percent on a hot day in urban traffic. In addition, the fuel loss from an automatic transmission is about 6 percent." The real villains, Train implied, were the idiots of Detroit who kept designing bigger cars. "The Chevrolet Impala weighed 4,000 pounds in 1958, but weighs 5,500 pounds now . . . A change of only 500 pounds in the weight of 1973 vehicles—from 3,000 to 3,500—can lower the mileage from an average of 16.2 miles per gallon to 14 miles per gallon—a decrease in fuel economy of nearly 14 percent. A thousand pound increase in weight, from 3,000 to 4,000 pounds, could lower gas mileage from 16.2 miles per gallon to 11.2 miles per gallon—a decrease of 30 percent."[5]

*

But blundering propaganda such as Mobil's did not hurt the oil industry's public relations efforts nearly so much as those damnable quarterly reports required by the Securities and Exchange Commission. Every three months, the companies had to confess that they were becoming remarkably richer. Profits in the first half of 1973, compared to the first half of 1972, were up magnificently. For example, they were up 443 percent—right: 443 percent—for Occidental; 143 percent for Standard of Ohio; 58 percent for Marathon; 51 percent for Atlantic Richfield; 48 percent for Exxon; 46 percent for Gulf; 43 percent for Cities Service; and so on. Some politicians fumed. Senator Jim Abourezk of South Dakota, who would be one of the most implacable critics of Big Oil over the next five years, sent a newsletter to his constituents listing the profits increase, pointing out that the nineteen largest oil companies paid an average of only 5.99 percent federal tax on their incomes (the lowest being Gulf's 1.2 percent and Mobil's 1.3 percent) and arguing that, as a result, they had put together such wealth as to make even states seem puny. "Exxon has assets of $21.5 billion. All of the real and personal property of South Dakota has an assessed valuation of $3.2 billion, roughly half of its true value. That is, Exxon could buy all the personal and real property of three states like South Dakota."

_____

5. Not once during the 1970s did the oil companies' propaganda ads blame Detroit's designs for even part of the gasoline supply problems. And not once during the 1970s or 1980s did the automobile companies publicly accuse the oil majors' soaring prices for destroying the U.S. auto industry's big-car dominance of the world market. The gentlemanly silence that prevailed between those two industries was eloquent.

Third-quarter reports were more of the same. Every company reported significant gains, but none could equal Occidental's 7,153-percent increase over 1972. Gulf was up 91 percent, Exxon 80 percent, and Mobil 64 percent. For the top ten, earnings were up an average of 52.1 percent.

"Somehow," wrote Ernest Holsendolph in the New York *Times,* "it didn't seem quite right, not when consumers were caught between the specter of scarcity on one side and the pressure of rising prices on the other. Assurances that high oil profits were good for the country, because they finance exploration and development, did not really suffice."

* * *

Environmentalists won one more battle, and then lost the war, over the Alaskan pipeline. On February 9, the seven-man U.S. Court of Appeals in Washington, D.C., agreed unanimously that the Mineral Leasing Act of 1920, which limits right-of-way over public lands to a width of twenty-five feet on either side of a pipeline, meant exactly what it said. The consortium of companies said they needed a right-of-way of at least 146 feet and had proposed to the court that the Interior Department's Bureau of Land Management be allowed to issue a permit exempting them from the statutory width. The consortium argued that the BLM had issued exemptions for many other pipeline routes and had in fact made a habit of ignoring the law. The appellate court rejected the proposition that an agency is "entitled to violate the law [if it does] it often enough." Furthermore, the court was extremely scornful of the effort to circumvent a congressional act. Reversing Judge Hart, of the lower court, the panel said: "These companies have now come into court, accompanied by the executive agency authorized to administer the statute, and have said, 'This is not enough land, give us more.'

"We have no more power to grant their request, of course, than we have the power to increase congressional appropriations to needy recipients."

But the court refused to rule on the touchier ecological issues, saying that they could be dealt with later on.

On April 2, the Supreme Court refused to take an appeal from this ruling. So the fight went back to Congress, and there the proponents of the trans-Canada pipeline as a substitute for the trans-Alaska pipeline went frantically to work again. (To say "trans-Canada" pipeline as though the proponents were suggesting that the oil be brought out of the ground and popped immediately into a pipeline on Canadian soil is misleading. If a trans-Canada pipeline had been built, the Prudhoe Bay oil still could not have reached it without first passing over a couple of hundred miles of Alaska.) Their main arguments were that the pre-Canada route across Alaska would be less ecologically damaging and would avoid the perils of tanker traffic on the coast; that a pipeline would ultimately have to be built down through Canada to handle the natural gas from Prudhoe Bay (both sides agreed on this), so it would be less expensive and more efficient to start out on that route; and that the oil would be funneling down where it was greatly needed—into the middle and eastern United States—not to the West Coast, where it wasn't.

Observers outside the industry could not understand why the oil companies said they wanted to bring the oil to the West Coast, for the West Coast was consuming about two million barrels of oil daily, 70 percent of it supplied by oilwells west of the Rockies, and unless those wells were shut down, it could not possibly absorb the 1.5 million or so barrels daily from Alaska. The only reasonable explanation for the oil companies' pitch was that they were not telling the truth, and that in fact they intended to ship the Alaskan oil to Japan—the country from which they had bought the pipe for the pipeline and which was always hard-pressed for oil, being dependent on the Middle East for more than 80 percent of its supply at that time. Sniffed syndicated columnist Joseph Kraft on March 25: "There is a question about whether Alaska oil really is going to the United States as claimed. Shipment from Alaska to the west coast falls under the provisions of the Jones Act, which stipulates use of American vessels and American labor for coastal shipping. The cost, accordingly, would be much higher than shipment in foreign vessels with foreign labor. So there is a widespread suspicion that, once the pipeline is approved, the companies will use the oil to make better profits in Japan rather than to alleviate the energy shortage in this country."

Suspicions were indeed widespread, and the reason they existed was that the oil companies had hardly been discreet about their plans. At first the Alyeska oil companies had been quite candid in saying they intended to sell some of the oil to Japan. Some oil executives were *still* candid about it. In an interview with the *National Journal*, Ronald H. Merrett, economics and supply coordinator for BP Alaska Inc., said flatly that perhaps by 1980 there would be half a million barrels a day surplus above what the West Coast could consume, and "then you reach the point where it's a matter of indifference, from the oil companies' point of view, whether we sell it to Japan or the West Coast." But such candor was unusual. Earlier, when the same philosophy was expressed by other oil company executives, conservationists and consumers raised hell at the idea of Alaska's wilderness being raped to give Tokyo more smog. When the clamor had reached a certain decibel level, the Alyeska executives began to pretend they hadn't said they would sell to Japan except, maybe, on a swap basis: shipping Alaskan oil to Japan and receiving an equal amount of Japanese-owned mideastern oil to bring to the East Coast of the United States. Later, the companies had figured out another pitch: juggling statistics in the mysterious way they had been doing for years, they claimed that West Coast production was dropping precipitously and that the region would thereby be able to absorb *all* Alaskan oil. Weighing that claim against previous production figures, it appeared to be a lie; but critics, who of course had no access to the companies' records, could not prove the lie.

In April, the Canadian route proposal began to pick up some momentum, with legislation introduced in both houses urging Nixon "to begin immediate negotiations with Canada" for a pipeline, and after the Supreme Court threw the issue back to Congress, the battle there began in earnest. Midwestern and eastern legislators sent up a bill aimed at forcing Nixon to enter into negotiations with Canada for a pipeline route; Interior Secretary Morton countered by sending a letter to every member of Congress saying the Canadian route was a lousy idea. Nixon's energy message to Congress on April 18 also touted the Alaska route over the Canadian.

There were deception and misleading arguments on both sides. Legislators from the Middle West and the East tried to argue that Canada was overwhelmingly enthusiastic about letting Alaskan oil come down through Canada. This was not quite the case. A strong current of nationalism was moving through Canada. Canadians were becoming increasingly offended by the fact that U.S. industries dominated their economy; Canada felt it had become a nation of branch offices. The oil companies were especially resented, for they controlled more than 85 percent of Canada's oil lands. On the other hand, while the Canadian Government had to respond to the nationalist fervor, it was also practical enough to know that only the U.S. oil companies could supply the kind of money needed to develop and transport oil from Canada's rich fields in the North. So Canada was truly open to proposals for the pipeline—cautiously, perhaps, but open nevertheless. The spirit was accurately conveyed on May 14 by Prime Minister Trudeau on the floor of Parliament: "Our policy is still to indicate that the Mackenzie Valley route is one which we would be prepared to consider if there is an application made in the proper form, and that we would be very happy to follow up on that."

The Nixon administration, on the other hand, argued that Canada really didn't want to have the pipeline routed down the Mackenzie Valley and that if such a pipeline was built by U.S. companies, Canada would insist on owning 51 percent of it.

Who was right? In June, the chairman of the House Public Land Subcommittee asked the State Department to find out definitely and to make a full report to Congress as to whether Canadian officials were resisting negotiation on the pipeline. In response to that request, the State Department cabled the U.S. embassy in Ottawa on June 8. The wording was so heavily weighted with political portents that it was clear what the State Department wanted in the reply. The cable read: "As the embassy is aware, the administration is seeking legislation which would permit early progress in the construction of the proposed trans-Alaska oil pipeline . . . It is apparent that some members of Congress remain unpersuaded by the administration's case. In this connection, the Department urgently requires your current assessment."

But the embassy folks in Ottawa refused to take dictation. On June 14, they reported to the State Department that Canadian officials were in a cooperative mood, that they would immediately and objectively consider an application for the pipeline project, that it was unlikely Canadian approval would take more than two years to obtain, and that the Canadian Government would not be unfair about sharing the use of the pipeline for U.S. oil. In short, the report was anything but negative.

However, when the State Department wrote to Congress on June 22, it ignored just about everything positive in the embassy's report. In fact, it might as well have not received the report, because the State Department's views in the letter were just the same as before: ". . . the Canadian Government has no strong current interest in the construction of a Mackenzie Valley oil pipeline" and, besides, there were worrisome rumblings of opposition from above the border: ". . . there appears to be increasing public concern in Canada for the environmental and native rights problems" that would arise from a pipeline. Moreover, the State Department neglected to mention one crucial point: Canada had indicated that it would not insist on 51 percent of the pipeline stock.

This misrepresentation of the case and withholding of vital information came just as Senator Walter Mondale of Minnesota was offering an amendment to the Alaska pipeline bill that would have postponed a final decision until the government made a full study of the Canadian alternative. Mondale's amendment was crushed (62 to 29) on July 13. Four days later, the Senate, still without correct data from the State Department, authorized construction of the trans-Alaskan pipeline by a vote of 77 to 20. An amendment to the bill, immunizing the project from further court challenges by environmentalists, was passed 49 to 49, with Vice-President Spiro Agnew casting the tie-breaking vote. Toward the end of the roll call, Agnew had slipped into the chair and was presiding. It was the first time in more than four years that he had cast a deciding vote.

Not until another two weeks had passed was it discovered that the Senate had been voting with faulty information from the State Department. Deputy Assistant Secretary of State Julius L. Katz said it wasn't intentional, but merely a "bureaucratic goof."

House passage, on November 12, was a cinch (361 to 14). By that time, the Arab embargo was in full swing and the politicians were ready to grasp at any oil supply, however distant in the future its flow might begin.[6]

***

The natural gas brawl was getting wild. Everyone was accusing everyone else of lying. Bureaucratic underlings feuded with their bosses, and their bosses retaliated. Agency investigators went out of their way to embarrass other agencies. And the basic questions remained unanswered: Were industry reserve figures accurate? (Once again, in 1973, as it had been doing each year since 1969, the American Gas Association reported another drop in proved reserves of natural gas.) Was the FPC selling out to the companies it was supposed to be regulating? How much deceit was involved in the rate increases that were costing consumers many extra billions?

The most spectacular FPC fuss of the year broke out when Morton Mintz, the Washington *Post* reporter who was such an aggressive investigator of the oil and gas industry that he made his editors nervous,[7] disclosed that a high-ranking Federal Power Commission official had tried to destroy documents relating to the claimed shortage of natural gas. According to Mintz, Lawrence R. Mangen, of the FPC's Bureau of Natural Gas, had ordered the papers destroyed. Mangen conceded his role in the effort, but said he believed he was doing exactly what the commission wanted; several of his superiors backed him up in this claim. Chairman Nassikas and FPC executive director Webster P. Maxson, however, accused Mangen of being in "direct violation" of FPC orders. Was he? There were suspicions that some of the top officials at the FPC were trying to make Mangen the fall guy. In any event, the destruction of the documents was frustrated, thanks to bureaucratic and military bungling: The documents had been torn up and taken to an army-base incinerator for burning—but the incinerator didn't work. So they were hauled back to the FPC and put in a safe. Just then, Senator Philip Hart subpoenaed them for hearings on the alleged natural gas shortage. FPC officials hurriedly pasted the documents back together. After looking them over and hearing testimony, Hart stated that the "so-called shortage . . . may be a hoax."

---

6. And however vague the supply might be. Early in 1973, Senator Jackson had been told by Interior that "approximately 24 billion barrels of crude oil in place had been proved on the North Slope of Alaska . . . and that the probable reserves of that region are many times greater." But, about the same time, Atlantic Richfield, one of the chief developers of the North Slope, was placing newspaper ads that told of only "ten billions of barrels of Alaska oil."

7. The Washington *Post* on December 23, 1972, began a long and strong advocacy of letting the oil industry charge anything it wanted to charge. In an editorial on that day, it said: "There is a tendency in our part of the country to assume that whatever is good for the oil-and-gas lobby must be disastrously bad for the rest of us. Deregulation of gas is an exception to this rule."

The Federal Trade Commission didn't use ugly words like that, but James T. Halverson, director of the FTC's Bureau of Competition, told the Senate Antitrust Subcommittee that an examination of documents obtained by subpoena showed that Gulf, Union, and Continental oil companies had submitted to the American Gas Association reserve figures "significantly lower" than the conservative estimates that the companies were using internally. In fact, said Halverson, the producers' internal records showed reserves up to 1,000 percent greater than the companies reported to the AGA. The AGA figures were used by the Federal Power Commission for setting higher rates. Halverson said that the AGA reporting procedure "could provide the vehicle for a conspiracy" to falsify data for profit. Nonsense, said the FPC, dragging out its own "independent" study to show that in fact the gas producers were *over*reporting the reserves by about 10 percent.[8]

It was a quarrel that wouldn't die, and it was impossible for the public to know which side to believe, because, as Senator Edward Kennedy remarked with awe after listening to witnesses pro and con, "It seems that there is a tremendous kind of juggling of figures and hiding behind a number of semantic differences" in connection with the data oil companies submit to federal agencies. The status and expertise of the accusers of the oil companies was impressive. There was no question about that. Nor was there any doubt about the substance of the evidence the accusers came up with. One had to take very seriously the charge by John W. Wilson, chief of the FPC's Division of Economic Studies, that at least thirteen major natural gas producers had grossly understated their reserves—in short, had lied. He was basing his charges on confidential replies by seventy-nine gas producers to FPC questionnaires. Among the highly suspicious conduct uncovered by Wilson: Five companies reported zero or virtually no reserves, and yet within a couple of months they were signing contracts to sell large amounts of the "nonexistent" gas. He said he could document numerous cases of that sort. FPC economist George L. Donkin charged that the top natural gas producing companies had spent nearly a billion dollars to lease more than eight hundred thousand acres off the coasts of Texas and Louisiana but were holding them out of production, presumably until the price of gas suited

---

8. The "independent" study was headed by Paul Root, a petroleum and geological engineering professor from the University of Oklahoma, a school heavily endowed with oil money. The study was designed by an "advisory" committee loaded with executives from Exxon, Gulf, Mobil, Texaco, and other majors. Howard Pifer III, a member of the Harvard Business School faculty and a "public" member of the study group, said that the 158 fields that were selected from a total of more than six thousand for the study "represented the least likely places to look for AGA underreporting," and Professor Root acknowledged that the 158-field sample was not set up to really check the accuracy of AGA's figures. Congressman John Dingell of Michigan, head of the subcommittee investigating the study, said it looked to him like "a put-up job."

them. Furthermore, said Haskell P. Wald, chief economist of the Federal Power Commission, the companies were being encouraged to strike by "public pronouncements" by "top Administration officials," including Nixon's own economic advisers and by several members of the FPC, who kept telling the industry that prices "were too low" and that they would do all in their power to raise them. (And raise them they did; in one 1973 case, the FPC allowed a precedent-setting 73 percent increase that gave a 48 percent return on equity.)[9]

Here was a remarkable sight: numerous top-level staff members from the FPC publicly—either in congressional testimony or in letters to members of Congress that they knew would be released to the press— saying, in effect, that the commissioners were dead wrong, in collusion with the industry they were supposed to be regulating, and fleecing the public. It was an impressive rebellion, especially on such occasions as the Senate Commerce Committee hearing in October at which FPC Chairman Nassikas testified that natural gas prices should be decontrolled, and then David S. Schwartz, assistant chief of the FPC's Office of Economics, marched right up to the witness table and testified that it was ridiculous to even consider deregulating natural gas prices. (Schwartz so outraged Senator Russell Long of Louisiana on that occasion that Long began shouting at Schwartz, saying that it was people like him who kept the natural gas people from tripling prices, as they deserved. "When they sell natural gas inside Louisiana, they can get more than 60 cents per 1,000 cubic feet," Long railed, "but when they sell it interstate, they can get only 22 cents. If you'd let us have a truly freely competitive system, all new gas could be sold at 60 cents. But you won't let them compete!" Schwartz coolly replied that because of interlocks and joint ventures "the claim of a competitive industry structure defies credulity.")

Nassikas did not take kindly to this insurrection. He wished for more discipline, more respect and support from the staff. But, aside from pride, what did it matter? After all, the Commission, not the staff, set the rates, and on that score the Commission was winning, hands down. And so was the industry. Part of the staff might love the consumers, but the consumers were losing badly. In April, the FPC announced that in a few months it would start setting national rates instead of regional for natural gas, and that the new procedure would bypass public hearings; it said the new rate-making method would take into consideration not only the cost of finding and drilling but also all sorts of vagaries, "numerous non-

---

9. The U.S. Court of Appeals for the District of Columbia set this increase aside on October 7, 1974, faulting the FPC for taking into consideration too many "non-cost" vagaries. In another gas decision, the Court scolded the FPC for its "what-the-market-will-bear approach," which violated the "primary purpose" of the 1938 Natural Gas Act: to "protect the consumer from profiteering."

cost factors, including supply and demand and consequences upon the
producing industry of the rate order." In short, the FPC was turning
rate-making into a subjective adventure. In May, the FPC by a 2 to 1
vote approved three long-term contracts at more than double the current
average price (Nassikas dissented! He said a 50 percent raise would have
been enough). It was the FPC's first use of yet another new rate-setting
gimmick ("optional pricing"), which allowed producers and pipelines to
decide what they thought the price should be, and then get the FPC's
virtually automatic approval.

These protestations of belief in freedom of speech to the contrary notwithstanding, Nassikas was apparently seething. Enough was enough.
The FPC staff was getting entirely too chummy with members of
Congress and taking the side of too many critics on Capitol Hill. He ordered that incoming mail from congressmen and senators to certain key
members of the FPC staff be intercepted and opened by his aides. When
this procedure was discovered, Nassikas excused it by saying that of
course he didn't pry into personal or confidential mail and that his intentions were simply to make sure that congressional members were well
served. Sometimes, he said, "important inquiries from members of
Congress were lost or delayed for inordinate periods of time in the
course of internal processing . . ." His explanation was not universally
accepted. Senator Jackson, the Senate's energy captain, accused Nassikas
of trying to prevent congressional committees from tapping some of the
expertise of the FPC staff—especially the expertise that disagreed with
Nassikas' policy. Nassikas had, among other things, forbidden FPC economist Schwartz from meeting with Jackson's staff to help them in their
energy study, and Nassikas conceded that his aides had "inadvertently"
opened a letter from one critical senator.

**

William D. Smith, a financial writer for the New York *Times* not given to
hyperbole, once assayed October 1973 as the month that "seems likely to
be remembered in history as a major turning point in world affairs. That
was the month when a group of 12 underdeveloped nations, the Organization of Petroleum Exporting Countries, began in earnest to turn the
world upside down." They did not do it alone. They got ample help,
directly or indirectly, from the oil companies and from the governments
of the consuming nations, particularly the United States. October was
the jumping-off point for the staggering price increases. Outwardly, the
major oil companies donned sackcloth and ashes, assuming the role of
martyrs. But, in fact, the long, painful road that lay ahead for consumers
was a road as golden for the companies as for OPEC. The more money
OPEC got, the more money the oil companies got. When the former
raised oil prices, the value of *all* went up—including the oil that the com-

panies already had in inventory and, more important, the oil that the companies had already found and would find everywhere in the world—while the cost of *producing* the oil already discovered would, of course, remain constant. There were other blessings that would fall to the companies. For one thing, down the road there would be—as there inevitably had been in the past—an oversupply of oil in the marketplace. When that day came, the oil companies would have these ruthless nouveaux riches as allies in the effort to prop up prices by slashing production and jiggering distribution. Best of all, after October, the oil companies were relieved of having to play the role of profiteering villain all by themselves. After all, were *they* to blame that the primitives of the Middle East were caught up in a frenzy of take-over and price gouging?

The assault on the West came about ostensibly as the result of a new outbreak in the war between Arabs and Jews. Syria and Egypt invaded Israel on October 6, the Jewish holy day of Yom Kippur and, a week into the war, the United States stepped in with arms and supplies to bolster Israel at a time when it was reeling and apparently on the verge of defeat. In retaliation, Saudi Arabia and most Arab states increased prices 70 percent and declared an embargo against the United States.

The White House pretended that the Arab boycott had caught it completely by surprise, that it hadn't the slightest inkling the Arabs might be preparing such mischief. In early September, for instance, replying to a query from Senator Clifford Hansen of Wyoming, Kissinger had said, "We have excellent relationships with our principal Middle Eastern suppliers of oil, Saudi Arabia and Iran, and we do not foresee any circumstances in which they would cut off our supply."

If he really felt that way, he was doubtless the only man in Washington to feel so. It was possible to believe that Kissinger and Nixon were actually caught off guard only if one were also willing to believe that they had, sometime early in 1973, stopped reading the newspapers and listening to their own diplomats or paying any attention to the counsel of the oil companies doing business in the Mideast.

Arab members of OPEC had been parading their strength, insulting the United States, and demanding more economic concessions, more support—at least neutrality—in their conflicts with Israel. It was generally known that Arab oil money had played a big part in the monetary crisis that forced a second devaluation of the dollar, in February; from somewhere in the Arab world—many believed Libya—had come half of the $6 billion that upset the Eurodollar market.

As for rhetoric, even the customarily courtly Saudis had begun to sound like tough guys. In March, when the Nixon administration sent out feelers to other industrial nations about coordinating their dealings with oil-producing countries—presenting a united front by stockpiling oil, sharing in time of need, etc.—Saudi Arabian Oil Minister Sheikh Ahmed

Zaki Yamani decided to interpret the Nixon plan as an act of belligerency and declared that ". . . if it is war they want, then war they shall
have . . . all civilization and industries of [consuming] countries will be
destroyed." But that was out of character for Yamani, so he hurried on to
say that ". . . definitely we don't want war and our policy is based on
cooperation." But not too much cooperation. In April, he was threatening
again. This time he warned the United States that unless it changed its
pro-Israeli stance, Saudi Arabia would not significantly expand its present oil production. (At the time, the Saudis were pumping about 8 million barrels a day; the United States was then hoping this would be
raised to 20 million by 1980.)

In April, Drew Middleton, of the New York *Times,* quoted "well-
placed sources" in Washington, London, and at North Atlantic Treaty
Organization headquarters in Brussels as predicting that pressures from
anti-American Arab radicals would result in an oil embargo for political
reasons. Nixon's own energy adviser, James Akins, warned of the embargo potential in his April article in *Foreign Affairs.*

It was generally known that the Saudi Arabian Government was under
growing pressure from radical Arab nations to stop being so friendly
with the United States. The radicals had been especially irritated by the
Saudi government's offer the previous September to enter into an exclusive Saudi-American oil arrangement under which the United States
would import all the oil Saudi Arabia wanted to sell and would permit
the Saudis to invest in the American oil market, in exchange for a guaranteed uninterrupted supply (Nixon rejected the offer). And yet the
Saudis resisted the radical pressure as best they could. Their need for
U.S. friendship was not only because this country was the world's largest
oil market but because the United States offered the Saudis protection.
Twice in the 1960s, the United States had sent in air squadrons to signal
its determination to preserve the Saudi regime. Though they were grateful for this, the Saudis had to consider the real possibility that if they
showed too much tolerance for Israel and sympathy for the United
States, their pipelines could be easily subjected to sabotage by Palestinian guerrilla fighters. As it was, the Saudi Arabian Government had
bought time by subsidizing the main Palestinian organization. But the
Saudis knew that more was expected from them, and so, after years of
benign neglect for the Arab cause against Israel, they had begun to
sound militant. In May, King Faisal ordered representatives of Aramco's
mother companies—Exxon, Mobil, Texaco, and Standard Oil of California—to meet with him for instruction in the matter. He demanded immediate action from them to help guarantee U.S. neutrality in the upcoming
war with Israel. If they didn't help, he said, "You could lose everything."
They agreed to do what they could. The most agreeable, because it was

the most dependent on Saudi Arabian oil, was Socal. Within a few weeks it would be in hot water with U.S. Jews because of a letter it sent to stockholders calling for Americans to give more support to Arabs' aspirations. (Actually, the letter didn't even mention Israel, much less say anything derogatory about it.)

Shortly thereafter, Aramco officials carried Faisal's message directly to the White House, to the State Department, and to the Pentagon. If they seemed ill at ease serving as messenger boys for a foreign—and sometimes hostile—government, they made no apologies. Joseph J. Johnston, a senior vice-president and director of Aramco, said, "All our operations are in Saudi Arabia. We have to follow the Saudi government's orders or get out. It's that clear-cut and getting out would do no one any good."

But King Faisal wasn't issuing his ultimata only in private. In June, he said publicly that the attitude of Saudi Arabia toward the United States in the future would depend on the United States "having a more even-handed and just policy" in the Middle East.

It was left to Colonel Qaddafi, however, to take the first "holy war" action. On May 15, four Arab countries—Iraq, Kuwait, Algeria, and Libya—staged a brief symbolic protest against the twenty-fifth anniversary of the founding of the State of Israel, and to the Western nations' support for Israel's continued existence. Typically, while Iraq, Kuwait, and Algeria shut down their wells for only one hour, Colonel Qaddafi closed Libya's wells for twenty-four hours and called for a complete shutdown of oil to the West. (Qaddafi was a superb symbolist, because everything he did—even though in substance it was no more disturbing than what Saudi Arabia or Iran did—had a specially irritating effect on Westerners. In this instance, the typical reaction came from a European oil company official, his voice shaking: "When a million little Bedouins in Libya have the power, by denying their oil, to paralyze the economy of a modern European nation of 50 million people such as Italy, that is a ridiculous situation, but that is where we are.")

Representatives of other oil-producing nations, however, said that Qaddafi was acting "prematurely." That did not mean they disapproved of Qaddafi's proposal, but only of its timing. Nor did their declaration soothe those nations that depended heavily on the Middle East for their energy and could recall that it had been the "premature" Colonel who showed OPEC the way to rebellion, in 1970. It had also been proved, as one oilman told the New York *Times*, "Whatever Colonel Qaddafi gets, King Faisal and the Shah will want, and more."

＊

The old pattern would be followed again in 1973. On June 11, Qaddafi nationalized the $140 million Libyan operations of Nelson Bunker Hunt, son of Dallas billionaire H. L. Hunt, saying, "The time has come for us to deal America a strong slap in its cool, arrogant face. American imperialism has exceeded every limit. The Americans support our Israeli enemy." This was the first time an Arab nation had used American foreign policy as its main reason for expropriation.[10] Of course if Qaddafi had not had that excuse, he would have found another. Nevertheless, the fact that he did select that excuse put more pressure on Saudi Arabia to act with equal religious fervor. In August, Qaddafi declared 51 percent of Occidental Petroleum forfeit to the state, and then, on September 1, tired of nibbling, he nationalized 51 percent of *all* oil companies operating in Libya, including more than twenty American. He also raised the price of oil to $6—double the previous rate.

Once again, the oil companies sent their elder statesman, New York lawyer John J. McCloy, to Washington to huddle with national security adviser Henry Kissinger and top State Department officials. What could they do to damp Qaddafi's zeal before it spread? The strategy they decided on was singularly unsuccessful. The State Department joined with Texaco and Standard of California in jerry-building a boycott, but the only result it had was (1) to force New York City utilities to pay nearly five times more for transporting substitute oil and (2) to divert oil marked for fuel-short New England to Communists in Eastern Europe. Even more ridiculous were the threats voiced by President Nixon, who, perhaps driven a bit balmy by the Watergate probe, announced in a press conference that if the Libyans didn't behave, the United States just might have to retaliate by not buying any more of their oil. It was an embarrassingly empty threat—most of Libya's prized low-sulfur oil went to European nations, and they were mighty happy to get it—and the oil companies quickly disassociated themselves from Nixon's position. As one oil executive told the New York *Times,* with an effort at sympathy, "I guess Mr. Nixon just didn't have his mind on the subject."

On October 8, Qaddafi's religious impulse reached Iraq, which announced the nationalization of the last major American oil holdings, because "Israeli aggression in the Arab world necessitates directing a blow

---

10. Here was a fine test of the oil companies' sense of ethics in the face of potentially great loss of wealth. Remember the "safety net" agreement of 1971, shortly after Qaddafi started acting up and the companies operating in Libya agreed to present a united front—the agreement that stipulated that if one company was nationalized, the other producers would contribute percentage shares of their Libyan production to help defray the nationalized victim's losses? Well, Hunt was part of that agreement. So, did the other producers unite behind him? Not so you could notice. Exxon and a couple of others stuck to the agreement, but most of them acted as if they had never heard of Hunt. Understandably, Hunt felt sold out. So in 1974 he filed the largest antitrust suit in history—claiming $13 billion in damages. The accused were Mobil, Texaco, Standard of California, Shell, Gulf, Occidental, Conoco, Atlantic Richfield, and Gelsenberg, of Germany. He charged them with trying to screw him out of his business in Libya. Some settled out of court, but most of the companies never paid a cent.

at American interests." By that time, Israeli and Egyptian troops were in combat. The Palestine Liberation Organization called on all Arab countries to use oil as a weapon in the war. But, for the moment, King Faisal—the one Arab the world was watching to see how he would respond—did nothing. He had cut off oil shipments for three months after the 1967 Arab-Israeli war, without much effect on the West. This time, it might be different. Hoping to use his oil power without actually calling for a shutdown, Faisal got Aramco's mighty four—J. K. Jamieson, of Exxon; Rawleigh Warner, Jr., of Mobil; M. F. Granville, of Texaco; and Otto N. Miller, of Standard of California—to send McCloy back to Washington on October 12, six days into the war, with another warning not to support the failing Israel. The memo, addressed to Nixon himself, was hand-delivered by McCloy to Nixon's chief of staff, General Alexander Haig. The memo ended with the judgment: "Much more than our commercial interest in the area is now at hazard. The real stakes are both our economy and our security."

If Nixon saw the message, he responded with a very odd silence.

On October 16, the producing nations, after a meeting in Kuwait, proclaimed their first unilateral price increase, an unprecedented rise of 70 percent. "From that time," Iran's Interior Minister Jamshid Amouzegar told a *Fortune* reporter, "the oil companies lost the power to determine price, either by themselves or through negotiations." The Arabs also announced a cut in production of 5 percent a month until Israel withdrew from occupied territory, but shortly thereafter they discarded across-the-board cutbacks, which would have hurt countries they considered neutral or friendly, and instead announced a total embargo on the United States and the Netherlands (also considered intolerably pro-Israel). By a strange coincidence, the announcement of the cutback on October 16 came only a few hours after foreign ministers of four Arab countries had met with Nixon and Kissinger in what the White House described as "a very good exchange of views." Apparently, if Nixon and Kissinger did not encourage the Arabs to go forward with their boycott, neither did they raise their voices in stern opposition, for without a tremor of hesitation the Arab states began cutting off supplies to the United States.[11]

---

11. If the Arabs hoped to frighten Americans into changing their traditional support for Israel, they failed. Two and a half months after the embargo went into effect, a Gallup poll found that 54 percent of those polled favored Israel over the Arabs in the conflict—up seven points from the support Israel got just before the war broke out.

While citizens in general reacted with little panic, corporations showed their usual wartime spirit by hoarding oil supplies. Many corporations bought larger storage tanks and leased thousands of railroad tank cars. J. R. Scanlin, president of General American Transportation Corp., said, in December, "We had about 3,800 idle tank cars [available to lease] a year ago. Today we have 700."

*

At this point, a puzzled observer can be excused for pausing to take stock. Surely all is not as it seems. On the surface, it would appear that the member companies of Aramco were desperately trying to persuade the suddenly blind and deaf Nixon administration to withhold aid from Israel lest such action deprive them of their holdings in Saudi Arabia and in other Arab countries. One might think that they were prescient in their alarm, for within a few weeks they would lose their majority ownership in Saudi Arabia; in mid-November, Faisal, who less than a year before had promised to wait until 1982 to take 51 percent control of Aramco, decided to do it right then instead. But were they really so worried about this? After all, the tearing up of contracts was nothing new, and the act rarely put the major oil companies out of business. Why, just the previous December their old friend Shah Mohammed Riza Pahlevi had summoned members of the Iranian consortium to his palace to inform them that, contrary to a promise he had made six months earlier to extend their agreement until 1994, he had no intention of doing so. The agreement would end in 1979, he said, when it came up for renewal. Then, growing more impatient, he had wiped out the consortium agreement in May and had established state control of the industry. But so what? The companies still had exclusive rights to oil production in Iran; they had become service contractors, perhaps not so profitable an arrangement as in the old days, but, given world conditions, it was much less wearing on the corporate psyche. An arrangement at least equally satisfactory would unquestionably be worked out with Saudi Arabia, for it had a much more stable and reliable government than Iran's. So the companies had nothing to worry about. Their importuning of the White House can be put down to nothing more than obedience to Faisal's instructions, a bit of corporate make-believe to maintain good relations with a monarch they intended to have profitable relations with for many years to come.

One might even be excused for wondering if the major oil companies operating in the Middle East did not in fact relish the thought of the embargo—which, as in 1967, was bound to be of short duration—and the blossoming prices that it would bring. Looking back over the long history of the oil industry, one searches in vain for even a single occasion when the Seven Sisters did not dominate U.S. foreign policy in the oil nations. Perhaps they were not empowered to *set* foreign policy in the Middle East, as some claimed, but they had certainly become, by default, an extension of the State Department. The majors had had carte blanche. At no time did the State Department seek, nor was it ever offered, a chance to sit in on contract negotiations that were crucial to U.S. economic security. The State Department did not even ask for detailed reports of what went on between the companies and the producing nations. That's the way it had always been, and would continue. A month into the embargo, Secretary of State Kissinger and other officials met with executives from eleven major oil companies to work out an arrangement by which the White House would ask Congress to exempt the companies from antitrust laws (as had occurred on other crisis occasions in the Mideast) so that the companies could join together as a secret ad hoc quasi government to work out some deal with the Arabs.[12] Once again, the U.S. Government was allowing the oil companies to be its representatives.

Considering all that, is it reasonable to think that if the oil companies had really wanted to head off the embargo, and if the Nixon administration had been convinced that its generous friends in the industry were really sincere in wanting to prevent the embargo, Nixon and Kissinger would not have set to work months earlier in an effort to dissuade the Arabs from using oil as a weapon? Or that Nixon and Kissinger would have given only slight consideration—much less a brushoff—to last-minute entreaties of the highest officials of the most powerful oil companies in the world? When were Nixon and Kissinger ever so churlish toward their patrons?

It's much easier to believe that oilmen told the Administration they were quite content to let the embargo come, happily anticipating the attendant profits, and assuaging their conscience with the knowledge that the interruption would hardly be enough to measurably slow the wheels of industry. Consumers would have to shoulder a much heavier economic burden, of course, but they would adjust. They always had.

(Nixon was obviously not much concerned about that. The White House was totally unprepared for energy inflation. Three months into the embargo, a congressional committee asked Herbert Stein, Nixon's chief economic adviser, to explain what the energy price changes would mean. He replied, "I'm ashamed to say, I can't answer the question." Whereas the White House at the first of the year had predicted that the general price index might advance three percentage points in 1973, in fact it advanced nine percentage points—carried upward by oil.)

---

12. Some congressional critics were extremely hostile to the suggestion. Senator Frank Church, chairman of the Senate Subcommittee on Multinational Corporations, charged that such companies as Exxon, Mobil, Gulf, Texaco, and Standard of California should no longer be viewed sympathetically, as "our" companies, but as "political agents of the Arabs' boycott," and that if antitrust laws are waived for the companies, then they should be considered "public utilities subject to government regulation."

Evidence that in fact the oil companies were agents of the Arabs came dramatically with the disclosure that the Aramco partners, on orders from King Faisal, had in November cut off fuel to the U.S. Sixth Fleet, in the Mediterranean, and to other U.S. forces around the world. The cutoff reduced supplies by 50 percent and brought about an unprecedented commandeering of some three hundred thousand barrels of fuel daily from domestic supplies.

In short, the crisis that had arrived with the embargo was mostly psychological, pumped into frightening configurations by government/ industry spokesmen. But there was no physical crisis. After all, U.S. dependence on Arab oil was marginal. The Arabs were supplying only about 6 percent of our total needs—an amount that could be easily made up by even a small increase from non-Arab Iran (our fifth-largest supplier) or Nigeria (our fourth-largest) or Venezuela (second-largest) or Canada (by far our most generous source of foreign oil), or easily compensated for by conservation so slight as to be no hardship.

*

So, to make a crisis out of a noncrisis, the government joined the oil industry in what they did best: juggling figures.

On October 12, just when King Faisal was issuing his last warning, White House energy adviser Charles DiBona (who would later become president of the American Petroleum Institute) announced that U.S. imports of Arab oil were averaging 1.2 million barrels a day. (Other experts said it was only 1.1 million a day.) Eight days later, the White House said we depended on the Arabs for 1.6 million barrels. Four days later, the White House said, oops, they really meant we were dependent on Arab production for 2 million barrels a day. Six days later—on October 30—the Nixon experts raised the floating figures to 2.5 million barrels. Early in November, the Pentagon took over the count and said the United States was dependent for 3 million barrels a day. Within one month the Administration's crisis figures had been stretched nearly 200 percent.

During this period, Senator Gaylord Nelson of Wisconsin complained to the press, "I sat through two executive sessions on the oil shortage with members of the White House energy office and they didn't know their ass from second base. First we were going to be short of oil by 6 percent, then it was 12, then 18, then 25. We don't know anything."

All such figures were beside the point anyway, for no matter what our dependence, we were being amply supplied. And so was the Netherlands, the only other nation specifically embargoed by the Arabs. Tanker traffic into Rotterdam, Europe's largest oil port, continued unchecked. The Dutch refineries were going full blast (or very nearly so; two months after the embargo, Shell's big Rotterdam refinery was running at 80 percent capacity, which was almost normal), oil and gasoline use continued at roughly normal levels, and there were no cutbacks due to a faltering fuel supply. In Italy, a nation the Arabs considered "friendly," an official groused to a *Business Week* reporter, "The damned Dutch probably have more oil than we do." Probably so. Executives at Royal Dutch-Shell admitted that the Arab embargo simply prompted them to shift around their world distribution pattern so that no feelings would be hurt. They sold Arab oil elsewhere and brought more Nigerian and Iranian crude into "embargoed" Holland.

Donald L. Barlett and James B. Steele, of the Philadelphia *Inquirer*, sifted through the shipping reports of Lloyd's of London, tracing the movement of tankers from Arab nations, and discovered that shipments from six large Arab ports picked at random were 31 percent *higher* during the last three months of 1973 than during a comparable period in 1972. They concluded, "The general picture that emerges from these statistics is that while there has been a cutback in oil production in Saudi Arabia, the Middle East cutback as a whole clearly is nowhere near as profound as suggested by the Arabs and government officials in Washington." If Americans had not been so frightened by industry advertisements and government pronouncements, they would have been able to figure out that so long as the producing countries permitted production, the oil had to go somewhere, and in the final analysis the producing countries had virtually no control over where it went, because the oil companies were still the principal marketers of the oil, and they maintained such an elaborate, complex marketing network from tanker to nozzle—with so many opportunities to shuffle the oil around from port to port, from refinery to refinery—that its ultimate destination was almost impossible for the Arab producers to ascertain. Oil, after all, does not carry a trademark. Who was to prove the origin of oil coming out of an Exxon tanker at dockside in Rotterdam or Bayonne?

Robert B. Stobaugh, coordinator of the Harvard Business School Energy Project, pointed out that the supposed crimping of shipments to the United States did not mean much, because "about half of the non-Communist world's crude oil production outside of North America is controlled by 18 U.S.-headquartered oil companies, principally Exxon, Texaco, Gulf, Standard of California, and Mobil. These firms, along with other big oil companies such as British Petroleum and Royal Dutch-Shell, can switch Arab oil to countries now using non-Arab oil, thereby making non-Arab oil available to the U.S."

One oilman described Aramco as analogous to the United Givers Fund. If the Arabs contributed all their oil to the companies with strict instructions not to give any of it to the United States or the Netherlands, "it's like giving to UGF and saying I don't want any of my money going to the Red Cross," he said. "Now the UGF might take note of your prejudice and not give all your money to the Red Cross, but somehow some of your money gets there anyway." Whatever their rascalities might be, the major oil firms proved the efficiency of their global marketing system. They became the rationers to the world, gathering and giving in such a way that countries favored by the Arabs got somewhat less than they wanted and countries despised by the Arabs got about all that they needed.

Anyway, it soon became clear that—except perhaps for Saudi Arabia and Kuwait—the other supposedly angry Arab producers really didn't care whether the embargo worked or not. Like the oil companies, their main objective was to make money. For example, Iraq, temperamental as always, announced an embargo of oil to the United States—and then increased production. And when Saudi Arabia tried to shame them, Iraq accused its Arab allies of "adopting an imperialist plan aimed at isolating Iraq." Unanimity among the Arab states was hardly the outstanding characteristic of the times. By December, it was known that the Arab embargo had sprung countless leaks—and the biggest leaker was none other than Colonel Qaddafi, who, for all his tough anti-imperialist rhetoric, was only too happy to sell out his brother Arabs. Nobody ever knew for sure why Qaddafi did anything, but in this instance he seemed to be doing it less for money than for revenge—revenge aimed, first of all, at Egypt. In 1972, Qaddafi had persuaded Egyptian President Anwar Sadat to agree, reluctantly, to a merger of their two nations by September 1973. The more Sadat heard of Qaddafi's demands for immediate war against Israel, however, the less he wanted to be permanently teamed up with him. But Egypt was financially strapped, and it needed the $150-million-a-year handout it was getting from Qaddafi—or it needed that much or more replacement money. With the merger deadline approaching, Sadat frantically flew off to Saudi Arabia and asked King Faisal if he would take over as Egypt's sponsor. Faisal agreed, and the Libya-Egypt merger was dead. Qaddafi, to put it mildly, was furious with Sadat and he didn't feel any too kindly toward Faisal. He became even angrier, if that was possible, when Egypt and Syria didn't take him into their confidence about their plans to attack Israel; and when he was also left out of the cease-fire talks, that was the last straw. For a long time thereafter, Qaddafi was so miffed that he refused even to attend meetings of the Arab states. He sold his oil to irritate both Egypt and Saudi Arabia. "Qaddafi does two things by selling his oil," one longtime Libyan observer pointed out. "He proves he's his own man to the rest of the Arab world and he shows the big oil companies that he can move his oil without their help."

And of course the United States could depend—for a horrendous price—on the Shah of Iran ("the nut," as William Simon called him), with his bottomless need for more money to finance his romantic "new Persia empire" dream of industrial development and military supremacy that would make Iran, he believed, one of the five most powerful nations in the world by the year 2000. Although a Moslem country, Iran is not an Arab country, and not only was it indifferent to the Arab-Israeli conflict, but it viewed Israel as a very good oil customer. Iran was, in fact, Israel's chief oil supplier. During the 1967 conflict and the brief Arab embargo of that year, Iran had also engaged in a most productive season of profiteering on the needy European market. And now it was ready to gouge again. In April of 1973, with the Arabian embargo already widely rumored as upcoming, Iranian Foreign Minister Abbas A. Khalatbary was asked what Iran, whose production was second in the Middle East only to Saudi Arabia's, would do if the embargo came about. "Our response might well be what it was in 1967," he said. And so it was. Iran increased production all that was needed to fill the Saudi Arabian-Kuwait vacuum; nevertheless, the need was so slight as to leave seven large Iranian oil fields shut down.

*

All in all, the United States and most other Western nations were sitting out the embargo so well as to make "crisis" seem the least appropriate word to describe the situation. "Charade" would have been better, and even "farce" might not have been farfetched, with crude-oil barges backed up along the Ohio River waiting to be unloaded—the storage tanks were already overflowing. Elsewhere there was the same bounty. In Maryland, a survey found that gasoline supplies were up nearly 17 percent in November over what had been available the year before. Virginia quit stockpiling fuel, because as one state official put it, "It appears more oil is available from the oil industry than we thought."

Apparently, from the position of the oil companies, their fright campaign was working a bit too well. Impressed by the new prices and nervous at the idea of being "at the Arabs' mercy" (Nixon's description at one of his press conferences), Americans were cutting back on their driving and turning down the heat. The result: by November, there was a remarkable 1.1-million-barrel-a-day drop in the nation's demand for petroleum. During the last week in November, demand dropped 1.9 million barrels a day. Unless government officials and the oil companies worked fast, there soon might not be even the vestige of a crisis to get excited about.

The most obvious evidence that there was no threatening shortage could be found in the actions of the White House and Congress, which surely would not have responded in so trivial and slapdash a fashion if they really had hard evidence that the United States faced what Senator Paul J. Fannin of Arizona called "a petroleum Pearl Harbor" or if they agreed with Senator Dewey F. Bartlett of Oklahoma that "If Saudi Arabia carries out its threat, the consequences will be a nightmare for the U.S. and other oil-dependent nations." Such statements were pure theater. So was the description of world conditions found in the *Oil and Gas Journal* of October 29: "Military and economic chaos beset the global oil industry last week . . . While the full effects of production cutbacks and embargoes on shipments would not begin to be felt for about a month—the average time for a Persian Gulf-west tanker voyage—government authorities in all the big consuming countries began preparing for the worst."

Very dramatic, but not true at all. The most noticeable thing about the actions of government authorities was that they did not prepare for more than a mild ruffle—which, in fact, was all that they got.

＊

Nixon's lack of action was nothing new. He had been bumbling along all year, lackadaisically issuing pep talks on the energy problem or shuffling the executive office's energy bureaucracy in the classical fashion, churning the water to simulate progress. Starting off in January, Nixon said he was naming a "counselor for natural resources" to be his chief adviser on energy matters. For that post he picked, to everyone's astonishment, Earl L. Butz, Secretary of Agriculture, who probably knew less about oil and gas than any other member of the Cabinet. Butz was expected to do the job in his spare time, while remaining as head of Agriculture. By late spring, that arrangement had become notably ridiculous. So, in June, Nixon decided that he needed a full-timer as energy adviser, and he decided it would sound nicely forceful if the new guy was informally referred to as the Administration's "energy czar." Not that he really wanted anyone with the independence of a czar. Nixon got the White House chief of staff, General Haig, to call Governor John A. Love in Colorado and offer him the czar's job. Love, in the last year of his third four-year term, was tired of being a lame duck and took the appointment, although he later admitted in bafflement, "To this day I don't know why they offered me the job." Love resigned as governor and Nixon sent a plane to Denver to fly him out to San Clemente, and he got to walk around the lawn at the Western White House while reporters and photographers recorded them in earnest conversation—presumably about the energy problem—and then Love was packed off to Washington to set up shop.

The talk on the lawn at San Clemente was the last time Love got to talk to Nixon alone, and he didn't get to talk to him even in company more than four or five times. As for the "shop" he was allowed to set up, that consisted of nine bureaucratic strangers and a complete lack of instructions on what he was expected to do. After the Israeli-Arab war broke out, Love wanted to move immediately to mandatory allocations of heating oil and some sort of gasoline rationing program. Nixon and his other advisers were dead set against anything that effective; instead they suggested that free-market price increases take care of the rationing—a program Love was opposed to. Also, at one point Love remarked, "With hindsight, I'm sorry we don't have that Machiasport refinery." Obviously, he wasn't a team player, so Nixon shuffled the bureaucracy in such a way as to force him to either get out or be made to appear a superfluous buffoon. Love quit on December 3, returning to Denver as bewildered as when he arrived in Washington five months earlier. Departing, he said it "has been difficult to do anything meaningful and even to get the attention of the President." The new "czar" would be under secretary of the treasury William E. Simon, named to head the new Federal Energy Office.

**

Nixon's—and presumably the entire Administration's—freedom from any sense of urgency, except to spread the kind of national nervousness that would aid in the acceptance of higher prices and fewer environmental controls, was especially evident in his energy speeches. The long-delayed speech in April was mostly a repeat of his previous pitches for higher "incentive" prices to encourage the oil companies to produce more of the energy they were sitting on. On November 7, a fortnight into the age of embargo, he came up with another energy message, this time including a hastily thrown-together package of solutions that included year-around daylight saving time, lower thermostat settings, lower environmental standards for air quality (to help factories and the auto industry), a reduction in highway speeds, accelerated licensing of nuclear plants, more leasing of federal offshore lands for drilling,[13] and a ban on utilities switching from coal to oil. Disregarding his own Transportation Department's estimate that the big trucks could save forty-seven thousand barrels of fuel a day by dropping to fifty miles an hour, Nixon proposed that the speed limit for cars be dropped to fifty but that the speed limit for trucks go no lower than fifty-five; the Teamsters were violently against going even that low, and they had put plenty of cash into Nixon's last campaign. In short, his solutions were for the ordinary citizens to be inconvenienced, be forced to pay more, while industry would be given special privileges. On that last point, he also suggested that oil companies be allowed to open up the government-owned Elk Hills naval oil reserves, in California, which the companies had been dying to do and which some observers said Standard of California was already doing—illegally.

That speech gave birth to "Project Independence," aimed, so Nixon said, at making the nation energy-independent by 1980—a goal that oil-industry executives, on whom the project would depend, immediately described as ridiculous. Kenneth E. Hill, a member of the National Petroleum Council, said self-sufficiency by that year was impossible, be-

---

13. That suggestion didn't go over very well with Senator Ernest Hollings of South Carolina, a key legislator in continental shelf affairs. He told the National Press Club in November that the number of "shut in" wells offshore had risen from 953 in 1971 to 2,966 in 1972, to 3,054 in 1973—all of which, he said, "could be developed immediately" and made the industry's claim to need additional offshore leasing nothing but a "fraud on the American public."

cause to achieve it would cost $70 billion a year for each of the next seven years, a price tag that the taxpayers would rebel at.

Typical of the skepticism aroused by Project Independence was David J. Rose's article in *Scientific American* in which he pointed out that to reach the goal on time would mean not only discarding environmental quality standards and allowing unrestricted strip-mining and accelerated depletion of known oil fields, but would also require too much from alternative fuels: "Between now and 1980 it will be virtually impossible to build more nuclear-power plants than those already on the drawing boards. It is also unrealistic to expect any substantial production of synthetic crude oil from coal or oil shale by 1980. It is estimated that to achieve a capacity of five million barrels per day of synthetic oil from these sources would cost $50 billion and take eight to ten years. Solar and geothermal energy can make no important contribution in the near future. And power from fusion reactors cannot be expected before the end of the century." In short, he felt Nixon was pipe-dreaming again.

Nixon's second postembargo speech, on November 25, covered the same territory, more or less; plus, it included proposals to close service stations on Sundays, curb outdoor lighting, and reduce the amount of gasoline distributed by refiners to wholesalers and retailers. But he nicely avoided suggesting that the military be required to cut back its extravagant use of oil.[14] (One B-52 carried enough gas to fill up 1,700 autos. Senator Proxmire of Wisconsin, who kept close tabs on the Pentagon through his Joint Economic Committee, said that a 50 percent reduction in military aircraft would, without endangering national security, save more than 200,000 barrels of oil a day. Proxmire brashly suggested that it certainly wouldn't hurt to ground the 178 personal planes used by top brass around the world. And although U.S. forces had pulled out of South Vietnam, the U.S. military was still sending twenty thousand barrels a day to the Saigon government of President Thieu.)

Some of the things Nixon proposed doing in his two November speeches required congressional approval. But some of them didn't. Through numerous, broad-based emergency powers previously granted by Congress, he already had the power to set up the one surefire method for living with shortages and spreading them evenly: rationing. Nevertheless, he ignored the authority already at hand and insisted that Congress grant him the *specific* authority to ration gasoline. The purpose

---

14. This was corrected later on by energy czar Simon, who did enjoy using his power. When domestic airlines came weeping to him about the prospect of having to cancel thousands of flights for lack of fuel, Simon diverted 1.5 million barrels of jet fuel from military to civilian use. Defense Secretary James Schlesinger protested that Simon was endangering national security and managed to have 600,000 barrels switched back to the military.

of the request was apparently to delay having to assume the responsibility and, if he should have to ration, to share the blame.

His request for rationing authority was a central part of the Energy Emergency Act of 1973. But the year ended with Congress still wrangling over it. The hang-up occurred because members of the House who didn't trust the oil industry tacked on amendments that would (1) prohibit the industry from making "windfall profits" and (2) require the oil companies to disclose the true size of their oil and gas reserves. Oil-state senators teamed up, with White House approval, in a filibuster to kill these provisions. They succeeded. At one point in the debate, Senate Majority Leader Mike Mansfield became so angry at the interference of the White House lobbyists that he shouted, "If we can't make up our minds by ourselves, I think we ought to consider the abolition of the Senate!" But the Senate didn't abolish itself; it simply adjourned for Christmas and went home—leaving the solution of the "crisis" to its frustrated colleagues over in the House, which was in a pitifully addled condition. One member after another got up and said he didn't even know what was in the energy bill they were voting on. The argument dragged on and grew louder. Many members were dressed in black tie for Christmas parties they were already hours late for. Finally, shortly after 1 A.M., Harley Staggers of West Virginia, chairman of the House Commerce Committee, which had handled the energy emergency legislation, admitted that "I don't know what's in the Senate bill either." But he certainly didn't like what he had heard was in it. "The Senate bill does not even allow us to find out how much energy we have. How can we vote for a bill that will leave us in the dark? How can we legislate without information?" His colleagues agreed that they couldn't. And so, hours behind the Senate, they quit too, one member shouting as they crowded out of the House chamber, "Merry Christmas! We've made asses of ourselves!"

They hadn't made nearly the asses of themselves that some members of the press had made of *them*selves. The Washington *Post*, continuing its crusade in support of higher prices as the solution, proclaimed editorially that for another fifteen cents a gallon, we could thumb our noses at OPEC. "At 60 cents a gallon [of gasoline], there would be, as the advertising agencies might put it, a special new ingredient in our gasoline that is absent from the 45-cent variety. That ingredient is independence. As the price of gasoline and all petroleum products rises, we are buying back our independence of supply and with it our independence of action in the world."

By that criterion, the oil companies were certainly doing their best to give us independence, for they were raising prices gallantly. Regular gas that had been selling at the pump for 37 cents a gallon in January 1973 was selling for 45 cents in December (super premium was selling for 54 cents). The average price of crude in the United States had risen from $3.40 a barrel in January to $6.31 at the end of the year.

Under Nixon's price control program, only old oil was controlled. Old oil was the volume of oil pumped from a well equal to what had been pumped in 1972. Oil in excess of that volume, or oil from wells brought into production after 1972, was "new" and the price was not controlled. New oil had gone up from $5.12 a barrel to $9.51 between September and December. But even old oil was jumping. In May it was selling for $3.90, and then the Nixon administration allowed it to climb another 35 cents. The $4.25 price lasted only until December, when another dollar was added to the price. (Internal government documents uncovered by newsmen more than a year later showed that White House economic adviser Herbert Stein had wanted to push the price of all oil, old as well as new, to $12 and that Treasury Department aide William Johnson had wanted $10 a barrel, but Cost of Living Council director John T. Dunlop would not agree to raising the price to more than $5.25 a barrel.) That dollar increase would cost consumers a mere $2.5 billion a year and was worth $30 billion to the oil companies on their existing inventory. As Senator George McGovern of South Dakota pointed out, the $1 increase was pure windfall profits for the major oil companies, for they owned 80 to 90 percent of the old oil, flowing from wells many of which had been brought into production five, ten, fifteen years earlier. The exploration costs had long since been paid for. More than $4 of the $5.25 was "pure unadulterated profit."

*

If America was going to buy its independence—as the *Post* proposed—it had a long way to go, for U.S. prices were tied to the soaring star of Islam. Thanks to the steadfastly fanatical demands of America's ally Shah Mohammed Riza Pahlevi of Iran, OPEC's new posted price—announced in the last week of December, to take effect on January 1—was $11.65 a barrel, more than 100 percent above the previous posted price of $5.04 set in October and a mere 470 percent increase in a year. It was hard to remember that only three years earlier, the price had been $1.80. The Shah said that he had permitted the posted price of $11.65 to rise no higher for the moment because of his feelings of "generosity and kindness." But lest he indulge the West with too much kindness, he was selling oil on the spot market as high as $17.34 a barrel. He was just doing it for our own good, the Shah said, teaching us to economize: "Eventually all those children of well-to-do families who have plenty to eat at every meal, who have their own cars, and who act almost as terrorists and throw bombs here and there, will have to rethink all these privileges of the advanced industrial world. And they will have to work harder . . ."

Though the Shah's action seemed to be based largely on emotion—distaste for the West, vengeance against the majors—there was in fact a good deal of cold calculation behind it. His experts had reconnoitered, to measure the enemy's reserve strength, to see what Iran could get by with, to see how vulnerable the West, and particularly the United States, really was. One of the persuasive discoveries they made was that the United States was just sitting on its coal. Amouzegar, Iran's Finance Minister in charge of oil policy, later told writer Anthony Sampson, "We were specially struck by the fact that in 1951 coal accounted for 51 percent of fuel in the United States, while in 1973 it was 19 percent." Now it was clear why the oil companies had bought a dominant position in the coal industry; it had given them the power to cut back coal production to the point that it was safe for their OPEC allies to raise prices endlessly. Big oil's flank attack on consumers through the mines had worked out beautifully.

Reportedly, King Faisal had not wished to raise the December prices nearly so much as the Shah demanded and had informed Kissinger that if the United States would apply restraining pressure on the Shah, the Saudis would do likewise, even if it meant endangering OPEC unity. Kissinger showed no interest in the plan. But such reports of the Saudis' reluctance have to be taken with extreme caution. In their more unguarded moments, they tended to sound like Sheikh Yamani, who said, "We are in a position to dictate prices, and we are going to be very rich."

And so were the oil companies. Fourth-quarter improvements over 1972 for the top companies: Exxon, 59 percent; Texaco, 70.1 percent; Standard of California, 94.2 percent; Mobil, 68.2 percent; Standard of Indiana, 52.8 percent; Gulf, 153 percent. Said Exxon chairman J. K. Jamieson, "I am not embarrassed."

Much later, after several years of sifting through accounts, federal investigators would uncover the reason for part of the oil companies' phenomenal profits: they were literally stealing from the public by overcharging. Estimates for the 1973–74 crisis period alone were conservatively set at $2 billion in overcharges. Most oil executives joined Jamieson in shrugging it off—nor did they ever repay more than a small fraction of their booty.

1974

"There is an underlying current I've seen time and time again of distrust of big companies and big operations and there seems to be a design to try to pull them down or cut them up into mincemeat . . ."

JOHN E. SWEARINGEN, *chairman, Standard of Indiana*

If reform was ever to be imposed on the oil industry, now was the time to do it. The national atmosphere was perfect. Every public opinion poll showed that the average citizen was convinced the crisis was trumped up to improve company profits. Rumors damaging to the industry swept the country. There were reports of scores of tankers anchored off the United States awaiting higher prices.[1] Senator John Tunney of California said he had heard many reports that storage tanks in the Los Angeles area were "filled to the brim," that the situation was "very suspicious." Senator Walter Huddleston of Kentucky said a member of his state's legislature had reported that all the land storage facilities were filled and that "the oil companies had the Mississippi River virtually clogged with barges loaded with fuel." Nixon's new Attorney General, William Saxbe, renowned for his sometime candor (he had once surmised that Nixon "must be out of his fucking mind"), admitted that the average American believed the oil companies were perpetrating a hoax and "as an average person, I share their view."

In an interview with Mike Wallace for CBS, the Shah of Iran suggested that the oil industry may have engineered gasoline shortages to increase their profits but that there was *not* a shortage of oil being delivered to the United States. In fact, said the Shah, the United States was getting "more oil than any time in the past." When Wallace asked if he saw fraud in the major oil companies' operations, the Iranian monarch replied with a slight smile, "Well, *something* is going on, for sure." Thomas Kauper, head of the Justice Department's Antitrust Division, said he and his investigators had not yet found "much hard evidence" of conspiracy, but he said he certainly wasn't ruling out the possibility and that it might take antitrust lawyers years to discover the truth. Critics too cautious to accuse the companies of outright fraud were perfectly willing to accuse them of exploiting the crisis. "Look at it like a war," said David

---

1. The rumors pestered Washington so constantly that at one point the Federal Energy Office assigned two hundred people over a fortnight, and at a cost of half a million dollars, to go out to see if they could find this idle fleet of loaded tankers. They reported back that it was a phantom.

Freeman, head of the Ford Foundation's energy study group. "Big oil didn't start the war, but they are war-profiteering."

Big oil was indeed doing splendidly. For 1973, the eighteen largest companies had reaped after-tax profits of $9.2 billion, an increase of 53 percent over 1972, leading the U.S. economy into the worst period of inflation in twenty-two years. Now and then, newsmen and congressional investigators uncovered some of the harsh methods used to make profits grow so robustly. For example, a subsidiary of Shell Oil was found selling heating oil for three times the price it had paid to import the oil.

Mind-boggling profits, revelations of price gouging, and rumors of supply manipulations put oil executives very much on the public relations griddle, and they didn't like it one bit. (See the Swearingen quote opening this chapter.) Unfortunately for them, every time they made great protestations of innocence and goodwill, more tainted money would float to the surface and everybody would keep gawking at it.

The aura of taint was heightened when Representative Les Aspin of Wisconsin, who was just the latest in a whole army of campaign-money sifters, released a 58-page study showing that oil company officials and principal stockholders, including the five Rockefeller brothers (Exxon), contributed $5,250,540 to Nixon's reelection campaign—contributions which, considering that the alternative candidate was George McGovern, were natural enough but still easily subject to the kind of interpretation given by Aspin: "The big oil companies have Mr. Nixon in a double hammerlock. After their massive contributions, there is little he can do to control them . . . It is now clear why the administration attitude has been so consistently anti-consumer and pro-big oil—the oil companies financed a big chunk of the President's last campaign." And—he might have added—the campaign before that, and the campaign before that, to the beginning of Nixon's career.[2] The major oil companies, which had raised gasoline prices a total of only 18 percent over the previous fourteen years, in 1973 alone hoisted them another 28 percent, saying that foreign crude prices drove them to it, and retail dealers—who liked to play the role of abused little-businessmen but usually were discovered to have as much larceny in their hearts as the oil giants—were adding their own techniques for fleecing customers. A nationwide survey by the Internal Revenue Service found that 20 percent of the gas stations were charging more than the price-control laws allowed. In some areas—notably southern California—the percentage of crooked filling stations was as high as 50 percent, the IRS said. Customers were being subjected to all sorts of insulting gimmicks. In Chicago, for example, a filling station op-

2. Aspin, a shark for publicity, actually was taking credit for nothing more than compilation. His basic data had come from Common Cause and General Accounting Office investigations.

erator charged the equivalent of a dollar a gallon by "giving" five gallons
of gasoline to any customer who paid $5 for a rabbit's foot. Other fast-
buck dealers would sell gasoline only to motorists who bought a hyper-
priced windshield cleaner or gasoline cans, or who bought "membership"
cards.

If the public was outraged by the attitude of some retailers (several
service station operators were [variously] shot, clubbed, knifed, and spat
upon),[3] they were even more outraged at the distant oil executives,
whom they could not get their hands on. Part of their outrage was undoubtedly caused by the feeling of helpless ignorance. Just what the hell
was going on? Although people in Boston and Philadelphia and New
York were having to scrounge for gasoline (on January 1, a 40-mile survey on Long Island found one station out of seventy-two doing business,
four lines deep; in New York City, motorists typically had to wait in line
three hours), it was plentiful in Seattle, Dayton, Dallas, and Denver
(yes, Denver, where shortages the previous summer had been among the
nation's most crucial). In fact, most of the West Coast's motorists were
on easy street. Then, why not in Oregon? There the supply of gasoline
was so short that Governor Tom McCall imposed an odd-even rationing
(motorists got to buy on alternate days, depending on the last digit of
their license number) and purchases were limited to ten gallons. Was it
true, as many Oregonians claimed, that the oil companies were making
an example of Oregon because it had some of the nation's toughest environmental laws?

Energy czar William Simon made a big production of the allocation
program launched in mid-January—limiting homeowners to only the
amount of fuel oil that would keep their thermostats at 6 degrees below
1972's settings; ordering refiners to cut gasoline production 5 percent
below 1972 levels to free more capacity for turning out heating oil and
industrial fuel; et cetera. Was he trying to kid somebody? The American
Petroleum Institute had reported on January 4 that inventories of most
refined products were higher than they had been a year earlier: middle
distillates (heating oils and diesel fuels) were a startling 28.5 percent
higher; stocks of gasoline and industrial fuel were slightly lower (4.4
percent); jet fuel was 15.6 percent higher. All in all, inventories of
refinery products were 9 percent higher than at the start of 1973. If the
industry's own trade organization would admit supplies looked at least

---

3. A Lexington, Mass., Texaco dealer complained: "They've broken my pump handles
and smashed the glass on the pumps, and tried to start fights when we close. We're all
so busy at the pumps that somebody walked in and stole my adding machine and the
leukemia-fund can." In Hartford, Conn., an Exxon dealer felt so threatened by his
customers that he barricaded himself in his station behind a tow truck, a blue sedan, a
panel truck, a purple Jeep, a red Volkswagen, a blue and white pickup truck, two garbage cans, oil drums, and a sawhorse.

pretty good, wasn't it possible that in fact the United States had plenty of oil and gas, but that it was being withheld from the market until prices went up further?

Why should the American people accept the API's statistics? It had lied before. How did the government know that the API wasn't lying this time? Simon admitted that nowhere in the bureaucracy was there an adequate reporting system of oil and gasoline stocks on hand and that the industry's inventory figures were "the biggest mystery of all." The prestigious Conference Board said it felt the Nixon administration was overstating the oil shortage by as much as 1.3 million barrels a day. Maybe Ralph Nader was right when he said that, far from being short, "this country is groaning in a sea of oil and gas." All the public knew for sure was that prices were going to keep right on climbing, soon and sharp. The new year had scarcely gotten under way when federal energy officials were predicting—on the advice of the oil companies—that gasoline, diesel fuel, and home heating oil would be ten cents higher by March.

*

That's the way things stood as Congress prepared to return to Washington.[4] If it really had in mind trying to reform the industry, it would never be more solidly supported by the public. And if it didn't want to reform the industry, at least Congress could wallow in front-page publicity as it pretended to try. Whatever their motivation, four congressional committees—two Senate, one joint, and one House—cranked up hearings for January. All were announced with stern piety. The House Select Committee on Small Business would hold hearings to determine whether the energy crisis was "fact or fiction." Senator William Proxmire of Wisconsin said his Joint Economic Committee would try to find out if the industry had been using "valid" statistics "for projection of energy shortfalls." Rosy-cheeked Senator Frank Church of Idaho was going to lead his Senate Foreign Relations Subcommittee on Multinational Corporations back through the thickets of the 1950s and 1960s to see what kind of skulduggery was behind the multinational corporations' Mideast operations. And Senator Henry "Scoop" Jackson of Washington, chairman of the Senate Permanent Investigations Subcommittee, said, ". . . the American people have a right to know the truth about the energy situation," and he was going to find out for them.

On behalf of readers who may be in suspense, let it be said at once that very little besides threats and posturing and lamentations came out of all these hearings. The January prediction made by Charls E.

---

4. The previous year, members introduced more than eight hundred energy bills. Most of them sank without leaving a trace.

Walker, a premier lobbyist with close ties to oil, proved to be solid: "When it all shakes out, I think we'll see a lot of rhetoric and some action but not that much in terms of radical change affecting the industry." Mark Lynch, who coordinated energy legislation for Nader's Congress Watch project, reluctantly agreed: "Although the climate is right to produce good legislation, I'm not that optimistic. There's not much leadership in the House in this area, and Senate liberals all seem to go their own separate ways." Still, there were pluses. Here and there the oilmen were subjected to some passing embarrassment. And, if nothing else, the hearings provided some good theater. In fact, the greatest piece of energy theater of the decade—better even than the President's war-equivalency speech three years later—was arranged, orchestrated, and conducted by Scoop Jackson, the Senate's Toscanini of energy, for three days, beginning on January 21, the day Congress started its new session.

For Jackson, it was a chance to redeem himself. Once a hero to liberals for his support of environmental legislation, Jackson had lost much of that reputation during the Alaska pipeline fighting in his Interior Committee. He was for bringing Alaska's oil to the West Coast, with much of it destined to be unloaded at ports in his home state. He was not loath to pull some fast tricks to support the oil companies. On one occasion he told several environmental organizations that they needn't send their spokesmen to one of his Interior Committee hearings, because the pipeline wasn't on the agenda, so they stayed away, leaving the field to oil lobbyists, who did show up and did talk about the pipeline. Well-publicized oil money, including some from Gulf's bad boy, Claude Wild, had occasionally fallen into his campaign coffers. (See WILD entry in the Appendix.) Here was a chance to wipe out some of the public's tarnished memories and to put on a good, old-fashioned Populist show. And why not? Already the press was calling Jackson (mostly for lack of competition at that early date) the front runner among Democrats for the 1976 presidential nomination.[5]

---

5. Of Jackson's credibility problems, Christopher Lydon mused in the New York *Times:* "Not the least of Senator Jackson's political hurdles may be reconciling his tone of shock and outrage before the oil executives . . . with his long familiarity with oil and his sometime closeness to the industry.

"His 1972 Presidential campaign, for example, received a $10,000 contribution from the Gulf Oil Corporation—an illegal corporate gift that was later returned. Last year Senator Jackson managed the bill that authorized the Alaska pipeline, a project dear to the industry.

"Yet if past performance is a guide, he will find ways of roughing up the oil industry in public now and again without breaking, or even concealing, a working relationship with industry leaders."

Lydon wrote that in February 1974. Later other contributions to Jackson uncovered in the Senate Watergate investigation included $225,000 from oil millionaire Leon Hess, board chairman of Amerada Hess Corp., who disguised his secret donations under the names of other persons, including an elderly widow in Florida; $50,000

And so to the same big, baroque Senate Caucus Room where the gray laundry of Watergate had been recently washed, if not exactly scrubbed, Senator Jackson now summoned seven representatives of the most powerful oil companies in the world (Exxon, Gulf, Shell, Texaco, Amoco, Mobil, and Standard of California), placed them under oath, and bade them sing.

He had told them to bring certain information about their profits and production with them, but they hadn't. How dared they disobey him? How dared they sit there looking so smug? Their profits were "obscene" and they knew it. They should be ashamed! They were guilty of "blatant . . . corporate disloyalty to the United States." On and on he raged, always well within range of the TV cameras.

He wagged his finger at them, waved documents at them, read scornfully from their newspaper advertisements, glared at them with his best heavy-lidded (he suffered from an ailment that attacks the eyelid's muscles), stony-faced manner, and in the remarkably monotonous tones that had made him infamous on the campaign trail, he demanded that they confess to the nation right then and there what rascals they were. Perhaps to his surprise, they did not confess. Indeed, they responded in a rather surly way, and no sooner had the hearings ended than they accused Jackson and his cohorts of "McCarthyism" and a "damn vendetta."

But in fact the seven oil executives, whatever their momentary discomforts, however many blustering insults they were subjected to, should have enjoyed the encounter, for the nine senators who confronted them spent a good portion of the time admitting that they were ignorant dolts. To hear the senators talk, they had only recently become aware that there were such things as international oil companies. These were, on the whole, the dumbest hearings on a major topic to be heard or seen on Capitol Hill in a decade, full of such ignorant examinations as this by Senator Abraham Ribicoff:

RIBICOFF: Exxon is part of Aramco [Arabian American Oil Co.], is it not?

ROY BASE (*senior vice-president of Exxon*): Yes, it is.

RIBICOFF: Is Texaco part of Aramco?

ANNON CARD (*senior vice-president of Texaco*): Yes.

RIBICOFF: Is Gulf part of Aramco?

Z. D. BONNER (*president of Gulf Corp.*): No.

RIBICOFF: Is Mobil?

---

from Walter R. Davis, an oil operator in Midland, Tex.; $15,000 from E. Edmund Miller of Beverly Hills, Calif., president of Time Oil; $8,000 from executives of Kerr-McGee, and $2,000 from Robert O. Anderson, chairman of Atlantic Richfield. Atlantic Richfield and Hess were beneficiaries of the Alaska pipeline Jackson fought so hard for.

ALLEN MURRAY (*vice-president of Mobil*): Yes.

Et cetera. Now, the membership of Aramco was not a closely guarded secret, and Ribicoff could have found his answers in the most basic petroleum encyclopedia. Other members of the subcommittee also pelted the cornered executives with trivial and silly questions, acting stunned and dopey when the oilmen responded with substantial data. (Not that much information of substance was forthcoming.) At one point, when the oil execs had led him up to his knees in the swamp of industry statistics, Jackson backed frantically away, saying, "I think I'll leave that to the CPAs."

Over and over again, the senators acknowledged that they were operating without even the most elementary information about the oil industry. For Jackson, chairman of the Interior Committee, a panel that should have regularly accumulated the most intimate data on the industry, it was apparently such a painful confession to make that he was driven into a poetic frenzy. He reached his peak in a Whitemanesque chant that could have been titled "The American People Want to Know," which was rhythmically a bit rough, but nicely impassioned.

"The American people want to know if there is an oil shortage.

"The American people want to know why the prices of home heating oil and gasoline have doubled when the companies report record high inventories of these stocks.

"The American people want to know whether oil tankers are anchored offshore waiting for a price increase or available storage before they unload.

"The American people want to know whether major oil companies are sitting on shut-in wells and hoarding production in hidden tanks and abandoned service stations.

"The American people want to know why oil companies are making soaring profits at a time when the government contends that only costs of production are allowed to be passed through to the consumer.

"The American people want to know if this so-called energy crisis is only a pretext, a cover to eliminate the major source of price competition—the independents—to raise prices, to repeal environmental laws, and to force adoption of new tax subsidies.

"The American people want to know why the oil industry benefits from special tax incentives that no other business or industry enjoys.

"Gentlemen, I am hopeful we will receive the answers to these and other questions before we leave here today . . ."

Challenging Jackson for the Subcommittee's poet-laureateship came the ranking Republican, Senator Charles Percy of Illinois, with his own, even more soaring refrain—"We Are Told"—of ignorance and confusion.

"The American public doesn't know who or what to believe. Should they believe a government which doesn't have the elementary information in hand to reach critical decisions? . . . We don't even know how much of a real energy crisis we actually have. Are there only scattered or regional shortages? Or as some have told me, perhaps we have a wholesale fraud being perpetrated on the American public . . . We don't know whether the situation is temporary or long-term. We do know we are wallowing in a morass of misinformation.

"We are told that there is no gas, but there is gas. No oil, but there is oil.

"We are told that the Arab embargo has reduced imports, yet the oil companies are generally reporting increased stocks over last year.

"We are told of empty storage tanks, yet many are so filled to the brim that incoming tankers can't even unload.

"We are told that there are no windfall profits at a time when third-quarter profits for the oil industry gushed to new peaks, with like results expected for the fourth quarter . . .

"We are told the American public will not tolerate excessive profits. Yet, when a windfall profits tax measure was on the Senate floor just prior to the recess, a filibuster led to its defeat.

"We are told that unemployment will not rise significantly. Yet, already, over 175,000 persons have been laid off . . .

"Is the energy shortage to be a kind of domestic Vietnam, where we are asked to sacrifice for a cause we are told is just but don't really know whether it is? Like Vietnam, in the face of inadequate and incomplete information, we appear hell-bent on total engagement of our troops—in this case one federal bureaucracy after another . . . It is almost as though the more bureaucrats you throw into the picture—to mandate, allocate, punctuate, and frustrate—the less likely Congress can be accused of sitting around doing nothing."

*

Oh, they were so unhappy. And angry. And suspicious. If their charges were repetitious, no more than the same old charges that had been floating around Congress and in some columns of the press for months, still they delivered their lines with surprising freshness. Senator Ribicoff's constituents in Connecticut, who had been having some rough times, were no doubt delighted to hear him sound lively for a change, accusing the oilmen of "causing a panic" to drive up prices, of participating in a "conspiracy with the Middle Eastern oil-producing states," and of cheating the United States of $3 billion a year in taxes.

But the oil executives had heard all those charges many times before and hardly worked up a sweat in making their ripostes. They were

polite, they were sympathetic, they seemed to be suitably hurt that anybody would think such things of them—and they were almost totally un-
cooperative. They said nothing would give them more pleasure than to
bring enlightenment to the Subcommittee and to the American people,
but they insisted that either the information sought had slipped their
minds or had never been lodged in their minds (they would try to supply some of the technical details later, by letter, they said) or was nonexistent. They weren't sure about their profits. They were hazy about their
taxes. They were hesitant to estimate reserves or the duration of the
shortage. They simply outmaneuvered the Subcommittee—and got away
with it.

Considering the importance of the problem, the stature of the
witnesses, and the eagerness of the senators to exploit the spotlight, the
hearings were stunningly unproductive of useful information. Their cli-
max was one big anticlimax, with Jackson on the last day admitting
morosely that he and his colleagues had gotten exactly nowhere. "The
one point that this hearing has brought home clearly," he said, "is lack of
timely, reliable, complete, and credible information about the energy industry. We do not have reliable current data on primary crude oil and
product stocks, and there is no usable information at all on secondary
stocks. Import statistics are covered with confusion and doubt. The
wholesale price statistics of the federal government regarding gasoline
and fuel oil are not believable or usable. We know almost nothing about
the international pricing and investment policies of the companies and
the tax benefits they enjoy. This is information that Congress needs in
order to legislate. This is information the executive branch needs regularly and promptly to discharge its responsibilities. This is information
which the American people need to dispel the cloud of suspicion and resentment that surrounds the present crisis."

Why was he crying? If Congress still operated in the dark, he carried
much of the blame. Early in 1971, he and Senator Jennings Randolph of
West Virginia had persuaded the Senate to launch a study of national
fuels and energy policy, and in the intervening years the Senate had held
twenty-nine hearings—many of them chaired by Jackson. The National
Fuels and Energy Policy study had produced a veritable bookshelf—
reprints not only of those twenty-nine hearings, but also of forty reports.
And yet these had all been handled so badly that none of the information needed in 1974 was available. Still, it was not too late. These hearings were supposedly called to make up for the deficiency. Wasn't that
why he had been browbeating the seven executives? He had the full
power of Congress—including its subpoena powers—to squeeze the information from them. But he hadn't used this power. Nor had he used
finesse, nor common sense. And so he had muffed the hearings.

One reason he had failed—and there were more than a few cynical

onlookers who thought Jackson wasn't nearly as unhappy about his failure as he pretended—was that he had structured the inquiry to get publicity, not information.

Oddly, the general press wasn't critical. Odder still was that the most
intelligent criticism came from one of the oilmen, Harold Bridges, president of Shell Oil: "Conducting the hearings with representatives of
seven competing companies appearing as a panel of witnesses, rather
than individually, was not the most appropriate procedure to be followed, particularly as each of the companies has its own unique operations, structure, problems and views."

With each member of the Subcommittee allowed only fifteen or
twenty minutes to ask questions, Bridges noted, a senator couldn't ask
any one witness more than two or three questions. And if Gulf gave a
general answer that didn't apply to Shell, that left Shell "faced with the
choice of either interrupting the questioner and infringing upon his limited time, or seeking in vain (as I found myself doing on several occasions during the hearings) to catch the attention of the interrogator by
raising of the hand. Such would not be the case if witnesses appeared individually."

An excellent point. Why didn't Jackson call them in one at a time, giving each executive one or two days of grilling, putting together a rich
profile of each company's operations? Why herd them in, all seven, kicking up dust and breathing hard, bawling and running in circles like cattle at a roundup? Because there is more drama to be had from seven
bulls in one ring. How vigorously bold Jackson could appear on evening
TV, confronting seven, yahooing his denunciations!

Because of Jackson's muddling of the event, even the few random
remarks of significance that came from the witnesses were lost to the
press, which hopelessly tried to weave seven strands together.

The two most interesting statements made during the hearings came
from Z. D. Bonner, president of Gulf. He said the Arab embargo "has
been called a blessing in disguise." Who called it that? The companies,
because it gave them an excuse to multiply their price by four? He admitted—probably the first time an executive of a major oil company had
made the concession in public—that "oil import controls were used as a
price control mechanism . . ." He made no mention of import controls as
a national-security device; he said it right out, simply: "price control
mechanism." Neither statement was picked up by the press. Neither
statement prompted follow-up questioning from the Senate subcommittee. Both statements just sank to the bottom of Jackson's themeless pud-
ding.

* * *

Of much more value were the hearings of the Senate Foreign Relations
Subcommittee on Multinational Corporations, which, with mountainous

piles of explicit details never before brought together for public inspection, revealed much of the melancholy history of the federal government's subservience to the major oil companies both at home and abroad over the previous four decades. The emphasis was on the postwar period: the secret arrangement by which the giant international companies were permitted to pay virtually no taxes to this country, the antitrust exemptions that allowed them to set up the Mideast cartel that worked against U.S. interests, the deliberate slowing down of production in the late 1960s that brought about the shortages of the 1970s, the blundering of State Department diplomats that played into the oil companies' hands, the unwillingness of Presidents to punish oil monopolies.

One of the most disturbing revelations of the Church hearings was the extent to which Western-owned oil companies had cheated Iraq. No wonder that country was so totally alienated from the United States. There had been a time when, if Iraq had been treated decently, she might have been as reliable a source of oil as Saudi Arabia. Practically speaking, the friendship of Iraq was as worthy of cultivation. Saudi Arabia was thought to have 150 billion barrels in reserve. But Iraq was presumed to have more than 100 billion—just how much more was uncertain because the oil companies that had exploited Iraq were accustomed to lying about that country's oil holdings. As for the character of Iraq, it was much more admirable than Saudi Arabia's. But not to U.S. militarists, not to the economic conservatives who had dominated U.S. foreign policy for years. Iraq was socialist and radical. Saudi Arabia was conservative and monarchical. Iraq was more interested in spending its oil riches on air-conditioned hen houses than on jet fighters. (By 1978, Iraq officials could boast, "We are now self-sufficient in eggs.") Any country that didn't prefer F-15s to hens was suspect to the Pentagon and the State Department. So, by our sullenness, we pushed Iraq into the Russian orbit.

The animosities between Iraqi and Westerner began many years ago. The Iraq Petroleum Company (IPC)—made up of British Petroleum, Shell, CFP (France), Exxon, and Mobil—set out in 1925 to control Middle East oil. They hoped to establish a steel-tight cartel that would dictate production and fix prices. The U.S. companies agreed to the cartel arrangement reluctantly. They preferred more-open competition, believing, correctly, that U.S. companies had superior manpower, technology, financing, and markets. But the will of Britain and France prevailed. Within a given area, said the negotiators (drawing the infamous "Red Line" around the old Turkish Empire), the cartel companies would act in unison. They would not set prices individually or challenge each other on an individual company basis. Iraq, of course, was caught within the Red Line Agreement.

On October 14, 1927, one of the most remarkable oil strikes was made, in northern Iraq. The first well, near Kirkuk, blew in at a rate of eighty thousand barrels a day. It was quite apparent from the very beginning that Iraq could become one of the world's great oil powers.

But it didn't. After Kirkuk, virtually nothing was developed for two decades. Throughout the 1930s and 1940s, the companies went through the motions of hunting for oil, but in fact it was all a put-on. Documents and memoranda uncovered in Senator Church's hearings laid out details of the fraud. Sometimes the companies dug wells that were so shallow they could not possibly have hit oil. Sometimes, despite every precaution not to succeed, they did hit oil; they would quickly cap these accidental discoveries, say nothing to the Iraqi Government, and quickly move on.

There were, to be sure, some extenuating circumstances. During the great depression of the 1930s, the world had more oil than it could sell, and if Iraq's oil had been brought onto the market, it would simply have sent the price of oil skidding to an even more ridiculous level. During the first half of the 1940s, World War II prevented development of the Iraqi fields. But *after* the war, the Iraq Petroleum Corporation was *still* reluctant to go after the oil that it knew to be there. Why? Simply because the companies preferred to market the oil they owned elsewhere and they didn't want Iraqi oil interfering with the market. U.S. companies preferred to pump from Saudi Arabia, where they owned 100 percent of the concession, than from Iraq, where they owned only 23.75 percent. And when the fields of Libya gave forth, the companies felt they had better pump there for all they were worth, not knowing how long Libya's unstable government would let them. And they preferred to pump in Iran because its oil, unlike Iraq's, was so convenient to transportation. Long accustomed to abusing Iraq, the companies continued to do so into the 1960s. But then Iraq began to rebel. Tired of being poor while it sat on an ocean of wealth, in 1961 it took away IPC's concessionary rights to all areas where it was not producing.

The U.S. members of IPC, Exxon and Mobil, let out a great wail and asked the State Department to intervene in their behalf. But, for once, an official of State refused to cover up for the exploiters. Under Secretary Andreas Lowenfeld's memorandum of December 11, 1961, suggested that the United States would be smart not to bring the matter up before some international body for adjudication, because the companies would probably be very embarrassed by the things Iraq could disclose. He said Iraq would not have much trouble showing that the companies had operated only to help themselves.

"A fairly substantial case," he wrote, "could be made (particularly in an arbitration) that IPC has followed a 'dog in the manger' policy in Iraq, excluding or swallowing up all competitors, while at the same time governing its production in accordance with the overall worldwide interests of the participating companies and not solely in accordance with the interests of Iraq."

"Dog in the manger" indeed. Following its seizure of the IPC concessions that weren't being pumped, the government of Iraq had sent out a team of geologists and petroleum engineers to see what the prospects for that area were. They found proof (according to Church's investigator) "that IPC had drilled and found wildcat wells that would have produced 50,000 barrels of oil per day [each]. The firm plugged these wells and did not classify them at all because the availability of such information would have made the companies' bargaining position with Iraq more troublesome."

In 1972, Iraq went the rest of the way and nationalized its oil.

*

In late March, at one of Senator Church's hearings on the multinational oil companies, an official from the General Accounting Office brought out charts, using figures supplied by the Arabian American Oil Co., that showed Aramco was riding OPEC's tail very profitably. Before 1973, the cost of producing a barrel of oil in Saudi Arabia had been about ten cents at most. In 1973, this cost jumped a couple of pennies. But at the same time the *profits* from a barrel of oil jumped from $1.23 in the preembargo part of 1973 to $2 in the postembargo part of 1973, to about $4.50 a barrel in the first part of 1974 (as of the Church hearings). Aramco Senior Vice-President Joseph J. Johnston, who was at the hearings as a witness, was asked several times what incentive Aramco and its owners (Exxon, Texaco, Standard of California, and Mobil) had to press for lower prices.

Johnston put his elbows on the table, cupped his hands under his chin, and stared at Senator Church for a long, long time. Finally he gave up. He couldn't think of any incentives.

*

Over the Church hearings hung the musty odor of old billion-dollar deals, bureaucratic chicanery, political collusion. It all seemed so long ago that the participants, like veterans of a guerrilla war convening to recall past mischief, now spoke openly of what had been done in secret. George McGhee, the Texas oil millionaire who had become a Mobil executive after leaving government, was there. He was the assistant secretary of state in Truman's administration who helped Aramco set up its awesome foreign tax loophole. Now he talked about it casually:

CHURCH: ". . . the effect of the decision was to transfer $50 million out of the U.S. Treasury and into the Arabian treasury. That was the way it was decided to give Arabia more money and to do it by the tax route. Isn't that correct?"

MC GHEE: "Yes, that is one way of looking at it . . ."

Senator Percy couldn't believe, or pretended he couldn't believe, that U.S. Treasury officials would watch so much money disappear right before their noses without complaining.

PERCY: "You would think there would be screams from the Treasury that is always looking for revenue . . . How much protest was there from the Treasury . . . ?"

MC GHEE: ". . . [T]he impression I had then was that no one objected to it."

The testimony revealed that as a result of the foreign tax credit allowance, none of the five largest U.S. oil companies had paid *any* U.S. taxes on profits earned overseas since 1962, and by 1971 they had accumulated tax credits worth $2 billion, which could be carried forward to cancel future U.S. taxes over a five-year period.

*

Some of the saddest testimony came in late February with the appearance of Leonard J. Emmerglick, who, as a special assistant to Attorney General James P. McGranery, had in the early 1950s led a grand jury investigation of the international oil cartel's antitrust violations. It appeared certain that the companies would face criminal charges. But eight days before he was to leave office, in January 1953, President Truman called Emmerglick and told him he had decided—"solely on the assurance of Gen. Omar N. Bradley"—that it would be detrimental to "national security" if the criminal charges were pursued. Truman—the World War I captain who claimed to distrust generals, the politician who had built his entire career around the reputation for being the champion of the little man, the President who ridiculed the frenzied anticommunists who had bedeviled his administration—succumbed to a five-star general who preached anticommunism on behalf of an oil cartel. What was the quid for the quo?

For his successor, Eisenhower, an open friend of the oil industry, the rest was simple. He changed the charges from criminal to civil and transferred responsibility of the case from the Department of Justice to the Department of State—the first time in history that an antitrust case was handed to State for prosecution. Seeing as how the Secretary of State was John Foster Dulles and the defense counsel for the oil cartel was Dulles' former law firm (Sullivan and Cromwell), the case was soon as good as dead.

*

Later in 1974, Senator Church discovered that the State Department was up to its old tricks. The Federal Energy Administration (FEA) was trying to do an updated study of the multinational oil companies. But the lawyer conducting the study had been asked to leave Caracas, Venezuela, by the American ambassador after officials at major oil companies expressed opposition to the study. Under State Department pressure, the FEA thereafter kept its investigators home. The interference infuriated Church. "I really don't know why they [the State Department] should be fronting for the oil companies," he said with rhetorical innocence. "Our hearings have revealed that the State Department knows next to nothing about oil and has no desire to learn. State Department policy has always been one of letting the oil companies handle oil. This is the policy that the department still adheres to." By the time FEA administrator John Sawhill was fired, later in the year, the study was comatose.

* * *

Even if the Church hearings hadn't reopened the old sores of the foreign tax credits, this would have been one of the big congressional quarrels of 1974. Nixon knew the battle was shaping up and placed himself from the first as being—hypothetically—on the side of reform. In his mid-January energy message, he asked Congress to reduce the amount of foreign "taxes" that the companies could count off directly against their U.S. taxes. But after Nixon made the request, nothing else was heard from him on the subject.

The usual critics, however, were not so quiet. Senator Proxmire attacked the credit as "the golden gimmick"—"a gigantic loophole that costs American taxpayers between $2 billion and $2.5 billion a year." Actually, Proxmire was understating the loss; it was closer to $3 billion. Senator Walter Mondale, citing a new Treasury study, said American oil firms used foreign tax credits to reduce their U.S. bills 75 percent in 1971. The next year, the companies had more foreign tax credits available than they could use in cutting their American taxes to zero, so they carried over the rest for use in future years. The "taxes" that came with the 1973–74 OPEC price surge were expected to increase the oil companies' foreign tax credits eightfold. It was beginning to look as though they might never have to pay more than a piddling amount of U.S. taxes again.

But nothing came of the demands for reform, and Senator Jackson's investigations subcommittee fittingly wound up the year by releasing a five-year analysis—1968 to 1972—showing that Exxon, Texaco, Mobil, Standard of California, Gulf, Standard of Indiana, and Shell collectively paid more than five times as much in taxes to foreign countries as they paid to the United States treasury ($10.3 billion versus $1.9 billion), that being the loss to U.S. taxpayers.

To lessen the public's unhappiness over oil profits, the Administration proposed that the oil companies be made to "plow back" excess profits into more exploration. But as financial writer Eileen Shanahan pointed out in the New York *Times*, "The problem with this proposal is that oil companies are already putting so much money into exploration and development—about $6.5 billion, as of 1972—that all large companies and most small ones could escape the excess profits tax just by continuing to do what they are doing."

***

Worldwide, there was no shortage of supply. The oil and gasoline were simply going most abundantly where the prices were highest. At the same time that many Americans were spending hours queued up for gasoline, Europeans were getting all they wanted—although paying more for it. That was the key: money. If a person, or nation, was willing to pay the industry scalpers' price, gas was available in abundance. When New Jersey politicians let it be known that they would patronize black marketeers to get gasoline for their fuel-starved constituents, they were besieged with offers of many millions of gallons of gasoline and crude oil. New Jersey State Senator Raymond J. Zane, after a week of negotiating with under-the-counter brokers, said he had learned from them that more than 700 million gallons of gasoline over just one February weekend were sold outside of regular distribution channels in the New York–New Jersey area alone. But the price was much higher than wholesale prices in the regular distribution channels. "There seems to be," said Zane, "a booming market."

The truth was, Americans were being subjected to hardships long after there was any rational explanation for such treatment. Even as early as the first of February, the wholesale supply of oil was beginning to stack up. The world price was beginning to break. Nigerian crude, which had been selling for $22.60 in December, couldn't be peddled for $14 a barrel in February. Iranian crude, which had sold for $17.04 in December, was selling at about $8.45 a barrel. Reporters wrote of tankers jamming into the Port of New York with their loads of crude that buyers had no immediate use for.

In March, the pretentious "embargo" was ended officially by OPEC—a meaningless gesture, since by then the world market was glutted. The Commerce Department released a previously secret report showing that, during the five-month "embargo," many millions of barrels of oil continued to flow into the United States from countries that were supposedly angry with us. Why had the report been hidden from the public for so long? To keep the panic—and the prices—up? No, no, said Commerce; the report had been withheld only because secrecy was "in the national interest."

Obviously, the problem that now faced the majors and their OPEC partners and their allies in the Nixon/Ford administration was to shore up prices by getting rid of the surplus.

*

This could be achieved (1) if the American people were shepherded away from such conservation measures as were being advocated by Sawhill, and by virtually nobody else in the Administration, (2) if we continued to favor OPEC and ignore the new sources of oil recently discovered in non-OPEC parts of the world, (3) if industry was discouraged from using more coal, and (4) if domestic supplies were *not* exploited as much as they could be.

Each of these steps was taken.

(1) In March, Nixon proclaimed that "the back of the energy crisis has been broken." Thereafter, all White House pressure for establishing a national energy policy evaporated. When the National Emergency Petroleum Act, which Congress had labored over since the previous October, finally found its way to Nixon's desk, it was emphatically vetoed, on March 4. The bill contained the sweeping authority that Nixon needed to order nationwide gasoline rationing and a wide variety of other conservation measures, and he didn't like those things at all.[6] (Nor did the President like the extremely modest pricing "rollback" provisions in the bill, claiming that they would discourage the domestic industry from hunting for more oil and gas and would "result in reduced energy supplies," which was nonsense, for it was very plain indeed that whether prices went up or down or stayed level, the domestic industry—bending to the will of the majors—had no intention of producing more than fitted into the long-range pricing strategy based on the appearance of shortage.)

Anyway, said Nixon, the supply situation was so rosy the legislation was no longer top priority. His pronouncements helped restore the national appetite for waste. With the White House whooping them on, U.S. motorists stepped on the gas with preembargo ardor. In early May, the Associated Press reported that nationally the average speed on most

6. Senator Jackson, who was the bill's chief sponsor in the Senate, looked upon the veto as a personal insult and took the floor on March 6 with a torrid counterattack. Referring to Nixon's claim that a rollback would hurt production, he declared:

"That assertion is preposterous. In February 1973, the domestic oil industry was producing 9.4 million barrels of crude oil per day at an average price of $3.40. In February 1974, it produced 9.2 million barrels a day at an average price of $6.95. So it is obvious that production was 200,000 barrels a day less than a year ago.

"Mr. President, crude oil prices have doubled, and crude oil production has not increased one whit. It is down.

"Let us look at the largest exempt category of crude oil. In February 1973, production from stripper wells [wells that could produce no more than ten barrels a day] in the United States was 1.17 million barrels a day, at an average price of $3.40. In February 1974, stripper well production was 1.15 million barrels, at an average price of $10.35. Prices have nearly tripled, and production is no higher than it was one year ago."

One reason Jackson was so mad was that he knew he and his allies didn't have enough strength to override the veto. And he was right about that.

highways was back to sixty-five to seventy miles an hour, the use of electricity was up, the use of public transportation was down. Many filling stations, which until recently had been open only eight hours a day or less and closed all day Sunday, were once again operating around the clock. "Clearly," said Sawhill in June, "the public has relaxed and isn't conserving energy the way they were. We are discouraged by the way energy demand has shot up since the end of the Arab oil embargo." Although high pump prices cut gasoline use 3 percent in the summer—the first summertime drop that anyone could remember—the resulting glut caused prices to fall 6 to 10 cents by autumn, and America's 100 million drivers began sucking it up again. Sawhill's successor as FEA administrator, Frank G. Zarb, reported that the last three months of the year wiped out the 3-percent decline of the summer, and at year's end Zarb reported, "Consumption is right back to where it was and is still increasing."

(2) Despite OPEC's obvious antagonism toward U.S. consumers, "our" oil companies increased their patronage of OPEC and turned away from friendlier sources. The majors' imports from Canada continued to fall, ostensibly because of a Canadian Government decision to conserve its energy for home use; but with U.S. companies—mainly the big international companies—controlling most of Canada's oil, it was safe to assume that the government's decision was largely determined by oil company influences. Also, if the companies had not been intent on keeping U.S. supplies at a vulnerably low level, they could have turned to other, new sources around the world. William Simon, now Secretary of the Treasury, using previously classified estimates made by the CIA, disclosed that twenty-six "significant, new oil discoveries" had been recently made in eighteen countries "all outside the boundaries" of OPEC. But the majors did not use these new sources with much enthusiasm.

(3) The coal industry—heavily dominated by oil companies, of course—showed little interest in enlarging its market. In May, the Federal Energy Office (FEO)—later the Federal Energy Administration (FEA)—estimated that if as many electric utilities as possible switched from oil to coal, the United States could save two hundred thousand barrels of oil a day. The FEO had pressured eleven power plants to shift from oil to coal during the embargo, but by late spring they were preparing to shift back. Why? Because the coal (oil) industry had increased its production by only about half as much as the FEO had expected. So long as coal supplies were uncertain, the utility companies could not be expected to make the change.

(4) At the same time that energy use rose sharply in the postembargo euphoria, the major oil companies quietly began to shut down domestic production. Claiming that they were hampered by a shortage of steel pipe, drilling rigs, and the like, oilmen—despite the huge price increases

allowed by the government to encourage new oil production—reduced production by 3.4 percent from the second half of 1973 to the first half of 1974 and then by another 3.7 percent in the remainder of the year.

Who were the villains behind this regressive development? In late January, energy czar Simon announced that eight large oil companies (he didn't name them) had stockpiled 74 percent of the tubular drilling goods held by the nation's oil firms. He said that the twenty-two largest oil companies had stockpiled 30 percent more tubular goods than their monthly average since January 1972. They were gobbling up the stuff— and hiding it away. Manufacturers and distributors of steel drilling goods reported that their inventories had dropped at least 60 percent below inventories in the year prior to the October embargo. Independent oilmen—wildcatters—who have traditionally found and developed most of the domestic oil fields, were being shut out by a lack of equipment. They accused the major firms of buying up and hoarding the available steel drilling products—and they were telling the truth.

The cutback in domestic production in fact flew in the face of the industry's own boasted potential. As Sanford Rose pointed out in the March issue of *Fortune:*

"The potential for rapid expansion of domestic oil output is apparently vast. Last year the American Petroleum Institute, the oil industry's trade association, reported that the companies could boost domestic production of crude on a crash basis by about a million barrels a day within three months—that is, we could raise output from 9.3 million barrels a day at the end of 1973 to 10.3 million barrels by March 31, 1974. This expansion could be achieved, said the API, 'with existing wells, well equipment, and surface facilities—plus work and changes that can be reasonably accomplished within the time period.' Even more important, the API stated that a crash program would not threaten the future productive life of existing oil fields."

That's not the way things turned out. When March 31 rolled around, the oil industry was not turning out an additional million barrels a day. It had cut *down* by 230,000 barrels a day.

Moreover, the industry began to cut back sharply on a worldwide basis, too. The most important drop came in August, when the four American companies of Aramco agreed with their Saudi partners to cut exports by 10 percent. By October, for the first time in seven months, worldwide production of oil matched demand. When that balance was struck, the industry not only successfully eliminated downward pressures on prices but, more important to the oil cartel, rescued OPEC from possible disaster. In July, *The Wall Street Journal's* James C. Tanner had written, "Knowledgeable observers are convinced that OPEC's major problem right now isn't whether to raise or lower prices but, rather, how to keep oil prices from crumbling without drastically cutting production.

If the problem isn't solved, some observers believe, OPEC could crash."

Within three months, the production cutbacks initiated by the major oil companies to fix prices had also gotten OPEC out of its bind.

⁎

Still, though OPEC had survived once more, the leaders of Saudi Arabia were convinced that it would be better strategy for the long haul if prices dropped somewhat right then, or at the very least, held steady. After all, OPEC production capacity greatly exceeded world oil demands. If further price increases drove consumer demands down farther, in turn forcing OPEC production down, where would the vicious circle end? By nature conservative, the Saudis preferred to ease up on prices until the condition of the world market became clearer.

Meeting with Secretary of State Kissinger in Cairo on October 14, Saudi King Faisal said that he would attempt to stabilize oil prices, if not push them down, but would need the assistance of the United States in exerting pressure on the Shah of Iran, who seemed adamant in his expansive greed. (This was the same pitch Faisal had made, without success, the previous October.) Kissinger promised to join King Faisal in this effort. But he did not do so. James Akins, then ambassador to Saudi Arabia, and Treasury Secretary Simon later asserted that Faisal's plan was undercut for foreign-policy reasons: Kissinger did not want to do anything to antagonize the Shah, who, he believed, was the linchpin in the United States' Middle East strategy.[7]

But crediting Kissinger with being motivated by foreign-policy considerations may be too kind. The real pressures came from the usual commercial interests. By December—after a total of four price advances by OPEC during the year[8]—executives of the major international oil firms were privately insisting that President Ford and Kissinger neither attempt to cut back OPEC imports nor force OPEC to lower its prices. Moreover, some of these executives were not bashful about making their opinions known publicly. For example, Harold J. Haynes, head of Standard Oil of California—one of Saudi Arabia's partners in Aramco— was quoted by the New York *Times* on December 8 as saying industrial

---

7. A year after Faisal's meeting with Kissinger in Cairo, Saudi Oil Minister Yamani wrote Simon, "I would like you to know that there are those amongst us who think that the United States administration does not really object to an increase in oil prices. There are even those who think that you encourage it for obvious political reasons and that any official position taken to the contrary is merely to cover up this fact."

8. Some of these advances were very cleverly done, in a public relations way. Instead of raising the "posted" price—the price that was so visible to the uninitiated public— OPEC kept raising its royalty rates, which were buried in a complex formula subordinate to the posted rates. The size of the cake remained the same, but OPEC's slice became increasingly larger—not to the disadvantage of the oil companies, however, for they simply recouped their rising royalty payments by raising their prices to the consumer, and, of course, by deducting the additional royalties from their U.S. taxes.

nations had to accept the prospect of "a long-term transfer of wealth to the oil exporters. I don't think there's any way to avoid it." Commenting petulantly on Secretary Simon's prediction of a break in world oil prices within the near future, Haynes said, "I don't think the consuming countries should be in a position of pressuring prices. We don't want an atmosphere of confrontation. We need to start working in an atmosphere of cooperation." He brushed aside questions about Saudi Arabia's reputed take-over of 100 percent ownership of Aramco (which some observers saw as mere paper shuffling), saying, "Who owns certain assets is not the important thing. The international oil companies still have a role to play in the Persian Gulf. The important things are access to oil and the incentive given us to go on producing it and developing new fields." All of which added up to insistence that Kissinger and everyone else in the U.S. Government back off, leave oil negotiations to the companies, as had been traditionally done, and swallow whatever prices and periodic blackmailing went with it.

Significantly, shortly after Haynes made his pronouncements on behalf of Socal and allies, the State Department floated a trial balloon—through a speech at Yale by Assistant Secretary of State Thomas Enders—for keeping oil prices at OPEC levels even if OPEC crumbled. The balloon ascended ahead of its time, and the general reaction around Washington was summed up by Congressman Henry Reuss of Wisconsin: "I just wonder what it shall profit the American consumer of oil if he is freed from the tyranny of the OPEC only to be ripped off by the U.S. oil companies." Reuss's statement was spoiled, however, by its naïve premise that the two forces were not roughly identical.

* * *

Oil company profits kept right on soaring, which was hardly surprising; the OPEC increase as of January 1 to $11.65 a barrel meant that companies were earning more than four times what they were earning in the early part of 1973. As for domestic crude, it was selling for prices from $5.25 (old oil) to $10 (new oil) a barrel, pumped from the same wells, by the same companies, that were producing it profitably in the spring of 1973 for $3.50 a barrel. It looked as though 1974 would bring as much corporate happiness as 1973. Of all companies, Occidental kept on getting the most lavish profits—up 718 percent in the first quarter. Exxon, the company everyone was watching, tried to avoid embarrassment by juggling its books: it reduced its true earnings by setting aside $400 million in the first quarter and counting this against "future taxes," and thereby claimed a profits leap of only 39 percent. Ordinarily a company does not reduce its earnings by a liability that hasn't yet occurred, but if Exxon had not done so, it would have had to acknowledge profits exceeding $1 billion for the quarter—a jump of 118 percent over earnings for the same period of 1973, a year that saw Exxon earning the largest annual profit ($2.4 billion after taxes) ever earned by any industrial company. As compiled by Chase Manhattan Bank, the after-tax profits of the top twenty-five oil companies rose from $6.4 billion in the first three quarters of 1973 to $10.3 billion in the first three quarters of 1974, even though the overall economy was showing a downturn of 3 percent.

Government economists (and oil executives) justified the higher profits as incentives for the companies to sink more wells.[9] And indeed they were pouring additional millions into exploration. But the flood of profits was so enormous that oil executives also indulged themselves—juicing up their own pay packages by more than 20 percent. The chairman of Exxon got an $81,600 income boost, making his total annual take $620,766. Said Senator John Pastore, "It was for a rise in the cost of living." There was laughter on the Senate floor. Senator Thomas Eagleton added, "He was having market-basket problems." More laughter.

The oilmen were also amusing themselves in sideline acquisitions. Gulf bought the Ringling Brothers & Barnum & Bailey Circus. Mobil bought Montgomery Ward. (To be more exact, it bought controlling interest in Marcor Corp., parent company of both Ward and Container Corp. of America.) Purchases of that sort hardly seemed to be aimed at supporting Project Independence. On the defensive, Mobil chairman Rawleigh Warner offered this excuse for diversification: "At one point there were 3,000 bills in the hopper in the Congress, all of them aimed directly at doing something dreadful to the oil industry. So we said, if we're going to believe these people, we'd better move out into a different direction."

*

9. Senator Jackson pointed out that increased earnings seemed to be having little comparable effect on production. Using figures on percentage increases (or, in one case, a decrease) in dollar net earnings from 1972 and 1973, and the percentage differences in barrels of oil products sold in the same period for the seven largest U.S. oil companies, Jackson concluded, "The whole story is that volumes went up very little but earnings skyrocketed. This is the heart of it."

	CHANGES IN NET EARNINGS	CHANGES IN OIL SALES
Standard of Indiana	32%	3%
Mobil	38.3	4.9
Shell	40.6	8.8
Texaco, U.S.A.	12.1	3.2
Texaco, worldwide	34.9	3.4
Exxon, U.S.A.	14.9	15.3
Exxon, worldwide	59.4	10.1
Gulf, U.S.A.	5.3	−4.8
Gulf, worldwide	60.1	5.9
Standard of Calif., U.S.A.	−0.4	3.9
Standard of Calif., worldwide	39.7	5.9

Good times for the oil companies meant very tough times for some parts of the economy. Utilities were struggling with 300–400 percent increases in fuel costs (investigators found some power companies paying as much as 80 cents a gallon for distillate oil that had left the refinery costing about 20 cents) and trying to pass those costs on to consumers. Consumers struck back by reducing use of utilities. The giant Consolidated Edison Company of New York, caught in the cost up / use down pincer, suspended payment of its quarterly dividend—the first time it had done that since it went into business, in 1885. Farmers were in trouble. Fertilizer prices were up 50 percent, because the cost of petroleum-based chemicals and natural gas used to produce fertilizer was up that much. Consequently, food prices saw their biggest monthly advances in a quarter century. Fuel, farm, and food prices pushed the wholesale index to its second-biggest one-month rise on record; the only bigger leap had been in the fall of the previous year. By April, auto sales in the United States were down 26 percent from the 1973 level and big-car sales were falling faster. Big cars had outsold the smaller cars 2:1 the previous October, but their advantage had fallen to 5:4 in November. By December 1973, the smaller cars had pulled even, and in January and February they had started moving ahead dramatically. The reason was obvious. The 1974-model autos averaged about 4,400 pounds—35 percent more than the foreign autos tested by the Environmental Protection Agency. The standard U.S. cars were traveling between eleven and twelve miles on a gallon of gasoline—37 percent less than the foreign autos tested by EPA (for that matter, U.S. cars were getting only about half the mileage they'd gotten in the early 1950s). Detroit was close to panic. FEO director John Sawhill said he sympathized but that actually gasoline prices were much too low and should be allowed to rise to at least 60 cents a gallon (an 8-cent increase). Senator Philip Hart, who pointed out that the 1973–74 energy price increases were already costing more on an annual basis than the Vietnam war, said Sawhill's view might be expected "from the president of one of the major oil companies, but coming from the director of the FEO—a body charged with protecting the public interest and not a group of stockholders—it is scary."

* * *

In fact, the conduct of the entire Nixon administration was pretty scary. Frantically trying to extricate himself from Watergate, Nixon couldn't be bothered with the energy problem. He left that to subordinates, and they bungled and quarreled endlessly. Was the nation faced with a critical long-term supply problem? Absolutely, said Simon. Not so, said Roy L. Ash, budget director; it was "manageable, one-time and short-term." Simon snarled in reply, "He should keep his cotton-pickin' hands off energy policy." Should the nation try for conservation through rationing, or

higher taxes, or higher prices? There were top officials in the Administration lobbying for each approach. To make matters worse, the energy
bureaucracy was a hive of incompetents, some of them borrowed from
the oil industry, some on loan from other executive departments who
were glad to get rid of them. The unwillingness of the energy bureaucracy to crack down on the oil industry made its rules and regulations
virtually meaningless. On February 1, the Federal Energy Administration ordered all refiners to share equally in the supply of crude oil, to
give the independent refineries a break; the international companies got
mad and cut their imports so that they wouldn't have to share; six
months later, Sawhill was complaining that the program (which had
been modified downward in May) still wasn't working worth a damn, because of "foot-dragging and calculated resistance" on the part of the majors.

Cloudy solutions floated back and forth across the landscape, and then
were blown away. In March, Administration officials said they were
seriously thinking about spending up to $100 billion to develop a synthe-
tic-fuels industry in the United States. (It would be several years before
that idea would pop up again—with a higher price tag, of course.) Not
even Carl E. Bagge, president of the National Coal Association, the industry's chief lobbyist, could get excited about such talk, though it would
mean the revitalization of his slumping industry. "All this stuff that the
public is being mesmerized with now," he said. "Liquefication and
gasification. You're not going to solve the problem by throwing billions
into coal research and development overnight."

"Project Independence," the complicated plan put forward by Nixon
in 1973 to make the United States independent of foreign oil by 1980,
had been repeatedly run through the computers and it still didn't make
economic sense. In March, the latest study by the Administration's energy experts found that even if the United States lavished $255 billion on
the Nixon plan between then and 1980, the nation would still be importing as much in that year as it had been in 1974. By September, Sawhill
(who was about to be fired) said he would "never advocate complete
self-sufficiency in energy for the United States." His coolness toward independence was understandable, seeing as how by that time estimates of
the cost of the program were bouncing between $545 billion (Federal
Energy Administration) and $700 billion (Federal Reserve Board).

*　*　*

Not content to squeeze the public by legitimate techniques, the oil companies were using some highly questionable—and sometimes downright
crooked—methods. Nobody knew for sure what profits they had reaped
illegally. In December, the General Accounting Office said it thought oil
companies might have overcharged by as much as $2 billion. The GAO

complained that it couldn't be more exact, because the Federal Energy
Administration, which was charged with regulating oil prices, was withholding information about oil company costs.

Perhaps one reason FEA officials showed so little enthusiasm for assisting the investigation was that many, if not most, of the FEA's senior
policymakers had held important jobs with oil and other energy companies before moving into their government jobs. Many of them intended
to return to those jobs after a brief stint with the government. Replying
to a demand for the information from Representative Benjamin Rosenthal of New York, the agency—which regulated industry prices and su-
pervised oil policy—supplied a list showing that more than one hundred
former oil-industry employees were on its payroll, fifty-nine of them in
key positions, ten in top-grade jobs. Among the topmost: Marmaduke R.
(Duke) Ligon, assistant administrator for policy, planning, and regulation. Before coming to government, he had held such posts as executive
assistant to the corporate vice-president of Continental Oil Co. Melvin A.
Conant, deputy assistant administrator for international trade and commerce. Conant came to the energy agency after ten years with Exxon,
part of the time as senior government-relations counselor for the Middle
East and Asia. Clement Malin, deputy director of the office of producer-
country affairs and emergency supply. He had worked for Mobil for ten
years. Philip L. Essley, deputy assistant administrator. He had worked
for Marathon, Skelly, and Sinclair.

This kind of coziness was so commonly found in the federal energy bureaucracy as to almost qualify as a tradition. The government would not
think of taking an important action without first consulting the oil industry. For example, in April, to nobody's surprise, the House Subcommittee
on Conservation and Natural Resources discovered that the U.S. Geological Survey had privately sought the advice of a committee of oil-
industry representatives before establishing regulations for offshore
drilling.

In September, Senator Lee Metcalf of Montana wrote Interior Secretary Morton to complain about the makeup of the National Petroleum
Council (NPC). Although a 1972 law required that federal advisory
panels be "fairly balanced in terms of the points of view represented,"
Morton's latest appointees to the NPC—all 21 of them—had close ties to
the oil industry. But that was nothing new. In fact, virtually all of the
134 members of the NPC were energy-industry officials, and some 70 of
them had contributed a total of $1.2 million to Nixon's 1972 election cam-
paign. There wasn't a consumer spokesman among them.

Criticism of the Administration's heavy reliance on ex-oil-industry bureaucrats became especially intense when congressional investigators
began looking into the background of a new regulation that permitted
major oil companies sharing crude oil under the mandatory allocation

program to recover their costs twice. "Double-dipping," it was called. Who thought up such an anticonsumer idea and foisted it off on the government? Many fingers were pointed at Robert C. Bowen, a Phillips Petroleum engineer on "loan" to the government through the Executive Interchange Program. (After serving his government, Bowen returned to Phillips.) According to Chairman Dingell of the House Subcommittee on Conservation and the Environment, which was seeking to discover the source of the regulation, Phillips got about $52 million in double-dip profits. However, even after an FBI investigation, authorship of the regulation was never pinned down, and the Justice Department said it didn't have evidence to bring conflict-of-interest charges against Bowen. Dingell accused Assistant Attorney General Henry E. Peterson, chief of the Criminal Division, of not pursuing the probe with much enthusiasm, and said Peterson's close ties with President Nixon raised questions about his "competence as an investigator." Peterson said Dingell was just a demagogue.

Sawhill tried to disassociate himself from the whole mess. As soon as the double-dip regulation was discovered, he protested that he was firmly against using oil company executives and would certainly see that nothing like that happened again. "It doesn't make sense to bring people from industry into a regulatory agency like ours where a potential for conflict of interest exists," he told the House Small Business Subcommittee. But later, after conferring with aides, an embarrassed Sawhill told the subcommittee that he had just learned the FEA was then using three other executives on loan from energy companies, including Mobil.

*

Some observers claimed that Phillips was also among those companies that profited the most from another government regulation: It permitted a 330 percent increase in 1973 on the price of propane, an energy source greatly relied on by rural poor people. While the eyes of the nation were mainly on gasoline and home heating-oil prices and government bureaucrats policed those markets most intently for middle-class public relations purposes, the rural poor—the kind of people you see off the highway, existing in tarpaper shacks and mobile homes—got little protection until Senator Jackson's subcommittee began uncovering a corner of the hidden scandal. Jackson said he found propane brokers "buying and selling large amounts of propane gas from one another, thereby driving up the price and gaining big finder's fees for themselves. In one instance, three brokers traded 14 million gallons of propane in a 24-hour period—and together they enjoyed a profit of $1.3 million."[10]

---

10. Here is an example of the kind of transaction Jackson ran into: Joseph Havens and Dan Duncan were owners of Enterprise Products Co., of Houston, a large propane wholesaler and a company whose net profits increased from about $306,000 in

Between January 1973 and January 1974, Amoco's propane gas prices had risen 354 percent; Exxon's were up 294 percent; Mobil's, 406 percent; Shell's, 406 percent; Warren Petroleum, a subsidiary of Gulf, had raised prices 367 percent. Jackson's investigators found a Tennessee family, not untypical, that lived on a Social Security pension of $165 a month and had been paying $30 to $40 a month for propane before the big price squeeze; now they were paying $100 a month. Senator Robert Dole said he had heard of families in his home state, Kansas, that were paying $200 a month for propane. Senator Ernest Hollings of South Carolina said some of his constituents were literally going through winters without heat. Arkansas poultry farmers were faced with an additional cost of up to $11 million for propane to heat chicken brooders; since they couldn't easily pass such a whopping addition on to consumers, some intended to let their birds die at the first cold snap.

***

The departure of Nixon and the elevation of Ford brought, if anything, only an extra dimension of confusion to the Administration's energy policy, or its absence of policy. The confusion was heightened by the fact that Sawhill was a remarkably straightforward bureaucrat with no head for politics, and he kept stumbling over the duplicities created elsewhere in the Administration, either by Ford himself or one of his top managers, especially William Simon. Sawhill made the mistake of thinking that these other fellows meant what they said, and very often they meant just the opposite—so when he attempted to go along with them, he found himself bumping into them instead. Too, he was hopelessly candid, as he proved at the very start of his FEA tenure, when he committed the un-

---

1972 to just under $6 million in 1973. Havens and Duncan bought two small retail-level propane distributorships, French L.P. Gas, of Malvern, Ark., and Holicer Gas Co. Inc., of Shreveport, La. Large-volume wholesale and brokerage transactions were then routed through these two companies, thus adding another markup in price. Jackson asked one of the owners about a transaction.

JACKSON: "Was the propane physically moved after the sale by Enterprise to Holicer? Was it physically moved?"

HAVENS: "The product was transferred to Holicer in underground storage."

JACKSON: "You are saying it was physically moved?"

HAVENS: "I am saying that the product was transferred in underground storage from Enterprise's inventory to Holicer's inventory."

JACKSON: "Where was Holicer's inventory?"

HAVENS: "Holicer's inventory was established at Arcadia, Louisiana."

JACKSON: "Where was Enterprise's inventory?"

HAVENS: "Arcadia, Louisiana."

JACKSON: "Why don't you say it wasn't physically transferred?"

HAVENS: "I am saying it was transferred. From a legal standpoint it was transferred from Enterprise to Holicer and subsequently transferred to American Oil (Amoco)."

JACKSON: "Let me ask the question again. Was the propane physically moved, not by paper, after the sale by Enterprise to Holicer?"

HAVENS: "No, it was not."

forgivable sin of criticizing Kissinger's lack of energy leadership. And his efforts at independent strategy, while very often logically sound, had a way of surfacing just in time to get tangled up with the counterstrategy of somebody—usually the President—who didn't take kindly to such accidents.

For example, Ford's WIN (Whip Inflation Now) message was already en route to Congress, containing a passage that rejected a gasoline tax, when Sawhill appeared on NBC's "Today" show and proposed a 20-cent-a-gallon tax on gasoline. Then Sawhill, responding to a query from Senator Jackson, said the United States did not have a clear policy to bring world oil prices down—a response that was made on the very day Ford went before the United Nations and called for lower OPEC prices.

The most confusing part of the Ford administration's energy policy was its intentions regarding oil price controls. Authorization for the controls would end on March 1, 1975, unless Ford persuaded Congress to end them prior to that date, or to extend them beyond that date. What did he have in mind? Sawhill was caught in the middle of that confusion, but, undeterred, he plunged ahead with suicidal boldness.

In mid-July, the Federal Energy Administration leaked to newsmen Sawhill's grand strategy for phasing out price controls. Decontrol would mean that two thirds of the oil being refined in this country would double in price, but Sawhill believed the increase—however disastrous for consumers—was justified as a way to protect the independent oilmen from unfair competition. Sawhill saw it this way: Under the two-tier system, the price of "old" oil—that is, oil from wells flowing before 1973—was controlled at $5.25 a barrel. Prices were not controlled for imported oil or oil from wells brought onto line in 1973 or thereafter. Most new oil and imported oil in mid-1974 was selling for slightly over $12. Some sold as high as $15. Most of the old oil was controlled by the major oil companies, so they were at a tremendous advantage. Their refineries were having to pay an *average* of about $8.70 a barrel for crude. The independent refineries were having to rely much more heavily on new and imported oil. Sawhill reasoned that if prices were decontrolled, old oil prices would climb to the level of new oil and all refineries would go into the marketplace on an equal basis.

As a matter of fact, to the last man, top officials in the Nixon administration and in the Ford administration wanted exactly what Sawhill wanted, and many of them wanted it for much less noble reasons than fair play for the independents. But Ford's strategists were aghast at Sawhill's timing. For political reasons, they did not want to get a public debate stirred up over oil pricing at that moment. The transition from one President to another was touchy enough without introducing another nerve-jangling issue. If they played it cool, maybe Senator Jackson would stop yelling about the likelihood that oil price decontrol would cost consumers $9 billion a year, and maybe House Democrats would stop trying to pass legislation to roll back prices (recently they had come within fifteen votes of achieving it). When things had settled down a bit, Ford would be only too happy to try to decontrol prices, but for the moment it would be wiser to pretend otherwise. So, a couple of weeks after Sawhill's leak, Treasury Secretary William Simon announced that "there is no economic justification for doing away with the $5.25 ceiling on old oil at this time. The two-tier price system is working, providing an incentive to bring out new oil at a higher price, and we should resist efforts to roll back that [higher] price. But we're *not* going to *raise* the $5.25 ceiling *or do away with it.*" That was the Administration's line, and poor Sawhill was made to toe it with an embarrassing recantation. Now he stepped forward and declared that decontrolling prices would deal a "severe blow to the consumers."

Secretary Simon's promise that the ceiling would not be raised was mere stage scenery. Despite public protestations to the contrary, Simon, head of the cabinet-level Energy Committee, did in fact favor decontrolling prices, and promptly. On September 8, the New York *Times* reported a "backstage power struggle" in which Simon and Interior Secretary Morton were pitted against Sawhill. Simon and Morton reportedly had ordered federal officials to start "devising a plan to phase out crude oil price controls by February." But Sawhill, a veritable Don Quixote, having been forced to recant on decontrols, was now stubbornly opposing them. But the results of the lopsided fight were inevitable. On October 29, Sawhill was fired.

Ford replaced him with Andrew Gibson, previously president of the Interstate Oil Transport Co., of Philadelphia, which bought and leased tankers to oil companies. He had also run the Maritime Administration for three years under Nixon. History had pretty clearly indicated that nobody could operate that agency without coming to terms with an army of lobbyists, including lobbyists for the oil tanker industry.

Consumer groups complained about the appearance of conflict of interest when it was revealed that Gibson would receive eighty-eight thousand dollars a year for the next ten years from Interstate Oil Transport. One senator said the payments amounted to the oil industry's "having a ring through his [Gibson's] nose." Ultimately Gibson asked that his appointment be withdrawn. Were there other rings through noses at the Federal Energy Administration? What about Melvin A. Conant, assistant administrator of the FEA? Conant (who had joined the FEA earlier in the year as director of its international trade office) was paid ninety thousand dollars for past services when he left Exxon to take his government job. An Exxon spokesman told *The Wall Street Journal* that the payment was to ensure that Conant didn't "suffer an economic pain" from becoming a public servant.

***

In one respect—in its determination to allow the majors to get their hands on federal property at cut rates—the Nixon/Ford administration was consistent, enthusiastic, and aggressive. In 1971, Nixon had appointed a task force to study shale lands in Colorado and estimate proper lease terms. The task force was headed by Hollis Dole, of the Interior Department (who, before the leases were sold, would move to Atlantic Richfield to head its shale division), and Reid Stone (who was with Atlantic Richfield before he joined the task force). After a two-year study, the panel set out six 5,120-acre tracts for leasing, and in January 1974, the first lease was sold to Gulf Oil and Standard Oil of Indiana for $210.3 million.

Interior officials clapped their hands and said they had no idea the lease would bring such a high price. But investigators for the House Select Small Business Committee discovered that, prior to the bidding, Interior had set $5 million—an incredibly low figure, less than one fortieth of the actual bid—as its "minimum acceptable bid." Did that mean Gulf and Standard of Indiana had been very generous in their bid? Not at all. For the investigators also discovered that the tract was so promising that the minimum acceptable bid *should* have been $515 million. Gulf and Standard of Indiana had gotten a $300-million windfall, at the very least. But that was just the beginning of their good luck. The tract was estimated to contain four billion barrels of recoverable oil. That worked out to 5 cents a barrel. But if they developed the tract promptly, the government would further reward them by front-end bonuses, reducing the cost to 3 cents a barrel. *New Republic* writer Peter Barnes toted up all the pros and cons and concluded: "If crude sells in the 1980s and 1990s for $10 . . . per barrel [about one third what it would be selling for, as things turned out], the Gulf–Standard of Indiana consortium that bid $210 million for four billion barrels could gross $40 billion on that tract alone."

The second tract of 5,120 acres was sold a few weeks later for $117.78 million to a four-company combine headed by Atlantic Richfield.

When committee investigators challenged John B. Rigg, Interior's deputy assistant secretary for energy and minerals, on the stunningly low "minimum acceptable bid," Rigg reportedly shot back that in his opinion it would have been in the national interest to give away the tracts, with "deep subsidies" to boot.

The Interior Department's willingness to set absurdly low values on federal land came as no surprise to the Small Business Committee. A few months earlier, its investigators had discovered that Interior had secretly appraised thirty-five offshore oil and gas tracts in the Gulf of Mexico at an identical $144,000 each. The appraisals had no tie to reality. One of the tracts later was leased for $91,617,000—roughly 635 times more than its appraisal—and another was leased for $76,827,000, about 533 times more than Interior's appraisal. These thirty-five tracts, with their comical evaluations, were among eighty-nine tracts that Interior had appraised at a total of $146,051,000. They were leased for ten times that much: $1,491,617,000. By radically underappraising the land, Interior cleared the way for accepting just about any bid that came along. Of the eighty-nine tracts, twenty-one drew only one bidder each. Interior accepted nineteen of these. Should it have held out for more-competitive bids? Congressman Dingell thought so. He pointed out that the record showed whenever Interior rejected a bid, it got an average price thirteen times higher the next time the land was put up for auction.

*

With the oil crisis clearing the decks for fast action, the Nixon/Ford administration was ready to start leasing offshore lands as fast as possible. Interior officials were, of course, eager to oblige in their usual fashion. In January, Nixon had announced that he wanted Interior to lease 10 million acres of outer continental shelf lands a year, beginning in 1975. Ten million acres, about twice the acreage of Massachusetts, was (1) ten times more than had been leased the previous year, (2) a hundred times more than had been leased in 1969, the year of the Santa Barbara spill, and (3) as much as the federal government had leased, in toto, from the beginning of offshore leasing in 1953 up through 1973. Characteristically, Nixon had decided to make the leap without doing what federal law required: file an environmental impact statement. In fact, he had made the decision without even talking things over with the Council on Environmental Quality, which was supposedly his chief adviser in such matters. After CEQ hurriedly got into the act and spent three months looking over the terrain, it leaked a rough draft of its study to the Washington *Post*. The rough draft's conclusion was that drilling for oil and gas off the Atlantic coast and in the Gulf of Alaska was an acceptable risk "under carefully stipulated and controlled conditions." So many members of Congress and local officials from the East Coast states and so many environmentalists in Alaska let out such an immediate, loud shriek of protest that by the time the official CEQ report came out, a week later, it had reversed itself in part. Now it said that any new offshore oil development should avoid the Atlantic coasts of Florida, Georgia, and Long Island, and the Gulf of Alaska.

But Nixon wasn't going to leave the great push to the next year. On March 28, the government accepted record-high bids—$2.16 billion—for drilling rights to some tracts off Louisiana, the biggest spread of offshore acreage offered in seven years. The Administration emphasized the amount of money pouring into the Treasury, but critics emphasized something else about the sales. Look at the winning bidders, said Dingell: Gulf, Mobil, and Texaco teaming up for one tract, Exxon bidding alone on another. It was the same old crowd. Where were the smaller companies, the independents? Shut out by the prices.

To Dingell, it was immediate proof of the problem his subcommittee was then investigating: the antitrust aspects of offshore oil development, and the collusion between the Interior Department and the big companies. Interior's leasing policies "appear to be deliberately rigged" in favor of the giants, he said. His investigators had prepared a good case in support of the charge, and they were getting solid support from the FTC's Bureau of Competition. Together they came up with evidence that, time and again, eight companies (and sometimes fewer)—Exxon, Mobil, Atlantic Richfield, Gulf, Union, Texaco, Shell, and Standard of California—had walked away with more than 90 percent of Interior's leases. Sometimes, though rarely, they bid independently; usually they teamed up in groups of three or four.

Some of the most damning congressional testimony came from Dr. John W. Wilson, formerly a top economist with the Federal Power Commission, who pointed out that ten of the sixteen major oil companies owned 80 percent or more of their offshore properties jointly with each other, that only two of these companies held as much as 25 percent of their leases independently, and that many had no independently owned leases at all. Said Wilson: "Of the eighteen largest major producers in the state of Louisiana, fourteen have five or more direct interlocks with the other seventeen. Continental, for example, has twenty-eight joint ventures with Atlantic, twenty-seven with Cities Service, twenty-seven with Getty, sixteen with Mobil, thirteen with Exxon, and eleven each with Amoco and Sun."

Facing that kind of teamwork, there was virtually no way independent companies could come up with enough money to offer a real challenge. The stakes were so high, they were simply shut out.[11]

To most critical observers, the vastness of the proposed acreage leases

---

11. The cause-and-effect was obvious, but only once had any official in the Justice Department ever seemed to recognize the connection, and that official was at such a low level that he was easily crushed by his superiors. His quixotic and historic effort was brought to light by Dingell. This is the story: In 1968, the Interior Department had accepted $602 million from two combines of oil giants for 92 percent of the leases in the Santa Barbara Channel. A lawyer and economist in the Justice Department's Los Angeles field office of the Antitrust Division launched a 20-month investigation, at the conclusion of which the Los Angeles office had recommended that a civil suit be filed to block joint ventures of that sort in the future, because they stifled competition. Many members of the antitrust staff felt that the suit would have had a good chance of success without even going to court, because the big companies would have surrendered to stiffer antitrust stipulations rather than undergo the kind of trial that would have opened their files to the public. But the antitrust soldiers never got to try their maneuver; generals in the Justice Department killed the proposed lawsuit in 1970.

was suspicious. There was no practical reason for pushing so fast, and there were many practical reasons for not doing so. The 10-million-acre idea, said David S. Schwartz, assistant chief of the FPC's Office of Economics, was "simply laughable . . . utter nonsense . . . a horrendous mistake," because the entire oil industry put together did not have enough spare drilling rigs capable of doing offshore work, or skilled manpower, to start working the leases soon.

Why the emphasis on the outer continental shelf, anyway? The U.S. Geological Survey estimated that more oil remained to be discovered in the lower forty-eight states than in Alaska and offshore *combined*. Nixon's officials tried to pretend that salvation lay offshore. "That's where the whole ballgame will be won or lost as far as our short-term energy supplies are concerned," said Interior Secretary Morton. In January, he informed Congress that his experts had assured him that out to a water depth of 650 feet there were 200 billion barrels of oil awaiting discovery. Why, off the Atlantic coast alone, he said, there were 48 billion barrels of oil. Here was the entire rationale for the 10-million-acre push. Oodles of oil was out there under water: let's go get it!

Unfortunately for the Administration's credibility, exactly two months later the Council on Environmental Quality released figures from the U.S. Geological Survey that showed Morton's figures were incredibly inflated. For the entire offshore area, said the USGS, the potential might be as low as 65 billion barrels, and the untapped Atlantic frontier out to a depth of 650 feet might contain only 10 to 20 billion barrels.

Who was trying to fool whom, and for what reason? Something odd was going on. The USGS got its data from the oil industry itself—so why the sudden outburst of pessimistic forecasts? Was it to make the risks seem greater and Congress more sympathetic to the oil crowd's efforts? (In 1975, the juggling of statistics would continue—and there would be better guesses as to why.)

*

Some critics felt that by coming onto the market with such a tremendous hunk of land, the Interior Department had no chance—and knew that it had no chance—to receive more than a fraction of the potential market value of the oil and gas resources, because the available industry funds would have to be spread so far. Another suspicion, voiced, among others, by FPC's Schwartz, was that Interior and the companies were working together in this way to get as much acreage out of circulation as possible, lest Congress become so radically wild as to actually pass the recently proposed legislation to create a Federal Oil and Gas Corporation (see Appendix)—a company that would enable the taxpayers' own representatives to go out and look for oil and gas, and not be at the oil companies' mercy. While the legislation had been written and pushed mainly by such liberals as Adlai Stevenson, Edward Kennedy, Philip Hart, George McGovern, and Walter Mondale in the Senate and John Moss of California in the House, it was also getting some support from people who were anything but liberal. Even that child of Wall Street, the early energy czar himself, William Simon, said he thought government oil explorations would be worth thinking about.

Senator Ernest Hollings, a southern conservative, also argued for government exploration. One of the Senate's experts on the outer continental shelf, Hollings hated the idea of the public's being panicked into giving away those lands until it knew what was there. A handsome, strapping South Carolinian who was noted for his sarcasm and loved to fire the last as well as the first shots in a civil war, he delivered heavy salvos in a National Press Club speech in November: "Look at this plan put forward by the major oil companies and Secretary Morton—better known as the team of Major Morton. They say the way to lick the oil cartel is to increase production. Lease 10 million acres on the Atlantic seaboard during the year 1975 and you will have the Arabs in a corner. What a cruel joke . . . With the lack of money in the United States, with the lack of drilling rigs and with the geological studies yet to be made, there isn't a chance of drawing a quart of oil from the Atlantic seaboard in less than six years . . . *Before we lease the Atlantic and Pacific to the oil companies, we ought to do some government-sponsored exploratory drilling . . .*"

By year's end, opposition to the giant leasing program was so intense and came from so many directions, and every action taken by the Interior Department was under such scrutiny from congressional critics and environmental groups, that President Ford, doubtless looking toward the 1976 presidential election, sent word through Interior spokesmen that he planned to sharply reduce the speed and scope of Nixon's proposed leasing program. Anyway, by then it was clear that the legislation to create a government oil corporation was at least momentarily stalled.[12]

* * *

The government-oil-corporation legislation was less a realistic hope than a symbol of the liberals' constant frustration. Always they were trying to work up some scheme for smashing the oil industry's concentration of

---

12. Wild leasing schemes would not be seriously pushed again until another Republican administration was in power. In 1981, Interior Secretary James G. Watt came up with a proposal to lease the next year not a trifling 10 million acres but *200 million acres.* He said it would be done "so we can inventory the land." Once again it seemed fairly obvious that, as in 1974, the Reagan administration's purpose was not to inventory the land or to get oil and gas from it, but merely to rush it into the hands of the major oil companies—to take it out of circulation until they could exploit it at their whim—or, at their whim, not exploit it at all.

power, and always they failed—though not for lack of evidence of the
virtue of their cause.

As if it weren't enough that the largest oil companies were tied together by oil and gas leases, joint ownership of production facilities, and
joint ownership of pipelines, they were also closely united through "communal" boards of directors. Was this legal? The Justice Department, the
Federal Trade Commission, and the Securities and Exchange Commission all had investigations underway in 1974 to determine if the in-
terrelated boards were in violation of the Clayton Antitrust Act. Though
written clumsily, the intent of the Clayton Act was clear enough: it was
to prevent the executives of supposedly "competing" companies from
getting together behind closed boardroom doors to work out deals that
would lessen competition and unfairly increase their profits. Obviously,
direct interlocks—the same person serving on the boards of two or more
competing companies in the same industry—are illegal under the Clayton
Act. That is a basic premise nobody disputes, and yet even on that point
some oil companies were casual scofflaws; in 1974 the FTC was obliged
to file complaints against half a dozen illegal director interlocks in the oil
business, and the Justice Department pounced on thirty oilmen who appeared to be in violation of the Act.

However, it was becoming increasingly obvious that some of the
closest and most intricate connections were not *directly* between oil companies' boards but *indirectly* via the boards of banks. These indirect interlocks may not have violated the letter of the antitrust laws, but they
certainly smashed their spirit. For example, as Senator Lee Metcalf
pointed out in a letter to FTC Chairman Lewis Engman, when the First
City Bancorporation called its board of directors together, one could see
gathered around the table executives from Exxon, a number of independent oil producers, El Paso Natural Gas, Texas Eastern Transmission,
Panhandle Eastern Pipeline, Brown and Root (a leading oil equipment
and services supplier), and such fellows as John Connally, whose law
firm represented several big and small oil companies. Metcalf asked
the FTC if that happy gathering looked like the right kind of "competition."[13]

---

13. A similar complaint had been made the year before by Dr. Wilson, chief of the
FPC's Division of Economic Studies, in an appearance before the Senate Antitrust
Subcommittee. Wilson pointed out that while federal law prohibits one person from
serving on two boards of companies producing the same goods or services, the oil
companies used a loophole. The law did not prohibit a "bridge" arrangement: two
officials from one bank, say, serving on the boards of "competing" oil firms. "For example," he said, "the most recently available evidence on corporate directors from the
banking community shows that, as of 1968, Morgan Guaranty Trust Company of New
York had its employees serving on the boards of Continental Oil, Cities Service, Atlantic Richfield, Belco Petroleum, Columbia Gas, Louisiana Land and Exploration Company and Texas Gulf Sulphur." Morgan also held stock in Texas Eastern Transmission
Corp. and Panhandle Eastern Pipeline as well as gas distribution utilities, Wilson said.

Some of the most aggressive antitrust work was at the state level. A New York State grand jury indicted seven majors for conspiring to rig the gasoline market. And in California, the legislature's Joint Committee on Public Domain finished a four-year study with the conclusion that seven oil companies—Texaco, Exxon, Union Oil, Mobil, Shell, Standard of California, and Atlantic Richfield—were tied together by "such a degree of intercompany cooperation in [California] crude oil markets as to make a mockery of the free enterprise system." The committee pointed out: the seven owned most of the state's pipelines and used this control to squeeze out independent producers; they controlled 42 percent of the oil produced in California, which was enough to give them control of the market; they produced 41 percent of their total California output cooperatively, enabling them to share inside information and data. Kenneth Cory, who had been chairman of the committee before being elected state controller, charged that the seven companies had cheated the state out of perhaps $170 million in four years through underpricing oil they pumped from state-owned land.

The beleaguered FTC still showed some signs of life, though it had only 18 lawyers (versus 144 company lawyers) pursuing the big antitrust case it had filed in 1973 against eight majors. (The National Association of Attorneys General offered to supply volunteer lawyers if the FTC got snowed under.) The FTC came forward in February with its first specific demand: the eight companies should be forced to sell 40 to 60 percent of their refinery capacity. This was generally dismissed as just another FTC bluff. But the FTC's statement did make one strong point, a point that would resurface with heavy proof in later years: the real kings of the oil industry, as several congressional investigations had already indicated, were perhaps not the oil companies, but the banks. The FTC suggested that the eight majors under attack were "to some extent . . . commonly rather than independently owned" by banks, and gave as its example: "Chase Manhattan, through various nominees, is both the largest shareholder in Atlantic Richfield and the second-largest shareholder of Mobil. Clearly it is not in Chase Manhattan's interest to promote vigorous competition between them." The FTC said one reason would-be competitors had no chance to buck the largest oil companies was that they couldn't get the proper financing from banks that owned the very oil companies they wanted to compete against.

* * *

Suddenly, in the midst of Watergate, the nation's No. 1 political scandal, there were reminders of history's No. 2 scandal, Teapot Dome (see Appendix).

In the early days of this century, when the Navy shifted from coal-fired to oil-fired ships, there was a constant worry that the fleet might run out of oil during a war. The fear was understandable, for the industry was even in those days raising the specter of dire shortages (see entry for *Early Fright Campaigns,* in the Appendix). So between 1912 and 1923, various Presidents set aside petroleum reserves on federal land—oil deposits to be tapped in national emergencies. Petroleum Reserve No. 1, set up in 1912, was Elk Hills, seventy-two square miles of rolling hills about sixty miles northeast of Santa Barbara. Petroleum Reserve (or just Pet, as they were fondly truncated) No. 2, set up the same year, was at Buena Vista, California. Pet 3, at Teapot Dome, Wyoming, was set aside in 1915, and Pet 4 on the Arctic coast, in 1923. Originally, management of these reserves was under the Interior Department.

But, from the very first, Interior showed an inclination to let private companies steal the oil, so President Wilson transferred jurisdiction to the Navy Department. Under President Harding, stupid and pliable, the reserves were promptly shifted back to the Interior Department, and Interior Secretary Albert B. Fall, in return for some hefty payoffs, signed secret contracts in 1922 to allow oil companies to start draining Elk Hills and Teapot Dome—from which the scandal took its name.

One result of the Teapot Dome tempest was that jurisdiction was again transferred to the Navy, which spasmodically fought off the continued efforts of oil companies to drain the reserves; but its vigilance was spotty. And besides, the Navy was still being betrayed by Interior; this could happen because even though the Navy Department owned the reserves themselves, the Interior Department still had jurisdiction over the land abutting the reserves. And that was a fatal vulnerability. Mother Nature does not pay any attention to surface boundary lines laid down by man; the pools of oil that underlie the Navy's reserves usually extend beyond the Navy's boundary and into strata underlying other federal lands or privately owned land. If wells are sunk into land just outside the Navy reserve and penetrate the transboundary pool of oil, there is nothing to prevent these wells from pumping off not only all the oil that lies beneath them but the oil beneath the Navy property as well.

There are only two ways the government can fight back: (1) it can create a buffer zone around the reserves, forbidding any private drilling within this buffer zone, and/or (2) it can drill "offset" wells to counterbalance the pumping of the private wells and at least try to get its share of the pool. In 1938, one-mile buffer zones were established around all of the Navy's reserves. The Bureau of Land Management (a part of the Interior Department) was ordered not to lease any of these buffer lands to oil companies, and the U.S. Geological Survey was ordered not to allow any drilling within two hundred feet of a reserve. So valuable was Pet 4, in Alaska, that a *two*-mile buffer was set around it.

However, all of these orders were violated with the knowledge of the Department of the Interior. Illegal as well as legal pumping in and around Pet 2 and Pet 3 was so heavy that by 1974 they had been virtually pumped dry. But they had never been so lush as Elk Hills and Pet 4. These were the treasures that the oil companies really lusted after, and for good reason. Elk Hills contained an estimated 3 billion barrels, which made it one of the nation's richest fields. Estimates for Pet 4 ranged up to 33 billion barrels—and higher—perhaps equal to the potential reserves in the Gulf of Mexico, which already was supplying the nation with a fifth of its oil needs.

The Bureau of Land Management, which determined the official boundaries for all federal properties, had already "mysteriously moved" (as Senator Stevenson put it) the boundaries of Pet 4 to allow oil companies to encroach and start pumping the Navy's oil. The Departments of the Interior and of Defense had also transferred some parts of the two-mile buffer zone to the state of Alaska, which promptly leased the transferred land to British Petroleum, Gulf, Mobil, Phillips, Texaco, Shell, and Occidental, allowing them to push right up against the federal lands and start pumping. In 1972, investigators from the General Accounting Office had found that this sucking around the edges threatened to seriously harm Pet 4. But instead of being embarrassed by these findings, the Nixon administration suggested that pumping both in and around the Alaskan reserve be *increased*. Moreover, they had a bold proposal for doing it: pump out the Elk Hills reserves, they suggested, and use the money obtained from selling that oil to step up drilling at Pet 4! Private oil companies, which would do the pumping and piping and selling for the Navy, would, of course, get a hefty share of the profits. At then prevalent prices, the Navy's oil was worth at least $360 billion.

Among the bureaucrats urging an accelerated program of pumping at Pet 4 was the Defense Department's Energy Task Group. The ETG had been organized by Deputy Secretary of Defense William Clements, Jr., of Texas. Coincidentally, Clements was chief stockholder of the Southeastern Drilling Company (SEDCO), an independent contractor that drilled offshore and onshore, laid pipelines, and gave engineering advice to all the major oil companies, including Standard Oil of California and those with heavy stakes in Alaska. When Clements was appointed to the Defense post, he kept his SEDCO stock but resigned as chairman of the board so as to avoid the appearance of conflict of interest. Some observers felt that hadn't been quite enough, since Clements' son continued to run SEDCO.[14]

---

14. Clements, the No. 2 official at the Pentagon, was also the target of a conflict-of-interest investigation in regard to arms sales to the Shah of Iran. Defense Department standards of conduct say, ". . . personnel are bound to refrain from any private business or professional activity or from having any direct or indirect financial interest which would place them in a position where there is a conflict between their private interests and the public interests of the United States . . ." Whose interests came first

Although the stakes were much higher at Pet 4, it was at Elk Hills that the most fascinatingly complex scheme of profiteering prevailed. At the center of it was Standard Oil of California.

When the Elk Hills reserve was set up, it surrounded some leases already held by Socal; the Socal leases constituted about 20 percent of the total. This, of course, made the Navy's lands vulnerable to being drained by the California giant. So the Navy tried to buy out Socal. Political pressures ruined this plan. Instead, the Navy had to settle for a joint operation. Socal was allowed to keep checkerboard sections in the northeastern quadrant of the 72-square-mile reserve, and in return for managing the reserve—which included pumping about twenty-five hundred barrels a day for test and maintenance purposes, keeping the facilities ready for quick wartime service—Socal was paid 20 percent of the proceeds. It profited not only from the sale of the oil but also from its transportation; the Navy leased Socal's pipeline to get the oil to market. And when the Navy wanted more exploration and development wells, who drilled them? Socal, of course, at $450,000 a well.

It was a sweet deal, but far from being grateful for these windfalls, Socal wanted more. And still more. Occasionally the Navy would take Socal to court in an effort to stop the company's pumping from wells that the Navy felt were in off-limits zones and were draining federal oil. But, lawsuits or no, the pumps kept pumping. None of this bothered the Interior Department. In December 1973, it admitted that it had known for twenty years that major oil companies were drilling illegally close to the reserve and draining it.

Despite the constant friction between the Navy and Socal, nothing seemed to jeopardize the company's peculiarly powerful position at Elk Hills. Moreover, it would become much more powerful if Nixon's plan to open up the reserve for full-scale pumping—the excuse was to ease the nation's "shortage"—was carried into action. If Nixon hadn't gotten the idea on his own, it would doubtless have been planted with him by such old friends as Otto Miller, chairman of Socal, who had given him fifty thousand dollars for his reelection in 1972, and David Packard, former deputy secretary of defense and member of Socal's board of directors, who had given Nixon eighty-nine thousand dollars.

---

with Clements? SEDCO had been in business in Iran for nearly two decades, chiefly in supplying oil equipment and know-how. In one drilling company, SEDCO was in partnership with a trust controlled by the Shah's family. Obviously, it would do Clements' company, and Clements himself, a great deal of good if he pushed Pentagon policies that the Shah favored—such as selling more arms to Iran, a policy that many observers believed had encouraged the Shah to raise oil prices, so that he could more easily afford the arms. In 1976, when the Senate Multinational Corporations Subcommittee was investigating Clements' involvement, he said in an interview that while he had taken no part in discussions of details, he had participated in policy discussions on arms sales to Iran.

Unfortunately for Nixon, he could not open up Elk Hills by presidential fiat, because in the aftermath of the Teapot Dome scandal, Congress passed legislation forbidding any oil to be pumped from naval reserves without the specific approval of Congress. Several embarrassments occurred in 1974 that made that eventuality seem remote. On January 11, Lieutenant Commander Kirby E. Brant, deputy director of the Office of Naval Petroleum Reserves, resigned rather than give his approval to further encroachment by oil companies upon the Navy's oil reserves. He was quoted as saying, "I have written my last lie" in support of the White House's policy. He said he knew if he stayed on the job the White House would expect him "to provide technical assistance in aid of the effort to destroy the reserves."

The dramatic impact of Brant's resignation had hardly begun to fade when U.S. District Judge M. D. Crocker, in Fresno, ordered Socal to stop pumping eighteen thousand barrels of oil a day from a field next to the Elk Hills reserve. That amount was equal to 12.9 percent of Standard's entire daily California production. At issue were ten wells drilled by Standard on its own land but part of an oil pool that also spread under the Navy's reserve. To prevent total loss of their oil, the Navy had had to drill four offset wells that it didn't want to drill. The Navy's unwanted oil was, of course, being sold through the ever-helpful Socal.

***

With the industry's reputation sinking lower every day, the oilmen and their allies increased their advertising campaign. Coincidental to the General Accounting Office report that the seven largest oil companies had spent nearly twice as much in the early 1970s on advertising as on research, Exxon launched an assault through the major newspapers and magazines by buying full-page ads headlined "Exxon plans to spend nearly $16 billion over the next 4 years to help get more energy for you." Texaco, smarting from charges that the oil companies were stashing away supplies to create artificial shortages, threw its net with full-page ads featuring a giant cartoon oilcan with the lid lifted and two men, leaning over the top, peering inside. The headline: "We're not holding back anything." But mostly the oil companies were sensitive about their profits. Shell Oil's full-page ads were headlined "How in all conscience can anyone call these excess profits?" While Mobil, with its customary twist, bought full pages in all major news outlets with the headline "Are oil profits big? Right. Big enough? Wrong." Its quoted authority for making that statement was the Chase Manhattan Bank, noted for its ties to the Rockefeller family and to the entire oil industry. As the New York *Times* pointed out in a business-section commentary, "Asking Chase's view of oil company profits is like asking Herbert Stein's opinion of President Nixon's budget message." (Stein was Nixon's chief adviser on budget matters.)

Although not even the industry's harshest critics suggested that the First Amendment did not cover its pronouncements, there were increasing questions about the legality of the advertisements for other reasons. It appeared that oil admen were trying to have it both ways: (1) On the one hand, they were claiming that their advertisements were not merely exercises in free speech but were business statements, the cost of which should be allowed as legitimate business expenses for tax-deduction purposes. (2) On the other hand, they contended that their "business" statements should not be subject to the Federal Trade Commission's regulations against false business advertising, because they were "idea" advertisements and not "product" advertisements.

As was true with many another important crusade during the 1970s, this one, challenging the oil ads, was launched by a small, poorly funded, public-interest firm. In this case, the gadfly was the Media Access Project, and its point man was attorney Harvey Shulman. He got Senator Hart's antitrust subcommittee interested in what Shulman called a "multimillion-dollar scandal involving the failure of the Internal Revenue Service and Federal Power Commission to enforce laws regarding the proper tax and accounting treatment of enormous sums of money spent for advertising." He was certainly not exaggerating about the money spent. Hart sent out inquiries; seven oil companies and a trade association—the biggest—admitted spending around $126 million on ads the previous year. (Shulman claimed they had actually spent twice that much.)

The IRS code was fairly easy to understand on this point. It forbade companies from deducting as business expenses any money spent for "lobbying purposes, for the promotion or defeat of legislation . . . or for the carrying on of propaganda [including advertising] relating to any of the foregoing purposes." Only Mobil conceded in its reply to Hart that most of its ads were not tax-deductible. The other companies played innocent. Exxon said its ads were just "goodwill" ads and therefore proper business expenses for tax purposes. Phillips, Shell, Atlantic Richfield, and Gulf offered the same argument. Texaco denied that any of its ads were political and said they were simply part of the company's "educational" effort to supply Congress with the kind of information it had been crying to get.

But a commonsense reading of the ads might easily have led one to conclude that they were indeed propaganda aimed at influencing legislators as well as the public. On January 18, for example, Texaco had placed an ad in the Washington *Post* warning congressmen that if they approved the "hasty and punitive" tax legislation that would be coming up for a vote within two weeks, they "would reduce the capital available to energy companies at the very time when their need for capital investment to supply consumer demand is at an all-time high." A Gulf advertisement proposed to anyone caring to read it, presumably including congressmen, that "Price controls over fuels should be eliminated . . . Tax incentives are needed in the form of credits for research . . . tax-free bonds for environmental protection facilities . . . Public lands should be made available for mining and drilling . . . We must permit offshore drilling . . . Strip mining must be permitted . . ." Et cetera. There were dozens of bills in Congress at that moment proposing the same things. An Exxon ad called for the deregulation of natural gas and for a modification of the Clean Air Act—both being heartily pushed (and fought) in Congress. A Phillips advertisement urged readers to let their congressmen know about auto emission standards—which Phillips left no doubt were evil standards.

If those weren't lobbying ads, if they were "business" ads, then why, asked Shulman, wasn't the FTC checking them for accuracy? It was quite obvious that some of the ads were of dubious accuracy. Some ads claimed that the oil industry was doing all it could to provide fuel for the United States. A solid court case could be built to prove exactly the opposite. Some ads claimed that the oil companies were doing their best to protect the environment. A stroll along the shore at many places on the Gulf would provide ankle-deep evidence to the contrary.

Utility companies were also under heavy fire from Shulman and Hart. And so was the FPC, for the Commission was supposed to make the utilities report political-ad costs as "nonoperating expenses." The utilities were spending around $89 million a year for ads (or at least that was what they spent in 1970, the last year for which figures were available), and *none* was being reported to the FPC as political advertising. Since they could count nonpolitical ads as part of their expenses and pass along the cost to customers, the utilities were, in effect, making their customers pay for being conned. The FPC was doing nothing about it. For example, American Electric Power Inc., a holding company for seven giant midwestern utilities, spent $2.7 million in 1974 on one ad alone, running it in most of the nation's major newspapers and magazines. At the top of the ad was a gimlet-eyed young man with the dress and air of those persons George Wallace used to call "pointy-headed intellectuals." The young man held a placard that read, GENERATE LESS ENERGY. In short, he was making an appeal for conservation. Underneath the young man, the American Electric Power Company gave its reply: "Sure. And generate galloping unemployment!" The ad went on to demand that legislators cut down the Clean Air Act "so that more of our coal may be burned." It also demanded the release of "vast reserves of U.S. Government-owned low-sulphur coal in the West"—which the major oil and mining companies were itching to get their hands on. If the legislators did not follow American Electric Power's advice, there would be "less production, fewer jobs, lower demand for products followed by still further diminished production and galloping unemployment until America is eventually reduced to the hard life." The theme of the ad: "Let's dig it."

If ever there was a bareknuckle lobbying effort on behalf of legislation to put money in industry's pocket, this ad would seem to have been it. Russell Peterson, chairman of the Council on Environmental Quality, protested to officials at American Electric Power that "the implied message of your ad is that persons who support energy conservation are pushing America into recession. This, if I may say so, can truly be labeled nonsense." But apparently Peterson was the only member of the Nixon administration who was offended by such lobbying at the taxpayers' expense, and after a sharp exchange of opinions between him and Donald Cook, chairman of American Electric Power's board, even that dispute simmered down. Neither the IRS nor the FPC ever treated the ads for what they were. Nor, of course, did the pitifully outmanned FTC, which, however, did have some employees who spilled over with noble intentions and pious outrage. "Our concern," said an FTC lawyer who conceded he had no power to do much about it, "is that the oil industry and its allies are able to spend tens of millions of dollars to promote their point of view, when it may be misleading. Without some opportunity for another viewpoint to be heard, the industry can create a crisis or turn it off, all over the world. I'm not saying that this is true with respect to the energy crisis, but it appears that at least some of the oil-industry claims warrant serious inquiry." By whom? Obviously not by the FTC.

* * *

OPEC's money machine was beginning to scare hell out of the banks. The 400 percent increase in oil prices between 1973 and 1974 sent an avalanche of money into the backward oil-producing nations so fast that they couldn't possibly absorb it, couldn't possibly spend it all. Except for Iran, the producing countries had no industrial base on which to lavish their new riches. Most of them had only the vaguest ambitions for industrial expansion. So most of their new income was surplus: income jumped from $29 billion in 1973 to $100 billion in 1974, surplus from $3 billion in 1973 to $60 billion in 1974—the rest being spent for goods and services. The only thing they could easily do with their surplus was to put it in the bank, or buy stocks and bonds, or buy property in the major industrial nations.

At first the bankers welcomed the new deposits. They expressed confidence that OPEC's surplus could be "recycled," one of those corporate terms that mischievously reduces the complex to the simple. By recycling, they meant: the big industrial nations would buy OPEC oil; then OPEC governments would deposit much of their surplus in the

Western-based international banks; the banks would lend most of the deposits to major industries or to "third world" nations and chaotically developing major nations, such as Italy, that were starving for energy; these borrowers would presumably use their loans to buy oil from OPEC, which would, again, deposit its surplus in the international banks, et cetera, et cetera—the money going around in this golden circle forever, with banks, oil companies, and OPEC profiting endlessly.

But as the OPEC surplus being processed reached staggering proportions, the banks got jittery. They realized they were riding a tiger. Most of the OPEC deposits were short-term. They could be withdrawn on short notice, ranging from twenty-four hours to thirty days. When many billions of dollars are at stake, it makes banks very nervous indeed to lend money out for several months or years when they know it can be called for at any time. That was the flaw in the recycling machine: by lending short-term deposits to long-term borrowers, especially to borrowers of dubious creditworthiness, the banks were vulnerable to a terrible squeeze if their OPEC depositors decided to make a sudden, massive withdrawal of funds.

By the autumn of 1974, the banks had begun to recognize a second serious threat: What if a major borrower from several of the world's largest banks ran up such a tremendous debt in trying to meet its energy needs that it decided it couldn't pay? And what if it, in effect, declared bankruptcy—refused to pay its foreign debts? (In December, the possibility of Italy's bankruptcy as a result of oil debts was openly acknowledged by U.S. officials.) Could such an act topple even giants like Chase Manhattan and Citibank? Quite possibly. And if they fell, the nation's—even the world's—banking structure would be badly damaged.

In short, along with enormous profits, the banks were facing enormous risks. The risks would become greater as the price of oil soared and the debts of industries and poorer nations mounted. In July 1974, a confidential study by the World Bank estimated that Arab oil-producing countries might have more than $1,000 billion—a cool trillion—invested in the United States and other countries by 1985, an amount that was ten times the total book value of U.S. investments overseas and a hundred times the value of all the gold held by the U.S. Government at the time. Much of this would be invested in real estate and government bonds and industrial stocks, but some of it would be deposited in banks. Could the banks risk such large deposits from such volatile depositors? Arthur Burns, chairman of the Federal Reserve Board, warned that the financial problems would become unmanageable if OPEC profits continued at their present level.

As they usually did in crises, the bankers wanted their governments to take the risk while they took the profits. In September, David Rockefeller, chairman of Chase, said he thought the responsibility for recycling petrodollars had to be shifted from commercial banks to government agencies. And Rimmer de Vries, a vice-president of the Morgan Guaranty Trust Company, warned in a speech in Beirut, "It should be made very clear that the international commercial banking system cannot be counted on to continue to increase its international intermediary role at the pace experienced so far this year . . . No private financial institution is willing and able to assume unlimited credit risks . . . [T]he less creditworthy borrowers will have growing difficulty in obtaining funds to finance their deficits. At some point, and for some countries, commercial credit may become virtually unavailable." In other words, the banks were angling for loan guarantees from the U.S. Treasury or from the World Bank, and if they didn't get them, they would close their purses to darkest Africa and murky Asia.

Throughout the year, finance ministers of the major countries were in a semicoma. In January, twenty of their cadre had met in Rome to talk about "reforming" the world's monetary system, but their discussion went nowhere, because, as they all knew, Arab and Iranian wealth made it impossible to write new rules for stabilizing currency values. With the Arabs destined to amass $50 billion . . . $70 billion . . . $100 billion— who knew what the future held?—every year, and with the world's monetary systems vulnerable to even a switch of $1 billion from one country to another, clearly they could swamp any system of fixed exchange rates.

Part of the OPEC surplus—the part that was making its most dramatic impact on the public's psyche—was going into the purchase of corporations and real estate, huge chunks of real estate. In July, Iran plunked down $100 million to purchase one fourth of the Krupp industrial empire, famed as the supplier of munitions for Germany's military adventures for more than a century. (Now Krupp was mainly involved in steel production.) In September, the sheikhdom of Kuwait, already heavily investing in U.S. stocks, spent $17.4 million to buy Kiawah, a South Carolina coastal island of 3,500 acres only twenty miles from the home of that great America Firster the late Congressman L. Mendel Rivers. For Kuwait, with its $10-billion annual income, the island was a mere trinket. By October, the largest office building in London was in Arab hands, and Arab agents were on the prowl in America, reportedly feeling out the possible purchase of two of the ten leading banks. In Atlanta, Kuwaitis were also underwriting a $100-million hotel/office complex.

U.S. reaction was not altogether friendly. For anyone who had recently filled up his tank, Arabs were understandably seen as the greedy enemy. Corporate executives were also restless, suspecting that the Arabs would not mind a sneak attack on management through Wall Street. OPEC's leaders tried to offset these fears with protestations of hardly believable innocence. A Commerce Department official returning from the Mideast said Arab leaders had ridiculed the idea that they were plotting to take over the biggest U.S. companies. He quoted one as saying, "Why should we take over GM? What would we do with it?" Saudi Arabia—with fewer than five thousand college graduates—could not, he implied, supply the managerial talent to run such a corporation. For anyone aware of the ease with which managers can be purchased, it was not a comforting argument.

The Arab real estate entrepreneurs were also trying to attract as little notice as possible. The broker handling the Kuwaiti Atlanta Hilton deal said, "The Arabs don't want to be discerned at the primary level. They are not investing alone, but are forming partnerships with Americans." This was true as far as it went (many Arab-American partnerships were being formed), but the Arabs were also buying many properties across the country—shopping centers, industrial buildings, downtown office buildings, apartments—using big U.S. banks as their purchasing agents. Secrecy and discretion were the rule.

But secrecy could not always be achieved. In November, it was revealed that, the previous spring, Arab investors had tried to buy controlling interest in Lockheed Aircraft Corp., America's largest defense contractor. Lockheed rejected the offer. Federal Reserve Board Chairman Burns said he thought the Arabs should limit their investments to outfits like Quaker Oats.

***

The Federal Power Commission spread flowers along the pathway of the natural gas industry all year. In February, it approved a price of 55 cents per thousand cubic feet for some Alabama gas. Never in its history had the FPC approved such a high price. Ironically, the split decision (3 to 2) found Chairman John Nassikas and Commissioner William Springer—both ordinarily on the side of higher prices—issuing a smoking dissent. Sounding like Populists, they charged the majority with capitulating to "the prescription of an industry-established price . . . rather than a just and reasonable rate by regulatory review." They called the decision "a travesty of regulatory justice." Just as ironically, one of the commissioners to vote for the Alabama rate increase was Don S. Smith, who had recently joined the Commission after a careful screening by consumer groups. How in the world had the majority arrived at 55 cents? The FPC staff had recommended 35 cents. Nassikas and Springer had recommended 41 cents. The administrative law judge who presided in the case had recommended 50 cents. But, for some reason, shortly after receiving a telegram from the producers (seven companies, including Exxon) requesting speedy action, the majority went to 55 cents. Although the rate decision applied to only one case, it signaled higher prices on a broad scale in the near future.

In June, the commission set its first national rate—the first national rate

ever; gone was the concept of setting prices according to various production costs in seven geographical areas—at 42 cents per thousand cubic
feet for new gas. Before that, the rates for flowing gas had ranged from
19.9 cents to 32.4 cents. Every penny increase meant another $225 mil-
lion from consumers' pockets every year. The FPC excused its action on
the basis of a "national emergency." The new rate brought the national
average—for old and new gas—to 28.39 cents per thousand cubic feet. A
year earlier, the price had been 23.81 cents. But the FPC wasn't through.
Six months later, it tacked on another 8 cents to the ceiling price for new
gas (and made it retroactive to January 1)—bringing the new ceiling to
50 cents.

Between the two escalations, consumers had won a symbolic victory,
which was the only kind they ever won. On October 7, the U.S. Court of
Appeals for the District of Columbia struck down the FPC's precedent-
setting 73 percent increase of May 30, 1973, in the notorious *Belco* case.
(That rate increase had pushed the price from 26 cents to 45 cents and
given Belco Petroleum, Texaco, and Tenneco a stunning 27.5 percent return on total investment.) But, because of the national rate increases that
were permitted by the FPC during 1974, the court's action had virtually
no influence.

On September 15, the General Accounting Office finished a 10-month
investigation of the FPC and issued a 115-page report that in any other
year might have shocked the public. But 1974 saw the culmination of the
Watergate scandal, and coming in the midst of all that, the GAO's report
got little attention. In effect, the GAO charged that the FPC had indulged in conflicts of interest while granting multimillion-dollar price increases with sometimes "improper" (a beautiful understatement) procedures.

The background was this:

The FPC's standards-of-conduct regulations, issued in 1966, forbade
employees to own stock in any company subject to FPC jurisdiction. In
addition to that flat prohibition, all employees at the Executive Schedule
level (presidential appointment) or in Grade GS-13 or above who were
the heads or assistant heads of bureaus and offices, section chiefs, etc.,
were supposed to reveal all their stockholdings within thirty days after
they started to work at the FPC, and they were supposed to make an updated report on June 30 of each year.

GAO investigators found that these regulations were widely violated,
that "for at least 3 years before our investigation, there had been a total
breakdown in the financial reporting and review procedures . . . We determined that in 1972, 111 of the 125 officials were required to file and
only 12 did and in 1971, 101 were required to file and only 10 did . . . As
of December 1973, 125 upper level officials were required to file annual
financial disclosure forms. Only seven had filed properly. Another 24

officials filed late but before our examination in November 1973. The remaining 94 had not filed when our review began . . . The disclosure forms filed in past years were not reviewed but merely placed in the officials' personnel records."

Among these key officials, the GAO had found nineteen who owned prohibited stock, including shares in Exxon, Union Oil, Standard Oil of Indiana, Texaco, Cities Service, Occidental Petroleum, Tenneco Oil, and Atlantic Richfield. The nineteen included seven administrative law judges, three officials in the Bureau of Power and two in the Office of Economics, and an engineer in charge of an FPC regional office.

Some of these officials had made no effort to hide their stockholdings. In the permissive atmosphere that prevailed at the FPC, the ownership was simply accepted as of no consequence. Five administrative law judges—the fellows who presided over quasi-judicial proceedings that helped determine company profits—did file forms that revealed prohibited stockholdings. But the FPC's Office of Personnel Programs did not order them to divest themselves of the holdings until the GAO's investigators began poking around.

Aside from the conflicts of interest, the GAO investigators were troubled by the FPC's "improper" use of claimed gas shortages to justify emergency natural gas sales at prices that probably were not "just and reasonable." They pointed out that the FPC had authorized ninety-six producers to sell gas at "emergency" prices—some as high as 75 cents per thousand cubic feet in areas where the normal ceiling was 26 cents—for periods of time that extended far beyond any possible "emergency."

Congressman John Moss, the permanent foe of Nassikas' FPC, tried in vain to stir up some passionate reaction. He demanded that the Justice Department look into the possibility of criminal prosecutions for conflicts of interest. Nothing came of that demand. The Washington *Post,* long an advocate of deregulating natural gas prices, used the occasion to suggest that since the FPC was doing such a lousy job it might as well be disbanded so that prices could rise and more gas would be discovered. Senator Philip Hart responded, in an op-ed-page piece, that there was nothing in the recent conduct of the industry to suggest that more natural gas would appear on the market for anything less than extortionate prices. "From 1972 to 1973," he wrote, "following industry promises for more production, the FPC allowed area-ceiling prices to double and emergency sale prices to triple—and new reserves in 1973 were one-third less than 1972. More recently, as the GAO reported, the FPC allowed emergency sales at prices in excess of 50 cents to increase flowing gas. Producers delivered only 14 percent of the gas they promised would be available at the higher price."

Why should they be expected to bring the gas onto market when all top officials in the Nixon/Ford administration had been saying that, at the first opportunity, they would let prices go as high as $1.80 per thousand cubic feet—nine times higher than the price when Nixon was first elected? Hart pointed out that the industry must be sitting on oodles of gas, just awaiting that happy day, for earlier in 1974 the Department of Interior had admitted that "of 103,502 oil and gas leases it has let, 94,224 are nonproducing. That's 91 percent."

Hart could also have pointed out that, only a few weeks earlier, some members of the FPC investigative staff had reported that thirteen pipelines held about 10 trillion cubic feet of offshore gas from the market in "shut-in" wells in 1972 and 1973—which was about half the amount the United States was consuming in a year. The pipelines had contracted for the gas but refused to connect the wells to their lines. The staff urged "an immediate, in-depth investigation into the reasons for the reserves being shut in . . ." The commissioners, always the gentlemen, thereupon wrote the pipelines for an explanation and patiently waited. They would still be waiting in 1975.

One reason the companies could get by with such high-handedness was that their power was so concentrated. When Hart called the degree of concentration "spectacular," he was not being excessive. "As of June 30, 1972, four oil companies controlled 92.3 percent of the uncommitted gas reserves onshore in southern Louisiana, 100 percent of the federal and state offshore uncommitted reserves in the Texas Gulf and 80 percent in the Permian Basin," our richest sources of natural gas. Where natural gas was concerned, four companies were a kingdom unto themselves.

1975

"There is a tendency around Washington to talk about oil companies as if they were something other than thinking, breathing, flesh and blood people."

FRANK IKARD, *president, American Petroleum Institute*

"The multinational corporations have done an extremely poor job of convincing the countries and the peoples of the world of their values."

CLIFTON C. GARVIN, JR., *chairman, Exxon Corporation*

From the beginning of his administration, in August 1974, it had been clear that President Ford intended to surrender to the energy corporations at the earliest convenient moment. But, with the aftermath of the Watergate scandal already making things more difficult for Republican candidates, it was obviously not a good idea to tell consumers they were going to be stuck with higher fuel bills, until after the November election.

With the new year, however, Ford wasted no time announcing his energy plans. In his 1975 State of the Union message, he said he intended to decontrol domestic oil prices on April 1, push for decontrol of natural gas prices, turn over federal lands to oil explorers in such quantities and with such rapidity that even the companies admitted they couldn't handle the turnover, roll back environmental regulations on the burning of coal, and go nuclear as fast as possible for the production of electricity.

Of all these actions, the decontrol of oil prices could be done the most expeditiously, and its impact would be the most severe. Ford had the power to remove oil price ceilings by presidential fiat unless blocked by either house of Congress. There was irony in his proposal. Earlier in January, Secretary of State Henry Kissinger had said the United States might have to go to war with some of the Arab countries if their pricing resulted in "strangulation of the industrialized world," and now here was Ford a few days later proposing gentle economic strangulation of the U.S. economy via domestic price increases. Decontrol of oil would of course have a ripple effect on the prices of coal and utilities and the price of everything that oil went into making. A Library of Congress study estimated that Ford's energy program would cost U.S. consumers more than $50 billion extra in 1975 alone if it was carried out on schedule; $11 billion of the cost would come directly from oil price decontrol during the first year.[1]

At first there seemed no reason to think decontrol would be delayed, and less reason to think that it would be blocked. Aside from a few partisan outbursts of dismay, Ford's oil price decontrol plan aroused surprisingly little resistance in Congress. At first.

To some extent at least, this was because the majority party in both houses was led by Democrats who were inclined to see things from the oil companies' perspective. In the Senate, the Democratic leader was Senator Mike Mansfield of Montana, the tenth-ranking oil-producing state, and the Democratic whip was Senator Robert Byrd[2] of West Virginia, the seventh-ranking natural-gas-producing state; of course, both Montana and West Virginia were major coal-producing states. In the House, Congressman Carl Albert presided as speaker and watched over the interests of Oklahoma oilmen. Albert had once boasted in a speech to the American Petroleum Institute that "nearly one half of the gas and one third of the oil produced in Oklahoma are produced in my congressional district." The energy states were doing quite well on the money committees. The House Appropriations Committee was run by Representative George H. Mahon of Texas; the Senate Finance Committee was headed by Russell Long of Louisiana. Until his headlined adventures with a stripteaser forced him into retirement, Wilbur Mills of Arkansas (ninth-ranking natural-gas-producing state) had run the House Ways and Means Committee. Over the years, Mills had carefully screened all members before they were appointed to Ways and Means to make sure they believed in tax laws favorable to oil and gas, and though he had been deposed, his influence lived on.

---

1. So what? asked the Washington *Post* in a proindustry editorial. What's a measly 11 billion a year? That—it argued—was no more than food prices had shot up, and "food prices ought to be a matter of as much social concern as oil prices. Decontrolling oil does not mean a great and unprecedented surge of inflation but rather more of the steady creep of basic prices that the country has been suffering for many months. The proper response is income support for the poor and the elderly, not sporadic attempts to hold down artificially the prices of a few selected items while ignoring others. Unfortunately, a majority of the House of Representatives has come to regard oil price controls as a moral imperative and a holy cause."

2. Richard Harris wrote in the August 7, 1971, issue of *The New Yorker* that although the traditional path of oil money to the finance committees of favored incumbents was through the office of Senator Russell Long of Louisiana, in the fall of 1970 a large amount of oil money was diverted instead to Byrd, so that he could make friends by dispensing it. Byrd wanted to unseat Teddy Kennedy in the race for Democratic whip. Harris wrote that Byrd "called in his IOUs from those he had helped" and that after the whip election—which Byrd won in the Democratic caucus by a vote of 31 to 24—Byrd's former administrative assistant, who was now working for the American Petroleum Institute, "telephoned at least two senators who were thought to have been for Kennedy . . . to thank them for voting for Byrd. Both men ran for reelection last fall, both were in deep trouble, and both won."

Besides these established allies, the oil industry and President Ford could depend on a mood of subtle panic in Congress. Members felt under intense pressure to come up with an energy program—even a lousy one. In the first weeks of 1975, the debate was seldom directed at the question of whether oil prices *should* be decontrolled but merely on what timetable. In 1974, nobody had sounded more militantly intent on controlling oil prices than Senator Henry Jackson; he had pushed hard for his rollback bill, but he had lost that fight, and now he seemed inclined to let others take the bruises for a while. If Jackson, the Senate's usual spokesman in energy affairs, was starting to be fatalistic about higher prices, where would the anti-Ford leadership come from?

*

It would come from a most unlikely source: the freshmen of the House, of whom there were seventy-five. To be more precise, it would come from five freshmen: Toby Moffett of Connecticut, Andrew Maguire of New Jersey, Jerome Ambro of New York, Herbert Harris of Virginia, and George Miller of California.

When the much-heralded post-Watergate class of "reform" congressmen blew into town, in January 1975, nobody (despite the ballyhoo that attended their arrival) had really good reasons for thinking they would be more effective than any other freshman class. During the first couple of months, except for dumping three House chairmen and instituting some procedural changes, they showed little inclination—or ability—to take on the old order. They seemed unable to get their strength organized around issues.

But, by March, that was beginning to change—at least for the five. By that time they were convinced that energy would be the big battleground of the decade, and they wanted to be part of the fight. In March, Congress, with the heavy support of the freshmen, had eliminated percentage depletion allowances for everything but the first two thousand barrels a day, phasing down gradually to the first one thousand barrels by 1980, with the percentage allowance moving down gradually to 15 percent by 1984. Liberals considered it a great victory, but there was some reason to question just how great it really was. Generally the majors were content to see the depletion allowance go, for, as mentioned in earlier chapters, it had become a public relations burden; besides, they were making so much from other tax loopholes they didn't need it.[3]

---

3. The reform cut out the majors entirely, but many middle-size and larger independent producers—on whom the nation depended for most exploration into new fields—were deprived of what was perhaps a justified incentive for risk. Momentarily it was feared that the reformers might have cut too deeply. Almost overnight, drilling rigs, which had been in critical shortage, began to stack up. There were 1,673 rotary

Whatever the merits of the depletion-allowance victory—a victory that was a slap in the face of the House leadership, which had opposed the reform—it gave the freshmen a taste for blood and rebellion. None developed a greater taste for it than the Five Freshmen, with their two natural leaders, Moffett and Maguire, who would remain key energy strategists in the House for the next five years.

Moffett was twenty-nine when he came down to Congress. Originally the family name was Mafouz—or at least that's how he tentatively recalls it; Lebanese; changed to Moffett on Ellis Island. He was born in Holyoke, Massachusetts. His father, once a truck driver for a brewery, had become caretaker for the brewery owner's huge estate on the banks of the Connecticut River. For the first fourteen years of his life, Toby lived like a rich kid. The brewery owner's wife treated him as her own boy. He'd go over and play in the big house with the glass-enclosed porch and the fountain and goldfish and parrot and the butler and cook—they were all "his." And when there were dinner parties for the governor and senators; he got to go over and watch and eat rich food. It was great. But then the brewery owner sold his estate, and Moffett's dad was back on the street, selling beer, and things weren't too easy after that. With good grades and considerable skill as a soccer player, Moffett got through Syracuse University on a full scholarship. After what he calls "a bad experience," he quit the Boston College Law School, where Father Drinan was then dean (Drinan later became a member of Moffett's energy subcommittee). He taught school in Roxbury's inner city, then became a sort of "youth expert" for the U.S. Commissioner of Education in both the Johnson and the Nixon administrations. But when the Cambodia invasion and Kent State assassinations took place, he called a press conference and resigned. Not long thereafter, Ralph Nader induced him to go to Connecticut to start a statewide consumer organization. Moffett hustled enough money to put himself on payroll at sixty-five hundred dollars a year and to hire four attorneys at five thousand dollars per. They organized people to protest their property-tax assessments; they did prescription drug surveys and got sued by the pharmacists; they picketed auto dealers who were cheating consumers. They also intervened in utility rate cases—an experience that got Moffett permanently hooked on the energy problem. As an experience in organizing, the consumer operation was invaluable for the fight Moffett was to take on in 1975.

---

drilling rigs at work when Congress voted the action against depletion; by May, the average dropped to a low of 1,571, and pessimism swept the fields. But then the industry bounced back; by December it was using 1,800 drilling rigs (the highest number in 14 years) and wound up drilling more wells in 1975 than in any year since 1966.

Andrew Maguire, thirty-five when he arrived in Congress, was an aggressive, exuberant egghead. With a B.A. in religion from Oberlin, a Ph.D. in government from Harvard, a book on Tanzanian politics (published by Cambridge University Press), a stint as adviser to Arthur Goldberg at the United Nations, three years under John Lindsay, directing a development project in New York City, and some fallow moments consulting for the Ford Foundation, Maguire seemed hardly the best bet to defeat three veteran Democratic politicians in the 1974 New Jersey primary (he won 50 percent of the votes in a four-way race and beat his nearest rival 2 to 1) and then go on to squeeze past incumbent Congressman William Widnall, who would have been the senior Republican in the House if he had won. Traditionally, it was a Republican district. Maguire spent about $150,000 for the primary and general elections of '74, which he admits was "a lot more than anybody had ever spent in that district before," but none of it went to television. It went into an elaborate canvassing campaign. He had three people going up each side of the street ringing bells. Maguire, trotting along behind, would climb the stairs at only those homes where people had told his emissaries they wanted to meet him. He says he went up to twenty thousand doors. In short, Maguire also came to Congress from rigorous training in organizing and one-on-one persuasion.

So closely did Moffett and Maguire operate together that Representative Harley Staggers of West Virginia, chairman of the House Commerce Committee, had trouble at first telling them apart—though in fact they look nothing alike, Moffett being handsome, swarthy, moody-looking, sort of a truncated Victor Mature type, while Maguire is tall, lanky, perpetually in motion, and gives off a conspiratorial static that was probably rather commonplace during the Easter Rebellion.

The Five Freshmen felt compelled to write their own energy program —against all odds—when they saw House initiative falling into the hands of oil legislators. Their suspicions were particularly aroused when a joint Senate-House task force on energy was set up to develop a plan for handling the crisis and Speaker Albert appointed Representative Jim Wright of Texas to be chairman of the House's part of the task force. Wright is a typically pushy, business-oriented West Texan, which is to say that he certainly has no grudge against the oil industry.[4]

---

4. In 1980 it was discovered that Wright had used his political influence in 1979 to help two oil groups, the Texas Oil and Gas Corp. and Neptune Oil, with whom he was associated in gas-drilling ventures, according to the Dallas *Times-Herald*. In a follow-up story, Spencer Rich, of the Washington *Post*, reported that Wright "scoffed at implications" that he had been invited "to invest in the two wells [both successful] as a payoff for political favors" done for the two groups. On behalf of Neptune, he had even gone so far as to intercede personally with President Anwar Sadat of

"When the Wright panel's energy proposals came out," Maguire recalls, "they struck some of us new members as being very little different from the Ford proposals. Shortly after that, Moffett and myself and Ambro and Harris and Miller produced our own energy program. We had invited ourselves to sit in on the Wright task-force meetings. We could see what was happening. It was tweedledum and tweedledee. Nobody was representing the consumer's side of the argument. We thought that was something terribly important to do, and so we produced our own program. This was about two months after we got to town, and in those days freshmen weren't taken very seriously. We had our own press conference. A lot of people turned out, but I think they said, 'Oh, well, these guys just want to get their face on the tube. There won't be much follow-through, because there rarely is.'

"Well, we were tenacious. We organized. One of the things that was characteristic of the group was that we spent an enormous number of hours on tactics and strategy and organization. This wasn't one of those operations where we just sent out press releases and attached hopeless amendments to bills we knew would never pass. *We organized.*"

*

Crucial to their effort was the enlistment of some senior members of high peer rating. By far the most important graybeard in their operation was the gentleman from Houston's Eighth District, Robert Christian Eckhardt, then sixty-one, who was known around Washington as something of a fey character. He idled away dull hearings by drawing cartoons. He injected Shakespearean quotes into his questioning of witnesses. He wore white suits and string ties and red vests and wide-brimmed panama hats and, thus attired, rode a bicycle back and forth to work at the Capitol. He was scion to an old Texas family (a Texas county was named after one of his grandfathers) but not to an old family fortune, because his Uncle Bob had blown that on oil speculations. Eckhardt was considered one of the smartest men in Congress, but at the same time he was never taken too seriously, was considered something of a political lightweight, which was probably a mistaken impression. He must have had some toughness, or craftiness, to have survived as a liberal in a state whose basic ideology was as conservative as Scripture. One reason Eckhardt managed to survive was that he had the ability to

---

Egypt. In 1967, Fred Graham, of the New York *Times,* had reported that Congressman Wright inserted a one-word amendment to the Clean Water Restoration Act that had made it virtually impossible for the Interior Department to police oil spills. His services to the oil industry, if great, were no greater than those of other oil-state politicians, and according to campaign records his rewards were no greater; but it didn't make him exactly attractive to nonoil-state legislators when the press reported that he got gifts from such sources as John Connally's law firm. For reporting these things, the press was denounced by Wright as "enemies of government."

make such philosophically complicated speeches that his audiences, if they managed to stay awake, probably could not tell for certain where he stood. Theory was his forte; he reveled in it; typically, in World War II, though he could not fly and was petrified at the thought of flying, he taught the "theory of flight" to Air Force cadets.

From juggling theories it was but a short step to juggling ideologies. Eckhardt was very tricky in that regard. He was a great civil libertarian on occasion, but he also voted for foreign aid to the Nicaraguan tyrant Somoza. If he was sometimes courageous in advocating liberal positions (such as the seating of Representative Adam Clayton Powell of New York) that most Texans found offensive, he also was pretty crafty at compromising—sometimes almost to the point of being a turncoat.

His talent for swapping off with some fellows of questionable character was first evidenced in 1948; already a leader of the labor-liberal wing of the Democratic party in Texas, Eckhardt joined with John Connally (whom he despised) and other conservative Democrats to prevent an investigation of the crooked ballots that that year elected Lyndon Johnson to his first term in the U.S. Senate. Eckhardt's excuse for doing this was that he had swung a deal with the Johnson gang to help the liberals fight off a Dixiecrat challenge at the state Democratic convention. Eckhardt always had a good excuse at hand. He was quick with "explanations" that sometimes strained credulity. One day, in conversation with a magazine reporter, Eckhardt said he thought Senator Russell Long was "the most dangerous son-of-a-bitch in the country." A couple of weeks later, when the reporter returned to Eckhardt and reminded him of what he had said and asked if he could be quoted on that, Eckhardt blandly insisted that he couldn't remember having made such a statement but that if he had done so, he'd simply meant that "Long is the most effective representative of the oil industry in Congress"—an evaluation that Long would have dearly prized.

In the energy complexities that followed 1975, Eckhardt would do things that appalled his claque of liberal supporters. In 1976, when liberals were making a valiant effort to break up the majors' vertical stranglehold over every part of the industry—from producing to retailing—Eckhardt fought the effort, with the explanation (best illustrated in a fawning speech he made to the International Association of Geophysical Contractors in Houston on May 21, 1976): "I am rather shocked that people in the oil industry are themselves rather shocked that I should adopt the conservative position of opposing divestiture. All of my decisions on oil and gas have stemmed from basically the same root and that root is grounded in somewhat conservative soil. The basic root assumption is that we should not violently wrench the economy . . ."

From that lofty position, he could, of course, jump either way. It was difficult to tell just how much influence the prevailing winds had on the

direction he jumped. In 1977, he was one of the chief sponsors of natural
gas lobbyist Lynn Coleman to become the Energy Department's chief
counsel; Coleman was a member of the Houston law firm of Vinson,
Elkins, Searls—John Connally's law firm—whose corporate gunwales were
awash with oil money. Coleman became Energy's counsel, and he
showed a unique lack of enthusiasm for prosecuting oil firms that
cheated and gouged the public, but Eckhardt (who, when he lost his
seat in Congress, would himself become lobbyist for a natural gas company) never once publicly criticized his chum for lack of vigor. Later, in
the battle over the deregulation of natural gas prices, Eckhardt deserted
his old liberal comrades of the '75 oil decontrol fight. And he was constantly running legislative errands for utility companies. In short, he was
a liberal who was much too slippery to be counted as an automatic supporter of liberal causes.

But this was, in fact, one of the strengths he brought to the freshmen's
side. He supplied them with the best that Congress would accept: jaded
idealism. The freshmen wanted to push a bill that would have extended
controls forever. He persuaded them that forever is a word that makes
Congress come down with palsy. To get the necessary support of moderates, some cutoff date had to be offered. The freshmen also wanted to
roll back domestic prices to 1973 levels. Eckhardt argued convincingly
that the times were against that much of a rollback. He escorted them
through the House's underworld of cynicism, caution, greed, and com-
placency, and showed them what they were confronted with. He
shocked them back to reality. But, at the same time, he freely offered the
oil expertise and the ties with the older members of the House that the
freshmen sorely needed and did not have. Maguire says, "The writing of
the 1975 legislation we pushed must be credited to Eckhardt. He put it
into legislative form, being the lawyer and the legislator that he was. He
was also the expert as to what the hell this kind of an oil field was versus
that kind, the declining ratios of production out of this kind of terrain
versus that kind. He knew all that stuff, which Moffett and I didn't know
then. He wrote our legislation. Eckhardt's problem was that he couldn't
translate the complexities of the bill easily enough so that other members
could comprehend it. Eckhardt would take a member aside and start
explaining the legislation and you'd see the guy's eyes glaze over and
then you'd try to talk to the guy later and give it to him in a way he
could understand."

Nor did Eckhardt have the slightest sense of organization. Despite his
amiable acceptance across a wide spectrum of ideology, he knew nothing
about building coalitions. Moffett and Maguire and their staffs did that,
working with public-interest groups, consumer groups, and labor and
business groups (whose jobs and profits depended on keeping energy
prices down). They helped organize what one lobbyist called "the most

unlikely, lusty alliance ever put together on Capitol Hill": Nader lobbyists, airline lobbyists, AFL-CIO lobbyists, truck lobbyists, teacher lobbyists, et cetera. Of course, the liaison might have come together even had Moffett and Maguire never reached Congress. As Roberta Hornig, of the Washington *Star,* reported at the time, the strange network of dissimilar lobbyists "was often formed in a most informal manner. Most of the time, one reports, it began with a 'how do your people feel about oil prices' along with a 'good morning' greeting as lobbyists passed each other in the halls. As each of them realized the strength of feeling, and the amount of it, they began coming together."

*

The Five Freshmen and Eckhardt had to decide two things before writing their price-control extension amendment: how long should prices continue to be controlled, and at what level?

They answered the first question arbitrarily: mandatory pricing for forty months after the law went into effect, after which the President could at his own discretion continue, or not, price controls until September 30, 1981. On that date, controls would evaporate. As one of Maguire's top staff members later explained the decision: "At the time, the whole thinking was, 'God, let's get ourselves to a Democratic administration.' We extended the cutoff far enough ahead to do that, at least. By virtue of putting in a light at the end of the tunnel, we could presumably round up some marginal votes—you know, people who weren't sure they wanted to favor controls forever—and at the same time get ourselves to a Democratic administration, which is to say an administration—or so we incorrectly presumed—that would favor some real, nonprice conservation. You have to remember the likely Democratic candidates at that point. Jackson was one of the leading candidates. Birch Bayh and Mo Udall were a couple of the others. They were all looked upon as Democrats who would be tough on the oil companies and put forward tough Democratic programs. Nobody at that time had even heard of Jimmy Carter."

As for the way they decided on the price-control levels to be proposed, Maguire recounts: "We started looking at the numbers. We started looking at what the oil industry had been saying prior to the embargo." They found that oilmen had been promising in 1973, before the embargo hit, that if they could just get something between $4 and $7 for a barrel of oil by 1985—*1985*—phased in gradually, they would be able to find and produce enough oil to put the nation on energy Easy Street.

"So then," says Maguire, "the question was, in 1975, What has changed? What has changed so dramatically that you are now telling us you have to have $11 to $12 a barrel in order to bring out of the ground that same oil you were talking about before? The answers they came up with weren't very good."

There had indeed been many public guarantees by oilmen that they could perform adequately for only a few more dollars.

Three years earlier (July 1972), *Business Week* quoted John G. McLean, chairman of Continental Oil Company, to the effect that if domestic crude prices should rise to $4 a barrel (from the then average of $3.40 per barrel), deeper drilling in older oil fields—tertiary recovery— would be economical, even though tertiary recovery is much more expensive than ordinary recovery of oil.[5]

In December 1972, the National Petroleum Council had estimated that if oil prices rose to $3.65 a barrel—that's right, $3.65—by 1975 and to $6.69 by 1985, this would give the incentive needed for "the highest drilling and finding rates." At the same time, the Independent Petroleum Association of America (IPAA) had stated that a price of $4.10 a barrel for crude would be adequate to assure the United States 100 percent self-sufficiency by 1980.

In 1973, witnesses from the American Petroleum Institute, testifying on behalf of the Nixon-Ford Project Independence, argued that if domestic producers could get $6.69 a barrel through 1983, our oilmen could supply us with all the energy we needed. In 1974, experts from the Federal Energy Administration trooped up to Capitol Hill to give the same prediction: $6 to $7 per barrel for new oil would do the trick very nicely, with $7.50 as the long-term price objective for domestic oil.

When Nixon, in March 1974, vetoed the Emergency Energy Act, primarily because it held oil prices to the $5.25–$7 vicinity, even *The Wall Street Journal,* a true believer in the mythical "free market," was prompted to editorialize: "Seven dollars [the Act's temporary ceiling price for new oil] is a price beyond the wildest dreams of oil men at any time up until last fall. At that price, incidentally, exploration and production go forward at the industry's full capacity. Beyond that figure, higher prices do not increase production incentives enough to justify the cost to the consumer."

In 1975, a staff study by the Federal Power Commission found that it cost $2.96 a barrel to produce old oil and $5.49 a barrel to produce new oil. That included such items as return on working capital, return on in-

---

5. When discovered, virtually all oil is under pressure, often from natural gas, which drives it through the strata and up the pipe. But as oil and gas are removed, the pressure decreases. When the pressure drops too low, artificial pressures must be introduced to drive the rest of the oil out. The first of the man-made efforts are called "secondary," the next are called "tertiary," but secondary and tertiary employ many of the same techniques, which include low-tension waterflooding (with detergent used in the waterflood to scrub oil out of the reservoir rock) and fireflooding, a technique whereby a slow-burning underground fire thins the oil and supplies the energy to push it to the producing well. Waterflooding, being much less expensive than fireflooding, is most commonly used in secondary and tertiary recovery.

vestment, royalty payments, income tax, cost of exploration, dry-hole drilling costs, et cetera, the whole works.

The IPAA's own figures showed that while the wholesale price of crude oil had gone up 68 percent between 1973 and 1974, the cost of doing business had increased much less. The price of oil-field machinery was up only 19 percent between the two years, the cost of well casing was up 23 percent, and oil-field wages were up only 10 percent. By the IPAA's own figures, the industry was in a better position to achieve independence for the United States than it had been in 1972, when $4 was seen as a sufficiently high price.

*

Using these, and other, industry statements from the recent past for their rationale, the Five Freshmen agreed on and Eckhardt wrote an amendment that included this pricing schedule: about 40 percent of U.S. production would be controlled at $5.25 a barrel; about 26 percent would be controlled at an average price of $7.50 a barrel; about 28 percent would get an average price of $10; and the remaining 6 percent would be controlled at $11.50 a barrel. The price would depend on whether the oil came from old wells, new wells, Arctic Circle wells, tertiary-recovery wells, marginal wells, or stripper wells—in short, whether the oil had started to flow in cheaper days, or was new, or was hard to recover, or came from wells that had almost played out.

The Eckhardt formula was much too elaborate ever to be understood by the press or by most members of Congress, though they did grasp its general weighting of old oil versus new and were willing to take on faith as an arguing point that the overall average price for domestic oil would come to something over $7. Wisely, the Eckhardt amendment's formula was greatly simplified before it became law. The final version set $7.66 as the average maximum per-barrel price for domestic oil. The FEA was free to leave old oil, about 60 percent of the total, at $5.25 and place new oil, about 40 percent of the total, at $11.28—or to raise old oil and lower new oil to any price in between, so long as the overall weighted average was not changed, and *so long as no oil was elevated from the $5.25 category unless there was a showing that to do so was necessary to encourage production.* If this last proviso had not been inserted, the FEA could have shortchanged—and probably would have shortchanged—independent producers, who were heavily engaged in the production of costly new oil, to the benefit of the major oil companies, who owned most of the old oil.

*

Putting together a price schedule that made sense wasn't enough. It had to be sold, and that wasn't easy.

Maguire again picks up the story:

"We were consistently told by all the old hands—the committee chairmen, representatives of the leadership, knowledgeable people who had watched Congress and the oil companies for decades—that we didn't have the chance of a snowball in hell. First of all, we couldn't get it through a subcommittee of the Commerce Committee—nothing had ever gone through before that represented a public-interest viewpoint; that if by accident it got through the subcommittee, it would be killed in the full committee; if by some unusual circumstance it got through the full Commerce Committee—perhaps because there were thirteen new members of the committee—it would get wiped out on the floor by a combination of Republicans and oil-state Democrats.

"Jackson was the lead person on the Senate side, but reluctantly. At first he was very cool. His initial attitude had been, You're just whistling in the wind. But when he saw our momentum, he got behind us . . . Jackson had been talking $10 to $12 a barrel and we got him back to $7 . . .

"We had to orchestrate meetings with Jackson in the early days, cramming them full of public-interest groups, consumer groups, labor groups, to make sure Jackson knew where the political coalition was going and how important it was for him to be there. Prior to the Ninety-fourth Congress, the chairman had the last word on everything. So there was no reason for Jackson to believe that this horde of new members would be any different from any other new group.

"This was an important influence in our relations with [Representative John] Dingell, too. He was a brand-new subcommittee chairman. He had been here fifteen to eighteen years and he was finally becoming chairman of the energy subcommittee of the Commerce Committee. He had lived through all those years when he had had to play the more traditional role of the junior member relative to the autocratic chairman. But now Dingell, the supposedly great liberal, had come into his very own chairmanship, and all of a sudden he discovered that his word was going to be evaluated on its merits by the new members of his subcommittee, of whom there were many . . . Dingell got a very, very quick case of chairmanitis when he took over that subcommittee. He thoroughly enjoyed wielding the gavel, being called over to the White House for meetings with the President, being the focal point for all the lobbying by the companies on this great national issue. This was *the* national issue of 1975 . . .

"Dingell had made his deals with the White House on the basis that 'We've got to have a bill.' That was the code sentence: 'We've got to have a bill.' . . . There were so many people in the leadership of the House of Representatives and the White House who didn't care *what* the national energy plan included, or whether it was a plan or not, or whether it was good for anybody or not, as long as they had something they could label 'national energy plan' . . . [Dingell said to us], 'There's no way the President is going to sign what you guys are for.' To which we always said, 'That's just the very reason we should fight as long and as hard as we can and not throw in the towel now, so that we can wind up with more than we would have otherwise.' Dingell's argument was always 'We've got to get this over with and not be grandstanding here and there' . . .

"On the day that Eckhardt's amendment came up in subcommittee, we had been in session all afternoon. We recessed at about six o'clock to reconvene at seven. We had Eckhardt's proposal before us, which Dingell was opposing. We were pretty confident that we could pass it by one vote. But Phil Sharp [Democrat of Indiana] had some reception that he had to attend. He didn't get back promptly, on the dot, at seven o'clock. Seeing that, Dingell called the subcommittee to order immediately. This was very unusual promptness. He had somebody call for the previous question, and then we voted on the thing. It failed on a tie vote—Dingell, knowing that it would fail, voting with us.

"Then, when Sharp got back, ten minutes later—and of course the subcommittee never acted with much punctuality and Sharp had every reason to believe it wouldn't matter if he was ten minutes late—we tried to bring it up again by various procedural devices, including changing the wording of the bill just a little. That's always acceptable. Taking X,Y,Z paragraphs out, et cetera. Dingell kept ruling it out of order. Some of us got so furious at the way the subcommittee was being frustrated by this autocratic chairman that I said to Dick Ottinger, 'What do you do in a situation like that?' and he said, 'You appeal the ruling of the chair.' I immediately appealed the ruling of the chair—just as Dick added, '*But you never do it, you never do it!*' Dingell went through the roof; he exploded. He stood up in his chair and brought the gavel crashing down and went into a tirade about my questioning the integrity of the chair and he would not tolerate it and banging and banging his gavel. So I said, 'I'd like to withdraw my motion.' That made Dingell explode again, 'The gentleman will *not* withdraw his motion!' There was a vote and there were a few mumbled no's."

So they failed in the subcommittee. This meant they had to bring the Eckhardt amendment before the full committee without the subcommittee's recommendations—a tremendous disadvantage. The Five Freshmen went to work on every member, lobbying and relobbying, playing every angle, calling in every IOU. It was so close that everything depended on the last vote, which was to be cast by Williamson Stuckey of Georgia.

"Stuckey had committed himself to me [says Maguire] the day before, that if his vote was needed, he would vote with us—you know the trick congressmen play: 'Well, if my vote is needed I'll be with you,' and 99 percent of the time they can slide out of it. There's usually a margin of more than one and they can do whatever they want to do. Stuckey had committed to me. He passed on the first vote. The first time around, he didn't vote. I got out of my chair—I spent less time in my chair during that meeting—here I am an absolute freshman talking with senior members about their votes on this thing we had worked up on the preceding days—I went over to Stuckey and I said, 'Bill, we need you. Now. This is the time. Now!' I was kneeling down beside his chair as he voted aye on the Eckhardt amendment. It was the vote we had to have. When it came to the crunch, Dingell had voted against us. [Commerce Committee Chairman Harley] Staggers helped us, but he didn't help us except with his vote."

In the floor fight, the Five Freshmen still had to contend with opposition from subcommittee chairman Dingell, and under ordinary circumstances that alone might have done them in, for the House tends to heed the advice of the chairmen of original jurisdiction. But the freshmen were able to bring in on their side enough key veterans besides Eckhardt —members like Brock Adams of Washington, Carl Perkins of Kentucky, and Henry Reuss of Wisconsin—to overpower tradition. Majority leader Tip O'Neill made a speech on behalf of the Eckhardt amendment, which, given the fact that House Speaker Carl Albert was very much against the legislation and O'Neill wanted to succeed Albert, was a reasonably courageous thing to do. On December 16, the House passed the energy bill by a vote of 236 to 160. In the Senate, where Jackson had whipped himself up for one more try, it passed two days later, 58 to 40. On December 22, President Ford reluctantly signed it into law. Trying to put the best face on a major defeat, he posed as the peacemaker—"The time has come to end the long debate over national energy policy"—and with an eye to his presidential campaign year just a few days away, he tried to claim a constructive role—"this legislation . . . puts into place the first elements of a comprehensive national energy policy."

Actually, he loathed the bill.

*

The Five Freshmen's crusade, once dismissed as silly and futile, had succeeded, after all. Few had expected it to happen. On two occasions during the year, President Ford had vetoed other energy bills sent up by Congress, and his vetoes had prevailed rather easily. There were no indications that the procontrol members of Congress could ever override a veto. In July, *The New Republic* had predicted: "The President's ability to sustain a veto probably gives him the power to negotiate a compromise extension bill very nearly meeting his own objectives." In late August, Charles Maxwell, whom the New York *Times* said "is considered by many to be the top oil analyst on Wall Street," had predicted that

Ford would whip Congress and that an Administration-shaped, long-term deregulation plan would be in place by November 1.

Why did Wall Street's expert turn out to be as wrong as *The New Republic*'s? Why did Ford, never timid about socking Congress with another veto, not kill this one with a veto, as he had the others? The probable answers are not to be found in any magic performed by the Five Freshmen. The fact is, they would not have come even close to winning if they had not had two forces on their side: the economy and, ironically, some of the major oil companies.

The majors? Yes, the majors. Or some of them. The smarter ones. Generally speaking, the international oil companies consider stability to be the most prized blessing that the gods can confer on the business world. To be sure, the majors also love higher profits, but unlike the tempestuous independent oil companies, who want everything they can get *right now*, the majors take the long view. Exxon and Mobil and their sisters are reasonably certain they will be around a hundred years from now, if they play things right, so why squeeze the consumer dry suddenly, and perhaps arouse him to dangerous reactions, when a more gradual squeezing would preserve stability in the system? Sometimes—overcome by greed, or misreading the public's tolerance, or convinced that the public is already so outraged that additional squeezing won't matter, or pressured by independent oil companies to join the looting—the majors choose profits over stability. But that is not a choice they like to make.

It was their great respect for stability that prevailed in the fight to decontrol oil prices in 1975. Here, they realized, was a dangerous situation. The Republican President and the Democratic Congress could stalemate each other, for each had great negative powers. Under the Emergency Petroleum Allocation Act of 1973, Congress had empowered itself (by a majority vote of each chamber) to block decontrol of prices by presidential fiat. On the other hand, it had become quite clear that Congress could not muster the necessary two-thirds vote to override a presidential veto of whatever action it took to continue price controls. The situation was explosive, because it was unpredictable. An extra shove from either side might, in the majors' view, carry things too far. They urged Ford to be cautious. Whereas he had opened the year talking about total decontrol, by early summer he had backed away from that position. Now he said he would allow all domestic oil prices to float up to $13.50 a barrel—about $2 a barrel more than imported oil was then costing and nearly *twice* as high as the Eckhardt average—with controls to be removed entirely at the end of thirty months.

After the House had killed that proposal, in mid-July, Ford took a group of House and Senate leaders for a dinner cruise on the presidential yacht *Sequoia* to discuss what kind of compromise might be accepted.

Apparently the advice he got wasn't very good, for when he sent another proposal to Congress, a week later—this one allowing the price of all oil to rise to $11.50 over a 39-month period—it, too, was killed.

As the tug-of-war between Ford and Congress continued, the majors became increasingly nervous. Judging from their public statements, they apparently feared that Ford just couldn't get through his head the value of stability; that no matter how compromising he might pretend to be, he really was still aiming for total and immediate decontrol. He must be checked. Indeed, here and there among the majors came surprising sounds of support—or at least what in that crowd could pass for support —for the Moffett-Maguire-Eckhardt bill. John Lichtblau, head of the industry-financed Petroleum Industry Research Foundation, spoke for this group when he said the bill "is not a very good law, but the nation and the industry can live with it. Some of the companies have indulged in a fruitless overkill campaign against it." He said also, "I don't think our domestic crude oil prices should be allowed to rise to OPEC levels." Rawleigh Warner, Jr., chairman of Mobil, said total decontrol of oil prices would cost consumers $8 billion a year and would be a "shock to America's fragile economic recovery." James Lee, president of Gulf Oil, said an end to price controls on crude would raise gasoline and home heating oil 7 or 8 cents a gallon (more than twice what the Federal Energy Administration had predicted), and "I don't think the market would support an immediate 7-cent increase." Harry Bridges, president of Shell, agreed that immediate decontrol could overnight kick pump prices up by 7 cents a gallon, and that would be not only bad for the economy but horrible for public relations. "I think that a lot of companies are mindful of the fact that too rapid a change might provoke a counterreaction they wouldn't like."

Their fears were justified. The mood of the nation—and the mood of Congress—was turning ugly. "Oil Industry, Used to Criticism, Finds Attacks Growing Fiercer After Energy Crisis and Price Rises," read an eight-column business-section headline in the New York *Times*. By summertime, the attacks were centering on what appeared to be another contrived effort to create profitable shortages. The higher postembargo prices had discouraged gasoline use, and by June there was a real glut, a glut so troublesome for the oil companies that they were forcing many of their dealers to stay open twenty-four hours a day. Normally when there had been an oversupply in the past, prices dropped. This time, however, prices continued to climb. Meanwhile, refinery output was cut back sharply: refineries were operating at 84.6 percent capacity on July 1, compared to 93 percent a year earlier.

Production in the field was being held back too. Walter S. Measday, chief economist for the Senate Antitrust Subcommittee, disclosed that surveyors of federal leases on Louisiana's continental shelf found that production there was less than half of capacity. Measday implied that in his opinion the oil was being held back to reduce the glut, create a shortage, and further drive up prices. All of these things were, of course, denied by the oil companies. Texaco, for example, took out a full-page ad on July 18 to respond to allegations made by Senators Jackson and Stevenson. The ad said no, no, no, and no. "First, Texaco has *not* manipulated its refinery output in order to raise retail gasoline prices. Second, Texaco has *not* forced its retailers to stay open 24 hours a day to stimulate greater gasoline sales. Third, Texaco has *not* managed its gasoline production in such a way as to turn an oil surplus into a shortage and drive prices up. Fourth, Texaco has *not* worked together with the FEA or in any manner with anyone in an effort to create a gasoline shortage." The real villains, said Texaco's ad writer, were government regulators.

Consumer quibbling was something, however, that the oil companies had become rather used to. They had learned that laws and regulations could break their backs, but words would never harm them. So what really troubled them in the bountiful autumn of 1975—and convinced them that Ford should *not* veto the Moffett-Maguire-Eckhardt bill—was an awesome occurrence in the Senate. To the oilmen's surprise and downright shock, liberal senators in October lost, only 54 to 45, on an amendment that would have forced the breakup of the twenty-two largest integrated oil companies into separate production, transportation, refining, and marketing components. The integration of those functions—called vertical integration—was the very foundation of the international oil industry. So long as they controlled every step of the process, from the well to the pump, nothing could seriously diminish their power to fix supply and prices. But if they had to give up any links in the chain, they might at last be subjected to dreaded competition and free enterprise. For the majors, vertical integration was considered an absolute must. Any challenge to it was a threat to their existence.

No legislative encounter in the 1970s had such a stunning impact on the psyche of the oil industry as that vote. The near miss was totally unexpected, like a lightning bolt from the blue.

＊

But in fact the majors should have been prepared for what happened. The cloud had been growing on the horizon for years. Among a small hard-core liberal coterie in Congress, the lack of competition in big business and especially in the oil industry had been a constant irritant. The most relentless pursuer of industrial monopolies was, of course, Senator Phil Hart, whose antitrust subcommittee had held many hundreds of hours of hearings to prove that the foundation for big business in this country was not free enterprise but economic concentration. His subcommittee's hearings on this problem extended to forty thousand pages in twenty-three volumes. His ambition was to pull down the giants in *every* industry and force a restructuring that would allow more competition, between smaller units. As for the granite-hard oligopoly that ruled the oil industry, he had said in 1973, "For my part, I have seen enough evidence to convince me that divestiture is the best step to take toward solving the energy crisis." But he was never able to get any action on his bills aimed at reforming the structure of big business; for a dozen years he had tried, but he couldn't even get them out of subcommittee, much less actually push them to the floor for a vote by the full Senate.

But circumstances in the first half of the 1970s shifted radically, in such a way as to make reform of the oil monopoly possible—not likely, to be sure, but possible—and the most profoundly influential change in the circumstances had come in reaction to the oil companies' new prosperity. It was very simple: so long as gasoline and heating oil were cheap, the public didn't give a damn whether the majors were vertically integrated or monopolistic, or not. The electorate was effectively soothed by 30-cent gasoline and 19-cent heating oil. But when prices began to move up sharply, in 1973, the public noticed the maddening profits of the industry and became "radicalized" overnight. Knocking the oil companies was no longer looked upon as simply liberal chic; it became a grass-roots sport. A lot of ordinary voters who hadn't cared at all started paying attention to the institutional issues raised by the control of oil, started asking questions about who *really* made foreign policy, who *really* made the nation's economic policy. The Church subcommittee's investigation into the multinationals released an incredible amount of stuff that gave substance to old suspicions. Previously, anyone who talked about the international oil cartel was dismissed as a paranoid pinko, but now came a flood of testimony from very legitimate and very establishment types that showed, right there on the record, that the cartel did exist. Suddenly, the oil industry was vulnerable.

Just how vulnerable, neither it nor its enemies had realized, however. Its enemies were as surprised at their near-success as the oil companies were. And the vulnerability would never have been discovered at all had it not been for a small—very small—group of senators who either were (1) naïvely hard-nosed or (2) so politically ambitious that they were willing to make headlines via what was generally seen as a hopeless cause.

Among the latter were Senator Birch Bayh of Indiana, a candidate for the Democratic presidential nomination, and Senator Edward Kennedy. Among the former were Senator Gary Hart of Colorado and Senator James Abourezk of South Dakota.

*

As the instigator, the catalyst, for the great divestiture drama that began in 1975 and spilled into 1976, Abourezk was probably the most important—just as he was certainly the least likely—leader among the leaders. If nothing else, it was because of him that the impulse to take on the oil titans originated not among the eastern elite and radical campus ideologues but out in the hinterland among very ordinary and very square folks. To be exact, the impulse was hatched on May 25, 1973, a few months after Abourezk became a senator, at a one-day Senate Interior subcommittee hearing he chaired in Sioux Falls, South Dakota. Dozens of witnesses came forward to complain, and for the most part they were small fry—farmers and truckers and little independent oil dealers, people with names like Erhard Phingsten and John Serbousek and Arthur Schlaiker—or they were officials representing those groups. Almost without exception they said they thought Big Oil was manipulating the market, that it was claiming false shortages to raise prices or to drive small competitors out of business. An independent gasoline marketer by the name of Russell F. Ripley came in and told how he had built up a string of thirty outlets for "Ripco" gas in the rural areas over the previous twenty-three years and how his supplier, one of the major oil companies, had just up and told him he couldn't have any more gasoline, which left Ripley with a wife and nine children to support and no business.

Now, in many states and to most U.S. senators, on-the-road hearings of that sort are no more than safety valves through which the folks back home can come in and blow off steam. But in a small state like South Dakota, where the frontier spirit is still pretty strong, the people who show up to testify usually know the senator by his first name and they are there to talk directly to him and by god they expect him to pay attention.

Abourezk—cigar-smoking (preferably Cuban), guitar-picking, soft-talking, tough, Jim to everyone, even to strangers—listened very closely. These were his people. He was at their level. Son of a Lebanese back-peddler, Abourezk was raised on the Rosebud Sioux Indian Reservation, didn't get around to college until he was twenty-six years old, put himself through law school as bartender and bouncer (the only bouncer at the American Legion Club who didn't have to use a blackjack, because he had learned judo in the Navy), earned a living as rancher, surveyor, civil engineer, and lawyer before jumping to the U.S. House of Representatives in 1971. There, in two years, he discovered that "idealism can't survive even one term in that place" and moved on to the U.S. Senate in 1973. He was known as one of the most down-to-earth (and financially poorest) members of the upper house.[6]

---

6. Regrettably, Abourezk left the Senate in 1979, after only one term, once again disillusioned, saying he was "glad to be leaving this chicken-shit place." Apparently Abourezk had no staying power. He was a political drifter. While he was in the Senate, he was one of the most courageously outspoken of the radical-liberals (not that he had much competition). He was extremely adept at using his many friends in the press corps to fight his battles. He was stubborn in a filibuster. But he was like a bar-

Angered by his neighbors' complaints, Abourezk returned to Washington determined to take on the oil companies. He called in two attorneys for advice: Martin Lobel, who had once been Senator William Proxmire's oil gadfly, and William J. Lamont, who had retired from the Justice Department after thirty years of total frustration in trying to get the antitrust laws applied to the oil industry. Lobel and Lamont suggested that Abourezk go the divestiture route. It had been more than thirty years since anyone had pushed an oil divestiture bill in Congress—not just tossed a bill into the hopper but actually tried to get other members to take it seriously. To be exact, the last attempt had been made by Senator Guy Gillette of Iowa in 1941. (Phil Hart's bills were aimed at restructuring big business generally, not oil specifically.)

As expected, Abourezk's bill got nowhere. One of his aides picked out twenty-eight senators he thought would be most receptive to the idea and for three weeks did nothing but make a circuit of their offices trying to get them to cosponsor the legislation. In the end, he got two, and one of them was the other senator from South Dakota, George McGovern, who could hardly have refused. During that doldrum era, Abourezk made a speech on divestiture to an executives' conference in Washington and, in the Q and A period that followed, a Texaco vice-president stood up and said, "Let's face it, Senator, there's nobody else in the Senate who thinks like you do, do they?" To which Abourezk replied, "Maybe not now, but maybe that will change."

*

He was right. The public distrust and dislike for the oil companies that had prompted him to introduce his legislation in 1973 had greatly increased by 1975. The United States was slipping deeper into the worst depression since the 1930s, for which the oil companies (with record profits) caught much of the blame. By the spring of 1975, API president Ikard complained, "The term 'big oil' is often spoken or written in a vituperative way that implies that these organizations are somehow soulless leviathans. . ."

Indeed that's exactly how much of the public had come to feel. A 1975 public opinion poll showed that although 81 percent of the people rejected the idea that the government should own all major industries, the people by a plurality of 44 to 42 percent believed that it would be a good thing for the government to take over ownership of oil and other natural

---

room brawler—good for a few wild punches, but he tired quickly. In that regard, he was certainly no Phil Hart. Abourezk quit the Senate just when its liberal group, badly depleted, needed him most. He became another Washington lawyer, another gun for hire. He hired his to Middle Eastern interests, including the Ayatollah's Iran, and launched some sort of outfit to quarrel with the press at presumed "defamations" of Arabs.

resources. They were so mad that they were willing to think dark thoughts of specialized socialism. And thoughts almost as dark were passing through several heads in Congress. Abourezk reintroduced his vertical-divestiture bill in February. He followed that up with a bill to require horizontal divestiture—forbidding oil companies from developing nonpetroleum energy sources, including coal, oil shale, geothermal steam, uranium, and energy from the sun.[7] Shortly thereafter, Senator Bayh came along with his own vertical-divestiture bill. Senator Kennedy offered a horizontal-divestiture bill. One of the most important in the growing group of dissidents was Senator Gary Hart of Colorado. He called himself a "radical free enterpriser." Industry's efforts to decontrol natural gas prices and allow them to be set by the "free market" triggered in him a fervor of economic fundamentalism—by god, yes, he was eager to put not only more competition into natural gas pricing but into the whole industry. Hart immediately became one of the most vocal prodivestiturites. Assuming this leadership role marked him, to be sure, as something of an upstart, for at thirty-eight he was a mere child of the Senate and he had arrived in that august body only nine months earlier. But he had become something of an expert in oil matters when he served as a special assistant to Interior Secretary Stewart Udall, and although he was indeed brash, he knew how to play the Senate game.

A lawyer who attended all the strategy sessions at the time says, "Jim [Abourezk] was the instigator, but he was a bull of a guy who would get excited and shout, 'Goddamn it, those bastards are ripping us off and we've got to do something about it.' Obviously, he is not one of the Senate types. Gary could very well be one of the Senate types. He is very low-key and very persuasive. Jim was the guy who started it [in 1973], but Gary was the guy who reworked it and I think was the key contributor in getting most of the support. I think Gary went around and said, 'Here's the evidence, here's why I think it's right, and gee, what have we got to lose anyway? It's probably not going to pass and it's a good public-interest vote.' The Senate understands that argument."

Although there was no visible evidence that the bill had great potential, the senators involved must have suspected that it did, for there were budding signs of jealousy as to whose name should go first on the bill. That was settled by putting first the name of the old antitrust warrior Senator Philip Hart, though in this fight he was the least active. He was dying of cancer.

The plan to bring their divestiture bill to the floor of the Senate was

---

7. Vertical divestiture was aimed at toppling corporations that controlled every type of service, from top to bottom, within the oil industry: production, refining, transportation, wholesaling, retailing. Horizontal divestiture was aimed at blocking oil companies from spreading out into allied fields.

announced by four of the group at a press conference on September 19. Only a handful of reporters showed up. Why should they? Of the four senators, only Phil Hart was considered a powerhouse, and he wouldn't be around much longer. Anyway, bad-mouthing of oil companies by liberal politicians around Washington was old stuff, and it had never come to anything.

The Hart/Abourezk group called several meetings with labor lobbyists and consumer lobbyists and asked for fast and heavy help, stressing the fact that they had less than a month to swing the votes. But, except for the Consumer Federation of America, the Communications Workers of America, the Independent Petroleum Marketers, and the National Farmers Union, few pitched in. As one of the Hart group later said, "The AFL-CIO sat on the sidelines, counting their pension."

If labor didn't take the move seriously, neither did management. Very few industry lobbyists bothered to ask senators for a negative vote. They were laughing right up to the time the votes were counted, on the afternoon of October 8, when they saw themselves escape by that narrow margin: 54 to 45. Indeed, a turnaround of *only five votes* would have given the victory to the Hart/Abourezk group. Industry had been taken by surprise, and Abourezk was probably close to the physiological truth when he declared with a snicker, "The oil industry has suffered a klong! Which is a medical term denoting a sudden rush of shit to the heart."

Two weeks later, another vertical-divestiture amendment lost, only 49 to 40, and a horizontal amendment lost, 53 to 39.

What had, at least momentarily, thrown the Senate into such a radical frame of mind? Were the Senators showboating? Whatever the cause, divestiture seemed a greater threat—however transient—than the continuation of price controls at a generous level.[8] That's why executives of the major oil companies, frightened as never before, urged Ford to go along with the energy bill Congress sent him. Better to accept it than to arouse the enemy further. And so he did.

***

Although it failed to remove controls, the Ford administration went out of its way to destroy the effectiveness of controls. It was the duty of the Federal Energy Administration to regulate prices of crude oil and petroleum products and to see that the companies didn't cheat the public. In December 1974, the General Accounting Office had made a study of the FEA's price enforcement activities and found them shot through

---

8. It wasn't too transient. The divestiture movement would reach its peak the next year. Most of the momentum would come in the Senate, but one influential member of the House, Representative Morris K. Udall of Arizona, told the National Press Club on April 22 that his presidential campaign from then on would ask the people's support of his intention to break up the oil companies both vertically and horizontally.

with favoritism, incompetence, and chaos. The GAO found that the FEA had no written guidelines or procedures for conducting audits of wholesalers, retailers, refiners, producers, or natural gas plants, and that it had no procedures for handling complaints from the public, no comprehensive policy for collecting civil penalties against companies that violated price regulations, and no written guidelines to assist FEA personnel in figuring out whether a violation was intentional or unintentional.

In short, the FEA had no enforcement policy. And it had virtually no enforcers.

That's what the GAO found in December 1974, and six months later, the Senate Subcommittee on Administrative Practice and Procedure found that nothing had changed. Its investigators reported that "for periods of from 2–3 months in March, April, and May 1975, there was only *one auditor* assigned to each of six of the 30 largest refining companies, including Exxon, the world's largest oil company."

Under pressure from Senate investigators, the FEA national office, on July 14, 1975, ordered the regional offices to double the number of auditors working in the seventeen largest refiners and to assign eight auditors to each of the six largest oil companies in Region VI (headquarters in Dallas). But as of September 30, Senate investigators discovered, only four to six auditors were working at each of these large firms, and of the forty-eight auditors assigned to these companies, sixteen—one third of the total—were undergoing "training" on that date, two and one half months after the national office directive.

Ralph Tippit, then the FEA's audit team leader at Exxon, admitted that on one audit he was allowed only fifty-four hours to complete work that he estimated should have taken seven hundred hours. He also admitted that, because of a lack of travel funds, he could not go to several locations where Exxon kept records that should have been inspected.

Major oil companies operated most of the natural gas plants. The GAO estimated that overcharging for natural gas might run as high as $1 billion. The FEA's refinery audit program called for thirty auditors to cover the gas plants, but as of the subcommittee's hearings, not one auditor had been assigned to that area.

Communication between the national office and regional offices was so bad that Washington didn't even know that only one FEA auditor was assigned to Exxon until six weeks had elapsed, and it wouldn't have found out then if the subcommittee's investigators hadn't asked about it. FEA administrator Frank Zarb said he was "shocked" to learn that only one man was watching Exxon.

An exchange between Senator Kennedy and Donald Mitchell, a former FEA auditor of independent crude oil producers, indicated that the lack of guidance and communication was intentional:

SENATOR KENNEDY: "Since there are thousands of independent producers, how did you and other auditors determine which producers to audit?"

MITCHELL: "I cannot say how others decided which producers to audit. I know in several instances I went to the Yellow Pages."

SENATOR KENNEDY: "The Yellow Pages?"

MITCHELL: "Yes, sir."

SENATOR KENNEDY: "Do you mean the telephone company Yellow Pages?"

MITCHELL: "Yes, Bell Telephone. You look under 'Producers' and go down the list and see what the name is."

SENATOR KENNEDY: "Did the national office give you this kind of instruction?"

MITCHELL: "I do not know what the national office did . . . Shortly after I went to Texas, I had to sign a written statement that I would no longer communicate with the national office."

Sometimes after FEA field-office workers had spent hundreds of hours investigating a violator, they found that their bosses back in Washington had worked out a settlement with oil company lobbyists and lawyers but hadn't bothered to tell the workers in the field.

The FEA admitted that it had only one ninth the number of personnel needed to enforce honest pricing. The skeleton crew reflected the FEA's intentions *not* to regulate. This was evident in confidential memoranda obtained by Senate subpoena. In February 1975, FEA's assistant administrator Gorman Smith wrote the regional administrator in Boston: "For some time—ever since late spring 1974—the Federal Energy Administration has been schizophrenic about its regulatory programs. The Administration's policy has been that we would deregulate the petroleum industry as soon as Congress would let us. *Budget and staffing decisions for regulatory programs have been made with that policy in mind.*" (Emphasis added.) In a March 4, 1975, memorandum to FEA's deputy administrator John A. Hill, Smith wrote: " 'Deregulation' has been the watchword, so why bother getting ready to regulate . . . ?"

At the subcommittee hearings, Paul Maloy, compliance and enforcement director for the Boston region, admitted: "There has never been any clear expression of the intent to have a strong compliance program . . . None of the auditors in the field believe that the agency wants to enforce its own regulations."

So they simply weren't being enforced. At the time of the subcommittee hearings, FEA had collected a mere $737,000 in penalties from retailers, wholesalers, and crude producers for violations totaling $87 million in overcharges. But these were all little guys: small retailers, small wholesalers, small producers. The penalties levied against them were trivial, to be sure, but they were still more than the big refiners were paying. The FEA found seventy-five cases of overcharging, totalling $267 million, on the part of major refiners, but it had collected not one penny in penalties from them.

Not only was the FEA refusing to do its own job, it was also trying to prevent other agencies from cracking down on oil company outlaws. This was discovered as early as May, when the House Commerce Subcommittee on Oversight and Investigation uncovered documents indicating that both the FEA and the State Department had tried to interfere with the Justice Department's grand jury investigation of charges that the city of Jacksonville, Florida, had been overcharged by $26 million during the six-month embargo. (The State Department got involved because some of its top officials were old friends of the accused company's lawyer.) The FEA never had favored the criminal prosecution of illegal oil profiteering, and although estimates of this activity during the embargo era ran as high as $3 billion, this was the first grand jury investigation of the problem. The FEA argued that the Justice Department should keep its hands off and leave such matters to the FEA for administrative correction.

The FEA was similarly slow to come to the aid of New England Power, which had bought oil in a deal involving the same company accused of overcharging Jacksonville. The New England deal was fascinating in one respect. As Michael Putzel, of the Associated Press, wrote, the fuel oil that first sold at less than $4 a barrel was finally sold to New England Power for $23.75, having "changed hands seven times between companies in four countries without leaving its storage tank in the Caribbean." It was all a paper shuffle. When New England Power, which was desperate for oil (this was during the embargo), complained to the FEA, wrote Putzel, the federal agency "said, in effect, 'Take it, or do without. You can argue about the price later.' . . ."

The FEA set up three investigations with fancy-sounding titles—Project Escalator, Project Manipulator, and Project Speculator—and boasted that it would force gougers to roll back prices, refund overcharges, and reduce illegal prices. But in fact they were getting refunds of only about $1 for every $100 illegally squeezed from consumers.

***

When President Ford told the nation, in 1974, he wanted to increase offshore leasing, some suspicious critics had argued that if too much land was put on the market at one time, the result would be a lessening of competition per bid and also a decrease in the size of bids. Senator Ernest Hollings, chairman of the National Ocean Policy Study, announced on January 27, 1975, that his investigators had found these suspicions to be well founded. He pointed out that a Gulf of Mexico sale "that was part of 1974's greatly expanded offerings resulted in over 33 percent of the tracts going to sole bidders. Furthermore, the average price per acre dropped substantially in 1974 as the number of acres offered increased."

Once again Hollings introduced legislation to require the government to explore the outer continental shelf before leasing to oil companies. He charged that the Department of the Interior, without having the slightest independent notion of the value of the offshore lands, was getting ready "to turn most of these offshore target areas over to industry through leases which have a built-in time delay of up to five years. Current regulations permit oil companies to sit on leases for five years before undertaking exploration, and they can wait for many more years before deciding to produce oil."

His bill got nowhere. But three things happened during the year that justified his criticism of the Administration's willingness to lease in ignorance.

First came a General Accounting Office report on March 20 that denounced Interior's leasing program as being based on "inadequate information and unrealistic assumptions." The GAO pointed out that although the Interior Department estimated that leasing 10 million acres annually until 1980 would bring on line an annual production of 7 billion barrels of oil in 1985, the Federal Energy Administration—using drilling rates, rather than acreage leased, as the basis for predicting production—anticipated only 1.5 billion barrels in 1985. The GAO said it believed that even *the FEA estimates were unrealistically high,* since they underestimated the lead times between discovery and production.

So who was right? Actually, nobody had even a good guess as to which agency was closest to being correct. Not even the experts knew what lay out there on the outer continental shelf, until they started drilling. This was proved when, in June, Exxon and its sixteen drilling compadres announced that they were abandoning exploration in the eastern part of the Gulf of Mexico, in the "Destin dome." Relying on seismic data, the oil companies had been so certain of the area's potential that two years earlier they had paid a record $1.4 billion to the federal government for drilling rights. But as of 1975 they had drilled nothing but dry holes—fourteen of them—at a cost of $1 million per. All told, the venture added up to the most costly failure in the history of oil exploration. It had only one moral: nobody can tell for sure where oil is until he drills for it.

More dubious expertise was offered by the U.S. Geological Survey in June.

Remember the USGS's 50 percent slash in offshore estimates in 1974? Well, that was just the beginning. Now the USGS was back with another stunning reduction. It cut its estimates of Atlantic offshore oil potential by another 80 percent. The decline was dizzying. In 1972, the USGS had said there were 114 billion barrels of discoverable oil in the Atlantic out to a water depth of 650 feet. The next year, it dropped its estimate to 48 billion barrels. Then, in March 1974, the USGS had cut this estimate to 10 to 20 billion barrels. Now it said that the Atlantic fields probably contained no more than 2 *to 4 billion barrels!*

The reduction in total offshore estimates was just as striking. Prior to 1974, the USGS had been saying that there was a total of 200 billion barrels awaiting discovery. In March 1974 they had dropped that to 65 billion to 130 billion barrels. Now they were whacking their estimates to 10 billion to 49 billion.[9]

Onshore, the same disappearing act was taking place. Whereas in 1974 the USGS had estimated that the nation's total onshore oil resources came to 135 to 270 billion barrels, now they estimated 37 billion to 81 billion; instead of the 1,000 to 2,000 trillion cubic feet of natural gas estimated in 1974, now the USGS estimated only 322 trillion to 655 trillion cubic feet.

What was going on, and why? Whatever was going on, one thing was certain: the oil companies were behind it. The USGS based its estimates, and always had based its estimates, primarily on figures supplied by the oil companies. The USGS didn't go out and drill wells; it did virtually no seismic work. It paid oil companies (or companies that worked for oil companies) to do some of the seismic investigation, and otherwise depended on handout information from the companies. So when the USGS said the potential reserves were disappearing, it was acting merely as a spokesman for the oil companies.[10] But what would be their purpose in spreading such profound gloom?

The answers to that were somewhat less certain. But some very good guesses could be made. One common guess among critics was that the USGS was rigging the system so that the oil companies could get by with bidding very low for the leases. After all, if there wasn't much oil and gas on the federal lands, they couldn't be expected to pay much for the

9. The low end of each new estimate, except those for Atlantic offshore areas, represented the amount of oil geologists were 95 percent certain could be found. The high end, except for the Atlantic, represented a 5-percent, "long-shot" figure. For its Atlantic estimates, the USGS was much more timid, using a probability spread ranging between 25 percent and 75 percent.

10. This was a role that some high officials at the USGS filled very comfortably, for many had come from the oil and gas industries and others intended to go into such employment after government service. Meanwhile, some USGS officials were betting their money on oil company prosperity, in what was clearly a conflict of interest. A report issued by the GAO on March 3 noted that despite the fact that by federal statute "no USGS employee may own an interest in oil or mining enterprises," there were flagrant violations. Among them, "an administrative geologist owned stock in 12 companies with oil or mining interest. A supervisory petroleum engineer, empowered to suspend oil company operations on leased lands if operations were not properly conducted, has owned stock in Mobil Oil Company, Standard Oil of California, and Standard Oil of New Jersey since 1971."

leases, could they? The Interior Department (of which the USGS was part) had often been accused of accepting bids at giveaway prices. The new reductions made it even easier for the USGS to place rock-bottom evaluations on the tracts to be leased and thereby excuse just about any bid as being "generous."[11]

There were prompt signs that the strategy was working.

In December, when leases for drilling off southern California were sold (which, if not further tied up in court, would end a six-year battle by environmentalists to block further drilling in that area), the bids were much lower than expected. The high-bid total was expected to hit $1.5 billion to $2 billion, but in fact the oil companies submitted high bids totaling only $432 million.

The low estimates of discoverable oil and gas had one other, psychological advantage for the companies: it strengthened their argument that the nation was running out of energy and that the government had better throw its lands open to exploration without regard to environmental problems.

* * *

If the naughty gods showered blessings bountifully on the major oil companies, so did the majors share their blessings with crooked politicians around the world. It had been going on for years, but only now, in 1975, did the full extent of the international payoffs begin to surface. Imagine how embarrassing it must have been to old John D. Rockefeller, wherever he was, when it was revealed that, over a 10-year period, Exxon had given $56 million to Italian politicians *including* members of the Italian Communist Party. After getting caught, Exxon chairman J. K. Jamieson admitted it was "a mistake" to try to hide the payoffs. Mobil also admitted to making $2.1 million in payoffs to Italian politicians and then falsifying its records to indicate that the money was spent for "advertising" and "research." Gulf chairman B. R. Dorsey admitted that his company had paid out nearly $5 million to right-wing parties in such places as South Korea and Bolivia. Actually—as subsequent investigations revealed —through the 1960s and early 1970s, Gulf channeled at least $12 million into foreign and domestic political pockets, including more than a hundred U.S. senators, numerous members of the House, eighteen governors, etc. Some of it was disguised by Gulf bookkeeping as "offshore exploration" expenditures. This was the first peek into Gulf's political mischief since 1973, when Claude Wild, Jr., a Gulf lobbyist, had admitted making

---

11. In the recent past, the USGS's evaluations had been downright ridiculous. On one Gulf tract it had evaluated at $38,833, the high bid was $32.2 million. Was this a lot, or a little? The USGS offered no sensible standard to measure it by. Obviously, th USGS's low estimates of discoverable oil and gas, coupled with its low evaluations, left the auctions to the mercy of the companies.

unlawful contributions to three presidential campaigns: Nixon's, Wilbur Mills's, and Henry Jackson's. (The Corrupt Practices Act makes it illegal for corporations to contribute directly or indirectly to federal political campaigns.) For committing that crime, Wild was fined $1,000 and Gulf was fined $5,000 by U.S. District Judge George L. Hart—a jurist noted for his sympathy for establishment malefactors.[12]

But the things that came to light in 1975 showed that the piddling political contribution Gulf and Wild were "punished" for in 1973 was not even the tip of the iceberg; it was only the sparkle at the top. (For a fuller account, see Appendix entry WILD, CLAUDE C., JR.)

Orin E. Atkins, chairman and chief executive officer of Ashland Oil, the nation's largest independent oil company, had also confessed in 1973 to making an unlawful contribution to Nixon's campaign, for which Atkins, a millionaire, had been fined $1,000. But that, too, turned out to be just the opening crack. In 1975, Ashland reluctantly surrendered documents to the Securities and Exchange Commission showing that it had laid out $1.2 million in foreign payoffs and illegal domestic political contributions. Like Gulf, it made a practice of "slopping both hogs," as the saying goes, giving to Democrats and Republicans, liberals and conservatives: buying Richard Nixon's Finance Committee with $100,000 and the Democratic National Committee with $30,000, buying reactionary Senator James Eastland for $5,000 and liberal Senator Hubert Humphrey for $11,914, et cetera, et cetera. Congressman Wilbur Mills was the conduit for $50,000 of Ashland's money, reportedly spreading it around among his needy colleagues in the House. Ashland also took CIA money for undisclosed purposes and allowed one of its officials to serve as a CIA spy for five years.

Although U.S. law does not forbid corporations from paying off foreign officials, Securities and Exchange Commission regulations require them to make a full accounting so that stockholders will know what the companies are up to. Most oil companies violated SEC regulations in this regard, and it was SEC investigators who were now uncovering their questionable activities. With the SEC closing in, some oil companies

---

12. Judge Hart was the chap who made the Alaska pipeline ruling. See the 1972 chapter. In 1974, when Harry S. Dent, Sr., President Nixon's top political strategist, pleaded guilty to aiding an illegal fund-raising operation, Judge Hart characterized Dent as "more a victim than the perpetrator" of the crime and let him go with one month probation. When former Attorney General Richard G. Kleindienst pleaded guilty, in 1975, to lying at his Senate confirmation hearing in 1972—conduct that the court of appeals equated with "dishonesty, fraud, deceit or misrepresentation"—Judge Hart let him off with a $100 fine and one month unsupervised probation (he could have been sentenced to $1,000 fine and one year in jail) and said Kleindienst's crime "reflects a heart that is too loyal and considerate of the feelings of others." Judge Hart also handed down kindhearted rulings at the 1975 bribery trial of former Treasury Secretary John Connally.

came forward and admitted political expenditures both at home and abroad that they had previously kept hidden. Cities Service Company, for example, in September announced that it had "discovered" that one of its overseas subsidiaries had made payoffs to foreign politicians.

Although there was some pretense of contrition—in December, for example, Exxon chairman M. A. Wright made a speech to the Chicago Rotary Club on "Restoring Public Credibility of Business"—the record proved that the companies did not feel sorry at all. Though Wild stepped down as Gulf's flamboyant lobbyist in 1974, he stayed on the payroll as a "consultant" for another $90,000 worth of service. Atkins remained as chairman of Ashland at $314,000 a year, with the board of directors unanimously praising him for "forceful leadership." William W. Keeler, another who pleaded guilty to making an unlawful contribution to Nixon and was fined $1,000, retired from the chairmanship of Phillips Petroleum in 1973 and was now being "punished" on a retirement pension estimated by the New York *Times* at $201,742 a year. In 1973, W. F. Martin was promoted to the presidency of Phillips, taking Keeler's place, and in 1975 he was still running the company, with the board of directors defending his questionable activities of the recent past on the ground that he was making money for Phillips. Martin, as Jerry Landauer of *The Wall Street Journal* described the messy affair, had become "involved, as senior vice-president, in a complex kickback scheme requiring overseas contractors to channel $2.6 million through foreign conduits for deposit in Swiss accounts; of this sum the company allocated $585,000 for political purposes. [Jerry Ford, Lyndon Johnson and Richard Nixon were among those who took the money.] Mr. Martin accepted the task in 1968 of 'monitoring' kickback payments from one contractor and he moved cash from Switzerland to company headquarters."

***

One of the routine oddities of the 1970s occurred in 1975: a ferocious natural gas "shortage" appeared, hovered over the nation through most of the year, and then disappeared—all with the credibility of a séance. But the industry had little credibility left to lose anyway, so it might just as well shoot for the extra profit. Its reputation, already in shreds, had sustained several serious rips recently when the General Accounting Office completed an investigation, in the fall of 1974, that indicated that the gas industry, with the collusion of the FPC, had, over a period of three years, reaped an extra and unjustified $3.3 billion. In a separate investigation, the GAO had discovered that one reason the FPC was so cozy with industry was that nineteen key officials at FPC owned petroleum company stock they were not legally permitted to own.

Having data of that sort to serve as context, informed segments of the American public were understandably dubious about all claims of a natural gas shortage and the need for higher prices to relieve it. Skepticism was so deep that mere full-page friendly apologies and explanations of the sort that had become commonplace in the *Times* and the *Post* were no longer having the desired impact.

So industry decided to get tough instead. It could do so in the natural gas arena without fearing the kind of political retaliation that was possible with oil. The natural gas industry, though controlled by the same majors and their allies, was structured differently. The threat of divestiture that momentarily hung over oil did not hang over natural gas. Here, industry could get tough with much less risk. And so, in the fall of 1974, it had begun to close the natural gas valve, and it continued closing it as winter moved into 1975. No longer did it rely on threats; now it was actually lessening the supply. If the public wouldn't accept higher prices happily and if Congress wouldn't consider total deregulation of prices, then industry apparently was ready for a showdown.

*

Typical of the action at the time was Transcontinental Gas Pipe Line Corp.'s brutal squeeze play on the East Coast. Transco—an interstate system that bought, transported, and sold natural gas to distributors in eleven states from the Gulf Coast to New York—served the residential needs of some 25 million people and of industries employing more than 1.25 million workers.

Many of Transco's customers literally depended on it for economic life. They became desperate when, in September 1974, Transco announced that during the winter months it would curtail deliveries by 20 percent. They became hysterical the next month, when Transco notified its customers of an additional system-wide curtailment of 33 percent. In southern New Jersey, for one example, unemployment was already hovering around 14 percent—double the national average—and these curtailments promised to wipe out twenty-five thousand jobs at eighteen factories in that area. At Danville, Virginia, the curtailments threatened to idle ninety-eight hundred people out of a population of forty-seven thousand. Danville ordinarily had an unemployment rate of about 4 percent, well below the national average.

But there were some highly suspicious aspects to all this, and they began emerging in 1975. New Jersey Representative William Hughes, for example, observed that "one of the great mysteries" was why Transco, the sole supplier of natural gas to Hughes's district, had to cut down on delivery even while sitting on 2.23 trillion cubic feet of available natural gas. The U.S. Court of Appeals noted that five years earlier Transco had reported the *highest proven reserves of gas in history*. So why was it now claiming that it would have to cut deliveries by as much as 50 percent? The Court ordered the FPC to investigate.

Performing in its usual fashion, the FPC, after investigating for a full year, found nothing wrong. But meanwhile, Representative John Moss, chairman of the House Oversight and Investigations Subcommittee, had uncovered data that pointed to a possible conspiracy. It seems that one big reason Transco hadn't had enough gas for the 1974–75 winter was that six wells on a Cities Service platform in the Gulf of Mexico were shut down for repairs at the worst possible time, depriving Transco of a crucial margin of supplies. The six wells constituted Block A-76, the fourth-largest producing field of some two hundred offshore fields supplying gas to Transco, and the largest producing offshore reservoir operated by Cities Service.

There seemed to be something funny about that shutdown. As far back as January 1974, one of Cities Service's natural gas wells had developed tube problems. By March 1974, the situation had deteriorated to the point that Cities Service notified Transco it might have to shut down some wells for repair. But the repair work wasn't started until September 20—just when natural gas demands began to move up for the winter—and it wasn't completed until mid-January 1975, a shutdown of 144 days. Why did they wait until the cold months to do the repairs? Why not get busy on the job during the summer months? Cities Service claimed that a workover rig was not available until August 29, 1974. But Moss's investigators went out in the field and talked to companies with workover rigs and found that suitable equipment had been available during June, had been offered to Cities Service, and had been rejected. The staff strongly suggested that the shutdown had been timed to create the kind of psychological strains that would make the public accept price deregulation.

If Transco needed the gas so badly, why didn't it complain about Cities Service's actions? Like other pipelines, it took curtailment of supplies without a whimper. They were not insisting on getting the gas they had contracted for. An investigation by the House Energy and Power Subcommittee in October found that *not one suit* had been filed by a pipeline company against any producer for welching on deliveries. The reason for this was, of course, pretty obvious: the pipeline companies and the producers were in business together, and they all wanted prices to go up. Representative Hughes explained the problem: "Transco, like many pipelines, is staking its future in joint ventures with major oil companies . . . in the federal domain this began in December of 1972 when the firm invested more than $57 million for a 19 to 25 percent interest in properties held with Shell. This year, Transco gained a quarter interest in a lease with Atlantic-Richfield, which cost the partners $1,125,000 as well as a 4 percent interest in a $4 million lease with Shell and a number of other joint investors. . . . What is wrong with these arrangements is not the legitimate and obligatory pursuit of new gas sources on the part of the pipelines, but the wedding of pipeline to producer interests. The producers want deregulation. *These joint ventures and community of interests perhaps help explain why pipelines like Transcontinental have not raised a hue and cry over the failure of producers to accelerate production from proven, known reserves."* (Emphasis added)

*

But disclosures of conflicts of interest and downright shady conduct no longer seemed to bother the natural gas producers and the pipelines; they were adjusting very well to playing the villain; what they wanted was more money, and never mind the public's opinion.

After the frightening experiences of the past winter, the people who depended on natural gas for their jobs were gun-shy. They began to shiver when, in the summer of 1975, there were new predictions of terrible shortages for the coming winter.

In July, President Ford told Congress they had better hurry up and decontrol natural gas prices, because otherwise shortages the next winter "will mean substantially less jobs" and "could interfere with economic recovery." On August 20, an attorney for the Transcontinental Gas Pipe Line Corp. told the FPC that it anticipated a gas shortage much more severe than that of the 1974–75 winter. A week later, Ford resumed his doleful chant. At a special White House meeting on natural gas matters with seventeen governors, he warned that nationwide there would be a natural gas shortfall of 15 percent and cutbacks of as much as 45 percent above the previous year, with some eastern states—notably North Carolina, Virginia, and Maryland—hit hardest. Since by law the household consumer must be served before the industrial customer, this forecast, if it came to pass, meant that many industries would be hit doubly hard and many thousands of people would be out of jobs.

As usual, the FPC exploited the atmosphere of panic by further undermining legal price controls. In the previous two years it had lost half a dozen court decisions, usually with the federal courts issuing scathing denunciations of the FPC's abandonment of its duty to defend consumers. In one case (*Public Service Commission, State of New York* v. *Federal Power Commission,* 511 F. 2d 338, 1975), the court had said that until Congress decided to decontrol natural gas prices, it was the duty of the courts to force the FPC to operate legally and "not abandon their responsibility by acquiescing in a charade or a rubber stamping of nonregulation in agency trappings." Unusually strong words, indeed. But the FPC no longer responded to insults. No sooner did the courts knock down one of its lawless decisions than the FPC blandly came forward with another. This time, as panic followed the pronouncements of imminent shortages, it ruled that hard-pressed industries could buy directly from producers at the wellhead without FPC price approval. It was, of course, a decision that violated the very statute on which the FPC was founded. The one dissenting commissioner, William L. Springer, accurately complained that, under the ruling, "someone who desires to purchase natural gas may go into the field . . . and pay whatever price the market will bear and transport it through an interstate pipeline. *This is exactly what the Natural Gas Act was intended to prevent.*" But the FPC majority ignored such complaints and offered their old argument that the higher prices would result in more supplies.[13]

The first deal struck under the new FPC arrangement was between Dan River Inc. of Danville, Virginia, a major textile manufacturer, to buy natural gas from a Texas firm at a cost nearly *three times higher* than the current price interstate pipelines were allowed to charge. Other industries were lining up to pay even higher prices.

The Washington *Post* admitted that the FPC ruling was a violation of the law but editorially praised it for that: "This new procedure would constitute an elegant evasion of the regulatory principle. But since the principle is a bum one and is creating serious trouble for industry in this part of the country, the evasion is useful and welcome."

*

With another round of frightening forecasts coming out of industry and the Administration every other week, Congress got scared. Most members seemed willing to capitulate to industry's demands; the principal dispute seemed to be over whether the gas prices should be freed from regulation partially and temporarily, or whether they should be freed wholly and permanently. Deregulation bills began whistling into the hopper. Other deregulation amendments entered Congress slyly, tied

---

13. The FPC's argument that decontrols would result in lush supplies was repeated so often—it was repeated every time the Commission raised prices, which was often enough—that it finally took on the sheen of a truism. But in fact it was quite inaccurate. History proved that supplies were most bountiful under controlled low prices, meagerest under semidecontrolled high prices. Senator James Abourezk made this point in a March 1, 1975, *Nation* magazine article: "The claim that regulation has not worked is a rewriting of history that assumes the public to have a very short memory indeed. From the advent of federal regulation in 1954 until 1969, the volume of natural gas sold in interstate commerce increased dramatically—from 5 trillion cubic feet in 1954 to 14 trillion cubic feet in 1969—and the largest portion of this growth occurred during 1961–1969, when the wellhead price was relatively stable, at approximately 17 cents per 1,000 cubic feet (Mcf). Though it is often forgotten now, natural gas was in oversupply as recently as the mid-1960s, after a decade of federal regulation. Thus for at least fifteen years, until 1969, regulation of natural gas prices by the Federal Power Commission did work to assure the nation an adequate supply of this basic energy source at a reasonable price . . .

"Beginning in 1970, the Nixon appointees on the commission accepted the oil industry's premise that the way to avoid impending shortages of natural gas was to allow higher prices; and when these higher prices led not to increased supplies but to even greater shortages the commission responded with still higher prices . . ." In four years it tripled the price of new gas—and the "shortages" were worse than ever.

onto bills that at first glance seemed only to relate to such arcane matters as the import duties on platinum and carbon. One deregulation amendment was tucked into a bill to provide for the duty-free entry of a telescope into Hawaii.

The Senate moved faster than the House. With fellows like Senators Russell Long and John Tunney hustling members, it passed, 58 to 32, a bill deregulating prices permanently, a move which, if seconded by the House, would cost consumers from $45 billion to $75 billion more for gas over the next five years, according to a Library of Congress study. Industry, of course, was ecstatic. David H. Foster, executive vice-president of the Natural Gas Supply Committee, a lobby, praised the Senate for its "courage."

But the House kept lumbering along at its customarily slower pace, and by the time Chairman Harley Staggers' Interstate and Foreign Commerce Committee was ready, in December, to vote on a piece of emergency legislation, the natural gas emergency had begun to disappear. On the West Coast, a sharp-eyed reporter began to notice the evaporation of the fraud. Wrote Bruce Johansen in the Seattle *Times,* November 27:

"The Great Natural Gas Shortage, announced with banner headlines during the summer and early fall, now appears to be dying with hardly a whimper."

Johansen saw the shortage as having been contrived to pressure Congress, and he squeezed a candid admission from an industry journalist on that point.

"Several months before the Senate vote," wrote Johansen, "the Federal Energy Administration, which favors decontrol, issued a report which said as many as 500,000 jobs might be lost to natural-gas shortages during the coming winter . . .

"After the Senate vote to decontrol gas prices, some F.E.A. officials began privately to recant some of their earlier dire predictions.

"Meanwhile, the *Pipeline & Gas Journal,* an industry magazine published in Dallas, had been playing a different tune all along.

" 'Unless the ice age returns this winter, United States gas-distribution utilities should be able to supply the critical residential and other top-priority gas needs of their customers,' Dean Hale, editor of the *Journal,* said in an article published about the same time the F.E.A. was predicting 500,000 lost jobs because of gas shortages.

" 'Overall, the gas industry is apparently well-prepared for the winter season despite press reports of "big shortages of natural gas," ' Hale wrote . . .

"Gas shortages this year are expected to be only slightly more severe than the average, according to the *Pipeline & Gas Journal,* which relies on the same industry statistics that are given to the government.

"Then what was the genesis of the F.E.A.'s alarming report?

"Stephen Reese, assistant editor of the *Journal*, said 'people [in the gas industry] open up more with us.'

" 'They [the industry] didn't propagate a series of lies to scare people . . .' Reese said. 'But if they think a little scare will get the Congress off dead center . . .

" 'There's gas in plenty of places. They've drilled wells and capped them,' Reese said."

*

The oil industry—taking full advantage of the recent FPC ruling that allowed 60-day "emergency" sales at unregulated prices—"discovered" it had plenty of gas, after all, to take care of everybody willing and able to pay uncontrolled prices. The states that once were threatened with great loss of jobs, now were merely threatened with extraordinarily high costs.

Consequently, Chairman Staggers and other members of his committee, recognizing that the issue of natural gas pricing was enormously complex and controversial, decided to put off any consideration of a long-term solution to the problem and to simply whip out some common-sense remedy to get the nation through the 1975–76 winter. It was also obvious, as Staggers told one reporter, that plenty of gas was available, so the problem was not an actual shortage of gas; the problem was how to meet the producer-hijackers' demands at a level sufficiently high to dissuade them from destroying the country—but to make the payoff on a temporary basis.

On December 2, Staggers' committee voted out just such a bill: it provided emergency methods for allowing job-stricken areas to buy gas at partly decontrolled prices. But it was a short-term bill. Staggers wrote to House Speaker Albert asking that the bill be placed on the "suspension" calendar on December 15 or 16. A bill placed on the suspension-of-the-rules calendar can be voted only up or down; it cannot be amended. Staggers wanted it that way because, if the bill were amendable, the oil and gas industry, through their many friendly members, would obviously have a chance to amend it to death. The industry wanted the Senate's total deregulation bill, not Staggers' temporary deregulation bill. Albert— coming to the aid of his oil pals—refused Staggers' request, ordering him to go instead through the Rules Committee and get the standard ruling to bring the bill to the floor. This would have meant his bill could be amended, so Staggers refused.

At that point, the Rules Committee—which was run by men whom Albert had appointed—took two drastic and highly unusual steps, both of them serious breaches of House protocol.

In the first place, the existing rules of the Rules Committee provided that no bill would be taken up that late in the session, or even be considered by the Rules Committee, unless it was submitted by the chairman of the committee having jurisdiction (in this case, Staggers) as an emergency matter. Staggers not only refused to submit the bill as an emergency; he refused to submit it at all through the Rules Committee. Nevertheless, the Rules Committee went ahead and scheduled the legislation for floor action, again on instructions from Albert.

In the second place, it is standard procedure for the chairman of the subcommittee in which the legislation originated to handle a bill on the floor. In this case, that would have meant Representative John Dingell, who was opposed to total deregulation. The Rules Committee ignored this tradition and adopted instead a rule with an extraordinary provision authorizing Speaker Albert to recognize *any* member of the committee—even a member who wanted to kill the bill—to bring the bill up for debate.

Representative Bob Eckhardt, who at that time (oil campaign money hadn't yet intimidated him) was still opposed to gas price decontrol, said Albert's betrayal of Staggers' committee's work was a rare performance of bad faith in an institution that holds tradition to be sacred.

"Members are usually very courteous to each other," he said, "and committees are punctilious in their interrelations. When customs of restraint and deference are flouted in so cavalier a fashion, one seeks an explanation."

Eckhardt's own explanation was that Albert's betrayal was merely the last act in "the stratagem of the oil and gas lobby"—a stratagem that moved expertly through several stages: from the panic raised by the industry and by the Ford administration with false warnings of a natural gas shortage, to a hurried manipulation of the Senate into passing a total decontrol bill, to the perversion of the House's rules. When many billions of dollars are at stake, the oil lobby is willing to neglect some of the niceties.

For the most part, the press had been silent about the natural gas confrontation or had given it the most cursory attention. Eckhardt tried to get the Washington *Star* to write something about Albert's misuse of the House rules, but the *Star*'s management turned him down. Over at the Washington *Post* the reception was even colder. As for the New York *Times*, there was some question as to whether anyone on its staff knew how to spell natural gas. In this fight, the public was strictly on its own. And the way the House showdown was being rigged seemed to indicate that only a miracle could stop permanent decontrol of gas prices. Meantime, there would be further delays on the vote, and the showdown would not take place until early the next year.

* * *

Since 1970, the Federal Trade Commission had been trying against great odds to see whether the American Gas Association's natural gas reserve reporting program was routinely distorted downward as a way to influence prices. Frustrated in its effort to get accurate data from the AGA, the Federal Trade Commission's Bureau of Competition tried to subpoena the books of the companies—Continental, Exxon, Gulf, Mobil, Pennzoil, Shell, Standard of California, Standard of Indiana, Superior, Texaco, and Union—that operated in the lushest fields in the nation, in southern Louisiana. The companies fought back in court, trying to quash the subpoenas, losing one round and winning the next (with the help of the same Judge Hart mentioned earlier in this chapter). As the court battle dragged out, four of the companies—Gulf, Union, Continental, and Pennzoil—began to supply some documents, but the other seven continued to balk. By 1975, the Bureau of Competition staff had collected enough information not only from cooperative producers but from other sources—the major interstate pipeline companies, the FPC, the IRS, and the U.S. Geological Survey—to convince it that, in the words of one staff report, "the AGA reserve reporting procedures are tantamount to collusive price rigging," and it recommended that the FTC file an antitrust suit against the AGA itself. When, in July, the FTC rejected this recommendation, it looked as though the investigation that had lasted four and a half years was as good as dead.

The Bureau of Competition tried to salvage some of its investigation by leaking the most fascinating portions to Congressman Moss's Oversight and Investigations Subcommittee. The Bureau of Competition staff had discovered that producers kept what were called "proved reserve ledgers." The FPC had never known about these ledgers when it was gaily raising rates. The ledgers, which contain a company's most conservative estimate of proven reserves, showed that the reserve figures which the AGA gave to the FPC for pricing purposes *were 24 percent less* than the companies estimated in their proved reserve ledgers.

In short, the companies were pulling the old trick: using two sets of books.

Moss's investigators picked up the crusade and carried on, though for the moment much of their work was aimed not at the companies but at the FPC, to show how dreadfully complaisant the FPC had been to the industry's misconduct. In July, Moss's staff put together this portrait of an agency gone to seed:

• The FPC's own staff, after checking thirty-one leases, concluded that the AGA's reserve estimates were 1.7 trillion cubic feet too low. An FTC recheck on the same thirty-one leases showed that the FPC staff had been too conservative—actually, the AGA figures were 2.4 trillion cubic feet too low.

The FPC did nothing about it.

• The U.S. Geological Survey had reported that of 1,068 tracts leased in offshore Gulf of Mexico since 1970, forty-eight were producing, one hundred and five were producible but shut in, and nine hundred and one had never been explored. Five years after being leased, they were simply being shelved, waiting for higher prices before the companies would sink a drill. In fact, in some instances leases had been held without production for thirteen years.

The FPC had done nothing to compel production and had not asked the U.S. Geological Service to require production, though it had the power to do so.

• In recent months, there had been a surprisingly rapid drop in the amount of gas delivered from the southern Louisiana fields.

The FPC had not sought an explanation.

• In the Natural Gas Act, Congress gave the FPC the same enforcement power it gave the Securities and Exchange Commission in the Securities Act of 1933. In an average year, the SEC was making about twenty criminal referrals to the Justice Department, recommending indictments against thirty-five potential defendants. Convictions were obtained in more than 80 percent of the SEC's cases.

The FPC had not made a criminal referral to the Justice Department since 1961.

The SEC was bringing about two hundred injunctive actions every year. Nobody around Washington could remember the FPC's *ever* taking injunctive action against a lawbreaker.

• The FPC was constantly propagandizing for deregulation of prices and misleading the public as to what such a move would cost. It estimated that the extra annual cost for deregulated gas would be only $1 billion. But this estimate was based on the idiotic assumption that contracts in force before deregulation would remain in effect *after* deregulation. In fact, every contract written since 1970 had contained a cancellation clause in the event of deregulation. The FPC's estimate also assumed that new supplies of natural gas would jump only about 50 percent in price. A more realistic forecast came with the revelation of a confidential internal memorandum from the corporate financial planning department of Getty Oil Co., which said that the wellhead price of natural gas would probably jump 400 percent within a year if decontrolled, with a resulting 10.7 percent increase in the average homeowner's gas bill. But the impact of decontrol on consumers' utilities bills was, in fact, the least significant burden and the least difficult to cope with. Much more burdensome were the indirect costs. Utility consumers could turn down the thermostats, insulate their homes. But what could the consumer do to compensate for the natural gas prices that went into food production—into fertilizer, into gas-driven irrigation pumps, into the operation of crop-drying machinery? Synthetic fibers are made from natural gas feedstocks and most clothing is made entirely or in part from synthetic fibers. Natural gas feedstocks go into plastics, many paper products, many de-

tergents used around the home. How does the consumer combat these indirect cost increases, even if aware of them, as most consumers are not?
The FPC acted as if these indirect costs—the biggest and most insidious
of the lot—simply did not exist.

In short, the Federal Power Commission had become a mockery of the
regulatory concept. When it operated at all, it usually operated to the
detriment of consumers.

But the pockmarked portrait that emerged from Moss's hearings in the
summer of 1975 was no longer of much concern to Chairman Nassikas.
By that time, he was on his way out, a lame-duck chairman, just hanging
around until his replacement was appointed.[14] He appeared before the
subcommittee with his usual attitude of certitude. The economic wreckage and social debris littering the landscape as the result of FPC rate increases did not trouble him, apparently. But he did make one admission
that was stunning. After presiding over many billions of dollars of rate
increases based on AGA figures, he now admitted to the subcommittee:

"I have been concerned for years about the facts and figures supplied
by the AGA." He admitted that there were "gross deficiencies" in the
American Gas Association's reporting program. Now that it was really
too late to hold him accountable to such doubts and suspicions—he was
admitting it.

Moss did not appear to be terribly grateful.

* * *

OPEC was stimulating a fascinating display of hypocrisy. On the one
hand, Henry Kissinger was mumbling a lot of nonsense about going to
war with OPEC nations if they brought on economic "strangulation." On
the other hand, quite a few former top officials—former Treasury Secretary John B. Connally, former Secretary of State William P. Rogers, former Attorney General Richard G. Kleindienst, former Defense Secretary
Clark M. Clifford, and former Vice-President Spiro Agnew—had gone to
work for the OPEC dollar in one way or another (attorney, agent, lobbyist, etc.). The height of irony was reached when, in February, only a
few days after Kissinger's oblique threats of military action against
OPEC, the Pentagon acknowledged that it was awarding a $77 million
contract to a Los Angeles firm to train Saudi Arabian troops in more
efficient techniques for protecting their oil fields. Were the Saudis potential enemies or not? "It's a bit confusing to me," said Senator Jackson.

---

14. Another notable departure in 1975 was made by FPC Commissioner Rush Moody,
Jr., the Texas lawyer who stepped down with a bitter denunciation of Congress for
failing to deregulate gas prices. Congressman Moss replied that since Moody joined
the Commission, in November 1971, natural gas prices had been raised from 19 cents
per 1,000 cubic feet to 58 cents, "with no appreciable increase in natural gas
supplies."

If the oil-producing countries were looked upon as enemies, you couldn't tell it by the performance of academe. In their characteristic way, colleges and universities across the country were lining up to beg for a handout from OPEC. The American Association of State Colleges and Universities said it would be happy to help Saudi Arabia develop teacher training programs for a mere $5.5 million. Georgetown University's School of Foreign Service said it hoped the Arab oil crowd would contribute half of the school's $6-million goal to finance an "institute for studies of Arab international relations and development." University of Indiana officials said they were looking for some educational (and financial) ties with Saudi Arabia. And so it went. As reports of white-robed emirs buying up golden toilet bowls and gawdy hotels floated around the campuses, the noble professors could not resist the call.

OPEC's successes stirred "oil experts" into a froth of wishful thinking. In January, the Brookings Institution, a private study foundation in Washington that frequently lends its scholars to the government, held an assembly of American specialists on energy problems and used the occasion to make public a 473-page report, *Energy and U.S. Foreign Policy*. The heart of the report was a prediction that OPEC would very likely disintegrate by 1978. Richard D. Erb, a fellow of the Council on Foreign Relations, predicted in the Washington *Post* that if OPEC raised its prices in 1975, "they will expose themselves to the very high risk that they will lose control of the price of oil within two years." Charles T. Maxwell, of the Wall Street firm of Cyrus J. Lawrence Inc., told the New York *Times* that "the world cannot live with the current level of oil prices and this is certain to be made clear to Middle East producers over the next year," with a slight drop in price coming in 1975 and "significant reductions . . . eventually." Unfortunately for their predictions, OPEC would in 1979 more than double the price of its oil.

*

From this distance in time, it might seem that such forecasts were ridiculously cocky. But in fact, there was good reason for such optimism, and the predictions might have been brought to fruition *if* the U.S. Government had used its splendid advantage of 1975—a real, honest-to-goodness oil glut—in a merciless assault on the OPEC stronghold.

To be sure, OPEC's leaders were still strutting about as if their position were impregnable. In an especially offensive interview with Oriana Fallaci, Saudi Arabia's Yamani boasted: "We can extract as much as 11 million barrels a day, but we are limiting ourselves to 3½. This makes us a power to be reckoned with both by producing and consuming countries. To ruin the other countries of the OPEC, all we have to do is produce to our full capacity; to ruin the consumer countries, we only have to reduce our production. In the first case, the price would fall noticeably;

in the second, the price would rise not by 35, but by 40, 50, even 80 percent. We can dictate our conditions to all, even within OPEC."

But very probably he was wrong about that. Because of the enormous glut of oil that existed worldwide in mid-1975, OPEC had had to cut production 30 percent below the preembargo production level and 40 percent below production capacity to keep prices from falling. In some OPEC countries, this was creating quite a strain. If Saudi Arabia had high-handedly increased its output, it easily could have triggered a rebellion among the less endowed producing nations. And if it had chosen to retaliate against the United States by further cutting its production, just how much farther could it have cut below 3½ million barrels and stayed in the game? (This interview with Fallaci was the first time Saudi Arabia had publicly admitted it had dropped so far below its normal flow of 9 to 10 million.)

Just how drastic the world's oversupply of oil was could be seen in the decline in the world tanker fleet. The glut had sent more than 10 percent of the tanker fleet to dry dock. Before the oil embargo started, in October 1973, spot-chartering (one or two trips) a supertanker for the 11,000-mile round trip from Rotterdam to the Persian Gulf hit a record cost of $8.8 million. By mid-1975, the spot-charter price for the Rotterdam run had sunk to $800,000. "These ships are being chartered for less than they cost to run," said William Slick, senior vice-president of Exxon. "I don't see how they can afford to operate."

The mood of the nation was such that the Administration would have had strong support if it had used the glut to fight back. More than a few leaders had come around to the belligerency of M. A. Adelman, professor of economics at the Massachusetts Institute of Technology, who for many months had taken the position that "the United States has no need for Arab oil," for it could buy a sufficiency from other oil-producing countries. He scorned "the eagerness of the United States to cooperate with the cartel" and saw it as a return "to the 1930s—the devil's decade, somebody has called it—when the nations of Europe each tried to deal with the tiger in the hopes he would go eat somebody else." Civilized countries, he said, could not negotiate successfully with barbarians. "The super-subtle diplomat is simply no match for the fellow who grabs what's within reach and then asks if you want to fight to get it." His solution: turn our backs on them. His was an extreme position, of course, but even the wobbly Washington *Post* was urging that the Administration sharply reduce imports by imposing a quota, thus helping to drown OPEC in its own oil. Others joined the call for bold action. In January, the Senate Foreign Relations Subcommittee on Multinational Corporations urged President Ford to initiate a mandatory slash of 15 percent in oil imports over a three-year period (this was 2½ times larger than the cut proposed by Ford) and to ration gasoline if necessary. The subcommittee's chairman, Senator Frank Church, suggested that we begin viewing the major OPEC nations as enemies, not as allies: "It is time we stopped viewing Saudi Arabia and Iran as pawns in the cold war with the Soviet Union. They have demonstrated that they have the will and the capacity to impose great economic harm on the oil-consuming world. Indeed, they have achieved a greater degree of destabilization in the West than the Communists have ever been able to achieve."

Support for this position came from an unusual source: the general board of the AFL-CIO, usually a cautious and even reactionary group. Meeting in emergency session in January, the labor fossils showed an unusual burst of spirit by calling for a *total* ban on oil imports from Arab nations that took part in the 1973-74 embargo. Like the Church subcommittee, the labor bosses also called for tough rationing at home to compensate for any resulting shortages. Criticizing Kissinger for "paying tribute" to Arab oil sheikhs by consenting to higher oil prices, AFL-CIO President George Meany said, "We will continue to pay until the United States deals with the blackmailers in the manner that they deserve. No tribute, no foreign aid, no trade, no jet fighters—nothing, until the blackmail stops."

In March, the New York *Times* reported that several high-ranking, dissident energy and defense officials had outlined an "alternate strategy" for winning freedom from the Persian Gulf *bandidos*. The proposal, barely disguised criticism of Kissinger's policy of playing along with Iran and Saudi Arabia, was for shifting our marketing emphasis to other parts of the world: to Venezuela, Mexico, Nigeria, and possibly Canada. Although at the moment Canada and Venezuela were cutting back sharply on their exports to the United States, the dissenters argued that relations could be improved and that with better relations and financial and technological help from the United States, we could get their cooperation. "If we devoted to Canada one tenth of the attention we devote to Iran and Saudi Arabia, we might get somewhere," one of the highest-ranking dissenters told *Times* reporter Edward Cowan. "In Venezuela, we have a real problem. The Venezuelans have a tremendous oil income rolling in and they have a conscious policy of using that dough to gain influence in Latin America. What do we do? We just let Venezuela fall into the sinkhole of policy we call Latin America. President [Carlos Andrés] Pérez is interested in the development of his country. We could be extremely helpful to him just as we are helping the Shah of Iran and the King of Saudi Arabia develop their countries."

But instead of trying to force OPEC to its knees, Ford, Kissinger, and the oil companies were going out of their way to prop it up and to sustain it through this period of strain. We were importing *more* from the Arab countries and Iran than ever before—from Iran, leader of the price gougers, we were importing *70 percent* more; we were importing 10 percent of our foreign oil from Iran.

There were, in fact, clear signs from the Ford administration that it did not want OPEC to lower its prices. In June, Ford said he thought another price increase of, say, 8 percent by OPEC could be "justified," although that little "justified" increase alone would add $2 billion to the nation's fuel bill.[15]

So it hardly came as a surprise that Ford and Kissinger received with such equanimity OPEC's 10 percent price increase, voted after a stormy session in Vienna, full of theatrics. Jim Hoagland, the wise reporter covering Middle Eastern affairs for the Washington *Post*, reported from Vienna:

"Suspicions have now arisen . . . that the United States does not in its heart of hearts want oil prices lowered.

"Sheikh Zaki Yamani, the Saudi petroleum minister, has told friends that the veiled threats against OPEC from Secretary of State Henry Kissinger and others serve only to increase the resolve of other OPEC countries to demonstrate their political independence by raising prices.

"Iran, a close ally of the United States, manipulates such statements to strengthen resolve in the camp of the price hawks, Yamani is reported to have said. He is also known to have said recently that high-level U.S. officials, including Kissinger, who visit Saudi Arabia have never seriously discussed lowering prices with him."

* * *

The financial world shivered slightly when, in February, Arabs bought controlling interest in the Bank of the Commonwealth, in Detroit, a bank that, though in deep financial trouble, had more than $1 billion in assets and fifty-seven branches throughout Michigan. It was Detroit's fourth-largest bank. The invasion of the OPEC money was just beginning. Where would it end?

In March, the International Monetary Fund reported that in the preceding year seventeen oil-producing nations took in $133 billion—giving them a trade surplus of $97 billion for 1974. By contrast, the United States, Canada, Japan, and the industrial nations of Western Europe wound up with a combined trade deficit for the year of $40 billion. George McGhee, a former under secretary of state for political affairs who had been at the center of the oil revolution, said of the transfer of

---

15. In July, the World Bank, under the presidency of that great populist Robert McNamara, tacitly gave its approval to OPEC price increases and suggested that low-income countries—which currently were being drained of $8 billion annually by OPEC—should pull themselves out of their economic crisis by exporting more goods. Like clay pots.

money from oil consumers to oil producers, "Nothing this drastic has occurred before in modern times, if ever."

The transfer of money meant also a transfer of power. When Secretary of State Kissinger said, in the fall of 1974, that military action against the oil producers was not out of the question, the Arabs pulled great hunks of their money from U.S. banks and transferred it to British banks—and with the transfer came a long slide in the dollar's value and a strengthening of the British pound.

What other political uses did the OPEC countries intend for their money to perform? Recently, it had been disclosed that several Arab countries were trying to exclude from underwriting syndicates some investment banks controlled by Jews here and in Europe.

According to Citibank's economics department, of the excess petrodollars that were accumulated by the OPEC countries during 1974, about $11 billion came back to the United States, $1 billion of it in real estate and other portfolio investments, about $5 billion in government securities, and the remaining $5 billion in bank deposits. In addition, OPEC already had an undisclosed deposit of billions in U.S. banks from previous years. As mentioned earlier, most of these deposits were in demand accounts—meaning they could be withdrawn on short notice. In turn, the banks had made billions of dollars in loans to needy nations on long-term bases. It was a touchy situation. What if the OPEC countries became angry and demanded their billions? Could the banks pay up? Just how dangerous was the situation?

Those questions could not be answered unless the federal government knew what concentration of OPEC money was held in which particular banks. In a series of hearings stretching from July through October, Senator Church's Multinational Corporations Subcommittee tried to find out. Senator Church, declaring that "we *have* to have the information," said he would prefer it if the banks divulged the information voluntarily, but that if they didn't, "we have subpoena powers." The threat didn't work. The ten largest banks, which were the only ones receiving the OPEC funds, flatly refused to divulge any information about their depositors, and officials of the Federal Reserve Board and of the State Department urged the subcommittee not to press the matter. Jack Blum, associate counsel of the subcommittee, acknowledged publicly that "we got these polite 'Thank you but no thank you's' from a few and an extremely impolite 'You can go straight to blazes' from the largest." Would Church carry out his threat and issue the subpoenas? No, that was just a bluff. And OPEC had a better bluff. It warned—or rather, Saudi Arabia and Iran, which controlled four fifths of the deposits, warned—that if the banks disclosed one single penny of their deposits, they would withdraw everything. Since that could easily have resulted in a catastrophe to several individual banks—three banks, First National City, Chase, and Morgan

Guaranty were believed to be holding 75 percent of the deposits—and perhaps a catastrophe for the banking system, OPEC's bluff triumphed. Church and his panel got nothing. Absolutely nothing.

Which left the United States Government in the peculiar position of operating in the dark as to how much control a group of hostile foreigners had over its banking system. The hearings ended with Jerome Levinson, chief counsel for the subcommittee, accurately describing a bomb that Congress couldn't even get its hands on, much less defuse:

"In a nutshell, my feeling is that we have a situation developing in which there is a very real possibility that it will blow up, and that once again people will say, Why didn't the Congress know? and the fact of the matter is this subcommittee made an attempt to know and then was told it is too sensitive for you to know; therefore, we don't know, and this subcommittee walked away from the problem.

"What is the problem? The problem is that there is a concentration of deposits from a few depositors in a few very large New York banks which are central and critical to the banking system, and these same banks are making very large balance-of-payments loans to oil-importing countries. In effect, those depositors have it within their power, as Governor Coldwell [Philip E. Coldwell, a governor of the Federal Reserve] told us in very elegant terms, to create an extremely serious disturbance in the U.S. financial system and, therefore, in the international financial system. If that occurs, the questions will be asked: How did it occur without anyone knowing that this situation was allowed to develop? Who allowed it to develop? Why didn't the Congress know it was developing? Why was U.S. foreign policy allowed to be subject to this vulnerability?"

The invasion of the OPEC dollars would become even scarier in the years ahead, and other hearings would be held, and no satisfaction would be gained from them.

1 9 7 6

"A billion dollars isn't what it used to be."

NELSON BUNKER HUNT

When, on October 9, 1975, the Senate had almost done the unthinkable, coming so close to voting for the breakup of the major oil companies, a stunned silence hung momentarily over the industry, and in the Petroleum Club of Houston, it is safe to conjecture, there was the smell of rich sweat.

Smug, arrogant, deceitful, dishonest Big Oil had always had its way in the past. Senator Adlai Stevenson summed up the history of its successes: "What has passed for an energy policy in the past was made in the boardrooms of the nation's major oil companies. Our national energy priorities have been based on the premise that 'What was good for Exxon is good for the country.'" Over the years, Big Oil almost always got the tax breaks it wanted, got the import quotas it wanted, got to rip up the ecology of Alaska the way it wanted, got to blacken our beaches with the kind of sloppy exploitation it wanted, got the prices it wanted. Stevenson was right: "Almost every time there has been a choice between what is best for big oil and what is best for the nation, big oil has won."

And then, suddenly, Big Oil saw in the Senate's divestiture vote the possibility—not certain by a long shot but strong enough to keep the boardroom lights on late into the night—that it just conceivably might not be able to withstand the battering ram of the vandals at the gate. Polls showed that the public—even if it didn't have the foggiest notion of what divestiture was all about—would approve congressional action to tame the oil companies. The belief that some real change was in the offing even began to take hold of top bureaucrats. John Hill, deputy chief of the Federal Energy Administration, predicted, "There's bound to be a major change in the structure of the oil industry within the next five years. Forces have been unleashed here that can't be stopped."

But the major oil companies were determined to stop them, or at least turn them aside, by brilliant deviousness. Inspired by the close call of October and convinced that they were fighting for their very Olympian existence (a conviction that was, as things turned out, hilariously inflated), the oil companies responded with unusual swiftness, resilience, and imagination.

Suddenly, the most important people in the business were no longer the geologists and engineers and tax accountants, but the Herb

Schmertzes, who were expert in propaganda. Industry was ready to fight with all the ballyhoo it could buy and to do it, for a change, efficiently. No more would it try, as in the rude old days, to convince Congress of the righteousness of its cause simply by hitting members over the head with satchels of campaign money. Gone was the clumsy era when it tried to convince the public it was doing a good job by offering a free kitchen glass with every fill-up. Big Oil was now prepared to be sophisticated and smooth and, well, "thoughtful." Most of the money would be stuffed this time not into congressional pockets but into the wallets of slick ad men and slicker lobbyists.

The affluence and the efficiency of the campaign that rolled through 1976 stunned some members of Congress. Said Senator Birch Bayh, another principal sponsor of divestiture legislation, "During my fourteen years in the Senate, I have never seen such an extensive, elaborate, pervasive, carefully orchestrated and costly lobbying campaign. There has never been a legislative issue in which an industry has resorted to such massive use of paid advertising to affect public opinion. It is really awesome." Just how costly it was, was anybody's guess. Martin Lobel, the lawyer who helped draft Senator Abourezk's bill, estimated that during the year following the October 1975 near miss, the major oil companies had spent "over 100 billion bucks. Oh yeah. Their stuff is everywhere. You take a look at this issue of *Columbia Journalism Review*. I flipped through it briefly and almost every ad in there was antidivestiture by one of the major companies. You take a look at TV. There hasn't been a news broadcast that I've seen that hasn't been sponsored by one of the oil companies. They do this institutional advertising, very low key, and they are the only ones who have that kind of bread to do that."

The intense concern, almost panic, of the major oil companies, launched them upon a diversity of counterpropaganda that at times was downright camp. Thus it was that Exxon put together a 3-act musical, *America's Way,* written around three principal characters—The Spirit of Bureaucracy, Exxon Oil, and Consumer—and had it performed in twenty cities to audiences (Exxon claimed) totaling fifteen thousand. The show, in Exxon's own words, was intended through "song and comedy and drama to prove how two invincible forces of good free enterprise and individual initiative created a spirit of achievement." It also was intended to prove, with a minimum of comedy, that divestiture was a bad, bad thing and quite contrary to the spirit of achievement.

But, for the most part, industry's effort was the standard approach: overwhelming their own employees and stockholders, as well as service clubs, newspaper and TV offices, et cetera, with written material, speeches, and personal visits. In midyear I asked the American Petroleum Institute to send me a sample of all the antidivestiture material it had sent out in the first half of 1976; I received a package eight inches thick weighing nine pounds. In July, the Washington *Star's* energy reporter Roberta Hornig did a survey and found that, among the majors, the most active propagandists had set up programs guaranteed to reach well over 6 million people. Exxon was typical in its elaborateness. It had held a total of 600 meetings with its 45,000 employees and 6,000 retirees, urging them to write their congressmen; mailed letters to its 650,000 shareholders and held 20 two-day meetings with its 23,000 dealers and jobbers to make the same appeal; 11 top Exxon officials had visited 43 newspapers and TV stations in 31 cities. Texaco, aside from making its pitch via brochures sent to credit-card holders and 371,000 stockholders and in meetings with its 70,000 employees, produced one of the cleverest antidivestiture television commercials. On it, the announcer piously intoned:

"To get you the gasoline and oil you need, a lot of complex pieces must come together very efficiently. Such as finding oil in places where no one has discovered it before, constructing huge pipe lines, building complex refineries . . . supplying these products to thousands of outlets in cities and towns and rural areas across the country . . . Fortunately, an oil company like Texaco is in all phases of the business so it can link the complex parts together efficiently and economically. It took a great many years to build this organization, and it's these various pieces working together that permits a company like Texaco to do its job for you."

At the time that ad hit the airwaves, the divestiture debate in Washington was in full voice; but Texaco very cleverly did not even use the word divestiture in the advertisement or allude even hazily to the legislation then before Congress, which avoided trouble with the Federal Communications Commission's "fairness doctrine." The doctrine is supposed to require stations to present both sides of controversial issues of public importance. Senators Abourezk and Bayh and Energy Action Committee Inc., a public-interest lobby, complained to the FCC that the stations should let them make a statement to balance the Texaco pitch. But the FCC turned them down. Even if the FCC had sided with them, it made its ruling—typically—too late to have done them any good, coming on April 12, 1977.

The industry propaganda task force was headed by H. J. Haynes, chairman of Standard Oil of California. The original budget was $1 million, but other millions soon followed. The task force met once a month at American Petroleum Institute headquarters in Washington, but the members could not give the time and the effort required, for they were, after all, simultaneously trying to operate oil companies. So they decided to bring in a full-time expert and ensconce him in a suite of offices at API, give him all the staff support and money he needed, and turn him loose.

Enter James B. Atkin, a blond, ruggedly handsome business blueblood with the perfect background and demeanor for the job. Son of a J. P. Morgan partner, schooled at the high Episcopalian prep Kent School and at the University of Virginia and its law school, he joined, in 1958, the San Francisco law firm to which he is still attached, Pillsbury, Madison, and Sutra, one of those modest little firms of about two hundred lawyers that help chart the legal destiny of such outfits as Standard Oil of California.

"I didn't have to sell the companies on the importance of this fight," Atkin told me when I dropped around in June to find out what he was up to. "I think every executive of every damn company is well aware of the consequences of this legislation.

"Business has been asleep while others have been questioning, attacking the role of business in our society. It takes a major issue, a major attack, like we are undergoing now, and business wakes up and says, My God, this is the product of neglect! We didn't pay enough attention to the fact that a number of people were questioning bigness, questioning why some business should be so large, asking if that is good public policy . . . I say, let's have it out in debate."

He obviously relished the showdown atmosphere. As for his present task, Atkin explained it as a simple matter of trying to prevent the company propagandists from duplicating each other and getting in each other's way. "What I try to do is to coordinate efforts between different companies. For example, if Mobil does a position paper on what dismemberment [industry spokesmen preferred that gory word to divestiture] will do to the financial community, there's no point in Exxon duplicating that." He said he tried to avoid the appearance of heavy-handedness. "If Exxon is in a position to send somebody around to visit the editors of the New York *Times* and other newspapers in that area," he said, "we'll let them do it and send Texaco's executives somewhere else. We don't want the executives of six different companies marching through the same newspaper offices."

But sometimes heavy-handedness did appear. Over in Charleston, West Virginia, Ned Chilton III, publisher of the *Gazette*, reported that the Kanawha Valley Bank, the largest bank in the state, gave a luncheon for civic leaders at the local country club and, at the suggestion of the oil industry (which picked up the bill), invited the treasurer of Shell and the treasurer of Exxon to address them on the subject of divestiture. The lecture, Chilton recalled, "was really kind of third-rate. If these guys are heavy hitters, shit, you and I are geniuses. Hell, it was just *dull*." Nevertheless, it was plentiful progaganda, quite enough for one day, so Chilton was somewhat amazed when, as he tells it, "I hadn't been back from that luncheon fifteen minutes and, I'll be a sonofabitch, in walks a guy from Atlantic Richfield, out in California. I said, 'Listen, old shoe, I've had it. I've been up there listening to your colleagues and that's as much as I can take.' So I walked him down the hall to talk to my editor. I'm not sure what position to take. The oil companies have lied to the American people so often on so many things that now, when they may be telling the truth, who can believe them?"

Atkin's crew of persuaders must have done something right; at the end of summer, only one newspaper in the country—the St. Louis *Post-Dispatch*—had come out editorially in favor of divestiture.

For dealing with members of Congress, Atkin insisted on a low-key operation. When Atkin himself approached a member of the federal legislature, it was in the shyest tones. He said he might say something like "Would it be helpful, Senator, if we sent you a two-page memo? Would it be helpful if we sent a guy around to explain how come a drilling platform costs seven hundred and fifty million bucks these days, and why, if you strip these companies down into thirds, in effect, the ability to raise that kind of money isn't going to be as easy as now?" Nothing pushy. Just a helping hand, holding out plenty of statistics, and accurate—by his standards. "My approach is, let's not bullshit anybody with distortions of numbers. Let's set this up like we were going to court. We've got to set it up so that the poor guy who gets his ass elected to Congress has an accurate presentation of the facts." And always the facts should be wrapped in true-blue Americanism. That last was terribly important to Atkin. He did not try to hide the fact that he thought the industry's enemies were trying to drive the nation into socialism.

But, again, in the congressional operation, one did occasionally hear rumors of heavy-handedness. There were reports circulating among Senate staff members, for example, that some companies told senators if they voted for divestiture the companies might have second thoughts about building refineries in their states. And of course there was always the ubiquitous campaign dollar out there, creating a certain atmosphere. As in North Dakota, for example: Senator Quentin Burdick, a Democrat who usually sided with labor and often with liberals, was up for reelection in 1976. Many of those who voted for divestiture were his ideological friends, but Burdick repulsed them and helped try to keep their legislation bottled up in committee. Now, why would he do that? One of Burdick's friends explained the senator's predicament: "Most people don't think of it that way, but North Dakota is a pretty oily state. The first time Burdick ran for the Senate, he got a substantial chunk of loot— like, a bundle—from the oil companies. I don't actually know if he's taking money this year. But I do know that the Farmers Union is the most significant political force in North Dakota, and the Farmers Union has a co-op that owns some wells and a refinery and pipelines and retail service stations. They get some of their crude oil from the big companies, and the big boys have told them if they support divestiture their crude supply will be cut off." (Burdick, informed of his anonymous friend's ap-

praisal of the situation, at first declined to comment, then acknowledged
that he had received oil money, including some for his present campaign,
but insisted that it was "nothing substantial." He also said he had voted
against divestiture solely because he was worried about the "legal problems" that would result from it.)

Part of the industry's soft sell was in trying to make it appear that *it*
wasn't doing the selling at all. For example, one vehemently antidivestiture report written by the Energy Policy Research Project at George
Washington University and published by the University was purchased
by the American Petroleum Institute (two thousand copies) and by
Mobil (one thousand copies) and mailed to members of Congress and to
editors. From all indications, the report was sponsored by neutral
sources. On the back of the title page was the acknowledgment "This
paper was written, in part, under a grant by the National Science Foundation, Office of Energy R. & D. Policy." The copies sent to members of
Congress were accompanied by a cover letter that stated: "For the past
year and a half, the Project has been funded *primarily* by the National
Science Foundation's Office of Energy Research and Development Policy." (Emphasis added.) Both statements were somewhat misleading in
what they omitted. While it was true that the Energy Policy Research
Project had received $130,000 from the National Science Foundation
through August 31, 1976, it had *also* received $125,000 from the oil in-
dustry. That wasn't mentioned.

*

On the prodivestiture side, outside Congress, there was not an impressive amount of organized effort and, by comparison, very little money. At
about the same time that the industry was marshaling its millions of dollars and its armies of executives for the big push, a few of its critics were
planning a contrapuntal organization called the Energy Action Committee. It was the brainchild of Harold Willens, chairman of the board of
Factory Equipment Corp., in Los Angeles. In more turbulent days, Willens was best known, at least in liberal circles, for his efforts on behalf of
George McGovern's presidential race and in opposition to the Vietnam
War. On Labor Day 1975, Willens invited to his Malibu home four
friends: actor Paul Newman; Leopold Wyler, chairman of the board of
TRE Corporation; Miles Rubin, chairman of the board of Pioneer Systems Inc.; and Stanley Scheinbaum, an iconoclastic economist.

All these men are millionaires; together they decided they could spare
$500,000 for a one-year trial subsidy of the newborn Energy Action Com-
mittee (EAC). Its patrons' goal, understandably vague, came down to
this, says Willens: "We didn't think the nation's energy policy should be
decided at the Houston Oil Club. We differ individually as to whether
vertical divestiture means anything. We all agree it is a crucial issue for

reminding Americans that too much power in too few hands is as bad in economics as in politics. We all agree that vertical divestiture was the right subject for the Energy Action Committee to seize upon. We put up the front money immediately because we wanted to test public reaction in an election year. The committee has made an incredible impact. I've given my time to public interest things for fifteen years and I've never seen anything go so far with so little money."

EAC's Washington lobbyist was James Flug, an aggressive young attorney who used to work for the Kennedys, Robert and Edward, and once had quite a reputation around town for his ability to bait the National Rifle Association with gun-control legislation.

Lacking an abundance of funds, he developed craftiness: petitioning the Federal Communications Commission for equal time under the Fairness Doctrine to answer the oil companies' TV ads and, in a superior outburst of nerve, writing Mobil to suggest that that company give free space in its advertisements to EAC's argument. Mobil PR boss Schmertz responded with a one-sentence letter acknowledging that the proposal was "the height of chutzpah."[1]

Flug, like Atkin, represented the power of blather, but blather achieves its power only if the blatherer convinces his audience that he represents a significant part of the population. Energy Action alone was nothing. But it claimed to speak for, and indeed in a general way did speak for, a number of organizational allies whose total membership was sizable. Such alliances actually mean very little in Washington unless their officials energetically get involved, and in this case very few did get involved in the lobbying. Among the organizations officially endorsing vertical divestiture were the AFL-CIO (16 million members), the United Auto Workers (1.5 million), United Steelworkers (1.3 million), National Congress of Petroleum Retailers (70,000 branded dealers), Consumer Federation of America (more than 30 affiliated groups), National Farmers Union (250,000 farm families), Independent Gasoline Marketers Council (3,000 independent marketers), Marine Engineers Beneficial Association (50,000 members), United Mine Workers of America (230,000 members), National Rural Electric Cooperative Association (1,000 cooperatives servicing 70 million consumers), and Communications Workers of America (650,000 members).

*

There was one thing that could be said categorically about the opposing sides: they offered plenty of diversity of opinion. And to make it all

---

1. Were Schmertz and Flug true antagonists, or were they just playing an ideological game, or what? Only they can say; but spectators were amused that in 1980 Flug took leave of Energy Action and Schmertz took time off from Mobil and both joined Edward Kennedy's campaign for the Democratic presidential nomination.

the more interesting, scads of experts could be found to swear to the conclusions of both sides. Economists Robert J. Samuelson and Neil H. Jacoby said it would be a mistake to break up the big oil companies. F. M. Scherer, the Federal Trade Commission's top economist, said it would be a good idea. So did Walter Adams, Michigan State University's distinguished university professor of economics, who sent Senator Philip Hart a letter, signed by 133 economists from colleges and universities across the country, in support of the divestiture legislation. Big Oil and its would-be divestors offered rival claims on just about every conceivable point. For example, Exxon contended that divestiture "could" increase unemployment by one million workers, reduce U.S. personal income by $50 billion, and reduce energy production by 4 million barrels a day. The supporters of divestiture, on the other hand, claimed that the resulting increase in competition would make the oil industry, and the entire U.S. economy, healthier than ever.

In short, if the general public had to depend on the experts for advice, there was absolutely no way for it to know, or even to guess, what the effects of divestiture would be. But there was something comforting about that, for since the experts pretty well canceled each other out, amateurs did not need to apologize for their own, freewheeling judgments of the opposing arguments, which took the following patterns.

BIG OIL SAID: Complaints about monopoly are nonsense. The industry isn't controlled, as our critics contend, by twenty companies. There's plenty of competition, with 10,000 companies producing oil and natural gas, 131 companies refining oil products, 100 companies transporting oil and natural gas by pipeline, 15,000 wholesale oil distributors, and 300,000 retailers.

And where are the "giants" they talk about? No one company controls more than 11 percent of any segment of the industry: crude production, refining, transportation, or retailing, and the top eight oil companies don't control more than 57 percent of any one of those fields. Compare that to other major industries. The top eight firms in steel control 65 percent of the market; motor vehicles, 98 percent; aircraft, 89 percent; tires, 88 percent. There is less concentration in oil than in at least twenty-five other major industries.

We don't try to squash competitors. Anyone with the money and moxie is free to jump in and hunt for oil and then go peddle it anywhere he wants. Small companies can still survive and grow big. Leon Hess started out with one tank truck shortly after World War II, and today Hess is so big that it would be one of the companies broken up by this legislation.

Moreover, America needs our bigness. Only big companies can afford to build the size refineries that are needed and take the kind of gigantic risks (and losses) that go with exploration these days. Let Atkin talk for us: "The typical efficient refinery for economics of scale is about 250,000 barrels a day and costs about $750,000,000. The thing that worries the whole damn industry is, you take the gutsy unknowns, and who can afford them? An Exxon guy told me what happened to them at the Destin Dome [a field off Florida, Mississippi, and Alabama]. The industry obviously thought that was going to be a hell of a place. So Exxon went in with others on bids totalling $700,000,000. On one tract alone it joined Mobil to bid $212,000,000—the biggest bid ever offered for a single tract. And what did they get? They got dry hole after dry hole. Nothing. One big bust. Who's got the bucks to afford that kind of failure?

"When we started drilling in this country—and this country has been explored and drilled more than any other surface in the world—we found the shallower wells, we found wells that were easy and not expensive in terms of depth. But we've pretty thoroughly worked that over. Now we're looking at places where you sometimes have to go down 15,000 feet and more. We've just recently developed the technology for it. I think Phillips just got through drilling a 30,000-foot well and found gas. You can do it, but for each foot after 15,000 feet the pressures, the temperatures are tremendous, the metal stresses are tremendous. It's a technology that costs lots of bucks. The question is, if you take away the ability to go out and borrow the money, well— If you look at the financial records of these companies over the past five or six years you'll see that historically they have operated on equity capital and used their earnings and stock issues to get the money to do their job. Now they are getting heavier and heavier into the debt market because, for various reasons, the money hasn't been coming in from sales. You break up the companies, and they'll have a much harder time borrowing."

And besides all else, we're efficient. That's why we are big. We knew how to do the job better than anyone else and as a result we just naturally grew in size. Don't punish us for our efficiency.

THE PRODIVESTITURE PEOPLE REPLIED: Never mind what share of the industry is controlled by the top eight. Let's see how much is controlled by the top twenty: about 84 percent of production, 96 percent of the crude-oil pipeline shipments, 80 percent of the refinery business.

The reason we should talk about the top twenty companies—not the top eight, and most especially not one particular company—is that any discussion is misleading and irrelevant that does not take into consideration all of the major international companies and view them as a confederation. The biggest companies do not operate independently. They operate, as Senator Abourezk has expressed it, "through a complex web of crisscrossing business deals that tie them together at dozens of points." They exchange oil, they exchange tankers, they share pipeline space, they swap refined products. Senator Philip Hart was not exaggerating when he said they "meet each other daily as partners in production, transportation and/or marketing."

That's why it is ridiculous to compare the oil industry to, say, the auto industry. For all their lack of competition, the auto makers do not share the same assembly lines, and in effect the oil companies do. Colorado Senator Floyd Haskell's Special Subcommittee on Integrated Oil recently completed a study that showed 68 percent of the major oil companies were operating their wells in partnership. Overseas their partnerships are even thicker.

It's this kind of cooperation, not their bigness, that has killed competition. The big companies have split up the retail market the way the crime syndicate used to split up Chicago. When the Standard Oil Trust was supposedly broken up, in 1911, the subdivided companies simply staked out regional territories to dominate, and four of those companies, though their names and shapes have changed with mergers, are as regionally dominant today as they were sixty-five years ago. Standard of Indiana is the leading seller in fifteen states in the Midwest and the Plains; Exxon is the leading seller in fourteen states and the District of Columbia, in the East and the South; Standard Oil of California is the leading seller in eight states in the Far West and the Southwest; Mobil is the leading seller in six states in the Northeast. It may be shuffled a bit, but it's the same deck old man Rockefeller was using.

The spirit of cooperation is best exemplified in the boardroom. Since its passage, in 1914, the Clayton Act has forbidden directors to sit on boards of competing oil companies. But they get around that, with hardly a break in the conversation, by setting up indirect interlocks: Mr. X will sit on the boards of Exxon and Chase Manhattan Bank, and Mr. W will sit on the boards of Mobil and Chase Manhattan Bank. Senator Haskell's subcommittee found that sixteen First National City Bank of New York directors were affiliated with seven oil companies, while over at Chase there were eleven directors from seven oil companies, and Chemical Bank had ten directors from eight companies.

It's probably reasonable to assume that these banks and their brother institutions, where similar interlocks exist, all of whom are heavy investors in the petroleum industry, will do what they can to discourage cutthroat competition and will serve as a clearinghouse for information that will enable all the major oil companies to cooperate for mutual profit.

As for industry's romantic suggestion that the little businessman can push in at a competitive level, Atkin's own estimates as to what is required for risk capital shows how ridiculous it is to suggest that the little operator could break into oil, or compete, at a significant scale or to an effective degree. Very few little operators have $750,000,000 to spare for a refinery. The standings of the big companies over the years tell the whole story of competition. The twenty largest companies in 1954 are still the twenty largest companies, though now three of the companies are tucked away in mergers with other companies on the Top 20 list. Where are the newcomers? Where are the little companies that fought their way into the ranks of the biggies in those years? For a full generation, and longer, the power of the twenty leaders has been such that "competition" meant only a jostling for space at the rail behind the eternal leader, Standard of New Jersey (Exxon).

Which isn't to say that big is automatically bad. It is simply to say that some bigness defies natural competition, and that if competition is to be established in the oil industry, it must be imposed from outside. And it must be imposed by legislation, rather than by taking the antitrust route through the courts; that route has never led to much success. Big Oil has merged time and again with a lessening of competition; it has conspired to fix prices; it has conspired to create artificial shortages to raise prices— and almost never has it been hindered by the Justice Department or the courts in these activities.

In any event, the purpose of this legislation is not to make oil companies weak. In the divested future, all the pieces of the dismantled majors will still be plenty big enough to rate high on the list of *Fortune's* 500. The new companies, though fractions of the old, will all be plenty big enough and stable enough to entice stockmarket investments. And why fear otherwise? After all, the crude oil will be there just as before, the refineries and pipelines, too, and above all, the marketplace will still be there, expanding in the same old, profitable way. In April, when the fight was really beginning to heat up, the investment house of Paine, Webber, Jackson & Curtis sent out a report on the probable impact of divestiture. It was written by Robert E. Golden, vice-president, research. He concluded:

"Fundamentally, the industry would be essentially untouched at the operating level. Supply and distribution people might have to work overtime a bit, but refineries and marketing operations would be virtually unaffected except for the added logistics problems. There is no reason to believe exploration or producing operations would be seriously affected either . . .

"In summary, shareholders would be affected primarily by their own fears. The industry's earning power shouldn't be changed seriously one way or the other. The only difference one year after divestiture would be the shareholder would have three (or more) pieces of paper representing his ownership of a predivested company, where before he had one. He would then have the ability to be a more selective investor—choosing from time to time, as fundamentals and market prices change, to increase or decrease his interest in exploration and production, or refining and marketing, or pipelines, or whatever. Today, he must take the bad with the good."

As for Big Oil's supposed efficiency, it is an efficiency based simply on the technique of monopolizing the raw materials. That's the real reason Big Oil is so adamant about maintaining vertical integration: it guarantees a supply of something to sell at the wholesale and retail levels. When there is a crunch—as in 1973—the first ones to feel it are the independent companies, who have no secure crude-oil supply. But if Big Oil's crude production is divorced from its refineries and if everyone has the same chance to buy, you will find the independent companies just as efficient as the majors. Or more so. Officials of Ashland Oil, for example, claim that they can spot any major company something like a dollar a barrel and still beat them on prices.

*

But after the Jacobys and Samuelsons on one side had squared off with the Scherers and Adamses on the other, and all the high-level economic arguments had been fired over the public's head, it became quite clear that the conclusion of this fight would ultimately be settled—if it ever got to the floor of the Congress—not by cool reasoning at all, but by the kind of gut emotions that the oil industry had always provoked. On the one side, the oil crowd was recruiting support with the suggestion that the industry's enemies were motivated by a kind of socialism that was foreign to the American way. The divestiture crowd also appealed to patriotism. It was an odd clash of interpretations of what, exactly, American-style free enterprise stood for.

His voice blending pity with censure, Atkin said, "I think there are an awful lot of people in this country who sincerely believe and question whether the structure of American free enterprise has served its purpose and who believe that we are now evolving into a new era where there is a need for democratization of American business—to have an environmentalist on your board, to have a representative of the federal government on your board, to get the *people* more involved in how business is run." That, says Atkin, "doesn't make sense to me, because what it points to is . . . socialism. I say, let's look at Great Britain . . ."

The appeal to patriotism from the opposite direction spilled into the closing pages of a very long study of the Petroleum Industry Competition Act of 1976 (the formal title of the divestiture bill), done by the staff of the Senate Subcommittee on Antitrust and Monopoly:

"However, in the end, the case for divestiture must rest upon a value judgment about the kind of people we want to be and the kind of society we want to have. The values at stake here are clear. We must ask ourselves whether we should do business in the world through the agency of private corporations endowed with governmental powers. As the history of the Iranian Consortium demonstrates, the international companies have, in effect, been given an exemption from our laws on the grounds that they have performed special governmental functions. The present status of the international companies can be compared to Burke's description of the East India Company as 'a state in the disguise of a merchant.' Their present status challenges our fundamental belief that all men and all institutions should be subject to law, that they should be equal before the law, that there should be no special exemptions for wealth and power, that our public affairs should be conducted by public officials who are responsible to democratic institutions.

"If it is true that we must have these gigantic corporations to raise capital for new energy, to plan our economic future, that 'regulatory' arrangements between unaccountable corporate oligarchs and bureaucrats are preferable to free markets, that our corporations must wield monopoly power to compete with monopolies sponsored by other nations, then we should give free enterprise a respectful burial and not disgrace an honorable—if much abused—concept by using it to camouflage a system of corporate socialism . . .

"Granted, divestiture provides no complete solution to the problem. It offers only a very reasonable chance for somewhat lower prices, but it's a measure we owe to the world to take."

As congressional reports go, that passage reaches a very high level of rhetoric. Those staff fellows were pouring their hearts into it. Never mind questions of efficiency, never mind questions of prices and profits—they admit they could make no predictions on that point. To them, divestiture had become an issue of pure patriotism and first principles.

The same stirrings could be heard in the comments of Senator Philip Hart. He knew he was dying, and so he also knew that the vertical-divestiture fight would be probably the last chance he would have of seeing one of his oldest dreams at least begin to take shape in reality. No one in Congress had fought longer and more tirelessly for economic competition in the marketplace. No one knew better than he how futile the whole long fight had been. If he had failed, now that he neared the end he could at least joke about it all in a wistful way—and hope, even more wistfully, but still with good humor, that the imperfect divestiture bill might bring about a splinter of reform. It wasn't that he was especially down on the oil crowd. He considered them as no worse than representative of big business generally.

These were the thoughts that came to the old antitrust warrior, looking back at his, and America's, failure:

"It happened in mid-sentence during a Senate antitrust and monopoly subcommittee hearing a couple of years ago: I went blank and couldn't think of a single example of a competitive industry. Stumped, I turned to the staff. No suggestions. I tossed the question to the audience—about

150 persons who work in industry or follow antitrust matters closely, or both. Silence.

"That memory comes back now because it seems to typify a problem of those who favor divestiture for the oil industry. We argue that this will bring consumers the benefits of competition. We get back blank looks.

"People are hard put to imagine what a competitive oil industry would look or act like. They are especially hard put to imagine how competition would affect consumers.

"Frankly, I should have realized long ago that murmuring 'competition' doesn't automatically bring blissful visions to consumers' minds. They don't often get a chance to see it practiced—even in this land supposedly dedicated to the free enterprise system.

"Every one of our basic industries—such as steel, autos, copper, computers, communications—are dominated by a handful of companies that are able to control their market instead of being controlled by it. In a country of more than three hundred thousand manufacturing concerns, two hundred control more than two thirds of total manufacturing assets . . .

"During the debate on the wisdom of divestiture for this industry, we are often asked: How much money will the consumer save? Frankly, I haven't the faintest idea. Nor, I am sure, does anyone short of God . . .

"But saving money is not the only benefit competition promises consumers. The almost universal trait of monopolists is their comfort. They don't have to hustle—and they usually don't. Therefore inefficiencies creep in; technological advances are slow to be made or implemented . . . On the average, the oil industry last year spent less than one half of one percent of sales dollars on research and development . . .

"Clearly, the only noticeable competition in the industry comes from the independents. The independents, not the majors, came up with new marketing techniques, such as unmanned 'gas-and-go' stations. Innovations like this and lower prices helped them capture about 25 percent of the market. That took a bit of hustling.

"Incidentally, after the subcommittee members thought about the competition question a bit, we did come up with a very good example of a competitive industry: the hand-held calculator industry. As you may recall, about five years ago, when they first began appearing, you had to pay $300 to $500 for a model that today sells for less than $100. And you can buy simple models for less than $10. What made the difference? Competition. That's what brought improvements in technology, lower prices, and a good deal of other benefits for consumers.

"Wouldn't it be nice to see a little of that in the oil industry?"

✲

Like so many other alarums of the oil decade, this one signaled a show-down that never occurred. For a while, things went very well for the divestiture crowd. They got their bill out of the Senate Judiciary Committee Antitrust Subcommittee by a vote of 4 to 3 on April 1. They got it through the full Committee by a vote of 8 to 7 (to the surprise of the oil lobby; Atkin conceded he had called that one wrong) on June 15. Three members—Senator Robert Byrd of West Virginia; Minority Leader Hugh Scott of Pennsylvania, the great friend of Gulf Oil; and Senator Charles McC. Mathias, Jr., of Maryland, said they didn't really like the bill but they thought it should get a chance for a vote on the floor.

But it still had a very long way to go. Not only would it have to pass the Senate, it would also have to be brought up and passed by two committees in the House—Interstate and Foreign Commerce, and Judiciary—and then go before the entire House. House hearings were not even scheduled. Passage by both House and Senate was very much a long shot. And even if the bill did get through Congress, it was sure to be vetoed by President Ford. Was there enough support for the bill in Congress to override a veto? Hardly.

Besides all that, by summer the divestiture leaders were beginning to fall away. Senator Hart was too sick to care anymore. Senator Bayh had tried to use divestiture to rally voter support for his presidential candidacy, but had failed, and seemed to lose interest. There were no divestiture leaders in the House. The bill's best friends were the opposition. As Paine, Webber's vice-president Golden observed, "In their near-panic efforts to kill the issue, the integrated oil companies could very well be providing it with new life . . . There is no indication that their [the Hart-Abourezk group's] idea is catching on or gaining momentum. No vote has been taken that suggests congressmen are swinging over on the subject. Still, anything can happen. The oil industry itself may promote divestiture just because it is so vocally denouncing it. Citizens who don't understand the issue, and couldn't care less, are being bombarded with industry propaganda which may, in the end, educate them enough so they feel they must choose a side. With so complex an issue, a little knowledge could be a dangerous thing and they could choose the wrong side (wrong from the industry's viewpoint). Their biases and prejudices may outweigh even the best evidence and logic, and the result could be a grass-roots clamor for congressional action."

It was an intelligent comment, but neither Golden nor the industry really need have worried about congressional action. The men who ran the joint were prepared to see that, despite all the rhetoric, no action would be taken. The bill had been put on the Senate calendar for August 23 to September 6. But it was taken off the calendar and never put back on. Why? Atkin gave a good explanation: "My understanding is that Mr. Mansfield—and I have never met the gentleman—does not like to send senators out to run for reelection burdened with a lot of controversial votes, as on abortion or oil divestiture."

Though nobody at the time could have foreseen it, and though most of the prodivestiture lobbies that worked so hard in 1976 were convinced that in 1977 they would have their chance, the subject of vertical divestiture was never again seriously raised in Congress. It died in 1976.

And yet, to read the Democratic party platform for that year, one could not have guessed that it was dead. The platform trumpeted: "It is increasingly clear that there is no free, competitive market for crude oil in the United States. Instead, through their control of the nation's oil pipelines, refineries and marketing, the major oil producers have the capability of controlling the field and often the downstream price of almost all oil. When competition inadequate to ensure free markets and maximum benefit to American consumers exists, we support effective restrictions on the right of major companies to own all phases of the oil industry."

There it was in print: the majority party officially on record favoring vertical divestiture. And yet the issue would never again be raised in Congress? Never.

But what about horizontal divestiture? Wouldn't Congress give that one a shot? Not even a blank. Which was a pity, for horizontal divestiture—forcing the oil industry to get out of and stay out of competing energy fields (coal, solar, uranium, geothermal, shale) in order to maintain competition—made a lot of sense, and it was easy to argue for. The argument against vertical integration is complex, arcane, difficult for the layman to hold on to. But the argument against horizontal integration is simple, logical, easy to see, easy to understand. In 1976, the oil companies controlled between 26 percent and 40 percent of coal production (the lower figure came from the Haskell committee, the higher from the United Mine Workers of America). Seven of the fifteen largest coal companies were subsidiaries of oil companies. The nuclear-energy industry was being swallowed by the oil industry, which owned about 30 percent of the uranium reserves in the mid-1960s and now owned between 50 and 55 percent. As Big Oil's ownership went up 60 percent, coal prices climbed 300 percent; there was probably a connection. As for shale and geothermal lands, virtually all of those leases had gone to oil companies.

In terms of legislative strategy, getting support for horizontal divestiture could have been reduced to one question: Do you want the same wonderful people who gave you the oil crisis to get their hands on coal and nuclear power, too? Energy Action Committee founder Willens conceded that he personally believed "horizontal divestiture is infinitely more important" than vertical. Vertical divestiture might have been a valid effort in 1938, when Senator Gillette first made the push, or in 1948, when Eugene V. Rostow argued for divestiture in his book *A National*

Policy for the Oil Industry, or even in 1965, when Senator Hart first offered a plan to break up the oil companies. But now, even supporters of the plan seemed to sense that they were pushing an idea whose time had passed, that vertical divestiture in the face of a fanatical OPEC might be too risky. But horizontal divestiture was just as clearly an idea whose time had arrived and was demanding attention with great urgency. Even the boilerplate authors of the Democratic platform sensed the difference. The portion on horizontal divestiture was much more emphatic:

"We also support the legal prohibition against corporate ownership of competing types of energy, such as oil and coal. We believe such 'horizontal' concentration of economic power to be dangerous both to the national interest and to the functioning of the competitive system."

Just how dangerous it was could be seen in an exchange that had taken place at a hearing of the Senate Antitrust Subcommittee. A key witness was C. Howard Hardesty, vice-chairman of Continental Oil Company, whose subsidiary, Consolidation Coal Company, had about 9 percent of the coal market—the largest share of any oil company.

At one point in the hearing, Senator Abourezk asked Hardesty:

"Say [there was] a public utility, or a private utility, that was thinking of converting to coal, if it could find coal at a somewhat cheaper BTU equivalent than it buys oil for. Would you tell your coal subsidiary—or would you permit your coal subsidiary to undersell your oil subsidiary?"

To which Hardesty responded, "No, sir, under no circumstances." And later he added, "We would not direct a coal subsidiary, a nuclear subsidiary, to have its price changed, modified in any way so as to either compete readily against or not compete against another form of energy. I think that broadly answers your question. We are not going to play one source of energy against the other."

So much for the chances of competition in a horizontally controlled energy world.

The main reason that neither vertical nor horizontal divestiture lived beyond 1976 was that the man who would be elected President that year did not believe in them.

So long as he was campaigning for the presidency, he put on the guise of a Populist; but, once in office, he wasted little time revealing his basic proindustry bias. Nowhere was this more clearly seen than in the evolution of his positions on horizontal divestiture.

A few days before the presidential campaign opened, with the Iowa precinct caucuses in January 1976, the consumer organization Energy Action pointed out in a Des Moines *Register* advertisement that Jimmy Carter was one of the five candidates who had failed to answer a questionnaire about his position on energy issues (ten other presidential hopefuls *had* answered the questionnaire). One of the questions asked of him had been, "Do you support or oppose legislative efforts in the U.S. Congress to prevent 'horizontal integration' and require major energy companies to divest themselves of such competing energy sources?"

Two days after Carter's silence had been criticized in that advertisement, he took out an even larger ad in rebuttal, explaining that he felt he needed more space to answer the questions than Energy Action had allowed him. He thereupon answered the questions at some length. In regard to horizontal divestiture, he said, "I support legal prohibitions against ownership of competing types of energy, oil and coal, for example." By the time the Democratic Platform Committee came out with its handiwork in June, Carter was in the saddle and his agents approved the platform before it was made public—including the firm statement in support of horizontal divestiture. In August, speaking to a luncheon set up by Ralph Nader, he again promised to try to get oil companies out of competing energy industries. Also in August, he told reporters at a news conference in his hometown of Plains, Georgia, he was disappointed that they had not asked him about his position on horizontal divestiture, because he considered it of vital importance.

Consumer groups that felt he would be their champion were, however, paying attention to him at the wrong moments. They should have been listening when, in July, he spoke to a group of a hundred thirty businessmen in Houston. Among them, of course, were many prominent oilmen. Carter promised them that he would never make "a decision of any sort of importance about energy problems," including taxes, regulation, and breakup of the industry, without "complete consultation with representatives of the [energy] industry." *That* was the promise he would keep.

Oilmen who knew Carter best weren't worried. Senator J. Bennett Johnston of Louisiana, touting Carter at a July fund-raiser in oil-rich Tulsa, Oklahoma, told his colleagues that while Carter "could conceivably be for horizontal divestiture," his commitment was of such a low level as to be hardly crucial. Johnston was so right.

* * *

The congressional advocates for natural gas decontrol were, after twenty years of trying, now poised for what they just knew would be the kill. How could they fail? The previous October, the Senate had passed a decontrol schedule. Everything had seemed to be firmly in place for House passage when Congress decided to quit for the year. Well, that had been a bit of bad luck in timing, but it was nothing they could not speedily compensate for, now that Congress was back.

Representative Robert Krueger, the handsome ex-English professor from Texas, had the support of a seemingly unbeatable coalition of Republicans and conservative Democrats for his own bill, which called for even more decontrol than the Senate version. Krueger's was the bill that the House Rules Committee, pressured by Speaker Albert, the Oklahoma peewee, had cleared for a House vote without its even being seen, much less studied, in a regular legislating committee. This was very unusual indeed. Quite heavy-handed. By allowing a shortcut, the Rules Committee insulted Chairman Harley O. Staggers of the House Commerce Committee and Representative John D. Dingell, chairman of the Commerce Committee's Energy and Power Subcommittee, who would ordinarily have processed the bill. (Staggers and Dingell would have probably killed Krueger's bill, too, which is why the oil-dominated Rules Committee allowed Krueger to skirt the normal procedure.)

Unfortunately for the congressional decontrol crowd, their strength was their weakness. They were too cocky. They offended the sensibilities even of many supporters. Lying and accepting bribes and other such mischief is frowned on in Congress, but it is not necessarily fatal to legislative schemes. Violating tradition—especially the tradition of showing respect for committee chairmen—is (or at least it still was in the mid-1970s) nearly always fatal to legislative connivings. If the rules were sacred, chairmen were even more so. The establishment must be protected.

Thus the preeminently establishmentarian Washington *Post* complained editorially on the day the decontrol bill was to come to a vote:

"Much as we support the deregulation of natural gas prices, we regret that the champions of this effort in the House have chosen to bring the issue to a floor vote in a decidedly irregular and peremptory way. In essence, the backers of decontrol have gotten tired of waiting for legislation to emerge from a Commerce subcommittee chaired by Representative John D. Dingell. Rather than exerting the usual kinds of gentle and less gentle pressures on the Commerce panel, the supporters of deregulation—with a crucial assist from Speaker Carl Albert—have decided to shove the committee aside . . . This approach has all the grace and subtlety of dynamite. Strictly speaking, it is not against the House rules, because the rules in such affairs are whatever a majority of the House will accept. But it is certainly at odds with every tradition of courtesy and deference to legislative committees. Indeed, it makes a mockery of the whole concept of delegation to committees, and ought to alarm not only congressional elders, but also the many newer members who have tried to make House panels more effective and informed . . .

"The power ploy is doubly ill-advised because it can only compound the rancor and suspicions already clouding the issue of decontrol.

"By resorting to such tactics, the backers of deregulation have hurt their own case and given their opponents new grounds on which to claim that dirty work is being done . . . Because the deregulation of gas prices will cost consumers some money, and especially because the lobbying by industry has been very high-powered, it is essential to enact this legislation in a way that the country accepts as orderly and fair . . . [I]t needs to be passed by the customary and conventional rules."

For the *Post*, which had been propagandizing endlessly for the decontrol of natural gas prices, to print that editorial must have been painful. The pain must have become excruciating when the *Post*'s editors actually saw their preachment have a crucial effect on the vote. Or perhaps it should be said that a combination of things appearing in the *Post* had a crucial effect. Though the newspaper's editors tried subtly to help the oil crowd, they could not control their own fine reporters. Late in January, the Washington *Star*'s gossip column "Ear" had commented, "What's that smell? . . . Is it true that the energy writer at another paper [there was only one other paper in town, the *Post*] has been warned to pursue his beat less energetically? Opposing the Company Line on deregulation of natural gas is probably naughty." Et cetera.

The *Post*'s reportorial tigers, ignoring pressure from above, kept digging, and what they turned up was often just too good for management to reject. And so it happened that on the day before Krueger's bill was to be tested in the House, the Washington *Post* reported that Krueger had received more than $200,000 in campaign funds in the second half of 1975, much of it from oil and gas interests. Krueger protested that the article was part of an anonymous campaign to smear him by suggesting—heaven forbid—that he had sponsored the bill in return for oil-industry campaign contributions.

Did the *Post* editorial and the campaign finance story hurt? Many thought so. *The Wall Street Journal* quoted one Democratic House leader as saying that the money story was "the decisive factor" in the outcome of the House vote "by lending credence to opponents' charges that his gas bill represented a windfall for the big-oil lobby."

For whatever reasons, the House's solid majority support for decontrol began to crumble. By the time that debate began, a number of congressmen who had previously been ready to vote for the Krueger amendment were looking for an excuse not to. They got that excuse in a bill offered by Representative Neal Smith, the Iowa Democrat. Smith's participation was part of the liberals' strategy. Actually, he served as something of a front man for Dingell. Dingell would have offered the bill, except that Dingell, who was often rather intemperate in debate, had irritated a number of Democrats with his stinging attacks (all of them quite justified) on Speaker Albert. Dingell felt it would be much wiser if he directed strategy from the background and let Smith offer the bill in his own name. The Dingell-Smith strategy was to seize the decontrollers' argument and turn it back on them, reasoning like this: If the objective of decontrol is to encourage, through higher prices, a more intense search for natural gas, then why not single out and favor those companies that were likely to use their extra profits in that fashion? In other words, why not dispense the blessings of decontrol to the small producers, the independents, the wildcatters, who historically were responsible for finding most of the oil and gas in this country and could be depended on to continue to do so in the future? Why decontrol prices for the major oil companies, who didn't need the extra profits anyway and were always very stingy about sinking their profits in further exploration?

The Dingell-Smith bill did exactly that: it continued price controls on the twenty-five major oil companies, which incidentally *owned* 70 percent of the natural gas, and decontrolled prices on about thirty-five hundred independent companies, which *discovered* most of the gas.

It was a bill that had something for everyone. The proposed decontrol of prices for small producers was aimed at luring the votes of moderates who believed the time had come for some loosening of the market. For liberals who wanted no loosening at all, the Dingell-Smith bill offered an appealing new wrinkle: an extension of federal price controls to intrastate sales (gas sold within the state where it was produced) as well as to the interstate market. And there was even a crumb for the oil crowd: the bill, while setting a generous base return of 18 percent on the majors' investment, allowed the FPC to consider "unusual circumstances such as higher-risk drilling" in setting even higher prices.

Supporters of the Dingell-Smith bill frequently laced their debate with citations from a couple of recent investigations that cast doubt on the industry's claim that only price decontrol could end shortages. What shortages? In January, John Galloway, a special assistant to Moss's investigations subcommittee, got wind of and obtained copies of several previously unpublished studies by the U.S. Geological Survey covering 153 fields of "unassociated" natural gas (gas found all by itself, not associated with oil) in federal waters off Louisiana. These were very important fields indeed, containing, according to the USGS, 67.4 percent of the natural gas reserves on the federal outer continental shelf. Galloway compared the USGS's findings with the reserve reports previously made public by the American Gas Association, and he found that the AGA had apparently underreported by 37.4 percent (14.8 trillion cubic feet of natural gas compared to 23.5 trillion cubic feet). The unreported gas—if it truly existed—would be enough to supply the nation's largest pipeline system, Texas Eastern, all it needed for eight years.

Galloway's findings were new in detail but not in thrust. Critics of the oil industry for at least five years had been claiming—and finding evidence to support their claims—that the gas industry was lying about its gas reserves. (The reputation of the industry was so notorious in this regard that, in February, Interior Secretary Thomas S. Kleppe, would say, "I'm convinced of the fact that there is natural gas in wells that were shut down that would bring a greater production at a higher price." But wasn't that extortion of a sort? Oh no, said Kleppe, that was just "free enterprise," and it was a matter that should be left up to the corporations. Trying to force the oil companies to produce more natural gas from private lands, he said, is "absolutely communistic in my books.")

The other investigation, also finished in January before Congress came back to work, was done by the General Accounting Office. It concluded that if gas prices were decontrolled, the cost to consumers over the next ten years would probably be around $75 billion and would immediately add nearly a full percentage point to the inflation rate, but that these extra profits would not arrest the rate of decline in production.

*

But since neither the gas industry's misrepresentations nor unjustified costs to consumers had ever aroused much outrage in Congress, the decontrol bill could be stopped, if at all, only by other events and tactics.

While Smith and others handled the sweet reason, Dingell handled the much more important element of timing. Shortly after 3 P.M., Dingell's lobbying allies—the trade-union and consumer-group lobbyists—passed the word to him that they felt they had cornered as many votes as they could at the moment. They warned him that he should not delay much longer in calling for a vote, because from then on any change would probably be an erosion of strength for their position. It wasn't so much that members would change their minds at once; it was simply that they were already beginning to drift away for a long weekend. The House was not scheduled to meet the next day, a Friday, and if the showdown was not contrived that afternoon, if it instead was postponed until the following week, the conservatives (many of whom had already disappeared) would be back in strength, and, besides, the long weekend would give the oil and gas lobbyists too much time to lean on wavering members. The vote should be called for *now*.

So, at 3:27 Dingell signaled that he was ready for the test of strength; he asked for unanimous consent to end debate on amendments to the Smith bill. And then the vote on the bill began. It came slowly. Many members on both sides held back to see which way it would probably go, hesitating to vote until they received some indication as to which would be the winning side. With four minutes left in the regular, 15-minute voting period, Smith was losing 112 to 116, but only 228 of the 435 members had voted. With one minute left, the oil crowd still hung on to an 8-vote margin. By now, the well in front of the Speaker's platform was jammed with more than 150 members, tense and noisy as the seconds ticked off. When the voting period expired, the count was a dead heat, 196 to 196, and with that there was a pellmell rush of voting, with congressmen hurriedly pushing their plastic voting cards into the electronic voting devices. The scoreboard fluttered and flashed, and then stood steady at 205 for the Dingell-Smith bill, 201 against it. Cheers and applause. Giddiness from the Left, disgust from the Right. The liberals, who only 48 hours earlier had themselves believed that victory was impossible, had pulled it off; 192 Democrats and 13 Republicans had voted with them, 84 Democrats and 117 Republicans had voted against them. The control of natural gas rates in interstate commerce would continue, at least for a while, for there wasn't the slightest chance that the conferees could figure out a compromise between the House and Senate bills that would be acceptable to both chambers. Krueger, the leader of the decontrol fight, knew what the vote meant. "I feel whipped," he said, trying to smile. "This legislation will not be enacted. Natural gas decontrol this year is once again stalemated."

*

The gloomy prospects were shared by oil supporters in both houses, but some were not yet ready to give up. On February 24, Senator Russell Long called a private conference in his office of oil-state heavyweights: including Senators James B. Pearson of Kansas, Lloyd Bentsen of Texas, John Tower of Texas, Henry Bellmon of Oklahoma, and Dewey Bartlett of Oklahoma, and Representatives Robert Krueger of Texas and Joe Waggonner of Louisiana. Also present was Federal Energy Administrator Frank G. Zarb.

After pessimistic remarks were batted back and forth for a while, the group agreed that the Senate decontrol bill, which they favored, should never be allowed to get into conference with the Dingell-Smith bill. They feared that the conference would be dominated by the procontrol crowd and that the compromise that emerged would make it much more difficult to pass real decontrol legislation later on.

They decided that there were only two routes to go: either let the whole thing die for 1976, or pass another proindustry bill in the Senate that might be taken up on the House floor without going through the Staggers-Dingell gauntlet.

They chose the latter strategy, and even tried to approach it with a dash of subtlety: Long stayed in the background. The less flamboyantly greedy members of the group, Pearson and Bellmon, plus Senator Paul Fannin of Arizona, were industry's front men in luring three unlikely allies—Senator Adlai Stevenson of Illinois, Commerce Committee Chairman Warren Magnuson, and Senator Ernest F. Hollings of South Carolina—into helping them construct a "compromise" bill. In May, the six emerged from their hideaway to present their baby: a "compromise" that would, among other things, immediately raise interstate "new" gas prices by 200 percent (to $1.60, up from 52 cents) on their way to total deregulation. David S. Schwartz, the former chief economist at the Federal Power Commission who had left that inhospitable clime to take a post at Michigan State University, estimated that the bill would cost consumers up to $12.5 billion a year.

On May 18, before consumer groups had a chance to gear up against it, the legislation "shot through the Senate Commerce Committee without benefit of a single hearing or a piece of testimony," in the words of Senator John Durkin of New Hampshire, the lone dissenter in the 16-to-1 vote.

Furor over the railroading turned into farce and the bill went nowhere. But never mind. The FPC was always ready to lend a hand when industry failed in Congress. So, two months later, the FPC—ignoring its own staff's advice that if the ceiling for new gas was raised to between 56 cents and 61 cents per Mcf it would let producers recover all costs and net 18 percent return on investments—set the ceiling for new gas at $1.42, nearly three times higher than the previous ceiling. To accomplish that neat bit of robbery, the commissioners not only accepted all the industry's cost and productivity information but tossed in a hypothetical income tax at the highest rate—although, in fact, many of the major producers paid no income tax at all. Never in its history had the FPC allowed such an enormous increase, and although the commissioners tried to soothe consumers by saying that the new rates would cost a mere $1.5 billion a year, the FPC's own staff assessed the probable impact at $2.25 billion a year.

A veritable army of consumer organizations, farm groups, municipal gas distributors, labor unions, and proconsumer congressmen joined in a lawsuit to overturn the FPC decision. Briefly they prevailed. On July 20, two federal judges temporarily blocked the FPC's order. Rattled by the fury directed against them, the power commissioners announced in September that they would hold new hearings on the price issue, but this was just a public relations gesture. After the hearings, the commissioners reaffirmed the contested price rates, and on November 9 a federal appeals court said the FPC could proceed as planned. Consumers had lost again.

**

Representative John Moss of California, one of those who sued, at least got some revenge on the FPC. His House Commerce Subcommittee on Oversight and Investigations issued a report ranking the nine major federal regulatory agencies. The FPC was put at the absolute bottom, with no competitors, because it had shown "flagrant disregard of its congressional mandate" to set "just and reasonable" rates, had failed to enforce delivery of natural gas to consumers, and had "displayed a conscious indifference to the public beyond comparison with any other regulatory agency."

At the time the panel's report came out, the FPC had become a way station for political gypsies. Three of the five commissioners—including the chairman, Richard L. Dunham, a former economist on Nelson Rocke-feller's staff—had held their posts for less than six months. The character of the commission was chillingly anticonsumer. One of the commis-sioners (and he was not out of place) was James G. Watt, later to make a mark as President Reagan's Interior Secretary.

Representative Moss threatened to try to impeach Dunham and Watt because he was convinced they had taken retaliatory action against two FPC staff lawyers—they got worse jobs—after they testified before Moss's subcommittee in early 1976 on alleged natural gas withholdings by Tenneco Oil Company and Mobil Oil Corp. It's a crime for federal officials to retaliate against subordinates because of testimony before congressional committees. Watt and Dunham denied wrongdoing.

* * *

The advocates of decontrol need not have been downhearted because of their defeats in the Democratic Congress; they would soon have a Demo-cratic President to help them to their goal. This, however, was not dis-cernible in the public remarks of candidate Jimmy Carter. On the con-trary, he spent the campaign year sounding like a militant consumerist. In January, to solicit votes in the Iowa precinct caucuses, he declared in a Des Moines *Register* advertisement: "I support legal restrictions to allow a 'reasonable profit' on oil and natural gas rather than allowing prices to be set without restriction." He said he favored deregulating price controls only on "that small portion (less than 5 percent) of pro-duction not under existing contracts" and that this deregulation should not exceed a trial period of five years.

His advice to the Democratic Platform Committee in June was a repe-tition of his January position: "For natural gas, we should deregulate the price of only that natural gas not currently under existing contract (less than 5 percent) for a period of five years. At the end of that period of time, we should evaluate this program to see if it increases production and keeps gas-related products at prices the American people can afford."

But October brought a lightning flash of the future. A letter—ad-dressed to the governors of Texas, Louisiana, and Oklahoma—began making the rounds of oil officials. The letter carried the signature of Jimmy Carter, and it was distributed from Carter's headquarters, but Carter aides would later imply that Carter did not have a direct hand in its production.[2] Whether he did or not, he clearly knew about its circula-

---

2. Apparently the genesis of the letter was this: At the Texas-Oklahoma football game in Dallas on October 9, Governors Dolph Briscoe of Texas and David Boren of Okla-homa were chatting with Democratic National Chairman Robert Strauss about the bleak prospects for Carter in their states. Briscoe and Boren said they couldn't very

tion and approved the effort to swing three doubtful states—Texas, Louisiana, and Oklahoma—into his column by giving assurance to those who feared his election might threaten their fortunes. (It helped him win Texas and Louisiana, but he lost Oklahoma.) The letter, dated October 19, promised, "I will work with the Congress as the Ford Administration has been unable to do, to deregulate new natural gas," and went on from there to praise the virtues of deregulation. He sounded as if he wanted to do it right then. What had happened to his five-year decontrol period for new gas? Once again, Senator Johnston seems to have known what he was talking about when he told his oil and gas colleagues in Tulsa in July, "I think we can get him to back off on that." By October, the backing off had obviously begun, and within a few months it would develop into a full-scale about-face.

* * *

Nothing Washington did seemed to go right. Everything the bureaucrats and their presumed bosses in Congress concocted under the rubric of Energy turned out to be stupid or chaotic or slightly crooked or baffling.

General Accounting Office investigators had found, in 1974, that there was total confusion in the gathering and analysis of energy data by federal agencies. In June 1976, the same investigators went back to see if there had been improvement. No way. They found 261 separate energy-related programs being administered by 44 federal agencies and bureaus, and no one agency—although the Federal Energy Administration was supposed to do it—was bringing together the disparate data floating around in all those corners.

New evidence of bureaucratic bias in favor of the oil industry surfaced all the time. Moss uncovered a memorandum showing that Lewis A. Engman, chairman of the Federal Trade Commission, had met privately in the summer of 1975 with lawyers of the American Gas Association—and 26 days later, the FTC decided (against the staff's advice) not to issue a complaint charging the AGA with supplying the government with faulty data. Engman hadn't done anything illegal, but his hospitality to the industry lobbyists certainly raised a question of propriety. Repre-

---

well campaign for the guy if he didn't come out for deregulation, so why not get him to sign a friendly letter with limited circulation? Right then and there they placed a call to Duke Ligon, an old friend, who had moved from a government energy job to become a high-priced oil and gas lawyer. Ligon spun off a quick draft of a letter, which, he later told Roberta Hornig, of the Washington Star, was supposed to be just a "starting point." He expected the Carter crowd to modify it considerably. Instead, they leaped to accept it as written, and Carter signed it without a quibble. After he won, he seemed to have temporary amnesia. Asked early in 1977 if Carter intended to carry out the promise, a top aide said, after a pause, "Well, did Jimmy write it in his own handwriting, or did he just sign a letter written for him by the staff or somebody else?" The implication was, apparently, that Carter hadn't known what he was doing.

sentative James D. Santini, Nevada Democrat, was one who wondered, "Who was in that private little get-together on behalf of the general public?"

With the coming of spring, a minor scandal blossomed at the Federal Energy Administration. On April 6 a sheaf of FEA documents was leaked to the House Commerce Committee's Energy and Power Subcommittee. Chairman Dingell had been trying to get the material for four months, since December, when it was learned that the FEA had paid $9,000 to a member of the American Gas Association to write a rough draft for a pamphlet—*The Natural Gas Story*—touting deregulation, and had allowed the AGA to dictate the wording of it. Dingell had demanded that the FEA send him its complete files on how the pamphlet was produced. And why. It seemed obvious to him that the FEA was teaming up with industry to influence the House to vote for deregulation when the issue came up, on February 5. Apparently fearing that release of the files would hurt their case before Congress, FEA officials stalled until after the vote. Then, when Dingell's side won, they apparently assumed that he would forget his request. He didn't forget. A very stubborn and hot-tempered fellow, he just got madder as the stalling went on.

In March, he phoned the FEA's general counsel and said the agency had better get that stuff over to his office immediately, or else. Thereupon, FEA officials began stripping their files of incriminating documents—including one that suggested the FEA "shove it to Dingell."

Unfortunately for them, the FEA's director of public affairs didn't like the cover-up that he was witnessing and leaked to Dingell the documents that had been taken from the files.

Dingell called the FEA brass before his subcommittee and denounced them for "a carefully thought-out scheme" designed to hide the government-industry propaganda effort. Deputy Administrator Hill admitted that he had made some "regrettable" decisions but tried to excuse himself with the heartrending complaint that the last six months had been a "very unfortunate period in FEA."

FEA officials were not so much repentant as they were unhappy at being caught. They locked the leaker out of his office, put him on six months leave without pay, and told him that when he came back he would be earning 40 percent less.

* * *

The Ford administration—and especially the FEA—was also embarrassed by the disrepute that was building around "Project Independence." To be sure, Project Independence was the flatulent brainchild of Nixon, but Ford had adopted it wholeheartedly. Nixon had promised that the various steps (higher prices, conservation, etc.) outlined in Project Independence would make the country self-sufficient in energy and down to zero imports by 1980.

At the time Nixon made that prediction, the United States was importing 2 million barrels of oil a day.

The goal proved to be a mirage. Even by the time the FEA published its first Project Independence report, in October 1974, it had stopped talking about the possibility of zero imports. It said it would be happy if imports didn't go above 3.3 million barrels a day by 1985. And now, in 1976, the FEA was saying that importation of 6 million barrels of oil a day could qualify as "independence."

The farce inspired this exchange between Senator Edward Kennedy and FEA Administrator Frank Zarb:

Kennedy: "Don't you think it about time that we stop using 'Energy Independence by 1985,' and that those words ought just to be tucked away in a safe pigeon hole and not be held out to the American people as a realistic policy objective? . . . Mr. Zarb, six million barrels a day is not energy independence."

Zarb: "If you want to change the terms and call it an 'embargo-proof economy,' that's all right with me, Senator. If you are defining independence as zero imports by 1985, that has never been the goal, at least as long as I have been in office."

Kennedy: "Well, it was not six million barrels, either. You have increased it by 300 percent since it was first announced. It started off with two million barrels, it is now six million barrels."

Zarb: ". . . we have not had exactly the swiftest public policy-making in the last year and a half, so, we had to slide a little bit . . ."

***

The endless flow of entertaining absurdities was perhaps best represented by the "entitlements" program, a part of the Energy Act of 1975. It had passed through Congress with, of course, noble reasoning; to wit: big refineries that had long-term contracts for cheap, "old" oil (much of it owned by themselves) would have a murderous advantage over the small refineries that had to rely almost entirely on the high-priced post-embargo oil. So, to even things out, why not make the big refiners with the cheap oil pay something per barrel to the small refiners that were stuck with high-priced oil? To transfer the money, the big companies would buy, and the small companies would sell, "entitlements" (just a bureaucratic word, concocted for the occasion, that had no real meaning). One entitlement represented the cost difference between a single barrel of low-cost oil and a single barrel of high-cost oil.

That amendment sailed through Congress under the saintly banner of "small business," a banner that any legislator just automatically salutes. And, as a matter of fact, a number of small refineries were helped. But the legislation had been written in such a fashion that some very big oil companies were profiting from it as well. Most were being helped by a loophole written into the legislation by a team of lawyers, the best known of whom was Joseph Califano. Companies that qualified for the loophole—and they included such hundred-million-dollar corporations as Pennzoil, Husky, Witco, and Charter—were exempt from paying for entitlements. The exemptions were worth millions of dollars.

The other kooky side to the entitlements program was that the companies judged small enough to qualify as *sellers* of entitlements included such giants as Atlantic Richfield, Ashland Oil, Standard Oil Company of Ohio, and Amerada Hess.

None of the "small" companies were raking it in like Amerada Hess, a poor little outfit that merely ranked as the nation's fourteenth-largest oil company. Hess was selling entitlements at a rate of $1 million a day to such corporate brothers as Mobil, Gulf, and Exxon. (By 1981, Hess would have received close to $1 billion in subsidies of this kind.)

Indeed, Amerada Hess had always received strangely favored treatment in Washington. The chairman of the company, Leon Hess, was a secretive fellow who stayed as far as he could from the press but was close to certain influential politicians and to officials at the Department of the Interior and at the Federal Energy Administration; one of the FEA officials who helped write the entitlements program was an adviser to Hess. But nobody in government seemed as friendly as Stewart Udall, who, as Interior Secretary in the 1960s, had granted Hess monopoly rights for importing quota-free oil from the Virgin Islands. His operation in the Caribbean was treated as "foreign" when that helped him, and it was treated as "domestic" when that profited him. As a "foreign" oil company, Hess was exempted from the Jones Act, which requires that oil shipped between U.S. ports must go in tankers manned by high-paid, U.S. seamen. On the other hand, because the Virgin Islands are a U.S. territory, Hess was treated as a "domestic" company for the entitlements program. And though enormously rich from refining and marketing, Amerada Hess was ranked among the "small" companies, because it owned few wells and bought most of its oil from foreign sources.

There was a moment when it looked as if Amerada Hess might lose its rich concessions. The Nixon administration in 1971 talked about canceling its refinery license for failing to live up to a couple of the original conditions laid down by Udall. But, in 1972, Leon Hess publicly gave $25,000 to Nixon's reelection campaign and—channeling some of the money through subordinates—secretly gave another $270,000. After that, no more tough talk was heard from the Nixon crowd.

(But Hess was generous to both parties. He loaned Hubert Humphrey $100,000 for his presidential campaign in 1968; he gave $225,000 to Senator Henry Jackson's unsuccessful presidential bid in '72.)

***

Speaking of campaign funds, Dr. Armand Hammer, chairman and chief executive of Occidental Petroleum Corp., on March 4 pleaded guilty to making illegal gifts ($54,000) to Nixon's reelection campaign. The 77-year-old oil maverick pulled out all the stops; he was rolled into the courtroom in a wheelchair, explaining to the judge that he had been suffering from dizziness and pain. His guilty plea made him eligible for a maximum jail stay of three years. He got a year's probation.

In fact, very few of the oil company criminals were suffering much. Bob R. Dorsey, kicked out as board chairman of Gulf Oil because of bribes Gulf paid to foreign officials while he headed the corporation, could take comfort in a $1.6-million lump-sum payment in retirement benefits, an annual pension of $48,158, a $16,330 savings bonus, $54,000 in accumulated vacation pay, and the chance to buy two hundred thousand shares of the company at a 20 percent discount—given by a grateful corporation.

Gulf stayed in the news. The corporation's bagman who had shuttled money from a Bahamas bank to Washington politicians was indicted for lying to a federal grand jury. In early March, Gulf made one of its most profoundly innocent gestures by asking politicians who had accepted its illegal campaign contributions to return the money. There was no rush to comply with the request.

New scandals seeped to the surface. Phillips Petroleum, which made at least $100,000 in crooked gifts to Nixon, announced that it would clean its management house. Tenneco stepped forward in February to admit that it had made a scattering of legal and illegal gifts to U.S. politicians and some $12 million in payments to useful foreigners over a 5½-year period.

There seemed to be no end to the accounts of oil money lavished upon Italian officials. Shell and British Petroleum admitted in April that they had paid about $6.6 million to Italian politicians between 1969 and 1973. They didn't say they were sorry. Exxon refused to name three countries where it had been paying off government officials, because, said board chairman C. C. Garvin, Jr., "we're still operating in these countries" with the help of some of those same lucky officials. As for the $50 million Exxon had given Italian officials, a special three-man committee set up by the corporation decided that no action should be taken against Exxon officials who had participated in the payoffs, because "what occurred was the result of errors of business judgment, not the result of lack of devotion to duty or to breach of faith."

***

The strength of OPEC was underscored on the very first day of the year, when President Carlos Andrés Pérez unfurled a red, blue, and yellow

Venezuelan flag over an oil well known as Zumaque No. 1–drilled in 1914 by Shell Oil—and with that symbolic act nationalized its oil industry, the largest single take-over of American property by a foreign government. The twenty-one companies and seventeen subsidiaries received a token payment of $1 billion total. Thus Venezuela ended sixty-one years of seeing its oil fields dominated by foreigners, most of them from the United States. Considering the fact that the idea for OPEC had been first pushed in Venezuela, the country had been remarkably slow in taking this final step—lagging behind most members of the cartel.

Executives of the multinational companies still tried to pretend that they had the situation under control. But Herbert E. Hansen, a corporate vice-president of Gulf, was candid enough to admit that "the ability to provide an orderly market for crude oil is the chief card the companies still have."

In Iran, there were ominous rumblings. The government claimed that it was rooting out widespread corruption, but there were no signs of any crackdown on the chief source of the corruption: the royal family. Dissidents claimed that the Shah had thrown one hundred thousand political opponents in jail and executed three hundred in the previous three years. Myriad stories of torture began to make news in the U.S. press, but mainly on the back pages of newspapers and not at all on television. Iran's economy was in trouble. The buying binge that followed the 1973–74 oil price leap had led to pitiful scenes of backwardness. Washington *Post* reporter Lewis M. Simons sent back accounts of Iranian ports that looked like "a spoiled child's playroom the day after Christmas, littered with too many expensive toys, many of them damaged or destroyed and discarded in dusty heaps." The "toys" were trucks and expensive machinery that just sat and rusted, because Iran did not have enough drivers for the trucks, and even if there had been drivers, it didn't have roads capable of taking so much heavy truck traffic. And if the machinery by some miracle could be transported to the site where it was meant to be used, said Simons, there weren't enough trained personnel, technicians, engineers, builders, or even trained laborers to put the machinery into service. The Shah's golden dream of a new Persian empire was dying in front of everyone's eyes.

* * *

The oil companies continued to crank out the advertisements that made them sound like history's greatest environmentalists. Phillips Petroleum hired a Dallas ad agency to produce a television commercial that would show how harmonious oil drilling rigs were with wildlife. There they were on the tube for all America to see: a deer, two cougars, and a golden eagle happily living in a northern Utah oil field. Newsmen discovered that these critters were tame and had been rented from a California game farm, to which they were returned after the cameras stopped rolling.

* * *

Meanwhile, on America's oil frontier, the Alyeska Pipeline Service Co.—the consortium of eight oil companies responsible for building the 800-mile conduit across Alaska—pushed its twenty thousand workers ten hours a day, seven days a week, to meet a mid-1977 deadline. Out of this "'77 or Bust" atmosphere came reports of fraud and dangerously sloppy workmanship. There were also indications that the government and the companies had conspired either to cover up the malfeasance or to silently ignore it, for much of it had occurred in 1975 and was only now coming to light.

From investigations by several congressional committees, this sleazy picture emerged:

Construction of the pipeline involved welding together 80-foot lengths of 48-inch-diameter pipe; the pipe was then either buried under permafrost and rivers or elevated above ground.

Alyeska had promised that somebody would inspect each and every weld as the pipe was laid in place. The inspecting would be done both by eyeball and by X-ray devices. The X rays were required to make sure that the pipe could withstand sufficient stress; cracks might cause the buried part of the pipeline to leak as much as five hundred barrels a day into the ground without being detected. A sudden rupture could spill sixty thousand barrels before being repaired. And the spilled oil could melt the permafrost and cause extensive permafrost damage.

Alyeska assured environmentalists that it was well aware of the dangers and that there would be plenty of inspectors on hand to make sure that the welding was done correctly. The Interior Department and the Department of Transportation promised to closely supervise the welding of the pipe as it crossed federal lands, and the Alaska Government promised to do the same for the 32 percent of the line traversing state land. About seven hundred government and private—mostly private—quality-control inspectors and X-rayers (radiographers) were supposedly hired to make sure everything went off smoothly, safely, and cleanly, and that the welding would be done with utmost care.

On paper, it sounded swell.

Pipeline welding began in the field in June 1975. Almost immediately, the operation fell apart.

For purposes of strategy, the generals at Alyeska mapped the pipeline in six sections. In July 1975, they ordered a routine spot check of the radiographs taken in Section 2. They couldn't believe what the check showed, so they ordered a complete audit of Section 2 radiographs. Sure enough: bungling and seeming fraud were all over the place. Over and

over, they came across X rays that had been done incorrectly, or welds
that had not been X-rayed at all, or welds whose X rays showed that
they were defective but had not been repaired. Could Section 2 perhaps
(hopefully) have been uniquely bad? Alyeska pushed on with an audit
of Section 3 radiographs. Again fraud and bungling were found everywhere. So Alyeska decided to doublecheck *all* 30,800 radiographs taken
in 1975.

Incredibly, it found 3,955 welds that were of questionable safety,[3] and
it went to work frantically to clean up the mess before the world found
out. The inspection records were in such disarray, however, that it wasn't
always clear whether the fault was in the weld or in the X ray; it *appeared* that 1,403 welds were questionable due to problems with the ra-
diography (the "problems" included the apparent theft of 400 X rays
from company files), and the other 2,552 welds were themselves botched.

Completing the nightmare: more than 1,000 of the questionable welds
were buried; Alyeska identified 1,015 as being "critical," which corporate
jargon identified as "those welds located in sensitive and/or very difficult
access related areas in which any remedial work will likely degrade the
end product quality and/or create substantial environmental concerns."
More simply, what Alyeska meant was that those thousand or so welds
were buried under 12 feet of permafrost (and many were buried in concrete) or under rivers.

What had gone wrong? For one thing, welding crews racing to meet
the 1977 deadline laid the pipeline so fast that many of the quality-control inspectors and radiographers couldn't keep up (some of the radiographers didn't understand their equipment). Radiographers sometimes
lagged behind welding crews by three miles, although the rule-book
limit was a half mile. So contractors employing the radiographers would
occasionally order them to cut corners and falsify their reports, and
hurry on. For another thing, the welding crews—under intense pressure
from Alyeska to get their pipe down on schedule—hated to have to go
back and correct defective work; when a quality-control inspector reported a faulty weld, he was often threatened with physical violence,
and sometimes actually mauled. That made them considerably less likely
to see faulty welds on the X rays.

And the final reason was that federal officials who should have been
policing the whole operation were not doing their job. The Department
of Transportation's Office of Pipeline Safety had *no* inspectors perma-

---

3. That number, 3,955, turned up in most news stories and became rather famous as
the scandal unfolded. But the true number may have been much higher. C. A. Champion, Alaska's chief pipeline inspector, told Roberta Hornig, of the Washington *Star*,
that Alyeska had to repair "around 6,000"—about one out of three—before it ever reported the "questionable" 3,955 welds.

nently assigned to the Alyeska pipeline. Deputy Secretary of Transportation John W. Barnum later admitted to reporters that "We don't know what has to be done to assure pipeline safety." The Interior Department was supposed to have a minimum of forty-four inspectors watching construction, but nobody ever saw them. Interior officials admitted that, with the pipeline nearly 70 percent complete, they had inspected only 3 percent of it.

Alyeska might have completed the pipeline without the shoddy work ever becoming a public scandal if a disgruntled radiographer, who had been fired by a subcontractor, hadn't gone to court to try to get his job back. In his suit, he listed fraudulent welding reports that he said his employer had forced him to sign. That lawsuit triggered press and congressional investigations. They discovered other failures.

Some of the aboveground pipeline—about half of the line was aboveground—was sinking, because the permafrost couldn't support the poles holding the pipe. Engineers who were not satisfied with the X-ray test (it did not show a weld's ultimate strength) subjected thirty-two randomly selected welds to what is known as a laboratory bend test; twenty-one failed the examination. At several river crossings, the pipe was so poorly laid that it broke loose and floated to the surface; when it was relaid, further serious damage was done to the river bottom—and federal inspectors were seldom on hand to enforce environmental restrictions. When state inspectors ran a hydrostatic test on a pipe section just east of Valdez, a 12-foot section split, "just like peeling a banana," Chief Inspector Champion said. The failure came when water was pumped through the line at only 187 pounds per square inch; the pipe was supposed to operate at 1,180 pounds per square inch.

The Ford administration had little interest in these findings. Its call for reform was perfunctory. The Department of the Interior hired Arthur Andersen & Co. to audit Alyeska's audit. When Arthur Andersen reported that it couldn't make sense out of Alyeska's haphazard bookkeeping, Interior just dropped the project. In July, when the welding scandal was making its biggest headlines, Ford felt obliged to dispatch a fact-finding force to Alaska, but they met for only two days in Anchorage, took a quick trip along the pipeline route in a helicopter, and then came home to say that everything looked remarkably good. Congressman Dingell, whose energy subcommittee had done some of the toughest probing and had been making some of the most sarcastic reports on the welding fiasco, appraised the trip as "little more than an administration public relations blitz," which was fair to say. Apparently, Ford's fact finders hadn't bothered to talk to the same people *Star* reporter Hornig interviewed in Alaska. She wrote: "One workman in the Alyeska camps said last week he had been sent out with a crew that was supposed to install an aboveground portion of the pipeline in a permafrost area just south of Fairbanks. 'You know what happened?' he asked. 'We got there and the supporting pipes weren't dug deep enough to support anything. They were also put in upside down. To top it off, when we checked we discovered the pipe had never passed inspection. Don't be surprised. This kind of thing happens all along.'"

If Alyeska's crews had been rough on the land when they first laid the pipe, they were downright brutal when they went back to correct the welds. Chief Inspector Champion, after making an airplane trip over the pipeline route in September, reported seeing about thirteen hundred 20-by-10-foot bell-shaped holes being dug or dynamited to get to pipe that had been buried beneath the ground in concrete. "In the Arctic," he said, "those holes should repair themselves in about ten thousand years."

And who would pay the bill for Alyeska's blunders? (For the welding errors alone, the cost would be $55 million; for repairing other construction foul-ups, estimates ranged up to $2 billion.) Spokesmen for the consortium acknowledged in October that they would try to pass it along to the consumer.

*

There was one other development related to the Alaska pipeline that promised to embarrass Alyeska and its Washington allies. This was the growing realization that they had been dead wrong to route the Alaskan oil to the California market. During the three years that environmentalists had tied up the pipeline in court, they had argued that one reason it shouldn't be built across Alaska to a Pacific port for transportation to California was that California didn't need the oil, but that the middle-western and eastern states needed the oil desperately. So why not build the pipeline down through the middle of Canada and let it spill into those areas? No, no, said Alyeska and their pals in Washington: the oil *could* be consumed in California. Definitely.

In 1973, Chairman Proxmire of the Joint Economic Committee put a series of written questions to Secretary of the Interior Rogers Morton. One of the questions was, "Given the Pacific Coast oil oversupply that is likely to occur if the trans-Alaska pipeline is built, as noted in your own economic and security analysis, did you evaluate how this oversupply would disrupt existing oil markets, forcing other oil sources out of the Pacific Coast market, and thereby imposing additional economic and national security costs on the nation?"

Morton's reply: "*There will be no oversupply of oil on the West Coast . . .*"

Three years later, there was clear evidence that Rogers had given a misleading reply and that Alyeska's bosses for eight years had been giving the government bad information. There *would* be an oversupply. For what Deputy Federal Energy Administrator John Hill called "a transi-

tional" period, which would last a long time, at least half the Alaskan oil
would have to go somewhere other than California, for that state had a
glut—partly because of conservation, partly because it was getting a substantial amount from Indonesia (considered a "safe" source, in that it
would not likely participate in any embargo), partly because California
was bringing in lots of continental shelf oil, and partly because Congress
had finally surrendered to the oil industry and was letting it dip into U.S.
Naval Petroleum Reserve No. 1, at Elk Hills.

If the oil didn't go to California, where would it go? To Japan? Japan
wanted it, and since 1972 the oil companies had been promising Japan
that it would get most of the Alaskan oil. But the notion of claiming an
oil shortage in the United States while at the same time exporting large
quantities to a foreign country was a public relations problem that no administration wanted to shoulder; in 1976 the Ford administration said absolutely no to the idea. About the only alternative left was to somehow
get the oil to the Middle West and the East, where the environmentalists
had been saying it should go all along, but the only likely way to get it
there was by setting up a relay of tankers through the Panama Canal:
taking it down to the Pacific side of the Canal in big tankers and then
pumping it into smaller tankers that could get through the canal—and
thence to Gulf ports for unloading into pipelines. At best, it would be a
real chore, and expensive, with the extra expenses being passed on to
consumers.

"It is somewhat troublesome," said Hill.

***

In March, Congress finally capitulated to the oil industry and passed legislation, which had been kicking around for several years, aimed at turning the naval oil reserves over to private industry. (See the chapter on
1974 for background.) Of particular importance was the 46,000-acre Elk
Hills Reserve, in California, which Standard of California had been slyly
draining for years, and the 23,700-acre North Slope Reserve No. 4
(Pet 4), in Alaska. Most of the immediate pumping would be done from
Elk Hills's 1.5 billion barrels. The legislation prohibited pumping from
Pet 4 unless Congress specifically authorized it, but that would be only a
matter of time. Meanwhile, the new law transferred Pet 4 from the jurisdiction of the Navy to the jurisdiction of the Interior Department—the
same move that had preceded the Teapot Dome scandal. The reserves at
Pet 4 were estimated up to 33 billion barrels, second only to the rich
lakes of oil beneath the Gulf of Mexico. The private oil companies had
lusted after Pet 4 for years. An unsigned memorandum had surfaced,
during debate on the bill, charging that it was part of a move to "turn
the naval petroleum reserves over to industry." Navy brass apologized,
saying the memo was the handiwork of an overzealous young officer.

But, in fact, history had shown that this was exactly what industry wanted, and the 30,000-acre Buena Vista Reserve, next door to Elk Hills, and the notorious 9,500-acre Teapot Dome Reserve, were proof of what happened when industry got its hands on federal lands: both of those reserves had already been pumped nearly dry.

＊＊＊

Globally, 1976 was the worst year the tanker fleet had ever experienced. Nineteen tankers were lost, and their wrecks spilled more than two hundred thousand *tons* of oil into the oceans and their tributaries. Of these disasters, the most impressive to Americans was the wreck of the *Argo Merchant*, on December 15. It was the biggest spill in U.S. waters up to that time, and it was a perfect example of the way an incompetent Coast Guard permitted defective ships and sloppy seamanship to mess up our waters (see Appendix entry on *ARGO MERCHANT*).

1 9 7 7

"If you are going to try to go to war, or prepare for war, in a capitalist country, you've got to let business make money out of the process or business won't work."

HENRY L. STIMSON

"This will be the Golden Age of the oil industry . . . It will be, for the next twenty years, a Golden Age for the industry that will rival, in many respects, the romance of oil of the past."

Energy Secretary JAMES R. SCHLESINGER

The winter of 1976–77 was a godsend for the natural gas industry. Beginning with an unseasonable chill in October, the weather deteriorated into the harshest temperatures in five winters. In some areas—West Virginia, for example—it was the worst winter in fifty years. The cold just hung there, and sucked away a six-month supply of stored gas in three and a half months. Supplies that should have been sufficient for both comfort and industry were needed for the former alone. By the end of January, eighty-nine hundred factories in the hardest-hit states had closed, laying off more than half a million persons. Before the gas supply caught up with the weather, more than a million and a quarter workers would be idled. Although in Georgia the weather was relatively mild, that state did not escape: thousands of mill workers were laid off when their industrial gas was shifted to needier areas.

It was the perfect setup for the gas industry to play what it had been regularly playing for half a dozen years: winter politics.

And it wasted no time. On the very afternoon of President Carter's inauguration, gas pipeline officials went to the White House to warn him of what they, having had a great deal of practice, portrayed as potential disaster unless prices were permitted to shoot up. Carter was easy to convince. A week later, he proposed (and Congress passed with giddy speed) his first piece of legislation: an emergency measure giving him authority to transfer gas from surplus to shortage areas and permitting pipeline companies to buy gas at any price—no ceiling—and pass the cost along to their customers. (As always, for customers who could pay "any price," there was no shortage.) The FPC implemented the new act with such gusto that gas suddenly appeared on the market at $2.25 per Mcf— 450 percent higher than interstate gas had been selling for a year earlier

—and FPC chairman Richard L. Dunham said he would allow the profits to roll in without the slightest challenge.

Within a matter of days, the frozen parts of the country were warming up with anger over fuel bills. In West Virginia, customers of Columbia Gas, the state's biggest supplier, were paying 200 percent more in heating bills than they had paid two winters earlier. General Public Utilities Corporation, which served parts of Pennsylvania and New Jersey, reported earnings up 67 percent over the previous year.

Greed was creating almost an underworld atmosphere. When local gas companies went into the marketplace to buy from the gas distributors, the rigmarole they had to go through, said Representative Clifford Allen of Tennessee, "sounds like dealing with a gang of illegal traffickers in dope and narcotics, rather than responsible businessmen." No exaggeration. One of Allen's constituents, James C. Cothan, executive vice-president of the Nashville Gas Company, told of the eerie experiences of his colleagues: "The producers are withholding gas from the market. There is absolutely no question about it. We have had members of our company in Houston, Dallas, New Orleans, off and on for the past couple of weeks, trying to find gas. And it is the strangest market I have ever seen. It is almost impossible to make contact with somebody who has gas to sell. You have to find a gas *finder*, or a gas broker, and this broker will make contact (and probably with somebody who will make further contact) and eventually you might find somebody who has gas to sell. You have no idea who it is or where it is."

That was the mood of suspicious cynicism everywhere.

＊

Along with the minority who were cold, out of work, and overcharged as a result of the gas cutback, a much larger number of Americans (as shown by an NBC poll) believed that the whole thing was a contrived emergency created by the oil companies for profit—an old, old belief that they had loudly enunciated in other years too. It was becoming a part of folklore. And once again, as was repeatedly the case in years past, government investigators came up with enough solid evidence to support the public's cynicism. Shortly after taking office, Interior Secretary Cecil D. Andrus assigned a 6-man team to investigate charges that gas had been deliberately held back from production. Two weeks later, the investigators gave a preliminary report: there was no production from reservoirs in four fields in the Gulf of Mexico with proved reserves of gas totaling nearly 1 trillion cubic feet. (The winter's shortage was something over 2 trillion cubic feet.) The leases in the four fields were held by the same old friendly crowd: Union, Shell, Gulf, Amoco, Continental, Exxon, Texaco, Tenneco, Pennzoil, and Phillips. The companies denied wrongdoing. A Gulf official called it all a "witch-hunt."

In March, Andrus did something very revolutionary: he ordered one company, Aminoil U.S.A., Inc. (a subsidiary of R. J. Reynolds Industries), to start pumping gas from its Gulf Coast site by the fall of 1978 or forfeit its lease with the federal government. Aminoil asked for a six-month extension to give it time to locate a drilling rig. Andrus said the company could have only four days. A rig was promptly found.

To understand just how unusual Andrus' actions were, one need only review the history of the relationship between the oil companies and the government.

There was nothing illegal about producers sitting on natural gas until the price was "right"—if the fuel they were withholding was under private land. But whenever they got a lease on federal lands, they promised to show "due diligence" in looking for fuel and getting it to market. The federal agencies policing the program had a very lax attitude toward that regulation. They usually interpreted "due diligence" to mean whenever it suited the producers. Federal Power Commission staffers on one occasion found producers sitting on 7 trillion cubic feet of gas that had been discovered on federal land. Nothing was done about it. The FPC knew that some of the dormant fields uncovered by Andrus' investigators should have been in production, but for years it had happily accepted the companies' excuses: Amoco, for example, said it couldn't *afford* the $1 million necessary to drill a new well; Texaco said it didn't have any available drilling rigs; etc. Any excuse was okay with the FPC.

The same lackadaisical spirit had pervaded the Interior Department. It had the power to cancel leases if a company didn't develop a field within five years, but no Gulf Coast lease had been canceled since drilling on federal offshore property began there, in 1954. In 1975, Interior Secretary Rogers C. B. Morton had ordered aides to find out why 980 billion cubic feet of proved reserves of gas in five offshore fields weren't under production. He said he had heard the companies were deliberately withholding production to drive up prices, and he wanted to find out if that was true. But he must not have been very interested, for the investigation was abandoned. Now House probers tried to revive it, summoning Interior officials in February to explain the inaction. Gosh, said the bureaucrats, they had forgotten all about it.

In another congressional investigation in February, House commerce subcommittee staff members charged that Texaco was withholding from production over 500 billion cubic feet of natural gas in two fields off the coast of Louisiana. Nonsense, said Texaco. But Texaco, Tenneco, and other big outfits did admit that billions of cubic feet of natural gas that could have been used to heat homes had been transferred for burning at their own refineries and chemical plants. Congressman John Moss's investigators accused Gulf of failing to deliver 625 million cubic feet of natural gas a day to the Texas Eastern Transmission Corporation, a pipeline that served sixteen southern and northeastern states. Moreover, they accused the FPC of knowing about it and letting Gulf get by with the breach of contract. The previous December, the FPC had ordered Gulf to deliver the gas to Texas Eastern immediately (which would have helped the winter crunch, of course) or pay damages. But Gulf appealed, and its case wouldn't come into court until warm weather. Said FPC chairman Dunham: "The FPC does not have immediate enforcement authority." FPC and Interior officials always sounded pitifully helpless.

*

The press did very little digging into the cause of the crisis. One of the better jobs was done by Jerry Flint, a New York *Times* reporter, though his late-blooming story didn't appear until March 20, weeks after the crisis had ended. Flint's target was the Columbia Gas System, the nation's largest integrated gas company: it not only bought and sold the stuff, but produced gas as well. Columbia serviced 10 percent of the nation's gas customers. With all its resources and facilities to draw on, why was it that the areas served by Columbia had suffered so much during the previous winter? Ohio had been particularly hard hit (45 percent of the nation's scarcity-created unemployment had occurred there), and it had been nip and tuck in some of the other states in the Columbia system: southern New York, Pennsylvania, West Virginia, Maryland, Virginia, Kentucky.

"Did the Columbia Gas System, through a series of management decisions, help turn a bad winter into a national economic crisis?" asked Flint. "There are indications that the answer is yes." In fact, a resounding yes.

Why was it that "in neighboring states such as Michigan, Illinois and Wisconsin—served by other companies—not a single worker was idled by curtailments in that February 4 week"? The answer, wrote Flint, lay in the fact that, during the previous autumn, Columbia had actually *sold off* gas that had been dedicated to the winter reserve. And when the company walked into its winter season, on November 1, with its storage reserves low, it did not demand that low-priority customers accept extra cutbacks. Gas poured from the company's storage, which by January 1 was down 100 billion cubic feet.

"One FPC official, who declined to be named, said: 'For that company to go into November 1 with an already drawn-down posture like that raises a lot of questions. Then to pull the guts out of it (the winter storage reserve) November 1 to December 1 and then to blast it open in December?'

"The official added: 'You must protect your storage. When you let people pull down your storage almost 100 billion cubic feet before January 1, you've got some serious questions about your business judgment.'"

The more important question was about the company's social conscience. As a business judgment, the decision to go into winter with a short supply proved to be, though disastrous for its customers, highly profitable for its shareholders. The company's fourth quarter indicated net operating income (after taxes but before interest) was $72.5 million, against $45.1 million for the year before.

Typical of the *Times*, this revealing story was not put on the front page, but on the first page of the financial section, where the ordinary reader would give it scant attention. Except for reporting hardships, the press generally fell flat. Charles B. Seib, the ombudsman for the Washington *Post*, correctly complained on February 11, "Was there a true shortage of natural gas, or was it a phony shortage engineered by gas producers who were out to break the price ceiling? That was the heart of the story in the Winter of '77, and the press only nibbled at it.

"We reported the charges and countercharges, what this expert said and what that study showed. But we showed none of the enterprise or commitment we would have shown if, say, a government agency had been holding back on the facts or if we were pursuing outright corruption.

"In the course of the past few weeks, I saw just two stories—one in *The New York Times* and one in *The Wall Street Journal*—that dug into what lay behind the withholding charge."

It was true. Reporters were willing, but their editors were weak—and the assignments, plus necessary expenses, just weren't forthcoming. But, of course, it must be said in the press's defense that this was not something that could be adequately explored by it alone. It had no subpoena powers. Only Congress could get to the bottom of the shortage. And Congress was acting its usual self.

* * *

Just how much vigor Carter intended to throw into the energy fight, and in what direction he intended to throw it, remained unclear for most of the year.

On February 2, he made his first television talk to the nation since his inaugural. In a middle-class imitation of Franklin Roosevelt's fireside chats, Carter sat in front of a fireplace and wore a cardigan sweater and grinned his way through his discourse in the contradictory style of a chatty, cheerful undertaker. He proclaimed that the energy problem was permanent, would not go away by itself, and required that "we all cooperate and make modest sacrifices." And just exactly what modest sacrifices did he have in mind? Specifics, he said, would come later.

They came two and a half months later. David Freeman (an energy adviser to the Nixon/Ford White House) and James Schlesinger headed up the small group that put the program together, operating in such secrecy—apparently nobody from Capitol Hill was consulted—that when the program emerged, it was automatically greeted with suspicion. What was this strange, Carterish thing? But, indeed, when all the piety and rhetorical frills were cut away, the heart of the program, its theme, looked very much like something that might have been borrowed from Ford's old files. And this was ironic, for in 1975, fledgling candidate Carter had told the Washington Press Club (July 11) that Ford's "disastrous" energy policy "is easy to describe—a large and sudden increase in the price of oil." Now it looked as though Carter had adopted the same policy. To be sure, Ford had proposed higher prices in the name of profits and Carter was proposing them in the name of conservation—but that was a fine point that consumers would not likely be able to appreciate.

On April 18, Carter went on national television to prepare the way for his program with what his staff privately called a "sky is falling" speech. Gone was the cardigan. No longer did he talk about modest sacrifices. Now he came on with his version of stern father and peacetime commander in chief: "Tonight I want to have an unpleasant talk with you about a problem unprecedented in our history. With the exception of preventing war, this is the greatest challenge our country will face during our lifetimes. The energy crisis has not yet overwhelmed us, but it will if we do not act quickly . . .

"Our decision about energy will test the character of the American people and the ability of the President and the Congress to govern. This difficult effort will be the 'moral equivalent of war'—except that we will be uniting our efforts to build and not destroy."

His goals by 1985 (which for some reason seemed to be a magical year for Presidents; Nixon and Ford had latched their energy programs to 1985 too): cut oil imports, then running at 8 million barrels a day, to 6 million barrels; cut gasoline consumption, then about 7 million barrels a day, by 10 percent; cut the annual growth rate in energy demand to less than 2 percent; establish a strategic petroleum reserve of 1 billion barrels, enough to last six months; increase coal production by about two thirds, to more than 1 billion tons a year; insulate 90 percent of U.S. homes and all new buildings; and extend solar energy, currently used on only five thousand homes, to 2.5 million homes.

And, oh yes, he promised that "we will monitor the accuracy of data from the oil and natural gas companies, so that we will know their true production, supplies, reserves, and profits." Lots of luck. How did he intend to do the monitoring? He didn't say, and in fact, from then until he left office, four years later, there was not one iota of improvement in the fumbling, blind, handout reliance on industry data that had been going on for years.

Two days later, in a speech to the joint houses of Congress, Carter gave details on how he intended to achieve his goals: He proposed a wide range of tax rebates for home insulation; heavier taxes to persuade utilities and industries using oil and natural gas as boiler fuel to switch to coal; taxes on gas-guzzling autos and rebates to persons who bought more-fuel-efficient cars;[1] a standby gasoline tax to use if consumption did not decline. Those were the relatively minor proposals. The major proposals were these: Carter would end the "cost of production" base for natural gas pricing (the system mandated by Congress, but regularly violated) in favor of incentive pricing. The price of new natural gas would be immediately raised to an extraordinarily generous $1.75 per thousand cubic feet; however, price controls (if such prices warranted the term) would not only be retained for interstate gas but extended to intrastate gas as well. As for oil, Carter proposed momentarily retaining the current price ceilings of $5.25 a barrel for old oil and $11.25 for new oil but heaping a wellhead tax on it to make it as costly to consumers as OPEC oil; over a three-year period, domestic oil would be allowed to rise to the world price level. (Obviously he had changed his mind since 1975, when he told the National Press Club, "The price of all domestic oil should be kept below that of OPEC oil.")

Those two items, much higher prices both for natural gas and for oil, were the centerpiece of his program. The industry would get considerably richer, the government might reap billions in taxes, and the consumer would be forced, by being punished at his pocketbook, to embrace conservation.

Consumer groups were confused and unhappy. Where was the Populist of yesteryear, the Carter they had grown accustomed to hearing during the campaign? Specifically, what had happened to his promised effort to crusade for horizontal divestiture? Had they been naïve to take him at his word? If so, they were not alone. Carter had led some very realistic newsmen to the same conclusions. In the January 9 New York *Times*, financial writer Steven Rattner had predicted: "Mr. Carter favors horizontal divestiture—prohibiting energy companies from owning competing forms of fuel—and the issue seems sure to be discussed early in the year."

But neither his moral-equivalent-of-war speech on national television nor his speech to the joint session of Congress two days later made any mention at all of horizontal divestiture. The closest he had come, in his speech to Congress, was one oblique suggestion that "strict enforcement of the antitrust laws . . . may prevent the need for divestiture." The White House released a "Fact Sheet" to accompany the speech. The Fact

---

1. In a typical industry response, General Motors chief economist Henry L. Duncombe, Jr., showed up in Washington to argue that if U.S. auto makers were forced to move too quickly to design and sell cars with better fuel economy, the American consumer just might stop buying American cars. With gas-thrifty foreign cars pouring into the country and finding a ready market, it was a puzzling argument.

Sheet only took notice of a vaguely troublesome "trend." It read: "Horizontal diversification by oil and gas producers, particularly into the coal industry, *has aroused fears* that the major firms will be able to restrict the development of alternative fuel sources. The existence of such power could be very detrimental to the nation as it increases its reliance on coal, uranium and renewable energy sources. The *trend* of oil and gas company entry into coal mining *merits continuous close attention.*" (My emphasis.)

It was a promise to watch, not act. Just whose fears had been aroused, he didn't say, but apparently Carter no longer shared the fears, for the Fact Sheet went on: "From information available at the present time, it does not appear that new laws mandating either vertical or horizontal divestiture are required in order to promote or maintain competition in the energy industries. That conclusion is subject to change. If it should appear that there are anticompetitive problems in the energy industries that cannot be reached under current laws, new legislation would be proposed."

Obviously, he was getting cold feet. Just how cold became unmistakably clear when, on April 29, nine days after his moralizing to Congress, Carter released his 103-page "National Energy Plan." In one paragraph, Carter succeeded in demolishing any hopes for bringing competition to the energy world. The crucial paragraph read:

"Traditionally, the structure of the coal industry has been extremely competitive. It is still relatively unconcentrated compared to industries such as steel and automobiles. Nevertheless, recent trends have caused legitimate concern. A total of thirty-two oil and gas companies accounted for 16 percent of total U.S. coal production in 1974, a 48 percent increase over their share in 1967. These companies accounted for more than 18 percent of coal shipped to electric utilities in 1974, a 27 percent increase over their share in 1967. In 1974, they held 5 percent of total U.S. coal resources, compared to 1 percent in 1967. These figures do not indicate that the oil and gas companies have a dominant position or even significant market power in the coal industry. But the trend of oil and gas company entry into coal mining and the companies' activities and performance merit continuous attention to make sure that a competitive industry does not become noncompetitive."

What had happened to the campaign promise to *prohibit* "corporate ownership of competing types of energy, such as oil and coal"? Ten months after being born, that promise was dead. By April, Carter had come full circle. From promising to press for horizontal divestiture in 1976, he was in 1977 defending the oil companies against charges that they suppressed competition. No longer did he see the existing horizontal concentration of economic power in coal and oil as "dangerous both to the national interest and to the functioning of the competitive system" (the platform's words); now he proclaimed that in fact corporate energy sources were "still relatively unconcentrated." But never mind the changes of ten months. What about the blindingly fast changes within the past few days? Whereas nine days earlier he had mentioned some people's "fears" of oil companies taking over the coal industry, now the fear was replaced by mere "concern." Whereas nine days earlier he had conceded that such concentration of power in supposedly competing industries could be "*very* detrimental," now he conceded only that it might be "detrimental."

Most amazing of all was Carter's false and misleading use of data. "[T]hirty-two oil and gas companies accounted for 16 percent of . . . coal production . . . In 1974, they held 5 percent of total U.S. coal resources . . ." What was Carter trying to pull? Were these just some of the grotesque errors that the nation would get used to in the years ahead, or was he trying to flimflam? Even the American Petroleum Institute admitted that concentration was much heavier. In an antidivestiture booklet published in 1976 (*A Critical National Choice: New Energy Horizons . . . or Horizontal Disintegration*), API said that *nine* oil companies owned about 20 percent of the nation's coal reserves and that they produced about 20 percent of the nation's total coal output. API further acknowledged that just *three* oil companies produced 14 percent of the nation's coal. Indeed, if captive production was excluded—mines owned mainly by steel and electric utility firms—the oil and gas companies' share of coal mined in 1975 came to 25 *percent*.

Anyway, for Carter to talk about the nation's total coal reserves (437 billion tons) was to play the oil companies' game. Much more relevant were the coal reserves currently in the hands of producers and destined for mining over the present generation (about 174 billion tons); of *that*, the oil companies controlled *nearly half*.

If Carter could ignore or misinterpret evidence of that sort, it was obviously no problem for him also to miss the significance of the fact that from 1964 to 1974 seven oil companies cornered forty-nine of the fifty-two patents for converting coal into synthetic gas and oil; that a dozen oil companies controlled about 51 percent of domestic uranium reserves, and that five oil companies controlled about 62 percent of domestic uranium milling. Kerr-McGee, ARCO-Anaconda, and Exxon were the first-, third-, and fifth-largest uranium producers.

Could the case for horizontal divestiture be clearer? Interior Secretary Andrus thought not. On a "Face the Nation" program, he said flatly, "I think that we are in danger of having large energy companies, and I would hate to see that. I think that we have to have competition, and between the forms of energy, if you're going to have any adequate price structure for the American people." In June, FEA Administrator John O'Leary testified at an antitrust subcommittee hearing, "We are into diminishing returns as a result of the spread of the oil companies into energy companies." And in August, the government's antitrust chief, John Shenefield, said at his confirmation hearings: "If I were a sitting senator and asked to vote on a law for [horizontal] divestiture, I would vote aye."

But nothing was heard from Carter. In September, Senator Kennedy and a group of other liberals introduced legislation *not* to force horizontal divestiture but simply to prevent *further* acquisition or ownership of coal or uranium assets by major oil or gas companies. The motive was not to strip down the oil companies but just to stop the *spread* of their ownership into competing energy fields until the Administration had completed its proposed study of the antitrust aspects. Said Kennedy when he brought his bill to the floor for a vote, "I should note that the Federal Trade Commission has for over five years been trying to do a report on the coal industry, but has yet to receive data from Exxon and Atlantic Richfield, so any conclusions that it draws can only be tentative. So long as the Administration allows oil and gas companies to continue to acquire coal and uranium while it studies the situation, it is likely to have as little success as the FTC in obtaining all of the necessary data. Time can only work to the advantage of the oil companies."

Carter gave no support to the Kennedy legislation, not even a rhetorical commendation, and the bill died, 62 to 30.

*

If Carter's turnabout on horizontal divestiture was shocking to consumer groups, at least they were not exactly unprepared for it. Even before Carter laid out his program in April, there were many signs that he was tiring of the Populist guise. Oilmen were noticeably gaining easy access to the White House. There was also reason to wonder just how much he wanted his energy program—as originally drafted—to succeed. When putting together the 283-page energy bill, he did not bring any member of Congress—not one—into consultation. And after his energy speeches, he became strangely quiescent. Where was the supposed crusader for energy reform? In the first week after delivering the bill to Congress, he made only two public statements on the issue, one of which was to a group of North Carolina schoolchildren. Indeed, for the next five months, while the oil and gas lobbies began working with a vengeance against the better parts of the bill, he did virtually nothing to use his massive propaganda powers to counterattack. And when the shredded energy legislation eventually bogged down in conference committee and Carter clearly needed any and every ally to salvage a piece of it, he still remained aloof from the conflict. As Representative John B. Anderson of Illinois, chairman of the House Republican Conference, pointed out: "Not once, to my knowledge, has the President ever pretended to take the minority conferees into his confidence or seek their help." But that's getting ahead of our story.

***

One of the Carter administration's biggest problems in pushing the energy program was exactly the same problem faced by other recent administrations: credibility. Despite his flamboyant display of piety, or because of it, everything Carter and his cohorts said about the energy crisis was subjected to the most skeptical scrutiny. And they didn't always come out so well.

The neutral General Accounting Office, which studied the plan carefully, admitted in July that it was bewildered by what Carter was up to. He had announced goals. He had also laid out steps for meeting the goals. But they didn't jibe. Comptroller General Elmer B. Staats called it "incongruous to submit a plan which is not designed to meet stated goals."

Carter's bill asked for "standby" authority to increase gasoline taxes 5 cents a gallon every year that national consumption exceeded a target level, with the possible increase totaling 50 cents a gallon. Critics smelled a mouse. Why was he trotting out that old, bruised idea? After all, the use of gasoline accounted for only 12 to 15 percent of our total energy consumption; and to achieve even a 10 percent reduction in gasoline use (a less than 2 percent reduction in overall energy consumption) would, many economists felt, require doubling the price of a gallon. A tax of that size would be catastrophically regressive on the poor.

Anyway, even a relatively small increase in the gasoline tax had been anathema in Congress for years, and every congressional leader now expressed dismay at the proposal. So why was Carter bringing it up? Strictly as a psychological gimmick, said Carter's advisers. "The American people have never believed in physical shortages," said James Schlesinger, and the proposed tax was to turn them into believers. But there were no clear indications that the Carterites expected the tax to pass. Many observers suspected it was offered as no more than a bargaining trick, something designed to be sacrificed, drawing the opposition's fire so that the rest of the package could slip through. It must not have been a very serious proposal, for Carter's strategists discarded the gas tax idea at the first grumble.[2]

Schlesinger was correct when he said that the American people doubted there were true energy shortages. Over the years, they had not believed the oil and natural gas companies, and their skepticism of

---

2. If Carter had really been serious about cutting down gasoline use, he would have sought authority to ration it. A poll of 1,814 drivers in October showed that 60 percent would prefer rationing to "considerably higher gasoline prices." Similar results were found in a number of earlier polls.

Carter's "shortages" was based on the awareness that, like the energy companies, he was simply trying to peddle something by frightening the public. He would have been more convincing if he had admitted that industry statistics were incredibly elastic, that fixing firm estimates of reserves was as difficult as pinning down a soap bubble. Top oil executives were becoming quite candid about that. How much oil and gas is locked inside the earth's crust? "It's like trying to guess the number of beans in a jar, without knowing how big the jar is," said Sheldon Lambert, who handled energy economic forecasts for Shell. Dale Woody, chief of Exxon's domestic natural gas operations, admitted, "Two well-qualified engineers can take the same raw data from a new field and come up with reserve estimates that may vary by more than 50 percent." Aside from the extreme differences in honest interpretation of the same data, there was also the problem of an inbred shiftiness on the part of oil people. They simply weren't very trustworthy: they loved to hide data from each other, to say nothing of their delight in confusing the government. As Interior Secretary Andrus put it in a moment of vexation, "Unless the government stations an inspector at every drill hole, every gas well and pipeline . . . every day, we'll never get completely accurate figures."

Given these handicaps, well known to the sophisticated public as well as to the experts, Carter would certainly have been more convincing in his claims of scarcity if he had made a serious effort to gather independent data. He had both the authority and the duty to do it.

The Energy Policy and Conservation Act (EPCA) of 1975 had mandated the government to set up an energy information and analysis office within the Federal Energy Administration. The law specifically ordered the energy information office to operate independently of the parent FEA, so that it could not be politicized. In March, J. P. Smith, a Washington *Post* reporter, neatly summarized the choice: "The Carter administration can now take two approaches to the battle of the numbers: it can, as the government has since 1946, continue to rely on the estimates provided by" industry. "Or it can exercise authority given it under two recently passed laws [not only EPCA but also the Energy Supply and Environmental Coordination Act of 1974] to develop its own base of independent reserve data . . .

"What course will Carter take?"

By the end of the year, the answer was shamefully clear: his bureaucrats would take industry's figures and, for political reasons, manipulate them into seeming even scarier than industry was wont to do.

In December a federal interagency group called the Professional Audit Review Team reported that in fact the Carter administration had totally politicized the energy information office, making it nothing more than "an extension of the energy policy and planning staff" headed by Schlesinger at the White House. Furthermore, the audit review team charged that the FEA had made twenty-one changes in the supposedly independent office's evaluations, jiggering the supply estimate down, the demand estimate up—"the increased gap between projected energy supply and demand translated into a greater dependence on imported oil, thus emphasizing the need to implement the President's energy plan."

Which is not to say that Carter was using panic statistics for the same reason that they were being used by industry. *He* wanted to paint a picture of *permanent* scarcity so that higher prices would be accepted as a way to force conservation. He believed, correctly, that about half the energy used in the United States was wasted. The propaganda of permanent scarcity was typically pushed by Schlesinger in an NBC interview: ". . . the United States will run out of oil and gas in the next thirty to forty years. We have a problem of conserving our supplies." But that was downright optimistic compared to what Carter told his television audience on April 18: "The oil and natural gas we rely on for 75 percent of our energy are running out . . . we could use up all the proven reserves of oil in the entire world *by the end of the next decade.*" (Emphasis added)

The *industry*, on the other hand, wanted to present a picture of *temporary* scarcity that could be changed into a panorama of abundance if only higher prices were given as incentive for exploration. Indeed, industry and its friends feared that Carter's use of their figures (promoting conservation with scarcity) might critically undermine *their* uses of the same figures (promoting profits with scarcity). Frank Ikard, API president, expressed this fear: "Some officials here in Washington have been making gloomy statements about our petroleum potential, and about whether the petroleum industry could really increase production if it were freed from government price-fixing and red tape. These officials say that there's not much oil and gas out there anyway, so what difference would it make if we got more reasonable rates of return?"

For industry, it was of crucial importance that the public be given hope for energy abundance in return for higher prices. Get rid of price controls, fellow citizens, and you can have all the energy you want! That was the message it wanted to get across. It abhorred Carter's pessimism, and—which was ironic, considering the source—accused him of deception. In one respect, this was a fair accusation, for his dire forecast was based on the silly assumption that the "proven reserves" would remain static: that the reserves already discovered were all that would ever be found and that higher prices and improved technology would not greatly expand the world's proven pool of recoverable oil.[3]

3. In fact, the very definition of "reserves" is that quantity known to exist and recoverable at current prices and with current technology. The "reserves" figure is always disappearing over the horizon as prices and technology change. It is very mis-

The oil industry was in general agreement that, given profit incentives and proper technology, there was *at least* twice as much oil awaiting discovery and recovery as had already been found. As for natural gas reserves, guesses as to the ultimate recovery were almost limitless. Even among the experts, there was some talk of a supply that could last for thousands of years. Such ecstatic predictions were used by supply-demand editorial writers to goad Carter and make fun of his long-faced predictions on oil and gas. "Mr. Carter apparently thinks the United States is running out of the stuff," said *The Wall Street Journal.* "If that were true, we might be as scared as he seems to be. But in the course of the debates on his plan, the President will discover that while we are now consuming 20 trillion cubic feet of natural gas every year and that—if prices were only decontrolled—we have roughly 20,000 trillion cubic feet of natural gas at hand, with some estimates that there may be 50,000 trillion cubic feet of it. That is, enough to last between 1,000 and 2,500 years at current consumption.

"The President's energy advisers know this. It was explained to them recently in a briefing by specialists of the American Gas Association. Experts in ERDA (Energy Research and Development Administration) have been trying to tell the White House too, but have been snubbed apparently on the ground that this news would take the sting out of the scare."

The *Journal* was even so rude as to call Carter's energy crisis "a snare and a delusion. Worse, it's a hustle . . ."

But the Carter crowd knew what they were doing. How could they sell their high-price energy program to Congress and the public if they acknowledged that in effect it amounted to paying ransom for a natural resource that was in enormously abundant supply but being held off the market by a rapacious industry? No way. Hard as it might be to peddle the program in the name of conservation, it would be infinitely easier than peddling it in the name of higher profits. Carter believed he had to use industry's figures to prove he was simply trying to sensibly ration a product that was rapidly disappearing. And he took a very unkind view of everyone in his administration who used industry's figures otherwise.

That was driven home in two celebrated cases. The first involved Dr. Christian W. Knudsen. Early in the year, ERDA had launched a study of natural gas reserves and put Dr. Knudsen in charge of the project. Up to this time, his superiors had thought so well of him that they had given

---

leading to use a "reserves" figure as though it were permanent. "Resources," on the other hand, is a word that embraces the future; it includes deposits known to exist but not yet recoverable, either because of technological shortcomings or because it would not be profitable to recover. Then, too, it is reasonable to speak of "potential" resources—not yet found, but on good evidence believed to be down there and someday recoverable.

him an award for outstanding performance. Apparently they thought he
was a team player—that is, they thought he would make this study con-
form to the Administration's desires. But Knudsen had the mistaken notion that he was supposed to produce an honest report. So, using data
supplied by industry and the U.S. Geological Survey, Knudsen's panel
came up with a projection that the United States would have an adequate and affordable supply of natural gas well into the twenty-first century. It concluded that we had much, much more gas than we had been
previously led to believe. If the report was released, it would be a blow
to Carter's crisis scenario. But Knudsen also was prepared to deliver a
terrible blow to industry's claims that abundance depended on much
higher prices. Indeed not, said Knudsen; in fact, according to his figures,
the cost of producing a thousand cubic feet of natural gas would average
no more than $1 until the end of the 1990s—and that would include a net
profit of 15 percent. *A mere buck per Mcf?* Why, that made even
Carter's proposed price—$1.75 per Mcf—seem ridiculously, absurdly gen-
erous, and industry was saying that $1.75 was a starvation proposal.
Behind Knudsen's back, his bosses launched another study group in
hopes that it could juggle statistics in such a way as to support the Administration's crisis position; after two tries, this shadow group managed
to put together an acceptable script. And thereupon, Knudsen was removed from his project and shifted to another job within ERDA, and
finally he was forced to resign.

When all this was inevitably discovered by the press, there were congressional hearings at which Knudsen's superiors admitted that there was
nothing wrong with his methodology or his figures, but that they felt his
conclusions, by contradicting industry's predictions, "would make ERDA
the laughingstock of the oil and gas industry." Two of Knudsen's bosses
may have been particularly sensitive to the feelings of industry, because
together they had a total of over sixty years' service as oil company executives and one was drawing more than $100 a day in pension from Stan-
dard Oil of Indiana.

The next victim of candor was Dr. Vincent McKelvey, director of the
U.S. Geological Survey. In 1971 he was not only promoted to chief geologist but, on the recommendation of the National Academy of Sciences,
he was appointed by Nixon to be director of the agency. Over the years,
he had received virtually every award a geologist can win, and although
the USGS directorship was a presidential appointment it was not looked
upon as a political so much as a scholarly job. In the 99-year history of
the Survey, there had been only nine directors. The truth was, few people had ever paid any attention to the USGS director, whoever he was.
Suddenly, however, the person in that job was viewed by the Carter administration as a highly important member of their propaganda team,
which is why they were very unhappy when, on July 13, in a Boston

speech, Dr. McKelvey made this comment about the natural gas supply:

"By far the greatest potential sources of natural gas are the geopressurized zones underlying the Gulf Coast region, both on- and offshore. The limited investigations that have been made of this region led to estimates of as much as 60,000 to 80,000 trillion cubic feet of gas dissolved in water at a ratio believed to average 25 cubic feet per barrel of water. This is an almost *incomprehensibly large number. Even the bottom of the range represents about ten times the energy value of all oil, natural gas, and coal reserves in the United States combined.*" (Emphasis added)

Wasn't he aware that this violated the Carter line? Didn't he know Schlesinger had taken the public position that such wildly optimistic predictions "seem to be based on smoking pot"?

Dr. McKelvey was fired as director.

***

There was also chilling evidence of Carter's anticonsumer bias in his restructuring of the energy bureaucracy. When, in August, Congress approved Carter's new Department of Energy, its thrust became immediately clear from the fact that he kept in power the same gang of proindustry policymakers who had previously been scattered among the old agencies—the FPC, the ERDA, the FEA, the AEC, et cetera. The only difference was that now, with these agencies absorbed into DOE along with functions previously performed by fifty other agencies, they would be hidden behind the deeper layers of bureaucracy and chaos that comes with cabinet status, and therefore more immune from inspection by press and public. Furthermore, the Department of Energy was largely manned by the dregs of other departments, which, when asked to let the new department have personnel they didn't need, naturally sent over their deadheads and timeservers. From the beginning, the Department of Energy was destined to exist in ignominy.

If the rank and file were castoffs, many top officials were very talented indeed, but of dubious orientation. To be the DOE's general counsel, Carter nominated Lynn R. Coleman, a member of John Connally's oil-rich law firm and Washington lobbyist for Houston Natural Gas Company. But perhaps the most unsettling step taken by Carter—a step that irritated most liberals and many conservatives—was his appointment of James Rodney Schlesinger to be Secretary of Energy.

*

Born in 1929, Schlesinger graduated from high school the year World War II ended; he was attending Harvard University while others fought the Korean War. His lack of experience with any of war's hardships may help account for the fact that he became so hawkish. With a Ph.D. in economics, he taught at the University of Virginia and published harshly anticommunist tracts until he joined the RAND Corporation, in 1963, where he became an expert on nuclear weapons and even more intransigent about the East-West confrontation. Schlesinger came to government with the Nixon administration, as assistant director of the Bureau of the Budget. His tough-guy posturing at first offended and then appealed to Nixon, and in 1971 Schlesinger was appointed chairman of the Atomic Energy Commission. He stayed eighteen months, and was best remembered for a typical act of zealotry: when conservationists objected to a proposed nuclear test on Amchitka Island, in the Aleutians, Schlesinger took his wife and two children along to watch the blast as a way of saying he was so certain of its safety that he would gamble their lives.

Intrigued by Schlesinger's published analysis of the Central Intelligence Agency as being too flabby, Nixon shifted him to the directorship of the CIA in January 1973. Some critics felt that Schlesinger politicized the CIA by suppressing those elements that in the past might have tended to disagree with the President. He was extremely unpopular with many CIA careerists, who rejoiced when, in July 1973, he became Secretary of Defense, replacing Elliot Richardson in the musical chairs Nixon imposed on his Cabinet. As head of the Pentagon, he had one theme (the Russians are coming) and one remedy: The United States must become the savior of the world. "The burden for the maintenance of free societies around the world can only be borne by the United States," he said. "There is no alternative. If the United States drops the torch, there is no one else that can pick it up."

His view of life prompted some to call him "The Prophet." He called himself "a revivalist." Although he was raised a Jew, Schlesinger as a young man was shaken by an experience that persuaded him to convert to Lutheranism. One who attended the University of Virginia with Schlesinger and later worked with him, said that he sometimes seriously believed he was "in contact with the God Almighty," that there were hallowed moments when he was receiving "the truth from the basic source."

Apparently he believed God had told him President Ford's policy of détente with the Soviet Union was wrong, and he expressed his disapproval to Ford so strongly that he was fired from his Pentagon post, in 1975. But Schlesinger's attitude appealed very much to Ronald Reagan, who used him as his military adviser during the 1976 primaries. When Reagan lost his bid for the Republican nomination, Schlesinger shifted his advisory support to Jimmy Carter, who believed that he, too, could talk with God. Carter was so grateful for Schlesinger's foreign policy coaching—Carter did better in his foreign policy debate with Ford than with any of the other debates—that he rewarded him with the secretaryship of the new Energy Department. Carter called it "my most important appointment."

It may have been his most disastrous appointment. From the beginning, Schlesinger would be distrusted by liberal congressmen (two dozen had written Carter in late 1976 asking that Schlesinger not be appointed) and by the vigorous consumer and environmentalist organizations. And why should they trust him? They could remember too clearly the way he had run roughshod over them at the AEC and of how, at the Pentagon, he had taken guidance in energy matters from his oil-soaked deputy, William P. Clements, founder and chief stockholder of SEDCO, the Dallas-based drilling company that was tied to the multinationals from the Arctic to Iran. How could they feel comfortable with a bureaucrat who could slide so easily from Reagan's camp to Carter's? Was that a forked tongue they detected? Could be. On the one hand, he claimed to be on the side of consumers, vowing to hold the line on price deregulation, but then, in Houston, he told three thousand oilmen, "The objective of the government is to make the American oil industry flourish." But if he was actively disliked by most liberal congressmen, he was not more than passively tolerated by many conservatives. He simply did not know how to get along with members. Said one member of the Senate Energy Committee: "Whenever he dealt with anybody he lost a vote." One day he came home from a protracted session on Capitol Hill to snap to his wife: "They're saying I'm arrogant. They're right, goddamn it. I am arrogant. I can't stand stupid questions."

For some reason, the political herd did not appreciate being called stupid by a maverick whose intelligence they didn't respect all that much. If they sometimes asked stupid questions, he could match them with stupid answers, congealed around such impenetrably fatty remarks as "We have no way of demonstrating the null hypothesis on that question." Schlesinger's encounters with politicians, foreign as well as domestic, were often memorably awful. When Mexico's Foreign Minister Santiago Roel and Petroleum Chief Jorge Díaz Serrano came to Washington, in December, expecting to get final approval of an already negotiated deal to sell natural gas to this country, Schlesinger brusquely reneged on the deal, said the price was much too high, and dismissed them. Outside, the Mexican officials complained of his rudeness. "For half an hour," one said, "he gave us a pompous lecture." That was Schlesinger, all right.

* * *

So fair was the weather prevailing in the House, that most of Carter's programs were accepted without major alterations. Although the House threw out his request for tax rebates to buyers of small cars (members feared the rebate would simply subsidize imports, which already had captured 18.7 percent of the U.S. market), it had, as requested, heaped heavy taxes on the buyers of Detroit's big gas-guzzlers.

Likewise, with some changes, the House approved the wellhead tax on oil to raise about $12 billion annually, with most of the money allegedly to be rebated to citizens who took steps to conserve energy.

The wellhead tax was looked upon as one half of the heart of Carter's package. The other half was the natural gas bill. It was extremely generous to industry. The current price for new gas was $1.42 per thousand cubic feet. Carter's bill would raise that immediately by 24 percent, to $1.75 per Mcf, and allow periodic increases to about $2.50 per Mcf by 1981. Old gas (gas brought into production before 1977) would remain under existing price contracts. The bill would, for the first time in history, extend price controls to intrastate gas—gas sold within the state where it was produced—but Carter's strategists presumed that the enormously higher prices would make controls acceptable to industry. Apparently the House thought so too, because this was the bill it passed.

The Administration's euphoria was understandable, because its victories came with a rush, in a group. Within a single week in early August, the Senate approved Schlesinger's nomination, Carter signed the Department of Energy into existence, and the House passed his energy package. Everything seemed to be going the Administration's way, and its optimism was contagious with the somewhat surprised press. Carter's public popularity was already dropping; the fact that he had succeeded in the House misled the press into thinking he was stronger than the polls suggested. *Time* magazine, among others, predicted that "the Senate is likely to act favorably" on Carter's energy bills when it returned after the August recess.

The Administration and the press were misled by the oil lobby's deceptive calm. It had not tried to block or significantly alter the energy legislation as it moved through the House, for it knew that its best chances lay ahead, on the Senate side and, after that, in conference committee. Anticonsumer forces were just warming up for an outburst of creativity.

These forces went far beyond the standard oil and gas lobby. Among its awesome allies were, for example, the "multipulps," such giant timber and paper-product companies as Georgia Pacific and Weyerhaeuser and Boise Cascade. The National Forest Products Association had a budget of $4.5 million; the American Paper Institute had a budget of $9 million. Hundreds of companies in just these industries alone were lining up side by side to fight for natural gas deregulation, for they used enormous amounts of energy and they wanted a secure supply at whatever the cost —which they could pass on to consumers anyway. As one oil lobbyist told Dan Morgan, of the Washington *Post*, "By ourselves, the oil companies can never win a fight in this town. That's why we rely on the users of oil to help us make our case on things like deregulation." The lumber outfits had made very generous contributions to such useful politicians as Senator Henry Jackson, chairman of the Senate Energy Committee; but since his home state, Washington, was so big in timber, who could accuse them of being out of line?

When the muscle of the oil alliance first showed its strength, in mid-August at Senate Finance Committee hearings, the White House strategists weren't paying enough attention. As one admitted, "We were all kind of happy and patting ourselves on the back for what we did in the House, and *they* were getting their act together."

It should have been obvious that the Senate would be bloodier. The quality of the Administration's enemies in the Senate was much more impressive than in the House, which had no pro-oil strategists to compare with Senator Bennett Johnston of Louisiana or his countryman Russell Long, the master tax juggler. As for allies, Carter had none so well placed in the Senate as in the House; and the liberals who would have fought for him were bitter at the White House's failure to consult with them. In the Senate, the leadership would not give forceful support. Majority Leader Robert Byrd of West Virginia, whose coal constituents were hardly distinguishable from the oil crowd, would never show aggressiveness but often reluctance in pushing the Administration's program; being a politician of notable vanity, Byrd would resent any effort Carter made to seek Senate allies except through him. The floor manager of Carter's natural gas bill was Energy Committee Chairman Jackson; he was still smarting from his defeat in the previous year's presidential primaries and would see no reason to get cut up on behalf of this upstart from Georgia. Jackson's control over his Energy Committee was less than impressive, to put it mildly; the committee was deadlocked, 9 to 9, on the natural gas bill, and this lack of endorsement was a heavy burden for the bill to bear when it reached the floor.[4]

The Senate Finance Committee effectively killed the other half of the heart of Carter's program by voting 10 to 6 on September 26 to reject the crude oil tax. Rebating the tax to consumers? A rotten idea, said Chairman Long; however, he might consider allowing the levy to be created if some of it—perhaps half? maybe all of it?—was turned over to the oil and gas companies to pay for exploration. Other oil senators agreed that was the only way to legitimatize the bastard. Consumer and labor organizations that had supported the crude tax in the House said this was an intolerable alternative. Caught in this cross fire, it expired.

---

4. The nine on industry's side were seven Republicans, Clifford P. Hansen of Wyoming, Mark Hatfield of Oregon, James McClure of Idaho, Dewey Bartlett of Oklahoma, Lowell Weicker of Connecticut, Pete Domenici of New Mexico, and Paul Laxalt of Nevada; and two Democrats, Bennett Johnston of Louisiana and Wendell Ford of Kentucky. Holding out for consumers were nine Democrats, Jackson, Frank Church of Idaho, Lee Metcalf of Montana, James Abourezk of South Dakota, Howard Metzenbaum of Ohio, Spark Matsunaga of Hawaii, Floyd Haskell of Colorado, Dale Bumpers of Arkansas, and John Durkin of New Hampshire.

*

But at least the death was swift and clean. What happened to the natural gas bill was messy indeed. Carter and his lobbyists had made the mistake of thinking it was an offer the industry couldn't refuse. It was certainly generous. But the industry did not want to be handed a fortune; in the best spirit of free enterprise, it wanted to be free of controls so that it could pillage and rob on its own initiative. By the middle of September, the Administration, finally aware that momentum on the natural gas issue had shifted to the opposition, began making frantic efforts to catch up. Carter and Vice-President Mondale started lobbying by telephone, and Energy Secretary Schlesinger on September 19 moved into an office off the Vice-President's reception room in the Capitol to grab members as they came by. But these steps were taken much, much too late. Only four days later, on September 22, the Senate prepared to consider a bill offered by Senator James Pearson of Kansas and Senator Lloyd Bentsen, Jr., of Texas to deregulate natural gas prices. It was the same bill the Senate had passed two years earlier. Senator Jackson moved to table it. His motion was rejected 52 to 46. If this was a true reflection of the Senate's mood, Carter's controlled prices were doomed.

At least they were certainly doomed unless Carter was given more time to lobby members, time to regroup his forces and concentrate the White House's influence, time to pressure three or four senators into changing sides.

To supply that critical time, Senators Howard Metzenbaum and James Abourezk decided to filibuster.

The public had already been introduced to Abourezk, the wild hare from South Dakota, in the divestiture fight. Metzenbaum of Ohio was a new face. Or almost. He had been appointed to fill a Senate vacancy in 1974 but was defeated that same year in the Democratic primary by astronaut hero John Glenn. A successful labor lawyer and millionaire (airport parking lots) with plenty of political training (he had been campaign manager for tough old Stephen Young), Metzenbaum tried again in 1976 and won.

But the "gruesome twosome" or "Israeli-Arab Alliance," as Metzenbaum and Abourezk soon were being called behind their backs, did not get off to an auspicious beginning. They had hardly launched their filibuster when cloture was voted. In other years, the Senate had allowed filibusters against civil rights and against consumer legislation to run on and on unhindered for days. Members on those earlier occasions had eloquently proclaimed the rights of their colleagues to orate endlessly. But this filibuster to protect the consumer was not at all popular, and cloture was easily voted on Monday, September 26. Thereafter, no member would be allowed more than an hour to talk and the Senate would refuse to consider any amendments that had not been introduced at the time cloture was voted.

However, those senators who thought that cloture would permit them to rush ahead to vote on the Pearson-Bentsen bill were still in for a disappointment. Metzenbaum and Abourezk had already introduced 508 amendments.

Five hundred and eight.

And such was the naughty temper of M&A that they intended to force the Senate to consider each and every one of those amendments. Having lost the traditional debate-style filibuster, they were now setting forth upon a new type of filibuster, not of debate but of parliamentary technicalities—the deadliest and dullest kind of legislative warfare known to man. On the very first day of battle, the Senate was forced to spend five hours and thirty-six minutes doing nothing but answer roll calls and quorum calls. Endlessly. In the more exciting moments, the Senate chamber was filled with the droning voice of the clerk reading every word of 20-page amendments.

As the Senate prepared grumpily for an all-night session on Tuesday, Majority Leader Byrd damned the filibuster as "outrageous"—an outburst amusing to those who remembered that the last time the Senate had held an all-night filibuster session was during debate on the 1964 civil rights bill and the senator who held the floor that night was a former Ku Klux Klansman, Senator Robert Byrd himself.

Night filibuster sessions are a serious test of ideological willpower. Given the proper cause to stir them up, conservatives seem to have that in abundance. Liberals do not. Senators as a genre do not like to sleep on army cots and cold leather couches, and be forced to wander around drafty chambers in their stockinged feet to answer quorum calls in the middle of the night, and do without their showers; liberal senators, being a tender lot, like it even less than most. They were becoming as snarly as the pro-oil crowd. Metzenbaum and Abourezk could count on between forty and forty-five senators for support of the spirit of their filibuster, but not of its fleshly sacrifices. Wandering out onto the Senate floor the next morning, one of their allies, Dale Bumpers of Arkansas, complained that he had had no more than an hour's sleep, that he didn't know anybody who had gotten more, that he didn't think he needed to undergo the torment of a filibuster to prove his manhood, that he was too groggy to vote intelligently and so was everyone else—"one does not have to be broken out with brilliance to know the mental condition of this body right now"—et cetera, et cetera, while all around him members in house slippers and sweat suits and wrinkled shirts yawned and rubbed their whiskered faces and nodded in agreement.

The growls from their rumpled colleagues had an effect on Metzenbaum and Abourezk. With less than a year of service, Metzenbaum was still thin-skinned enough to feel the chill. And Abourezk, who fancied himself a tough maverick, apparently wasn't as tough as he thought. He acknowledged, "It is not very pleasant to be put in a position of protest. There are all kinds of peer pressures."

They felt especially isolated because, although their filibuster was designed to save Carter's program, they received absolutely no encouragement from the White House. They were operating in a vacuum. Here was a bizarre situation indeed: two shavetails holding the fort for a general who apparently had lost the ability to command. Senator Long could not resist the temptation to mock them. "So far," he told the Senate with a smug smile, "we do not know whether the President of the United States is for the filibuster or against it. All we know is that the President wants us to vote on his side. Whether that means it is the filibusters' side, nobody knows . . . I understand what the President's position is and the filibuster is probably closer to his position than mine. But I am curious. What does the President think about the filibuster, that we ought to get on with the business or keep filibustering here forever?"

Feeling abandoned, Metzenbaum and Abourezk succumbed to the blandishments of compromise. When Senator Jackson offered legislation that would raise the price of new gas to $2.03 immediately, gradually increasing to $3.36 by 1985, they said they would go along with that and end their filibuster if the Jackson offer was agreeable to the rest of the Senate. It was much, much too high, but they would accept it.

Metzenbaum laid out their position: "Senator Abourezk and I . . . do not approve of the $1.42 price that is presently in the law. We do not approve of the increase to $1.75 that the Administration proposes. But we went along with that in committee in an effort to bring the matter to a resolution and also to include intrastate gas. We certainly do not agree and do not approve of the $2.03 figure that is included in Senator Jackson's proposal . . .

"Having said all of that . . . we are prepared to support the compromise in an effort to break the stalemate—not because we approve of it, but because we think that is far better than total deregulation."

But pro-oil members were not ready to compromise. It was evident now that the filibuster would dribble out, fail. And just what did they mean to do when that moment came? They had in mind, said financial writer Hobart Rowen, "one of the boldest and biggest steals of all time." Lest his readers think he was exaggerating, Rowen suggested they review the history of natural gas pricing: "Not content with a price increase for new gas of 445 percent from 1972 through 1976, the industry in reality is seeking to get the equivalent of the monopoly price of oil, as set by OPEC: $2.50 to $2.75 per thousand cubic feet.

"That would give the industry a price increase of 2,000 percent—yes,

20 times the 13- to 14-cent price at which it was making a good profit in 1968 . . ."

Rowen reminded his readers that "every added penny on the gas price per thousand cubic feet costs consumers $200 million. Every dime costs $2 billion. Yet, in an effort to stave off the greedy drive to total deregulation, hard-pressed Democratic senators are giving away dimes and quarters like chicken feed . . ."

The hemorrhaging of billion-dollar dimes and quarters might have been stopped with assistance from the White House. Instead, the White House was about to double-cross the fighting liberals.

On Friday, September 30, Majority Leader Byrd said he was opposed to any White House intervention. But over the weekend several Senate leaders—including Minority Leader Howard Baker and Finance Chairman Long—took Byrd aside and laid down the law: he would have to show more strength, get nastier, manipulate the rules to shut up the dissenters, if he hoped to adjourn the Senate on schedule at the end of the month. That did it. Nothing was so sacred to Byrd as a tight schedule. Counseled by Long, he emerged from this meeting with a scheme that would require the assistance of the White House, and the White House— contrary to Schlesinger's assurance to Abourezk as late as Saturday that he and Carter "would stay out of the Senate's internal fight"—was only too eager to cooperate. The success of Byrd's ambush would depend on Vice-President Mondale, the Senate's presiding officer.

*

Late Monday morning, the rumor went through the Senate galleries that Mondale would take the chair—something he rarely did—and make a series of parliamentary rulings to break the filibuster. When the rumor reached Metzenbaum, he scurried over to Mondale's office. Mondale said he was too busy to see him, so Metzenbaum went back to his seat on the floor. Within five minutes, Mondale entered the chamber. When Metzenbaum approached, Mondale told him, "Howard, I'm sorry I couldn't see you. The majority leader wanted me to take the chair right away. But don't worry, we've got the votes."

Got the votes for what? It was a puzzling remark, but not puzzling for long.

Byrd, demanding recognition, asked Mondale if he didn't think it was the presiding officer's responsibility to take the initiative in ruling out amendments that he considered to be dilatory or out of order for other reasons. He moved that Mondale assume that duty. Abourezk saw immediately what was coming. Ordinarily it was left to other senators on the floor to raise objections that an amendment was out of order; if the presiding officer took the initiative, he could flatten a filibuster on his own without following the normal, time-consuming routine. Abourezk objected to Byrd's motion. His objection was tabled by the Senate, 79 to 13. Now it was clear what Mondale had meant when he'd said, ". . . we've got the votes."

Quickly the Vice-President ruled three dozen M&A amendments out of order before Senate liberals—enraged by the tactics—brought Senate business to a standstill with shouted insults and threats. Senator Paul Sarbanes of Maryland accused Byrd of trying to "establish a dictatorship." Senator Gary Hart of Colorado denounced Mondale and Byrd for a "sophisticated steamroller." And so on. And on.

Metzenbaum and Abourezk had 243 amendments left. Whether or not Mondale would have had the gall to continue ruling them out of order in that way will never be known, because he didn't have to. The White House had taken the spirit out of the filibusters. At 6 P.M. they announced they were quitting. Said Abourezk, "We were defending the public position of the Administration, and the Administration pulled the rug out from under us. Since I've been in politics I've been told that governments lie. One thing I never thought would happen is that Jimmy Carter would lie. Nixon had his enemies list; Carter has his friends list."

*

The following day, the Senate passed—50 to 46—the Pearson-Bentsen Act. Sixteen Democrats and thirty-four Republicans voted for it; of the Democrats, twelve were from the South and Southwest. If the bill was given only a passing glance, it would not have appeared to decontrol natural gas prices for another two years. That, however, would have been a false interpretation, for the bill permitted prices to shoot up during those two years to $2.48 per Mcf—70 percent above the current price ceiling and 42 percent above the limit proposed by Carter—and since this was even higher than the prices then obtainable in the privateering intrastate market, the bill did effectively decontrol gas prices at once.

Or it would, if it survived the conference committee.

Carter called the Senate bill "unacceptable" and "unfair" and "an injustice to the working people of this country." But if he actually felt so strongly about it, why had he undermined Metzenbaum and Abourezk? The White House's liberal lobbyists—that is, those persons (Anne Wexler, Stu Eizenstat, Kitty Schirmer, etc.) it believed would be most credible among liberals on the Hill—passed the word that the job had been done on Abourezk and Metzenbaum in order to move the battle to the conference committee. Cathy Hurwit, policy adviser for the House Government Operations energy subcommittee, later recalled, "They told us, 'When we get to conference, we'll be with you; but we have to get the bill out of the Senate.' Who is 'we'? Schlesinger, O'Leary, Carter. 'Trust us,' they said; 'once we get it out there we're really going to be tough. We're really going to support the House.' At that point, those of us on this side really began to smell a rat."

What had Carter achieved in the Senate that gave him the idea that the conference could salvage anything resembling his original program? What pieces of the Carter energy program had the Senate left intact? Nothing. Both the tax and the nontax features had been destroyed or changed beyond recognition. Senator Abraham Ribicoff of Connecticut asked a White House aide, "Shouldn't the President admit his energy program is in shambles? All the indications are it's just not going to fly . . . Shouldn't the President and Schlesinger go back to the drawing board and come up with a new program?"

Psychologically and tactically, it couldn't be done. Carter had publicly stated that energy was "the most important domestic issue that we will face while I am in office" and that the program presented to Congress was the program he would stake his reputation on. As one of his political operatives put it, "If we fail on this, we fail completely." Carter could not turn back. And he had no fancy strategy for going ahead. So he resorted to the kind of heavy rhetoric President Kennedy had used against the steel industry fifteen years earlier; only, he was no Kennedy. The U.S. oil companies, Carter told a press conference in mid-October, were seeking "the biggest rip-off in history,"[5] were trying to "rob" consumers, were guilty of "potential war profiteering." He pointed out that in 1973, just before OPEC imposed its oil embargo and sharply raised prices, U.S. oil and gas companies had an income of $18 billion. Under his proposed program, Carter said, that figure would increase to $100 billion by 1985. But, he said, the oil and gas companies were demanding legislation that would yield $150 billion in revenues by 1985. "Our proposal, if adopted, would give the oil companies the highest prices for oil in all the world. But still they want more—the oil companies apparently want it all."

He was, if anything, understating the case. But heavy rhetoric was not enough to pull his troops together in Congress or rally public opinion. Polls showed most people felt he was losing his grip. He would have to become more personally involved. He had planned to visit nine countries in eleven days, starting November 22, but he obviously needed to win more friends in the Senate than in Nigeria or Poland. So he called off the trip (no President had canceled a major announced trip overseas since anti-American rioting by students in Japan had forced Eisenhower

5. The ripping was taking place even under the present price structure. Profits for the first half of 1977, compared to five years earlier, were up thusly: 77.4 percent for Exxon; 177.4 percent, Indiana Standard; 100.8 percent, Standard Oil of California; 70.2 percent, Mobil; 54.9 percent, Gulf; 321 percent, Atlantic Richfield; 240 percent, Phillips; 160.6 percent, Conoco; 153.6 percent, Sun.

to cancel a trip to that country in 1960). The calendar was beginning to mock him. Once, he had thought he would get his energy program out of Congress by October 1. Now his aides were telling him to expect the bill to land on his desk "to the tune of Christmas carols." But that, too, was an unrealistic hope. The conference committee was obviously in no hurry. It was deadlocked on the natural gas issue. Both sides, as Congressman Toby Moffett of Connecticut, leader of the liberals in conference, said, "are in an ass-kicking mood." Recalling that period, Moffett now explains the reasons for the liberals' irritation. "Keep in mind, the liaison and lobbying by the White House and by the Department of Energy was pathetic—inefficient, didn't know what was going on, didn't know what their position was, double-talk—give us one position over here and then another position over there. Did they favor this amendment or didn't they? You'd never know, couldn't get a response. And also there was a great deal of resentment over here [in the House] because Schlesinger just took his cues from the Senate, just dealt with the Senate. Here we were, giving the President 85 percent of what he wanted, putting our asses on the line, and they [White House lobbyists] are over there taking their cues from the guys who gave them 15 percent of what he wanted and took three months longer to do it."

Did Moffett mean that Schlesinger and the Senate were working together, that Schlesinger in effect was working with the enemy? "Yeah, they were working together. But what happened was—this guy is the worst political poker player who ever served in government. I mean Schlesinger . . . Well, all you have to do is give the guys over there [in the Senate] the signal that you're a pushover and that you're not that devoted to your own plan and they are going to steamroller right over you. And that's what happened."

If you want the other side to win, you're not going to try to be a good poker player, are you? "Let's put it this way: if your heart's not in it, if you don't really believe in your own hand, you're more likely to throw it in early. They [Carter, Schlesinger, et al.] killed us from around November on by making it very clear that they weren't going to hang in there when it got tough."

*

The mood of House members became even uglier and less cooperative after Schlesinger, answering newsmen's questions on November 21, said he thought Carter would be willing to compromise the $1.75 gas price upward to, oh, say about $2. When that hit the papers, Carter's congressional allies were appalled. Speaker O'Neill phoned Schlesinger to warn that if he didn't stop popping off in public, House liberals might get so mad they would vote against the conference report. Congressman Thomas Ashley of Ohio, who had chaired the House ad hoc energy committee, said he felt betrayed: ". . . the House fought hard for a good bill and I don't think it is helpful for Administration officials to publicly pull back from what we fought so hard to win." But Schlesinger was only telling the truth. Carter—though he hadn't wanted it known so early—was perfectly ready to accept just about anything called an energy bill. Meanwhile, he continued to pretend to be steadfast. On December 2, he called three dozen liberal congressmen to the White House to assure them that Schlesinger "is not authorized by me to depart from the Administration position without specifically coming back to me and getting my approval for it." He further vowed that before he gave such approval to Schlesinger, he would consult with them.

A few days later, a brigade of liberal congressmen trooped back to the White House for another presumed showdown with Carter and Schlesinger. Moffett recalls: "We sat in the Cabinet Room and it was a real show of strength. We laid it out for him: 'We are the people who voted for your plan in August. We are the people who swallowed the natural gas thing [the price increase] when we didn't want to. We urge you not to cave in.' Once again, Carter gave us assurances. It raises some interesting questions. Did Schlesinger have Carter's authorization to deal over there in the Senate as he was doing? If he did have the authority, how come Carter was telling us he wouldn't change his position?"

Is it fair to say, judging from the assurances Carter gave at those two meetings, that either the President was lying through his teeth or Schlesinger was betraying him? "It's one or the other, isn't it?" said Moffett. "There's another possibility: that the President didn't understand what in hell was going on."

Congressman Andy Maguire of New Jersey also has vivid memories of the meeting: "We told Carter and Schlesinger, 'We'll work with you, but you got to tell us you will stick with this plan, because we are putting ourselves out on a limb. Look how far we are compromising our position to make this thing work.' I put this directly to Schlesinger. There had been reports in the press that Schlesinger had been negotiating on the Senate side and had been saying that the price of natural gas might have to go way, way up to around $2. So I said to Schlesinger, 'Can you assure us that this is where you are going to stick [at $1.75]? What is the President's position? Are you going to move off this the next time we turn around?' I don't know exactly how I put it, but that was the thrust of my question, and he said, 'YES! a dollar seventy-five, and at most a minor, minor adjustment in that.' There was no way to interpret what he said except maybe at *most* a dollar eighty-five.

"Twelve or fifteen of us had a press conference after meeting with Carter and Schlesinger. We had to talk our way into the press room, because [Jody] Powell and the other guys were not at all interested in having us hold our own press conference at the White House. But we did.

We stood up on the stage after Powell had his say, and I said that Schlesinger had made these commitments.

"Yeah, we got the commitments, all right. We walked out, and three days later we read that Schlesinger was again giving away the horse on the Senate side."

                        *

Carter's December promises to the House liberals were similar to the moonshine he had distributed in October to liberal senators when they met with him at the White House and begged him to stick with them in the fight and not negotiate on the sly with Senator Long. They, too, had received Carter's assurance that he was on the square, that he had not been dealing with Long, and that he would indeed frequently confer with them.

The promises may have been made sincerely, but they were not honored. Carter rarely touched base with the liberals; his lobbyists constantly negotiated with Long and his allies, especially with the other senator from Louisiana, Bennett Johnston, who was showing extraordinary talents as a negotiator—"Cool Hand Luke" and "Swamp Fox," the liberals dubbed him with grudging admiration. Long's conference committee on energy taxation was supposed to be reconciling differences—if possible—between the wellhead tax on crude oil passed by the House (at Carter's request) and the energy trust fund for producers (a $42 billion tax break for the oil industry) passed by the Senate. But instead of pressuring Long for a compromise, White House lobbyists secretly agreed to go with the trust fund. The Administration finally became rather blatant about this bit of hypocrisy. One Monday, Schlesinger assured a group of proconsumer congressmen and lobbyists that the Administration was opposed to creating a producers' trust fund from crude oil taxes. But, on Wednesday, Assistant Treasury Secretary Laurence Woodworth (who had been a top aide to Long before he joined the Carter administration) told tax conferees that the Administration did "not oppose the trust fund as such." And apparently that was indeed the new Carter line, for Transportation Secretary Brock Adams was out lobbying for the trust fund. (When this was called to Schlesinger's attention, he replied, "That's news to me. He shouldn't be.")

                        *

But if Carter was caving in, so were key liberals, especially among the House negotiators. This became increasingly evident after that cold, rainy December 14 evening when Carter summoned to the White House eight Democrats: Senators Jackson, Wendell Ford, and Johnston, and Congressmen Staggers, Dingell, Ashley, Moffett, and Eckhardt. Schlesinger was of course also there. Carter, as Moffett recalls, said, "All right, enough is enough. You've been on gas for three months and there is no progress. I want you to work something out." He wrapped that little message up in the usual gauze of patriotism: he had rescheduled his trip abroad for the end of the month and he made it sound as if the President would go naked among foreigners if he couldn't say that he had his energy package virtually in his pocket. Then the Capitol Hill politicians got up and made conciliatory speeches, and everyone began feeling chummy, and four hours later the foxy Senator Johnston had just about sold everyone his plan. "I don't remember the details," says Moffett. "I thought maybe I could buy it, but it was very generous. I was feeling guilty as hell even being in the room discussing it."

The next day, Senator Jackson went back to the White House to talk with Carter again, and came out saying he thought it might be a good idea if the antideregulation forces modified their stance to permit phased deregulation over a five-year period, accompanied by much higher prices en route to decontrol. It was Johnston's plan all over. Looking a bit abashed, Jackson told reporters he was only offering the compromise suggestion to get the conferees off their deadlock.

Now that the proindustry members of the conference had the liberals sagging, they felt they could complete the job much better in private. Usually the eighteen Senate conferees and the twenty-five from the House had met openly in the House Commerce Committee hearing room, perched high on a dais and forced to speak into microphones for all the world to hear. But Congress was in recess now. Most of the conference committee had, like the rest of Congress, gone home for the long Christmas holidays. Why stay in the chilly big room and feel lonely? Ah yes, why indeed, asked Senator Johnston as he suggested he and his fellow conferees "shut this conference down and meet somewhere" in private. The others agreed. So, on December 15, the day after the chummy White House session, they moved into a third-floor room in the Capitol. There they could be alone, where the chairs were deeply cushioned and the mahogany table was covered with soft brown felt and the smoke from Johnston's Grenadier cigars floated fraternally through the air.

It was a tight little group. Instead of the full complement of forty-three conferees, usually there were no more than a dozen. Should an outsider have looked into the room, he might have thought, from the people there, that the third-floor gathering was suffering from the customary ideological split. But, as one participant told Peter Behr, of the Baltimore Sun, "In that room there is no dissension at all." That was not quite accurate. But the quarrel had become mushy. "Behind closed doors," says Moffett, "just about everyone began talking about the need to create the image of solving the energy problem. It is very important to understand how much of a factor this was, how much of a factor it became with our House conferees and with Jackson and the Senate conferees. The conversations behind closed doors were just filled with references to the dollar evaporating on the world market if we didn't give the *impression* that we were doing something. This is very touchy for me to be saying it, but it's the truth; this was the talk, time and time again: 'We have got to get a bill, *any* bill, because it's important to create the *image* that we're doing something.'"

❖

Snowed by Carter, that may have been what most liberals thought was the main objective, but the steelier conservatives never lost sight of a very special kind of bill, and therefore they prevailed. After wrangling for fourteen hours behind closed doors, the surviving negotiators (eight from House, three from Senate) emerged shortly before midnight, December 20, to say that they had come to a conclusion: a majority was ready to recommend to the full, 43-member conference a compromise proposal that was, in fact, just a dressed-up version of Johnston's old plan. It went like this:

On February 1, 1978, the price of new gas would jump to $1.75 and move upward steadily at a regular rate of inflation-plus-4.5-percent every year until the end of 1983. By then, prices were expected to be above $3 per Mcf. Then the price-control program would be removed entirely and replaced by what was called a "floating cap." The "cap" would float upward as prices continued to rise. Supposedly it would prevent gas prices from rising more than 15 percent a year, but since the cap was tied to free-market levels, it really was no price control at all.

In short, the conferees had cooked up a bit of sleight of hand: by giving the free market the designation "floating cap," the Johnston crowd hoped to talk House members into accepting it as a continuation of meaningful price controls.

In their third-floor hideaway, they had great success. Lud Ashley, chairman of the Ad Hoc Energy Committee, went for it (no big surprise: Ashley had become very close to Schlesinger and to Charls Walker, the eminent Texas lobbyist). So did John Dingell, chairman of the House Energy and Power Subcommittee (again, no great surprise, for Dingell had reportedly met with Johnston privately on December 7 and given his approval). So did Bob Eckhardt, and that was something of a surprise, for Eckhardt had fought vigorously on the side of consumers only two years earlier to extend energy price controls.[6] Among the House group,

---

6. Eckhardt would be back on the side of consumers when Carter set out to lift oil price controls in 1979. But, at the moment, Eckhardt was very much on industry's side. He not only supported phased-in decontrol but was instrumental in getting the legislation out of conference committee. At one point, in fact, he had the vote—or at least he later claimed to have had the vote—that could have killed the legislation in conference. Instead, he used his vote to save the bill. Indeed, Eckhardt might be con-

only Moffett voted no. Of the three senators present, Johnston and Ford were of course very hot for the proposal, and Metzenbaum just as predictably against it, saying, "The prices to consumers would be just as high as if controls were lifted. This is an appropriate plan to be considering during the Christmas season. It has a lot of giveaways in it." By this time, Senator Jackson had flown off to Seattle to be with a sick relative. When he was told of the decision by phone, he said he didn't like the sound of it—but the basis for his disagreement was narrow, focusing only on the definition of "new" gas, which he thought was too generous. If that was all he had against the plan, the future looked bleak for proregulation members. But, in the meantime, Jackson's opposition would be enough to kill the compromise. When it was put to the full Senate panel of conferees, sixteen voted against it—some because it was too tight, some because it was too loose—and only Johnston and Ford voted aye. As for the full panel of House conferees, they didn't even bother to vote.

So the third-floor roost had produced, after all, nothing but what would come to be known as "the Christmas turkey." Carter would ring out 1977 with no more of an energy program than he had taken office with, and negotiators would return to Washington at the end of January to indulge in more of what one reporter called "the moral equivalent of chaos."

***

The trans-Alaska pipeline opened for business on June 20 with a flick of a switch. Oil started flowing at the rate of 1.1 miles an hour toward the port of Valdez, nearly eight hundred miles away. If all went well, the crude would complete the trip across the state in a little more than a month and would be shipped to California by late August. But, of course, all did not go well; like everything relating to the pipeline, there were hitches. Within the first twenty-eight days, the line was shut down thirteen days because of cracks in the pipe, faulty valves, and an explosion that destroyed a pump station, killing one worker and injuring five others.

Some people in Washington would probably have been happy if the

---

sidered one of the most valued allies of the natural gas crowd throughout these negotiations, since his reputation as a consumer advocate equipped him to serve as a Judas goat to lure other liberals into supporting decontrol. His lapse from liberalism made life easier for him in his next election. In 1978, his opponents found the energy cash spigot half shut. In the general election, his Republican opponent, the same man who had raised $201,372 (66.5 percent of his total campaign chest) from oil people in 1976, was cut back to a mere $39,084 (28.5 percent of his total) from oil people. At the same time, Eckhardt, who had never before gotten more than pocket change from that crowd, raised a magnificent campaign fund of $284,242 for the 1978 election, and this included, for the first time in his life, a sum of oil and gas money worth mentioning: $32,756, or 11.5 percent of his total.

explosion had put the pipeline out of commission for a year or two. Except to the oil companies, the Alaskan crude's coming to market brought little joy. The worrisome question of where to use the oil was no longer hypothetical; now it was real, and federal officials were no closer to an answer. Five years earlier, Nixon's Interior Secretary, Rogers C. B. Morton, argued that the trans-Alaska right-of-way was justified because the "North Slope oil will be a timely contribution to the needs of the West Coast." He had been dead wrong. The West Coast was now faced with a glut of oil—a glut which, as *The Wall Street Journal* recently reported, "was foreseen years ago, even before the pipeline route was selected, and could have been averted. One oil company source says privately that his company has believed strongly from the beginning that not all of the Alaskan oil could be used on the West Coast." Now that the error was so evident, some of the Nixon crowd were willing to admit it. Not long before the pipeline opened, Russell Train, who had been Nixon's Environmental Protection Agency chief, was asked if it had been wise to route the oil across Alaska instead of down through Canada to the midwestern market. He answered, "The nation probably made the wrong decision." In fact, the nation hadn't made the wrong decision. The Nixonites and the oil companies had.

But it was too late for second thoughts. Regrets would not make that 500,000-barrel-a-day surplus disappear, nor would remorse ease the embarrassment faced by the Carter administration. Since they were trying to pass an energy program based on the premise of shortage, the West Coast glut posed what Schlesinger called "political problems and problems of symbolism."

The Alyeska oil companies were still hot to sell the oil to Japan—they were already selling 51 billion cubic feet of Alaskan gas (liquefied) to Japan every year—but in July, Carter decided that at least for the moment he didn't want to have to explain to the American people why he was allowing Alaskan oil to go to Japan during an "energy crisis" at home. Schlesinger (who favored selling the oil to Japan) told newsmen Carter had decided against it "partly on political grounds, partly for other, technical reasons."

With the door closed on the Far East, Standard Oil of Ohio, which owned most of the surplus, proposed shipping it from Long Beach, California, to Midland, Texas, through an existing natural gas pipeline that would be modified to carry oil. From Midland it would be piped into the Midwest and the East. California environmentalists wouldn't stand for the proposal, and they got support from Governor Jerry Brown. They feared that the transfer of oil from tankers to pipeline at Long Beach would result in some spills and the emission of enormous amounts of fumes. The California Air Resources Board said that under "best case" circumstances, there would be about eleven hundred forty pounds of emissions per day, equivalent to the exhaust from thirty-eight thousand cars, and under "most probable" circumstances nearly eighty-one thousand pounds of emissions a day, equivalent to the exhaust from 2.7 million autos, which was exactly what the Los Angeles basin did not need.

Meanwhile, there was the little question of unethical business practices. In March, the Alaska Pipeline Commission (APC) charged the Alyeska Pipeline Service Company with trying to foul up its investigation of Alyeska's claimed construction costs. The APC suspected that Alyeska had padded its costs by millions—perhaps billions—of dollars to avoid paying fair royalties to the state. Alyeska would be allowed to charge the North Slope oil companies (which, in fact, *were* Alyeska, since they owned the pipeline) a tariff for transporting the oil, based on pipeline construction costs. The higher the costs, the higher the tariff; the higher the tariff, the less taxes and royalties the oil companies would pay to the state. The suspected scheme was that simple. But proving it was another matter, for, the APC complained, the companies were frustrating the investigation by withholding pertinent data.

Then, in June, the Justice Department joined the fuss by charging that if the pipeline rates were allowed, the oil companies would reap $900 million in overcharges in one year—a nice, 40 percent return on equity.

***

Awed by the sudden onslaught of economic forces that were beyond their comprehension, America's politicians and journalists continued to interpret OPEC as a kind of Shiva: both Preserver and Destroyer. It was an almost mystical interpretation. There was indeed evidence that the same OPEC actions that were imperiling our economy were also, in a perverse fashion, giving it an advantage—at least in competition with other industrialized nations: rather like the advantage a person of robust physique would have over persons of weaker physique in a poison-drinking contest.

Reporters William Greider and J. P. Smith made this point in a Washington *Post* front-page story on July 10. The headline was a jewel of candor: "A Proposition: High Oil Prices Benefit U.S." The Greider-Smith elaboration: "The United States is stronger today in the world than it was five years ago, thanks partly to OPEC's fourfold escalation of crude oil prices . . . [S]ince the takeoff of oil prices in the fall of 1973, America's economic stature in the world has improved dramatically, reversing a long decline, while our competitors (and friends) in Western Europe and Japan have suffered." The United States' share of manufacturing exports in the world had been declining for fifteen years; since OPEC's price revolution, our share had been increasing. The dollar was stronger, by 11 percent, compared to the currency of other industrialized nations. "Since 1974, more than $100 billion a year has flowed to the

OPEC nations in oil revenues from all of the consumer nations, but the largest share has flowed back to the United States in trade, investments, arms sales and development contracts." Before 1973, our economic growth rate was slower than the average for the 24-member Organization of Economic Cooperation and Development; now it was above the average.

Had we become addicted to the poison? *The New Republic* told of a meeting at which several top economists had urged Energy Secretary Schlesinger to take advantage of the current softness in the crude market to loosen OPEC's price stranglehold. Schlesinger reportedly replied: "It would work. But do we dare let it work?"

The economic benefits that flowed, relatively, to the United States were like the deceptive blush that accompanies high fever. Even to talk of the appearance of health was sick. Irving Kristol correctly observed the various ways that U.S. leaders had tried to rationalize what was happening. Many bankers, he wrote, had smugly announced "that the 'recycling' of OPEC's newfound wealth is proceeding better than had been anticipated, and that the economics of the problem are quite manageable. This, of course, is economic nonsense. Why should we be pleased that Saudi Arabia buys our goods with our dollars, instead of burying those dollars in the sand? Is it easier for us to produce goods than to print dollars? Is it cheaper?

"What the bankers seem unable to realize is that we are talking about a net transfer of real wealth—a levy, a monopoly tax—and that whether we transfer this wealth in the form of goods or dollar bills is of no economic significance to the nation as a whole (even if it does make a difference to bankers). As a matter of fact, that very term, 'recycling,' helps disguise the economic reality of the transaction that is taking place. The word, as originally applied to problems of pollution, signified a process that produced a net economic gain—what had been waste matter was now being converted into a marketable commodity. But as applied to our relations with the OPEC countries, it obscures the fact that we are talking simply about their gain and our loss."

*

Bankers (and arms merchants) were indeed the chief beneficiaries of what Kristol called "the OPEC connection." A veritable flood of new business had come their way. They were rolling in "recycled" dollars from OPEC, and to make sure they would not be regulated in the way they exploited their new wealth, America's biggest banks were opening branches in Europe—the Eurodollar market being notoriously a black market, which existed because it was unregulated.

U.S. banks' foreign branches now had total assets of over $160 billion, having nearly doubled in five years. The banks were making massive loans to countries that needed money to pay OPEC: Britain and Italy had run out of private credit the previous year, and Portugal, Spain, Greece, and Turkey were also heading into credit trouble because of their oil bills. Among the banks' steadiest and most desperate customers were the less developed countries (LDC's), which since 1973 had borrowed $100 billion—a bill that would continue to grow, a bill that they would never be able to pay, a bill that ultimately the developed nations would have to quietly pay off lest a series of LDC collapses topple the international banking system. In September, the Senate Subcommittee on Foreign Economic Policy, having completed a study of OPEC fallout, warned, "An international debt crisis . . . is coming to a head."

If government leaders weren't sufficiently intimidated by the oil companies and the banks, they were additionally handicapped in coping with the problem by the fact that the old Communist specter still shaped foreign policy. *The Wall Street Journal* noted that "the ascendancy of foreign policy over energy policy has continued. One senior Carter administration official who also served in the Nixon and Ford administrations [Schlesinger?] declared recently that 'the rise in prices is unpleasant, but it isn't intolerable to our society. We need to preserve our access to the Persian Gulf so that the Soviets don't get control of the oil tap. Therefore, it isn't wise to risk alienating the Saudis just to knock a few bucks off the price of oil."

***

In June it was discovered that the Aramco partners—Exxon, Texaco, Mobil, and Socal—had paid no U.S. taxes on $2.8 billion in profits from their Saudi Arabian operations in 1975. (The oil companies' tax shuffle was always a couple years late being discovered.) The House Government Operations Subcommittee on Commerce, Consumer and Monetary Affairs later broadened the study and accused the Internal Revenue Service of permitting all U.S. oil companies operating overseas to escape $7 billion in taxes since 1974. The loss had arisen from a questionable interpretation of the venerable IRS rule that royalties paid by American companies to Saudi Arabia and other oil-producing nations were taxes, not operating expenses, and therefore could be fully subtracted from corporate taxes owed to the United States. In contrast, payments to landowners in the United States and Canada were considered by the IRS to be royalties and therefore merely deductible as normal business expenses. The difference? A Treasury official explained: "A royalty payment is deductible from income, whereas a foreign tax credit is an offset against the United States income tax. Thus, for a taxpayer whose marginal rate of tax is 50 percent [meaning all the big oil companies], a credit is worth twice what a deduction is worth."

To be sure, the tax gimmick had been around a long time (see chapter on "The Company Cartel"), dating back to the 1950s, when Saudi Arabia demanded more money and the oil companies persuaded U.S. officials to permit the establishment of the "foreign tax credit" as a way of making U.S. taxpayers foot the additional largess to the Saudis. But there was always an aura of shadiness, if not downright lawlessness, hanging over the deal that bothered many of the more conscientious IRS officials. After the OPEC oil embargo and price increases of 1973 and 1974, the Government Operations subcommittee report said, ". . . numerous field auditors raised technical-assistance questions with IRS headquarters in Washington regarding the propriety of permitting continued foreign tax credit claims by United States oil companies . . ."

Still, the IRS dawdled. Despite a tougher tax law, passed in 1975, that made it possible for the IRS to crack down on the foreign-credit loophole, top IRS officials, being unaccustomed to treating oil people roughly, hadn't decided by the end of 1977 whether or not to use the law.[7]

When the tax-credit issue was raised, Aramco officials claimed harassment, of course. One grumped to financial writer Rowen, "This thing has been beaten to death for years. If someone tried to figure out the best way of driving American companies out of the Middle East, and turning it over to the Dutch, the French, and others, they couldn't find a better way. The whole thing astounds me."

Critics of the industry were, on the other hand, astounded that although the issue had indeed been beaten to death for years, the abuse of tax laws was more alive than ever. Proof of that came in October with a report from Library of Congress researchers that because of loopholes and write-offs, the *maximum* tax rate paid on oil and gas operations came to only 17.2 percent, compared to the 48 percent statutory rate that most corporations were faced with. And for the smaller companies that still qualified for the oil depletion allowance, the effective tax rate dropped to minus 3 percent—meaning they got money back from the Treasury. Complaints of that sort flew out of Washington as regularly as the seasons, however, and probably left little impression on the jaded public.

Likewise, the public must have felt it was listening to a broken record when the Federal Energy Administration announced in April that twenty oil companies had overcharged the public $336 million by inflating imported crude oil costs. It was indeed an old charge, merely increased by $51 million since it was first made, in 1975.

---

7. In January 1978—five years after its field auditors raised the question—the IRS would issue a ruling prohibiting the deduction of most royalties as tax credits. But the ruling was not to go into effect until July 1, 1978. The House Commerce, Consumer and Monetary Affairs Subcommittee charged that because of the delay in the effective date for the new ruling, the Treasury stood to lose $2 billion.

*

One of the roguish mysteries of the year came to light in June, when the FEA announced that nearly 40 million barrels of low-priced oil had just vanished—poof!—the previous year, only to reappear as oil costing twice as much. The legerdemain was obviously used to beat price regulations.

"Old" oil—oil from wells brought into production before 1972—was by law not supposed to sell for more than $5.25 a barrel. New oil sold for about $11 a barrel.

The FEA kept records of all purchases of oil at wellhead. It also kept a record of refined oil. FEA officials began to notice that the amount of old oil refined was considerably less than the amount of old oil purchased at wellhead. About 108,000 barrels of old oil were "disappearing" every day somewhere between well and refinery. A comparison of the same records showed an almost identical amount of "new" oil mysteriously turning up at the refineries, although there was no evidence that it had ever been pumped. Obviously, an illegal switch of identity. The additional cost to consumers was more than $200 million. Were federal officials upset? Not much. FEA Administrator John F. O'Leary described the oil companies' desire to make $11 a barrel instead of $5 "a human tendency." Actually, it was the FEA's incredibly complicated operating procedures that made it easier for the companies to twist the law; the crooks could hide their tracks in those twenty thousand pages of FEA regulations.

*

It wasn't a happy year for Gulf Oil. A U.S. district judge in Pittsburgh fined the corporation $36,000 for giving free (illegal) trips to a federal tax auditor who was responsible for reviewing the company's books. The fine didn't hurt, but the publicity did. Just as Gulf seemed about to pull out of the mud left from the Bob Dorsey political payoff era, it was shoved back. Another shove came at a House committee hearing at which new evidence was presented that, contrary to its claim, Gulf had not been innocently "forced" to join a worldwide uranium cartel that drove up prices. Committee chairman Albert Gore, Jr., got kind of sarcastic with the Gulf witnesses, telling them that they were trying to play the part of "some kind of corporate Patty Hearst: you were forced to do this and only afterward did you develop an enthusiasm for the task."

* * *

In July, a special panel headed by Securities and Exchange Commission enforcement chief Stanley Sporkin issued a report denouncing the Federal Energy Administration's efforts to regulate the oil industry as a "dismal failure." In a letter accompanying the report, Sporkin said, "Unfortunately, to date the FEA's efforts to secure compliance from our nation's major refiners have been a failure. There are entirely inadequate audit resources and no lawyers assigned on a full-time basis to any of the major refiners. Given the size of the problem, the limited work that has been done to date, and the enforcement problems that necessarily accompany any attempt to remedy aged violations, a major new undertaking is required."

Recommended was the establishment of an office with the specific duty to catch the violators and make them pay up. On December 4, Paul Bloom was named to head the new Office of Special Counsel for Compliance. A pudgy, mustachioed optimist, Bloom plunged in. Only nine days after his office was officially launched, he subpoenaed financial records from all 34 major refiners. He was bearing down on the biggest of the lot in hopes that any decision reached there could be applied to the rest of the industry. "We have 65 people at the Exxon site every day," Bloom said, "and they are poring over microfilm machines, practically going blind." He had the authority to hire 613 lawyers and auditors, which was none too many, considering the tricks that the oil companies knew how to play. In the previous three years, the Federal Energy Administration had not completed even one audit of the 34 major refiners. The oil companies pieced out a starvation diet of data to the auditors, feeding them just enough to keep them going but never enough to let them finish their work. By statute, Bloom was forbidden to let that happen to him. He was supposed to complete all field audits and launch all necessary enforcement actions by 1979. Could the golden fleece be found in such haste?

1978

"In many cases I feel more at home with the conservative Democratic and Republican members of Congress than I do with the others, although the others, the liberals, vote with me much more often."

JIMMY CARTER'S diary,
January 19, 1978

"Politics, so far as mobilizing support is concerned, represents the art of calculated cheating, or, to be exact, cheating without really being caught. Slogans and catchphrases, even when unbacked by the commitment of resources, remain effective instruments of political gain. One needs a steady flow of attention-grabbing clues, and it is of lesser moment whether the indicated castles in Spain ever materialize."

JAMES R. SCHLESINGER
(as a senior official with
RAND Corporation in 1967)

President Carter's search for an energy policy continued to be marked by milestones of ineptness and confusion, much of it originating with Energy Secretary Schlesinger and his jerry-built department. While the executives of the major oil companies had become moderately enamored of Schlesinger, realizing that he was on their side, many independent oilmen viewed him with deep suspicion, feeling, as Joseph Walter, chairman of Houston Oil & Minerals Corp., did, that Schlesinger was "completely unqualified, transparently deceitful, and tricky." Many consumer groups and liberal congressmen agreed with that assessment, and several times during the year such senators as Metzenbaum and McGovern went on television or took the floor of the Senate to demand that Schlesinger quit or that Carter fire him. *Fortune* observed that "practically no one in Washington has a good word for Carter's energy chief," but this missed a crucial point: he did have supporters in important places. Two of the key energy negotiators, Congressman Thomas Ludlow Ashley and Senator Henry Jackson, were buddies of Schlesinger's. Jackson, who loved Schlesinger's hawkishness, was virtually his patron. *U.S. News & World Report* quoted an opponent of the Administration's energy policy as saying, "Schlesinger is the best thing we have going. We can count on him to make a major blunder about once a month."

Polling one hundred key people—including White House aides, members of Congress, career bureaucrats, and citizens who deal with the government—*U.S. News* found that of the twelve cabinet departments, Energy was ranked next to the bottom in efficiency. Partly, Schlesinger's low popularity rating was due to his celebrated insolence. To all criticism he had one of two responses: "Horseshit" or "Bullshit." Five years earlier, Governor John Love of Colorado, the first energy "czar," had operated with a staff of ten. To be sure, he had done a very poor job indeed; but, considering everything, Love's 10-man staff hadn't done as poorly as Schlesinger's twenty thousand employees (plus a hundred thousand contract workers who don't show up in personnel figures) operating with a budget of $11 billion. Both sides seemed to agree on the DOE's character. William T. McCormick, vice-president for policy analysis at the American Gas Ass., said that even DOE officials "will privately admit that it is a zoo." James F. Flug, director of Energy Action, the public-interest lobby, described DOE as "utter chaos . . . There are people with nothing to do, people who don't have bosses, bosses who don't make decisions because they don't know if they're coming or going." Some observers believed that Schlesinger's heart was still at the Pentagon and he detested DOE. His lackadaisical effort at management seemed to indicate it. To all appearances, he didn't give a hang about the Department's reputation. A fellow reputed to be a Republican hatchet man was fired at the Department of Transportation; Schlesinger—something of a Republican hatchet man himself—hired him immediately and gave him the sensitive job of director of administration, from where he supervised all manpower, budget, and operations at DOE. Later, congressional investigators accused the fellow of falsifying his employment record (he claimed to be "business manager" for Kansas, but investigators said he had only been a clerk at a Kansas orphanage), but Schlesinger shrugged it off. Actually, the temper of Schlesinger's DOE was such that an orphanage clerk would have fitted in rather well.

The only thing lower than the Department's morale was its efficiency. With little to do, and with few supervisors interested in seeing that they did it, DOE's employees sat around gabbing on the telephone endlessly. Investigators would find (in a very fragmentary study) during 1978 that DOE had made more than a quarter of a million dollars' worth of unnecessary long-distance calls—seventy-four thousand such calls, all told. The son of one DOE official billed the Department for a 129-minute phone call to Key Largo, Florida. When asked about it, the official explained that his son was "an unpaid consultant." Another DOE official, getting bored, would ring up a friend of his—a sidewalk artist in Crystal Bay, Nevada—at a sidewalk telephone booth and chat for half an hour at a time. Meanwhile, the mountains of paper grew more mountainous, while industrialists and consumers trying to get a straight answer from DOE fretted and fumed and waited.

More confusion originated with Schlesinger's stubborn adherence to a propaganda line that was fast becoming ludicrous. Carter's moral-equivalent-of-war speech had included the prediction that the world would begin to run out of oil by the mid-1980s. This was greeted by wide skepticism at the time, and by 1978 skepticism had reached flood tide. Oil specialists, oil companies, and most international economists now openly scoffed at the idea. It wasn't just that the world was presently experiencing an oil glut (that was embarrassing to the Carter "crisis" scenario, but all conceded that the glut was temporary); it was that clearly encouraging developments were taking place: Mexico's oil potential was now known to be much greater than originally thought, perhaps greater than Saudi Arabia's; Communist China was thought to have large oil reserves, and it had asked Western help in developing them; technological advances were beginning to pay off everywhere with surer and speedier exploration. Now it was plain, too, that Carter had built his crisis on deception and bad data. He had, for example, used Central Intelligence Agency information to forecast that by 1985 the Soviet Union would be requiring oil imports of up to 4.5 million barrels a day, much of it drained from "our" source in the Middle East. The Soviet figures were essential to Carter's crisis forecast. Early in 1978 it was learned that the CIA's figures were faulty in a number of ways, chief among which was its failure to take into consideration the U.S.S.R.'s enormous natural gas supply, which could be substituted for oil. "An honest mistake," said the Senate Select Committee on Intelligence, the CIA's apologist, but many—remembering that Schlesinger had once headed the CIA—wondered if this was not another example of the Administration's politicizing the agency through selective (and twisted) use of its information. Others, remembering that, at the start of the decade, the CIA had forecast a steady decline in oil prices, conceded that the supply forecast could be just part of the agency's generic stupidity. As for Mexico's oil supply, Richard Halloran, of the New York *Times* reported that "administration officials now privately concede that they let the Mexican potential go unpublicized because calling attention to it would have undercut the urgency of the President's [call for war] in the energy crisis."

But Schlesinger refused to budge. In fact, he plunged deeper into pessimism. The outlook for the oil supply, he said, "is bleaker than it appeared a year ago," "probably a little grimmer than we thought." Was there no relief in sight? Alas, said Schlesinger, "At the present level of consumption, we have to discover a new Saudi Arabia every five years. That's just not in the cards." And what about the current oil glut? That, he said, "is an illusion."

But the developing natural gas glut was certainly no illusion. The "shortage" of the previous winter had already turned into an oversupply, particularly in the producing states, where prices weren't controlled. While producers waited for their pals in Congress to deregulate interstate prices, 87 percent of newly discovered gas was staying within the state where it was found, and it was in such bountiful supply as to be a headache. Intrastate prices, though still about 25 percent higher than interstate, were beginning to soften because of the glut. So the Texas Railroad Commission—which did not regulate prices so long as they went up—stepped in to regulate supply so that prices would not go down. It ordered a cutback in production.

Naturally, this was a bit embarrassing to oil and gas lobbyists on Capitol Hill who had argued that industry wanted interstate prices deregulated, as they were in the intrastate market, only so that the companies could get out there and produce like crazy and compete like crazy—even if it did mean a drop in prices, yes sir, because competition was the American way. The Texas cutback didn't help their credibility along that line. Nor did the jargon they used to disguise what was happening. Dale Woody, head of Exxon's domestic natural gas operations, avoided using the word glut. It didn't sound nice. He preferred to say that industry was having a problem of "overdeliverability."

*

In this situation, the Administration revealed its willingness to reverse itself with stunning rapidity. In his energy speech the previous year, Carter had firmly stated the need to wean industry away from the use of natural gas. It was too precious an energy to be burned in boilers, he argued, and therefore he was prepared to give an extra 10 percent tax credit (with Congress' approval) to factories that switched from oil and natural gas to coal. He also asked Congress to levy a hefty tax penalty against those industries that didn't switch. That's what he had said in the spring of 1977. But by early 1978 the Administration was growing noticeably less enthusiastic for its own proposals. Carter officials rarely mentioned the tax credit and tax levy to reduce industrial use of oil and gas. And at the end of the year—after the natural gas fight was over and consumers had been screwed—the Administration would reverse the field altogether. On November 16, Schlesinger removed the pipe from his mouth and uttered a remarkable reversal: "Firms that have shifted off natural gas will be encouraged . . . to shift back [to gas] rather than burning imported oil." And a couple of weeks later: "Although the Administration remains committed to the use of coal instead of oil or gas in new boiler facilities over the longer run, over the course of at least the next several years, existing industrial and utility facilities will be provided every encouragement to burn gas instead of oil." Incredible! The ink in Carter's signature on the natural gas bill would be hardly dry before they were admitting that the "price incentive" argument had all been a put-on. The gas was on tap all along, in glut proportions.

But that admission didn't come from Carter and Schlesinger until the end of the year.

* * *

The backroom alliance between the Department of Energy and the oil industry was revealed with exactness in May, when the press got hold of an internal memo written by American Petroleum Institute lobbyist John Iannone in which he boasted of receiving numerous copies of confidential draft regulations affecting industry profits in advance of some DOE officials, of being invited to review DOE documents before they were turned over to the agency's own general counsel, and of being offered a chance to "review" a DOE letter to Senator Kennedy before it was sent. Iannone also claimed, among other things, that DOE officials had asked him to "revamp" an advisory committee "to make it more producer oriented."

Senator Metzenbaum wasted no time launching a subcommittee investigation that turned up other memos showing that Iannone had had the same relationship with DOE throughout 1977, too. "Received advance notice of possible refiner overcharges resulting from interpretations of definition of transactions," read a typical entry in the October 1977 report. "This gave the companies advance warning to prepare rebuttals." "Received advance verbal notice (approximately three weeks) of extension of price freeze through August 1977 . . . In addition, received advance copy of written notice to the Federal Register on this." "Obtained an advance copy of the gasoline decontrol proposal before it was released for public hearings." "Obtained an advance copy of the proposed gasoline price monitoring system, as well as all internal correspondence on the subject." Et cetera, et cetera.

A Library of Congress study done at Metzenbaum's request estimated, according to the Senator, that one of the leaks "could be worth $500 to $600 million a year to industry." Industry denied it.

At hearings before the Senate Energy and Natural Resources Committee, DOE witnesses paraded up to confess that, sure enough, they had sometimes been unethical and certainly unprofessional in the way they handed out confidential documents to industry lobbyists. From their testimony, it was also plain that the DOE had no security regulations at all to protect its rule making and that important documents were left lying around DOE offices for any passersby to pick up and read. Officials admitted that it would be easy not only to read them but to carry them off.

The rationalization of DOE-industry teamwork was typified by this exchange between Senator Metzenbaum and J. Peter Holihan, industrial specialist in the Division of Oil and Gas, Office of Resource Applications, at the DOE:

SENATOR METZENBAUM: Mr. Iannone also testified at the June 16 hearing that you gave him advance copies of two different drafts of proposed amendments to subpart K of the mandatory petroleum price regulations . . . Did you, in fact, give him advance copies of those drafts prior to their release to the public, Mr. Holihan?

HOLIHAN: Yes, sir.

METZENBAUM: On whose authority?

HOLIHAN: I was having a little problem with one technical matter in the rule making, and Mr. Iannone stopped by and I asked him if he could help me with this matter.

METZENBAUM: There are twenty thousand employees at the Department of Energy?

HOLIHAN: Yes, sir.

METZENBAUM: Not one of those employees could help you with the technical problems you were having and you needed, instead, to go to the representative of the American Petroleum Institute in order to get the technical matters resolved; is that what you are testifying?

HOLIHAN: I didn't go to Mr. Iannone. It just happened coincidentally that I was working on the rule making. I was asked to comment on the rule making and he did stop by.

METZENBAUM: And you were having some technical problems and you asked him about them, rather than going to somebody at the Department of Energy?

HOLIHAN: Yes, sir.

Consumer activists were furious that they had not had equal access to the documents. Administration officials tried to soothe them. David Bardin, administrator of DOE's Economic Regulatory Administration, called in a group of the consumer spokesmen and admitted that he did have "a serious leak problem . . ." Mark Green, of Congress Watch, the Nader outfit that had first uncovered the Iannone memos, came out of the meeting unplacated. "He said he was disturbed," Green reported, "but he sure didn't act it."

**

When last seen, the House-Senate natural gas conferees were a raggletaggle bunch dispersing at Christmas after Senator Jackson, chairman of the Senate group, had telephoned from the West Coast that he didn't like the final compromise proposal. Actually, he wasn't very unhappy with its provisions; he simply didn't want to accept it, because he had had precious little to do with cooking it up. That bruised his vanity.

And his vanity was no small influence in the shaping of this legislation. Jackson obviously was one of the most powerful members of the Senate, and yet he had reached that point in his career when it was plain—after thirty-seven years in Congress—he had nowhere else to go. The presidency? The voters had repeatedly indicated their coolness to that. The Cabinet? If he had rejected Nixon's offer of perhaps the most important chair, at the Pentagon, what else was there to consider? Nothing. At sixty-six, he was stuck in the Senate, so he would make the best of it by seeking to revive those moments of glory he had achieved in recent years. Mostly they had been the result of militant positions he had taken on behalf of consumers. At the end of 1973, for example, a year in which he had scourged the major oil companies for their part in the quadru- pling of oil prices then underway, a year in which he had flatly accused the oil companies of creating bogus shortages, the Gallup poll found that Americans ranked him among the ten "most-admired" men in the world.[1] It was heady stuff. And since the oil quarrel had proved previously to be a path to glory, he would use it for what it was worth once more. He had the rank and he intended to pull it. At the moment, he was sulking be- cause of the central role played in the Christmas negotiations by Senator Johnston. Testy, thin-skinned, egotistical, and not nearly so wise on en- ergy matters as he thought himself to be, Jackson was not the easiest fellow to work with, but Carter had to.

On January 6, Secretary Schlesinger, accompanied by FERC Chair- man Charles Curtis and several other DOE officials, flew secretly to Palm Springs to confer with Jackson, to court him, flatter him, and (it was hoped) convince him to support a compromise that looked as though it might get through Congress. In short, they gave him the any-bill-will-do argument. And since they asked him nicely, he said he was willing to co- operate. But he was firm about one thing: he wanted to be acknowl- edged by all sides, including the President, as the No. 1 negotiator. No more spreading around the glory. Carter, who also coaxed Jackson by telephone, laid it on thick and told the press that Jackson had assured him of his, in Carter's words, "redetermination to exert his own leader- ship and profound influence to bring about a resolution of the present deadlock."

Proconsumer conferees—sensing that Jackson's eagerness to "cooper- ate" and Carter's burst of cheerful predictions that "something can be worked out soon" presaged capitulation—were dealt another stiff blow on January 12, when Senator Lee Metcalf of Montana died.

Until now, the Senate conferees had been split 9 to 9, half wanting total deregulation, half wanting a continuation of price controls. Metcalf had not only been on the consumer's side, he had been probably one of the most militantly proconsumer senators in the conference, along with Metzenbaum and Abourezk. Would Jackson now ask the Senate to ap-

---

1. Under (in descending order) Henry Kissinger, Billy Graham, Richard Nixon (then up to his armpits in Watergate), Gerald Ford, George Wallace, and Ralph Nader.

point a like-minded replacement? No, he decided to let the new imbalance stand, 9 to 8 in favor of deregulation.

His willingness to "cooperate" was further illustrated when top Senate staff members of the conference committee brought out a proposal, prepared at Jackson's direction, that in broad principle was the same plan he had rejected at Christmas. There were, however, two significant differences, one serving Jackson's vanity—that is to say, whereas the Christmas plan was credited to Johnston, this plan carried the imprimatur of Jackson—and the other serving the oil and gas industry. The Johnston plan for phased deregulation would cost consumers about $13 billion more than the bill approved by the House; the Jackson plan would cost about $15 billion more.

Obviously, the oil and gas crowd had won him over by playing on what Carter called Jackson's "leadership and profound influence." He was beginning to take the lead for *their* side, and he would continue to do so, despite the stupidity of the Republicans in the conference committee who sometimes stepped on his ego by showing their counterproposals to oil-company officials—who indiscreetly quoted them around Washington—before showing them to Jackson. He would get temporarily huffy when that happened.

*

But Jackson had some selling to do. First he had to sell a majority of the Senate conferees before he could even begin to work on the full conference, and the Senate conferees weren't all that easy to persuade. At the time he began his campaign, in January, he faced a majority that one way or another wanted no compromise: they were dead set against permitting deregulation ever, or they were dead set against allowing regulation to continue even a day longer. At the outset, only six of the seventeen senators were willing to compromise up or down. The negotiations continued for the rest of January, through February, and into early March—all the meetings held in secret—before Jackson had a package. Emerging in shirt sleeves from the smoke-filled room on March 7, Jackson announced, "We're no longer deadlocked. We're moving toward an agreement." Two hours later he had it, but only barely, with nine others deciding to go along with him, some of them as grudgingly as Senator Dale Bumpers, who grumped, "If I had my druthers, I wouldn't draft this bill. But compared to the alternative of doing nothing and letting the government raise the price ceiling to this same level without the power to allocate intrastate gas in an emergency, it's not bad."

On the other hand, three who voted against it—the irrepressible Metzenbaum and Abourezk, along with spunky John Durkin of New Hampshire—announced that in their opinion the Jackson compromise was not only bad, it was terrible—"capitulation to the natural gas industry"—and by 1985 would cost the American people $23 billion more than the House bill, not the $15 billion estimated earlier.

The Jackson compromise would remove price controls from new natural gas in seven years. Even if sluggishly achieved, that's decontrol. Decontrol was supposedly a dirty word with Carter, wasn't it? Less than five months earlier, speaking to an audience in Norfolk, Virginia, Carter had promised that because the Senate bill decontrolled gas prices, he would never, never accept it or anything like it. "I hate to veto a bill that a Democratic Congress passes, but you can depend on it, I'll protect your interests—you can count on that—when the bill comes to my desk." When a House subcommittee had barely voted for deregulation in 1977, Carter denounced the oil-gas interests for pressuring the subcommittee to act against the public. Considering such actions and statements from the recent past, was it not reasonable to expect Carter to oppose the Jackson compromise of phased deregulation? It might have been reasonable, but it would have been wrong. On March 9, Carter welcomed the Jackson compromise by saying that of course he could accept gradual deregulation. Skipping his remarks of 1977, he went back to the hocus-pocus statements of the 1976 campaign to explain his switcheroo, specifically referring to the letter to the governors of Texas and Oklahoma promising, "I will work with the Congress . . . to deregulate new natural gas." Never mind that he had repudiated that letter in 1977; now he was reviving it. Now he said that he was ready to honor "a campaign statement and commitment of mine, that I thought natural gas should be deregulated. In my speech to Congress last April 20 [his energy message], I repeated this hope, and I think that a long phased-in deregulation process without shocks to our national economy would be acceptable." He was not recollecting accurately. In his April 1977 speech to Congress, he had said nothing about wanting to deregulate gas pricing; he had said he wanted to raise natural gas prices from $1.42 to $1.75, extend interstate price regulation indefinitely, and extend price regulations to the intrastate market.

The fact was, Carter had taken so many positions in the previous three years—for deregulation, against deregulation, for phased deregulation—that nobody knew where he stood on anything. Said Representative Dingell, "I don't know what to believe." The smartest thing to believe was that Carter would accept anything remotely resembling an energy bill, no matter what it gave away.

*

And the pitiful part about it was that by surrendering on deregulation, he got nothing in return. Apparently he had hoped that by knuckling under on gas, Senator Long would let him have the other centerpiece of

his energy program, the domestic crude oil tax. That had been on a back
burner since November, where it was placed by Long, who said he
wanted to see what happened to gas decontrol before he let the Finance
Committee even consider the tax. It was a treacherous ploy, as Carter
discovered. On March 7, the very day Jackson announced he could count
on a majority support among Senate conferees for his phased-deregula-
tion compromise, Long had lunch with Carter and told him that the
crude oil tax "could not be passed by the Senate, as of now, under any
imaginable set of circumstances." He said to even talk about the tax was
"beating a dead horse." So much for trading off with the Louisianian.

But Jackson's job was far from over. Having prevailed 10 to 7 within
the Senate conference, he now had to help bring that splintered group—
whose majority might fall apart at any moment—together with the
twenty-five House conferees, who were split 13 to 12 in favor of continued regulation, and help persuade a majority of the *entire* group to go
along. He was walking a heavily mined field; every step was fraught.
Aside from those diametrically positioned in regard to whether there
should be controls of any sort, there were those who were willing to
decontrol but passionately favored a few pennies less or more. Then
there was the question of how much, if any, above the inflation rate gas
prices should be allowed to rise each year until decontrolled. The matter
of how to define "new" gas was enough to start a full-scale war within
the conference. And there was the matter of what date decontrol should
start, if it started at all—two years in the future? five? seven? seven and a
half? There were determined advocates for each date, and billions of
dollars turned on the question, on every question. Then too, some of the
conferees were willing to decontrol but didn't want to give their consent
until the crude oil tax (despite Senator Long's pronouncement of its
death) was passed.

Given the legislative complexities, the multiplicity of egos and short
tempers, the diversity of the home interests represented by the conferees,
it was little wonder that Jackson insisted on keeping the conferees behind closed doors while the negotiations went on. It was also understandable that Jackson arranged the conferences so that some members—
such "troublemakers" as Abourezk—couldn't attend. Since the previous
Thanksgiving, in fact, the energy negotiations had virtually all been done
in secret. Quiet dickering, Jackson felt, would work better than public
wrangling and showboating.

Understandable or not, however, it was a clear violation of congressional rules. Both Senate and House rules require open conferences unless there is specifically a vote to close them. In mid-March, David
Cohen, president of Common Cause, ran into Jackson in a Capitol hallway and upbraided him for negotiating in secret. They almost came to

blows as Jackson began shouting, "I don't need Common Cause to tell me about morality."[2] But Cohen was not the only one offended. Key congressmen of all ideologies were ticked off. A month later, Representative Toby Moffett teamed up with Representative Clarence J. Brown of Ohio—a Republican who favored immediate deregulation—to try to pry the conference open in a clever, backhanded way. If they had introduced a resolution commanding the conferees to meet publicly, it would have seemed redundant, because the rules already commanded public meetings; they might have lost the vote. So they introduced a resolution to *close* the conference, hoping of course that it would be defeated, and it was, 371 to 6. Thus the standing rule of the House was reaffirmed: "Each conference committee meeting between the House and Senate shall be open to the public except when the House, in open session, has determined by a roll-call vote of a majority of those Members voting that all or part of the meeting shall be closed to the public."

Resolution or no, the secret meetings persisted; Jackson and Ashley and the other conspirators insisted that they really weren't conferences, but merely informal discussions, and therefore not in violation of the rules. But the stealthy, surreptitious, clandestine atmosphere certainly indicated otherwise. The negotiations were conducted in a Capitol hideaway approachable only through a maze, so remote as to require a map almost.

Richard Corrigan, of the *National Journal*, described the secretiveness:

> If you wanted to find out how President Carter's energy program was doing one year after he sent it to Congress, here is what you had to do:
> Go to the third floor of the Capitol on the Senate side, walk through the

---

2. A few weeks earlier, Common Cause had irritated many congressmen and most oilmen in another way, by suggesting that the energy industry was employing some very unscrupulous lobbying tactics to bend the Carter energy program to its own end. Its investigation found: Only one out of every ten energy-related organizations with Washington representatives registered with Congress as a lobbying group. Only about 35 percent of the individual lobbyists hired by these organizations registered with Congress as lobbyists. Energy lobbyists were obviously lying about their expenditures. For example, while seven of Mobil's lobbyists registered as individuals, the only expenses reported by them for the first nine months of 1977 were $24,975 in salaries received for lobbying and a total of $796 in lobbying expenses. "Mobil Oil spent $4 million on advocacy advertising in 1977. Mobil placed full-page newspaper ads throughout the country with clip-out coupons for readers to send members of Congress. Despite the obvious effort to get readers to communicate their views to Congress, a Mobil spokesman told Common Cause that the advertisements were not designed to generate lobbying, but simply to educate people. Mobil is not a registered lobbying organization." Common Cause pointed out that "the two largest oil and gas trade associations, the American Petroleum Institute and the American Gas Association, both of which have $30 million annual budgets, reported spending only $274,900 and $28,684, respectively, on lobbying during this nine-month period."

swinging doors of the Senate Document Room, breeze past the gate where
people wait for copies of bills, go straight ahead and up a ramp, turn right
into a long dingy hallway, proceed through the hall and down a short flight
of steps, turn right at the first landing and go up two steps, take a quick
right and left around a corner and climb three steps into a spacious corridor
painted aquamarine, move up to the second paneled door on the right, num-
bered S-334, and wait, and wait, and wait for somebody to come out and
tell you what was going on inside.

There are easier ways to get to this room, known to those who frequent
the back alleys and private elevators of the Capitol honeycomb, but this
route proved to be the most dependable for this wayward correspondent.

No matter how you got to the door of S-334, you could not get inside unless you carried the proper credentials. Most—though by no means all—of
the Senate and House energy conferees were welcome, as were the Secretary of Energy and his associates . . . But the press and the public were
barred, because the people inside had concluded that government in the
sunshine has its limits, and besides, they would have you believe, these conferences were not conferences at all . . .

Maybe this is the only way to get things done in Washington, but if energy is the most important domestic issue of this generation, as the President
has been saying, the political process should function so that the nation can
see what is going on, and the process, by its secrecy, should not invite com-
parisons to the workings of a substandard small-town zoning commission.

And to make the general atmosphere all the more tasteless, President
Carter—who had previously made a policy of staying out of the conferees' business—chose this occasion to butt in by approving the closed
meetings on the ground that "the time for [public] posturing is over" and
also because the public was, in his opinion, too stupid to know or care
what was going on, anyway—". . . not one in a million people" would
understand the complex issues, he said. To show his approval for negotiations being secret and limited to only the most "cooperative" conferees,
Carter invited a select group to meet privately with him and with Schlesinger at the White House for three days.

The odd couple, Moffett and Brown, were among those excluded, and
they did not go quietly. Congress, Moffett advised, "should resist any
President's attempt to institutionalize closed meetings by moving them to
the White House." Brown added, "Deals should not be made by a few.
We should say to the conferees: Come back to the Hill, where the House
and Senate belong and the press and public can see what we do. Then
when decisions are made the public will have some idea how they occurred."

On April 12, Carter met with Brown and other Republican House conferees who had been shut out. He apologized, said it wasn't his idea to
exclude them, and offered to accept even a Republican plan for deregulation. He was passing the hat for contributions. After the meeting,

Brown told reporters, "He said he would support, in effect, anything that came out of the conference."

*

On April 20, the anniversary of Carter's energy speech to Congress, the President scolded the federal legislators for "wasting twelve months of precious time," and the rump conference pitched in with extra enthusiasm in an effort to come up with something on the memorable day. They didn't make it, but almost. They worked from 2 P.M. the twentieth until 2:30 A.M. the twenty-first, took off for a snooze, reconvened at noon, and at 1:25 P.M. reporters outside the locked door could hear clapping and cheers. Senator Jackson soon appeared to tell the television cameras, "We have, with all our differences, been able to merge these differences into a bill [on natural gas decontrol] for the first time in thirty years."[3] He was slightly in error. Eighteen years earlier, Congress had passed a natural gas decontrol bill that President Eisenhower felt compelled to veto, because it came to his desk bearing the stink of bribery. So Jackson was twelve years off on that one; and he was also off by a mile to suggest that the conference committee, not to say Congress, was in agreement; this was just the *rump* conference, and even its members were still packing knives. With an uncharacteristic smile on his face, Secretary Schlesinger stepped before the cameras and declared, "Peace is at hand." There was laughter from the reporters, but they didn't realize just how funny the remark really was.

*

Wednesday, April 26. This was the day the full conference was supposed to meet in public to ratify the agreement. But the meeting was canceled. The latest head count showed that two House conferees who had been expected to support the compromise—Representative Henry Reuss, Wisconsin Democrat, and Representative James C. Corman, California Democrat—had had second thoughts. Corman said he was afraid that if they passed the gas pricing first, the crude oil tax would be forgotten. Reuss said he was afraid passage of the gas proposal would force passage of the crude tax, and he was against it. Damn! Carter and Schlesinger got on the phone to Corman, but he wouldn't budge. Carter began trying to recruit a replacement from among the other House holdouts. He tried Representative Charles Vanik, Ohio Democrat, but ran into a stone wall. "Deregulation of gas won't save one drop of oil," said Vanik. "I wouldn't vote for it if it was deregulation by 2085 instead of 1985." He tried Representative Charles Rangel, New York Democrat, but

---

3. The compromise provisions set a maximum price for new gas in interstate commerce at \$1.93 per Mcf; the current price was \$1.42; the ceiling price would rise about 10 percent a year until controls were removed, in 1985.

Rangel said nope, "From what I hear, the consumer gets the short end of the bargain." And so it went. Meanwhile, over on the Senate side, more trouble surfaced. The filibuster veterans Metzenbaum and Abourezk met with Senators Durkin and Donald W. Riegle, Jr., of Michigan, and staff aides of several other Democratic senators to map plans for another filibuster if the gas bill ever came back to their side. "My office, and Senator Abourezk's as well, has been receiving calls from other senators expressing willingness to join," said Metzenbaum. "If there is a filibuster, it will be more than a two-man filibuster. There have been indications that Republicans might be willing to join," though of course only to embarrass the Administration or because they wanted immediate deregulation, not because they opposed higher prices.

April 28. With timing that some skeptics interpreted as an effort on the part of the Administration to make the oil companies seem more deserving of the riches of the natural gas bill, Interior Secretary Cecil Andrus released results of the study, begun shortly after Carter took office, to determine if the oil companies were producing all the natural gas they could from five of six large offshore fields in the Gulf of Mexico. At the time the study was launched, many parts of the nation were suffering from lack of gas, and critics—repeating a charge that had become commonplace in and out of Congress—said the companies were withholding offshore gas to force up prices. The investigators' preliminary findings, in April 1977, were that there was no production from reservoirs in four fields in the Gulf with proved reserves of gas totaling nearly one trillion cubic feet. At that time, John F. O'Leary, deputy energy secretary, had said there was "no question" that some energy companies were withholding gas, awaiting higher prices. But now, a year later, just in the nick of time for the PR-starved oil companies, came the much more detailed study purporting to show that the oil companies were producing all the natural gas they could. But the investigators had concentrated on the older, thoroughly developed fields—fields that accounted for only 16 percent of the 1976 gas production in the outer continental shelf—and did not try to find out whether the newer fields were being developed as fast as they could be. The companies hailed the report as vindicating their protestations of innocence, and Andrus said it "cleared the air," but he also conceded that the study in no way settled the debate.

May 3. On the eve of the second public meeting of the conferees this year, Senator Long said that maybe he had been hasty, maybe there was a slight chance that the crude oil tax could be passed. Obviously this was meant to dupe members like Corman, but Long had by now become such a transparent trickster that nobody paid any attention to him.

May 4. The second public meeting of the full conference committee was actually held! And what a hysterical waste of time it was! Most of the one and a half hours was used by conferees who had been excluded from the negotiations to tell those who had put the bill together privately what a rotten bunch of scofflaws they were. Everyone had a good time shouting. And when they weren't screaming imprecations at each other, they were asking questions that showed just how little most of them knew about what was going on. During the discussion of special price provisions for gas extracted from tight sand, for instance, the commonest question was, "How tight is tight?"

May 9. Senator Long's trick having failed to win over the no-gas-pricing-without-crude-taxing members, the Administration went for the holdouts like Reuss, who didn't want a crude tax. Shortly before noon, House Speaker Tip O'Neill, taking his cue from the White House, agreed to break off the crude oil tax from the rest of the energy package—in other words, to kill it. Reuss said that with that decision by the Administration, they could count on his vote for gas pricing.

White House lobbyists were jubilant. Reuss's vote should put them over the top! At 2 P.M., the House conferees met to vote on the measure. But . . . two of the conferees were missing! Where the hell were Charles Wilson, the stringbean from East Texas, and Joe D. Waggonner, the hard-shell conservative from Louisiana?

The answer to that riddle was supplied a half hour later, when Wilson and Waggonner turned up at the White House to tell Carter that they had decided, after soulful consideration, to oppose the compromise, because they felt it mistreated Texas and Louisiana gas producers. Thus ended the 204th day of deliberation, as much—well, almost—in a muddle as ever. Why was it that every time the House vote reached the needed thirteen, it fell apart again? Carter's problem was that being so close to agreement in the committee, he was more vulnerable to blackmail than if he had been four or five votes away from success. Every time he reached the magic number, another conferee who wanted to squeeze something out of the bill—or obtain a favor of some other sort from the Administration—would drop off until the payoff was made. It was happening on the Senate side, too.

Cathy Hurwit, a House energy adviser who was in the middle of it all, recalls, "These guys like Charlie Wilson and Bennett Johnston, who were in an excellent negotiating position, got a lot more than they thought they were going to get. What would happen at the end is that in these closed sessions, so-and-so would get up and say, 'I've been in this from the beginning and what we've achieved is great. But if I don't get this particular language to suit my consumers back home, or my producers back home, count me out.' And because it was one vote either way, they'd get it. This was happening until the very last day. In fact, it continued to happen right down to the day when they actually signed the draft language."

This sort of dickering, this ransoming of votes, went on not only within

conference but, as Wilson and Waggonner showed, even more successfully if taken to the White House. Wilson and Waggonner got what they
wanted; it took a couple of weeks of bluffing, but in the end they won an
alteration to the bill that made it easier for producers to wiggle out of intrastate contracts to take advantage of price increases.

For pure gall, however, the prize had to go to Wilson. He went outside
the energy debate, outside even of the domestic realm, to pluck a concession in foreign policy from Carter on behalf of Wilson's "constituent"
dictator Anastasio Somoza, whose family had controlled Nicaragua for
forty-two years. Because Somoza was reputed to be a pretty cruel fellow,
Carter was holding back $12 million in aid that had been earmarked for
the impoverished Central American country. Wilson, the most active and
vocal member of the "Nicaragua lobby" in Congress, let Carter know
that if he wanted cooperation on, among other things, the energy bill,
he'd better cough up the $12 million. So Carter did.

❋

May 24. On this, their 219th day of haggling, with a 10-to-7 vote
among Senate conferees, the deed was done. The day before, the House
group had voted 13 to 12 for it. Abourezk called it a "rape" and a "rip-
off" of consumers. From the other trenches, Senator Dewey Bartlett of
Oklahoma damned the bill as a cowardly evasion of the "free-market,
free-enterprise way." But, harsh words notwithstanding, the vote finally
stood. The conference committee was through.

What kind of job had they done? Had consumers been well served?
Not by a long shot. President Carter's bill had been anticonsumer
enough, but Congress had somehow managed to inflate that characteristic to monstrous proportions. According to the DOE's comparative
analysis, the original House bill (essentially Carter's) would have made
residential users of natural gas pay $2.89 per thousand cubic feet in 1985.
Under the bill first passed by the Senate—a bill backed by the oil and gas
industry—the residential user would have paid $2.92. But under the com-
promise bill just passed, the residential user would pay $3.28. Incredibly,
the conference committee had managed to exceed—*greatly* exceed—even
the generosity that the oil lobbyists had been willing to accept. Instead
of compromising the House and Senate versions, striking at least a
gloomy medium, the conferees had succeeded in going far above *both*. If
it hadn't been going to cost consumers many billions of dollars, it would
have been farcical. Carter's original bill looked *pro*consumer by comparison. After the DOE analysis came out, Senator Jackson said: "I never
pretended that the compromise is perfect."

❋

While Congress waited around for the rough compromise to be
polished and reduced to semiliterate legislative language, a chore that

would take more than two months, experts picked their way through the specifics to discover just what the conference committee had wrought. Some surprising and unpleasantly duplicitous features began to emerge.

For one thing, the Administration's professed priorities for allotting natural gas had been turned on their head. Back in the spring of 1977, when Carter sent his energy bill to Congress, he declared that its various pricing, taxing, and conservation features were all aimed at favoring homeowners over industry in the use of natural gas. The shrinking supply of that precious energy, he said, would be preserved primarily for use in homes and in commercial establishments; industry, with its gluttonous furnaces, would be coaxed and driven into giving up gas for coal. In the summer of 1978, the Administration—or some parts of it—were still pretending that this was their goal. Said Schlesinger's press aide Jim Bishop on July 29, "That's the heart of the Carter policy. Gas is going to be reserved for the homeowner." Perhaps Bishop wasn't pretending. Perhaps he just didn't know any better. The energy legislation that had emerged from conference was indeed a confusing mess; experts couldn't always agree on what it said. But, in any event, Bishop was dead wrong.

It was quite true that the *original* bill sent to Congress by Carter would have favored homeowners in the allotment of gas. Under *that* bill, it was expected that residential-commercial consumption of natural gas would increase 8 percent and industrial consumption would probably decline slightly by 1985. But, under the bill that had just emerged from conference, and which Carter was willing to accept, the results would be quite different. Indeed, the DOE's own Energy Information Administration reported in July that as far as it could tell, the results of the compromise bill would be to raise prices so much that residential-commercial consumption would probably *decrease* 4 percent while industrial use would *grow* by perhaps as much as 14 percent by 1985. In short, the conferees had completely reversed Carter's plan. Historically, industrial users had been allowed to buy natural gas at a much lower price than homeowners; it was part of the "cheaper by the dozen" idiocy that had prevailed in the energy marketplace for years. Carter's original bill was to end this industrial favoritism. But, in the secret backroom bargaining, the conferees had preserved the bargain rates for industry, and Carter's conservation plans were fated to go up the big industrial stacks. And he no longer seemed to care. He had long since reached the "any bill" frame of mind.

*

During the months of formal bill writing, support for the legislation rose and fell on a daily basis. There was never any certainty it could be passed. Indeed, there were periods during August when its passage seemed highly unlikely. "It's being widely advertised as being dead," said Congressman Dingell, "and I'm not prepared to accept that. Yet it seems every time we turn around we've got fresh troubles."

It was inevitable. The pressures were coming from too many directions to allow peaceful passage. Reuss, for example, though he had given assurance of his support for the bill in May, was getting uncomfortable. On August 3, one of his aides said Reuss now had "grave misgivings." He was under heavy lobbying from some home-state officials like Charles J. Cicchetti, chairman of the Wisconsin Public Service Commission, who begged Reuss not to sign, because the compromise bill "would be an economic catastrophe for Wisconsin's industry, result in a loss of jobs and create economic hardship for residential gas consumers." Cicchetti predicted the typical household bill might be several hundred dollars a year higher. Carter phoned Cicchetti and tried to persuade him to back off, but with no luck. Other bleak prophecies came from the likes of Kathleen F. O'Reilly, executive director of the Consumer Federation of America, who said that by 1985 the compromise bill would push gas prices 1,608 percent above what they were in 1970, hurting poor folks the worst, because "the lowest 10 percent on the economic ladder spends a ten times greater proportion of its income on home energy consumption than does the top 10 percent."

Reuss, a will-o'-the-wisp liberal, was impressed. He was also impressed by the potent labor-union coalition that had been formed to fight the bill: the "Citizen-Labor Energy Coalition," headed by William W. Winpisinger, the feisty president of the International Association of Machinists and Aerospace Workers,[4] who, with his usual decorum, denounced the bill as an "insidious private tax that takes money from the pockets of the people and puts it into the over-bulging coffers of the oil and gas industry" and warned that it would produce "the worst scandal on the American energy scene since the Teapot Dome scandal of the 1920s."

Worn down by bombast, Reuss began complaining that the 170-page bill, the finished product, seemed to be violating the spirit of the compromise committee's rough version in such ways as to make the costs more burdensome to consumers than previously agreed to. He didn't say he wouldn't sign, but he certainly sounded as though he would prefer that the bill just magically vanish.

From the other side came intense opposition to the bill from some oilmen who figured that if the compromise wasn't passed, then Congress would decide to get rid of the whole problem by simply decontrolling

---

4. Other unions in the coalition were the United Automobile Workers; International Association of Sheet Metal Workers; American Federation of State, County and Municipal Employees; United Steelworkers of America; Oil, Chemical, and Atomic Workers; Retail Clerks; Communications Workers of America; Amalgamated Clothing and Textile Workers Union; and the National Football League Players Association.

prices immediately. To these fellows, high on greed, the compromise bill was obnoxiously cheap. These were not the majors—the majors took the long view of profits and were delighted with the compromise—but the independent producers, who were now clomping through the corridors of the congressional office buildings dressed like Marlboro machos. Their new demands of winner-take-all, now that they seemed destined to win, put some of the most loyally pro-oil senators in a curious bind: Johnston of Louisiana, for example, had been one of the principal creators of the deregulation bill under consideration; he had helped fashion it in a way that he thought was overwhelmingly generous to the industry. And now he was being told by independent oilmen—the most powerful oil bloc in his home state—that it wasn't enough. He was flabbergasted. Speaking to a group of gas producers in Houston in June, Johnston lobbied frantically to revive support among independents for his compromise bill. "I tell you this," he said, "compared to the President's program, compared to the House bill, compared to what we feared, and frankly, even compared to what we had hoped, this is a *magnificent* bill." He boasted that of the ten goals most important to the producers, "we achieved what we were trying to achieve on each of those ten."

But, with a primary election contest facing him in September, Johnston was willing, somewhat sheepishly, to unsay in August what he had said in June. Now, having looked over the 170-page draft bill, said Johnston (echoing Reuss, though from the opposite perspective), he had decided that the committee staff drafters had played around with it too much and had "substantially" altered the agreement made in May in such a way as to hurt producers, so he could no longer support it. He was assisted in his moment of embarrassment by his chameleon colleague Russell Long, who declared that ". . . now they'll either have to go back and rewrite that thing the way it was supposed to be written or I don't think they are going to have a bill." It was not always possible to take Long seriously, nor was it possible to tell which way he would jump next. But Johnston's support from another Louisianian, Representative Waggonner, was critical indeed, for Carter had seemed to need Waggonner's signature on the compromise, just as he needed Reuss's, to get the required complement. With both Waggonner and Reuss defecting, it seemed, as of Thursday, August 17, that the gas bill was once again down the drain.

But no legislation that lousy ever dies, so by the end of the week it had once again been resurrected. Carter regained the required majority among the thirteen House conferees by obtaining signatures from Representative Corman, the California Democrat, and Representative Rangel, the New York Democrat. Previously opposing the bill, they were now won over by an amazing lobbying effort. First came pressure from

Secretary of the Treasury W. Michael Blumenthal and Federal Reserve
Board Chairman G. William Miller (Fed chairmen virtually *never* lobby
for a White House bill; they consider it déclassé). According to Blumenthal and Miller, the fate of the nation hung by the gas bill; well, almost. And last, they said with a straight face, the value of the dollar
hung by it, and if the dollar sank, so would the national economy. Bread-
lines and bankruptcies were the theme of their dirge. Then more pressure came from House Speaker O'Neill, with his honeyed tongue promising rich blessings in the offing if they proved to be team players. And
then they were summoned to the White House for an evening chat with
Himself, Carter, who pulled the old oriental line of the great loss of face
he would suffer around the world if he failed to obtain passage of a bill
that had been his top priority for more than a year and a half. Whether
or not Carter also promised pork was never determined, though some
cynical observers were convinced he had.

At that point, only ten of the required thirteen House members had
actually signed. Giddy with attention, Corman and Rangel now promised
that if one other conferee agreed to go along, they would too. As it happened, Representative Wilson—who often managed to hold off in major
legislative fights until his support could be redeemed in great wedges of
pork—had left his signature on a blank piece of paper, with the assurance
that the paper could be pasted onto the conference report if twelve other
names were obtained. With that, Wilson flew off to Texas. Shortly after
midnight, the White House cornered him there by phone, and the deal
was completed. So much for the House.

*

Meanwhile, the Senate side had been pumped up again in a somewhat
crude fashion. Shortly before meeting with Corman and Rangel on
Thursday night, Carter had sat down for some horse trading with Senators Pete V. Domenici, Republican of New Mexico, and James A.
McClure, Republican of Idaho. Both emerged from the meeting saying
they were prepared to go with Carter. Now Carter had the bare minimum of Senate signatures he needed. What Domenici got out of it was
never made known. But McClure was as talkative as he was tickled. He
had gotten Carter to promise, in writing, that the Administration would
spend heavily over the next three years for the development of breeder
reactors.

In making this commitment, Carter went 180 degrees away from his
often stated—fervently stated, *piously* stated—opposition to breeder reactors because they produce large amounts of plutonium "waste" that can
be used to make atomic bombs. The deal didn't do much for Carter's
fast-fading reputation as an idealist ("backdoor maneuvering," said
Ralph Nader), and it did even less for his reputation as a politician. It

was a stupid swap, and if he had pulled the trick earlier, before the prodecontrol bill had reached its present momentum, he would probably have had no chance at all of passing it, for the McClure deal grossly offended one man he ordinarily could not have risked offending: Senate Republican Leader Howard Baker of Tennessee. Baker was furious. He had been a supporter of the gas bill. Now he opposed it hammer and tongs. It seems as how the only breeder project under way at the time was, and had for years been, the Clinch River program, in Tennessee. McClure's home state, Idaho, had had a small, experimental breeder project in the 1950s. The way Baker read the Carter-McClure agreement, it would halt work at Clinch River and, well, reading between the lines it looked to Baker as if the breeder work would be shifted to Idaho.

Baker had been of enormous help to Carter in passing the Panama Canal treaty. He could have been as useful in rounding up reluctant Republicans to support the gas bill. Instead, on September 7, Baker formally withdrew his support of the bill, thereby guaranteeing that most Republicans would join him in an effort to scuttle it.

But, by that time, the Carterites had managed to beg and browbeat enough support, particularly from big-business lobbies, to turn the trick. Until late August, the major steel companies opposed the bill. Then White House lobbyists passed the word that if steel flip-flopped, it would be rewarded with a variety of tax relief and federal aid. Flip-flop it did, pronto. The textile industry opposed the bill until, in August, Carter's special trade negotiator, Robert Strauss, told the textile people that he would be going to Japan soon to talk about restraining Japanese textile exports to the United States. Textile flip-flopped. With similar lollipops, the White House persuaded several key outfits, such as General Motors and B. F. Goodrich, which had opposed the bill, to at least shift into neutral.

Right and left, some of the opponents stood firm; the American Farm Bureau did; so did the AFL-CIO; so did the United Auto Workers. The Machinists' Winpisinger not only stood firm but announced that no member of Congress who voted for the compromise would get a penny of campaign funds from that union's $600,000 war chest. Seldom does a union cancel support of friendly members on the basis of a single vote, but Winpisinger said, ". . . we are fed up with posturing politicians who come around, seek our support, our money, our votes and then when the criticial issues are up for a vote they see fit to horse-trade and swap votes on the issue." (He was true to his word, and the aid the Machinists withheld from such hard-pressed liberal Senators as Dick Clark of Iowa and William Hathaway of Maine surely contributed to their defeat.)

*

Doubtless, the swing of big business contributed the final momentum Carter needed. But it would be too simple to assume that big business came around to his side solely from promises of financial benefits, and it would be similarly unfair to assume that the now noticeably shifting mood of Congress resulted solely from horse trading and lobby pressures. It seems more reasonable to assume that both business and politicians were motivated by at least some small degree of pity and embarrassment for the President and his henchmen—and for the nation that was trapped with such bumblers. For seventeen months, the Carterites had performed clumsily, with naïveté and juvenile trickiness. The energy program that the President had offered in the spring of 1977 was now actually unrecognizable—it had started out as a procoal program and had now become a progas program—and yet Carter continued to pretend it was just the program he had wanted all along. Shamelessly, he now publicly urged that politicians and public should not pay attention to the "details" of the program but should keep uppermost in mind only that if *a* program were not passed, there would be a harsh impact on U.S. prestige, credibility, leadership, solvency, military strength, and so on. "The posture," as columnist James J. Kilpatrick noted at the time, "smacks of panic—the panic of a spinster who has to have 'a' husband."

But there was a certain logic to Carter's plea for everyone to ignore the details of the bill. It was an incredible mishmash; so much so that the 170-page bill was accompanied by a 130-page report that was intended to explain what was in the 170 pages. It was full of language such as: "This special rule limits the operation of indefinite price escalator clauses in existing intrastate contracts for which the contract price on December 31, 1984, is higher than $1.00 per MMBtu's so that the contract prices may not exceed the new gas ceiling price as of January 1, 1985, adjusted by the monthly equivalent of the annual inflation adjustment factor, plus 3.0 percentage points."

It was a piece of legislation to conjure up visions of a bureaucratic madhouse. After studying the early drafts of the bill, Sheila S. Hollis, director of the Federal Energy Regulatory Commission's Office of Enforcement, sent a private memo to her boss, Charles B. Curtis, FERC chairman, saying, "The proposal is so complex, ambiguous and contradictory that it would be virtually impossible for this commission to enforce it in a conscientious and equitable manner . . . The provisions are so involved that OE fails to understand how any reasonably accurate assessment of the price and revenue impact could be made . . . Put another way, the bill is not necessarily a 'good' bill or a 'bad' bill; it is merely impossible to administer conscientiously."

Later, when her memo was leaked to the press, she altered her judgment. But she shouldn't have.

Even more embarrassing were the contortions of Energy Secretary

Schlesinger. The previous year, he had insisted heatedly that raising the price of gas higher than $1.75 per thousand cubic feet would be a senseless gift to the industry, since $1.75, he said, would induce maximum production. Now, less than a year later and with the compromise bill offering *much* more than $1.75, he was insisting just as hotly that the higher prices would result in higher drilling rates and "more gas in the interstate market." Indeed, now he touted gas as the great substitute for oil; some days, he said the replacement of oil with natural gas would come to five hundred thousand barrels a day, and on other days he grandly predicted a savings of a million barrels a day, and sometimes he even shot up to 1.4 million barrels. If anybody was still listening to him, it was only in amazement.

Whether from pity or federal payoffs, big business did begin to pitch in on Carter's side to such an extent that the climate around Congress changed radically during the first days of September. On September 1, an Associated Press survey of the Senate found 32 favoring or leaning toward the gas bill, 35 opposed or leaning against it, and 33 undecided. An AFL-CIO lobbyist put the count at that time at 35 in favor or leaning in favor, 42 against or leaning against, and the rest undecided, but he conceded that the White House's stepped-up lobbying campaign was making headway with industry executives.

*

And liberals were beginning to crumble. Those opposing the bill were dealt a stiff blow on September 8, when Senator Edmund Muskie of Maine announced that he was joining the Carter camp. His reasons for doing so seemed all to be rooted in mental exhaustion and confusion. "No one really knows what will happen to energy prices and supplies if we pass the bill," he said, "or even if we defeat it." Abourezk was shaken by Muskie's defection, saying, "Not since 'Bloody Monday,' September 27, 1977, when the Carter administration switched sides and ran a deregulation spear through its own supporters, have I been as disappointed." (Apparently the earlier trauma had addled his mental calendar; Bloody Monday was on September 26.)

On the same day as Muskie's defection, the League of Women Voters announced its endorsement of the natural gas bill, making it the first major consumer-oriented organization to do so. Key governors—Julian M. Carroll of Kentucky, William G. Milliken of Michigan, Brendan Byrne of New Jersey, Richard Lamm of Colorado, and Dixy Lee Ray of Washington (all Democrats, except for Milliken)—left a conference with Carter to announce their support. On September 13 and 14, six liberal senators—Adlai Stevenson of Illinois, Thomas Eagleton of Missouri, Thomas McIntyre of New Hampshire, Patrick Leahy of Vermont, and John Culver and Dick Clark of Iowa—who the previous fall had voted to continue price regulation for natural gas, announced that they were switching to support phased deregulation. While Senator Baker's opposition meant that most Republican senators would oppose the bill, the announcement on September 15 by Senator Ted Stevens of Alaska, assistant minority leader, that he would support the bill as "the best we can do," meant that Carter could count on at least a handful of Republicans to do as Stevens was doing. Actually, what changed Stevens' mind was the Administration's pitch that passage of the bill would make it easier to finance a natural gas pipeline from Alaska, Stevens' home state, to the hungry markets of the Midwest. At the time of Stevens' announcement, an Associated Press survey showed that Carter was now virtually out of trouble in the upper chamber: 48 senators for or leaning toward his bill, 39 opposed or leaning against, and 13 still undecided. If the survey was accurate, Carter had to squeeze only 3 more from the uncommitted ranks to win. Senator Metzenbaum grimly insisted that "the battle isn't over yet," but now it was clear that he and Abourezk and their allies had virtually no chance.

Everything hinged on the possibility of a filibuster. If they could persuade the Senate to leave the rules flexible enough to permit a filibuster, then they would indeed have a chance, for Carter's new supporters were neither enthusiastic nor loyal. But the Senate did not leave the rules flexible. It did, however, give the dissenters a generous, if finite, period in which to whip up support for killing the bill. They could talk their heads off during that period, cajoling, shaming, threatening, pestering, but at a given time they would have to shut up. It sounded fair, and it was fair; but in effect it was just a nice way of disarming them. The agreement was that on Tuesday, September 19, the Senate would vote on the motion to send the bill back to committee to be gutted of its pricing provision. If that motion passed, the bill was effectively dead. If the motion failed, debate would be resumed for another week, during which time other recommittal motions could be made and voted on. But on September 27, if the dissenters hadn't managed to swing a majority to their side, and few thought they would, then the tournament would come to an end: on that date the conference bill would be voted up or down, and that would be that.

*

The Tuesday vote was 55 to 39 against recommitting the bill. When Senator Jackson, floor leader, said the vote proved the bill "is no longer in danger," Metzenbaum glumly agreed, "I'm not so sure he's wrong." But Metzenbaum still refused to give up. He said he knew of at least five senators who could be dislodged from Carter's ranks if "we find a motion to recommit that has broader appeal." But his side could not find it. A second motion to recommit was defeated, 55 to 36, on Tuesday, September 26, eve of the final vote. There were no switches.

On Wednesday, it slid through, 57 to 42,[5] and Carter hailed passage of the butchered legislation as a "remarkable demonstration of leadership" by his congressional allies. Jackson, one of those remarkable leaders, added lamely that the bill was "the very best we could get under existing circumstances." Whatever that meant. And the Washington *Post*, while admitting that the legislation it had supported in all its variations was "a tortured compromise," tried to put the best face on the Senate's achievement by praising "the Senate's bipartisan center" for rescuing the energy issue "from the zealots and ideologues on both sides"—among whom it singled out Metzenbaum and Abourezk and Kennedy on the left, Barry Goldwater, Lloyd Bentsen, and Bennett Johnston on the right: strange allies, said the *Post*, who had conspired against "the national interest." The editorial was a suitable envoi to one of the Senate's less attractive legislative struggles.

Now it was up to the House.

---

5.   57-TO-42 ROLL-CALL VOTE ON MEASURE

Here is the 57-to-42 roll-call vote by which the Senate approved the natural gas compromise.

Democrats For

Allen (Ala.)	Inouye (Hawaii)
Bumpers (Ark.)	Jackson (Wash.)
Burdick (N.D.)	Leahy (Vt.)
Byrd (W.Va.)	Magnuson (Wash.)
Cannon (Nev.)	Matsunaga (Hawaii)
Chiles (Fla.)	McIntyre (N.H.)
Church (Idaho)	Melcher (Mont.)
Clark (Iowa)	Morgan (N.C.)
Cranston (Calif.)	Moynihan (N.Y.)
Culver (Iowa)	Muskie (Maine)
DeConcini (Ariz.)	Nunn (Ga.)
Eagleton (Mo.)	Pell (R.I.)
Ford (Ky.)	Randolph (W.Va.)
Glenn (Ohio)	Ribicoff (Conn.)
Gravel (Alaska)	Sparkman (Ala.)
Hart (Colo.)	Stennis (Miss.)
Hatfield (Mont.)	Stevenson (Ill.)
Hathaway (Maine)	Stone (Fla.)
Hodges (Ark.)	Talmadge (Ga.)
Huddleston (Ky.)	Williams (N.J.)

Republicans For

Case (N.J.)	McClure (Idaho)
Chafee (R.I.)	Packwood (Ore.)
Danforth (Mo.)	Pearson (Kan.)
Domenici (N.M.)	Percy (Ill.)
Griffin (Mich.)	Stafford (Vt.)
Hatfield (Ore.)	Stevens (Alaska)
Heinz (Pa.)	Thurmond (S.C.)
Javits (N.Y.)	Young (N.D.)
Mathias (Md.)	

Democrats Against

Abourezk (S.D.)	Johnston (La.)
Anderson (Minn.)	Kennedy (Mass.)
Bayh (Ind.)	Long (La.)
Bentsen (Tex.)	McGovern (S.D.)
Biden (Del.)	Metzenbaum (Ohio)
Byrd (Va.)	Nelson (Wis.)
Durkin (N.H.)	Proxmire (Wis.)
Eastland (Miss.)	Riegle (Mich.)
Haskell (Colo.)	Sarbanes (Md.)
Hollings (S.C.)	Sasser (Tenn.)
Humphrey (Minn.)	Zorinsky (Neb.)

Republicans Against

Baker (Tenn.)	Hayakawa (Calif.)
Bartlett (Okla.)	Laxalt (Nev.)
Bellmon (Okla.)	Lugar (Ind.)
Brooke (Mass.)	Roth (Del.)
Curtis (Neb.)	Schmitt (N.M.)
Dole (Kan.)	Schweiker (Pa.)
Garn (Utah)	Scott (Va.)
Goldwater (Ariz.)	Tower (Tex.)
Hansen (Wyo.)	Wallop (Wyo.)
Hatch (Utah)	Weicker (Conn.)

Not Voting

Helms (R-N.C.)

*

But there, too, the climate had changed. The proregulation forces who had carried the House rather easily in 1977 no longer had the support of the Democratic leadership; Tip O'Neill et al. had deserted them. Which is not to say that the proregulation forces could not swing a majority of the House against the gas pricing provisions; it is only to say that they could not—and they knew they could not—swing a majority against the energy bill *as a whole*.

To understand their problem, one must go back to the beginning, in 1977. In the House, the Carter energy program was split into four bills: conservation, utility reform, coal conversion, and natural gas pricing. The House passed all four bills and sent them to conference committee. In the Senate, the Carter energy program was never split up; it was handled as a whole, and that's the way it was sent to the conference committee and returned to the Senate; *and it was this whole that the Senate had now approved and sent to the House.*

The only hope that the proregulation forces had was to block the bill's being considered in this way and to persuade the House instead to vote on Carter's energy package once again in four parts. As a matter of fact, in making this demand the proregulation forces were upholding normal House rules: the House had passed four bills, it had sent four groups into conference—it should now give final votes on four bills.

If it were done otherwise, the Rules Committee would have to approve. Dingell and Ashley went to the Rules Committee and did ask for approval to combine the bills into a single package. Those who were in the Rules Committee say that the decision was made clumsily in a classic legislative storm—chaotic, impassioned. Congresswoman Shirley Chisholm of New York became so confused that she voted the wrong way, to combine the bills. Then she said, "Wait a minute—I don't understand what's going on." She switched, voting to consider four separate bills. With her vote, the proregulators—the Moffett crowd—had won. But only momentarily. The Carter forces took old Representative Claude Pepper of Florida aside, and they took Representative B. F. Sisk of California aside, and they talked of wondrous things, and when the Rules Committee reconvened the next day to reconsider—behold, the proregulators had lost.

This left them with only one more chance. They had to go to the floor: they had to persuade the House as a whole to override the Rules Committee and consider the bills separately.

Moffett, the hardest fighter of them all, picks up the memory:

"We lost by a vote. One vote. That was the greatest disappointment of my adult life. Not just because we lost—you learn how to lose a little bit —but because they got to my friends, some of my dear friends.

"Rick Nolan [of Minnesota] came to me and I could just tell by looking at his face—this was, like, the day before the vote—and I said, 'Rick, you wouldn't do that to me!' And he said, 'Look, Mondale fathered me politically.' I said, 'Rick, you can't vote for deregulation!' He said, 'I can't help it—I'm sick about it but—I can't sleep at night, I'm sick about it, I feel dirty and evil but I made a commitment.' And Downey [Thomas Downey of New York]—he sort of jokingly said to me, about a week before the vote, almost as an aside, 'The President asked me if I would be with him on the gas thing and I said yeah.' And I said, 'What!' He wanted to get on Ways and Means—that's what they used on him. He was on Armed Services and he wanted to get on Ways and Means."

When it was suggested that the manipulation of Downey sounded like a shafting by Tip O'Neill, Moffett went on:

"Of course. I had to work against the speaker once they put the bill together, once the deal was cut. He was doing the same thing as everybody else; after that whole horrible period of much of '78 when everybody was trying to get 'a' bill, he was trying to get a bill. I kept saying to him, 'You can have a bill—pass the other three parts. They're very good pieces.' The leadership worked their tail off on this thing; they had never put out an effort like that before."

And then came the moment of defeat. "Bob Carr [of Michigan] stood in the well with the vote 206 to 206 and me two feet from him saying, 'Bob, don't do it.' He wouldn't even look me in the eye. Carr had been one of those guys who was patting me on the back, saying, 'Great job, keep it up,' taking my handouts and saying, 'This is terrific.' And now he wouldn't even look me in the eye. I said, 'Bob, will you look at me?' He's taller than I am. But he's fingering the card, and O'Neill has got the gavel ready. And he writes his name on the card and throws it in.

"I was devastated emotionally. Carr was a friend—his girl friend was killed in an auto accident my first year here, and George Miller and I rushed to the hospital and spent twenty-four hours with him, straight. He's been to my place in Connecticut. But we're not close anymore.[6]

"That whole episode devastated me. The fact that those guys—we'd sit around at night over at Downey's apartment, night after night, week after week, month after month. 'What can we do to change this place? We need more people like us! . . . What can we do?' The whole liberal

---

6. At the end of the roll call, the vote was tied. Over the next five minutes there was great confusion as members voted and changed their votes. Some believe that it wasn't Carr but Representative Thomas R. Evans, Delaware Republican, who cast the 207th vote against Moffett's side. Jimmy Carter's diary entry for October 13, 1978, notes: "This day has been a nightmare. . . . The crucial vote on energy was 207–206, with the last-minute support of Republican Congressman Tom Evans, who just cracked up afterward when I called him on the phone. The abuse he received from the Republican leadership was excessive, to say the least. Tom had promised me in the Oval Office yesterday that he would vote with us, but it was very difficult for him to keep his promise."

thing, right? I said to Tommy [Downey]—he avoided me for two days after the vote, but he finally came up and said he had to talk to me, and I said there was nothing to say. He said, 'Let me just say it wasn't anything corrupt.' He said, 'I didn't sell out.' I said, 'Tommy, I want you to know that I would never suggest that. I don't think you're that way. It would be incredible for me to suggest that you sold out. The fact is, you are a weak son of a bitch. And you will have to live with that. I don't want to hear any more shit about what we have to do to change this place! The biggest domestic issue you faced and you flunked the test. So don't tell me . . .'

"I just couldn't believe it. I was absolutely shattered! I walked out of the chamber—like I didn't even know where I was. Walked out to the steps, a beautiful day, walked across the driveway to the Library of Congress and started shaking. Finally, I just put my face up against a tree and cried for about twenty minutes. I was living this thing. Pete Starke and a lady I go out with came over and grabbed me and took me over to Pete's house about a block away and we sat in the backyard. Dellums came over. This was when we were in session around the clock. I came back to vote, but I stayed until about midnight. It was like a wake. People came by to pay their respects. We were so shattered as a group. Everybody was shattered—not so much about losing the vote as about what had happened to our group."

Between fifteen and twenty members (depending on who was doing the counting) that the Moffett crowd thought they had commitments from defected.

* * *

The year saw considerable action on the shady side of the street. Paul Bloom, enforcer at the Office of Special Counsel for Compliance, which had been set up in 1977 to crack down on oil rule violators, levied his first fine in July: $52 million against Ashland Oil. If the fine survived a court test, then Bloom was expected to start socking it to thirty-three other oil companies in the same way. He talked of making them cough up at least $1 billion in overcharges, and that was just for starters, "just the tip of the iceberg," said Bloom, compared to what he intended to do later. Most of the overcharging uncovered by his six hundred accountants and lawyers was allegedly the handiwork of Exxon and Texaco.

Some of the overcharging was innocently done—the result of confusion caused by the DOE's complex rules—but Bloom was discovering that a great deal of the overcharging had been deliberate, the oil company executives figuring that they would never be caught and that if they were caught the penalties levied by DOE would be small enough to make their crime pay very well. Which wasn't so dumb. Late in July, Gulf Oil was allowed to pay the government $42.2 million to settle claims that it had overcharged customers $79.9 million. Bloom said he hoped the settlement would set a precedent for settling other cases—meaning, apparently, that the government would be happy to settle for 50 cents on the dollar. A Gulf executive said the penalty would not affect the company's earnings and that the fine would be taken from a reserve fund, which Gulf had been building up for several years and which more than covered the fine. Did this mean that Gulf had anticipated being penalized?

*

More evidence of the industry's intentional carelessness toward price regulations surfaced in a Union Oil Company internal memorandum. The memorandum, from Thomas B. Sleeman to other company executives, advised: "It would not be good strategy to request an FEA [Federal Energy Administration] interpretation. Rather, we should file our next reports using interpretation 2"—meaning, Union should translate the price regulations more generously to itself, because "The worst that can happen is they will force us back to No. 1"—an interpretation Union officials acknowledged was "supported by a literal reading of the regulations. No price reduction would be required." In short, Sleeman was urging that the company not ask the FEA for guidance in how to comply with the law, but to conduct business as though the regulations allowed much more generous pricing than a literal reading of them would indicate. DOE attorneys said the memo indicated that much of the industry's claimed confusion over price regulations was a profitable farce.

*

The first criminal felony charges of overpricing brought pleas of nolo contendere from Continental Oil Co. and two smaller Texas firms, Foremost Oil Co. and M&A Petroleum. The indictment charged that, during the oil crisis of 1973, Conoco schemed with M&A and Foremost to sell refined oil at prices higher than permitted by law, after which the transaction was reported fraudulently to the Federal Energy Office. The lawbreakers agreed to pay the government $3.1 million.

In August, an oil-industry conspiracy case ended in Baltimore federal court with convictions of seven companies. Five other companies were acquitted. The conspiracy, which lasted from 1967 to 1974, involved price fixing of more than 17 billion gallons of gas.

In New Orleans, two giants of the offshore oil industry—J. Ray McDermott & Co., of New Orleans, and Brown & Root Inc., of Houston—pleaded no contest to charges that from 1960 through 1975 they had conspired to rig prices and squeeze out competitors. Each company was fined $1 million, which, given the profits they had been making, was the equivalent of a $5 parking ticket to you or me.

＊

Meanwhile, the search for the "missing" oil went on. As mentioned earlier (see the chapter on 1977), the DOE was unable to account for up to two hundred thousand barrels of old oil that was "disappearing" from the government's accounting system each day. The discrepancy was measured by comparing the amount of old oil purchased at the wellhead with the amount of old oil that arrived at the refinery. It was believed that the old oil was being fraudulently recertified as new oil to make higher profits. (By federal regulations, old oil, meaning crude oil from domestic wells in production before 1972, could sell for no more than $5.25 a barrel; new oil could sell for uncontrolled prices, which went as high as $13.50 a barrel.) Consumers had been cheated of at least $2 billion over the previous four years in this fashion.

The technique for achieving the fraud came to be known as "daisy chains." A daisy chain was a series of bogus resellers or brokers. The background for the scheme was this: Historically, there was only one transaction between oil field and refinery; the refiner simply bought directly from the producer. The only exception to this rule was oil in small fields, which didn't justify pipeline connections and was bought by brokers who usually trucked their mom-and-pop purchases to refineries and resold it. Before the 1973–74 Arab embargo, there weren't over a dozen resellers of this sort doing business in the United States. But, following the embargo, when a ceiling was placed on "old" oil to prevent the industry from exploiting the market unmercifully, almost overnight an army of bogus "resellers" sprang up. By 1978, there were more than five hundred of them, often going into business with no more than a one-room office and a telephone—which was enough equipment to turn many of them into millionaries overnight. Unlike the old, legitimate resellers, who actually bought oil in the field and trucked it to refineries, these fellows never left their desks. They simply inserted themselves between the producer and the refiner to rig prices in midstream. (Not that the producers and refiners were innocent of what was going on; indeed, many of these "resellers" were owned by, and were fronts for, the producers and refiners.) Sometimes dozens, scores, of resellers would handle the same oil (on paper) before it reached the refinery. And of course, at each transaction, the price would go up. Somewhere en route, usually early on, the oil would often be recertified—"flipping the price," it was called—as "new," thereby moving the price-rigging to a higher stratum altogether. From refinery to outlet, the process was repeated. Refineries that were in on the racket did not sell their products—as they would have prior to 1974—directly to legitimate customers such as utilities. Instead, they now sold through another series of "resellers."

Legitimate buyers who were part of the daisy chain apparently didn't mind being cheated, because they simply passed on the overcharge to the public.

The House Energy and Power Subcommittee staff, in December, issued a memorandum accusing the DOE of collusion in allowing "these schemes to continue and proliferate. There is evidence in DOE internal files that indicates top officials had been aware of this criminal activity as early as 1975—nearly three years before the first case was referred to the Department of Justice for criminal prosecution."

*

In May, the Justice Department charged Gulf Oil with conspiring with other uranium producers to drive up the price of "yellowcake," the raw uranium used to make fuel for nuclear power plants, from $6 to $41 a pound. But the wages of sin are less for corporations than for individuals, so the charge against Gulf was only a misdemeanor, punishable by a fine of up to $50,000; if it had been considered a felony, the fine could have been $1 million. In December, Gulf pleaded no contest—guilty—and was rewarded by the federal judge by being fined only $10,000.

*

Limping past its fifth anniversary, on July 18, was the pathetic *Exxon* suit, filed in 1973 by the Federal Trade Commission against the nation's eight largest oil companies for allegedly monopolizing the oil business east of the Rockies. At the rate it was going, the suit would probably never be brought to trial. Every time the FTC's small legal staff asked the oil companies to supply documents, the oil companies would complain to the commission that the request was too burdensome, and months of haggling would ensue. This had happened over and over again, and as yet the FTC's lawyers had not received even one of the documents that they had requested. The glacial pace of the lawsuit was taking its toll on the agency's legal staff; the two lawyers in charge of the case quit in mid-1978.

And the practices that prompted the lawsuit in the first place were continuing.

***

Why did the oil companies need increasingly higher prices? Oh yes, to finance exploration for more oil. It was hard to remember their explanation, because they kept pumping money into projects that had nothing at all to do with finding more oil. In March, Superior Oil Co. bought Hecla Mining Co., one of the ten largest U.S. copper producers. Three months earlier, Exxon had announced that it would invest $1 billion in Chile's La Disputada copper mine. A few months earlier, Atlantic Richfield paid $700 million for Anaconda Co. Indeed, over the previous fifteen years, the big oil companies had been quietly funneling a great deal of their profits into an effort to corner the copper market, and they had made great progress toward that end. *Barron's,* the financial weekly, reported that oil companies now controlled 40 percent of the domestic copper industry; they owned, or had major interests in, six of the thirteen largest U.S. copper companies, which accounted for 95 percent of U.S. production. It was a good time to buy, for copper stock was selling for about 50 percent of replacement value. Copper prices were depressed, but oil company executives admitted that they were buying into copper for the long haul, not for short-term profits. Why, the day might come when they would have as much domination of copper as they had of oil. It was an industry they would feel at home in: copper had a depletion allowance too.

***

It was becoming clear in subtle and not so subtle ways that Saudi Arabia would displace Iran as the American linchpin in the Persian Gulf. For several years, Iran had been the largest single purchaser of American military equipment in the world. Since 1972, its purchases of military hardware had increased eightfold. The number of Americans servicing Iran's military programs had doubled. It had become the region's superpower, militarily. But with that status had come a growing desire for independence from Washington. The Shah was getting uppity. That, plus stories flowing from Iran about a plague of political repression and even torture, did not sit well with the Carter administration (which claimed to base its foreign policy on "human rights"). Anyway, on the scale of necessary allies, Iran was slipping. Although still a very important source of oil, its production was no longer vital to U.S. welfare; and besides, Iran had shown a predilection for not only gouging Western consumers to the utmost but, worse in the eyes of the U.S. Government, showing a fickleness toward the needs of the international oil companies.

So it came to pass in 1978 that the Middle East arms debate in Congress was not over whether too much military equipment was being sold to Iran, but whether a rather small package of arms should be sold to Saudi Arabia. At issue were sixty F-15 planes, which the Saudis obviously sought not so much for military advantage as for political prestige among their Arab neighbors, most of whom were already nicely outfitted with French and British fighters. The Saudis also wanted the planes as a gesture that the U.S. Government loved them. "We place great importance and significance on this transaction," said Saudi Oil Minister Sheikh Ahmed Zaki Yamani. "If we don't get it, then we will have a feeling you are not concerned with our security and you don't appreciate our friendship." Meaning what? Clearly meaning that if they didn't get our planes, they might not be so enthusiastic about pumping oil and supporting the dollar. "You need us more than we need you," he said. On that,

Carter was apparently in wholehearted agreement; White House spokes-men put it around Capitol Hill that he considered this the most impor-tant arms transaction that he would make during his administration. Is-rael, of course, was adamantly opposed to the sale. The strength of its lobby was notorious. To overcome it, Carter put together an arms pack-age for all sides and the middle: not only the sixty F-15s for Saudi Arabia, but fifty F-5E fighter-bombers for Egypt and fifteen F-15s and seventy-five F-16 fighter-bombers for Israel. He did not need approval from Congress, but the sale could be blocked within thirty days after official submission of the package if both houses adopted resolutions op-posing it. On May 15 Carter won; a Senate move to thwart the sale was defeated 55 to 44. It was an ironic victory for a President who took office promising to make arms sales less important in U.S. foreign policy. Said a White House aide, "The Senate has made the political judgment that the Arabs should be treated as friends, not as enemies or adversaries, and that this is compatible with our firm commitment to Israel." The New York *Times* called it "a watershed on Mideast." Some observers called it a dangerous shell game.

*

It was just as well that the United States was shifting its affections from Iran to Saudi Arabia, for the gloriously chaotic and megalomaniac empire of the Shah was about to be destroyed. Washington, for all its vaunted spies, did not see it coming. Repeating the error they made in judging the situation in Vietnam, U.S. officials could not believe that an impassioned people could rout such a heavily armed government. In twenty years, the Shah had bought $36 billion in arms (half from the United States)—frigates from Holland, tanks from Britain, submarines from West Germany; and his air force—ah! his resplendent air force flew 141 F4Es, 64 F-14As, 20 F-14s. He had 220,000 in uniform, with 300,000 more in the reserves. Could such a mighty military machine be stopped by a mere mob of holy men and peasants and shopkeepers? Our most ex-perienced observers thought not.

Former CIA director Richard Helms, who was ambassador to Iran when Carter took over, reported the Shah completely in charge of the domestic situation. His successor, William Sullivan, a veteran of the for-eign service, did the same. Relying on such appraisals, Carter, visiting in Tehran at the turn of 1977-78, gave a toast that included a bit of unin-tentional graveyard humor: "Iran, because of the great leadership of the Shah, is an island of stability in one of the more troubled areas of the world."

Just how wrong he was, was revealed within a matter of days. Iran's Moslem clerics were already stewing over the Shah's sharp cutback in their subsidies—payoffs, really, for the clergy was the only group likely to give him trouble. They had the grass-roots organization that could stir the masses. Lately the clergy had become unhappy, and had voiced their unhappiness. They were offended by the revolutionary modernization of Iran that the Shah had brought about since the quadrupling of oil prices, in 1973. They complained about the passing of the old ways; they complained about his having taken away much of the clergy's property and power; and they complained that to silence their complaints the Shah had cut their payoffs. But instead of falling silent, they complained more loudly. From abroad, in exile (where the Shah had chased him in 1963), came the especially irritating complaints of Ayatollah Ruhollah Khomeini. In retaliation for that irritation, the Shah's claque made a terrible mistake: On January 7, it forced the Tehran daily *Ettela'at* to publish an article attacking Khomeini as a homosexual, a flunky for British imperialists, a false Moslem, and a dupe of communism. The hysterically unrestrained tone of the article so enraged the clergy—who felt that not only Khomeini but all members of their brotherhood, moderates as well as radicals, had been slandered—that they cried out for a show of public opposition to the Shah. On January 7 and again on January 9, there were large demonstrations in the holy city of Qum. The crowds clashed with police, and in the second demonstration police were so foolish as to kill six of the demonstrators. That act tapped a well of rebellion that would ultimately wash the Shah out of Iran. Thereafter, violent demonstrations came with the regularity of a heavy pendulum. As soon as the mandatory mourning period over the deaths in one demonstration had passed, a new demonstration would fill the streets in some city, or in several cities at once, and there would be new deaths, and a new mourning period, and then the crowds would pour into the streets once more. After six months of that, the intermittent periods of quiet disappeared and violence was constant. The more repressive the Shah's secret police and military became, the more the people of Iran fought back. Old political and clerical enemies suddenly found themselves allied in the fight against the Shah.

By December, it was clear that without direct U.S. assistance—and possibly even with U.S. assistance—the Shah, once presumed to be impregnable, would fall and would be replaced by the Ayatollah Khomeini. Carter's spies had been wrong from start to finish. Central Intelligence Agency director Stansfield Turner conceded his agency's blindness: "What we didn't forecast was that . . . a 78-year-old cleric who had been in exile for fourteen years would be the catalyst that would bring these forces together, and that we would have one huge volcano—a truly national revolution."

*

That wasn't the only bad news from the Mideast. In December, OPEC ended an 18-month price freeze with the announcement that prices would rise 14.5 percent in 1979. Most Western sources had been predicting a much lesser increase: somewhere between 5 and 10 percent. Their hopes had been based on Saudi Arabia's repeated promise that it would not permit other members of OPEC to go higher than that range. But when the 13-member organization had ended its 2-day huddle in Abu Dhabi, the Saudis had agreed to the 14.5 percent jump. Asked why he had gone along, Saudi Oil Minister Yamani, with well-practiced sorrow, responded, "I tried my best to make it a little bit lower. I truly wanted something lower than that. I was hoping for 5 percent, in fact. But the market today is in a unique situation, particularly because of the shortage caused by the Iranian situation, and it is difficult to hold prices down under such circumstances." The West had heard that line before—he had tried his hardest, but . . .

As a matter of fact, Iranian crisis or no, the world at the moment was experiencing an oil glut, which partly was the result of a slower world economy; the consumer nations had never fully adjusted to the drag of the heavy OPEC price increase of 1974. Also, there was more oil coming in from new fields in the North Sea, from Alaska's North Slope, and from Mexico. OPEC's premier position had begun to slip, just a little. The increase in non-OPEC oil was enough that the interruption in Iran's flow was not critical at all. On that point at least, Yamani was just plain lying.

* * *

Pipelines, those buried skeletons of the oil industry, stirred a couple of brief outcries of fright. But few people paid much attention. After all, pipelines are out of sight, so why worry?

In April, the General Accounting Office gave one reason for worrying: pipeline leaks were killing about fifty people and injuring about three hundred fifty every year, not to mention the loss of energy and resulting environmental pollution. The GAO noted in its April 26 report that the Office of Pipeline Safety Operations (OPSO) had failed to issue safety regulations governing all hazardous material that pipelines carried; that it failed to enforce penalties against safety violators; that the federal pipeline safety program had had a permanent director only three of its ten years, and that the OPSO employed only thirty-seven persons— which, though absurdly few, was fifteen fewer than it was authorized to hire—to oversee the 1.7 million miles of pipeline carrying gas and other hazardous materials.

*

In June, Senator Kennedy's Antitrust and Monopoly Subcommittee offered another reason why the public should worry about pipelines, though the subcommittee was concerned not with gas pipelines but with those carrying oil and refined oil products: gasoline, jet fuel, kerosene, and distillate fuel oil. The subcommittee staff pointed out that the top twenty oil companies own the pipes that move 96 percent of the nation's crude oil and 80 percent of all petroleum products. Just the four largest oil companies carried 48 percent of the nation's crude. This "control over pipelines yields the power of life and death over independent producers," said the staff. That may have been a slight exaggeration, but it was certainly true that the pipeline-owning oil companies used their facilities to control prices and to dominate independent producers through what is called a "natural monopoly."

The natural monopoly grew out of the fact that pipelines have the greatest cost efficiency and the most profitable economies of scale. Pipelines offer by far the cheapest overland transportation—much cheaper than either railroad tank car or truck—and even where there is waterborne competition, the pipelines of larger diameter are cheaper.[7] It costs 75 percent more to ship oil products by tanker than by pipeline from the Texas-Louisiana Gulf Coast refining area to cities in the middle Atlantic states. The cost differential is so great that independent companies can submit to unfairly high charges by the pipeline companies and still do better than if they shipped by tanker, so they submit and don't complain —being afraid that if they did complain their products would be kept out of the pipelines altogether. Of course, every penny of overcharge they pay to use the pipelines puts them at a marketing disadvantage to the oil companies that own the lines.

They have good reason to be afraid. History has shown that the majors can find a method to block some independents from using the pipelines, no matter what price they are willing to pay. It's illegal, but that doesn't seem to matter. Pipelines are common carriers, required by law to do business with all shippers; it's a law pipeline owners regularly ignore. The Interstate Commerce Commission, which is supposed to enforce the law, claims it knows of no independent shippers that have been denied access. Strictly speaking, they have a point; but the ICC knows very well that there are many ways to say no without actually saying it. As the Kennedy staff noted, "Multiple logistical and practical problems rather than outright denials have preserved these pipelines for the almost exclusive use of major oil companies."

Assistant Attorney General John H. Shenefield, testifying at the June

---

7. The diameter is crucial because pipeline capacity varies with the square of the radius of the pipe; that is, a 36-inch-diameter pipe will carry nine times as much oil as a single 12-inch-diameter line, or three times as much as three separate 12-inch lines. Since construction costs, for the most part, reflect a more linear progression, the shipment cost per unit declines if pipeline size increases (assuming the line is fully utilized).

28 Kennedy hearings, agreed that by failing to provide proper storage facilities, by offering only inconvenient routings and worse shipping schedules, and by imposing all sorts of onerous rules on the independent shippers, "the vertically integrated pipeline company has at its disposal a variety of subtle operational means short of outright access denial" to shut out the independent competitors. Shenefield admitted he wasn't sure that *"closer* regulatory scrutiny" would stop the abuses, but, he added wryly, "it is clear that most of the abuses have never been the subject of *any* regulatory scrutiny."

Holding virtually exclusive ownership over the most cost-efficient mode of transportation, the major integrated oil companies naturally use the pipelines to turn a tidy profit. They always have charged monopoly rates. Even at the depths of the Great Depression, pipelines were earning extraordinary before-tax profits, on depreciated investment, of up to 34 percent! In recent years, the Interstate Commerce Commission, which is supposed to keep rates at a fair level, has made a few flabby rulings aimed at "fairness," but the companies have nicely ducked them by juggling their rate formulas in such a fashion that almost nobody can understand them.

If the big oil companies make monopoly profits with their pipelines, why don't they build enough of them—and of a sufficient size—to take care not only of all their needs but of those of the independent producers, too? The most obvious reason, of course, is that the big oil companies feel under no obligation to make life easier for the independents. But secondly, it benefits the big producers to have some oil transported by the more expensive methods, because *that is the oil that sets the market price.* In other words, even if it costs 20 cents a barrel less to ship by pipeline than by tanker, the oil will still come out of the pipeline and go on the market at the same price as tanker oil. The market price for *all* oil reflects the *highest* transportation cost. Those companies fortunate enough to ship over the pipeline, rather than by tanker, will simply pocket an extra 20 cents on each barrel they sell. This rule of the marketplace is so important to the big companies that even if they drove all independent producers out of business, they would want to ship some of their *own* oil to market by one of the more expensive methods in order to peg the market price of oil at the higher rate.

Which brings us to this question: If there aren't enough oil-company-owned pipelines to take care of all the potential customers, and if pipelines are so profitable, why don't more independent pipeline companies move in on the market? Why doesn't the industry attract more investors who are not in the oil business but are simply interested in making money in the transportation business? Can't independent pipeline companies, unaffiliated with oil companies, successfully compete with the pipelines owned by oil companies? It's very, very difficult. Earlier it was pointed out that the twenty largest oil companies own the pipelines that carry 96 percent of the crude oil and 80 percent of oil products. If you counted not only those large oil companies but *all* oil companies owning pipelines, you would find that they control the lines that transport 98.6 percent of all crude and 86.9 percent of all oil products—leaving a pitiful 1.4 percent of crude and 13.1 percent of products for the independent lines. There are a number of reasons why the independent lines have so much trouble competing, but the main reason is that the oil companies don't have to get all their profits from the pipelines they own; what they fail to earn there—or what they might lose there, if competition, by some miracle, became real—they can make up "upstream," in the sale of their crude, or "downstream," in the sale of their products. Independent pipelines have only the one source of income, which means that they are very, very vulnerable to competition from the whipsaw pricing of the oil-company-owned lines.

Is there a way out of this dilemma? Certainly, said the Kennedy subcommittee staff: force the oil companies to get out of the pipeline business. Here was a modest—and time-honored (three generations old)—proposal. They weren't suggesting that Carter go all the way on vertical divestiture; they weren't asking him to send up legislation breaking the oil companies into separate production, transportation, refining, and marketing companies. All they wanted him to consider was one of the oldest reform proposals on the books: forcing the oil giants to unload their pipelines.

From the Justice Department's antitrust chief, Shenefield, came support, up to a point. After distinguishing between "prospective divestiture" (forbidding future oil-company investments in oil pipelines) from "retrospective divestiture" (requiring the sale of pipelines already owned by oil companies), Shenefield said he felt that "the benefits of prospective divestiture are great, and its social costs are small." He was more cautious about retrospective divestiture. But his caution seemed downright brazen compared to the response of the Department of Energy and the Office of Management and Budget (read Schlesinger and Carter). They were not in favor of the Kennedy proposals even a little bit. An OMB official explained, "The rest of us aren't absolutely sure there is a problem." Alvin L. Alm, the assistant secretary for energy policy, added the classic bureaucratic kiss-off: "We think a lot more study needs to be done."

* * *

The last good turn of Senator Lee Metcalf, the Montana Populist, before dying in January was to oversee the completion of a study of interlocking directorates among U.S. corporations. Published in April, it was the first comprehensive study of this pernicious practice in ten years. The Clayton Act of 1914, made it illegal for business competitors to have direct interlocks on their boards of directors. That is, it is illegal for the same person to sit on Exxon's board of directors and on Mobil's board of directors. But that is a prohibition that is easily circumvented—and has been consistently circumvented over the years—through *indirect* interlocking directorates: A man from Exxon and a man from Mobil will sit on Citicorp's board of directors, where, it is easy to imagine, they will discuss industry problems to their mutual benefit. If interlocking directorates are widespread—and they are—then the potential for abuse is obvious. Stated by the Metcalf study, it comes down to "the danger of a business elite, an ingrown group, impervious to outside forces, intolerant of dissent, and protective of the status quo, charting the direction of production and investment in one of several industries. Such an elite may be spawned by the concentration of key directors of major firms on a single board where they directly interlock, or by the distribution of such key directors among various other boards where they indirectly interlock their companies."

In short, directors from "competing" corporations use third-party boardrooms to meet and discuss how to avoid competition and how to screw the public. They especially like to get together on the boards of big banks and other lending institutions, such as life insurance companies. Metcalf's staff found this kind of chumminess:

Exxon had two directors—one its chairman—sitting on the board of Citicorp, the nation's second-largest bank, alongside directors of Mobil and Standard of California. Other energy-related companies on the Citicorp board were Halliburton (Brown & Root), Texas Eastern Transmission, General Electric, Stone and Webster (engineers), and Westinghouse.

Over on the Chemical New York Bank's board, Exxon, Mobil, Atlantic Richfield, Standard of Indiana, Amerada Hess, and Aramco could talk things over through their directors.

On AT&T's board, there were Exxon, Mobil, Texaco, and Continental Oil directors.

At Chase Manhattan, David Rockefeller's hangout, Exxon was linked with directors of Standard of Indiana, Utah International (mining and shipping subsidiary of General Electric), Allied Chemical, Cities Service, and the Rockefeller Family Associates.

At Metropolitan Life, Exxon had ties with Atlantic Richfield and Phillips Petroleum.

On Equitable Life's board, there were directors from Exxon, Mobil, and Continental Oil. Also, supplying another indirect interlock for the oil companies, there were directors from Chase Manhattan and Citicorp.

Ironically, the most intricate opportunity for a summit discussion on energy was not a financial institution, but a seemingly innocuous heavy-machinery manufacturer, Caterpillar Tractor, whose board included directors from Exxon, Mobil, Shell, Standard of California, and Atlantic Richfield. Chemical Bank, where four majors met, was also directly interlocked with Caterpillar. Similarly, AT&T, IBM, and U.S. Steel—whose directors were companions with the oil companies at the previously mentioned financial institutions—were on the Caterpillar board.

But that, said the Metcalf study, wasn't the end of the web, by a long shot. "Mobil met Shell on the board of General Foods. Mobil connected with Texaco on the board of American Express, and with Atlantic Richfield through Time, Inc. Shell interlocked with Gulf Oil on the board of Ampex Corp., and Standard of California met Atlantic Richfield on the board of Carter Hale Hawley Stores. Standard of Indiana interlocked with Mobil on the boards of Eli Lilly and Bell & Howell."

Metcalf's staff also found other channels between the oil companies. For example, Exxon's chief auditor was Price, Water-House & Co., which also audits Royal Dutch Petroleum, Standard of California, Gulf, Standard of Indiana, and Shell, as well as Caterpillar. Also, Exxon's lead investment banker was Morgan Stanley, which was also—coincidentally?— the principal investment banker for Mobil, Standard of Indiana, Texaco, and Shell.

All of which, wrote the subcommittee staff, raised some rather fundamental questions, to wit: "To what extent do these extraordinary corporate linkages provide a mechanism for stabilizing prices, controlling supply, and restraining competition? What is the effect of major energy-company interlocks on industry attempts to influence government policies? What is the impact of the energy companies' potential boardroom powers to influence decisions on the kinds of energy-consuming products and services marketed by major companies with whom they interlock? [That is, what kind of regressive plots for auto styling were hatched between Exxon, Mobil, and Texaco on the one hand and General Motors and Chrysler on the other when they met on AT&T's board?]

"They are questions which have yet to be answered."

They never were answered. One sign of the oil companies' influence was that Congress simply ignored the Metcalf report.

1979

"I wasn't prepared for 5,500 women to literally boo at the answer I gave on why there was a gasoline shortage."

CLIFTON GARVIN, *chairman of Exxon,*
after appearing on the "Phil Donahue Show"

"A bitter joke here [in Washington] holds that the solution to the energy shortage is to tell half the Department of Energy to stay home on even-numbered days and the other half on odd-numbered days, and then dismiss the half that come to work."

RICHARD HALLORAN *in the*
New York Times, *July 16, 1979*

In his State of the Union message to Congress, in January, President Carter, with his usual foresight, glided over the nation's energy problems in thirteen words. In a way, it was a good decision. The less he said, the less he would arouse suspicions. Unfortunately for him, he could not continue to be that circumspect for long. Before the year was out, he would have many thousands of words to say on the subject—some pleading, some scolding, most of them confused and confusing—and most Americans, as polls repeatedly showed, would believe very few of the words he spoke. He and his aides would make so many mistakes in handling the energy complexities, and would spread so much misinformation and so many falsehoods about what was going on, that his credibility would sink nearly as low as Nixon's in the butt-end days of Watergate.

The way he handled oil price decontrol didn't exactly bolster his credibility.

Domestic oil had been under price controls since August 1971. In 1975, President Ford wanted to lift the controls but was prevented from doing so when Congress, goaded by militant freshmen in the House, passed the Energy Policy and Conservation Act. It kept controls in place until at least June 1, 1979, at which time they could be removed, or continued, at the President's discretion. If he took no action to remove them, they would automatically live on until September 1981.

At the time the Act was being fought through Congress, in 1975, Carter, then an obscure candidate for the Democratic presidential nomination, indicated he thought controls of some sort should be kept in place forever. He said then that he opposed letting world market prices dictate domestic oil prices. "The price of all domestic oil," he had told the Washington Press Club on July 11, 1975, "should be kept below that of OPEC oil." The next year, as a better-known candidate, he promised to oppose deregulation of both oil and natural gas prices.

Of course, as we have seen abundantly, he did not hesitate to go back on his promise regarding natural gas controls, but even during the long struggle in Congress over that issue, he and his aides had more than once suggested both publicly and privately that if the Administration was successful in raising natural gas prices it would be disposed to keep an even tighter lid on oil prices. This was being said, of course, as a way to soften opposition to gas decontrol.

Even into the spring of 1979, White House officials were still pretending, in their dealings with procontrol members of Congress, that Carter was sympathetic to their position on oil. He was no longer promising to continue controls, but neither was he saying he would lift controls. He left the impression of being still "undecided" and open to all arguments.

It was hard to understand how Carter thought he could get by with such deception. Meeting with European heads of government in Bonn in 1978, he had promised that he would raise U.S. domestic oil prices to world levels by 1980. This promise was no secret; it was reported in the press. Likewise, in October 1978, some of Carter's energy advisers assured oil-state legislators that he fully intended to decontrol prices at his earliest opportunity, June 1, 1979. Energy Secretary James Schlesinger certainly made no effort to disguise Carter's intentions; testifying before the Senate Energy Committee on March 1, 1979, he said flatly, "It has been the objective of this administration to get to world prices [OPEC prices] . . . the means are less important than anything else."

Nevertheless, despite these declarations of intent, Carter apparently thought it was good strategy to pretend that he still had an open mind. To promote the illusion, he invited a group of procontrol congressmen to drop by the Oval Office to give him their thoughts on what he should do, and on several occasions in late March he sent his domestic-affairs adviser, Stuart Eizenstat, and Eizenstat's assistant, Kitty Schirmer, to Capitol Hill to meet with key energy legislators and solicit their views.

At a typical meeting in Toby Moffett's office (Moffett had moved up to the chairmanship of the House Subcommittee on Environment, Energy, and Natural Resources), Eizenstat and Schirmer would sit down with, say, Moffett, Andrew Maguire, Albert Gore, Jr., of Tennessee, Bob Edgar of Pennsylvania, Edward Markey of Massachusetts, and Thomas Downey. In one form or another, the question Eizenstat always put to the group was simply, "Should the Administration phase out price controls on oil?"

Since every member in the room was widely known to favor continuing controls, the question was frivolously rhetorical; the unanimous response was "No." One by one, around the room, the congressmen carefully enunciated the various arguments for their position, arguments that had become virtually rote—raising U.S. prices would just encourage OPEC to raise its prices; there was no assurance that the oil companies would use their higher profits to hunt for more oil, etc., etc.—and Eizenstat cocked his head and listened to each man with seeming raptness, as though he were hearing it all for the first time and was very impressed by it. Actually, he knew their reasoning as well as they did. Some members had heard that Eizenstat's personal view for most of the preceding six months had been close to that of the Moffett/Maguire coterie but that he had lost the battle inside the White House to Schlesinger and had accepted the "practicalities" of decontrol.

Eizenstat was not a very good actor. His polite listening fooled nobody. Maguire recalls: "I told Toby that it was clear as a bell to me that the Carter crowd had already decided they were going to go with a decontrol proposal and that the only question was how they could best dress it up to isolate the liberals. At those meetings with him, we were still arguing conservation strategies, still arguing about the proper price for old oil, considering how little it cost to bring it out of the ground, still talking about why a windfall profits tax was a futile effort, and so on. But it was clear to us that they [Eizenstat and Schirmer] were not talking about whether or not the control law should be extended, but were talking about different degrees of phasing out controls—in short, that the ball game was really over by the time they met with us, and that we had lost."

April 5 was the day the ax fell. That evening, Carter would go on television to announce his new energy plan. A few hours before air time, Schlesinger and Alfred E. Kahn, director of the Council on Wage and Price Stability, went to the Capitol for a perfunctory briefing of key members on what the President would say. Gone was the contrived atmosphere of rapprochement, gone the "let's hear your side" chumminess. After making their statements, Schlesinger and Kahn went through a stiff, brisk routine of asking for questions. But any questions that sounded even mildly critical were dismissed with curt responses, sometimes one-word responses, often (as was later discovered) inaccurate answers. They weren't there to plead for legislation; the President didn't need legislation to decontrol oil prices; he had the power to do it by fiat and he intended to do just that—ah, Schlesinger was obviously relishing the moment, cramming it down the throat of these legislators whom he had felt forced to treat with some amicability during the natural gas fight. Not even the old patsy Speaker O'Neill could get a civil word out of him. Schlesinger's performance, says Moffett, was "arrogance at its ripest."

*

Carter's message to America was, in part, this:

"Our nation's energy problem is serious—and it's getting worse . . . The energy crisis is real. I said so in 1977, and I say it again tonight, almost exactly two years later. Time is running short . . . We are wasting too much energy, we are buying far too much oil from foreign countries and we are not producing enough oil, gas and coal in the United States . . . Just ten years ago, we imported hardly any oil. Today, we buy about half the oil we use from foreign countries. We are by far the largest customer for OPEC oil, buying one fourth of that foreign cartel's total production . . . This growing dependence has left us dangerously exposed to sudden price rises and interruptions in supply . . . In the last few months, the upheaval in Iran again cut world supplies of oil, and the OPEC cartel prices leaped up again . . .

"Federal government price controls now hold down our own production and encourage waste and increasing dependence on foreign oil.

"Present law requires that these federal government controls on oil be removed by September 1981, and the law gives me the authority at the end of next month to carry out this decontrol process. In order to minimize sudden economic shock, I have decided that phased decontrol of oil prices will begin on June 1 and continue at a fairly uniform rate over the next twenty-eight months.[1]

"The immediate effect of this action will be to increase production of oil and gas in our own country . . .

"As government controls end, prices will go up on oil already discovered, and unless we tax the oil companies, they will reap huge and undeserved windfall profits. We must impose a windfall profits tax on the oil companies to capture part of this money for the American people. This tax money will go into an Energy Security Fund, and will be used to protect low-income families from energy price increases, to build a more efficient mass-transportation system and to put American genius to work solving our long-range energy problems . . ."

He admitted that phased decontrol would add to inflation in the short run, but he insisted that "the actions I'm taking tonight will help us to fight inflation" in the long run by raising prices so much that it will force down consumption, and when consumption drops, "the foreign oil cartel will then find it harder to raise prices."

Again he acknowledged that "decontrol could . . . further inflate the already large profits of oil companies. As I have said, part of this exces-

---

1. Under Carter's plan, 80 percent of the nation's old oil—oil from wells that went into production prior to 1972—would jump from $5.85 a barrel to $13 a barrel on June 1. In later stages, it, along with the other 20 percent of old oil, would be allowed to climb to world market prices. As for new oil, from wells completed since 1972, it would rise from $13 to world prices, in steps, beginning January 1, 1980. Oil discovered after June 1 would immediately be eligible for world prices.

sive new profit will be totally unearned—what is called a 'windfall' profit. That is why we must have a new windfall profits tax to recover the unearned billions of dollars, and to ensure that you—the American people—are treated fairly.

"I want to emphasize that this windfall profits tax is not a tax on the American people. It is purely and simply a tax on the new profits of the oil producers which they will receive but not earn.

"Even with the windfall profits tax in place, our oil producers will get substantial new income—enough to provide plenty of incentive for increased domestic production. I will demand that they use their new income to develop energy for America, and not to buy department stores and hotels, as some have done in the past."

He closed with the usual litany of threats about forcing thermostats up in summer and down in winter, and the usual *Popular Science* promises of a wonder age built on shale and solar energy. But the heart of his message was up front: decontrolled prices for sure, and a windfall tax maybe.

*

As usual, the public received Carter's warning about the energy crisis with a cynical yawn. A New York *Times* / CBS poll taken after the speech put this question to the people: "President Carter has told us that we are running out of oil and natural gas. Do you think things are as bad as the President said, or do you think it is not as bad as all that?" Only 32 percent said they believed him; 57 percent said they did not. (It was the same statistical response to the same question posed after Carter's "moral equivalent of war" speech, in 1977.) Replies to another question showed how little faith the public had in Carter's ability to maintain fair play in the marketplace. Asked if they thought the government could prevent the oil companies from making a killing on decontrolled oil prices, four out of five of the people polled said they were convinced that the government could not.

If the general public was mostly mute, except as it spoke through opinion polls, individual critics with access to political forums and the press responded volubly and endlessly. Scarcely an item in Carter's program escaped bitter denunciation.

There were the expected broadsides from Moffett ("He has declared war on consumers") and Maguire (". . . unconscionable posturing. He stands up before the American people and says, 'I'm going to fight the oil companies,' and then he gives them exactly what they want"). Congressman Bob Eckhardt, who, after defecting to industry's side during the natural gas fight was now back on the side of those trying to preserve controls on oil, asked, "Why, when real earnings of oil companies are going up and real earnings of individuals are going down, should there

be such a transfer of money from people to oil companies? If it be conceded that it would be good for people to drive less, does it follow that
the oil companies . . . should be permitted to tax them until they behave
properly? I think not. But high energy costs . . . are just such taxes, the
receipts from which go into the coffers of private corporations who are
royally rewarded for making us be good!"

Senator Edward Kennedy, who was preparing to challenge Carter for
the Democratic nomination, launched his assault on Carter with his famous "fig leaf" speech to the American Society of Newspaper Editors, in
New York City, on April 30: "The overbearing power of the oil lobby
has exerted its influence in two new and unacceptable ways. First, it has
intimidated the Administration into throwing in the towel without even
entering the ring on the issue of oil price decontrol. And second, it has
also intimidated the Administration into submitting a token windfall tax
that is no more than a transparent fig leaf over the vast new profits the
industry will reap." (A few hours later, Carter held a press conference in
which, of course, he was asked for rebuttal. He said of Kennedy's remarks: "That is just a lot of baloney.")

Supposedly the tax would confiscate half the difference between controlled prices and decontrolled prices. The figure of 50 percent sounded
good. But, on closer inspection, the Carter tax proved to be puny indeed.
Even the Washington *Post*, which editorially supported decontrol, was
offended by the deception. It complained in a May 3 editorial that its
"heart sank" as it watched the Carter tax formula come "inching into
view." What a letdown! "By even the most sympathetic reckoning, the
tax would take not half but somewhat less than one third of the profits
generated by the first stages of decontrol." *Post* reporter Art Pine observed: "Although the president made a big show of doing battle with
the oil companies—and with supposed other 'critics' of his new plan—the
measure's tax bite is so modest that almost no one really opposed the legislation except for a handful of liberals who think it ought to be tougher.
Even the oil industry isn't fighting the measure seriously. One oil industry executive confessed last week his company was grunting about it
merely to save face for Carter and House and Senate lawmakers—to
avoid pushing them into a really serious tax." *Fortune* magazine chuck-
led at the big oil companies' pretended outrage over the tax. "The
[proposed] tax burden doesn't seem as terrible as some oil-industry
spokesmen would have the world believe. Orin Atkins, the chairman of
Ashland Oil, which has little crude production of its own, says that if
Congress enacts decontrol and the windfall tax the majors will cry all the
way to the bank . . . Wall Street analysts say decontrol, coupled with
the tax, will help the majors achieve earnings growth of 15 to 20 percent
a year, enough to put them in the 'growth stock' category." *Fortune*
predicted that the eight largest oil companies, which had earned a mere

$9.33 billion in 1978, would enjoy a "rather sensational" leap of at least 30 percent in earnings if Carter's decontrol tax plan let prices go up to even $19 a barrel.

Many criticized Carter for not using the lush profits of decontrol for negotiating with the oil bloc in Congress—if they allowed the windfall tax to pass, *then*, and only then, would he lift the ceiling on prices. Why not? After all, everyone agreed that the windfall tax was anything but harsh: if the oil bloc was smart—and it was—it would have jumped at the offer. This strategy had been pushed by some of Carter's aides, principally Eizenstat, but Schlesinger had wanted decontrol pronto and without any strings, and Carter, as usual, went along with his Energy Secretary. In effect, Carter threw the burden of getting the tax through Congress on the people. If they didn't want to see the oil companies walk away with unjustified billions, they'd better lean on their congressmen—*he* wouldn't, except for a little Populist showcase rhetoric now and then. In his April 5 speech, he had told Americans, "As surely as the sun will rise, the oil companies can be expected to fight to keep the profits which they had not earned. Unless you speak out, they will have more influence on the Congress than you do . . . Please let your senators and representatives in Congress know that you support the windfall profits tax—and that you do not want the need to produce more energy to be turned into an excuse to cheat the public and to damage our nation." It was absurd to suggest that a letter-writing campaign could counterbalance the oil lobby; the public's opinion had never come close to offsetting oil money in Washington, and Carter must have known that what he was proposing was hopelessly naïve. Once decontrol went into effect, it would be terribly difficult to get any meaningful windfall tax through the oil-dominated Congress.

Many were also angry at what they considered Carter's insulting effort to put a benign gloss on the oil companies' profiteering. Toward the end of the speech, he had promised to use the windfall tax money for an Energy Security Fund, which would pay for "sound strategy of energy research and development," by which he meant designing more-energy-efficient cars and buildings and appliances, "turning coal into clean gas, liquid and solid fuels," learning "how to use our immense reserves of oil shale," encouraging "even more rapid development and use of solar power." Oh, swell! How lucky Americans were going to be! All those marvelous technological developments could be had if consumers simply coughed up, say, an extra $50 billion a year to the oil companies so that the federal government could make the companies chip in, say, $10 billion to the Energy Security Fund. Churlish critics, however, pointed out that this was a costly and circuitous way to do it. Why pay the oil companies $40 billion a year to be tax collectors? That's what the IRS was paid to do. If controls were kept on oil, consumers could be hit with an extra $10 billion in income taxes for the Energy Security Fund and they would still be $40 billion better off. Or, if the purpose of raising prices was to lower consumption, as Carter claimed, why not keep a lid on crude prices and slap a dollar-a-gallon federal tax on gasoline? "That," as Tom Wicker pointed out, "would give the windfall not to the oil companies but to the government, and insure funds for energy research and development and for adequate rebates to the poor. The Congressional Black Caucus estimates that under Mr. Carter's [windfall tax] proposals, rebates will compensate low-income families for less than a third of the estimated $326 annual increase in their energy costs."

In any event, one thing was certain: the oil companies wouldn't be hurt by the windfall tax. *They* wouldn't suffer. John E. Swearingen, chairman of Standard Oil of Indiana, appraised the situation very accurately: "For a president who ran on a platform of never lying to the people, he certainly seems to be stretching truth to the snapping point. He knows full well that his windfall proposal is an excise tax—truly a sales tax—that will be paid by the public."

*

There were other claims in Carter's energy speech that, if dissident experts were correct, also stretched truth to the snapping point.

• To illustrate why it was so vital for the United States to gain independence from foreign oil imports, Carter had said, "In the last few months, the upheaval in Iran again cut world supplies of oil . . ." The true situation was this: When the Shah's regime collapsed in early January and he fled the country, Iran's oil exports were disrupted for a couple of months, and when exports resumed they were only half as large as before the revolution began. On the surface, that would appear to have been a moderate blow to consumers everywhere, for Iran had been supplying 10 percent of the world's oil needs and 5 percent of U.S. imports. Using these statistics alone, Iran's cutback would seem to have left the world short by 5 percent, the United States short by 2.5 percent—certainly a manageable shortage, but still a shortage.

Carter and Schlesinger had immediately seized the occasion to spread fear. In early February, Schlesinger warned that the Iranian cutback presented a crisis "more serious" than what the United States was subjected to in the embargo of 1973–74. For the next two months, he and Carter continued to claim that the Iranian disruption had left the non-Communist world short by 2 million barrels of oil a day, the United States short by five hundred thousand barrels and creeping toward eight hundred thousand. This was the propaganda line that Carter used in his energy speech. Were he and Schlesinger telling the truth, or were they, as Congressman Gore charged, seizing "upon the Iranian cutoff to build support for a dramatic increase in domestic energy prices much as the Johnson Administration seized upon the Gulf of Tonkin incident to wrest from Congress a carte blanche approval of his war policies"?

Apparently it was the latter. Carter and Schlesinger knew—for the CIA had told them—that throughout the Iranian cutback, world oil production was higher than ever: in January, 60 million barrels a day, or 5.8 percent higher than for the same period in 1978; in February, 60.3 million barrels a day, 4 percent above the previous year. Although at the time Carter made his energy speech the March figures weren't in, experts believed they would show a similar increase. Using CIA statistics as well as their own expert guesses, the DOE estimated that worldwide crude stocks for the first quarter would be 4.317 billion barrels, compared to 4.276 billion in 1978. The Iranian disruption had been more than offset by sharply increased production in Saudi Arabia, in the North Sea, and in Third World countries outside OPEC. (Oil production in non-Communist countries, according to an August report in the authoritative *Platt's Oilgram News*, was up 5.8 percent for the first half of the year.) Admittedly, previous CIA figures for oil production around the world had sometimes proved to be way off the mark; nevertheless, the DOE and Administration officials had always relied on them, and it seemed quite odd that Carter and Schlesinger now ignored them and went off with analyses of their own, based on data that were pulled out of the air.

But even without the increased world production, the United States was apparently in good shape. In March, Schlesinger's own deputy, John O'Leary, had reported that U.S. oil consumption had dropped between seven hundred thousand and eight hundred thirty thousand barrels a day as a result of switching to other fuels and because of conservation. That would offset even Schlesinger's worst-case scenario from the Iranian cutback. (Schlesinger was infuriated by his deputy's upbeat report. Shortly after it was quoted in the press, Schlesinger went before a House subcommittee and just flatly denied that O'Leary had ever said such a thing. There was one easy way to find out: ask O'Leary. But when the subcommittee suggested that O'Leary be brought before them to repeat or deny the newspaper quotes, Schlesinger said O'Leary was out of the country and couldn't be reached; exactly where, he wasn't sure; maybe in the Bahamas. "He seems to be on a boat and unavailable.")

• Carter said the increased profits to the oil companies were needed as an incentive. Critics were swift to suggest, however, that if the oil companies weren't willing to hunt for oil at the present prices, they simply weren't very eager to hunt for oil.[2] On June 15, Senator Thomas Eagle-

---

2. Proof of the fact that they weren't eager to hunt for oil could be found in a western area called the "Overthrust Belt," which some people considered potentially the

ton released a study, based on Securities and Exchange Commission data, showing that during the previous year sixteen major oil companies had marked up domestically produced crude by an average of 389 percent. "During 1978," Eagleton reported, "Pennzoil spent an average of $1.20 to produce a barrel of domestic crude. Its average selling price was $10.03, for a markup of $8.83, or 736 percent. For all sixteen companies, the average production cost was $1.83 per barrel, the average markup was $7.11 per barrel, and the average sale price was $8.94 per barrel.

"Who can read over these figures and then seriously suggest that the oil companies need to make even more money on domestic crude? Who in these inflationary times can seriously suggest that we ought to raise Pennzoil's markup from 736 percent to as much as 1300 percent or 1400 percent? But that is just what decontrol will do. After decontrol, Pennzoil still will be pumping that oil for $1.20 per barrel, but they will be selling it for $16 or more." (He was conservative; within two years they would be selling it for twice $16.)

Who could seriously suggest it? Carter could. And he was doing it not only in the face of those 1978 profit figures but in the face of earnings for the first quarter of 1979 that were up as much as 102 percent. That was for Exxon, whose first-quarter profit of $1.925 billion was the greatest single-quarter profit any corporation had ever reported. Other majors had been similarly blessed from January through March: Texaco's profits up

---

richest oil reservoir in the lower forty-eight states. The Rocky Mountain Oil and Gas Association predicted that the Overthrust Belt would prove to contain *twice* as much oil and gas as Alaska's Prudhoe Bay. And yet the developers of Prudhoe Bay were putting *fifty-four times more* oil and gas on the market. How so?

Joseph Albright, of the Cox Newspapers, dug into the matter and came up with these findings:

Most of the land was owned by the federal government and leased through the Interior Department. But the law—dating back to 1946—was so written that the oil companies could lease the land, for $1 an acre, and just sit on it. And that's exactly what the nineteen companies holding leases to two million acres were doing.

Albright found that Exxon, for example, held 202 leases covering 230,147 acres and, as of autumn 1979, had drilled only one well on its property. Exxon was the second-largest holder of federal leases. The largest holder, Louisiana Land and Exploration, as of late 1979 had not applied for any permits to drill on its leased 314,343 acres. Albright, after checking more than 50,000 land and drilling documents, reported that "98 percent of the leased land [is] untouched" by "Louisiana Land and Exploration, Exxon, Chevron, Shell, Texas Pacific Oil, Hunt International and 13 other companies."

Moreover, the laws were written in such a way as to permit the oil companies to tie up the land indefinitely. "These leases run for at least 10 years," wrote Albright. "A company can get an automatic two-year extension by sinking a drill bit as late as the last day of the lease. A two-year extension can be obtained by pooling a group of leases into a drilling unit."

Ironically, if the companies should succeed in finding oil, they automatically could obtain—through a permanent extension of the lease—the power to hold it off the market for years.

97.6 percent; Shell's up 67 percent; Amoco's up 64.5 percent; Gulf's up 56 percent, et cetera. They needed more incentive?

• Which brings us to the heart of Carter's energy message: the promise of more production. That's what it supposedly all boiled down to: freeing ourselves from dependence on foreign oil by a dramatic increase in the production of our own oil and by the development of a bountiful synthetic fuels program paid for by taxes on crude. Thus, directly and indirectly, all hopes for independence were tied to increasing the production of crude, and decontrolling prices was supposed to bring about that increase. It was the *only* excuse for price decontrol; if it did not result in independence from OPEC, then decontrol would mean nothing but more profits for industry. Nothing but that.

Most experts were confident that his promised freedom from OPEC would never be achieved. Robert Baldwin, president of Gulf Refining and Marketing, said, "There's no way, for any amount of money, that you can reverse the decline curves on crude oil production in the United States. I don't care if crude oil goes up to $100 a barrel." Robert Stobaugh, director of the Energy Project, at the Harvard Business School, pointed out that "the amount of drilling and exploration work has gone up roughly 70 percent since oil prices started jumping up in late 1973," and "despite that, our reserves continue to fall and, except for the blip caused by Alaska, so has our production." Pointing out that two million wells have been sunk in the United States, four times the number in all other non-Communist countries combined, he figured "the chances of finding a really big field are quite remote. The rest are ragtag." Gulf Oil's chairman, Jerry McAfee, said, ". . . we'll do well just to stay level in domestic oil output during the next decade," and John F. Bookout, president of Shell, agreed, adding that even if decontrol were instantaneous and not phased, and even if there were no windfall tax, it was "unlikely" that U.S. production would show "substantial improvement" by 1985, if ever. And Charles T. Maxwell, a partner and principal oil analyst at Cyrus J. Lawrence Inc., widely regarded as one of the most prophetic observers on the energy scene, went into some detail when asked by the New York *Times* if raising the price would result in more oil and gas. "There is," he said, "a strong geologic case in this country for higher prices allowing us to develop larger supplies of natural gas, particularly from the deep zones of 15,000 feet and below, which is the frontier of natural gas exploration. I don't expect the higher prices of oil to operate in the same way, however. There is very little oil to be found below 15,000 feet. As you drill for oil and gas, which are found together, what you may find at 5,000 feet would divide out to about 90 percent oil and 10 percent gas. At lower levels, a marked switch begins to occur. Everything you're likely to find from 19,000 feet on to theoretical limits will be predominantly gas."

Ah, pity the poor President. The whole world seemed to feel that his predictions of independence via domestic production were so much hot air. But surely he had support from his own Cabinet? Alas, no. Treasury Secretary W. Michael Blumenthal conceded publicly that there was "no assurance" the higher prices would necessarily result in more oil exploration, and Transportation Secretary Brock Adams added his doubts: "I don't think there's going to be a great deal of additional production. I just do not feel in the United States that you're going to produce that much more oil." Blumenthal and Brock were fired a couple of months later; White House aides explained that the President felt they had been "disloyal."

Notwithstanding Carter's rhetoric to the contrary, he couldn't really have believed the United States would win independence from foreign oil any time soon. Behind the rhetoric were hard statistics that his own advisers, principally Schlesinger, had been confronting him with: an additional seven hundred fifty thousand barrels a day was positively the most the United States would get as the result of decontrol, and it wouldn't be in the pipeline until 1985. The Congressional Budget Office disagreed, estimating instead that an additional four hundred thousand daily barrels was the most he could hope for. But even assuming that Schlesinger was right for once, seven hundred fifty thousand barrels a day would be less than 4 percent of daily consumption. Independence from foreign oil could hardly be built on such a piddling addition. And look at what Americans would pay for the minuscule domestic buildup! Assuming that oil prices doubled by 1985 (a safe assumption), the difference between controlled and decontrolled prices would mean that U.S. consumers would be paying $265 for each of those seven hundred fifty thousand additional barrels daily—sixteen times more than OPEC was then charging for its oil. Some bargain!

*

Considering the many features of the Carter oil decontrol plan that were patently proindustry and of dubious advantage to the needs of the nation generally or of individual consumers, one might suppose that he wouldn't have gotten by with it. But who was to stop him? The law giving him power to decontrol beginning June 1 had been on the books for four years. If Congress wanted now to renege on that power, it would have to pass legislation extending controls; what's more, realistically it would have to do so before June 1, for once the price lifting went into effect, the complexities of starting from scratch and writing an entirely new commercial arrangement, of writing *re*control legislation—which meant dragging out once again all the old arguments over whether, and under what conditions, to control prices on old oil, new oil, stripper oil, oil below fifteen thousand feet, offshore oil, Alaskan oil, and so on dizzyingly—would discourage Congress from doing so, even if a majority wanted to, which always was much in doubt. Passing an extension of *existing* controls, however difficult to do, would be duck soup compared to writing *new* controls. But the extension would have to go the regular route, through subcommittees and committees on both sides of Congress, then through a conference committee that was bound to be badly divided, and then back to both houses for a final vote. All within less than two months?

It would be all but impossible. Congress was addled, if not exhausted, by the bickering and stewing that had gone on since the 1973–74 embargo. For half a dozen years, it had been constantly under pressure from new crises, real and contrived. It had been buried under conflicting statistics and arguments from the oil companies, from the Energy Department, from their own committee investigations, and from consumer lobbyists. In such an atmosphere, Carter and the oil companies seemed likely to win not by superior virtue and logic but simply by default.

And even if all else had been equal, the proindustry character of the Senate would have guaranteed victory for Carter. Polls showed sixty-five senators favored decontrol. To be sure, Senate Energy Committee Chairman Henry Jackson, though an ally of Carter's in the natural gas decontrol fight, did introduce legislation on April 10 to extend mandatory controls on oil for two years, but that was a pro forma move; early in the year, White House aides, nosing around on the Hill to learn if their scheme could be frustrated, had been assured by Jackson that there wasn't a chance that an order to decontrol could be reversed. Nevertheless, having lost status with consumers in the natural gas struggle, Jackson apparently felt obliged to put up a show on oil; and besides, he was irritated at Carter for insulting Congress and the public by saying decontrols wouldn't raise gasoline prices more than 4 or 5 cents over the next couple of years. (Carter had accepted American Petroleum Institute estimates.) Nonsense, said Jackson, gasoline prices would go up at least 15 or 20 cents by 1981. (They would, in fact, go up that much by the end of that summer.[3]) Jackson had more than a dozen cosponsors for his bill, but it promptly sank out of sight on the Senate side, where its opponents included Senate Majority Leader Robert Byrd, who, as soon as the bill was introduced, indicated what its fate would be: "I would hope it would not get anywhere," he said.

If it did get anywhere, It would have to be in the House, where identi-

---

3. The Administration was full of misleading cost data. When he first announced his phased decontrol plan, Carter said it would cost consumers only $16 billion more from June 1979 to September 1981, when decontrol became total. But, a year later, Energy Secretary Charles Duncan admitted they had been in error in their prediction; the extra cost to consumers would actually come closer to being $47.4 billion.

cal legislation was introduced by a coalition of House liberals, a coalition that included not only veterans of the 1975 oil controls fight, such as Moffett and Maguire and Eckhardt, but also such spunky newcomers as Albert Gore, Jr., and Edward Markey and Thomas A. Luken of Ohio.

The House group tried to whip itself into combat readiness by recollecting how they had won in '75 over great odds. "They told us we couldn't keep controls on then, but we showed 'em, eh, fellows?" But it sounded hollow. The mood was very different now from what it had been four years earlier. Democrats taking on Republican Ford was one thing, but now they had to fight a President of the majority party, of their own party, a President, moreover, who had proved in the natural gas fight—unlike Ford—that he was willing to accept the political unpopularity that came with decontrols.

Moffett told reporters, "Like Jackson, we're not extremely optimistic."

*

Still, for a brief time it seemed the House antidecontrol forces just might develop the momentum they needed. Their big break almost came —but didn't—on May 2. Not only did the Moffett-Maguire forces have to fight the White House, they also had opposition from Representative John Dingell, chairman of the energy subcommittee where the legislation originated. Dingell, as other occasions had shown, was an unpredictable fellow. He opposed the liberals in the oil fight of 1975, supported them in the natural gas fight of 1978, and now was opposing them again. A prickly, stubborn, vain chairman, Dingell stood in the liberals' path as stolidly as Carter. The Moffett strategists had tried to go around him, bringing up separate antidecontrol legislation in such a way that it could circumvent Dingell's subcommittee and be handled through another subcommittee. But Dingell had blocked them on that. So their final tactic was to attach an antidecontrol amendment to an Energy Department annual authorization bill (that is, their amendment would have made it unlawful to spend any Energy Department funds to implement decontrols) —not the easiest method for launching a crusade. It was this amendment that came up for a vote on May 2 in the House Commerce Committee.

White House agents had swarmed over the committee room, buttonholing members with what they believed to be overkill lobbying. White House lobbyist William H. Cable later acknowledged that the Administration thought it had at least twenty-four votes sewed up—the procontrol forces would probably not get more than fifteen votes, and under no circumstances more than eighteen. But the final vote was 21 to 21. A tie vote meant that Moffett's crowd lost, but it also meant that the Administration had been dealt a stunning psychological defeat. The underdogs' achievement roused a brief flurry of spirited support in the rest of the House. Speaker O'Neill, who had previously maintained a lardy neutrality, stated publicly that if he had been on the committee, "I would have voted with Moffett." He also predicted that if the liberals got their bill to the floor of the House, the vote would be very close. But Cable disagreed: "If they can't pass it in the Commerce Committee, the most sympathetic place in the House for the idea of extending controls," he said, "then they can't pass it anywhere." And he was, it turned out, quite right.

Although on May 24 Moffett went on to the Democratic Caucus, the forum in which House Democrats thresh out their policies, and won formal approval, two to one (138 to 69), of a resolution calling for extension of controls, the resolution had no legislative force and no persuasion with Carter, who shot off a memorandum: "Any thoughts that such votes will change the president's policy are completely misdirected."

Sixty-two Democrats who supported the resolution followed it up with a letter to Carter asking that he at least postpone decontrols until the House and Senate had a chance "to act on oil pricing policies."

Carter ignored the request. Time had run out for the rebellious liberals, and the decontrol program began phasing in four days later.[4] But, in winning, what had Carter lost? Congressman Markey said Carter's rebuff showed that he was "completely at odds with what his party stands for." Moffett went farther: "In my part of the country, Carter's decontrol program has made him a dead politician . . ."

*

Dead—perhaps not yet, but certainly dying, and the energy mess was a principal reason. It was still much too early to measure the effect of decontrols on the public's psyche, but it was not too early to tell the effects of other developments, primarily the gasoline shortages and price increases at the pump.

Indeed, by June the United States was suffering by far the sharpest gasoline shortage in the world. For the first time in history, the Automobile Club of New York advised members to stay home for the weekend, and elsewhere auto clubs were preaching the doctrine: drive no more than one tank's distance from home.[5] Diesel fuel was also scarce and

---

4. Although House liberals lost this effort to extend controls to 1981, they had already achieved a great victory for consumers. In the three and a half years that their controls were in effect, they saved consumers about $66 billion, or 34 percent of what they would have paid if prices had been decontrolled in 1975. (This estimate is based on the difference between the price of controlled oil and the price of stripper oil, which was not controlled during that period.)

5. The shortage did not hurt DOE's bureaucrats, however; they continued to burn 11 million gallons a year. Nor did the Air National Guard—which burned 57 million gallons a year—have to cut back on its weekend games. As for favored members of Congress, not only did they not have to wait in line for gasoline, they got it at cut rates, from their own pumps in the basement of the Capitol. News photographers who came by to record the lucky fellows were angrily shooed away.

sometimes even more expensive than gasoline. Independent truckers, hardest hit, pulled a nationwide strike, with serious disruptions in the shipment of foodstuffs. Truckers who defied the strike were frequently shot at or had their tires slashed. Under orders from the Independent Truckers Association, twenty-eight big rigs slipped into Washington just before dawn on May 31 and double-parked in front of the White House, threatening to stay there, and even expand their invasion fleet to tie up Washington traffic, unless they got more and cheaper diesel fuel.

The Administration's political nerves were apparently sedated. Considering the fact that polls showed a Republican candidate could knock off Carter in 1980, he and many of his aides were incredibly indifferent to the public's reaction to the long lines, closed stations, and higher prices. In July, economists at the Department of Energy put their calculators together and discovered something that the motoring public had known all along: waiting in gas lines was damned costly and wasteful— $200 million a month in lost time and more than $100 million in gasoline burned as cars idled. (Seymour Zucker, economics editor of *Business Week*, told the House Oversight and Investigations Subcommittee that by his reckoning the cost would be much higher: $2.4 *billion* in lost time and $320 million in wasted gasoline for every month the nation's motorists had to sit in line.) And yet the Administration never seriously considered using a system of coupon rationing—Schlesinger said the estimated cost, $1 billion a year, was too high—although polls regularly showed motorists would have preferred rationing to waiting.

The gasoline shortages were never *proved* to be the result of a conspiracy on the part of the oil companies, or on the part of the Carter administration, or both; but gradually, over the rest of the year, a retrospective picture was pieced together that clearly revealed actions *resembling* a conspiracy. For the oil companies and their refiners and dealers, the motivation was obvious: big bucks. In the early days of the gas lines, in April and May, many Americans would have agreed with Frank Collins, an official of the Oil, Chemical and Atomic Workers International Union, that the reduction in gasoline supplies was "to put the thumbscrews on for decontrol." But even after phased decontrol had begun, on June 1, shortages still occurred. Why? One of the more obvious reasons was to force the government to lift price ceilings on gasoline, which *was* still under controls.

For the Administration, whose incredibly bad decisions contributed so much to the gasoline shortages and rising prices, the motivation was not so clear. Perhaps it was another part of its effort to force conservation via economic pain. For Carter, conservation was a chance for him to appear, in the eyes of other world leaders, to have the situation well under control—something he had seldom seemed to achieve in the past. At a meeting in Tokyo with our major economic allies, Carter had urged them to cut back consumption 5 percent and had promised to make the same cuts in U.S. consumption—one way or another. Helping to rig shortages and raise prices was one way.

*

In any event, whatever the motivations, this is how the shortages and stunning gasoline price increases in the late spring and early summer of 1979 came about:

1978 Background: OPEC and the U.S. oil industry had moved into 1978 with a surly attitude; high oil prices had resulted in worldwide economic stagnation; oil inventories everywhere were at glut level. It was a deceptive situation, made more deceptive by the oil producers, who set about throwing the world off guard. In June 1978, Ali Attiga, secretary general of the Organization of Arab Petroleum Exporting Countries, told a group of European businessmen that they needn't worry: there would be no more shocking upward movement of Arab oil prices for at least the next ten years. He talked as though the marketplace had tamed OPEC. Most world leaders took the bait, happily accepting the assurance without question. The Trilateral Commission, made up of corporate and government bigwigs from the major non-Communist nations, issued a report concluding that it seemed "unlikely that there would be any sharp and sudden upward movement in real prices of oil for at least the next 10 to 15 years."

However, when the Iranian revolution began, in December 1978, interrupting its oil exports, other OPEC nations seized the occasion by cutting their own output and raising oil prices 14.5 percent—only the first of several heavy increases over the next year.

Meanwhile, U.S. companies were up to their own strategy. They began drawing down inventories. By the middle of 1978, the nation's gasoline inventory was at its lowest level in three years, and the companies held it at that level—a level too low to permit any extra demands—for the rest of 1978. (Asked later to comment on this drawdown, Energy Secretary Schlesinger said with his usual passion, "That was regrettable. It was an error in judgment.")

Coincidental with the refinery drop was a cutback in domestic crude production. Just as the Iranian revolution began, crude oil production in the United States suddenly went into its sharpest decline in seven years. And the decline continued through April. One would never have learned about the cutback from the American Petroleum Institute, however; statistics released by that lobbying group nicely covered up what was going on. But Associated Press reporters, finding that "API's projections have consistently overstated domestic production in recent months," went on to dig up the true production data, and concluded that "the virtually unnoticed and still unexplained domestic dropoff plus changes in

American refinery operations cost the United States more gasoline than the widely blamed cutback in Iranian imports." When AP completed its exposé, DOE experts admitted that the drop in production was "strange" but indicated their faith that industry had an explanation. It did. Oil company brass said the decline was because of "extreme cold weather" and "heavy rains," which caused pumps to break down and interfered with trucking from remote wells. But AP reporters went back to the weather records and found that in the seven American oil-producing areas that accounted for three fourths of all production only three had had cold weather or heavy rains. In short, the domestic production cutback seemed to have been planned.

Panic Buying. No sooner had the Iranian fuss gotten under way than Schlesinger began making his dire warnings, which had the effect—some believed it was the effect he desired—of frightening many industries and businesses into stockpiling oil and drawing down frantically on the already barely adequate stocks of gasoline, thereby helping to create the very shortage they were mistakenly trying to escape.

Although in fact the United States was importing more oil in January and February, during the Iranian shutdown, than it had imported during the same period in 1978, major oil importers pretended that the Iranian "shortage" that Schlesinger kept talking about was real. It was the excuse they gave for slashing the amount of gasoline they supplied to their retail dealers. But General Accounting Office investigators, looking into the economic effects of the Iranian cutoff, reported on March 5 that the companies that depended on Iranian oil for only 2 to 4 percent of their supply were curtailing gasoline sales to their dealers by 10 to 15 percent. (Actually, some of these companies were cutting dealer supplies by as much as 30 percent.) The GAO sleuths called it "puzzling."

The Disappearing Crude. Not only was more crude oil imported during the two months of the Iranian shutdown, more was imported—9 percent more—during the whole first six months of 1979 than had been imported during the same period of 1978; indeed, some companies were importing a great deal more: Gulf up 23.5 percent for the first six months, Mobil up 17.9 percent, Exxon up 15.5 percent. It was certainly a strange "shortage."

The whole situation was pockmarked with oddities. If more crude came into the country, where was it used, where did it go, what happened to it? How could such heavy imports be followed by gas lines, especially when nationwide demand for gasoline was up only 3 percent? (The statistics showing the abundance of imports were not released until August, long after the gas lines had disappeared.) No industry spokesman could explain. "Where did the oil go? You've got me bothered by the fact that I don't have a satisfactory answer to the question," said Anthony L. Seaver, Exxon International's manager of planning.

One place that a considerable amount of oil from *some* sources *did* go —was back overseas. A CIA study showed that in the first five months of the year, at a time when the Administration was deploring our oil scarcity, U.S. companies exported more oil than they had in either of those glut years 1977 and 1978. In 1977, exports had ranged from only 192,000 to 288,000 barrels daily; yet now, in 1979, during the alleged U.S. pinch, the companies were sending out of the country from 329,000 barrels daily in January to 445,000 barrels daily in both April and May, according to the CIA. More in, more out—what a queer shuffling!

The Refinery Slowdown. Just because crude oil is available does not mean gasoline will be available. The production of gasoline is not an act of God, but an act of boardroom decision, and if industry brass decide that it is more profitable to let crude oil sit in storage rather than refine it into gasoline and other by-products, then sit it does. Many observers both in and out of government were convinced that oil supplies were being withheld from the market to promote tighter market conditions and higher prices. Alfred F. Dougherty, Jr., director of the FTC's Bureau of Competition, was one who publicly made that accusation. Proving it, however, was another matter, for *all* of the government's information on oil stocks and production was obtained from either the American Petroleum Institute or from the companies themselves. So it was impossible for government officials to keep on top of what was happening as it happened.

How much crude oil was backed up? At the moment, nobody but the oil companies knew, and what they said was not exactly reliable. But, throughout the spring months and into early summer, it was definitely known that the oil companies were sharply curtailing gasoline production. Indeed, for the first five months of 1979, refineries ran at an average of only 85.8 percent capacity, compared to an average of 91.2 percent during the last six months of 1978. Some experts believed that if refineries had operated at just 90 percent of capacity up to the start of the vacation season, there would have been no gasoline shortage.

Schlesinger hadn't helped matters by urging the oil companies in April to decrease gasoline production and turn to the production of home heating oil to ensure enough for the following winter. It was a bubble-headed suggestion that only added to the suspicion that the Energy Secretary had something in mind other than making life easy for motorists. "It doesn't make sense," commented Lawrence Goldstein, senior economist of the Petroleum Industry Research Foundation, "to maximize middle distillate [including heating oil] production at the outset of the driving season."

Nor did Schlesinger seem much perturbed that the refineries were poking along at such a low level of gasoline production. On the first of May, he said that if they didn't pick up their production rate within the

next few weeks, he would have the refiners in for "polite conversations."
If he did have them in subsequently, the conversations must indeed have
been polite, for production remained very low. In the middle of June,
with fuming consumers lined up at gas stations and threatening to shoot
each other as well as the attendants, Schlesinger held another press conference, at which he admitted that while oil imports were rising, refinery
production was again falling. Yes, yes, he admitted, it was "irritating,"
and he intended to continue exerting "moral suasion." Not all refiners
were loath to produce gasoline, he said; the medium-sized refiners were
"moving through every barrel they can," but not the big guys. Then,
why not embarrass them by getting specific about which of the majors
were holding back? Oh, no, he said, "it would be inappropriate to name
them."

Summoned to Capitol Hill and berated by a number of committees,
Schlesinger finally agreed to take action. He threatened to use his allocation authority to withhold oil from refineries that weren't producing
wholeheartedly and assign the oil to refineries that were. The threat
didn't last long. Ten days later, he said he had decided not to use his
allocation authority, because the multinational oil companies he punished
might retaliate by withholding oil from the United States and selling it
elsewhere. Thundered Representative Benjamin S. Rosenthal, chairman
of a consumer subcommittee: "This 'blackmail' threat by the U.S. multinational oil companies . . . calls for a vigorous response . . ." It was a
rather naïve outburst, seeing as how Congress had not yet responded
vigorously to anything relating to energy since the first oil well was struck,
in Pennsylvania in 1859.

Was Industry Hoarding? From the moment the shortages began to appear, there were suspicions—and evidence, in some cases—that the oil
companies were, one way or another, holding back their supplies until
prices were forced up. The first sharp shortage of gasoline occurred in
California in late April, with nine counties—where 10 million of the
state's 15 million drivers lived—turning to odd-even gasoline rationing.
Incredible: California? The state that only a few months earlier was turning away the 400,000-barrel-a-day glut of the Alaska pipeline? How in
the world could California have developed a shortage so fast? "I wish I
knew," a federal official told the New York *Times*. "This is a strange situation." Steve Shelton, executive director of the Southern California
Service Station Owners Association, added, "I'm as puzzled as anyone by
some of the things that are going on." (Suspicions of industry hoarding
were so strong in California that Carter ordered an investigation in May;
in August the DOE said it could find no evidence of dirty work.)

Then, just as swiftly, the California shortage disappeared and the District of Columbia area was mysteriously afflicted. In June, with long lines
at the pump because gas supplies to area service stations had been cut

back by 25 to 30 percent, a DOE audit showed that in fact the major oil company storage tanks in the area had received 5 percent *more* gasoline than during the same period in 1978. Were the companies holding back? It certainly looked that way, but Schlesinger said the brimming storage tanks were perhaps being misinterpreted. Maybe, he said, the gasoline was in transit. He didn't seem especially eager to unravel the mystery, and he refused to order emergency allocations for the capital area, which already had moved into the odd-even rationing system.

When the mysterious shortages moved into the New York-New England area, new questions were raised—and never answered. When, on July 2, the Italian-manned tanker *Texaco Hannover* pulled up to Texaco's Eagle Point refinery (the company's third-largest refinery), at Westville, New Jersey, to deliver seven hundred fifty thousand barrels of crude oil, it was instructed to wait at the dock for three days to unload the cargo, because the refinery's storage tanks were filled to the brim with 1.8 million barrels of crude oil. Nor was Texaco's seam-popping supply singular. Other companies were similarly blessed. Al Grospiron, president of the oil workers union that represented seamen on Mobil tankers, charged that Mobil's storage tanks were filled, up and down the East Coast. A tanker seaman told House Commerce Committee staff members investigating the gasoline shortages, "We knew that the tanks were full, and we'd go into town [New York City] and see the gas stations closed, and people told us there was no fuel."

Grospiron also made the interesting accusation of "hoarding on the high seas." He charged that for several weeks during the gas crisis Mobil's tankers were under orders to reduce speed, lollygagging along for nine days between Beaumont, Texas, and Boston, a trip that ordinarily required no more than five days. Tankers that normally would have loaded in sixteen hours, said Grospiron, were taking up to four days to fill their tanks.

All the causes of the gasoline shortage and price escalations were never uncovered, and such uncovering as did occur was usually months late in coming, and then hedged and smothered in bureaucratese.[6]

* * *

Watching the oil producers cream off heady profits, the nation's 171,000 service [sic] station operators threatened to strike if the DOE

---

6. In mid-September, the DOE ended its preliminary investigation of the hoarding charges with the conclusion that industry was innocent. It could hardly have come to any other conclusion, for the investigation was based entirely on information supplied by the suspects themselves. In July 1980, both the Justice Department and DOE finished further investigations into the charges, and again the conclusion was that the oil companies were blameless; both departments continued to use the Iranian cutoff as the (discredited) cause for the shortages.

didn't let them join in the looting. The Carter administration, eager to use gas prices as a conservation weapon, was happy to oblige. Indeed, acting on the assumption that Carter would soon end gasoline price controls, the DOE had begun dismantling its gasoline price enforcement branch at the first of the year. Thereafter, although price controls were still on the books, all semblance of law and order in pricing was gone.

Since 1973, dealer profits had officially been limited to a national average of about 9 cents a gallon above what dealers had to pay wholesale plus taxes. Then, in July, the DOE changed the rule to allow dealers a 15.4-cent margin per gallon, on top of wholesale prices plus taxes. On December 15, the margin was raised to 16.1 cents a gallon.

That's what the rule said, but it was just for show. Throughout the year, dealers everywhere were cheating like crazy—some by as much as 30 or 40 percent above the legal limit—and DOE made virtually no effort to crack down on the violators. Indeed, at the same time that its audits were uncovering a 43 percent rate of price violations among retail dealers, DOE was cutting out two thirds of its enforcement personnel. A New York State legislative committee found that nearly 60 percent of the gasoline stations surveyed in New York City were charging more than the federal maximum prices; it accused DOE of engaging in "a shameful cover-up of its own ineptitude." Actually, DOE wasn't trying to cover up its ineptitude; it was being inept right out in the open. In July it ruled that as of August 1 all stations must post their profit margins and maximum selling prices; but the day before the ruling was to go into effect, DOE backed down, saying that so many dealers had complained about being forced to inform the public of legal prices that it had decided they could ignore the new posting regulation if they would promise in writing that they were complying with price controls.

In June, the DOE had predicted that gasoline prices would go up about a nickel a gallon by the end of summer. They went up 16 cents— making the total increase 33 cents since the first of the year. And only about one third of that could be blamed on OPEC price jumps. The rest of it was the fruit of homegrown greed and of DOE regulations that were so cockeyed and so weighted in favor of industry and against the consumer that they invited profiteering.

*

There was, for example, the "Tilt Rule." Here's how it worked: About half of every barrel of crude is refined as gasoline (the other half going into what's called middle distillates—such as home heating oil and diesel fuel—and into heavy fuel oil). In the early part of 1979, the refiners went to DOE and complained that they needed more capital to generate unleaded gasoline, of which they had managed to create a shortage by operating refineries far below capacity. DOE was sympathetic and decided to "tilt" more profits into gasoline as an incentive to refiners to invest more money in gasoline refining apparatus, rather than in the production of other oil products.[7]

The tilt was made by permitting refiners to pass through 55 percent of the crude oil cost in the price of their gasoline, even though they were actually using only 50 percent of the barrel for gasoline. Thus, a 10 percent bonus. And everyone, from refiner to dealer, got to reap the same bonus.

The Tilt Rule went into effect on March 1 (having been rushed into law without the 30-day waiting period customarily set aside for public comments). But it was made retroactive to January 1. Why? Douglas G. Robinson, DOE's second-ranking regulatory official and the fellow who wrote the rule, later admitted there was "absolutely no justification" for making it retroactive. By doing so, DOE had simply handed the oil industry an extra bonus of hundreds of millions of dollars.

Additionally, the Carter administration had misled consumers about the cost of the Tilt Rule. At the time it went into effect, Administration officials predicted that the rule would cost motorists an extra 1.6 cents a gallon at the pump in 1979 and slightly more—maybe 1.8 cents a gallon— in 1980. All told, the rule was supposed to be a gift of no more than $3.7 billion for the oil industry in those two years.

But no sooner had Tilt gone into effect than the oil companies raised gasoline prices not the predicted 1.6 cents but 4 to 6 cents. That was the immediate raise, and more, much more would follow over the next two years. Instead of soaking the consumer a mere $3.7 billion as a result of Tilt, industry would take away at least four times that much.

Had the Carter administration just made a bad guess? Robinson conceded that in fact the Administration's experts knew they were misleading the public. "It is fair to say that we had some indication at that time [of the rule's probable impact] . . . and the decision makers were aware of that at the time, but that did not dissuade them from going ahead," he told Washington *Post* reporter Patrick Tyler in August.

And what did the consumers get for the extra billions they paid? Nothing. Extra gas? No. Not a drop.

Herbert Bruch, technical director for the National Petroleum Refiners Association, said Tilt was "a nice thing to have" but he didn't think it

---

7. "Tilt" was a misleading word. It sounded like an economic seesaw that raised gasoline prices only as prices on the other end of refining, for heating oil and diesel, went down. In fact, these middle distillates, deregulated three years earlier, had been going up in price steadily and would continue to go up, whatever happened to gasoline prices. A study of profits at only nine refineries showed that they had reaped $481 million more from the sale of heating oil than they would have earned if controls had been kept on. The deregulation of middle distillates was also the reason diesel fuel had soared to $1.13 a gallon by the summer of 1979, sending truckers into a tantrum.

would provide enough incentive to build more refining capacity. From its beginning, the program had been nothing but a profitable charade.

Another of the energy bureaucracy's clever gimmicks for funneling money to industry had been concocted after the 1973 shortage but was only now paying off. Ostensibly to protect consumers, the government had set a ceiling on profits on all commercial activities from refiner to filling station. But that didn't mean dealers (and refiners and middlemen) would always be able to charge the full ceiling price, for in the years ahead there would be periods of glut that would force prices down. Indeed, that had happened, and consumers had thought they were benefiting from the bargain prices. They just didn't know what lay ahead, thanks to a clause energy bureaucrats had slipped into the law saying that, during the glut years, dealers (and refiners and middlemen) could keep a record of all the gasoline they sold at below-ceiling prices, and when the next fuel crunch came along, they would be allowed *to raise prices above the ceiling as much as necessary to recover what they had "lost" to consumers during those "bargain" sales.* That time had now arrived in the spring of '79, and dealers were taking advantage of the bizarre ruling by gouging away. Most of them were doing it illegally, however, for few dealers had actually kept records of the gas they had sold below ceiling prices since 1973. They were just guessing wildly, tacking on everything the market would bear.

The results of the proindustry regulations were pretty impressive. A typical high-volume station in the Washington, D.C., area, for instance, that had sold 137,000 gallons of gas in January and made $7,188 in profits was selling only 90,000 gallons in July but profiting by $11,429. The days when most retail gas dealers were "little merchants" was long gone. In such metropolitan areas as Washington, D.C., a typical Amoco or Shell or Exxon dealer was making well over $100,000 a year. The pickings were so bountiful and so easy that Exxon's eastern-region public relations manager quit his $60,000-a-year job to become an Exxon dealer in Baltimore. Sure, he said, he expected to earn more than $100,000 a year at his filling station, but, he added, "the dealer is better off portrayed as the struggling businessman."

*

As the dealers' profits soared, service deteriorated. To hell with the customer's comfort. A survey of a group of New York City service stations in June found a typical one open only 27.2 hours a week—down from 109.8 hours a week the previous September. It wasn't that the dealers were short that much gas (nationally, they were getting about 20 percent less than normal in June); they had simply found it much easier to let the public line up for blocks before opening for business.

This casual approach to hours only heightened, of course, the public's nervousness. The more they had to line up, the more desperate they felt and the more willing they were to pay scalper prices. Indeed, such was the oil industry's overwhelming victory in this psychological war that consumers actually became so *grateful* for being allowed to buy gasoline at any price that they opened their wallets without looking. Writer Fred Powledge, looking back with wry bitterness from the vantage of July, told readers of *The Nation* how brainwashing happened to him:

> I know the precise moment when I became a victim of the energy crisis. It happened late in May in a large off-brand gasoline station in one of the suburbs east of Los Angeles. [He had been touring the country, moving westward, gathering material for a book.] All across the country, and especially as the weekends drew near, I had been fearing the sort of crisis I had heard about: the closed gas stations, the exhausted allotments, the buck-a-gallon gasoline . . . but I didn't see an abnormally closed station until I hit Phoenix. Even then the stuff was available if you looked around a bit.
>
> And then, on that afternoon in May, I pushed my way through an evil mixture of smog and dust storm into the suburb east of Los Angeles, and I left the interstate in search of gas. The tank was a quarter full. And it appeared that only one gas station, a Texaco, was open. I got into the line. After I had moved forward two car lengths, a process that took perhaps eight minutes, the operator walked over and told me, with what I was pretty sure was a touch of pleasure, that the station was closing after it had served the fellow ahead of me. I could feel the panic setting in. Nothing very dramatic, just a combination of emotional and physical feelings that meant panic.
>
> I drove slowly down the boulevard, looking for a cheap place to spend the night. The trick, my California friends had told me, was to get your gasoline first thing in the morning, and that was what I'd have to do. And then I saw the other station. It was open and pumping. I pulled in, warily because of what had happened minutes before. I rolled down the window and asked the operator if it were true that his station was open. "Sure it is," he said with a big grin.
>
> "No catches?" I asked.
>
> "No catches," he said. "Take all you want until it's gone."
>
> I filled the tank and cracked a few jokes as I paid him and pulled out of the station. I glanced at the fuel gauge and saw the needle all the way over on the right, and it made me feel good. The sensation, I am embarrassed to admit, was almost utter joy; it was close to the cliché about a "new lease on life." A replenishment of my mobility was what it was. I realized that now I could go another 200 or so miles; that I was not going to be forced by an empty fuel tank to spend the night in this dreary neighborhood of chain restaurants and tract housing and silent, empty gasoline stations . . .
>
> As I eased back on the freeway that would take me there, I realized that I had never noticed what that tank of gasoline had cost. And I always pay attention to such matters. Such had been the nature of my panic that I had been grateful, eager for any gasoline at all—and at any price per gallon. And

that, I think, is when I became a victim of the energy crisis. I had willingly participated in the . . . geographically *floating* gouge, engineered by the oil industry, almost certainly with the collaboration of the Federal Government through its Department of Energy and most likely with the help of the Department of Justice. The managers of the U.S. cartel and their underlings in Washington know very well how to create panic among motorists . . . To get us to the point where we'll give up anything, in dollars and in governmental control, just to get the freedom that goes with a full tank of gas.

＊ ＊ ＊

On May 31, the eve of the beginning of phased oil price decontrol, President Carter invited a number of oil company executives to drop by the White House to discuss their mutual problem: public relations. In a way, it was a strange invitation, coming from one who had recently been the source of much of the oil executives' bad press; Carter had been going around denouncing them for "price gouging" and of plotting a "massive rip-off of the American people." These were accurate appraisals. So why was he now calling them in for a chummy 90-minute talk (a talk that was so chummy he refused to let photographers take pictures of the meeting)? Because Carter was smart enough to know—and even if he hadn't been smart enough, every public opinion poll would have informed him—that in the public's eye it was difficult to tell where the villainy of the industry left off and the villainy of the government began. As Carter informed the oil execs at that meeting, "We're all in this together," in the public's perception.

The companionship hardly benefited either side; each in its own way contributed to an appearance of deception and duplicity. The most generous contributions, of course, came from industry. The public may have been baffled by the complexities of imports and production and price regulations (though probably no more baffled than the experts), but it had no difficulty understanding the plain arrogant statements and the plainer arrogant gestures, both the product of the dumbest public relations effort ever made, or not made, by a major industry. Edwin McDowell, of the New York *Times*, perfectly captured the daffiness of industry's actions:

> With motorists all along the Atlantic Seaboard lined up hoping to buy gas, a senior vice president of the Atlantic Richfield oil company told the San Diego Financial Analysts Society, "It's a great education process for East Coast residents to have to wait in gasoline lines as Californians have done," because it will force them to drive less.
> When the daughter of a Mobil executive vice president and director was married in New Canaan, Conn., early last month, the town's only Mobil gasoline station, which normally closed its pumps at 11 a.m., was open from 6:30 p.m. to 10:30 p.m.—hours that coincided with the reception for 200

guests. Company officials vigorously denied any connection between the two events.

At a time when oil companies are bending every effort to convince the public that their profits are not only not obscene but inadequate, the Exxon Corporation has begun a tender offer of up to $1.17 billion for the Reliance Electric Company of Cleveland. During a similar period of public mistrust and suspicion of oil companies, the Mobil Corporation, in one of the largest acquisitions on record, purchased the giant Montgomery Ward retailing company for $1.8 billion.

For these and other reasons, Big Oil is embroiled in a crisis of public and political confidence. They are the people you love to hate. Oilmen are perceived as liars, cheats, profiteers and worse. They have made many mistakes and paid for a number of them, yet they have been pilloried as well for things they haven't done. The majority of Americans simply don't believe their denials, in part because industry pronouncements are so often tactless and their timing so frequently inept.

In *Fortune* magazine, Edward Meadows wrote with puzzlement about the industry's "almost paranoid view of the mass media," which left the oilmen "almost stonily uncommunicative and helplessly inarticulate" at the very moment in history when they needed to be glibly persuasive. Meadows noted that when NBC aired an hour-long energy special on June 3, the network included interviews with government and OPEC officials and consumer lobbyists but could not coax the chief executives of Mobil, Exxon, Shell, Texaco, Gulf, ARCO, Amoco, or Aramco to appear, and that Charles DiBona, president of the API, "also refused to take part—finally relenting only after the program's producer threatened to leave an empty chair on the set and read off the names of the companies that had refused to participate."

*

Why the fortress mentality? Why did the oil executives withdraw sulkily into their own circles? The same questions could be asked of Carter and his innermost clique. It all conveyed an atmosphere of irrationality, which was considerably heightened in early July, when Carter abruptly canceled a nationwide address on energy and retired to Camp David. He gave no reason for the cancellation. A White House official conceded to *The Wall Street Journal* that it was a "bizarre situation." Carter's aides said they didn't know when he would return to the White House or if he intended to reschedule the speech. One got the impression that balloons were bouncing off the ceiling, and the press corps got caught up in the spirit. One of Carter's press aides complained, "I've been asked whether the President's freaked out; if we're installing rubber wallpaper in the offices; if there's been a coup, and that sort of thing."

No, none of those things. Carter had just discovered that his energy ship was sinking; his decontrol "victories" had left him with holes in the hull and leaden ballast—at least in political waters. No one on his staff saw the situation so clearly, or summarized it so accurately, as Eizenstat in a memorandum to Carter.

First he ticked off the signs of damage: The truck strike was continuing; gas lines were prompting violence—"a recent incident in Pennsylvania injured 40"; inflation was up dangerously, and no wonder, since "gasoline prices have risen 55 percent since January"; "Congress is growing more nervous by the day over the energy problem . . . members are literally afraid to go home over the recess, for fear of having to deal with very angry constituents"; DOE was under fire for "conflicting signals and numbers"; Maryland was suing the Department for misallocating gasoline; and "other states can be expected to shortly follow that politically popular route."

In short, said Eizenstat, the Administration's energy position was a disaster. "It is perhaps sufficient to say that nothing which has occurred in the Administration to date—not the Soviet agreement on the Middle East, not the [Bert] Lance matter, not the Panama Canal treaties, not the defeat of several major domestic legislative proposals, not the sparring with Kennedy, and not even double-digit inflation—have added so much water to our ship. Nothing else has so frustrated, confused, angered the American people—or so targeted their distress at you personally, as opposed to your advisers, or Congress or outside interests. Mayor Koch indicated to me . . . he had not witnessed anything comparable to the current emotion in American political life since Vietnam . . .

"You must address the enormous credibility and management problems of DOE which equal in public perception those which State or Defense had during Vietnam."

If Eizenstat's appraisal was on target, his suggested solution was laughably off: blame OPEC. "Use the OPEC price increase as the occasion to mark the beginning of our new approach to energy. It must be said by you—and by us—time and again publicly to be a watershed event. We must turn the increase to our advantage by clearly pointing out its devastating economic impact and as the justification of our efforts against the OPEC cartel and for increased domestic production of all types. We have provided you with a tough statement that will accomplish those ends, and buy us a week or so before the public will expect more specifics . . .

"With strong steps we can mobilize the nation around a real crisis and with a clear enemy—OPEC."[8]

---

8. Within four months Eizenstat was so mad at the major oil companies that he was almost willing to forget his advice. Eizenstat wrote a memo on October 29 in which he noted, "Increases in the price of crude oil by the OPEC nations can account for much less than one-half of the price increases so far this year in refined petroleum

*

But Carter thought he had an even better scapegoat: the American people. He would address them as the erring children of Israel who had allowed their heads to be turned away from right thinking, away from commitment to "higher things," who had turned to golden idols and away from the Word as revealed through Carter. And so it came to pass that after a suitable period of meditation at Camp David with leaders of business, labor, government, academe, and religion—all summoned to the presidential retreat to give him of their thinking—Carter came down from the mountain at last and on July 15 went on national television to deliver the delayed message.

"Ten days ago," he said with even more earnestness than was his custom, "I had planned to speak to you again about a very important subject, energy. For the fifth time I would have described the urgency of the problem and laid out a series of recommendations to the Congress. But as I was preparing to speak I began to ask myself the same question that I now know has been troubling many of you: Why have we not been able to get together as a nation to resolve our serious energy problem?"

His answer: Americans had lost confidence in themselves, had lost faith in their institutions, in their government. No, no, it was not the venality of the oil companies and the cupidity of Congress and the stupidity of the Administration that were to blame. No, the trouble was that the American people were just a bunch of lousy skeptics. But he would forgive us for that and give us another chance to believe: "The energy crisis is *real*. It is *worldwide*. It is a *clear and present danger* to our nation. These are the facts—and we simply must face them!"

Naturally, he also followed Eizenstat's advice to give OPEC a dig—"It [OPEC] is the direct cause of the long lines which have made millions of you spend aggravating hours waiting for gas"—but, for strategic purposes (he was begging Saudi Arabia to increase production, and he didn't want to offend them), he went rather lightly on that line. Instead, he pushed on with his theme of energy as a new patriotism, if not a new theology: "On the battlefield of energy, we can win our nation a new confidence—and we can seize control of our common destiny . . . The solution to our energy crisis can also help us conquer the crisis of the spirit

---

products . . . Gross margins for refiners increased 6.9 percent during the three months ending in March, 15.7 percent during the three months ending in June, and 37.4 percent during the three months ending in September (these are actual increases, not annual rates) . . . From April through August, energy alone added about five points to the CPI [Consumer Price Index] . . . There are indications that some major oil companies tried to cover up the size of their third-quarter profits . . ." But apparently Eizenstat thought it wiser to go on using OPEC for the villain, for he withdrew the memorandum.

in our country. It can rekindle our sense of unity, our confidence in the future, and give us a new sense of purpose."

Unfortunately, the weapons he hauled onto "the battlefield of energy" in that message did not exactly kindle the nation's imagination. But one of the weapons certainly kindled suspicions of a new sellout.

"To give us energy security," he said, "I am asking for the most massive peacetime commitment of funds and resources in our nation's history to develop America's own alternative sources of fuel—from coal, from oil shale, from plant products for gasohol, from unconventional gas, from the sun. I propose the creation of an Energy Security Corporation to lead this effort to replace 2.5 million barrels of imported oil per day by 1990 . . . Just as a similar synthetic rubber corporation helped us win World War II, so too will we mobilize American determination and ability to win the energy war. Moreover, I will soon submit legislation to Congress calling for the creation of this nation's first solar bank—which will help us achieve the crucial goal of 20 percent of our energy coming from solar power by the year 2000. These efforts will cost money—and that is why Congress must enact the windfall profits tax without delay."

*

Ah, it sounded swell, just as it had when Nixon tried to hatch the syn-fuels program. Finally, the United States Government was going to get the long-dormant shale-oil program rolling, was going to utilize the world's richest coal reserves. And it was going to let nothing stand in its way. Right? Well, not quite. On somewhat closer inspection, the Carter synthetic fuels program was obviously nothing but the old Nixon-Ford plan warmed over. It was also obviously a method for giving the major oil companies further assurance that they would continue to control the nation's energy future. The nation's shale, coal, and uranium were of course dominated by the majors. The synthetic-fuel patents were owned mostly by the big oil companies. For years, Exxon had owned the only viable coal liquefaction process, but had shown no interest in using it to ease the nation's energy problems. Even if the U.S. Government picked up the development tab, how seriously would Exxon—or the other majors —want to produce "alternate" energies, to compete with oil? And if they did decide to squeeze oil from shale, and gasoline and gas from coal, what guarantee would there be that they would be willing to sell it for less than cutthroat prices? After all, as TVA chairman S. David Freeman had pointed out a few weeks earlier, the entry of the oil companies into coal and uranium had resulted in "monopoly pricing"—coal and uranium prices jumping 500 percent since 1970.

In an effort, quixotic, as everyone knew, to keep the synfuels monopoly out of the hands of Big Oil, Senator Kennedy and Congressman Morris Udall cosponsored the energy antimonopoly bill of 1979, which would prohibit the nation's sixteen largest oil companies from acquiring any company with assets exceeding $100 million. Although the bill would also block the acquisitions of department-store chains and circuses, it was primarily aimed at preventing further oil company purchases of coal companies. The Administration was extremely cool to the bill, not only because Carter hated Kennedy but because most of Carter's aides agreed with Energy Deputy Secretary O'Leary's appraisal that the expansion of the coal industry "will have to be done by managers who are now almost entirely associated with the oil industry." Carter had come a long way from his 1977 campaign promises to fight for horizontal divestiture.

There was another point made by Carter in this part of his speech that some observers whose memories went back to the pre-World War II years considered indiscreet, not to mention tasteless. This was Carter's likening of his proposed Energy Security Corporation to "a similar synthetic rubber corporation [that] helped us win World War II." He was referring to the Rubber Reserve Co. In 1941, when our supply of natural rubber was cut off by the Japanese, the federal government gave the Rubber Reserve Co. $750 million with which to build synthetic-rubber plants. And who was to run the show? Standard Oil of New Jersey—Exxon—that's who. Which was ironic, to say the least. For the previous decade, Standard had been in a cartel relationship with I.G. Farbenindustrie—the industrial base for the rise of Nazi Germany—and during that time had worked closely with Farben in the development of synthetic gasoline and synthetic rubber, the two commodities most needed for rebuilding the German war machine. At the same time, the Standard Oil - I.G. Farben cartel worked effectively to prevent the development or production of any substantial amount of synthetic rubber in this country. And thus the United States entered World War II perilously short of rubber—a handicap that remained for the first two years of the war. (See Appendix for STANDARD OIL AND THE NAZIS.)

Did Carter seriously think that Standard Oil had changed its attitude toward profits versus national interest, and that it and the other major oil companies would produce synthetic fuels even if they interfered with the companies' own plans? Apparently he did, and so also did Congress. After rejecting an amendment that would have blocked the participation of the eight largest oil companies in the federally subsidized synfuels program, it went on to authorize $19 billion as a starter for the Synthetic Fuels Corporation (originally called the Energy Security Corporation). The gigantic cash machine would be primed, not surprisingly, by general-revenue funds, not by the windfall profits tax. That hadn't even been passed as yet.

And now that the machinery was set up, were Exxon and the other majors demonstrating great eagerness to get started on synfuels? To the contrary. Speaking to a group of a thousand Wall Street executives convening in Boca Raton, Florida, Clifton C. Garvin, Jr., chairman of Exxon, said that *if* the federal government offered what he called "modest economic incentives"—such inducements as an investment tax credit of 15 to 20 percent, production tax credits of $2 to $3 a barrel, and an accelerated depreciation program—*maybe* the industry might consider pushing synthetic fuels. Sure, he admitted, there was enough oil in shale and coal to make the United States independent for the next 150 years, but "we are not going to take our shareholders' money and invest it if we don't see a chance for a decent return." He didn't explain what he meant by decent. Exxon's report for the third quarter, just ended, showed that its profits, compared to 1978, were up 120 percent to a record $1.15 billion—the first billion-dollar quarter in the company's history. Wasn't that decent enough?

***

Angry because gasoline prices were even nominally still under control, the oil companies made up for it with some extra gouging in the heating-oil market. Heating oil had been decontrolled since 1977. In that year, the average price was 46 cents a gallon, roughly 100 percent higher than before the Arab embargo of 1973. With decontrol, it had moved up gradually to a national average of 53.7 cents by January 1979. But, by the early fall of 1979, it had soared another 50 percent—pushing past 80 cents a gallon—and the oil companies admitted that more increases were on the way. Between January and September, the cents-per-gallon spread between the refiners' selling price and their crude-oil costs had doubled. Each penny of increase resulted in about $200 million more profit every year. For low-income families, it meant severe hardship. Studies had shown that in the winter of 1978–79, before the latest sharp round of increases, the poor were already paying as much as 40 percent of their income to stay warm, and in the coming winter, said Deputy Energy Secretary O'Leary, stating the obvious, the "cruel choice between food and heat" would press down on them even harder.

And the most infuriating thing about the gouging was that it wasn't even being done in the name of scarcity. There was plenty of heating oil.

So what were Carter and Congress going to do about it? Reimpose price controls? That was the last thing they had in mind. On the theological side, Carter suggested that the oil companies show humanitarian price restraint; on the practical side, he asked Congress to allocate money to help poor people pay their fuel bills come winter. In November, Congress obliged by voting $1.35 billion in emergency assistance. Which meant that middle-income taxpayers would be asked to pay twice for heating oil: once for the oil used in their own homes, a second time for the oil used by the poor.

***

Finally, the twins of piety fell out. Secretary Schlesinger had been an albatross from the beginning, but President Carter had been steadfastly loyal to him. As late as March, he was still giving his Energy Secretary an unequivocal endorsement. When Senator Dennis DeConcini of Arizona and six other senators took the floor to demand that Carter fire him, the President sent DeConcini a letter saying Schlesinger had his "full trust and confidence." Carter appended a handwritten postscript: "He has a very difficult job and needs all the help and support he can get. He's got mine." But with his own popularity polls sinking to the level of Nixon's during Watergate, it was a loyalty Carter would not afford to continue. Politically, Schlesinger was a Typhoid Mary. He was seen as the embodiment of the Energy Department, and the Energy Department was generally judged to be the most chaotic, the most blundering, the most useless pit in darkest Washington. As Eizenstat had noted conservatively in his memo to Carter, the Department suffered from "enormous credibility and management problems." The department was seen by many critics as nothing but a shill for the oil industry.

In May, investigators for the General Accounting Office concluded that the Federal Energy Regulatory Commission—a part of DOE—was not trying to stop the decades-long practice of major oil companies charging illegal rates for their pipeline services, a practice through which they had extorted hundreds of millions of dollars. The GAO pointed out that the Interstate Commerce Commission had made absolutely no effort to regulate pipeline profits in the seventy years it was supposed to be policing them, and that when the regulatory chore was passed on to FERC at the founding of the Department of Energy, in 1977, the tradition of regulatory indifference was continued. FERC, it charged, "has not addressed many questionable pipeline practices and presently has no plans to do so." In fact, it was totally unequipped to do so, because it has "not established criteria for determining the justness and reasonableness of oil pipeline rates."

Deputy Inspector General Thomas S. Williamson, Jr., concluded an investigation showing that the department "maintained a double standard of access to information that favored the American Petroleum Institute over members of the public," and he expressed fears that the public would lose "confidence in the integrity of DOE's procedures for rule-making and policy formulation."

Was there any more confidence to lose? Hardly had the DOE issued its report clearing the oil industry of hoarding gasoline than reporters discovered that the clearance was based on information supplied by the American Petroleum Institute and oil companies; the DOE had done no independent investigating. Even the notoriously corrupt Small Business Administration worked up enough nerve to criticize DOE, accusing it of teaming up with the major oil companies to force thirty thousand small gasoline dealers out of business over the previous five years, seventy-five hundred of them during 1979.

Most repugnant of all was the DOE's growing reputation for indifference to industry's criminal activities. Although federal policy required that any department having "reason to suppose" that it had evidence of criminal activity must submit its evidence to the Justice Department, the energy bureaucracy almost never did. In May, General Accounting Office investigators surveyed the history of the DOE and its predecessor agencies and concluded that it was an almost unbroken record of misfeasance. From 1974 through 1977—four years laden with oil corruption—the energy bureaucracy had not referred a single criminal case to the Justice Department. Since 1977, DOE had referred nine cases to Justice, but, because the DOE had sat on the cases for one to three years, one had already been invalidated by the statute of limitations and others were built on evidence grown cold. The DOE's own inspector general, J. Kenneth Mansfield, conceded that programs involving billions of dollars were receiving only "glancing" audits and that rampant fraud was going "undetected, unprevented and unpunished" (and yet DOE's current budget request would reduce its staff of auditors from six hundred to two hundred fifty).

Two months earlier, at the opening of hearings covering the official topic "White-Collar Crime in the Oil Industry," Energy and Power Subcommittee Chairman John Dingell pointed out that ever since the 1973 Arab embargo, the oil companies had been enjoying "a number of well-recognized schemes to cheat on oil prices and to violate criminal laws prohibiting unjust enrichment and fraud," and that "millions of taxpayer dollars have been spent by the Departments of Energy and Justice to ferret out fraud and abuse in the oil industry," but that "these efforts have resulted *in exactly one successful criminal prosecution*—the chairman of the board of Florida Power." (Emphasis added)

•

Still, by far the most troublesome of the schemes was the "daisy chain" (see chapter for 1978), by which, through an incredible bit of paper-shuffling, "old" oil was changed into "new" oil—with a fraudulent upgrading of price by as much as $8 a barrel.

The major companies were rarely detected as part of the daisy chains, but they were often suspected of at least tolerating their existence.

Joseph D. McNeff, a thoroughly frustrated DOE investigator, told Dingell's subcommittee: "By these two stratagems [daisy chain brokerage both before and after refining] the major companies have been able to raise the general price of fuel to its present artificially high level, insuring that when controls are removed they will not have to boost their prices even more dramatically and suspiciously."

Was the DOE or the Justice Department interested in the daisy chain fraud? Congressional staff investigators thought not. Many honest officials in the DOE itself had their doubts as well. For example, when McNeff was a DOE investigator in Houston, he began to suspect that the national office and the Justice Department were covering up for oil industry criminals. On June 5, 1978, he flew back secretly to Washington to meet with Dingell's staff; after that, he said, "the head of the Houston FBI office called me in and berated me for going to an outside agency and asked me what I was now going to do for a living . . ." Then McNeff was transferred to DOE's Dallas office, where once again he found that investigations were being covered up. For a while he wasn't allowed to work on anything, he said, but finally he was given one criminal case. That one, however, was enough. In developing it, McNeff said, he stumbled upon a cabinet that had been locked for a year or two, and in that cabinet he found "incriminating evidence" pointing to "all the old familiar daisy chain people, dozens and dozens of them . . . I don't know how many chains, a hundred chains, within that one case." After which, he said, "I started looking at some other file cabinets which nobody looked at for two or three years." However, when his superiors found out what he had uncovered, said McNeff, he was told to give back the files.

If what McNeff reported was true—and several other DOE investigators backed him up at least in spirit, if not always in detail—it would appear, as Congressman Dingell put it, that consumers were being victimized by an "institutional coverup" that was due either "to intentional malfeasance or bureaucratic ineptitude."

And what was the DOE's malfeasance or ineptitude costing consumers? Everyone talked in terms of many billions of dollars. But billions is too vague a figure to interest the ordinary consumer. Congressman John Conyers of Michigan, chairman of the Subcommittee on Crime, who was cochairing the investigation with Dingell, said he thought the government was "sitting on top of the largest criminal conspiracy in American history," but that was also too grandiose a description to hit home. It was all brought down to the lunch-bucket level in an exchange between Conyers and Marvin L. Rudnick, the U.S. attorney who had prosecuted the Florida fraud case.

Conyers asked, "Isn't it fair to say, Mr. Rudnick—and I am aware that this is an estimate—that perhaps as much as 60 cents of every 90 cents that Americans pay at the gas pump is traceable to profits from white-collar crime that might be analogous to the daisy chain type activities?"

Rudnick replied: "Last week I went to a pump in Tampa and filled up my car at 92.9 cents . . . I think you can make some speculative estimates that possibly . . . two thirds of that money could be the subject of that type of crime."

At the moment, the only major enforcement actions that the Energy and the Justice departments could point to were the indictments of two relatively minor companies—Uni Oil Inc., of Houston, and Ball Marketing Enterprise, of Lafayette, Louisiana—and several of their officials for allegedly overcharging by $3.8 million in a daisy chain transaction. DOE General Counsel Lynn Coleman boasted, "This tells the oil industry we're serious about seeing the energy laws enforced." But these companies were small pumpkins. What about the other $500 million to $2 billion cheated by others on the daisy chain during the past year? What about the big companies? Did he also intend to tell the majors that they were "serious"? Not likely. As J. A. Conales, a U.S. attorney in Houston, had told the Dingell subcommittee: "I don't think we are ever going to get to the majors. The only major that has been convicted [Conoco] we convicted only because they turned themselves in. That is the only reason we convicted them."

*

Of course, Secretary Schlesinger was not solely responsible for all of DOE's floundering and blundering. But, with the political roof falling around Carter's ears, he had to get rid of the man with the title that went with the mess, so on July 20 he let Schlesinger go, replacing him with Charles Duncan. Although Duncan was a former deputy defense secretary and former president of Coca-Cola Co., it was unlikely that he could do much to hurt the DOE.[9]

On the other hand, it was soon evident that Duncan would also *not* be the man capable of improving its reputation. In November, the staff of Alfred Kahn, the White House's anti-inflation adviser, reported that throughout the year a "handful" of major oil companies, by withholding cheap foreign crude from their regular customers, had forced them into the high-priced spot oil market, which "had the double impact of driving up prices for both domestic crude oil and refined products." After leveraging prices in this way, the majors, with their cheap oil, moved in to make a double-whammy profit. The staff proposed a number of remedial actions to block the leveraging and drive down prices, but neither the DOE nor the White House showed any interest in them.

* * *

Though the majors escaped being caught in the daisy chain naughtiness, they were exclusively the target of Paul Bloom's investigations into other types of overcharging. Bloom, you will recall, was the ebullient head of the Office of Special Counsel, set up with about six hundred employees

9. Ten days before Schlesinger left, his deputy, John O'Leary, resigned effective September 4. O'Leary was replaced by John Sawhill, who had been federal energy administrator during the 1973–74 embargo.

at the end of 1977 to uncover violations of the DOE's extremely complex regulations. But the probe was not aimed at criminal violations; it was not directed at what popularly would be considered crookedness; it was out to uncover profits earned wrongly through the *misinterpretation* of DOE's rules. Bloom's was a gentlemanly game of tag, and to make it all the more gentlemanly, he chose as his first opponents not the scruffy independents but the fifteen largest oil companies. At year's end, with his audits of these companies virtually complete, he toted up nearly $10 billion in overcharges. "This," said Bloom, who had a great talent for making headline statements, "is the largest offensive and counteroffensive in the history of the United States Government."

But accusations put no money in consumers' pockets. How much refund of that $10 billion would the ordinary home and auto owner get? Precious little. Most of the accused companies denied any wrongdoing; if they resisted through the courts, there was little hope of the cases ever being resolved to the benefit of consumers. A few companies admitted overcharging and agreed to make refunds, but these would total only about $650 million. Some of the methods of refunding hardly seemed like refunding at all. Phillips Petroleum, for example, promised to make a $200 million settlement. But, of that total, $100 million would be spent on increasing domestic exploration and development—a "punishment" that surely benefited Phillips. Another $75 million of the "refund" was not a refund at all, but simply an agreement not to raise prices by that much, and Phillips acknowledged to reporters that it hadn't intended to charge ceiling prices, anyway. Another $22 million was to be spent buying crude oil on the open market, which would be added to some of Phillips' own crude oil to produce more heating oil for its customers. In short, DOE was simply asking Phillips to increase its business. The final $3 million would be the only direct repayment, and it would go to some of Phillips' biggest customers.

Consumer organizations viewed the refund process with considerable bitterness. "If these [$650 million] in settlements are any indication of what is to come," said Ellen Berman, executive director of the Consumer Energy Council of America, "consumers will never see most of the $10 billion they have been overcharged. As usual, the oil industry has come out on top, showing it pays to violate the law. These settlements assure the industry of at least a 90 percent success rate in illegal overcharges." By her reckoning, of the $650 million in settlements, "a whopping $475 million would be retained by the offending company and will never be received by consumers. Another $114 million would go to middlemen and jobbers, either directly or through a claims procedure." Less than 7 percent of the total, she argued, would go directly to consumers in the form of low-income heating assistance and reductions in the price of gasoline at the pump.

Many remembered President Carter's pledge in April to "channel the tens of millions of dollars we are already winning . . . into further energy assistance for lower-income citizens," and wondered what "winning" he could possibly have been talking about.

***

Mexico, which had stumbled on vast petroleum reserves in 1977, continued to show its traditional inability to develop the new resources without messing things up. On June 3, as the government oil company, Petróleos Mexicanos (Pemex), was bringing in a test well in Campeche Bay, a spark from an electric motor ignited leaking fuel. The explosion ruptured a pipe. And that was the beginning of the world's biggest spill. Before the well was finally brought under control, nine months later, it had spewed 134 million gallons of crude oil into the Gulf of Mexico. The goo spread eight hundred miles to Texas and there deposited tar balls and other mementos on one hundred forty miles of Texas beach. Mexico, which was incensed that the United States said it expected reparations, didn't seem to give a damn about the mess; it was only interested in the evidence of booty. "It [the massiveness of the spill] goes to show how rich that oil field is," said Miguel Tomassini, a spokesman for Pemex. Instead of rushing to plug the well, Mexico decided it was easier to just lie about it. After the spill had been going for seven months, Mexico said they had reduced the flow to two thousand barrels a day or less. But an expert from the Massachusetts Institute of Technology said the well was actually still gushing about fifty thousand barrels of oil a day.

Senator Lowell Weicker, ranking member of a Senate energy subcommittee, raged, "The truth is not in 'em . . . If it were not for being on our knees in front of anyone that has oil, we would have told them long ago to shape up." Weicker said a Coast Guard reconnaissance plane flew over the busted well area in mid-December and that "absolutely no cleanup effort was visible." Others, too, were angry, as evidenced by the fact that the U.S. Government, fishermen, shrimpers, and tourist businesses filed $370 million in lawsuits against Mexican and American contractors involved in constructing the test well.

A month after the Mexican blowout, something occurred that everyone had been dreading since supertankers came into vogue: *two* of the giants, fully loaded, collided. It had never happened before. At 7:15 P.M. on July 19—long before nightfall—the *Aegean Captain* and the *Atlantic Empress* ran smack into each other when they were sailing about eighteen miles northeast of Tobago (an island near Trinidad). One might have supposed that since each ship was longer than three football fields and higher than a nine-story building, they would have spotted each other in time. But they were Liberian- and Greek-registered, which meant their crews were not the ablest. By the time they did see each other, they were only six hundred feet apart—hardly enough, considering that supertankers of that size, traveling at twenty knots, would require about fifteen miles to come to a halt.

So they hit. And if the worst had happened, if they had both spilled everything, the ocean would have been richer by 3.2 million barrels of oil (enough to take care of about one fifth of one day's consumption in the United States). Instead, they lost 1.6 million barrels—still enough to make it history's second-largest spill, behind the Mexican blowout. Hardest hit was the *Atlantic Empress,* which lost twenty-seven crewmen and half its cargo; it hung onto the rest, thanks largely to heroic salvage crews, who (without life jackets) spent days scrambling around on its slippery decks listing at 15 degrees, spreading foam.

All in all, the amount of oil spilled or accidentally burned in 1979 was 56 percent greater than in 1978, according to the Center for Short-Lived Phenomena, in Cambridge, Massachusetts. The Mexican disaster accounted for 40 percent of the total. But tanker spills alone were up 42 percent, the Center reported. Worldwide, the spills resulted in the known deaths of two hundred fifty people and the estimated deaths of more than fifty thousand birds and two hundred seventy thousand fish.

In Massachusetts, there was one group who cared mostly about the fish statistics. The fishermen who worked the Georges Bank area, which stretches from fifty to two hundred miles offshore and constitutes an area of eleven hundred forty square miles southeast of Cape Cod, were up in arms at the idea that Interior Secretary Cecil D. Andrus planned to sell oil leases to twenty-two thousand acres of Georges Bank. Similar plans had been made by Interior in the past, only to be beaten down by the fishermen's public relations campaign that made it all seem a showdown battle between food and energy, between the little Gloucester fishermen whose legends began with the Colonies and, on the other hand, the big, impersonal oil companies. Angela Sanfillip, president of the Gloucester Fishermen's Wives Association, sounded the typical complaint: "We have been accused of being selfish, but we are holding on because we are producing something more important than oil: food. Do we have to destroy every place that exists to find more oil?"

Indeed, Georges Bank as a whole was an enormously productive protein factory, providing 17 percent of the world's annual commercial fishing harvest. Of this, the editorial writers who supported the fishermen made much, while emphasizing that the area to be leased might provide only a relatively trifling amount of oil and gas.

But this did not tell the whole story, and Andrus refused to surrender to the sou'wester-enthralled editorial writers who opposed the leases. To the Washington *Post*'s editorial "No to Georges Bank," he responded in part: "The *Post*'s argument that the 150 million barrels of 'estimated' reserve in the tracts proposed for leasing equals 9.5 hours of U.S. energy needs every year for 20 years or eight days of current U.S. consumption is misleading. If one were to use this approach to present the other perspectives, it could also be argued that the total protein value of all the fish on the Georges Bank would provide only four meals for every American. This kind of argument proves nothing."

As for the *Post*'s concern about a Bay-of-Campeche-like spill in the Georges Bank area, said Andrus, there were at that time more than 2,400 drilling rigs and pumping stations on the outer continental shelf producing "more than 292 million barrels of oil, or 9.3 percent of U.S. domestic oil, and nearly 4.4 trillion cubic feet of natural gas, or 22.4 percent of U.S. domestic gas. Yet there were only two oil spills last year of more than 50 barrels, the larger one being only 135 barrels. Since 1971, there have been only six spills [from drilling or pumping] of more than 1,000 barrels, all in the Gulf of Mexico and none from exploratory drilling operations. And the number of small spills, averaging only one or two barrels, has declined over the last eight years."

Obviously, Andrus was going ahead. On December 18, the big oil companies sent their agents to the Rhode Island Veterans Auditorium, in Providence, to be on hand for the opening of the bids. For $827,832,853—about $200 million more than Interior had anticipated—they got their leases. But they also got something else. From the balcony above, angry fishermen threw down plastic bags filled with crankcase oil, sometimes with considerable accuracy, and then took their departure via a fire escape.

***

Some day the oil industry should build a monument to Jimmy Carter for the favors he did them in 1979, with disastrous results to his own career. Launching the phased decontrol of oil prices on June 1 was, of course, the first great favor; but just as financially beneficial to the industry was his taking such actions as to guarantee that Iran would no longer supply oil to the United States. This encouraged OPEC to complete the most extravagant price increases since 1973–74—and those increases would be reflected in domestic prices as they were transformed into world prices via Carter's decontrol program. It was a beautifully circular economic arrangement that left U.S. consumers gasping with something less than admiration.

On January 16, Shah Muhammad Riza Pahlevi had flown from Iran on what he called an "extended vacation" but which in reality was permanent exile, for within a month the 37-year-old monarchy he left behind was in rubble.[10] The supporters of Ayatollah Ruhollah Khomeini took

10. So much for the "genius" of Henry Kissinger. He was the fellow, remember, who persuaded both Nixon and Ford to take a soft attitude toward OPEC because Saudi

over, and in March, after many years of exile, the Ayatollah himself returned in triumph. At this point, Carter decided quite correctly that the best course to follow was for the United States to wash its hands of the Shah and to establish at least the appearance of neutrality toward the revolution that was taking place, in the hopes that trade might be continued. Carter's old buddy from Annapolis days CIA director Stansfield Turner established the Administration's note of realism when he said, on ABC's "Issues and Answers," that the Shah's government had turned out to be a lousy ally, because "it couldn't stay in power," and that if Khomeini established a stable government, "it's quite possible" the new Iran would turn out to be a good ally.

Privately, Carter had his minions inform the Shah (momentarily stranded in Third World countries) that he would not be welcome in the United States until things had cooled down in Iran. Carter had been warned by the CIA that if the Shah was allowed in, the militants might storm the American embassy in Tehran. Nervous embassy officials passed word to the State Department that they feared that reaction too. So Carter made up his mind: no Shah.

It was a smart decision, but it hadn't been cleared with the right people. David Rockefeller, chairman of Chase Manhattan Bank, and Rockefeller's protégé, Henry Kissinger (a Chase consultant), and New York attorney John J. McCloy, a former chairman of Chase Manhattan who for years had been godfather and chief counselor to the Seven Sisters, were determined to get their old friend into this country, no matter what the consequences—or perhaps because of the probable consequences—and get him in they did.

(Rockefeller's eagerness to help the Shah was quite understandable. Chase Manhattan had always held the largest share of Iran's deposits, mostly in Chase's London branch. In addition, much of the Shah's personal fortune was deposited with or managed by Chase, and although most experts doubted that the Shah's fortune was anywhere near the $20 billion figure claimed by the Ayatollah, it was believed to be well into the billions—quite enough to make Chase tremble, if not close its doors, should the Shah, deciding that Rockefeller wasn't trying hard enough, pull out his money.)

Rockefeller picked a doctor from a medical center heavily endowed with Rockefeller money and sent him off to Mexico, the Shah's latest haven, to examine the ex-monarch, ailing with cancer, and declare whether or not he was getting the right treatment. If he wasn't, should he come to the United States for better treatment? The doctor was not an expert in cancer; he was an expert in tropical diseases. But his conclu-

---

Arabia and Iran were pro-Western and it was worth paying them whatever price they asked, because we could depend on them for a politically stable source of oil.

sion was prompt and not at all unexpected. Only the United States, he
said, had the facilities that could help the poor fellow. Bowing to these
pressures, Carter said that for "humanitarian" reasons the dying Shah
could come; and so, on October 22, he arrived.

Twelve days later, the U.S. embassy in Tehran was seized and its employees taken hostage. That, of course, was the end of trade between the
two countries, and on November 13 Carter made it official, banning
Iranian oil imports.

The absence of Iranian oil should have made no great difference; the
cutoff of its supplies at the first of the year had been easily offset by imports from other countries. It could just as easily be offset once more, for
Iran was supplying only about 4 percent of our oil needs. For both countries, it was more a symbolic rebuff than anything else.

But the oil market, like the stock market, is a creature of spooks. It
breeds hobgoblins and thrives on fairy juices. Shortages that do not exist
are eagerly conjured up, and whispered about, in such a way as to keep
the market jumping. Thus it was that even before the embassy fell and
we split officially with Iran, oil buyers around the world began to hoard.
It was a strange and illogical action, for the global supply was to the
brim and the world's biggest oil customer, the United States, had actually begun to trim consumption. The market atmosphere should have
been one of calm, of moderate bidding. Instead, the big oil companies
and their customers were scrambling around, buying frantically, bidding
up the price to ridiculous heights, and squirreling it away in all available
containers, as though the last twist was about to be taken on the cosmic
oil tap. Asked to explain their actions, industry executives talked with
wild-eyed vagueness about the "possibility" that OPEC might cut back
production in 1980, and the very mention of Iran seemed to frighten
them. "All you need is resumption of the Iranian revolution and you've
got a shortage," said Charles DiBona, president of the American Petroleum Institute. This was foolish talk; there was consensus among most
experts that, with world consumption declining, neither Iran alone nor
any likely agreement among OPEC would result in a serious supply reduction. The only thing the industry faced was a psychological "shortage"—which was the kind it loved the best. And so, when the Iranian
cutoff did in fact come about, buyers were seized with another layer of
self-induced panic. And OPEC, watching all this silliness with what must
have been great satisfaction, was ready to round out the year with yet
another demand.

***

Hard as it may be to remember such tranquillity, there actually were
long stretches during the 1970s when OPEC left its prices pretty much
alone. So shocking was the price jump from 1973 to 1974 that we tend to

think of OPEC throughout this decade as acting with all the ruthlessness of, oh, say a John D. Rockefeller. But such was not the case. Its most acute ruthlessness was limited to 1973 and 1979-80. The price per barrel of light crude oil leaving Saudi Arabia on January 1 of the years from 1973 to 1979 was as follows: $2.41 in 1973, then up, up, up, up to $10.95 in 1974; after which the world was so stunned and depressed that it cut back consumption enough to force a slight decline, to $10.46, in 1975. The next three years showed only modest increases: $11.51 in 1976, $12.09 in 1977, $12.70 in 1978.

The year 1979 opened with a Saudi barrel costing $13.34—hardly a bargain, considering the fact that the oil was costing Saudi Arabia between 25 cents and 30 cents per barrel to produce, but by the end of the year it would be looked back on as a bargain indeed.

In June, the thirteen petroleum ministers of OPEC met in Geneva with greed on the agenda, and they handled the topic with their usual agility, meaning that the price policy that emerged was total chaos. "I am sure," said Saudi Arabia's Sheikh Zaki Yamani, as he explained the new pricing system to reporters, "right now you are already confused." It was the only thing he said that made sense. Roughly, very roughly, the new prices ranged from $18 to $23.50, which was expected to take $6 billion more from U.S. consumers annually. The upper price was supposed to be a "ceiling," but it wasn't. One third of all the oil sold by the OPEC partners was being sold on the spot market—six times the normal amount. Spot sales were for one cargo only. For these random deals, the sky was the limit, and in mid-1979 the sky reached to such unbelievable zeniths as $35 and $40 a barrel. (Before the year was over, it would go even higher.) When the OPEC ministers first met in Geneva, they said they wanted a firm agreement to end the hysterical spot-market gyrations. But no such agreement was reached, and as Venezuela's Minister of Energy and Mines, Humberto Calderón Berti, admitted, "The situation is out of control."

As it turned out, *only* Saudi Arabia held its oil to $18 a barrel for the second half of the year, and it did so with increasing irritability. Understandable irritability. Saudi Arabia had held its price down as a public relations gesture, expecting that the lower price would be reflected at the gasoline pump and motorists would learn to love them. That rather remote possibility was scuttled by Saudi Arabia's biggest buyer, Aramco (Exxon, Mobil, Texaco, Standard of California). Sure, they had shaved a couple of pennies from gasoline prices in this country, just enough to beat their competitors (who were paying $24 and more to other OPEC members) but not nearly as much as the Saudis' $18 price would have permitted. Elsewhere around the world, the Aramco quartet trimmed prices not at all. Yamani, watching his public relations pipedream disappear into Aramco's cash register, complained to the Carter administration that U.S. motorists weren't reaping the blessings he had planned. Getting no satisfactory response from Carter, Yamani announced in early December that Saudi Arabia was raising its price 33 percent and making it retroactive to November 1, hoping thereby to recoup about $2 billion that Aramco had walked away with.

With even Saudi Arabia, which loved to pose as a moderate, in this frame of mind, the outcome of the OPEC meeting in Caracas, in December, was naturally rapacious. The stated objective of the meeting was to decide on a new base price. But avarice kept the conferees apart. No matter how high a base price was proposed, there were some members who thought they could get even more from the industrial nations. The latest Iranian panic swirling around the U.S. embassy in Tehran, a crisis only a few weeks old, gave them confidence on that point. So, after four days of fruitless searching for the highest common gouge, the ministers went their separate ways with as many separate prices in mind.

Saudi Arabia's price, usually considered the benchmark of moderation among the major exporting nations, was $24—a mere 100 percent increase over the previous December. Other nations left the parley with official prices as high as $30 a barrel. But none of that pointed to any stability whatsoever, for the OPEC ministers had not had time to get home and unpack before four members—Venezuela, Libya, Indonesia, and Iraq—raised their own prices 10 to 15 percent above what they had set a few hours earlier in Caracas. What Calderón Berti had said after the Geneva meeting in June was even more applicable now: The situation *was* out of control.

* * *

Did anybody have a plan for fighting back? If anybody in government had, he succeeded in keeping it a secret. But a couple of imaginative ideas did pop up from the grass roots. Farmers' pickups began blossoming with bumper stickers demanding "Cheaper Crude or No More Food." Administration officials tried to laugh it off as a silly suggestion. Threaten to stop shipping wheat to the OPEC countries if they didn't drop their oil prices? It would never work, said the Carter crowd. But Dan Morgan, author of *Merchants of Grain* and one of the country's top experts on the world grain trade, said, ". . . the idea deserves more serious consideration than Washington has given it." He pointed out that OPEC's wheat imports, growing at a record pace, already accounted for 14 percent of the entire world wheat trade and that OPEC was dependent on the United States for half of the wheat it needed. OPEC's biggest oil producers, all of whom considered wheat a staple of their diet, were especially dependent on us; of the three hundred fifty thousand tons imported by the Saudis, two hundred fifty thousand came from the United States; of the 1.5 million tons imported by Iran, 1.2 million came from the United States. "Given the fact that U.S. food is feeding Iranians," Morgan wrote in the Washington *Post,* "the Ayatollah's rantings against the United States seem particularly ungracious. A countersqueeze using U.S. food might show us what the Ayatollah is really made of."

But to use wheat as a weapon would have meant having a federal marketing board that would set the prices, make them stick, and handle sales to other countries. The multinational wheat dealers—who controlled grain as tightly as the Seven Sisters and OPEC controlled oil—were of course fanatically opposed to the U.S. Government taking action on behalf of consumers in this way, so Carter didn't even consider it. Nor did Congress.

The other bold grass-roots idea—no, action this time—came from the International Association of Machinists and Aerospace Workers, which went to court seeking a preliminary injunction against OPEC for price fixing and other antitrust violations. It also filed a lawsuit seeking damages for the inflation and unemployment that OPEC price fixing had inflicted on the U.S. economy. (Similar suits were filed by the cities of Cleveland, Los Angeles, New Haven, and Pueblo, Colorado.) The union's legal pleas were considered by U.S. District Judge Andrew Hauk in Los Angeles.

There was legal doctrine for the suit. The Foreign Sovereign Immunities Act of 1976 declared that foreign states were not immune from suits in U.S. courts for commercial activities that affected this country's economy. In passing the Act, the House of Representatives issued a report specifically stating that the new law applied to the oil traffic.

Although the lawsuit seemed as unlikely to connect as a drunk's haymaker, it was taken seriously enough to provoke consternation in the White House and great bustling in the Justice Department. What if the union actually got a favorable decision! Philip Taubman, of the New York *Times,* said top officials told him they were "concerned that an injunction against OPEC could prompt Saudi Arabia to withdraw billions of dollars it has invested in United States Treasury notes to prevent the assets from being seized by court order to secure payment of damages if the machinists' union wins the case." They were also afraid, he said, of an oil boycott in retaliation. Why, the White House was so alarmed that it even considered filing a "friend of the court" brief supporting OPEC, but finally, as one official recalled, decided that "it would kill us with the public to have the government siding with OPEC when people are waiting in lines and paying $1 a gallon for gas."

They needn't have worried. Judge Hauk, showing the venerable ability of judges to read headlines, ruled that OPEC couldn't be sued for price fixing. "If you define the acts shown by the evidence as being strictly a getting together to fix prices to rip off the world," he declared, "you get a different view than if you say that to preserve their natural resources they got together." He said he preferred to think the Mideast brigands were just interested in preserving their oil, not in making a lot of money, and he said it with a straight face. One thing the judge did do for America. He enriched the language with a new name. He kept calling the defendants "the OPECers."

* * *

If the doubling of OPEC prices in 1979 was a melancholy development for the lowly consumer, it was downright scary for some of the world's largest banks.

But fright, as the reader will doubtless remember, is something that the big banks had been feeling for several years (see the chapters for 1974 and 1975). The reasons for their black and jumpy mood in 1979 was the same as before, only more so.

The first reason had to do with the towering surplus of OPEC dollars, a problem of financial bloat brought about by backwardness. If the Middle East nations were industrial nations, they would have no trouble spending the riches reaped from oil; as soon as it came in, they would spend it on machinery and plant expansion and roads and sewers and all the other things that go into keeping the wheels turning in a civilized society. But they were neither industrial (though the Shah, in a painfully clumsy way, had tried to be) nor civilized. They were primitive lands that could not possibly spend all their riches on constructive things. So, after buying another covey of U.S. fighter planes and building some more gold-lined bathrooms for the palace and buying a few more mansions in Beverly Hills and subsidizing a few more brothels in Cairo and Paris, the new Croesuses of the Middle East had nothing left to do with their money but stick it into banks or blue chip corporate stocks or U.S. Government securities, the solidest investment in the world.

When world oil prices made their first great surge, in 1973–74, the bankers said not to worry, that OPEC's profits would be easily "recycled"—by this (as we have previously explained) they meant that OPEC nations, being unable to spend much of their loot, would deposit the bulk of it in the Western-based international banks; the banks would then lend the money to industries or to oil-consuming nations, who would hand over the loan to OPEC for more energy; OPEC would again deposit this in the Big Oil banks, et cetera ad infinitum, with the money going in a circle.

But this was a tricky game the bankers were playing. After all, the countries to whom the banks were lending money to buy oil did not have the best credit ratings. How much debt could some of the grubby nations support? The big bankers had been whining about their risk since 1974, and every year their peril had grown. As of the middle of 1979, our big banks had lent needy foreign nations a total of $258 billion, of which $41.6 billion was owed by Asian countries, $3.6 billion by African countries, and $33.8 billion by Latin American and Caribbean countries. What if some of those nations, weary of struggling with their "recycling" oil debts, were to say, To hell with it, leaving the biggest U.S. commercial banks holding such a pile of worthless IOU's that they themselves went bust? Of course, if the bankers had really wanted to avoid the risk, they could have cut the circle by refusing to take OPEC deposits. But those billions were irresistible. The bankers, like drunks turned loose in a warehouse of whiskey, went on sopping up the stuff they knew might kill them.[11] The recycling, and the whining about dangers, continued. What happened in 1979 would again multiply the problem. OPEC's latest price increases were expected to give the oil-producing nations at least a $130 billion surplus from 1979 and 1980 production alone, with other huge surpluses in the years ahead. Far from being delighted to wallow in such deposits, now the oil bankers were afraid they might drown in them. The money glut—and the accompanying Third World debt—threatened to become unmanageable. "Increasingly," wrote Ann Crittenden, a financial reporter for the New York *Times,* "individuals close to those [money] markets are warning that the private banking system may not be able to handle the new stresses." One who had known the stresses and been complaining about them since 1974 was Rimmer de Vries, senior vice-president and chief international economist for the Morgan Guaranty Trust Company (one of the top three repositories of Arab money), who now warned that the financial community "may be on the brink of severe trouble" caused by "bloated balance sheets."

The banks—and government officials—were also scared, as they had been for six years, about the possibility that the big Arab depositors might, in a snit, withdraw their money too suddenly. "Just the fear that they might withdraw gives them significant leverage," a State Department official told Judith Miller, of the New York *Times.* "We have added a second layer of potential vulnerability—dependence on Arab Petrodollars—to our initial dependence on their oil."

The source of the problem was the *concentration* of deposits. If there were hundreds of big Arab depositors and if they had put their money in dozens of United States banks—really spread it around—there would have been no great threat, for an avalanche of withdrawals could not

---

11. There was plenty to sop up. Typical income changes among the richest OPEC nations were these: Saudi Arabia's 1972 income was $4.5 billion; its 1979 income was about $63 billion; Iran, $3.6 billion in 1972, $31 billion in 1979; Iraq, $1 billion in 1972, $26 billion in 1979; Nigeria, $1.8 billion and $20.6 billion; Libya, $2.5 billion and $18 billion; Algeria, $1 billion and $10.3 billion; Kuwait, $2.4 billion and $16.4 billion.

have affected any one bank in a devastating way. But that wasn't the way things were. There were only a handful of really significant Arab depositors, and their deposits were concentrated in a handful of the largest New York banks, whose financial health was—is—crucial to the U.S. banking system. Some experts believed that 90 percent of the OPEC money could be found in the vaults of only six banks: First National City Bank (Citicorp), Chase Manhattan Bank, Morgan Guaranty Trust, Chemical Bank of New York, Manufacturers Hanover Trust, and Bank of America.

So long as that concentration existed, the great danger of what one or two major Arab depositors might do to the banking system by destroying a keystone bank was both psychological and real. The psychological danger had surfaced in the fall of 1978, when a rumor spread along Wall Street that Kuwait—a piece of sand about the size of Connecticut, with a population of less than Baltimore—had withdrawn a huge deposit (the rumor ranged from $1 billion to $2 billion) from Morgan Guaranty. On the world monetary market, the dollar was already looked upon as a soggy piece of merchandise. International bankers were dumping it in large quantities and turning to harder and more stable currencies. The rumor of Kuwait's pullout triggered a new wave of dumping, which finally reached such proportions that it had the effect of a run on the currency, and for a moment the nation's economy teetered on the edge of what *The Wall Street Journal* later called a "19th-Century-type of financial panic."

We did not fall over the edge, only because the Administration rushed in desperately and bought $30 billion worth of dying dollars on the world market, thereby making it seem that our currency was worth having. The price of the dollar stabilized for the moment, and the panic was past.

What made the episode so frightening to the financial world was that the rumor *was* only a rumor—Kuwait had *not* withdrawn a bundle from Morgan Guaranty. But if a mere rumor could have such shattering results, what would an actual withdrawal of billions of dollars do?

It was a situation in which blackmail could flourish, the type of blackmail that had occurred across the border, in Canada. When Joe Clark became Prime Minister of Canada (briefly), in 1979, he said he intended to move Canada's embassy in Israel from Tel Aviv to Jerusalem—a gesture that pleased Canada's Jewish voters. But it enraged the Arabs, who threatened to withdraw their money from Canadian banks, dump their Canadian money holdings, and cancel proposed investment in Canadian industry.

Clark quickly backed down.

If Canada, where the Middle Eastern oil producers had invested a relatively trifling amount, was vulnerable to such blackmail, where did that leave the United States? The truth was, nobody really knew—or if they knew, they weren't saying—and yet there was no possible way that the government could prepare a strategic defense against financial blackmail by the Arabs unless the government knew how much money the various oil-producing nations had on deposit both here and in the banks' foreign branches. In 1975, Senator Frank Church had threatened to use subpoenas to get the information, but under pressure from the banks he backed down. In 1979, Representative Benjamin S. Rosenthal, whose Consumer and Monetary Affairs Subcommittee did a badly organized investigation of OPEC influence, also threatened to dig out the information with subpoenas, but he also backed down. The bankers simply refused to divulge the information, and got by with it. Profits before patriotism. The Arabs wanted secrecy, and the bankers were all too willing to oblige—for a price. As Hans Angermueller, vice-president and general counsel of First National City Bank once told a Senate committee trying to pry the amount of the Arab deposit out of him: "We wonder if in a balance of risk against reward it is worth subjecting the major U.S. international banks to losing their OPEC customer relationships in order to glean some knowledge of where . . . the world's petrodollars ended. We think the balance should run against running that risk."

And so the federal bureaucrats were left in stupefying ignorance, illustrated by this exchange between Representative Rosenthal and C. Fred Bergsten, assistant secretary of the treasury for international affairs:

ROSENTHAL: "Is there anybody in the United States Government who knows how much the OPEC countries have invested in U.S. securities, in U.S. banks or U.S. resources? Is there anybody in the U.S. Government who knows that?"

BERGSTEN: "There would be no one who would know, Mr. Chairman . . ."

ROSENTHAL: "What is the outer limit of your best upper guesstimate including direct, indirect, hidden, or anything you want—covered, uncovered—anything, altogether?"

BERGSTEN: "Gee, I have not put those numbers together."

And he was talking not only about bank accounts or government securities, but commercial investments, stocks and bonds, as well. J. Dexter Peach, of the General Accounting Office, admitted, "The government has no record of how much portfolio investments in a U.S. sector or industry is being held by OPEC."[12]

---

12. Some sharp observers believe the government's secrecy was one of the self-defeating reasons it felt pressured to admit the Shah. Claudia Wright, Washington correspondent for the *New Statesman,* of London, wrote on April 7, 1980, in *Inquiry* magazine: "The U.S. Treasury knew it was entirely possible that since 1974 the Shah had accumulated an enormous and secret stock of government securities, but because of

Of course, some of the OPEC invasion was known. It was known that in addition to hotels and cattle ranches and clothing manufacturing plants and trucking firms and all sorts of other enterprises, the OPEC barons now owned all or part of the Bank of Commonwealth, in Michigan (a bank that Rockefeller's Chase had tried to prop up with a $20 million loan; when that failed, they called on their Arab friends for help), the Main Bank of Houston, the National Bank of Georgia, the Union Chelsea National Bank, in New York, the First National Bank of Hialeah, the Security National Bank, and the Bank of Contra Costa, in California—but that list, everyone knew, was ridiculously incomplete. Senator H. John Heinz III of Pennsylvania, a member of the Senate Banking Committee, warned in August that if all the currently proposed bank acquisitions were approved by the Federal Reserve Board, "foreign-owned bank assets will soar to more than $95 billion—almost 10 percent of the total bank assets in the United States." Because of the various techniques for hiding ownership, it was impossible to know just how much of the control would rest in the hands of oil-producing nations. But one thing was certain: the danger came not only from OPEC governments but from individuals, the superrich princes living in those Arab nations. "With the tens of billions of dollars in surpluses being accumulated by OPEC states," said Heinz, "the prospect of private citizens of those countries buying our major banks has become very real. In 1978, for example, the SEC charged four Arab businessmen with violations of securities laws for secretly attempting to acquire control of the $2.2 billion Financial General Bankshares, a Washington, D.C.-area bank holding company. It seems likely that the prospect of both direct and indirect financial and political influence will convince more wealthy Arabs that American banks are promising investments."

The willingness of the Arabs to toss great gobs of money around to buy influence was indicated on two occasions as the year closed. On December 28, the International Business Machines Corporation announced that it had borrowed $300 million, at 10.8 percent interest, from the Saudi Arabian Government. It was thought to be the Saudis' biggest investment in an American corporation.

A few weeks earlier, Prince Abdullah Ibn-Abdel Aziz, a deputy prime

---

the Treasury's own rules about secrecy there was no way to tell. It knew also that he had the option of 'rolling over' these securities (repurchasing them as they reached their maturity) or alternatively, demanding cash and withdrawing his investments altogether. It was widely believed within the administration that a Saudi decision to pull out of treasury notes between November 1977 and August 1978—estimated to be a movement of approximately $11.7 billion—had produced the serious run on the dollar of late 1978. Without knowing with certainty the value of the Shah's portfolio, U.S. Treasury officials could have feared that it was at least the size of that of the Saudis, and possibly, even larger."

minister and commander of the Saudi National Guard, said in an interview with the Jordanian newspaper *Al-Rai* that his nation's efforts to buy its way to the top of the heap sometimes ran into problems. "We would have liked to control all influential news media in the world," he said, "but will the proprietors of these media be ready to sell? Our frequent attempts in the past have been negative."

* * *

The propaganda flag raised by the Carter administration over the natural gas decontrol fight was already in tatters. The Administration had warned legislators that they *must* raise prices to get more gas, that the nation might never again have enough of the precious fuel, that gas companies should stop signing up new household customers, and that for factories and utilities to burn natural gas would be like burning mahogany in the fireplace. Industrial customers, the Carter crowd warned, must turn away from natural gas and go back to old, reliable coal.

That's what Carter had been saying when he first hit Washington, in 1977, and it was what he had still been saying when, in the fall of 1978, he signed the Natural Gas Policy Act, to decontrol prices, and the Power Plant and Industrial Fuel Use Act, mandating that utilities switch from gas to coal.

And yet less than sixty days after that signing, the White House was complaining about a "gas bubble"—surplus—of one trillion cubic feet and acknowledging that the bubble might last at least two or three years. Energy Secretary Schlesinger in January wrote state regulatory commissions urging them to encourage more residential hookups to natural gas systems. The same month, in a speech to Wall Street oil analysts, Schlesinger said, "Although the Administration remains committed to the use of coal instead of oil or gas in *new* boiler facilities over the longer run, over the course of at least the next several years, existing industrial and utility facilities will be provided every encouragement to burn gas instead of oil."

To complete the irony, DOE soon changed the formula by which natural gas prices were being decontrolled; to encourage industrial users to slop up the surplus bubble, the formula was rewritten so that they would have to pay less and homeowners more.

1980 ETC.

"[Price] decontrol, by itself, is not a comprehensive energy program."

WILLIAM P. TAVOULAREAS, *president, Mobil Oil Corp.*

Having been increasingly abused as the Oil Decade unrolled, Americans moved into the 1980s poorer, more confused, and much more cynical.

Except for the same old, stolid reliance on "marketplace forces" dominated by the same old, giant oil firms that most consumers had learned to distrust with a passion, federal politicians arrived in the 1980s with no more of a national energy policy than they had had in the 1960s. Or in the 1920s.

Despite the energy crises that pockmarked the 1970s, they had obviously failed to learn enough from adversity to construct a plan to meet future emergencies. The guiding assumption of the decade—bequeathed to the future—was that if even greater wealth was transferred from all other segments of the economy to the oil industry, then consumers would conserve in response to financial pain and the oil companies would produce more in response to greed, and together they would thereby lift the United States toward reasonable independence of foreign energy suppliers. That was the rationale for price decontrol, but it was as naïve as it was brutally deceptive;[1] the economy was permanently crippled, but independence remains as elusive as ever. In 1973, we were importing about one third of our oil; ten years later, we were still importing about one third, but with one terrible difference: whereas in 1973 nearly all of our imports came from friendly Western Hemisphere nations such as Canada, in 1983 much was coming from hostile nations in the Middle East. The money we spent for energy security had been not only wasted but perverted.

For producers and hucksters of energy, however, the decade had turned out to be exactly what Secretary Schlesinger promised President Carter would help it to become: "a second golden age," an era symbolized by Exxon's becoming in 1980 the first industrial company in U.S. history to have 12-digit sales—that is, sales of *one hundred and three billion, one hundred million dollars* ($103,100,000,000).

---

1. Former President Carter and some of the officials who helped him carry out his energy program, such as former Deputy Energy Secretary John O'Leary, now admit that they did not come even close to realizing the terrible consequences of the energy price increases they pushed. But apologies don't help much.

The Carter administration had promised to protect consumers from industry predators, but of course it did not. The windfall profits tax, proposed by Carter on April 5, 1979, finally cleared Congress on March 27, 1980, and he immediately telephoned those fabulous friends of oil, Senate Finance Committee Chairman Russell Long and Senate Majority Leader Robert Byrd, to thank them for this "good news for the country and for the whole world."

Actually, the only group that could call it good news was the oil industry, which had achieved a whopping victory. Of course the new law, however bogus it was, did give federal politicians something to brag about in an election year. Carter lost no time using it that way, declaring the law to be the Administration's "most significant domestic accomplishment and the most important energy bill ever to emerge from Congress." A more accurate assessment was given by Senator Daniel P. Moynihan, New York's rude pixie, who, on the last day of Senate consideration, observed, "We're not doing anything very serious here today, we all know."

Why was Carter so happy? How could he pretend to call this law *his?* He had sent Congress a bill that would have presumably taxed away $280 billion of the estimated one trillion dollars industry would earn by 1990 as a result of oil price decontrol. (Although 1990 was the arbitrary date used by Carter to construct his tax formula, actually he wanted, or said he wanted, the tax to be permanent.) He had asked that half the tax be used to develop synthetic fuels, 17 percent of the tax be used to help poor people pay their fuel bills, and the rest be spent on such things as mass transit and tax credits for filling the chinks around loose windows.

The bill that emerged from Congress, and that Carter hailed as something of a Mosaic tablet, was considerably different. Its tax harvest would be at least $60 billion less. Instead of being a permanent tax, it would be phased out over a 33-month period beginning January 1988. Instead of going into a special trust fund, the tax money would disappear into general revenues. And the dispensing of the money would be significantly different from Carter's plan. The most important change made by Congress was to relegate the Energy Security Corporation, which would oversee the synfuels program, to a minor role. Instead of reaping *half* the projected $227 billion in taxes, it would get something around $20 billion—maybe. Indeed, just about everything in the bill turned out to be "maybe," for while Congress had set guidelines directing how the money should be spent—including 60 percent of the taxes for income tax reductions (mostly for business, little for individuals) and 25 percent for energy aid to the poor—these were only suggestions, not binding. Also suggested was that businesses receive $8.6 billion in energy tax credits and that homeowners receive a piddling $600 million in credits for taking conservation steps.

Using the new law as a measure, one might fairly conclude that industry's purchase of politicians had paid off handsomely. In the 1978 election, which shaped the windfall-tax Congress, oil's political action committees (PACs), as well as the industry's executives, directors, and lobbyists, had chipped in $3.9 million in congressional races. (That was the recorded amount; but it is a rule of thumb that unrecorded contributions equal those that are on the record.) In the House, the effect of these gifts could be seen in the key vote on an amendment that was backed by the oil lobby and offered by Jim Jones, the Oklahoma Democrat. It passed, 236 to 183. Those who voted for it had received an average of $6,032 from oilmen in their latest campaigns; those who voted against the amendment had received an average of $932.

As always, the oil lobby had been particularly generous with members of the Senate Finance Committee, breeding ground for tax loopholes: twenty members of that committee had received $600,000 in their 1978 campaigns, and the money was still rolling in (especially to the campaign treasury of Chairman Russell Long). A grateful and eternally expectant industry turned 1980 into another good year for sympathetic members. Russell D. Hemenway, director of the National Committee for an Effective Congress, said his organization's study of one hundred ninety oil and gas PACs found $6 million flowing to House and Senate candidates that year, and, he added, the oil crowd "certainly got their money's worth the day the tax bill passed. We have always known that the big oil boys are smart investors, and they've proved it again."

No doubt about it, the footprints of the oil lobby and the doodling of Chairman Long were seen all over the bill that went to Carter for his signature.

The synfuels generosity of Carter's original legislation had been aimed at the major oil companies: they were the only ones with the experience and coal-shale-uranium reserves to handle the program swiftly. But that didn't mean they were enthusiastic about the idea, not even if supported with federal subsidies. Now that they had finally driven crude-oil and natural gas prices so high, why would they want to develop competing fuels that would inevitably drive them down again? So there was no reliable constituency among the majors for Carter's synthetic program. As for the independent oil companies, they opposed the program. They stood to benefit very little from the Energy Security Corporation handouts, and they were understandably displeased with the idea of paying windfall taxes that would go to the majors' synfuel plants. Which is why Senator Long, himself an independent oilman coming from a state where the independent oilman was king, helped do away with all but a token amount—if $20 billion can be called only a token—for synfuels, and threw the rest into a kitty for business in general, as tax breaks.

Although the windfall levy was supposed to fall with biblical impartiality on the just and unjust alike, in fact it emerged from Congress with a heavy bias in favor of the independent oilmen and against the majors. For example, under the guidance of fellows such as Long and Senator Lloyd Bentsen of Texas, Congress dropped into the bill an item to guarantee the independents a depletion allowance equivalent to a 22 percent deduction against the gross income from the first thousand barrels a day —a gesture to the "little" oil companies that would cost the federal government a mere $13 billion.

One thing was very, very certain about the new law: individual consumers did not stand to gain much.

*

A year after the windfall tax took effect, the Internal Revenue Service admitted that things weren't going so well.[2] IRS had received less than half the taxes Congress had anticipated, and the new Reagan administration had made certain, by drastically reducing the number of IRS personnel assigned to police the program, that collecting the tax would become increasingly difficult.

At the end of the second year, collections were down again by about 50 percent. What had gone wrong? To a lesser extent, the trouble was a falling market: a drop in production and sales meant less profit to tax. But the main reason for the wretched results was collusion between government and companies. The Reagan administration, which did not believe in the windfall tax, was indifferent about collecting it.

***

When collusion was the game, the Interior Department's U.S. Geological Survey was always among the top players. It had had decades of experience at turning its back on crookedness, and investigations launched in the 1980s showed that its expertise had not lessened at all with the passing years.

The USGS was supposed to be collecting royalties of 12½ percent for oil produced on federal land and Indian land. The General Accounting Office, Congress' investigative arm, reported in 1981 that because of "serious financial and other management problems," the USGS couldn't be sure it was collecting the right amount of royalties from oil companies, let alone know what portion of the royalties should be allocated to the windfall profits tax. "Hundreds of millions of dollars" were at issue, said the GAO. For traditionalists, it was perhaps comforting to know that the

---

2. One of the built-in, but never publicized, defects of the tax came to light at the end of fiscal 1981, when George Ross, chief tax spokesman for the Treasury Department, announced that of the $23.3 billion in windfall taxes levied against the oil companies, the government realized less than half—to be exact, $9.5 billion. Said Ross, "You have to remember that the oil companies can deduct the tax from the income tax they pay. In this case, the deduction is $13.8 billion."

USGS's incompetence had continued into the 1980s and would no doubt continue forever. A lucky thing, too, for what would the GAO do if it had to stop issuing periodic reports of USGS malfeasance and non-feasance? Some traditions die hard, and this one went back a long way.

The Mineral Leasing Act of 1920 gave the Department of Interior responsibility for managing the development of mineral resources on public lands. Interior's Bureau of Indian Affairs and Bureau of Land Management were put in charge of leasing the lands for exploration and development; the USGS was given responsibility for overseeing actual operations on the lease site.

All of which, for the first four decades, was so much theory; in actual practice, the oil companies literally ran the program themselves. Nobody in government paid the slightest attention to what was going on.

Then, in 1958, the GAO made a cursory investigation and was horrified. It found that the USGS had no idea whatsoever as to whether the oil companies pumping from federal and Indian lands were paying the proper royalties; its formal report warned that a "number of serious deficiencies exist in royalty accounting"—which, in the GAO's conservative language, meant that the USGS's bookkeeping was in complete shambles. The investigation was, of course, ignored by Congress.

In 1964, the GAO investigated again and found the same conditions; 1972, ditto; 1976, ditto; 1979, ditto. All the while, the value of the oil was skyrocketing and the loss to the federal government, to state governments (states receive half the royalties from federal lands within their boundaries), and to Indian governments was now being talked about at the "hundreds of millions of dollars" level, which was the phrase used in 1981. To be a bit more exact, the GAO guessed that governments and Indian tribes would lose 10 percent of their rightful royalties—which, in 1981 alone meant a loss of $650 million—so long as cheating on royalty reports and outright theft of oil continued.

For years, the Justice Department had run halfhearted civil investigations and the FBI even less-enthusiastic criminal investigations into the mess, with no results. But now, with the larceny reaching the level of super bucks and with the Reagan administration facing the biggest deficits in history, the White House had to at least pretend to go after this lost income, so it ordered Interior Secretary James G. Watt to do something. Watt, being a natural-born bureaucrat, launched still another investigation. However, it must be admitted that this was better than the usual. As such outfits go, the special, 5-member commission Watt appointed, in July 1981, was truly blue-ribbon.[3] It had to be listened to

---

3. The Commission on Fiscal Accountability of the Nation's Energy Resources was made up of Chairman David F. Linowes, a former chairman of the American Institute of Certified Public Accountants' Trial Board and a frequent government trouble-

with respect, even if ultimately ignored. The report it handed in, in 1982, was appropriately bleak.

What the Commission found was this: Stealing via false reporting could be as high as 10 percent; outright physical theft of oil could run as high as 6 percent. So governments and Indian tribes could be losing a total of 16 percent (not just the 10 percent previously estimated by the GAO) of their rightful income from oil. And that was a conservative guess; it could be higher.

The Commission found "that the nation's collection of oil and gas royalties is on the honor system. The government has no way of verifying independently how much oil and gas are taken from leases on federal and Indian lands." Everything was being left to the whim of the producing companies. If they lied, there was no way to catch them, because "there are no internal controls."

The Commission reported that "oil and gas lease accounts kept by the USGS . . . are so out of date and filled with errors that, as the USGS itself has said, the balances shown are virtually worthless . . ."

A full 73 percent of the accounts showed that the producers owed the government money. Late payments had been the rule for at least twenty years, and yet not until July 1981 was interest charged for late payments; the loss of interest alone came to more than $1.6 million in 1980. "It is remarkable," the Commission observed with awe, "that USGS royalty collection functions at all, considering that there are virtually no teeth to the system. Meaningful penalties are rarely imposed . . ."

Even if the USGS had wanted to police the industry, it couldn't have. "In 1982, there were 63 USGS field inspectors for 17,522 onshore leases and more than 55,000 wells." Many remote leases were never inspected.

As for the outright pirating of oil, that was so easily accomplished that nobody had any solid measure of it. David Linowes, Commission chairman, said, "We have no handle on how much is being stolen, but we've been told that as soon as it gets dark, the trucks begin running through the oil fields like it's midtown city. If they see the feds coming, they shut off the valve and get onto a state road [where federal law enforcement authorities have no jurisdiction]. They find the cracks."

Many of the wells, of course, are remote and unattended. Oil pumped from them is usually stored in a battery of easily accessible tanks. H. P.

---

shooter; Michel T. Halbouty, former president of the American Association of Petroleum Geologists and a top oil producer; Mary Gardiner Jones, a former Federal Trade commissioner and president of the Consumer Interest Research Institute; Charles J. Mankin, director of the Oklahoma Geological Survey and former vice-chairman of the National Academy of Sciences' Board of Mineral and Energy Resources; and Elmer B. Staats, who, as comptroller general of the United States, had presided over most of the GAO's investigations of the royalty chaos.

Walter, a USGS engineer, told the Commission, "A typical tank battery can contain two hundred barrels of oil on a lease site. That's like putting a $5,000 bill on the ground and putting a rock on top of it. There's nothing in the world to keep a crook from driving up and stealing that oil."

Royalties are paid according to how much oil is metered at time of sale. But if the oil is diverted through another pipeline before it reaches the meter, it can be safely sold on the black market, right? Right. Some producers, eager to avoid the windfall and other taxes, were suspected of bootlegging their own oil in this way. "The USGS rules are intended to guard against diversions of this sort," wrote the Commission. "But the USGS inspection program of September 1980 and January 1981 showed the rules are often violated." And the USGS was clearly indifferent.

Equally indifferent to the theft of oil were the big companies, though they were often the ones being ripped off. Officials of six major oil and gas companies and three large independent crude-oil producers talked with the Commission; none was upset by the stealing. As the Commission pointed out, "Even very substantial losses due to theft may be acceptable, from a cost-effectiveness point of view, to corporations which are among the largest in the world. Six oil companies are among the top ten industrial companies in the United States; their 1980 sales ranged from $26 billion up to $103 billion. By way of comparison, California, the most populous of the 50 states, had a budget of $22.4 billion in 1980. For a company taking in $25 billion a year, losses on the order of $25 million, for example, would amount to only one tenth of one percent of sales."

But, for taxpayers, the lost royalty on that $25 million comes to $3.1 million.

The Commission estimated that for the decade of the 1980s, the producers would pay more than $90 billion in royalties—if they wanted to. If they didn't want to, if they wanted to juggle their books instead, or if they wanted to bootleg part of their own oil, or if they wanted to skip the expense of policing their leases and let thieves haul away some of it, then the loss to taxpayers would, or might, total as much as $1.35 billion.

As of 1983, no enthusiastic crackdown was in sight.

* * *

Efforts to uncover all the overcharging that had gone on since 1973 and to return the money to consumers ended in frustration with the Carter administration and shifted to farce with the Reagan administration. Producers, refiners, pipeline operators, brokers, middlemen, retailers—all had their special ways of cheating, and all had been successful. Never before had crime paid so well and with so little risk. Few were caught and virtually no one was punished, as Representative Bob Eckhardt discovered in hearings he conducted as a finale to his political life. (A flood of oil money swamped him in the 1980 election.) He and his Subcommittee on Oversight and Investigations concentrated on one of the variations of miscertification. This one had to do with stripper oil.

During all the years that other oil prices were controlled, the product of stripper wells (wells that produced less than ten barrels a day) was not. It could be sold at world prices. The favoritism was logical, being aimed at encouraging producers to squeeze the last drop from old wells. If stripper oil had been controlled at "old" oil prices, it could have commanded only about $6 per barrel, hardly enough to tempt producers to keep the wells flowing. But, as world prices shot up, stripper wells became quite profitable, and by the end of 1979, with world prices hitting $34 and up, stripper wells were little gold mines. (The term "stripper" might seem to imply that only a small quantity of oil, nationally, was at issue. In fact, for some time, stripper wells were supplying about 15 percent of all U.S. oil.)

The stripper price exemption obviously invited cheating. Eckhardt's staff calculated that enough old oil had been miscertified as stripper during 1979 and the first half of 1980 to put $1.5 billion in somebody's pocket. What were Department of Energy enforcers doing to crack down? Eckhardt haled DOE officials to Capitol Hill to ask them.

His question was simple enough: "Now, has any individual served as much as one day in jail for any type of willful violation of DOE petroleum price and allocation regulations?"

Carl Carrollo, solicitor in DOE's Office of Special Counsel for Compliance, gave an equally simple response: "The answer to that, I think, is no."

In all those years, not one single white-collar criminal had spent a day in jail for robbing consumers by miscertifying stripper oil? No, not one. But Carrollo, to laughter in the committee chamber, promised, "I will keep looking."[4]

***

---

4. Usually the DOE failed for lack of trying, but sometimes it also had bad luck. Among the many brokers suspected of juggling labels was one Robert P. Sutton, a secretive oilman from Tulsa. Allegedly, IRS records showed that in 1975, before he became a broker, Sutton had a total income of $7,998 and paid $541 in taxes. Then he set up two reselling operations, BPM (Bob's Petroleum Marketing) Ltd. and Scurry Oil Company. By 1980, his companies were reselling an incredible $2.7 *billion* worth of oil and turning a $43 million profit. In 1981 a federal grand jury in Tulsa indicted him for fraudulent mislabeling that resulted in overcharges costing consumers between $2 billion and $4 billion. Not even the giant companies had been accused of mispricing so much oil.

If an oilman must stand trial for fraud, Oklahoma is by far the best place for him to be; in that state, judges are notoriously sympathetic to anyone who handles crude. And so it came to pass that Federal Judge James Ellison, ruling that the government hadn't prepared its case as tidily as he thought it should, dismissed all charges of oil mislabeling against Sutton.

And what about the final score on Paul Bloom's efforts? That depends on whether the score is measured by symbolism or substance. Considering the enormity of the task confronting him when he took the job of DOE's special counsel, in 1977, he must be judged to have done a good job, at least symbolically. He had joined a DOE that was operating in an atmosphere of collusion and lethargy. "We found," he recalled in 1980, "that some [DOE] auditors—that is, those assigned to individual refineries to collect data—had moved television sets into their offices and spent the day watching game shows and soap operas. Once a week a guy from the company would hand them an envelope and that would be their report."

Bloom had changed all that. But he and his staff of six hundred had *not* fulfilled their assignment, hadn't come close to policing all the companies they were supposed to police: two hundred refiners, nineteen thousand crude-oil producers, and twenty-five thousand wholesalers. Nevertheless, by concentrating on the largest fifteen refiners, they at least had uncovered pricing violations that added up to some $10 billion, and by the time he left office, on January 19, 1981, Bloom had negotiated the "return" of more than $1 billion in settlements, of a sort. When a coalition of consumer, labor, and public-interest organizations filed a lawsuit against DOE, in October 1981, they protested that "only about $100 million—or less than one percent of the total allegations—has been set aside for consumers, either for refunds or indirect benefits.[5] DOE's overcharge settlements represent a monstrous consumer fraud. The settlements are heralded with great fanfare, but, in fact, most of the agreements allow the offending refiner to keep the lion's share of the overcharged funds. DOE has hardly made a dent in the $10 billion in overcharges."

Quite true. In fact, with one pronouncement, President Ronald Reagan had straightened out the slight dent left by Bloom. In negotiating "repayments" (the word belongs in quotes because rarely were the companies actually asked to repay what consumers had paid them) of overcharges, Bloom had been most successful at getting the companies to promise that they would, for a given period of time, charge a certain amount less than they otherwise *could* have charged under the federal oil price control program. These agreements, which totaled hundreds of millions of dollars, would work, however, only so long as there was an absolute ceiling

5. On the very day he left office, Bloom gave $4 million to four charitable groups—$1 million each to the Salvation Army, the National Council of Churches, the National Conference of Catholic Charities, and the Council of Jewish Federations—with instructions to give the money to "the most acutely needy." The money had come from a settlement with Amoco. It wasn't much, but among overcharge payments that actually found their way back to the man on the street, it was one of the larger amounts. The Reagan administration immediately took steps to make it less. Ruling the disbursement "unauthorized," it forced the organizations to give back one million dollars.

by which to measure the reductions. In other words, if Company X agreed that its punishment would be to sell crude oil for six months for 10 percent less than the ceiling, the punishment could be measured only if the federal ceiling was known to be, say, $33 a barrel.

As soon as Reagan was sworn in, however, he decontrolled oil prices[6] and, with that one action, wiped out and made meaningless all settlements of that type; for what did 10 percent of the-sky's-the-limit come to? It was impossible to measure.

Of course, there were many other overcharge cases that had not been settled when Reagan reached Washington; indeed, of the $10.8 billion in alleged overcharges, about $9.4 billion were still pending. Nothing had been done, for instance, to collect the more than $1 billion each that Exxon, Texaco, and Gulf were accused of improperly charging. And what did Reagan intend to do about it? That became clear enough when his administration proposed slashing DOE's bill-collecting budget by 80 percent. That, plus laying down an edict that pending audits and lawsuits against all companies must be completed within one year—an impossibility—prompted the accurate judgment from ex-counsel Bloom: "What this amounts to is amnesty for the oil industry under the guise of budget-cutting." So many nasty remarks were made by Democrats on Capitol Hill that Reagan decided not to slash the enforcement budget by more than 50 percent, and his Energy Secretary, James B. Edwards, promised with all the firmness of a former dentist, "There will be no amnesty for any oil company, large or small."

However, that promise didn't jibe with policy statements made in 1982 by Rayburn D. Hanzlik, chief of the Energy Department's Economic Regulatory Administration. (Hanzlik, before coming to the Reagan administration, had been a legal adviser to an Alaska oil refinery project.) Hanzlik was bothered. Where did the public get the idea that the major oil refineries had bilked the public of more than $10 billion over a seven-year period? "Grossly inflated," he said. What about the General Accounting Office's own estimate that the overcharges totaled $13 billion? No, no, "grossly inflated," said Hanzlik. Well, how much wrongful costs *had* been passed on to the public during those seven years? Hanzlik, with a straight face, replied that he didn't think they had gotten away with more than, oh, say, $1.5 billion to $3 billion.

---

6. By shortening Carter's phased-decontrol program by eight months, Reagan put an estimated extra $10 billion in the oil industry's kitty. Not exactly to pay him back, but to show their appreciation, some of the good old oil boys chipped in $270,000 in March 1981 to help redecorate Ronnie's and Nancy's living quarters in the White House. Some of the givers, alas, displayed a short memory and fickleness. Carl Anderson, an Oklahoma City oilman, for example, donated $10,000 with the explanation that Reagan had a more favorable attitude toward the energy industry than Carter. Fiddlesticks! No matter how favorable Reagan's attitude might be, it could not possibly be more generous than Carter's.

He added that his agency, obviously already dead in spirit, would be officially out of business before the year was out, if he had his way.

Thus ended the most elaborate, the most ballyhooed consumer-protection project of the energy decade.

***

The dazzling days between 1973 and 1980, "when oil prices and profits seemed to be on a never-ending rise," as James E. Lee, chairman of Gulf Oil, described them, created unhealthful illusions and resulted in a few disasters and near disasters.

Marvelous examples were found in the nations touching both of our borders. Mexico could not wait to cash in on its enormous new oil discoveries, so it began mortgaging the future, borrowing heavily from foreign banks, especially U.S. banks. And these banks, assuming, as Lee put it, that the rise of prices would never end, lined up for what they perceived as the very profitable privilege of lending to Mexico.

By the time the oil market had begun to sicken, Mexico was the biggest debtor in the developing world—in hock to the tune of about $81 billion, of which about $22 billion was owed to U.S. banks, including more than $1 billion each to Chase Manhattan, Citibank, Manufacturers Hanover, and Bank of America.

In 1982, Mexico took in only $12 billion from the sale of oil, which was about half of what was expected, and oil sales were supposed to be the foundation of the nation's economy. Everything went to pot; the peso was rapidly becoming worthless; the nation seemed to be on the verge of bankruptcy. So the United States stepped in with loans to help prop it up —which is to say, our government lent money to Mexico so that it wouldn't have to default on its loans, causing massive problems, to say the least, among the banks of this country and its industrialized allies.

One might have expected such bungling from Mexico; it has seldom done anything right. But why was Canada in trouble—sophisticated Canada, which seems less a foreign country than an extension of the United States?

The source of its problems, or at least one of the principal sources, was this very closeness—or at least Canada's reaction to it. Many Canadians were fed up with being treated as an extension. Nothing irritated them quite so much as having U.S.-based companies overwhelmingly dominate their energy industry.

Although the province of Alberta, where most of Canada's oil and gas seems to be, was perfectly happy to go along with the heavy U.S. investments, many central government officials of a more nationalistic sort, including Prime Minister Pierre Trudeau, were not. So, in 1980, with Canada still riding high on a wave of oil income, Trudeau announced his National Energy Program. It discriminated against foreign-owned firms by giving subsidies to oil companies that were more than 50 percent Canadian-owned; also, the new law allowed the Canadian Government to seize (with compensation) a 25 percent interest in all production on federal lands.[7]

Trudeau's government, listening to euphoric stock-market analysts and blowhards within the oil industry, projected that world oil prices would continue to rise every year and by 1986 would reach $62 a barrel. With that kind of bonanza subjected to Canadian taxes, Trudeau believed, he could underwrite the Canadianization of oil and all other key industries. Indeed, he was gambling *everything* on the belief that prices would continue to climb; the taxes from them would be the underpinnings for his entire economic strategy of nationalization.

His vision of Canada's future, at least in the oil business, was epitomized by Dome Petroleum Ltd., the largest Canadian-owned oil and gas company; and the spirit of Canadianization was personified by John P. "Smilin' Jack" Gallagher, chairman and founder of Dome. Gallagher was a wildcatter deluxe. He had ultimate faith in Canada's energy future and in Dome's future (he took his salary in Dome stock). In the hysterically optimistic last years of the 1970s, he bought up other oil companies and so much exploratory land (15 million acres) that within forty-eight months Dome's assets jumped from $1 billion to $9.4 billion—making it one of Canada's most asset-rich companies. It was Canada's largest gas producer. It controlled the only pipeline link between the oil fields of Alberta and the big markets of eastern Canada. It was the premier explorer in the Arctic seas. Dome, in short, was looked upon as the shining example of the success that can come to a company owned by Canadians.

But, like Trudeau's program, Dome's plans all rested on continued ris-

---

7. The move toward seminationalization of the industry was understandable, considering the outlandish percentage of Canada's industry—not only oil, but all industries—that was owned by Yanks. Still, it was also a bit unfair. Until the 1940s, Canadian oilmen had been unsuccessful at finding a major field. They had spent a great deal of money in the search and were beginning to despair. Needing outside financing to continue the gamble, they literally begged U.S. oil companies to come in. The government of Canada joined the plea. And so they came—and conquered. At 3:55 P.M. on February 13, 1947, oil erupted in a snow-covered grainfield eighteen miles southwest of Edmonton, Alberta, at Leduc No. 1 well, owned by Imperial Oil Ltd., a subsidiary of Standard Oil of New Jersey. That was the beginning of Canada's energy life. In 1946, the year before Leduc, Canada produced only enough oil and gas to fill 11 percent of its domestic demand. In twenty years, it was producing 90 percent of domestic requirements. U.S. investors were crucial all the way. Typical was the experience of John C. Rudolph, one of Canada's luckiest wildcatters and discoverer of one of the major oil pools in Alberta. When Rudolph set out to raise $7.5 million to organize his second oil company, he recalls, "We spent four hard, long arduous months trying to sell this thing in Canada. Then we broadened this thing to the United Kingdom and the United States and we sold this thing in five weeks. That kind of risk capital just isn't available in Canada." Having used U.S. money to arrive at the door of energy independence, Canada now moved to squelch its partners.

ing prices. Even stable prices would not have been enough. And when prices actually began to fall, in 1981, Canada's dream of a prosperous Canadianization and Smilin' Jack's dream of becoming the Rockefeller of the Arctic seas began to evaporate. By 1982, with Dome's stock sliding from 21 to 2½ within a year, there was even doubt about the company's survival. There were also doubts about the survival of four major Canadian banks that had loaned Dome billions. And if Dome went under, Trudeau's nationalistic energy policies would probably sink too, from shame.

**

The startling thing about these developments in Mexico and Canada was that the governments of both nations made their mistakes with the encouragement of bankers, who themselves stood to lose billions of dollars from the errors they financed. Bankers, of course, are notoriously dumb. But in this case they must have been acting on the advice and counsel of the largest oil companies. As we have already seen, the boards of directors of the world's biggest banks are crowded with officials from the biggest oil companies. They are thick as thieves, and their prosperity lies in not steering each other wrong. We must assume that the major oil companies had told the banks that prices would indeed continue to climb forever, and therefore their loans were in no danger at all.

How could the oilmen have been so wrong? How could they have been so in error about the market and the world's economy that they would see their forecast blow back in their faces within twelve months? The answer is simple: oil experts aren't nearly so smart as they think they are. They never have been. Clifton C. Garvin, Jr., Exxon's chairman and chief executive officer, tells the truth when he says, "Predicting the course of events is like trying to tattoo a soap bubble."

By the 1980s it had become plain enough that price and supply predictions by experts shouldn't be taken too seriously. RAND Corporation, in 1981, using oil company statistics, estimated that the United States has a domestic supply that could last for twenty to forty years. On the other hand, the Heritage Foundation's energy experts, also using oil company statistics, estimated that the United States has enough oil to last forty-six to seventy-four years. Neither prediction was of any consequence, one way or the other, because predicting the future of oil and gas has become about as frivolous as a parlor game.

The fog hung over price predictions as well as supply predictions. On August 24, 1980, that fine financial writer Hobart Rowen, of the Washington *Post*, after making a broad sounding of the experts, said, "Everyone expects the cartel [OPEC] to force an additional real price increase of 2 to 3 percent a year for the next ten years or so." Almost exactly two years later, on August 29, 1982, the New York *Times* trotted out its financial writer Douglas Martin to tell us, "There is scant chance, according to many analysts, despite OPEC's best efforts, that oil prices, adjusted for inflation, will increase over the next decade and perhaps beyond."

* * *

Supposedly the idea behind raising the price of oil and gas was to instill enthusiasm in the oilmen to go out and discover just how much energy was down there, and bring it up. A few oilmen, a few of the traditional wildcatters, really did mean to keep their promise to make fair use of their decontrolled profits. Greed was an integral motivation for them, but it was a productive greed. They wanted more money—and more, and more—because they honestly wanted to use it to squeeze every drop of oil from the earth or from under the ocean, from however remote or inaccessible an area, sincerely believing that with luck and a few more billions of dollars they could—contrary to the forecasts of establishment geologists—find enough lush new pools to make us independent of OPEC.

But this frontier spirit was rare. Most oilmen did not want consumers to supply them with a bigger grubstake so that they could go farther afield to explore. They wanted to get rich without risk. This was certainly true of the international oil companies. In 1980, the top twenty spent the largest part of their spare cash on nonpetroleum investments: buying into beef processing, paperback books, shipbuilding, real estate, trucking, fertilizer, data processing, life insurance, medical equipment, television, and other industries that had nothing at all to do with bringing oil out of the ground.

In 1978, the top twenty oil companies and their affiliates spent a little over half a billion dollars buying other companies. By 1981, that expenditure had multiplied twenty-four times, to more than $12 billion. When they lusted after more oil, they went the safe way—merging with or buying up other oil companies (while the Justice Department Antitrust Division paid no attention); the preferred tactic, of course, was to buy undervalued oil companies—what cynics called drilling for oil on the floor of the New York Stock Exchange. When Mobil tried to buy Marathon, in 1981, for example, *The Wall Street Journal* reported this comment from a Wall Street analyst: "Marathon's shares recently had traded at such low levels relative to their underlying value . . . that a takeover is an opportunity . . . The cost of finding oil is $12 to $15 a barrel. By buying Marathon at $85 a share, Mobil can buy it at about $3 to $3.50 per barrel."

These multibillion-dollar purchases of course did not add one ounce of oil to the nation's reserves. They did not enlarge the pie; they simply rearranged the way it was cut.[8]

---

8. A couple of the noteworthy acquisitions were the purchase of Belridge Oil by Shell

To be sure, the majors were buying up a great deal of land, but apparently only to sit on. Between 1976 and 1980, they increased their undeveloped landholdings more than 40 percent, but they increased their developed acreage by less than 3 percent. After a study of the way that sixteen majors had spent their loot, the consumer-oriented lobby Energy Action concluded, in late 1981, "Decontrol and higher OPEC prices have more than doubled the funds available to the major oil companies over the last two years. Yet, despite a domestic drilling boom that the industry's public relations apparatus never tires of publicizing, only one fourth of the additional funds available to the companies is being spent to find oil and gas in the United States."

On the surface, it might have appeared that industry's failure to take up the slack was not from want of trying. For a while, oilmen were sinking wells furiously, more than sixty thousand wells in 1980—more than twice as many as were sunk in the early 1970s. But behind those statistics was a caution approaching cowardliness. These weren't Dad Joiners or Smilin' Jack Gallaghers, hunting new fields; they were hunting the quick and certain buck. Most of the drilling was of development wells—wells sunk near existing wells, where chances of a dry hole are much lower. Two out of three of the new wells were paying off, but because they were tapping old sources, they weren't paying off as wells used to. The average potential payoff for a successful well even as late as 1977 was 90 barrels a day; in 1980, with the touted "risk-takers" going for the sure thing, the average potential had dropped to 62.1 barrels.

So the promise that rising prices would result in the security of larger reserves had turned out not only to be false, but one that the oil industry was clearly making no real effort to live up to. To be sure, it could be said—and apologists for the industry did say—that hunting new fields was becoming more difficult, simply because such profuse exploration had taken place over the decades. No country in the world had perforated itself with so many wells: 2.5 million. Two of every three oil wells drilled in the world had been drilled in the continental United States. In the nation's lushest county, Plaquemines Parish, Louisiana, more oil and gas wells had been drilled than in all of the Middle East. More wells had been drilled in Arkansas than in all Africa. "The petroleum industry is gradually running out of ideas as to where oil and gas may still be found in the United States," oil expert Richard Nehring argued, "not because of lack of creativity and imagination, but because of the increasing exhaustion of geological possibilities." Maybe. But the

---

on December 11, 1979, for $3.6 billion cash, the largest acquisition up to that date; the purchase of Texas Pacific Oil by Sun Company on September 15, 1980, for $2.3 billion cash, the second-largest business transaction in U.S. history to that date; and Occidental Petroleum's purchase of Cities Service for $4 billion in 1982, making the combine the eighth-largest oil firm in the United States.

statistics indicated that the oilmen weren't even *trying* very hard. While the crude-oil price soared 1600 percent in the decade, the number of *exploratory* wells in the United States had risen only 10 percent. Anyway, when the oil companies had pleaded with Congress for price decontrols, they had said nothing about running out of places to look. To the contrary, they made America sound virtually like virgin land.

*

If further evidence was needed that U.S. energy policy was still being made at industry's cash register and not in response to national and consumer needs, that evidence surfaced when the price of oil began to drop, in 1981. From the very first softening of prices, oilmen began sticking their rigs under wraps. Even though 1982 prices were still so high that a new well could recover all costs in six to nine months (compared to three-to-five-year payouts prior to the first big price jump, in 1974), the rate of drilling declined more than 30 percent. For years, the big companies had been finagling to get the outer continental shelf opened up; *That's* where the future lies, they had said. Well, with the coming of that fanatical free-enterpriser Interior Secretary James Watt, it *was* opened up wildly, irresponsibly, for them to come and take whatever they wanted. But oil companies took only 29 percent of the offshore offerings in 1981—down from the 50 percent they had snapped up in 1979 and 1980, when prices were exploding. Watt's proposal to open one billion offshore acres to leasing over a five-year period suddenly drew less than rave responses from oil's boardrooms. Whatever enthusiasm the oil execs did muster was due only to the new giveaway inducements. In pre-Watt days, the government decided which tracts to put on the auction block; Watt changed the routine to allow the companies to bid on *any* unleased tracts in vast designated areas. In May 1983, for example, he opened 40 million Gulf of Mexico acres to bids—ten times the usual government offering—and begged the oilmen to take their pick at bargain prices. It was an offer they couldn't refuse. They swooped in and took 656 tracts for $3.47 billion—a new auction record for offshore Gulf leases. The previous record had been set in 1980, with $2.7 billion paid for 147 leases. Watt boasted, "We have demonstrated that the marketplace is the right place for decisions to be made regarding allocation of natural resources." Actually, he had only demonstrated that oilmen know a sucker when they see one. The average price paid for the 1983 leases was less than one third the price per lease at the 1980 auction. And having cornered their bargain acreage, the oilmen showed no urgency in moving rigs into position. Their leases allowed them five to ten years for that.[9]

9. By the way, remember the fishermen of Georges Bank? They won. In the fall of 1982, after drilling eight very expensive dry holes, the oil companies pulled out of those fishing grounds and didn't sound eager to come back.

Why the sudden reversal of activity and enthusiasm? It was true that the world, wallowing in a recession, temporarily had cut its oil purchases; and in the United States, the world's biggest oil consumer, conservation measures were beginning to work. New cars were averaging twice as many miles per gallon as they had gotten in 1974. Consumption of all petroleum products in 1982 was down 22 percent from what it had been three years earlier. So, naturally, prices were down.

But this wouldn't last forever. The American Petroleum Institute reported that half of the drop in U.S. consumption in 1981 was in residual oil, used primarily by industry. Obviously, when the economy bounced back, that reduction would quickly be wiped out. As for gasoline prices, motorists apparently were getting used to paying well over a dollar a gallon (full-size and intermediate cars accounted for 53 percent of sales by American auto makers in 1982, up from 46 percent in 1981). Peering into the future through smeared binoculars, the Department of Energy predicted in the spring of 1982 that gasoline would be selling for more than $5 a gallon (adjusted for expected inflation) within ten years; if DOE's prediction was 100 percent exaggerated, which was always possible, it would still mean that gasoline prices were going to stay on the escalator.

So there was no sound, long-range reason for industry to begin retrenching; it was simply responding with its usual economic myopia. On the other hand, there was every reason for the oilmen to show *extra* aggression at this moment if, as they had once claimed, they seriously wanted to free us from dependence on an unreliable and hostile source of oil. Isn't that what they had always said? Give us more money so we can find oil to free you from the blackmail of OPEC. Yes, that is exactly what they had said. Well, now was their chance. Rocked by the world recession, OPEC reduced production one third below the 1979 level to shore up prices, but it didn't work, and panicky members started cutting the best deals they could make on the side. Staggering into 1983, beset by internal bickering, OPEC was forced to cut prices and again cut production. Man oh man, here was the opening! It might be futile to hope that in the long haul the United States could free itself from at least partial dependence on Middle East oil, but it would not have been futile to seize this depressed moment—one of the few moments in recent years when buyers, not sellers, were king of the world market, perhaps one of the last lulls before the start of what former CIA director Stansfield Turner forecast as a "vicious struggle" for oil and other precious resources in the 1980s—to subject "OPECers" to the savagery of some good old-fashioned capitalistic price wars. Now was a magnificent time for U.S. oilmen to *increase* exploration and development, and increase them again, to flood the market, forcing OPEC prices down farther, poisoning the cartel with further disunity.

What a pipedream! The suggestion that we hunt-and-pump our way to some glorious revenge could be offered as a serious scenario only if the companies on whom we rely to search for and produce oil had the same objectives as the American people and only if those companies really wanted to break OPEC's back. But why would they want to break the back they had ridden to riches in the 1970s, a back that perhaps could, with a little pampering through hard times, carry them farther?[10]

If OPEC prices were to drop to $20 a barrel, or $15, carrying domestic oil prices down with them, most consumers would rise early in the morning to spend the whole day rejoicing. So would many have-not nations, whose energy debts of the 1970s have pushed them toward bankruptcy and whose bankruptcies would drop the world into an economic pit— something that by late 1982 was seen as a distinct possibility.

But oilmen, and consultants who hold the hands of oilmen, and some of those charming fellows who used their government positions to help boost oil prices to their impossible levels in the first place, see things differently. In January 1983 former Energy Secretary James Schlesinger removed his pipe and uttered comments that were worthy of him: "The United States should not be engaged in attempting to bring down the cartel or break oil prices . . ." Peter Walters, chairman of British Petroleum, warned that a sharp drop in world oil prices would be "disastrous." Oil consultant Walter Levy said $20 oil "would be an outright catastrophe." John Lichtblau, one of the best-known oil economists, talked nervously of the need to take steps to guarantee that there would be no sudden price decline.

If OPEC prices were to fall to a certain level, well . . . some experts began talking about the need for, or the likelihood of, another import quota, or the imposition of a tariff, as a price-fixing apparatus to protect the domestic oil industry.

Writing in the December 21, 1981, *Newsweek,* saucy Christopher T. Rand, author of *Making Democracy Safe for Oil,* suggested, "In 1959,

---

10. The symbiotic skulduggery between OPEC and the major oil companies has always been accepted as a matter of course by our government. As the U.S. State Department's Bureau of Intelligence and Research pointed out in 1977, "because of their vertical organization, the international oil companies presently are important to OPEC's survival. These companies provide a cartel-like marketing mechanism that allows easy pass-through of crude oil price increases" and "provides crucial expertise to keep national oil companies operating effectively." In return, the companies get "secure supplies to feed their downstream investment." The Bureau predicted (it didn't take much insight to do so) that "if OPEC members continue to market most of their crude oil through the multinational companies, the threat to the cartel is fairly low."

Despite the tribulations of recent years, this restless love affair has not cooled. And although the independent oil companies have less to do directly with OPEC, their passion for the cartel's prices is no less ardent. After all, the best guarantee of high domestic prices is high OPEC prices.

President Eisenhower, faced with a growing world oil surplus, imposed a stiff oil-import quota system that lasted until the price of foreign oil began to rise above domestic prices again in 1973. President Reagan may have no choice but to follow suit . . ."

And what would be the rationale for keeping prices high? Fellows such as Levy and Lichtblau and Walters and Schlesinger offered humanitarian reasons. They would rescue the poor bankers who made bad loans to oil companies and oil-producing nations. They argued that high prices are a good-neighbor policy, propping up the crooked government of Mexico and the bad guessers of Canada. They argued that maintaining high oil prices would make us nicer citizens—more eager to conserve. Low prices would send us back to lives of profligacy and dissipation. In other words, we should continue submitting to impoverishment for our own good.

But another old faithful reason was also heard again. To let oil prices get too low, said William Brown, director of energy and technological studies for the Hudson Institute, would be a "threat to national security." Ah, yes. As prices sagged into the 1980s, one began to hear that magic phrase more often: price-fixing in the name of "national security."

Rhetorically, at least, the Oil Decade had come full circle.

* * *

Attaining independence through new crude-oil discoveries might be an impossible dream, but if the formula was expanded to include synthetic fuels—especially oil squeezed from our vast shale deposits, oil and gas rendered from our equally vast coal deposits—surely independence could be just around the corner, couldn't it?

This was the note struck by President Carter when he promised that "just as we harnessed American dedication and brainpower to put men on the moon," this country would achieve energy independence "through technology." It was the note struck again in the summer of 1980, when he signed into law the last major piece of his energy program, the Energy Security Act, through which the government intended to spend $20 billion in loans and price guarantees to produce the technological magic. "This," said Carter at the White House signing, "is a proud day for America. The keystone of our national energy policy is at last being put in place."

If synfuels were the keystone, then the entire edifice was fated to fall, not necessarily because the concept was in error,[11] but because the

---

11. Many environmentalists thought the program was replete with mischief, partly because synthetic-fuel plants would leach water needed for farming. But largely their complaint was that nobody knew what effect synfuel wastes would have on human beings and animals. For this group, a *Science* magazine cover became the battle standard; the cover showed a cricket with an extra pair of eyes—the cricket, while an embryo, had been exposed to synfuel wastes.

Many liberals were also against it for humanitarian and ideological reasons. Bob program would be in the hands of the oil industry, and the oil industry had proved over many decades that it did not want to bring synfuels into the marketplace in significant quantities—at least not yet, and probably not for a long time.

But the bleak destiny of Carter's synfuels program could hardly have been anticipated, for, at the moment, some of the big companies' rhetoric was matching his own. They were, of course, ambivalent, almost schizophrenic on the subject: they blew hot and cold. Exxon, for example, had been cool to synthetics in 1979, but only a year later, perhaps intoxicated by the prospects of a billion-dollar handout, it sounded very up. One of its public relations booklets had acknowledged that, until we develop alternative fuels, "the United States economy will be hopelessly hostage to any foreign producers wishing to exercise the power of embargo on oil shipments to gain political ends"; but America could take cheer, because by Exxon's reckoning there were enough known recoverable reserves of coal and oil shale in this country to provide synthetic fuels equal to *one trillion barrels of oil,* and *that,* said Exxon proudly, as though it were about to plunge into synthetic production, is "three times as much energy as the U.S. Geological Survey estimates can be provided by the country's remaining proved and undiscovered reserves of oil and gas. And it's enough to sustain a synthetic fuels industry producing 15 million barrels of oil a day for 175 years." Fifteen million barrels of oil a day, as it happened, was more than twice as much as Saudi Arabia was producing in 1982.

Looking at Exxon's incandescent figures, one could realistically assume that we would soon be able to laugh in the face of all those sullen "OPECers." All it would take was corporate enthusiasm, and Exxon, for the moment, seemed to have plenty. Carter's goal, as outlined in the Energy Security Act, was to produce the synthetic equivalent of five hundred thousand barrels of oil a day by 1987, and then—if all the environmental and economic and social wrinkles had been ironed out—to add another $68 billion to the program and aim to produce 2 million barrels of synthetic fuels a day by 1992.

Nonsense, said Randall Meyer, president of Exxon USA; why settle for such a modest goal? The nation, he said, should shoot for a 15 million-barrel-a-day goal from synthetics. Sure, it would be expensive, but so what? "The investment total required to reach such a volume is stagger-

---

Eckhardt said the Synthetic Fuels Corporation arrangement reminded him of the alliance between industry and government under Nazi Germany. Richard Ottinger, chairman of the House Energy Conservation and Power Subcommittee, said, "The existence of the Synthetic Fuels Corporation today only confirms the most cynical view of the federal government. For while we make low and middle income Americans suffer increasing hardship in the name of economic recovery, we give out billions of dollars in loan guarantees to Exxon, and Texaco, among America's richest corporations— billions for uneconomic ventures that the private sector won't finance."

ing," he said, "almost $800 billion in 1980 dollars. This expense would be spread over thirty years or more, however, and *is within the capabilities of private companies.*" (Emphasis added)

Exxon certainly seemed to be getting into the spirit of the Carter program when it announced, on May 12, 1980, that it had acquired control of the Colony shale project, in Garfield County, Colorado, and in league with Tosco Corporation would be producing forty-seven thousand barrels of shale oil a day by 1983.[12]

It appeared that Exxon was at last willing to put the government's money where its mouth was when, in 1981, it asked for and was granted a $1.1 billion guarantee for the notorious Colony project, the largest synthetic-fuels pilot plant in the nation, which had been floating on the horizon like an elusive *Flying Dutchman* for decades, borne along by gusty promises but always just out of reach of fulfillment. Did the $1.1 billion grant mean that finally Exxon would bring the project into commercial production?

The answer to that came ten months later. The roller coaster of enthusiasm had hit bottom again, and Exxon president Meyer announced that his company was pulling out of Colony, because the drop in crude-oil prices had made it no longer attractive. For years, this was the excuse oil companies had given for doing nothing with the shale lands they had leased. Exxon was not alone. Gulf, Standard of Indiana, and Mobil were also slowing down or shutting down their shale experiments. Some companies—Standard of California, for instance, one of the biggest leasers of shale land—complained that the government wasn't offering enough incentive. No, billion-dollar loans and price guarantees weren't enough. They wanted tax credits, too, for their shale work.

But what about making oil and gas from coal? Didn't the industry want to do that? After all, they owned plenty of coal, didn't they? Ah, yes. The ten oil companies with the largest energy reserves—Conoco, Exxon, Phillips, Mobil, Occidental, Sun, Texaco, Shell, Atlantic Richfield, and Standard of Ohio, in that order—together own an estimated 15 billion barrels of crude oil, which equals a little less than one third the amount of oil controlled by Saudi Arabia. *But* these same companies own coal reserves *equivalent to 191 billion barrels of oil,* enough to keep

---

12. Philadelphia *Inquirer* reporters Donald L. Barlett and James B. Steele, in a series about the mirage of synthetic-fuel production in this country, commented on this point: "Ambitious as Exxon's plans might sound, they are actually rather modest. A thriving shale oil industry in Scotland, for example, has produced as much as 67,000 barrels of shale oil a day." They added wryly, "Of course, that was back in 1915." Barlett and Steele also pointed out that twice before in the previous sixteen years, oil companies—the first time, it was Standard Oil of Ohio, in 1964; the second time, Atlantic Richfield, in 1969—had bought into Colony with a great fanfare of promises, only to pull out silently within a couple of years.

OPEC away from our doors until the second half of the twenty-first century.

And even though the major oil companies were spending virtually nothing on developing synthetic techniques (at the end of the 1970s, Mobil was spending two tenths of 1 percent of its revenue on research), actually they didn't have to. The techniques had been perfected long before, and Exxon, a leader in the field, had never tried to hide the fact. In 1929, Standard of New Jersey told its stockholders that "it is now shown to be practicable to convert coal into liquid hydrocarbons at a cost which, although above prevailing oil prices, is not prohibitive." But nothing happened. Several times in the intervening half century, Exxon publicly confirmed its ability to produce gasoline from coal "commercially"— meaning it could be done at a profit. Still nothing happened. In 1980, the year Carter signed the Energy Security Act, Exxon declared that "much synthetic fuels technology . . . is now ready for commercial use . . . and the domestic resource base is adequate to support a very large industry." Still, no action.

The technique of coal conversion is no secret. The government has for thirty-five years been spending hundreds of millions of dollars on synthetic-fuel experiments, and it has had some promising results.

The government-subsidized plant that opened in Louisiana, Missouri, in 1949 succeeded in converting coal to a variety of petroleum products, including gasoline, using techniques that Standard Oil of New Jersey had learned from its German partners. But for some reason it was shut down in 1953, despite the fact that officials at the Interior Department were convinced that if the government pushed ahead, "the production of two million barrels" daily of synthetic fuels—which by coincidence was the same amount Carter would deem a suitable goal for the 1990s— would be possible within "a period of four to five years."

Another dozen pilot plants were established; but it seemed that the more successful they were, the more likely they were to be shut. As America entered the 1980s still talking about the potential of synthetic fuels, still talking, always talking, about the desirability of gaining energy independence, only five of the dozen plants were still operating, none with much encouragement from either industry or the federal government. Typically, Reagan appointed Edward R. Noble, an Oklahoma oilman, to chair the Synthetic Fuels Corporation. Noble had headed the energy-transition team that advised Reagan to kill the SFC. Noble's chairmanship ensured a kind of lingering death. He said his only interest in synfuels was to keep just enough pilot plants going to show OPEC that we had the technology at hand and could use it if they got nasty. He also favored backup synthetic plants in case of war. But as for producing a significant amount of synthetic fuel to compete with crude oil and natural gas, Noble said he wasn't interested.

And neither were the companies. In 1982 the Synthetic Fuels Corporation voted to give away $10 billion for synfuels development, including $3 billion for shale oil. There were no takers. In fact, two and a half years after Carter set up the SFC with its pot of gold and promises that the rainbow would be showing up soon, that agency had not funded one single synthetic fuel project.

The reason, which was obvious enough, had been explained for his denser colleagues by Senator Pete V. Domenici of New Mexico during congressional debate on Carter's SFC bill: "The fact is that under present energy economy conditions, it is simply more profitable for companies to keep their resources in the ground, watching them increase in value, and take their profits from conventional crude oil and natural gas. They wish to develop synthetic fuels at their own speed and under conditions they dictate."

Half a century of history supports that observation.

***

In 1980, the Corporate Data Exchange Inc. issued a marvelously rich lode of information about the 142 largest U.S. energy companies (*CDE Stock Ownership Directory: Energy*). Try as one might to avoid such ugly thoughts, one could not read the CDE directory without suspecting that there just might be a few tiny breaches of antitrust laws, some mischievous collusion, some conflicts of interest, in all the tightly braided knots recorded within its pages. The editors of the directory, after heaping up their evidence, concluded that "a group of fifty institutional investors control at least 15 percent of the stock of the top thirty-eight energy conglomerates." To talk of fifty institutional investors, however, is to avoid the chilling aura of concentration that permeates the CDE directory. In fact, a handful of financial institutions—banks and insurance companies, mostly—are running the energy show.[13] The CDE found that in the ten largest oil companies, the top five stockholders together owned from 8.56

---

13. One need only look at half a dozen banks to see what's going on. Citicorp is among the top five stockholders of Atlantic Richfield, Conoco, Phillips, Standard of Indiana, Standard of Ohio, and Getty Oil. (Dropping into the second tier of five, it is No. 6 at Exxon, No. 8 at Texaco, No. 8 at Marathon, No. 8 at Union Oil.) Chase Manhattan is among the top five at Exxon, Standard of California, Conoco, Standard of Indiana, Sun Oil, and Mobil. (It is No. 10 at Atlantic Richfield.) Bankers Trust of New York is among the top five stockholders at Conoco, Mobil, Getty, and Sun. (And No. 8 at Exxon, No. 10 at Standard of Indiana, No. 9 at Amerada Hess.) Manufacturers Hanover is among the top five at Texaco, Atlantic Richfield, Phillips, Exxon, and Standard of California. (It is No. 9 at Standard of Indiana, No. 7 at Amerada Hess, No. 6 at Getty, No. 10 at Superior, which is the largest independent oil company in terms of reserves, No. 9 at Union.) J. P. Morgan, parent of Morgan Guaranty Trust, is among the top five at Mobil, Marathon Oil, Superior, and Exxon. (It is No. 10 at Cities Service.) Chemical Bank of New York, aside from being the top stockholder at Ashland Oil, is No. 6 at Atlantic Richfield and Cities Service, No. 9 at Standard of California, No. 7 at Superior, and No. 10 at Exxon.

percent (Texaco) to 80.68 percent (Shell), with the average being 23.6 percent. Bear in mind that the House Banking Subcommittee on Domestic Finance "presumes" that control of 10 percent of a corporation's stock equates with control of the corporation, that as low as 5 percent qualifies for control, and that even 1 or 2 percent of ownership offers "tremendous influence."

If that web of ownership does not work toward nullifying competition within the industry, what in the world would? And yet when the CDE directory was issued, it was followed by a strangely muffled response. William Winpisinger, president of the International Association of Machinists and Aerospace Workers, asked, "Where is the cry of protest?" Where, indeed? Even the best of the daily press gave the report only a few inches, and promptly forgot it. Television gave it no coverage at all. Winpisinger, perhaps the most colorful of current union leaders, was thought by many to be excessive when he said, "The CDE study makes it clear that what we have in America is a vast in-house energy and financial conspiracy that makes the Mob look like a bunch of amateurs." Conspiracy is a word sophisticates prefer not to use; but, in fact, with the CDE directory at hand, it is easy to use the word without apology. The interlocking nature of U.S. capital at the top, as shown in its pages, can hardly be accidental or innocent.

Not only is the intense concentration seen in stock ownership, but in the sharing of lawyers. The CDE's "Index of Legal Counsels / Washington Reps" discloses, for example, that Howrey & Simon represents no less than six major oil companies: Exxon, Gulf, Mobil, Shell, Tenneco, and Texaco; that Covington & Burling represents Atlantic Richfield, Standard of Ohio, and Superior; that Mobil and Cities Service share the confidential legal talents of McClure & Trotter, et cetera. The oil companies claim competitiveness and independence, but their most confidential trade information is cared for by shared lawyers.

The CDE findings indicated that antitrust enforcement by the Justice Department and the Federal Trade Commission is puny, at best. It was a conclusion reached again in 1981 by that remarkable team of reporters Donald L. Barlett and James B. Steele, after a year-long study of the oil industry for the Philadelphia *Inquirer*. "Government antitrust lawyers," they wrote, "have routinely attacked those oil industry mergers that would have little effect on consumers, while rubber-stamping mergers— especially the acquisition by oil companies of firms that own competing fuels—that could cost consumers billions of dollars . . . Today, oil company holdings of coal reserves may be counted in the hundreds of billions of dollars, when calculated at the current world oil price.

"The coal reserves of one company, Phillips Petroleum—which ranks 12th among all oil companies in sales—are worth $1 trillion, based on the world price of oil. That is equal to 24 General Motors Corps. and Du Pont Cos. combined.

"Even though coal and oil compete for some of the same markets, the Justice Department has brought *no antitrust charges against oil companies that have purchased coal companies.*" (Emphasis added.)

Nor had Justice brought any antitrust charges to block oil company acquisition of uranium mines, shale lands, or solar-energy companies. Interestingly, those two concrete watchdogs of antitrust, Justice and the Federal Trade Commission, had shown the same kind of indifference to oil companies' buying up copper companies (see chapter on 1978), a phenomenon that continued in 1979, when Standard of Indiana bought Cyprus Mines for half a billion, Standard of California bid $4 billion for the remaining 80 percent of Amax (it had bought 20 percent in 1975), and Standard of Ohio bid $1.7 billion for Kennecott, the nation's largest copper producer, in 1981—thereby placing more than 55 percent of domestic copper-mining capacity in the hands of oilmen.

By 1982, the likelihood that the Federal Trade Commission would ever seriously crack down on oil-company mergers seemed more remote than ever. Loaded with Reagan appointees committed to allowing free rein to "market forces," the FTC in 1982 issued a 298-page study in which it recommended "against any legislative ban on oil-company mergers" because mergers have had "no significant adverse implications on the state of competition in the industry."

But the end of antitrust enforcement against Big Oil was best measured by the death—so expected as to be scarcely noticed or mourned—of the FTC's suit aimed at breaking up the nation's eight largest oil companies. Called the *"Exxon case,"* although in fact seven other companies were also targeted, the lawsuit was recognized from the beginning as probably hopeless; but it had been, since being filed in 1973, the flag, the last-ditch symbol, around which oil critics had rallied. These were realistic critics, though. Senator Phil Hart, who had goaded the FTC into its lawsuit, predicted at the outset, "We won't get a verdict—and relief—for eight or ten years. FTC has to prove not just monopoly power, but anticompetitive behavior. This will mean a search of millions of documents to confuse everyone." (See chapter for 1973.) Well, here it was eight years later and there was no verdict and no relief, because the case was still at the pretrial stage, and the FTC staff officially recommended killing the suit, because it felt the case "could continue without a final judgment . . . until fifteen to twenty years after the filing of the complaint," which would mean sometime between 1988 and 1993. The staff said the oil companies had swamped it in millions of pages of confusing documents and had hampered the case by subpoenaing "massive" amounts of documents from many government agencies, an effort that was calculated to result in never-ending litigation over the question of whether the companies were entitled to the information, and *those* cases would all have to wind their way through court before the government could get on with its original antitrust suit.

The end came as no surprise. The FTC simply didn't have the heart or the money or the personnel to wage such a long-term battle. Oil executives estimated that legal and related fees had, since 1973, cost the eight companies a total of at least $100 million—which was less than one of the defendants, Exxon, had earned every single week of 1980.

***

The Department of Energy, having undergone ten major reorganizations since it was established, in August 1977, entered the 1980s as disorganized and floundering as it had begun. Virtually none of its twenty-eight major departments, which were broken down into more than a hundred subdivisions, could do anything right. It was still storing, at an annual cost of a quarter of a million dollars, such useless documents as a 1975 pamphlet entitled *Why an Energy Crisis?* and handing out grants for such frivolous projects as a study on how to transform whey, a cheese by-product, into alcohol fuel; and though it had twenty thousand employees of its own, among whom presumably there were a few experts, it was still hiring outsiders to do its thinking (for example, Harvard University was paid to do a study on "Energy and Security" in 1980, and the RAND Corporation was hired for a study of energy futures in 1981).

So, naturally, nobody much cared when President Reagan, having campaigned with a promise to disband the DOE (which would make it the first cabinet department ever formally killed), took such steps as to throw the despised department into further disrepute. He appointed Dr. James B. Edwards, oral surgeon and former governor of South Carolina, to be Energy Secretary. Edwards immediately declared his chief purpose was to preside over DOE's demise, and some critics felt that by merely filling the top job he might have some effect toward that end. A White House official told *The Wall Street Journal*, "I alternate between thinking that it was a horrible appointment or that it was somebody's stroke of genius. You couldn't have picked a better person to downgrade and diminish the job." Of course, Edwards also had his supporters. In any event, he probably did as well as any secretary could do with a department that was hopelessly fragmented, that had no White House support, and that was constantly being undercut by David Stockman's trickledown apaches at the Office of Management and Budget.

***

Whatever his inadequacies, Secretary Edwards could at least claim to have carried out one of his responsibilities better than any of his predecessors: filling the Strategic Petroleum Reserve. When Edwards got to Washington, the reserve contained only 112 million barrels, only slightly more than 25 percent of what Ford and Carter had grandly predicted would be in the reserve by 1981; if Middle East imports were disrupted, as they had been three times in the previous six years, the stockpiled oil could have taken up the slack for only eighteen days.

Within Edwards' first year, the reserve supply was more than doubled, enough to balance a loss of imports for five weeks. But nothing ever went right at the Strategic Petroleum Reserve, and at that point another handicap came into the reckoning: shortage of space. The General Accounting Office announced in 1982 that even if there was no further slippage in the storage construction schedule, space would be so skimpy that "at best the Department of Energy will be able to achieve an average fill rate of 189,000 barrels a day."

By this time, the government had dropped its reserve goal from one billion barrels (which had become an embarrassing impossibility, it seemed) to only 750 million barrels; but if the GAO was correct in its prediction, it would take another eight years to store even the lesser amount.

Such endless errors and pessimism had become routine. The history of the Strategic Petroleum Reserve since Congress established it, in 1975, was one long, scandalous bungle (see Appendix entry for STRATEGIC PETROLEUM RESERVE), which was all the more baffling because, from the very moment the stockpile was proposed, it had received the support of every energy policy expert; all agreed that a large reserve stockpile of oil was the *only* way to cushion the shock of OPEC's periodic embargoes and production retrenchments. Yet neither Republican nor Democratic administrations had made much effort to fill the reserves on schedule.

The Presidents could not have been careless from lack of warnings. The Persian Gulf nations had repeatedly proved their irresponsibility, and sometimes treachery, during the 1970s; and officials who were supposed to have some foundation for making intelligent judgments said the 1980s would hold more of the same. In 1980, outgoing CIA director Turner said, "All the obstacles to securing a stable flow of oil from the Persian Gulf will be magnified" in the coming decade. At the same time, the Senate Energy Committee, having completed an intensive inquiry into the geopolitics of oil, concluded that "an oil supply interruption of a major magnitude is a virtual certainty at some time within the next decade." At an American Enterprise Institute energy security forum in 1980, participants generally agreed with the gloom, if not the specifics, of panelist Senator Bill Bradley of New Jersey when he predicted that oil-supply interruption was "a one-in-two probability in the next three to four years," and the threats of the future would arise not merely from political pique or political blackmail aimed at the industrial nations, not from the quarrels of the major powers or from the standard Jew-Arab conflicts, but from fresh jealousies and quarrels between the producing nations themselves. These indeed might be the most devastating, for the Persian Gulf was being roiled with new fanaticisms. In the past, when Moslems quarreled, they had not even considered cutting their opponents' oil arteries. But the Iran-Iraq war that broke out in late 1980 showed that the new fanatics would spare nothing. The Iraqis and Iranians clobbered each other's major oil facilities.

Notwithstanding all the arms we had sold and were selling to Saudi Arabia, that nation was not immune from the kind of military assault that could put her out of business for many months. What if that happened? Since Saudi Arabia supplied the bulk of our Persian Gulf oil, what would happen to our economy if the Saudis were shut down for, say, a year?

A Congressional Budget Office study concluded that if that should happen, the gross national product would drop $150 billion, inflation would jump to 25 to 30 percent, and unemployment would hover around 15 percent—in short, that there would be a depression.

Considering the dire possible results of a Saudi cutoff, the Strategic Petroleum Reserve was obviously the cheapest kind of insurance. (As Senator Bradley figured, "Every barrel of oil that goes into the reserve now is worth, assuming a reasonable probability of a supply interruption, $280 in gross national product loss averted.")

Logic, however, had never been very good at filling the Strategic Petroleum Reserve, and by 1982, with memory of the last Middle East interruption growing faint and with the Administration badgered by deficits, Reagan and his crowd (though they were eager to spend $180 billion for defense) began to look for ways to avoid spending even $3 billion a year to fill the SPR's storage salt domes.[14]

And then, as befitted the history of the program, it was discovered that something was amiss at one of the storage domes near Baton Rouge, Louisiana, in caverns presumed to contain 44 million barrels of high-grade crude oil. Apparently beginning as early as 1977, somebody or some corporation—or several—in the chain of suppliers had been selling slop to the government. It was believed that within that one dome perhaps as much as 20 percent of the stuff the nation was saving for an emergency was waste oil, similar to cast-off crankcase oil.

The patriots of the oil industry had risen to the occasion once again.

* * *

14. Fortunately for the SPR, Mexico, as mentioned earlier, moved to the edge of bankruptcy in 1982 and the United States had to step in with a few billions to keep her from defaulting on her loans to our banks; in return, Mexico agreed to pay us back in cheap oil for the reserve.

Between 1972, the last preembargo year, and 1981, the beginning of a sharp recession largely created by higher oil prices, the top twenty oil companies increased their profits 404 percent, or 188 percent when corrected for the inflation they helped bring about.

The amazing prosperity of the oil industry during the decade was achieved, however, at a terrible price to the rest of U.S. industry, as well as to the nation's normal growth pattern. For most consumers, both individual and industrial, the Oil Decade developed into a horror story. One way or another, the horror for individuals was in the disappearance of comfort. For pensioners forced to choose between heating and eating, comfort was replaced by downright pain. For others, there was the psychological trauma of being scolded for living by standards that political and industrial leaders had told them to expect as their due. From the end of World War II until the oil price revolution began, in the 1970s, Americans had a steadily improving standard of living. They earned more for their work every year and they had more left over to spend on fun and gadgets and cars. But then, battered by direct and indirect waves of inflation caused primarily by a 1200 percent rise in energy prices during the decade,[15] Americans' standard of living was left in shreds, and to compound the shock, their leaders now began to blame them for being "wasteful" and to lecture them on the new patriotism of living at uncomfortable temperatures. With the cost of energy distorting the cost of everything, the traditional assurance that everyone but the very poorest could afford a reasonable amount of luxuries was hard to cling to.

Consider what happened to "discretionary income," the amount of the paycheck that is left over after basic necessities such as food, fuel, shelter, and medicine are paid for. In the 1960s, discretionary income increased 78 percent; but during the Oil Decade it increased only 16.7 percent; and if inflation is taken into the formula, workers began the 1980s with less to spend on the nonnecessities than they had in 1972.

Worst of all, there was no justice to the impact of energy prices. Some Americans were reduced to lives of desperation, some were merely inconvenienced. To be sure, at the end of the decade, the upper crust was spending considerably more, for example, to send their sons and daughters to Ivy League schools, and a significant part of the increase could be traced to oil prices. A. Bartlett Giamatti, president of Yale, said energy

---

15. As the decade ended, the impact of energy prices accelerated. An extensive study undertaken by Dr. Milton Lower, economist for Congressman Dingell's Subcommittee on Oversight and Investigations, found that "directly and indirectly, energy price increases accounted for over 38 percent of total U.S. inflation in 1979" and "for nearly 36 percent of the continuing inflation experienced by the U.S. economy." More important, the subcommittee investigation found that energy prices were almost wholly responsible for the *momentum* of inflation increases during the 1979–80 period, a momentum that sent the recession cartwheeling into the next decade.

costs there shot up 800 percent during the 1970s and had increased 48 percent just between 1980 and 1981. At Brown, energy costs were up 40 percent—from $5 million to $7 million—even though Brown itself generated a third of its electrical power and had installed nine thousand storm windows.

These extra costs no doubt caused some unhappy mutterings in Scarsdale, but the fact was, as economist Lester C. Thurow discovered, that the energy price increases of the 1970s fell with *seven*fold more harm on the poorest 10 percent of the population than it did on the wealthiest 10 percent.

The Energy Department estimated that at the end of the decade, middle-income families (meaning families with an average income of $20,196) were spending 5.1 percent of their income on energy, or if gasoline was counted in, 13.2 percent. Poor folks (families with incomes around the $4,000 level) were spending 21 percent on heating and other household energy bills, 35.7 percent counting gasoline. To keep their expenditures even at the crippling 35.7 percent proportion, the poor were consuming less than half the total energy used by the average U.S. household.

Naturally, the DOE's bureaucratic advisers did not suggest making the oil companies come to the relief of the poor. They suggested instead that Congress, which was spending $1.8 billion to help the poor get enough household energy in 1980, should increase this expenditure to at least $3.5 billion to offset rising oil and gas prices; which meant, of course, that the major portion of the burden would be placed on middle-income taxpayers. The DOE did not figure that additional tax cost into their middle-income energy bill.

But of all the pain that the Oil Decade brought to individual consumers, none was so traumatic as the forced end of America's great love affair with automobiles. Average Americans could no longer afford to maintain those wonderful rolling mistresses the size of a bedroom. The price of gasoline crammed consumers into dinky vehicles that swapped twice the fuel efficiency for half the comfort and safety.

Even sadder was the disappearance of those once-sacred trysting places—service stations, *real* service stations, where Americans could give all sorts of fond attention to their machines, and most of it free. Oil companies who controlled retail outlets worked with efficient diligence to make everything more Spartan and less convenient. First of all, they reduced almost by half the number of places Americans could buy gasoline. Whereas in 1972 there were 220,000 service stations, ten years later the number was down to 148,000. Income was soaring at the remaining stations—$500,000 in 1980 at the average station, compared to $430,000 in 1979—not only because there were less competition and higher prices but also because service stations no longer offered service. At the end of the decade, Americans were buying 70 percent of their gas at self-serve pumps, and it appeared likely that oil companies would eventually force them to buy all their gasoline in that way, because virtually all stations being built were of the gas-only genre (no bays in which to grease and work on cars, no rest rooms); and with companies raising rents and reducing profit sharing, established dealers were being forced to fire employees and convert to gas-only operations. Vic Rasheed, of the Service Station Dealers of America, was not exaggerating when he warned, in 1982, that "the motoring public is really in danger of not having a place to take their car when they need emergency service. The oil companies are no longer interested in repairing motorists' flat tires, leaky radiator hoses, broken fan belts and other emergency services." The average car on the road, he pointed out, was seven years old.

Gone, or going fast, was the attendant who could tell why your motor sputtered; who—not for an extra 8 cents a gallon but simply from gratitude for your business—checked your battery, oil, and tires, washed your windshield, and was capable of telling you how to get on the nearest interstate. In one short decade, America had seen the mobile attendant replaced by a zombie perched in a kiosk behind a cash register (and often behind a bulletproof window) who took your money with the sullenness of a Murmansk peasant. In such a hostile environment, the concept of "service" had become grotesque. "These days," as Fern Schumer wrote in the Chicago *Tribune*, "service is the attendant coming to your car to collect $20 for the tank of gas you pumped yourself. Of course, he was nowhere in sight 10 minutes before when you rattled every lever on the pump trying to get the gas to flow. Or when you were topping off the tank, causing it to overflow and spill all over yourself and the car. There you stood in a puddle of $1.28-a-gallon gas, a testimony to the economics of self-serve."

*

If the decade was traumatic to individual consumers, however, it was possibly even more traumatic to nonenergy industries. Traditionally, this country has supported a highly diversified and healthy industrial base. Manna from free enterprise had always fallen over a wide plain. After 1973, however, it fell mostly on the energy industry, and only the oil and gas companies grew fat.

In the decade prior to 1973, our gross national product increased at an average annual rate of 4.2 percent. By the early 1980s, it had slumped to 2.4 percent. Largely, the decline was the result of an alarming transfer of wealth away from autos and steel and the like, and into one industry: oil. Some feared it was turning the United States into a banana republic, in which economic well-being rested ultimately on "banana oil," not on industrial excellence. Prefacing the House Oversight and Investigations

Subcommittee's 1981 report on the changing distribution of industrial profits, Michael F. Barrett, Jr., staff director, pointed out: "Four of the five largest U.S. industrial companies are oil companies. The twenty largest oil companies are among the fifty largest industrial companies in the U.S. This is significant because in 1970 the situation was very different. This shift into energy exploitation has reduced the U.S. to the status of a lesser-developed country. We are a net exporter of food and raw materials, such as lumber and coal, and we are a net importer of value-added products such as machine tools."

Oil companies' profits accounted for 40 percent of *all* profits earned by U.S. manufacturing firms in 1980. Their profits were up 30 percent, while the rest of the economy was virtually stagnant. Of the profit increase reported between 1978 and 1980 by *Fortune's* 500 largest U.S. industrial firms, 98 percent—*$19.2 billion out of $19.6 billion*—went to the 56 oil and gas companies on the list. Among *Fortune's* 1000 largest industrial corporations, the 82 oil and gas companies creamed off 96 percent of the profit increase: *the other 918 companies split the remaining 4 percent.* It was a stunning performance, but not so surprising when one realizes that Exxon alone came within $300 million of equaling the profits of *all* of *Fortune's* Second 500.

Which helps to explain why the 1970s saw such a precipitous drop in the gross national product. U.S. plants and machinery were getting old and outdated. But money to expand and rebuild can come from only two sources: external borrowing and internal profits. Incredibly high interest rates inhibited borrowing, and the oil and gas industry had a corner on the internal cash flow. Or so it seemed. In 1980, the big four auto makers together generated less money from their operations than did Gulf, the sixth-largest oil company. The five biggest steel companies, which account for the vast majority of all steel production in America, generated less funds internally than Phillips Petroleum, and Phillips was just the fourteenth-largest oil company.

If nonenergy industries paid several hundred percent more for energy, or, out of anxiety caused by oil and gas shortages in the past, switched their plants to coal, these expenditures contributed not one iota to their productivity; they simply sucked away billions that could have helped make those industries more competitive with their rivals abroad. Bankers Trust Company estimated that in 1980 the nonenergy industries spent $25 billion—or 12 percent of all outlays—juggling and redesigning their energy facilities (switching from oil to coal, etc.) and that "the nonenergy sector underinvested by $50 billion or so in 1980," because the oil price revolution had "drained consumer purchasing power, disrupted international trade, provoked economic dislocation and accelerated inflation. Naturally, business investment slacked in this environment."

***

The permissiveness of the Federal Power Commission that had cat-apulted natural gas prices to such heights in the early and mid-1970s was still at work in the 1980s. Only, now it was the result of the Federal Energy Regulatory Commission, the five-member commission that took the place of the FPC when the Department of Energy was set up, in 1977. The Federal Energy Regulatory Commission's acronym was appro-priate; it was expert at "FERCing" consumers.

Passage of the 1978 Natural Gas Policy Act (NGPA), after that long, nasty congressional fight, had falsely left the impression that the pricing of natural gas had been settled once and for all. In fact, industry had no intention of quitting the fight so long as a few dozen more billions could be wrung from gas consumers, and FERC was solidly on industry's side.

At the time the NGPA was passed, about 60 percent of the gas on the market was new gas, but of course this percentage would increase as the old fields played out; they were expected to be gone by the early 1990s. Under the NGPA's provisions, the price of most "new" gas (reserves dis-covered after 1977) was supposed to rise 4 percent more than inflation each year until 1985, at which time controls on new gas would disappear entirely. But one segment of new gas—that which was produced from depths below fifteen thousand feet—was favored with immediate deregu-lation, as an incentive to producers to go out and try to find the hard-to-get stuff. (By 1982, this deep gas was selling for prices 400 percent above the market average.) As for "old" gas sold on the interstate market, its price increases were supposed to be held to about the same as the rate of inflation even after 1985, and until the old gas was depleted. This was simple economic justice; after all, producers needed no "incentive" to bring it to market. Its development costs had been paid for years be-fore.

The NGPA was a complicated pricing program, which made it suscep-tible to all sorts of proindustry juggling by the federal energy bureau-cracy, and indeed this did occur regularly. Thanks to the FERC way of handling the NGPA, wholesale gas prices were 1000 percent higher in 1982 than they had been ten years earlier, and scalping at the retail level was even more brutal. Pipelines in cahoots with the big producers helped keep prices up; Columbia Gas Transmission passed up a bounti-ful supply of natural gas offered by small producers at $2.50 to $3 per thousand cubic feet and instead bought huge amounts from the big producers costing up to $8 and $9 per Mcf, claiming "contract obliga-tions." FERC didn't seem to mind in the least.

The average price of natural gas doubled during the first three years that the NGPA was in effect, but gas producers didn't think that was generous enough. They wanted *immediate* decontrol of *all* gas, old and new. Holders of the largest reserves—names the reader is thoroughly fa-miliar with by now—were particularly eager to get rid of the price con-

trol on old gas, for its profits were the purest gravy. A detailed study by
Ann K. Lower and a team of researchers from the Consumer Federation
of America concluded that if natural gas prices were decontrolled as of
1983, over the next fifteen years "the top 20 natural gas producers will
reap a $68.3 billion windfall from their sales of old gas to the 15 largest
pipelines" and "the top 5 producer companies will each gain $5 billion or
more under such a scenario."[16] Moreover, that was just the profits that
would descend on them from the decontrol of *old* gas.

Reagan came into office promising to get rid of gas controls. But he
ran into an economy that was crumbling from the rise of oil prices, and it
would clearly be rash to ask Congress to give consumers another dose
with decontrolled gas. So, after a few months of hesitation, he decided
against going that route—for the moment. Instead, he loaded FERC with
commissioners who could achieve nearly the same results quietly, piece-
meal.

Named to chair FERC was Charles Butler III, a native Texan who
had practiced law with Baker and Botts, one of Houston's largest firms,
and with Kendrick, Kendrick and Bradley, a Dallas firm; his work included cases for natural gas producers and natural gas pipelines. Splitting up those legal tours with long periods on the staff of Senator John
Tower, the Texas Republican, Butler had a hand in both Tower's constant proindustry legislation and in the 1980 Republican platform's anti-
regulation plank.

He was, obviously, a natural. And he performed accordingly. While
Reagan waited to carry his case to Congress, Butler and his fellows,
without fanfare, issued rulings that automatically raised natural gas
prices to lush heights. Critics charged he was achieving back-door deregulation; this was hardly an extravagant accusation, for the price of both
new and old gas was being bid up so high that, as Butler conceded, on
average the price was about the same as if no controls remained.

FERC had come a long, long way from Congress' mandate that natural gas prices should meet a "just and reasonable" standard.

And were the new prices bringing abundant supplies to market? Not
so's the General Accounting Office could notice it. The GAO reported in
1981 that "production continued to outpace additions to proven reserves,
and, therefore, reserves continued the post-1975 decline, but at a somewhat slower pace." Not that the gas wasn't out there to be found. The
problem was a lack of enthusiasm. In some of the richest basins, drills
have been sunk in only 3 to 15 percent of the terrain.

---

16. The twenty top natural gas producers, which control 72.3 percent of old gas, are
Mobil, Exxon, Texaco, Gulf, Shell, Tenneco, Standard of Indiana, Standard of Califor-
nia, Phillips, Atlantic Richfield, Getty, Cities Service, Union, Superior, Sun, El Paso,
Conoco, Pennzoil, Marathon, and Columbia.

The reason, of course, was that to bring too generous an amount to market too fast would hurt prices. So the producers continued to sit on their leases. And even where they had found promising pockets, they let it stay underground. The House Subcommittee on Fossil and Synthetic Fuels discovered in 1981 that many producers had capped their gas wells —the history of the early 1970s being repeated—and were waiting for higher prices. Even more dramatically in defiance of national needs, some producers were simply flaring old gas—burning it right at the well, wasting it, rather than bringing it to market at prices they didn't like— the history of the 1920s and 1930s being repeated.

* * *

Although the temporary decline in oil prices in 1981 and thereafter put some restraint on the predatory inclinations of OPEC, the treasuries of that cartel had already bought so heavily into Western business activities and had invested so deeply in U.S. private and government securities as to convince some observers that nothing would stop them from trying to exert permanent political influence, which is to say blackmail, in our affairs.

Treasury Department figures showed that, by 1981, OPEC countries were buying 20 percent of the total equities in U.S. corporations purchased by *all* the countries of the world, and that the oil exporters owned 30 percent of *all* foreign holdings of U.S. Treasury securities.

In October 1980, *Business Week,* alarmed by the potential that came with the doubling of prices within the previous twelve months, warned that "the Arab nations of OPEC are building a new international banking system that threatens to capture control of the world's financial resources in the 1980s in the same way they took control of the world's energy resources in the 1970s. While the different pieces of that Arab banking system are only now being put into place, it is already clear that the OPEC money weapon will join with the OPEC oil weapon in giving the Arabs unprecedented sway over the economies and the politics of the West."

When such observations are made about the Arab "banking system," they are meant to include much more than merely banks and more than merely banking. The entire governmental wealth is involved, and each transaction is judged by what it can accomplish for an OPEC nation's political welfare as well as for the profits that are likely to ensue. "So intertwined are the political and economic motivations behind Arab bank lending and investing that it raises eyebrows worldwide," *Business Week* continued, "when Kuwaitis buy 4.9 percent of nearly all of the top 20 U.S. banks, a big chunk of Eastern Air Lines, a large percent of the equity in Texaco, Getty Oil, Mobil, and even Exxon."

Kuwait, second only to Saudi Arabia among OPEC producers, got another round of attention in 1981, when the Chicago *Tribune* obtained confidential documents that permitted it to detail—for the first time publicly—an OPEC nation's U.S. holdings. The panorama was stunning. The record showed, for one thing, that Treasury and other government officials had lied to the American public when they gave assurances that OPEC investments were mostly in short-term money-market securities such as Treasury bills.

In fact, if all OPEC investments were like Kuwait's—and there was every reason to suppose they were (although one couldn't be sure, because the U.S. Treasury tried to keep the information secret)—then the very heart of U.S. business and banking was already well skewered.

The documents obtained by the *Tribune* showed that Kuwait had invested more than $7 billion in U.S. businesses, including from 1 percent to more than 2 percent of the common stock in such major corporations as Hewlett-Packard, American Express, General Mills, Ralston Purina, American Home Products, Eli Lilly, Johnson & Johnson, Merck, Burroughs Corp. Digital Equipment, Honeywell, IBM, Caterpillar, General Electric, Federated Dept. Stores, K Mart, J. C. Penney, and Union Pacific Railroad. One of its largest holdings was 1.7 million shares of AT&T.

Additionally, it held significant amounts of stock—though not as much as *Business Week* claimed—in eighteen banking institutions, including BankAmerica Corp., Chase Manhattan, Continental Illinois, Manufacturers Hanover, and Mellon National.

It also owned enough shares to have a strong voice in stockholders' meetings at Schlumberger, Atlantic Richfield, Conoco, Kerr-McGee, Phillips, Standard of Indiana, Standard of Ohio, Standard of California, not to mention a few million shares in such companies as Hughes Tool, Halliburton, Exxon, and Superior Oil.

Perhaps, as financial writer Dan Dorfman suggested after viewing the Kuwait portfolio, "there's a genuine danger of the oil-exporting nations' gaining control, or, at the very least, a strong influence, over some of the leading U.S. companies." Perhaps not. But in any event it was certain that governments of countries around the Persian Gulf who haven't the foggiest concept of democracy today can boast of an inordinate influence on the economic decisions, and to some extent the foreign-policy decisions, of the world's oldest democracy.

Whether it has been for the better or worse is something that will be more clearly seen at some future date, but there can be no question of the drift in the 1970s of U.S. favoritism in the Middle East away from Israel and toward the oil-producing states.

***

EPILOGUE

"It's no trick to make a lot of money if all you want to do is make a lot of money."

MR. BERNSTEIN, in *Citizen Kane*

L'envoi

Remember our glory years? They weren't all that long ago. In the early 1950s, the United States was oil king of the universe. Texas alone produced twice as much oil as the U.S.S.R. and more than all the Middle Eastern countries combined.

Times have changed a bit. Now the Soviet Union is the world's No. 1 producer and we couldn't get along without heavy Middle Eastern imports. The United States is thought to have less than 5 percent of the world's remaining proven reserves of crude oil, and few in the business think there are great reservoirs down there still to be discovered. At any price. Such is the slump here at home that the experts say anyone born in the 1930s who lives a normal life-span will probably see most of the wells in America come to a wheezing halt as the fields run dry.

All in one lifetime.

Americans are not going gentle into that good night. We are falling into the energy void with confusion and loud recriminations and complete lack of grace. We are also going with the knowledge that we have been suckered.

By whom? By the oil companies themselves, of course. We (by which I mean our politicians) indulged them, we spoiled them, we left energy matters up to them. And they let us down. Always. Big Oil was allowed virtually to write its own tax code, and it responded by cheating us of many, many billions of dollars; it treated environmental laws as no more binding than grocery-store handbills; it was allowed to gang up secretly to devise better ways to screw the consumer and to merge and remerge with total indifference to antitrust laws; and when confronted with price ceilings, the tiger, with smiling impunity, crapped in our tank. At home or abroad, Big Oil played by its own rules—and was reluctant to give us even hints as to what they were. John J. McCloy, Big Oil's troubleshooting attorney, made more Middle East foreign policy in the postwar period than did the U.S. State Department. Senator Stevenson was so right: "Almost every time there has been a choice between what is best for Big Oil and what is best for the nation, Big Oil has won."

It has won for a number of reasons, but most of them have to do with their money and our lethargy and venality. They have so much money that when B. R. Dorsey, chief executive officer of Gulf, was asked how he could *not* have known his subordinates had spent $10 million in illegal lobbying, he could answer in all innocence: "Senator, this is a relatively small amount . . . $10 million is not really a very large amount. It does not stand out" on the corporation's books.

The oil crowd has won because Congress—probably not so much because it is bought off as because it simply prefers to follow the line of least resistance—has responded to the industry's generosity by permitting it, in essence, to set up its own bureaucracy within the federal government. As we have seen, those who presumably are the "regulators" of the industry often are alumni of the industry. Every time some political gadfly forced the Federal Energy Administration or the Department of Energy to divulge the professional background of its policy-making officials, the public learned that dozens—scores, hundreds—of them had migrated only recently from the warm nest of the oil industry. Did I mention that Senator James Abourezk had the General Accounting Office check the backgrounds of eleven agencies that had responsibilities over oil-industry affairs, and found two hundred and one former oil-company employees and affiliates in top-level positions in the federal agencies— and that didn't count the employees in two agencies that refused to answer the GAO's inquiry? Exxon, the largest oil company, was the one most frequently represented with former employees.

(Tired of being embarrassed by such disclosures, the Department of Energy later put a ban on the release of such data either to politicians or to newsmen; if you go through the publicly available biographies of its top officials on file at the DOE's press office today, you will find hardly a one who seems to have ever heard of petroleum before reaching Washington, much less have earned an income from it.)

As seen again and again in this spotted history, by far the most effective weapon the oil industry has used in frustrating federal regulators and manipulating federal politicians is its total domination of information. In the years when the Federal Power Commission was making at least vague gestures toward setting natural gas rates, the Commission relied almost solely on information supplied by the industry as to how many wells were available and how much gas could be counted in reserve. When the U.S. Geological Survey makes its predictions about probable oil reserves, it relies primarily on information supplied by the oil companies. Generally speaking, the Department of Energy and its predecessor, the Federal Energy Administration, have gone to the industry's chief lobby, the American Petroleum Institute, for oil statistics. So we have really never known where we stood. We still don't know.

The government's ignorance was not compulsory during the 1970s. It didn't have to let the oil industry corner all the information. Congress had a wide range of alternative courses to take. It could have (as the AFL-CIO suggested) nationalized the oil and gas industry, thereby coming into possession of all the industry's secrets in one swoop. Congress, of course, would never do anything that drastic; but at least—as several anything-but-radical members of Congress suggested from time to time—it could have financed exploration parties of its own, to go out and drill holes in the ground and find out what, and how much, is down there in a few key areas.

Although Senator Long hates the idea of the government's doing such a thing as exploring for oil, he nevertheless admits the soundness of the principle. Borrowed statistics won't get the job done; geological hypotheses based on past experience may be useful, but they are still guesswork. Truth lies in the drill bit. As Senator Long once put it, "Until one has explored, there is no reason on earth to assume one acre of land is any better than any other acre of land anywhere on earth." You'll hear that from any aggressive oilman, Indiana Standard's John E. Swearingen, for instance: "I don't know that all the easy oil has been found . . . And there is no way of knowing if there is oil or gas there until you go out and drill a well to see."

Most of the unexplored land in the United States is in the federal domain, so the government's oil explorers would not have had trouble getting permission. And 98 percent of the federal land has never been explored. A dozen Spindletops may be out there waiting to be found. Or perhaps the nation is truly running dry. We will never know for sure until we find out independently of the oil companies. Which means, now that the big fight is over, that we will probably never know.

Our ignorance has left us addled by the advice and predictions of the "experts," experts such as Walter J. Levy, who, in the Summer 1981 issue of *Foreign Affairs* ("Oil: An Agenda for the 1980s"), spread his little cup of gloom: ". . . there is no realistic prospect that either the major industrialized countries or the less developed countries can become anywhere near self-sufficient or reliant on non-OPEC sources." Since Levy gets his information from the same crafty fellows who supplied the information on which the government built its energy policies of the 1970s, one may fairly wonder if he knows what he's talking about. If sinking wells is the only way to really know where the oil is, experts share with the rest of us the darkness of our future. How does former Energy Secretary James Schlesinger know, as he said in his farewell speech to the National Press Club, "The OPEC nations possess some 80 percent of the Free World's proven oil reserves—and that percentage is likely to increase"? It's that kind of airy "expertise" that made the Oil Decade so memorable. The fact is, if this country, where so many wells have been sunk, is still a mystery, the underdeveloped parts of the world are immeasurably more mysterious. Nobody knows what the poorer nations have to offer, because, though they account for about half of the world's prospective reserves, they have been tested by less than 5 percent of the exploratory drilling. Mobil walked away from a dry hole in Libya; Occidental came along and discovered oil within a mile of Mobil's abandoned rig and developed a field flowing eight hundred thousand barrels a day. The smart guys in the oil companies aren't always so smart, which in retrospect makes our government's goggle-eyed belief in them and their satellite "experts" all the more galling.

*

If our federal officials were a pushover for the oil industry, it was because they wanted to be. They didn't care. They didn't try. They certainly didn't lose for lack of power. Congress—and if empowered by Congress, the bureaucracy—has the power to do anything it wants to do. Since 1906, the Interstate Commerce Commission (ICC) has been empowered to prevent the oil companies from using pipelines to create a monopoly situation. Never in all those years has the ICC been anything but what one historian called "relatively passive" in the employment of this power. In fact, the ICC has not used that law at all. The law is still on the books, still unused.

Antitrust "enforcement" has been a bad joke. Economist Robert Lekachman reminds us of what was supposedly the greatest antitrust victory, and weighs its results quite accurately: "In 1911 the Department of Justice won a famous victory against Standard Oil, the tyrant of its industry . . . Was anyone better off after the 1911 court victory? Well, yes. The lawyers for both sides." Too true. No real precedent was established. The giants are still suppressing competition, and Washington does nothing.

By 1980, it was plain that the nation might as well lay a wreath on the Sherman Antitrust Act, of 1890, and the Clayton Act, of 1914, which, though still on the federal books, are effectively dead and buried. Though meant to protect us from such evils as monopolies, unfair mergers, price fixing, divvying up of markets, interlocking directorates, insider deals—all the devices that industrial gangs use to lessen competition or exploit lack of competition—the laws, because they simply are not enforced, do more harm than good, by giving the appearance of protection that does not exist. The two agencies with antitrust responsibility—the Justice Department and the Federal Trade Commission—are quite obviously indifferent. But so is Congress and so, for the most part, is the press. Trust crimes seem to arouse no anger, though they are the most radically destructive of free enterprise and are the most profitable crimes of all.

The CDE directory of stock ownership in energy companies, pub-

lished in 1980, was just the last of several powerful investigations that
showed the anticompetitive tendencies of oilmen. Others, mentioned in
this book, were Senator Lee Metcalf's report in 1978; the Senate Interior
Committee's *Structure of the U.S. Petroleum Industry*, in 1976; the
Metcalf-Muskie joint *Disclosure of Corporate Ownership*, in 1974. And
what was their combined impact? Nil. Coming with the regularity of
waves, the reports were full of dramatic revelations and warnings, full of
evidence of trust violations, and yet probably not more than three dozen
persons—a generous estimate—in the entire country even thumbed
through these fascinating staff studies. Certainly they resulted in not
even the faintest quiver of a reform nerve anywhere in government, for
the antitrust movement, if it ever could be said to have truly lived, is
long dead.

＊＊

This book's emphasis might lead one to suppose that federal officials and
federal politicians are peculiarly susceptible to industry's wiles. Not so.
State officials roll over just as fast. All the mistakes and improprieties and
stupidities and conflicts of interest that have marked Washington's handling of the oil industry are embedded, down to the deepest fossil, in the
history of Texas oil politics. Indeed, they were there earlier, and more
abundantly, more shamelessly. Considering the fact that until the 1970s,
and for the previous four decades, Texas was the preeminent producer of
oil—dishing up 35 to 45 percent of the nation's total output each year—
one might have reasonably expected the Texas Railroad Commission,
which supposedly regulated the industry, to take more than a parochial
view of its duties. But seeking the fast buck for Texas—and to hell with
the rest of the nation—was its guiding principle, because the Texas Railroad Commission was, and is, *part* of the industry it supposedly regu-
lates. If the fast buck required grotesque inefficiencies and criminal
waste, that was okay with the Commission. For decades, the Commission
permitted the state's fields to be depleted by a frenzy of wasteful competitiveness—"pumping contests," so to speak. Many fields quickly lost
pressure, wells stopped flowing, and boomtowns became ghost towns.

The Commission's handling—or nonhandling—of natural gas was, in a
way, even more deplorable. When oil is found, it is, to varying degrees,
found in association with natural gas—casinghead gas, as it is called. For
many years, this gas was just burned off at the wells, wasted in flame,
and according to oil historian David F. Prindle, "Motorists could drive
for hours at night in parts of Texas . . . and never have to turn on their
automobile lights, because the casinghead flares illuminated the country-
side." This was taking place years after a method for reinjecting casinghead gas into its original rock formation was available; if the Commission
had required its use, not only would the gas have been saved, but the

pressure would have been preserved to such an extent that the amount of oil taken from the field would have multiplied by four.

For all that waste, we're paying today.

The point is that, whether we're talking about the conduct of the industry at the state, or national, or international level, it has seldom, and usually only by accident, based its actions on what is best for the American people. When that grand old rascal Cornelius Vanderbilt exclaimed, "Law! What do I care about the law! Haint I got the power?" he could have been expressing the creed of the oil industry. It has obeyed the law only when it was profitable to do so; otherwise, it relied on power.

Why didn't the American people force the oilmen to behave? If the final power in this country rests with the people, why didn't we make them produce our natural resources at a pace and at prices that were best for the nation as a whole? Democracy may be more defective than we have previously allowed ourselves to think. Or perhaps the terrible problems of the 1970s simply came upon us too fast and overwhelmed us before we realized that that particular crop of politicians had no desire to protect us. If we had had better politicians, well, maybe . . . But now it's too late. Now we can only ruminate over how it all should have been handled. Let me suggest as a theme for such ruminations this remark made by—surprise!—an oilman, Thornton Bradshaw, of Atlantic Richfield: "The whole energy situation is too important to be left to the oil and energy industries, the same as war is too important to be left to the generals."

Too bad that idea didn't grab us—*really* grab us—about fifty years ago. Or even ten.

ANDERSON, ROBERT B. Under President Eisenhower, Anderson was one of the principal architects of the highly controversial oil import program that existed for two decades thereafter. He was also perhaps the most important member of Lyndon Johnson's "shadow cabinet," LBJ's No. 1 financial adviser (not to be confused with Robert O. Anderson, of Atlantic Richfield).

Anderson's career is swathed in that unique kind of piety and worldliness so common to old-fashioned rich Americans. Tall, lean, mild-mannered, scholarly, Republican, deeply religious (he sometimes kept a picture of Jesus on his office desk), no breath of scandal ever touched his name. And yet he mingled with the sporting crowd, the speculative money crowd, and talked their language. Many years before, he had been on the Texas Horse Racing Commission. In that position he had become a close friend to one of Texas' wealthiest families, a horse-loving family, an oil-rich family. When pari-mutuel racing was closed down in Texas, this family hired him to manage half a million oil acres, and he served his masters so well that the oil community took him to its breast and made him president of the Texas Mid-Continent Oil and Gas Association, one of the most influential oil lobbies in the world.

Among the many intimate friends he made was fellow Fort Worthian and legendary oilman Sid Richardson. Ultimately, Richardson would be influential in sending Anderson to Washington to take care of things for the oil fraternity.

Richardson had the power to name oil's ambassador to the Eisenhower Cabinet because of a strange bit of luck that had begun to evolve shortly before World War II. Richardson and Bill Kittrell, a kind of protégé of Sam Rayburn's and a well-known man about Texas, and President Roosevelt's son Elliott were keeping each other company on a train trip to Texas. One night, as the train rocked and clacked through the darkness, the three men became bored and conversation flagged, so Richardson suggested that Kittrell go back to the chair car to see if he could round up somebody to make a fourth for bridge.

After a few minutes, Kittrell returned with a round-faced young army colonel by the name of Dwight Eisenhower.

Before the train trip ended, Richardson and Eisenhower were fast friends. They kept in touch. After the war, when both parties were trying to get Eisenhower to become their presidential candidate, Richardson began putting the heat on Ike to run, and to run as a Republican. He used both religion and the purse in his argument. For his religious lobbyist, Richardson picked the evangelist Billy Graham, whom he had secretly been patronizing for several years with both money and introductions into rich circles. First Richardson got Graham to write General Eisenhower, who was still heading things at SHAPE, in Europe, and tell him to run. And then Richardson paid Graham's way to Europe to personally preach Republican duties to Ike. Not willing to leave the matter to chance or divine intervention, Richardson (accompanied by General Lucius Clay and George E. Allen) then went to Paris himself to assure Ike that if he got into the presidential race he could count on plenty of Texas oil money —including a good piece of Richardson's personal pile. Eisenhower especially appreciated the Texas oil money, because most of the Oklahoma oil money went to Taft.

Just how much of Richardson's own pile went to Eisenhower has never been disclosed, but apparently it was enough to make him grateful. On Richardson's recommendation, Eisenhower named Anderson Secretary of the Navy, on February 4, 1953. (It's interesting how many secretaries of the Navy came from landlocked Fort Worth over a brief span of time. In 1961, John Connally, who had served as Sid Richardson's attorney and would later be executor of Richardson's estate, was named Secretary of the Navy. When Connally retired after a few months to run for governor of Texas, he was replaced by another Fort Worthian, Fred Korth. Of course, Texas oilmen did appreciate that sort of thing, for not only did the Navy lease valuable lands—Teapot Dome and Elk Hills, for example—to favored oil firms, but it is one of the largest consumers of oil.)

Anderson moved from Navy Secretary to assistant secretary of defense, but then he retired, late in 1955, to pluck some of the wealth that was passing him by in private business. But he left government with strong assurances from Eisenhower that ultimately he would be called back to serve in a more powerful role. In conversation with both Richardson and Anderson, Eisenhower said— and repeated on several occasions—that he thought Anderson would make a swell running mate in 1956, replacing Richard Nixon, of whom Eisenhower had confided to Emmet Hughes, "I just haven't honestly been able to believe he *is* presidential timber."

But Anderson was not so certain of his own merits. He knew he was not the political type—he looked and acted like a banker, or a professor, and Eisenhower's confidence in him did not deceive him into thinking that he would be equally appealing to the party's politicos or to the public. Moreover, as he reminded Eisenhower, he was politically inexperienced. The more he protested, the more Eisenhower pushed him toward preparing himself for the higher role. He urged Anderson to make himself better known, to accept every speaking engagement that was offered. Eisenhower liked Anderson's conservatism, his knowledge of international finance, his alliances with the southern wing of the GOP, and of course his deep roots in the oil fraternity. To bolster his own arguments, Eisenhower got General Robert Wood, once the czar of the Sears, Roebuck empire and still a powerful voice of the right wing (chairman of the America First Committee), to encourage Anderson's interest in the vice-presidential spot.

Meanwhile, Richardson, excited by the thought of his political protégé only one heartbeat from the presidency—a thought made more thrilling by Eisenhower's heart attack in 1955—kept pressing Eisenhower for more and more assurances. His courtship of Eisenhower took on an exotic flair as the campaign neared; shortly before Christmas 1955, Richardson flew back to Washington in his private DC-3. The plane was loaded with quail, ducks, steaks, and other rich delicacies for the President. On this occasion, Richardson and Eisenhower came to a fairly firm agreement that Anderson would indeed be Eisenhower's running mate the next year.

By now Anderson himself was almost persuaded that it would be a good idea. However, there was one final hurdle in his mind: money. He did not feel eager to sacrifice himself simply to help others in the oil industry by going back into politics for four years—banished from all those wonderful opportunities in private business. He would feel better about making the sacrifice, however, if he had, say, a million-dollar capital-gains nest egg to make up for what he would lose.

That was no problem for Richardson; he arranged the million dollars in a complicated oil deal affecting several companies. I obtained details of the arrangement in 1963 from an attorney of a medium-large oil company that had been seriously harmed by the oil import program that Anderson later helped set up. He passed along to me a note penned on personal stationery by J. Edwin Hill, who had died in January 1960. (He also supplied me with supporting courthouse documents.) Hill was production manager and an officer and director in Richardson's corporate empire. Oilmen usually do not tell tales on each other, but, for some reason, after Richardson had died and shortly before his own death, Hill, at the urging and in the presence of the old friend whose name cannot be revealed here, wrote out in longhand the source of Anderson's good fortune, as well as the agreement between Richardson and Eisenhower. At the time I received the Hill note, I was working in Texas for Time-Life. At first its editors claimed to be intensely interested in the Richardson-Anderson transaction, but in the midst of my development of the story Lyndon Johnson became President, and for some reason Time-Life decided not to use the material. In 1967 I included the material in *The Accidental President*, a biography of Lyndon Johnson.

This was Richardson's method for putting a cool million in Anderson's hands, as detailed by Hill:

1. Stanolind Oil Company, Kirby Oil Company, Phillips Petroleum Company, and Sun Oil Company held farm-out property belonging to Richardson in Texas and Louisiana.

2. Richardson asked those companies to assign a royalty interest to F. J. Adams, a Fort Worth oilman who had been a vice-president of Gulf Oil Corporation. Adams's role was simply that of a go-between.

3. Adams assigned his royalty interest to Anderson for one dollar and "other valuable interests."

4. Anderson sold his interest in the property to Dalada Corporation for $900,000, half cash, half from future earnings. (Dalada was run by Toddie Lee Wynne, an old friend of Richardson's.) Also, Anderson had already earned $70,000 in production before the sale.

5. Finally, Perry Bass, Richardson's nephew (John Connally's law partner), bought back Dalada's interest.

Thus the property completed its merry-go-round, with Anderson supposedly grabbing the golden ring—$970,000—as it went past.

Three years after I disclosed Hill's memo, in *The Accidental President*, the Washington *Post*, on July 16, 1970, finally got around to publishing an account of the same episode, using the same material. Its version, however, states that Anderson received only a little more than a quarter ($290,000, to be exact) of the planned $1 million. But the *Post* did manage to get the accurate drift of the event, stating that "Just before he became Treasury Secretary in 1957 and a central figure in policy-making to protect oil prices, Robert B. Anderson completed a deal with some oil men to pay him nearly $1 million," of which a good portion "depended in part on the price of oil." There was nothing illegal about it. But there was certainly a question of good taste and fair play.

Unfortunately for these schemers, the GOP's party bosses decided not to go along with Eisenhower's desire to have Anderson on the ticket. At the time of Eisenhower's heart attack, 61 percent of the public said they wanted Richard Nixon to replace him—if Ike had to have a replacement. Clearly Nixon was a name that was well known and was a name that could probably be parlayed into succession by the party in power. The name Anderson rang no bells with the public. The political professionals did not want him, and they persuaded Eisenhower to stick with Nixon.

For the moment, it appeared that Anderson's windfall would not pay off for anybody but himself. Had the scheme been in vain? Wasn't there still some highly useful place he could be stuck in the Eisenhower regime?

Yes, indeed there was. On the urging of Richardson and of Senate Majority Leader Lyndon Johnson, to whom Eisenhower was much in debt for the way Johnson had botched the Democrats' presidential campaign in Texas in 1952 and 1956, Eisenhower named Anderson to be his Treasury Secretary. On June 21, 1957, ten days after disposing of the gift oil property mentioned above, Anderson told the Senate Finance Committee that he held no property that would conflict with his public duties as Treasury Secretary.

A few weeks later, Secretary Anderson was appointed to a cabinet committee to "study" the oil import situation.

Out of that study emerged a program that heavily benefited the major international oil companies. To benefit from the import program, a company had to own a refinery. This automatically excluded most, though by no means all, of the so-called "independent" domestic companies. Superior Oil Company, for example, had extensive oil holdings in Venezuela but owned no refineries; so it was forbidden to bring in even its own oil from those Venezuelan fields. The program played right into the hands of the major, international oil companies, all of whom are well set up with large refineries. At the time the oil import program was imposed by President Eisenhower, only one hundred fifty companies had refineries. But, since import quotas were linked to the amount of domestic production and domestic refining, the largest companies got the biggest imports. Twenty oil giants brought in 85 percent of the foreign oil.

Among these was Standard Oil of Indiana. If you refer back to step No. 1 in the Richardson formula for placing $1 million at Anderson's disposal, you will see that Stanolind was among those who helped. Stanolind, which was later absorbed by another Standard subsidiary, Pan American, was at that time a wholly owned subsidiary of Standard of Indiana. Although Standard of Indiana had little overseas oil holdings, it had major refinery facilities. So it became one of the top six to benefit from the import program and used this windfall to invest in 'overseas oil properties. Within a few years, it moved from being a company with virtually no foreign holdings to one of the largest overseas oil explorers.

ANTITRUST. Standard Oil—which, despite the elaborate duplicity that depicts it as several entities, can be considered as one—has amply demonstrated that when corporations achieve a certain level of giantism they are forever beyond the control of any one government. The history of antitrust in this country is largely a history of Standard Oil's success as an outlaw. The world's first great trust, Standard Oil has defeated all efforts to cut it down to a politically manageable size.

By 1880, hardly fifteen years after John D. Rockefeller had entered the oil business, he controlled 90 percent of the nation's refinery capacity, controlled nearly as high a percentage of the nation's pipeline network, and owned tank car companies and oil exploration and production companies. His various enterprises, some retail, some wholesale, were scattered over many states. The flagship of the Rockefeller empire, Standard Oil of Ohio, a joint-stock company organized in 1870, itself had assets in thirteen states and several foreign countries by the end of its first decade of operations.

Because controlling interest was held by such a small number of persons (five men owned four sevenths of the stock in all the companies), there was naturally a high degree of centralized management at Rockefeller's headquarters, 26 Broadway, New York City. But it was not centralized enough to suit Rockefeller. Decision making was still too scattered for his taste. And besides, it was dangerous for Standard Oil of Ohio to own, as a corporation, property in other states. There was always the danger that these other states—Pennsylvania had already made the effort—might try to tax Ohio Standard not only on the business it did within their borders but on its entire corporate value.

Some new entity was necessary to bring all the Rockefeller interests together, to assume the management responsibility for all the companies and at the same time carry out this function one step farther removed from the omnivorous tax-minded legislatures. The objective was to consolidate, simplify, and obfuscate.

So, in 1882, Rockefeller and a small circle of business associates set up the Standard Oil Trust Agreement. Legally, the trust did not exist. It was not chartered with any state. The name of the trust was not a matter of record anywhere. It was just what its founders called it, no more and no less: an agreement.

Under the agreement, the forty-two stockholders of the forty Rockefeller companies turned over their stock to the nine trustees of the Standard Oil Trust and in return received certificates in the trust. In turning over their stock, the other stockholders also turned over total control to the trustees. The nine made the bylaws; they created all management committees and appointed their members; they elected their own replacements, on the rare occasions when that was necessary; and of course they elected the directors and officers of the subordinate companies. All earnings went first to the nine trustees, who then divvied up the pot to the certificate holders.

Actually, the concentration of power was no greater than before the trust but was simply formalized in a new way. As Ralph and Muriel Hidy point out in *Pioneering in Big Business* (p. 49), "The same group of individuals, who had formerly held authority as the largest stockholders in the various companies in the Standard Oil alliance, now held it specifically as trustees. The Trust Agreement made possible the easy transfer of holdings, kept all operations from the public gaze, and was in itself a major step toward the more efficient administration of the integrated petroleum enterprise."

No doubt the trustee arrangement increased efficiency. But because the operation of the trust was secret (its trustees pretended that no such thing existed), and because the new efficiency resulted in more ruthlessness as well as a stunning new level of profits, Rockefeller's clique became a unique magnet for the public's darts. In their attraction of hatred, the Standard Oil crowd was different only in degree. The public generally looked upon all big business as the enemy. Industry's Gilded Age of the 1870s and 1880s stirred deep negative feelings. The kings of capitalism were, quite properly, held to be responsible for the periodic financial depressions that shook the lower strata of society. William Jennings Bryan and Populism took wing. Bigness became anathema. Much of the popular hatred was directed at the railroads, which had been the most openly corrupt. And when the public thought of the railroads, it naturally also thought of Standard Oil, whose monopoly of refining came about largely through its manipulation of rail rates. The flame of every kerosene lamp reminded households across America that they were at the mercy of one man.

"Between 1872 and 1892 the Standard Oil combination came to stand before the bar of public opinion as the epitome of the evils of Big Business," write the Hidys (p. 201). (Actually, it held that position at the bar long after 1892.) During those years, the public was abused by trusts in steel, in tobacco, in sugar, in salt, in meat, and in whiskey. Unconscionable profits were squeezed from consumers by the secret division of markets, by phony shortages, by price fixing of various sorts, by destroying would-be competitors through underhanded practices. In such an era, why did Standard Oil stand out? The public hated all trusts, but, for some reason, perhaps because of Rockefeller's ostentatious piety, it particularly hated the Standard Oil Trust.

This national antipathy for railroads and Standard Oil was largely responsible for goading Congress into establishing the Interstate Commerce Commission, in 1887, to control the railroads, which it failed to do, and three years later for Congress' passage of the Sherman Antitrust Act, to control Standard Oil, which also was never accomplished. Allan Nevins notes in his biography of Rockefeller, "In the discussions of the bill both inside and outside Congress the Standard Oil Trust was naturally treated as the principal culprit. [Senator John] Sherman [of Ohio] himself remarked: 'I do not wish to single out the Standard Oil Company, which is a great and powerful corporation, composed in part of citizens of my own state, and some of the very best men I know of.

Still, they are controlling and can control the market as absolutely as they choose.'" (*John D. Rockefeller*, Vol. II, p. 136)

The Sherman Antitrust Act cannot be rated as the most polished piece of legislation ever to emerge from Congress. It was, in fact, a typically jerry-built piece of law, as might be expected from the way it was put together. As one student of the law has observed, ". . . the bill which was arduously debated was never passed, and . . . the bill which was passed was never really discussed" by Congress.

The Sherman Act imposes two types of restrictions. It prohibits any person or group of persons from monopolizing, or conspiring to monopolize, any part of the country's interstate commerce. It also prohibits "restraint of trade" through such actions as group boycotts, the division of markets, the artificial restriction of production, or price fixing.

Federal officials displayed little enthusiasm for using the new trust-busting law. Long before the U.S. Justice Department showed any inclination to move, Ohio's attorney general, David K. Watson, despite powerful pressures from such Republican party leaders as Mark Hanna (see entry in Appendix), petitioned the Ohio Supreme Court to dissolve the Standard Oil Trust for being in violation of state conspiracy laws.

On March 2, 1892, the Ohio Supreme Court ruled that Standard Oil was indeed the illegal tool of an outlaw organization whose goal was to monopolize nationally all elements of the oil business. The Court ruled that Standard Oil of Ohio had to sever its ties with the trust; it forbade the trustees from having any control over Ohio Standard's affairs.

The ruling did not break up the Standard Oil Trust. It simply ended—or attempted to end—the trust's management of the one company, Ohio Standard. However, eight days after the Court's decision was handed down, Rockefeller announced that because he did not want to contend with further public hostility, he would voluntarily do away with the entire trust arrangement with all his companies.

In fact, no significant changes were made. Only the superficial nomenclature was altered. The old trust's "Executive Committee" shed its name; now its members, the same handful who ran the old trust, pretended that there was no formal organization among them at all, even though they continued to operate under the same roof, at 26 Broadway. They insisted that observers should not jump to conclusions from that; they were merely intimate friends who chatted from time to time on business matters. No longer the "Executive Committee," now they were informally referred to as "the gentlemen upstairs."

Not only did Rockefeller fail to carry out his promised voluntary dissolution of the trust, he also continued to break Ohio law by having the trust-in-other-guise continue to run Standard Oil of Ohio. The trustees had superficially obeyed the Court's order; they had exchanged their trust certificates for stock in Standard Oil of Ohio (and they had also exchanged their trust certificates for stock in the other Rockefeller companies). But the result was that the same half dozen people who owned majority interest in the trust now owned majority interest in Standard of Ohio and the other companies. Ownership was back to what it had been in pretrust days, but this was exactly what it was during the trust era, too. Nothing had changed. There had been a mere shuffling of papers.

When evidence that the old trust was still alive in different guise and still running Standard of Ohio was laid before Ohio Attorney General Frank Monnett, in 1897, he promptly went before the State Supreme Court and charged that Standard Oil of Ohio was in contempt of the Court's 1892 ruling. He pointed out that the trust's nine trustees were now managing all the Standard companies, including Standard of Ohio. But Monnett failed to prove his case. He failed largely because when he tried to subpoena records and books that would prove Standard of Ohio was still part of the old, monopolizing ring, the records and books were mysteriously lost in a fire before they could be presented. The nastiness of the case was heightened when Monnett accused Standard officials of offering him a $400,000 bribe to drop his charges. But he could not prove this, either.

By 1899, Rockefeller had decided he needed a new way—a holding company—to cloak his operations and to confuse the public into thinking that real changes were finally going to be made.

Standard Oil of New Jersey, which had been one of Rockefeller's companies (but not the largest) from the trust era, now became the empire's centerpiece because of its propitious location in a state that took a most casual attitude toward the conduct of holding companies. Jersey Standard would thenceforth be the big mother. In her corporate arms she would hold the other companies, and they would all be guided to their familial destiny by the same inner circle that had been running Standard Oil affairs for years.

But the new arrangement did not bring peace. The public was not fooled. In the early 1900s, dozens of lawsuits were filed against Standard Oil—in Kentucky, Kansas, Missouri, West Virginia, Texas, Maryland, Ohio, and Arkansas—charging monopolistic practices. These were all merely warm-ups for the big battle that began in November 1906, when the U.S. Government went into federal circuit court in St. Louis and accused Standard of New Jersey, Rockefeller, six other directors, and various corporate entities within the holding company of being outlaws, in myriad gross violation of the Sherman Antitrust Act. They were charged with slashing prices only to drive out local competitors, after which they raised their prices higher than ever. They were accused of setting up phony companies as "competitors" with Standard, of spying on real competitors and engaging in business espionage, of offering secret rebates in such a way as to undermine the market for others, of threatening the customers of competitors—all aimed at monopolizing the industry. The government's prosecutor was Frank B. Kellogg, who gained such fame from this case that he went on to win a seat in the Senate; later he was Secretary of State (under Coolidge and Hoover, during which time he demonstrated that he could also be the friend of Big Oil).

Before the battle was over, four hundred witnesses had trooped forward to fill twelve thousand printed pages with testimony describing sometimes the evils and sometimes the wondrous ingenuity of Standard and its executives. On November 20, 1909, the federal judges in St. Louis unanimously agreed that the oilmen were guilty.

Standard appealed to the U.S. Supreme Court, of course, but the evidence of guilt was just too overwhelming for even that business-oriented body to ignore. The Court handed down its decision on May 15, 1911: upholding the lower court's decision and ordering the dissolution of the holding company; the twenty-nine subordinate companies were ordered to operate independently of Jersey Standard and of each other.

But, at the same time, the Court enunciated its "rule of reason" with regard to restraint of trade by large corporations. By this, the Court apparently meant that the government should try to restrain only corporations that attempted "unreasonable" restraint of trade, while overlooking "reasonable" restraint of trade. If it didn't mean that, what did it mean? It was a ruling of such vagueness that, as Associate Justice Harlan pointed out in dissent, his brethren had opened a breach in the antitrust law wide enough for virtually all monopolies to slip through. Matthew Josephson accurately observed, in *The President Makers*, that although Standard Oil cried persecution, it paid no fine and none of its corporate evildoers was ever put in jail. Furthermore, ". . . the companies that suffered from dissolution decrees, reappearing eventually as separate entities, worked together as a 'community of interests,' and maintained secret price agreements as harmoniously as ever . . ."

Spectators who had hoped that the Court's decision would damage the old monopoly were sorely disappointed. Standard stock soared in value. When the dissolution forced the opening of some of Standard's books to the public, and investors for the first time got a glance at the inside of the empire, they saw that Standard's financial value was far, far greater than the secretive Mr. Rockefeller had pretended. Within a few days, shares that had previously sold for $100 were selling for $700.

Once again, the legal effort to change Standard Oil had illusory results. Once again, as had happened after the trust suit, the biggest stockholders in the holding company became the biggest stockholders in the new, "independent" companies. Rockefeller alone held more than one fourth of the stock in these companies. The corporate directorates were controlled by the same people, and although the Court had specifically ordered them not to consult with each other in the operation of their various Rockefeller firms, there was no way to prevent this happening. Corporate fraternalism prevailed, as always.

In 1915, the Federal Trade Commission, which had been established the previous year to help the Justice Department police antitrust violations, looked into the results of the 1911 ruling and found that the interrelationship of the Rockefeller companies through stock ownerships still curbed competition within the industry; and after another investigation, in 1922, the FTC once more concluded that "an interlocking stock ownership in the different" Standard companies "has perpetuated the very monopolistic control which the courts sought to terminate."

In 1940, Congress itself investigated the situation and reported that the Rockefeller family, either by individual ownership or through trusts and foundations, controlled more than 20 percent of the stock in Standard of New Jersey, more than 16 percent of the stock in Standard of New York, more than 11 percent of the stock in Standard of Indiana, and more than 12 percent of the stock of Standard of California.

As for the Court's impact on Standard's bigness, that was quite the opposite to what reformers had hoped. Standard of New Jersey—later under the name Esso and now Exxon—would remain the world's largest oil company. Indeed, if anything, the Court's dissolution order in 1911 had the same effect on Standard as the god Cronus' swallowing of his children: when he was forced by Jupiter to disgorge them, the children themselves became gods. Giantism today is the mark of not one Standard company but a family of companies. Two that were once subordinate to Jersey Standard—Mobil (known first as Standard of New York, or Socony, then, through merger, as Socony-Vacuum, later Socony-Mobil, and now just Mobil) and Standard of California, better known by its trade name, Chevron—soon joined the ranks of giantism. Writes Anthony Sampson, "These three daughters of Rockefeller, Exxon, Mobil and Socal, were all for years afterward called the Standard Oil Group and accused by their many critics of acting in unison. The suspicion was hardly surprising; they all sold their oil at the same price, under the same Standard name, their directors were old Standard Oil men, and their principal shareholder was still John D. Rockefeller. In later years . . . these three sisters were to come together in their operations abroad—linking hands, now in one place, now in another, as in an intricate square dance. The indignant denials of collusion were not very credible after the record of mendacity and secrecy of their ugly parent." (*Seven Sisters*, p. 37) Later, by a crafty exploitation of the Eisenhower-imposed oil import program, Standard of Indiana, known at the gas pump as Amoco, would join the Standard giants. (See the *ANDERSON* entry in the Appendix.)

Although the percentage varies slightly from year to year, Exxon, Mobil, Standard of Indiana, and Socal usually own more than 32 percent of domestic reserves, hold more than 30 percent of domestic refining capacity, and make more than 26 percent of all retail gasoline sales.

While it is quite true that, because of the entry of many more companies into the marketplace, competition has increased in the oil industry, it is not the kind of competition that benefits the consumer's pocket. Allan Nevins once pointed out that "the competition which resulted has been primarily a service competition, not a price-competition. Reduction of charges, all factors considered, has been illusory. Any motorist who finds at his crossroads four service stations of four different companies, selling substantially the same gasoline at precisely the same prices, and battling for trade by variations in washroom facilities, has reason to ponder upon the proper limits of competition." (Op. cit., p. 609) Sadly, not even that competition remains. Nevins made his sarcastic observation in 1940; today, all washrooms are the same: filthy. In the service-competitive era, oil companies based national advertising campaigns on friendlier service. The service-competitive era is gone, and the price-competition era never really existed.

*

So the application of the antitrust laws to the oil industry as a way of promoting competition has been disappointing at best, fraudulent at worst—and the worst has generally prevailed. But the ritual of pretending to "get tough" with the oil industry by threatening it with antitrust prosecution is something that federal regulators feel obliged to go through periodically. It is a ritual something like a rain dance, except that the rain dance is sometimes followed—whether by accident or divine assistance—by rain. Nothing ever falls after the antitrust dance.

The ceremony was performed again in 1938, when Congress appointed the Temporary National Economic Committee to make "a thorough study of the concentration of economic power and its detrimental consequences." Based on mountains of data supplied by the TNEC, the U.S. Justice Department filed an antitrust suit in 1940 against the 22 largest oil companies, 379 of their subsidiaries and affiliates, and the American Petroleum Institute. There were so many defendants and they were charged with so many violations of antitrust law that the government's case came to be known as the "Mother Hubbard" suit. Our entry into World War II the following year gave the Justice Department an excuse for delaying action in the name of "national security." The case was revived in a most desultory fashion by government lawyers in 1945, but whatever enthusiasm they had was quickly squeezed out of them by pressures from the oil industry's lobbyists, and the case was quietly dropped in 1951.

However, just as the Justice Department was preparing to surrender, the Federal Trade Commission was cranking up its own investigation. In 1949, the Commission ordered its staff to investigate the international oil cartel. The staff's report—which was the first and only significant study of the global cartel —was issued on August 2, 1952, by the Senate Small Business Committee, with the committee's chairman, Senator John Sparkman, making the grandiloquent and altogether false pronouncement that the study was being released because he and his colleagues believed "it is the basic philosophy of the United States to oppose vast monopolistic concentrations of economic power."

The FTC study proved that for at least two decades seven international oil companies—five American (Jersey Standard, Standard of California, Socony-Vacuum [Mobil], Gulf Oil Corporation, and The Texas Company [Texaco]) and two European-based companies (Anglo-Iranian [British Petroleum] and Royal Dutch-Shell)—had a virtual lock on the world's production, refining, transporting, and selling of oil.

The staff found that "in 1949 the seven international petroleum companies accounted for more than one-half of the world's crude production (excluding Russia and satellite countries), about 99 percent of the output in the Middle East, over 96 percent of the production in the Eastern Hemisphere, and almost 45 percent in the Western Hemisphere. If United States production is excluded, their share of the output of the rest of the Western Hemisphere is 80.5 percent." The staff investigators found that "the seven international oil companies controlled, in 1950, almost 57 percent of the world's crude-oil-refining capacity. In the Western Hemisphere, excluding the United States, they held more than 75 percent; and in the Eastern Hemisphere, 79 percent. Excluding the capacity of the United States and that under Russian control the seven international companies owned more than 77 percent of the rest of the world's crude-oil-refining capacity."

Even more significant, the FTC staff believed, was the seven-company cartel's control over the world cracking capacity. It noted that ". . . the cracking process enables a refiner to obtain a greater quantity of higher-valued products (for example, gasoline as compared to residual fuel oil) from a given quantity of crude than can be obtained by the straight-run distillation method of refining . . . Moreover, it is only by using cracking processes that the petroleum industry is able to produce high-octane gasoline and many of the chemicals which are the basic raw materials for synthetic rubber and many plastics. Thus the cracking process has made the petroleum industry an important supplier of products to other industries, and the concentration of control over the world's cracking capacity thereby affects a broader segment of the world economy than control over crude-refining capacity."

The seven giants were found to own 47 percent of the cracking capacity of the United States, 53 percent of the Western Hemisphere's, 84 percent of the Eastern Hemisphere's, and 55 percent of the world's. If the United States and the Soviet Union were excluded, they owned 85 percent of all cracking facilities in the world, compared to their ownership of 77 percent of the crude-refining facilities.

As for transportation, the staff reported that the seven companies owned at least 50 percent of the world's tanker fleet.

The conclusion was obvious: the price-fixing power of these seven companies in the world's oil market was "unchallengeable." It was a power (the staff proved by many previously unrevealed documents) that had been used for at least two decades to monopolize foreign production and to fix prices by manipulating both foreign and domestic production and by restricting imports for the same purpose.

The FTC's case was so stunning and so persuasive that President Truman had no alternative but to order the Justice Department to start antitrust action against the international oil cartel. He issued his order on June 23, 1952.

But almost immediately thereafter, he began to cave in. Less than seven months later—on January 12, 1953—he ordered the Attorney General to drop the criminal charges and continue the prosecution only as a civil case, thus assuring the executives of the oil companies that they would spend no time in jail.

A few days later, President Eisenhower took office. Always a friend to oil interests, one of his first actions was to pronounce the policy of his administration as being "that the enforcement of the antitrust laws of the United States against the Western oil companies operating in the Near East may be deemed secondary to the national security interest . . ."

This "national security" pronouncement placed the matter directly in the hands of the National Security Council, which, on August 6, 1953, took the extraordinary step of transferring from the Justice Department to the State Department primary jurisdiction over the cartel case. Never before had the Secretary of State been given jurisdiction over an antitrust case. The reason for this strange transfer, which was guaranteed to cripple the case beyond recovery, has never been explained, but John Blair, who was on the FTC staff that drew up the famous report, later pointed out (*The Control of Oil*) that Secretary of State John Foster Dulles' former law firm, Sullivan and Cromwell, had been retained as defense counsel by some of the cartel members. Dulles, of course, was, aside from Eisenhower, the most powerful member of the National Security Council. Later, the NSC ordered the Justice Department to drop all charges against the cartel relating to joint production, joint refining, joint storage, and joint transportation. With this prohibition in effect, the federal prosecutors had little chance to build a case on marketing alone. Fifteen years and three Presidents later, the cartel case was finally and secretly closed (January 28, 1968). No penalties had been applied, and no changes had been forced upon the cartel's operation.

There have been a few other desiccated and melancholy antitrust cases involving the oil companies. Their outcomes—if they ever went so far as to have something that could be called outcomes—were sometimes instructive. For example, in 1957 the Justice Department sued twenty-nine U.S. oil companies for raising their prices in collusion during the Suez crisis. A federal grand jury handed down price-fixing indictments. There was plenty of juicy evidence; the feds even had wiretap transcriptions showing that the oil executives plotted their price jumps. But then something remarkable happened: the case was transferred from Alexandria, Virginia, to Tulsa, Oklahoma. It is a state where profound sympathy for oil companies can be commonly found, even in the hearts of judges, and Judge Royce A. Savage was no exception. He dismissed all antitrust charges. A few months later, he resigned from the federal judiciary and accepted the offer of a vice-presidency with Gulf Oil Corporation. Gulf had been one of the defendants in the antitrust suit.

Another instructive case was concluded in 1969, when Jersey Standard, Mobil, and Standard of Indiana were convicted of violating federal antitrust laws and fined $300,000. The moral of that lesson, as Morton Mintz and Jerry Cohen pointed out (*America, Inc.*), is that the fine came to only one tenth of 1 percent of their total net incomes in the preceding year.

ARGO MERCHANT. The 640-foot tanker ran aground on the Nantucket Shoals on December 15, 1976, creating the United States' biggest ocean mess. Heavy seas pounded the *Argo Merchant* to pieces, and her cargo of 7.6 million gallons of gooey No. 6 fuel oil spread into a hundred-mile slick that immediately began to threaten one of the world's best fishing grounds, the 10,000-square-mile plateau known as Georges Bank. As it turned out, the fishing area was not nearly so harmed as had been feared. After all, as tankers go, the *Argo Merchant* was a squirt—a mere 18,700-ton ship. What would happen to America's fishing areas if the supertankers—the 200,000-ton to 555,000-ton ships—began to break up off our shores?

This misfortune also pointed to two dangerous defects in tanker traffic: (1) the lack of stringent international safety regulations and (2) the sloppy attitude of the U.S. Coast Guard.

The 23-year-old *Argo Merchant* was a rust bucket. It had been flagged as a dangerous and defective ship by the Coast Guard when it had made a previous trip to the United States; indeed, it had been banned from the port of Philadelphia. But here it was nonetheless, legally afloat and fully loaded and plowing U.S. waters once again, despite its past record. And what a record it was!

In the previous twelve years, the *Argo Merchant* had been involved in nineteen major "incidents," including collisions with docks and other ships and two previous groundings. One of its more illustrious trips had required nearly eight months from Singapore to the West Coast of the United States. En route, there were three engine-room fires, requiring her to be towed back to Singapore; on her fourth attempt, her engines broke down and she had to be towed to Osaka, Japan, for more repairs. As she limped onto the high seas once more, her boilers again broke down and she barely made it into Honolulu Harbor for further repairs. No sooner had she cleared Honolulu Harbor for the last leg than her electrical system collapsed and she had to return to Honolulu for further repairs.

The *Argo Merchant*'s previous two groundings had been off the Borneo coast in 1969 and off Calabria, Italy, in 1971.

But, of course, a ship does not fall apart, founder, and run aground on its own. It takes a lousy captain and crew to finish the job.

The ship's owners, a group of Greeks, claimed that the *Argo Merchant*'s captain, George Papadopoulos, was in his room asleep when the ship went aground, at 6 A.M. But Captain Papadopoulos said he was not only on the bridge but had been there all night.

It might have been better if he had been in bed, for during his extended watch on the bridge he had managed to get the ship twenty-four miles off course. How had he accomplished this in such well-charted waters? First of all, as the Captain later admitted at a hearing, his ship carried no long-range navigation equipment. Second, his gyrocompass was broken—registering six degrees off true. So this forced the helmsman to steer by magnetic compass, which is not nearly so reliable as a gyrocompass. Third, the Captain had not had an accurate celestial fix on his position for more than fifteen hours. And fourth, the water-current charts he was using were November's, not December's, and this made a great difference. In fact, Greek merchant mariners were noted for their sloppy seamanship, so Captain Papadopoulos was simply maintaining an ancient tradition.

When the *Argo* struck the shoal, the Captain had slammed the engines into full-speed reverse. This started the ship to shaking so violently that a valve broke and water poured into the engine room. The weight of the water in the engine room hopelessly locked the ship onto the shoal.

Such accidents could happen to ships flying under any flags, of course. But, at the moment, it appeared that ships flying Liberian flags were strangely susceptible to accidents.

Of the nineteen tankers that sank in 1976, the *Argo Merchant*'s year to go down, eleven, as it did, flew the Liberian flag. Many of the great messes of recent history had been made by Liberian-flag ships. Two days after the *Argo Merchant* foundered, the 810-foot Liberian-flag tanker *Sansinena* blew up in Los Angeles Harbor while her tanks were being cleaned, killing nine and injuring fifty. A week later (on December 24) the Liberian-registered *Oswego-Peace* spilled two thousand gallons of oil in the Thames River near Groton, Connecticut. Three days later (December 27), the Liberian-registered *Olympic Games* ran aground in the Delaware River near Philadelphia, spilling 133,000 gallons of oil and fouling the shorelines of three states. Et cetera, et cetera. The *Amoco Cadiz*, which ran aground and broke up off the coast of France in March 1978, spilling 1.3 million barrels of crude oil (the worst tanker accident up to that time), flew the Liberian flag; so did the infamous *Torrey Canyon*, which ran aground fifteen miles off Land's End, England, in March 1967, spilling 830,000 barrels—giving the world its first hefty taste of supertanker pollution. (When oil of that quantity is loosed, the problem is almost too great to contemplate. Seven months after the *Amoco Cadiz* spilled its cargo, the cleanup was still going on. Ten thousand people were employed to do it. The special horror was in the emulsion of oil and water—called "mousse" —that more than doubled the weight and volume of the original oil. There was enough mousse from the *Amoco Cadiz* spill to fill 17,000 railroad tank cars, if they had been handy.)

Bad as things were, it was really remarkable that they weren't worse, considering the potential for trouble. James J. Reynolds, president of the American Institute of Merchant Shipping, in a letter to the Washington *Post* on January 1, 1977, reasonably argued: "It is not generally known that this nation daily imports about 7.3 million barrels of crude and petroleum products, practically all of it brought in over the seas by tankers with very few spills or incidents. That translates into about 307 million gallons imported per day (42 gallons to a barrel) or on a yearly basis the astronomical amount of about 112 billion gallons. This tremendous movement means that a virtual armada of tankers is constantly plying the seas every day and night into and out of the ports of the United States . . . Without meaning to ignore the ugliness of any oil spill, I suggest that the *Argo Merchant* and *Olympic Games* incidents add up to a minuscule spill when considered as part of the tremendous flow of oil continually entering this country . . ."

The potential for trouble was also greatly augmented by the poor seamanship and poor equipment of foreign shippers and the craven guardianship of the United States Coast Guard.

It was hardly surprising that Liberian-flag ships figured so often in maritime tragedies. Nearly a fifth of the world's 5,311 tankers then flew the flag of Liberia, a tiny nation in equatorial West Africa, which, ironically, made Liberia's tanker fleet the largest in the world. (Later, Liberia's percentage of the world's fleet would increase.) Since Liberia could hardly be considered a maritime nation, the heavy registry was a bit of economic fakery.

The Liberian flag is called a "flag of convenience." Some of the biggest oil companies in the world register their fleets in Liberia (or in Panama, or Greece, or some of the other nations that take an anarchistic view of ocean commerce). They do it to save money. U.S. law requires ships registered in this country to hire U.S. crews. Italian crews cost half as much; Greek crews cost only one third as much, and Chinese crews can be hired for even a bit less than one third U.S. rates.

By registering under a flag of convenience, shipowners not only save millions of dollars a year in salaries, they also are able to duck most—and sometimes all—U.S. income taxes on their "foreign" shipping profits.

And, of course, nations like Liberia and Panama and Greece have such low safety standards that shipowners can keep truly hazardous vessels on the high seas making "just one more trip" over and over until something horrible occurs, like the wreck of the *Argo Merchant*. The United States was especially vulnerable to the traffic of rust buckets, because it had no deepwater ports on either the Atlantic or the Gulf coast, and only a few on the West Coast, that could handle the new, 200,000-ton supertankers. So shippers sent their oil to the United States in the smaller tankers—80 percent arriving in ships of under seventy thousand deadweight tons—and it was this breed that contained the old clunkers that could fall apart at the drop of an anchor. Shortly after the *Argo Merchant* accident, Jesse Calhoon, president of the Marine Engineers Beneficial Association, complained (partly, of course, because the foreign-flag ships were costing his union jobs), "We are the garbage dump for the tankers of the world." There was an element of truth in what he said.

But we needn't have been. Much of the blame lay with the United States Coast Guard, which had, under pressures from the shipowners, shirked its duty in the worst way.

Vernon A. Guidry, Jr., a reporter for the Washington *Star,* dug into the Coast Guard's records in 1976 and discovered that although that agency is mandated to investigate every oil spill, in fact it was not investigating 15 percent of the major spills, not investigating 13 percent of the medium spills, and not investigating 32 percent of the minor spills (a category that some environmentalists would argue does not exist, since all spills do ecological damage). He found that the Coast Guard was spending ony 4 percent of its operating budget on a marine-environment protection program. He found that during a recent three-year period, the Coast Guard assessed penalties in fewer than one third of the spills, and that although the assessments totaled $9.4 million, the Coast Guard collected only $4.3 million. Moreover, the average penalty had fallen from $1,143 in 1973 to $674 in 1975.

There were other signs of the agency's shiftlessness. In 1972, Congress had empowered the Coast Guard to unilaterally impose safety standards on all ships entering U.S. waters and to bar tankers that did not comply with the standards. But the Coast Guard did not use these powers, because, as its commandant, Admiral William O. Siler, told the Senate Commerce Committee, he and his fellow officers did not want to "cause trouble." Instead, the Coast Guard adopted the relatively lax international standards already in use.

At the time of the *Argo Merchant*'s sinking, the Coast Guard had been working for many months on a new set of regulations that, among other things, would have required for the first time that ships coming into American waters have such basic equipment as magnetic compasses, depth finders, and radar. Not until after the sinking stirred public anger—and then only because of the personal intervention of Transportation Secretary Brock Adams—were these regulations established as law. Also as a result of the *Argo* sinking, the Coast Guard instituted its Tanker Vessel Inspection, a program that required foreign-flag vessels to submit to detailed checks of their structural soundness and firefighting and cargo-handling equipment. Previously, only ships carrying volatile cargoes, such as liquid natural gas, had had to open their holds to safety inspectors.

But there were still gaping loopholes in the Coast Guard's protective screen, even under the new regulations. Some of the trouble could be blamed simply on lack of manpower. With hundreds of foreign-flag ships entering U.S. waters every day, it would have been impossible, even with the best of will, to give them all a sharp inspection. The Coast Guard's Norfolk office, for example, had a staff of thirty-two inspectors who were responsible for all ports in Virginia and most of North Carolina. They were able to board and cursorily inspect only one of every four foreign tankers that entered Hampton Roads, Virginia, one of the major U.S. ports on the East Coast.

There was no way for the Coast Guard to discover the dangerously decrepit vessels until they reached port; the guardsmen could hardly pounce on every ship as soon as it penetrated the three-mile zone. And yet, having said that in defense of the Coast Guard, one must point out that it often failed to spot, and impound, the rogue vessels *after* they reached port. For example, the Coast Guard had to be held responsible for the presence on the high seas of the Liberian-registry tanker *Golden Jason*, which, one month after the *Argo Merchant* disaster, broke down on its way to Newport News and had to be towed into port. En route from Jacksonville to New York, the *Jason* was filled with 9 million gallons of crude oil and could have turned into a worse polluter than the *Argo* if the seas had been rough. What condition did the Coast Guard find the *Jason* to be in? Its engines were, obviously, worn out completely, and so were its boilers. Its lifeboats were inoperable. Its emergency fire pump was broken. Its anchor had lost so much chain that it could not be safely used. A Coast Guard commander gave this description of the *Jason's* electrical system: "They'd put in an extension cord and run it a half mile down the ship." Some Coast Guard officials who inspected the *Jason* after the breakdown said they could not understand how such a ship could even sail.

But the moral of the story is that the *Golden Jason* presumably would not have been sailing up the coast with its time bomb of oil if the Coast Guard had been on its toes. Before its breakdown cruise, the *Jason* had been out of service for almost a year in Jacksonville, Florida. At no time during that year did the Coast Guard send an inspector aboard. So, although the ship's owners intended to take the *Jason* to Spain and dismantle her for scrap iron, they decided to load her with oil and make one last coastwise trip. Because the Coast Guard had failed to visit the *Jason* during that year and discover her condition, it almost became the East Coast's worst spill.

The Coast Guard's collusion with the oil industry was further illuminated in 1975, when Senator Lee Metcalf disclosed that the Coast Guard's decision not to require double bottoms on the tankers that would transport Alaskan oil down the coast was made on the advice of a study group that included the American Institute of Merchant Shipping (the tanker lobby) and the American Petroleum Institute (the oil lobby), but that when the Coast Guard's final report was published it somehow neglected to mention where the advice had come from.

EARLY FRIGHT CAMPAIGNS. The history of Big Oil's fright campaigns can be traced deep into the nineteenth century, but for the sake of brevity let's start with World War I.

1914-18

Britain had just converted her navy from coal to oil, so it was absolutely vital that her supply of oil be uninterrupted. Obviously, she was ripe for plucking. All our oilmen needed to do was to present a picture of scarcity. This was easy to arrange. In 1914, Standard Oil, monarch of world oil, supported by statements from the U.S. Bureau of Mines (always in industry's pocket), announced that the United States was down to its last 5.7 billion barrels of oil reserves—scarcely enough to last out the decade—and after that there would be no more. Oil had clearly become a precious commodity. Up, up went the price.

Later in the war, after the United States had entered it, the oilmen decided to continue the claim of great scarcity in order to win a tax advantage: the oil depletion allowance.

Previously, the federal income tax law had treated oilmen like other businessmen. The money they spent exploring for oil, digging wells, building refineries and pipelines, et cetera, was considered ordinary business expense; and if they could prove that their wells were about to run dry, they could receive a very modest depletion deduction—5 percent of gross income—which was the same kind of tax benefit that a farmer could get if his land was being eroded by a river. The declining production of a well was at that time viewed as nothing more unfortunate than the depreciation of factory machinery, and oil was viewed as no more sacred a commodity than, say, overalls or paint.

But, using the war as a vehicle for their propaganda, the oilmen sought in 1918 to obtain special privileges. They asked that, in the future, they be permitted tax deductions—depreciation—based not on the cost of a well but on "the present fair market value of the oil." It was a license to rob the U.S. Treasury, but the oilmen asked it in the most patriotic way: give us that advantage, they said, and we will go out and find enough oil to win this war, no matter how long it lasts.

Oil, crucial to the Allied effort, was, they swore, fast disappearing, and no time should be lost passing this incentive tax.

The leader of oil's patriotic fright campaign in Congress was the great Republican mountebank Boies Penrose, who had first won his seat in the U.S. Senate by bribing the Pennsylvania legislature with a half million dollars (this was before senators were popularly elected) and went on to become the most powerful political boss of his era. An elephant of a man with an appetite to match (typical dinner: a dozen oysters, chicken gumbo, a terrapin stew, two ducks, six kinds of vegetables, a quart of coffee, and several cognacs), he was almost as well known in the whorehouses of Pennsylvania (some of which hung his photograph in the parlor) as he was in the council chambers of the mighty. Penrose was The Great Fixer of his day, and his success on this occasion was doubtless made easier by the use of funds from his oil patrons (John Archbold, of Standard Oil, for example, was known to have given him $25,000 on one occasion).

The following exchange, on October 11, 1918, was a typical piece of Penrose orchestration:

Oil Policy Administrator Mark Requa: "Forty percent of the oil is exhausted . . . The United States imported 30 million barrels from Mexico last year."

Senator Penrose: "Is not the fact that we are dependent on a foreign nation for a very large percentage of our consumption a reason for providing in this revenue bill some means of stimulating the American field as much as possible during this war period?"

Requa: "I think it is necessary."

Exactly one month after that exchange, the war ended. But such was the hysterical momentum that had launched the bill in the first place, it could not be stopped, and in December 1918, it was passed overwhelmingly.

The oil companies immediately began abusing the new law; the very next year, Gulf, for example, claimed depletion allowances equaling 449 percent of its net income. As this scandal grew and spread, public outrage pressured Congress to put a ceiling to the thievery; so, in 1926, leaders of the industry, fearing that reform might get out of hand if they did not head it off, proposed that Congress limit depletion deductions to 25 percent of their gross, which could allow 50 percent of their net income to be tax-free.

The House used the suggested figure, 25 percent, but the Senate, apparently not wishing to appear niggardly, set the limit at 30 percent. The conference committee split the difference, and thereby that infamous figure, 27.5 percent, came into existence.

1920–28

Our big companies, particularly Standard Oil, were running into stiffer competition overseas. Britain and France, for example, had teamed up to exclude U.S. companies from the Middle East. U.S. companies decided to stir up public opinion in such a way that it would be easier for the State Department to step in and help them get foreign leases; so the industry's propagandists began to circulate rumors once again that we were running out of oil. The U.S. Geological Survey—drawing its information, as always, from the oil companies—told the New York *Times* in early 1920 that "the position of the United States in regard to oil can best be characterized as precarious." Four months later, Dr. George Otis Smith, director of the USGS, warned that within the near future "Americans will have to depend on foreign sources or use less oil, or perhaps both." Two months later, USGS officials predicted that "unless our consumption is checked, we shall by 1925 be dependent on foreign oil fields to the extent of . . . possibly as much as 200 million barrels of crude each year, except insofar as the situation may . . . be helped to a slight extent by shale oil. Add to this probability that within five years—perhaps three years only—our domestic production will begin to fall off with increasing rapidity, due to the exhaustion of our reserves . . ."

Oil industrialists began planting stories with the press that when our oil reserves were gone we would be at the mercy of the British, an ungrateful lot who had been saved by U.S. oil in World War I but now only waited for a chance to scalp us at the pump. These rumors were so successful that there was actually serious talk in Washington about having to go to war with Britain.

Once again, it worked. Seeing the U.S. State Department and the U.S. Congress carrying the oil companies' flag so militantly, and seeing the American public's angry and fearful mood, the British, after six years of negotiation, capitulated in 1928, giving up 24 percent of the stock in the Iraq Petroleum Company to Standard, Mobil, Texaco, and Gulf. Thus the U.S. giants cracked the Middle East.

The British had not been fooled by all the talk of "running dry." E. H. Davenport and S. R. Cooke, two British writers, observed wryly in *The Oil Trusts and Anglo-American Relations* (Macmillan, 1924), "There is this strange habit peculiar to the American oil industry which one should observe in passing. Although it doubles its output roughly every ten years, yet it declares every other year that its peak of production has been passed and that its oil fields are well nigh exhausted. . . . Nevertheless new pools are continually producing wells brought in to replace those declining, and each year the total output turns out to be surprisingly greater than the year before. One cannot doubt that the lugubrious prophecies of American oilmen are in some way related to the wish for higher prices." And the wish to expand their overseas operations.

1928-35

Joining forces to obtain concessions in the Middle East was only part of the U.S. majors' objective; the other half was to reach an agreement on restricting foreign production in such a way as to support prices. This was achieved at the infamous conference at Achnacarry House, in Scotland, in 1928, where officials of Standard Oil, British Petroleum, and Shell met for a spot of grouse shooting and also, not incidentally, to devise a plan for limiting the worldwide output of crude. The world was enjoying an oversupply, and all signs pointed to a continuing glut (world production had risen 17 percent in 1927; storage stocks were at an unprecedented level, and prices were tumbling). The Achnacarry agreement would help stop that.

But it wouldn't help the astonishing overproduction in the United States. Not only were U.S. prices being driven down (20 percent down in 1927), but there was excruciating waste.

*

Fields were being pumped so furiously that they lost much of their gas pressure; only a fraction of the oil was brought to the surface that would have been recovered if the fields had been developed at a sensible pace. It was estimated by experts that in 1927, in the Burbank field, in Oklahoma, failure to maintain proper gas pressure resulted in the loss of at least 20 million additional barrels of oil—$36 million in revenue—from that one field alone, in that one year. But the independent operators, the wildcatters, were intoxicated with the notion that the oil would never run out, that there was always more to be found, lush fields of it, just over the next hill. So why be cautious? Many of them favored pumping the limit, no matter what it did to gas pressures and no matter what the resulting oil glut did to prices.

The independents were not trying to build long-term global empires. They simply wanted the excitement of the wild and risky hunt, hoping for immediate riches, which they were willing to gamble on another hunt. It was a colorful and romantic point of view—but it chilled the major, integrated firms (who had much to lose, for fourteen of them already controlled nearly 60 percent of the proven domestic oil acreage). They knew that the only dependable riches were built on market stability, that stability in prices could be achieved only by regulating production, and that this must be done either through private agreements—as at Achnacarry—or by public regulations. They much preferred the former, but since there were far too many independent companies and they were far too anarchistic to reach agreement on self-control, public regulation would have to do.

At the moment, regulation depended on such agencies as the Oklahoma Corporation Commission and the Texas Railroad Commission, but they were filled with hacks, and their enforcement powers were so limited that when they set a suggested ceiling on reduction, it was commonly ignored. The majors wanted to change that; they wanted to give these agencies rules of iron.

But instead of being honest about it, instead of explaining to the public that the chaotic production hurt company profits as well as ruined fields, the majors used their standard tactic: a fright campaign. In 1929, the Federal Oil Conservation Board, dominated by majors, warned that the United States was "exhausting its petroleum reserves at a dangerous rate." It advised cutting back production in the United States and bringing in all the foreign oil possible, particularly from South America—where the independents were almost nonexistent but some majors were strong. (The most important foreign source of oil in this hemisphere was Venezuela, where the biggest producers were Standard and Gulf—the latter company being controlled by the family of Andrew Mellon, who was then Treasury Secretary and the most influential aide to President Hoover, as he had been earlier to Coolidge and Harding—three Presidents who were virtually on call to the oil industry.)

The majors' worries turned into downright panic after October 30, 1930, the day that the irresponsible and irrepressible wildcatter Columbus M. (Dad) Joiner brought in a well on the Daisy Bradford farm, near Kilgore, Texas. The oil world would never again be the same. That discovery well opened up the East Texas field, the richest the world had ever known. And it brought in a horde of other adventurers. By the end of 1930 there were 3,540 wells in East Texas (by the end of 1933 there would be 12,000) and they were producing a million barrels a day. Quickly, the market came apart.

The thing about the East Texas plunder that frightened the majors so much was that they had had very little to do with the discovery, owned few of the leases, and certainly had little control over the total production.

So they mounted a pious campaign for conservation, and they had their friend Secretary of the Interior Ray Lyman Wilbur declare, in 1931, "We must import as much foreign oil as possible to save our domestic supply"—

foreign oil owned by the majors to save domestic oil owned by the independents. Naturally, the small operators paid no attention to this plea and went right on pumping like crazy. So the majors gave them a marketplace lesson by slashing the price they paid for crude to 10 cents a barrel. What could the independents do about it, since the majors, owning most of the pipelines and refineries and retail outlets, were the principal buyers? And yet, those independents who recognized the destructiveness of riotous production could not afford to quit pumping unless their neighbor, and their neighbor's neighbor, ad infinitum, agreed to do so too. So they all went on pumping madly away, for pennies, creating economic chaos and forcing the Texas legislature to pass, in 1933, a "market demand" law; production of oil within the state would thereafter be "prorationed" by the Texas Railroad Commission; which is to say producers would be permitted to operate their wells a predetermined number of days each month, according to what the "market" (that is, the major oil company buyers) desired. And since Texas was by far the most productive state, its price of oil pretty well determined the national price—and to some extent, the world price.

Two years later, at the behest of the majors, Congress passed the Connally "Hot Oil" Act, prohibiting interstate shipment of oil that had been produced in excess of what the majors (or, to be formal about it, the state commissions they controlled) said should be produced, and establishing stiff penalties for those who broke the law.

Thus the majors had reached their goal: a politically approved technique for fixing domestic prices. After that, when they wanted to create enough of a scarcity to bolster prices, they simply placed smaller "buy" orders, and the Texas Railroad Commission (and similar agencies elsewhere) ordered lower production.

Years later, U.S. Senate investigators would acknowledge the obvious, that the "prorationing" and "hot oil" acts had been passed not for conservation—not to preserve a national resource as long as possible—but as a crucial part of what the investigators called "a perfect pattern of monopolistic control over oil production and the distribution thereof among refiners and distributors, and ultimately the price paid by the public." In victory, the majors became so cocky that they became candid. W. S. Farish, chairman of the executive committee of Standard Oil of New Jersey, told a congressional committee, ". . . the whole idea of conservation and stabilization of the industry [that is, stabilization of prices: price fixing] . . . to my mind are synonymous terms; they mean practically the same thing."

From the mid-1930s until the early 1970s, the Texas Railroad Commission was the chief regulator of prices in this country.[1]

---

1. The TRC has always operated in a cocoon of conflict of interest. Its officials are elected; theoretically, Texas voters could create a commission that would take a critical view of the oil industry and a sympathetic view of consumers, but this has never happened. It has never happened because, although the oil industry is not capable of buying elections outright, it is quite capable of tilting elections with so much money that the outcome is virtually guaranteed. Presumably this has always been done. There is proof it was done in the 1960s and 1970s, for University of Texas Professor

FEDERAL OIL AND GAS CORPORATION.   Most of the early suggestions for getting the government into the oil and gas business were made for anything but radical purposes, and never were they made with the idea of competing with private enterprise. In 1913, when the fleet was being converted from coal to oil, the Navy wanted the federal government to get into the oil business simply because it felt that a government-controlled supply would be more reliable in time of war than a private source would be.

The next serious proposal came in 1920, and it was meant to be an element of economic warfare—or retaliation—against Britain. Anglophobia was running pretty high (we had supplied Britain virtually all her refined petroleum needs during World War I and she had repaid us after the war by banning U.S. oil companies from holding development leases anywhere in the Empire), so Senator James Phelan of California, in May 1920, introduced a bill (S. 4396, 66th Cong., 2nd sess.) which would have set up a government-owned corporation to explore for oil in foreign countries. It would have been called, appropriately, the United States Oil Corporation. Phelan's hope was that a government oil company would be able to give stiffer competition to the British and the Dutch (the latter also barred U.S. oil concessions in their colonies) than private companies were giving. But the oil companies, fearing a federal foot in the door, succeeded in having Phelan's proposal shelved.

Nothing was heard of the proposal after that until World War II put tremendous strains on the oil industry. As Michael B. Stoff points out in his fine little book *Oil, War and American Security* (Yale Univ. Press, 1980), "The invasion of North Africa had driven Allied demands for American petroleum sharply upward in 1942. By 1943, two out of every three tons of cargo shipped to American forces were petroleum or petroleum products. At the same time, the Germans had captured the oil of Rumania and two of the most important Russian fields. It seemed likely that the reserves of the Middle East were their next target. With German submarines disrupting shipping from the Caribbean to the United States and with Pacific oil in the hands of the Japanese, the possibility existed that all the Allied nations might become completely dependent on the United States for oil." The drain on us was so heavy that there were oil and gasoline shortages in this country in 1942 and 1943. The oil industry was unable to keep up with the demand; by the end of 1943, proven reserves had fallen for the first time in a decade.

David F. Prindle did a study of those decades (*Petroleum Politics and the Texas Railroad Commission,* University of Texas Press, 1981) and found that a Commission candidate endorsed by the oil industry usually received about twenty times more in campaign funds than all his opponents combined.

And then, just to make sure that none of these hand-picked chaps goes off on a wild streak of independence and causes trouble, the industry prevails upon the legislature to cripple the Commission with lack of funds and a skeleton staff. At the time of the slant-hole scandal of the 1960s (many oilmen in East Texas were caught burrowing under their neighbors' property with slanted holes and stealing oil), the Commission had only three field inspectors—one tenth as many as they had hired in the 1930s. Also in the 1960s, when the gas utilities were tricking consumers into signing up for gas the companies didn't own, the Commission's Gas Utilities Division employed eight people to keep an eye on two hundred and five companies. Impossible. And that's exactly the way the industry wanted it to be.

This was the tense atmosphere in which the State Department's Committee on International Petroleum Policy (CIPP), created in January 1943, went to work. Its assignment was to appraise the foreign oil problems that we could probably be facing after the war and to recommend whatever steps would be necessary to guarantee an abundant foreign source to supplement our domestic supply.

Prior experience having shown that private companies could not be relied on to put national interests ahead of profits, the CIPP recommended that the government establish a Petroleum Reserves Corporation, owned by the government and directed by representatives from the State, Navy, War, and Interior departments, to acquire its own overseas oil supply, specifically to buy oil from Saudi Arabia.

Harold Ickes, Interior Secretary, loved the idea—only, he didn't think it went far enough. To say that Ickes distrusted oilmen is putting it mildly. For several years, he had been trying to persuade Roosevelt to undercut their influence on the foreign oil scene by getting the government into the business as an active participant: not merely as a buyer of oil but as an explorer for oil and a producer of oil. He wanted the U.S. Government to own an oil company, just as the British Government did. He thought he saw his chance when, in 1943, Standard of California and Texaco, then operating in Saudi Arabia under the name California Arabian Standard Oil Company (Casoc), ran into trouble.

As mentioned earlier (see the chapter on "The Company Cartel"), when World War II cut off most of Casoc's market, the company was hard pressed to pay the profligate Saudi King Ibn Saud enough royalties to keep him happy. That was when officials of Casoc—which in 1943 would be renamed the Arabian American Oil Company (Aramco)—came to Washington with proposals for obtaining illegal lend-lease money for Ibn Saud. Desperately, they even suggested—a strange suggestion, coming from oilmen—that the United States Government itself buy oil products from the Saudis, just to keep the Arabs in pocket money until Casoc/Aramco could resume its full-scale oil shipments after the war.

Casoc officials took their proposals to Ickes and asked his help. He may have sounded sympathetic, but in fact he was delighted to learn that the oilmen were in a bind and vulnerable. He hurried to capitalize on the situation.

It was at that point that he proposed that the United States Government buy Casoc.

His proposal won surprisingly strong support. By mid-June 1943, the following officials had endorsed the creation of the Petroleum Reserves Corporation, for the purpose of acquiring oil leases in foreign countries: James F. Byrnes, director of the Office of War Mobilization and Roosevelt's adviser on domestic affairs; Frank Knox, Secretary of the Navy; Henry Stimson, Secretary of War; Herbert Feis, chairman of the CIPP; Robert P. Patterson, assistant secretary (later Secretary) of War; Abe Fortas, then an Interior official; Cordell Hull, Secretary of State; and others, including the future Secretary of Defense James Forrestal and a host of Pentagon brass.

Few projects with such potent godfathers have failed.

The Petroleum Reserves Corporation was chartered on June 30, 1943; President Roosevelt named Ickes to be its chairman and at the same time ordered negotiations to begin immediately for the purchase of Casoc's stock in its entirety.

The United States was about to take the radical step of becoming the proud owner of an oil company with vast holdings in Arabia.

Or was it? Well, no, not quite. Standard Oil of California and Texaco simply refused to sell Casoc's stock. Would they consider selling, if not all of it, at least 51 percent? No. Would they consider selling 50 percent and letting the government be an equal partner? No. Would they sell, say, a third of the stock? No. They wanted the government's help, but they didn't want its partnership. All of Ickes' proposals ran into a wall of no's.

So he tried to get tough. Casoc wanted to build a new refinery in Arabia but needed U.S. Government financial aid. At first, when Ickes thought he had a good chance to buy Casoc, he indicated his approval for the loan. But when Socal and Texaco turned him down, he canceled the refinery loan.

Temporarily, that seemed to soften Socal and Texaco. They reentered negotiations and began sounding as though they might be willing to sell a one-third interest in Casoc, after all. They named a price ($40 million). Ickes agreed. But then, with the flimsiest of excuses, Socal and Texaco *doubled* the price. Ickes felt he couldn't justify spending $80 million, so the deal fell through, with Ickes complaining that the companies had just been stringing him along.

Still, he was determined to get the government somehow into the oil business, because he was convinced that, by his doing so, it could, in the postwar world, prevent the multinational companies from manipulating prices and supplies to the detriment of the people. "If we can really get away with it," he wrote at the time, "the Petroleum Reserves Corporation can be a big factor in world oil affairs and have a strong influence on foreign relations generally."

The companies knew this as well as Ickes did, and they were determined that it not happen. As Michael Stoff points out, "The reluctance of Socal and Texaco to give up possession of their property was but a small measure of the industry's unwillingness to give up the initiative in framing national policy for foreign oil. Ickes' doggedness reflected his intention to see that initiative placed in public hands."

He would try a different approach. He would try to get the government to build a pipeline in Arabia. This would put the government squarely in the middle of the oil business but without engaging in the kind of production competition that so frightened the private companies.

Virtually all of the Washington officials—including President Roosevelt—who had favored buying Casoc now threw their support to the pipeline idea. But the oil companies, and their friends in Congress and the press, were just as wholeheartedly against it. Oil-state congressmen denounced it as another of Roosevelt's socialistic schemes. The president of the Houston Oil Company called it a "fascist" plot. The 66-man Petroleum Industry War Council—made up entirely of executives from the major oil companies—not only opposed the idea but recommended that Ickes' whole oil bailiwick, including the Petroleum Reserves Corporation, be immediately disbanded before it thought up any more mischievous ideas. Industry's fear, as Stoff explains, was that "through the pipeline agreement the government could influence directly the production, marketing, and pricing arrangements throughout the Middle East and the world."

Industry's resistance paid off. By the middle of 1944, the pipeline proposal had become buried in the broader postwar oil policy negotiations with Britain; and Roosevelt, his body and spirit failing, was no longer able or willing to fight for the project. So it died. And nothing like it was ever again able to muster strong support in Washington.

HANNA, MARCUS ALONZO (MARK, or "DOLLAR MARK"). When oil companies set out to buy politicians, they cannot do it as simply as a farmer slops hogs, bucketing out the money and yelling soooo-ey. The money must be channeled carefully to the politicians who can do them the most good, and it must be channeled with at least a touch of decorum. As in many other aspects of the industry, it was Standard Oil that blazed the trail of political bribery. So lushly did Rockefeller's company pay off politicians that jokes were made of it. In the 1880s and later, it was said that Standard "did everything to the Pennsylvania legislature except refine it," and Standard's generosity in the Ohio, New York, and other pertinent legislatures, and of course in Congress, was similarly welcome.

The most successful collector and dispenser of political bribes in the latter part of the nineteenth century was Marcus Alonzo Hanna, the political boss of Ohio—a state as crucial to national politics as it was to the Rockefeller empire. Hanna was also the creator of William McKinley (that is, he bailed McKinley out of bankruptcy in 1893 and then financed his rise to the White House, in 1896, to become a rubber stamp for big business).

Hanna—a crass, dictatorial, bullet-headed, blunt-spoken coal and iron magnate—had power over the Republican Party, and over all national politics, "such as no other man in our history has had" (in the words of Theodore Roosevelt). He was as responsible as any one person for what Henry Adams saw as "the final surrender of the country to capitalism." It was a tribute to his power that trusts flourished at the turn of the century. Men feared him, because he knew how to use money to buy the nation's political apparatus. He got the money he needed by forcing it out of the business interests who would benefit from his efforts. He levied heavy "dues" against all the big businessmen of his day; none was asked to ante up more heavily than the Rockefeller interests.

Thanks to a man who worked at the Standard Oil headquarters in New York and frequently lost at crap shooting, we know some of the details. Needing more money for his gambling, he rifled Standard's files for letters and sold them to the Hearst newspapers.

None of the letters involved Rockefeller himself, though he must have known what was going on. Several of the letters were either to or from one of Rockefeller's oldest associates, Standard vice-president John D. Archbold. The letters indicate that Archbold had a real feeling for the sport. Nor was he stingy. The letters show, for example, that he processed $44,500 through Senator Joseph B. ("Fire Engine Joe") Foraker of Ohio to pass around among senators willing to help fight antitrust legislation.

But Archbold's most luxurious relationship involved Hanna, who was always forthright, telling Archbold in one letter, "I am 'holding the bag,' and this is going to be an expensive campaign."

The first written evidence that has come down to us of Standard's willingness to buy politicians is in one of these stolen letters. It is from Hanna to Ohio Attorney General David K. Watson, who had just embarked upon an effort to have the Standard Oil Trust broken up for being in violation of Ohio's conspiracy laws.

Hanna made it clear to Watson that if he continued to pursue that course, he would be deprived of Standard's generosity and could ruin his political career. Hanna threatened, probably at the urging of Standard Oil executives, with whom he was in constant contact: "There is no greater mistake for a man in or out of public place to make than to assume that he owes any duty to the public or can in any manner advance his own position or interests by attacking the organizations under which experience has taught business can best be done. From a party standpoint, as in the line of political promotion, I must say that the identification of your office with litigation of this character is a great mistake . . . The Standard Oil Company is officered and managed by some of the best and strongest men in the country. They are pretty much all Republicans and have been most liberal in their contributions to the party, as I personally know, Mr. Rockefeller always quietly doing his share . . ."

REGULATION–NATURAL GAS. Until 1918, the production and distribution of natural gas was largely an intrastate problem and was confined almost entirely to the Appalachian field: western Pennsylvania, parts of Ohio, Kentucky, and West Virginia.

Then, in 1918, the great (more than one million acres) field in the Panhandle of Texas began to come in. It was soon the largest source of natural gas in the United States. Over the next decade, other abundant reserves were discovered, in Louisiana, in California, elsewhere in Texas, and especially the Hugoton, southwestern Kansas, field.

But there was a problem getting the gas to market. Pipelines in the early days were leaky, easily ruptured. That changed in 1926 with the invention of the seamless pipe. After that, the nationwide distribution of natural gas expanded steadily but not exactly swiftly. (The expansion did not keep up with the production of gas. In 1933, the daily waste of natural gas in the Panhandle field alone—waste through actual blowing into the air of excess production—equaled a billion and a half cubic feet, which was an amount sufficient to supply the needs of all domestic and commercial users in the entire United States.)

There was practically no market outlet for the gas produced in the Texas Panhandle until a group of gas-property owners banded together and built a pipeline to Chicago. But first, to guarantee their supply, they acquired most of the Panhandle leases (to be exact, 62 percent). Other groups were doing the same thing elsewhere: acquiring a majority of the leases in a field and then building pipelines to often distant markets.

As of 1936, 11 holding-company groups owned 38,093 miles of the more than 50,000 miles of pipeline in this country—about 76 percent. Of these 11, the 4 largest were The Columbia Gas & Electric Corporation (a Morgan group), which owned 24 percent of the pipeline mileage; Cities Service Co. (the Doheny group), 14 percent; the Electric Bond & Share group, 10 percent; and the Standard Oil Company of New Jersey, slightly under 10 percent. Owning 58 percent of the total pipeline mileage, these four companies also produced 67 percent of the natural gas, and they controlled two thirds of all the natural gas sold in interstate commerce.

The pipeline companies had to report their business to the Federal Trade Commission, but the FTC had no power to regulate them. Here was a commodity, selling interstate for more than $350 billion a year, subject only to the whims of an oligopoly. The concentration of market control, with the same companies dominating both production and distribution, created a great deal of public unhappiness. There was a general feeling of helplessness. If no agency of the federal government was empowered to regulate interstate distribution and rates, neither could state or local agencies get much of a handle on the problem. Nor was there any prospect of relief from the courts. In 1934, the United States Supreme Court (*Kansas State Corporation Commission* v. *Wichita Gas Company,* 290 U.S. 561) ruled that the commerce clause of the Constitution forbade states from trying to regulate the price at which a pipeline company could sell gas for resale if the gas had been transported from another state.

This ruling triggered efforts in Congress to close the regulatory gap. As originally drafted, the Public Utility Holding Company Act of 1935 (the Wheeler-Rayburn Act) had included the pipelines. But the natural gas companies fought it so hard—they especially disliked features of the bill that would have made the pipelines common carriers and would have controlled the price of gas sold to industrial customers—that the pipeline title was removed from the bill before passage.

But Congress was whipped into a new spirit of reform in 1936 with the release of a study by the Federal Trade Commission that charged, among other things, that a few large holding companies controlled virtually all of the pipelines in America, that they had divvied up the nation and had allotted "territorial rights" to each other for certain areas. Within a given area, a holding company exercised a monopoly. When independent groups, attracted by the large profits they saw being made, tried to buy natural gas from producers and build lines into the territory of one of the large holding companies, the holding company would either destroy the smaller competitor through price wars or buy it out.

Going back through the congressional hearings and floor debates of those years, one finds countless tales of injustice to support the FTC's findings. The big companies were indeed dividing up the market in violation of the Sherman and the Clayton antitrust acts. Columbia's pipeline from the lush Panhandle fields passed only sixty-eight miles northwest of St. Louis. St. Louis attempted

to have the 68-mile gap closed—and got Phillips Petroleum to offer to build it—
so that it could tap into Columbia's pipeline. But Columbia refused to furnish
natural gas to St. Louis even if the spur line was built for them, because they
did not want to "raid" the territory assigned Jersey Standard and Electric
Bond, two other of the big four interests.

Residents of West Virginia were paying 35 cents per thousand cubic feet
(Mcf) for gas produced in West Virginia. But the same gas, piped just a few
miles over the border into Virginia, was selling for $1 per Mcf. Virginia had no
authority to fix the price of gas transported from West Virginia; and of course,
the same sort of dilemma was faced by all state and local authorities. Only the
federal government can regulate interstate commerce. Indeed, there were some
situations of a specially mocking nature. For example, gas produced in the
Panhandle of Texas was transported across a part of Oklahoma and back into
Texas, and thereby became "interstate" gas—immune from price regulations of
the Texas Railroad Commission. There were also terrible inequities in the
differences in the prices charged for interstate natural gas that went to industry as compared to that bought by household consumers. Gas piped out of the
Texas Panhandle to the city of Chicago sold to households for as high as $1.50
per Mcf but as low as 9 cents per Mcf when sold to industrial concerns. It was
commonplace for the companies to lose money on industrial sales and then
force household users to make up the difference. The pipeline companies
could, moreover, sell at one wholesale price to one industry and another price
to another industry. They could charge one wholesale price for residential gas
in one community and, ten miles away, put twice or half the price on the residential gas in another town. When state governments or city councils asked
the pipeline companies to show their books to prove that their prices were
justified, the pipeline companies would refuse—and invariably be upheld by
the federal courts—on the grounds that no arm of government below the federal government had the right to intrude on their interstate business.

Finally, in 1938, after another complicated redrafting of the legislation,
Congress passed the Natural Gas Act (without a dissenting vote in either
house), giving administrative powers over the interstate natural gas industry to
the Federal Power Commission. (The intrastate market was exempted by silence, and in 1954 Congress passed an amendment specifically exempting intrastate sales from FPC jurisdiction.)

A reading of the Natural Gas Act clearly shows that it was passed to provide natural gas at the lowest possible rate that would allow the companies a
fair profit based on the cost of the gas. "Just and reasonable" rates were mandated by Section 4 (a) of the Act. As the Supreme Court later said, "Protection of consumers against exploitation at the hands of natural gas companies
was the primary aim of the Natural Gas Act."

The Federal Power Commission, which was established in 1920 but didn't
have much work to do except regulate the small amount of interstate electricity, was given the job of enforcing the Natural Gas Act. The FPC was a
five-member commission of staggered terms, with no more than three members
from the same political party. Its members were usually not of the most impressive quality, but even if they had been made up of mental giants, they

would have been confronted with a most imposing task, for, in the first place, the Natural Gas Act was ridiculously vague.

Just whom and what was the FPC to regulate? Pipelines, that was for sure. Pipelines were the obvious villains. And the producers of natural gas who were affiliated with the pipelines were also obviously part of the price-gouging industry that the FPC was to protect the public from. But what about the independent gas producers—the thousands of oil and gas companies that sold their product to, but had no formal connection with, the pipeline companies? They were several steps removed from the consumers. Were these independent gas producers also to be regulated in regard to the price they placed on the gas they sold to the pipeline companies? In short, did the Natural Gas Act authorize the FPC to set "wellhead" or "field" prices as well as pipeline prices charged for wholesale gas? Since the pipelines were only the middle conduit between producer and local utility, it made sense to assume that the Act intended the FPC to regulate prices all the way back to the producers, but the wording of the Act was not clear on that point.

So, choosing the easy way of avoiding a collision with the oil and gas industry, the FPC decided that the Act did not authorize them to set wellhead prices. At first this decision made little difference to the consumer, for in the 1930s and 1940s the field price of most natural gas was ridiculously low—some selling for 2 to 3 cents per Mcf. Even into the 1930s, natural gas was still largely an unwanted product. In those days, nobody went looking specifically for it; it was obtained only as an accidental by-product of the search for oil. Many oil explorers and producers felt there was too much natural gas, looked upon it as a nuisance, and felt that venting it or burning it as a waste product right in the fields was a practical and sensible way of disposing of it. State conservation laws put an end to most of this waste in the 1930s, but natural gas was still not looked upon as a prized commodity, and producers generally felt that any price they got was gravy.

However, with the completion of the big pipeline systems, after World War II, natural gas use soared and so did the field price charged by independent producers. It became evident that if the regulation of pipeline prices was to mean anything, the price of the gas at the wellhead, on which the pipeline prices were built, would also have to be regulated. Local utilities got tired of having to keep raising their customers' rates. They asked the FPC to take charge of all rates, from wellhead to local wholesale, and the pressures on the FPC to bring some order to the chaotic market became so intense that in 1947 it almost aroused itself from its customary lethargy. In that year, the four commissioners (the FPC was one short of its usual number) divided over the question of whether to take control of producers' prices. (Commissioner Leland Olds's vote, to regulate producers, was probably responsible for his bureaucratic death by character assassination.[1]) Congress, very much under the

---

1. Son of a former president of Amherst College, Leland Olds graduated from that school magna cum laude in 1912, went into church social work, then into the ministry (Congregationalist) in a low-wage section of Brooklyn, then became disenchanted with the sluggishness of organized religion and began to teach in college, at the same time working for liberal New York politicians. From 1922 to 1929, as a labor editor

control of oil-state legislators, refused to settle the question. And so it was left to the courts.

When Phillips Petroleum, the largest independent producer, raised its prices for interstate gas, the state of Wisconsin and the cities of Milwaukee, Detroit, and Kansas City, Missouri, banded together to challenge Phillips' action. Once again, the FPC ruled that it had no jurisdiction over independent producers. The FPC's ruling was appealed to the courts, where it was reversed first by the D.C. Court of Appeals and later, on June 7, 1954, by the U.S. Supreme Court, which said, in effect, "We don't know what statute you guys have been reading, but the Natural Gas Act tells us, 'How the hell can you control or regulate a national industry if all you are going to regulate is the transportation of it and not the price of the product itself?' You guys better get about your business."

For a moment, it seemed that the FPC's sixteen years of nonenforcement of the Natural Gas Act's spirit had come to an end. But in fact there was much more of the same stretching ahead.

The FPC continued to balk. On March 21, 1955, a commission majority, in a letter to the chairman of the House Interstate and Foreign Commerce Committee, urged that Congress nullify the Supreme Court's decision and exempt independent producers from the Natural Gas Act. The next year, the gas producers themselves got into the act by spreading money around Congress so lavishly and so carelessly, in an effort to pass a law exempting them from regulation, that a major scandal occurred: On February 3, 1956, Senator Francis Case of South Dakota got to his feet, cleared his throat a few times, and told his Senate colleagues, "I rise to make a difficult speech . . ." He told of how a lobbyist for Superior Oil Company had dropped off an envelope fat with cash at the office of a friend of Case, with instructions that it be given to Case for his "campaign." It was, said Case, "the largest contribution I could remember for any campaign of mine." Was it an effort to bribe Case to get his vote for the natural gas deregulation bill? Many in Washington thought so. There were rumors of gifts from other companies for other members, too. (A former long-

---

for the *Federated Press,* he wrote some fiery editorials deploring the inequality of the distribution of wealth. Typical of his complaints circa 1927: "President Coolidge with his share of U.S. Steel stock is entitled to about $900 of the 1926 profits. An unskilled worker in the steel mills would have to work more than 2,000 hours to earn as much for his family as Coolidge gets without a stroke of work." He denounced class exploitation and America's "dollar empire."

In 1939 President Roosevelt appointed Olds to the Federal Power Commission. During the ten years he sat on the FPC, he was credited with saving consumers a quarter of a billion dollars in rate reductions, and he introduced into regulation practice the concept of rates based upon the number of dollars actually invested, rather than upon what the market would bear. The natural gas industry chafed under Olds's presence on the FPC, and though he was twice successfully reappointed, on his third time up, in 1949, Senator Lyndon Johnson—citing some of his two-decades-old writings for the *Federated Press*—portrayed him as a dangerous left-winger (this was the McCarthy era) and persuaded the Senate to reject his nomination. The Milwaukee *Journal* saw the situation correctly: "Natural gas, and natural gas alone, is the point at issue in the outrageous attack on Olds' nomination. Communism and all other charges are pure smear tactics."

time lobbyist for Superior Oil Company told me, five years after this took place, that he had accompanied Congressman Sam Rayburn to his home in Bonham, Texas, where Rayburn cleaned out his dresser—every drawer stuffed with cash from oil and gas companies—and packed this into a suitcase, which he set between his knees on the train ride back to Washington.) Their generosity backfired. So loud was the editorial outcry that although Congress passed the deregulation bill, Eisenhower felt obliged, to protect his reputation, to veto the tainted legislation. (He did so grudgingly, for he was himself greatly indebted to oil executives for "campaign" contributions.)[2]

However, although the gas producers lost that legislative round, they in effect won the fight, because the FPC was on their side. Laws that call for regulation are worthless if the official regulators refuse to enforce them, and that's exactly what the FPC did. It did nothing. For the six years from the Supreme Court's ruling, in 1954, until the end of the Eisenhower regime, in 1960, the FPC's regulatory record was a blank. It spent the first five years simply trying to figure out a way to regulate producers' rates. It assigned one of its hearing examiners, Joseph Zwerdling, to work up a scheme for doing it. In 1959, he came in with a plan that was spread over ten thousand pages. The commission spent the next year reading and mulling over Zwerdling's proposal, which came down to this: Regulate each company as if it were a utility. Find out how much it cost the company to produce gas, and then give it a reasonable rate on top of that cost. *Each* company? Each company *separately?* There were thousands upon thousands of gas producers out there. The FPC decided that it simply couldn't be done; to be exact, the FPC estimated that if it tried to set a rate for each individual company, in separate cases, it could triple the size of its staff and still not finish the task until the year 2043. Zwerdling's plan was junked. Six years had been lost. Partly because of its failure to implement the Supreme Court's 1954 ruling, the Eisenhower-era FPC was appraised by James Landis, former Harvard Law School dean, as "without question . . . the outstanding example in the Federal government of the breakdown of the administrative process."

The Eisenhower FPC did do one thing. At the very last minute, it cooked up one other scheme for regulating rates, a scheme it bequeathed to the incoming Kennedy FPC. The new plan was to cut up the nation into twenty-three geographic areas and set uniform prices for all producers within each area.

By comparison with the Eisenhower FPC, the Kennedy FPC, chaired by

---

2. This wasn't the only time that Superior Oil executives had given abundantly to a politician with disappointing results. The same Superior Oil lobbyist told me that at a small luncheon in Los Angeles during the 1960 Democratic convention, old man Keck, a founder of Superior, turned to Congressman Wright Patman of Texas, sitting beside him, and said, "I gave Lyndon $200,000 to make his race for President, but I told him I did *not* want him to accept the vice-presidential nomination. I don't want him to keep the money if he does that. You don't think he would accept the vice-presidential nomination, do you?" Of course Johnson did accept the nomination, and, said the lobbyist, laughing, he doubted very much if Keck ever saw his money again.

Joseph C. Swidler, seemed downright revolutionary, at least on the surface.[3] When the Swidler commission got in place, it found a backlog of four thousand suspended pipeline rate increases. The increased payments had been held in a kind of escrow, waiting for a final ruling. These cases were wiped off, but *not* as the result of the creation of a logical formula by which rates could be established in the future. They were taken care of simply by negotiated settlements. As Louis M. Kohlmeier, Jr., a *Wall Street Journal* reporter with considerable experience as a regulatory-agency watcher, explained in his book *The Regulators:* "The FPC split the difference. Of some $420 million annual rate increases then pending, the pipeline companies for the future were allowed to retain $205 million and roll back their rates to the tune of $215 million a year. Of the nearly $1 billion by which the pipeline revenues had been increased up to 1960 by the annual rate hikes, the companies refunded $658 million to their local distributing and industrial customers and they kept a roughly equivalent sum."

It took no great talent to split the difference in this way. Wiping the backlog off the books maybe was a good idea, and it had a certain public relations value. But it did nothing to establish an efficient rate-setting technique *for the future*. That problem found the Swidler commission just about as sluggish as its predecessor. Not until August 1965 did the FPC finish the first of its area rate cases—the Permian Basin case—and its findings ran to a mere thirty thousand pages. The ruling was of course challenged by a number of Permian Basin producers, including such biggies as Jersey Standard and Texaco, but three years later the Supreme Court upheld the FPC. So there it was: Sixteen years after the Supreme Court in *Phillips* had ordered the FPC to get cracking, the first rate ruling had been finished. It was hardly an auspicious beginning. At any rate, it would take until at least the end of the century to complete rate settings for the other twenty-two areas.

David Freeman, who was Swidler's assistant in those days, recalls the setup: "When Joe [Swidler] came in as chairman, in '61, we found that the commis-

---

3. Hoisting Swidler into the chairmanship wasn't easy. Lee C. White, who succeeded Swidler in the post, recalls how it was achieved: "When Kennedy named Swidler to be chairman, everybody said hooray. That is, everybody except the old chairman, Jerry Kuykendall, a sweet guy who said, 'I hate to be a horse's ass but my lawyers tell me that the way the statute reads, the President doesn't have the right to name a new chairman unless there is a vacancy in the chairmanship, and my term runs for two more years. The way I understand it, my chairmanship runs until my membership ends.' President Kennedy said, 'Jesus Christ, doesn't anybody around here do any staff work?' Nick Katzenbach was in the office of legal counsel and he comes up and says, 'Mr. President, you'll probably lose this in the district court and probably in the court of appeals but the Supreme Court will probably uphold you.' And Kennedy said, 'You must be out of your goddamn mind to think I'll go to the Supreme Court with this crummy little thing.' So we sat around, Ralph Dungan, Katzenbach and myself (I was on the White House staff then) trying to figure out how to get the old guy out. We had mental pictures of the GSA coming in and taking Kuykendall's stuff out in the dark of night—*a la* Sewell Avery—but finally Everett Dirksen broke the log jam and told Kennedy that Kuykendall would remain as chairman for three months and remain as a member for two months, and then leave." White said he didn't know what Kennedy gave Dirksen in return for his help.

sioners had no personal staff. Separation between staff and commission was so complete there was sort of a wall between them. And actually at the commission meetings, the commission hadn't even been letting the staff into the room, except when they would call in a particular staff member they wanted some information from. That was one of the problems of the commission in the late '50s." Swidler changed that. The commission and the staff became tightly coordinated, with Freeman acting as the key go-between.

Swidler, a proconsumer activist, had the advantage of being given by Kennedy a commission he could dominate. Freeman: "We had a unique situation. Kennedy appointed almost a new commission and we were a team in '61. Joe Swidler, Charlie Ross, and Dave Black. At the beginning, Howard Morgan was there and then Black took his place. Joe was in a kind of unique position most of the time. There were two people who were a little to the left of him, either Ross and Morgan or Ross and Black. And then there were the other two members, O'Connor [Lawrence J., Jr.] and Woodward [Harold C.] and later O'Connor and Bagge [Carl E.], who were a little bit to the right. So Joe could cast deciding votes any way he wanted to. In the four years we were at the commission, Swidler dissented in only one case. We had to remember we couldn't take the other commissioners for granted, but it was a unique situation where the chairman's office not only had administrative control of the staff but, in terms of the voting positions of the commissioners, we could pretty much chart the thing the way Swidler wanted it, in almost all cases."

But even the FPC's small successes irritated the industry and its allies in Congress. Pressure to go easier began to build. Freeman (now boss of TVA) recalls: "Oh, god, the pressures were tremendous. Albert Thomas was chairman of our appropriations subcommittee. He was a congressman from Houston. He approved our budget each year. If you want to read some blistering hearings, get the record of one of the hearings in '63-'64, just before Thomas' death, when Joe Swidler was testifying. Mr. Thomas was dying of cancer and in great pain, so I don't want to be too harsh on him, but he was mad! Joe had rolled back some of these prices and had closed some of the loopholes. The transcript that's printed is rough enough, but you should have been there. It was an open hearing, and you should have seen the transcript before it was edited. I mean, I've never seen anybody treated with the contempt and meanness that Joe was treated by Albert Thomas. It was a wonder to me that Joe was able to sit there and take it. It was such a rough session that Mr. Jonas, the Republican from North Carolina, who had been an old-time critic of Joe when Joe was general counsel of TVA and they had fought the public/private power battles— I remember Mr. Jonas pulled a cigar out of his pocket, leaned across the table, and handed it to Joe just as a friendly gesture, as if to say, 'You've really been catching it.'

"One reason Thomas was so furious was we had foiled the industry in a series of cases involving in-place sale of gas. When we got to the commission, we found that the producers had developed a very ingenious loophole to avoid the *Phillips* case and the entire wellhead regulation. What they had developed was a system whereby instead of selling gas to the pipelines, they sold leases, and they sold the gas 'in place' on those leases, and then the pipelines would

pay for it over a 20-year period. That way, they were able to get a whole lot
more money for the gas and there was an old Supreme Court case that held
the sale of a lease was not subject to regulation by the Federal Power Commission. So we found all these big gas reservoirs being sold under this device.
Well, we weren't exactly stupid as lawyers and we could see that if this precedent were followed, we'd be regulating a trickle of gas and the bulk of it
would be sold, unregulated, at much higher prices. We instituted proceedings
to assert our jurisdiction over these in-place sales and we were skillful enough
as lawyers to be successful. We finally won it in the Supreme Court. Well, the
result was there was a good deal of hard feelings." (Q. They hated your guts?)
"Yeah, that's about the size of it. And we instituted these area rate proceedings and we cut out all of these thousands of individual producer cases. What
upset industry so much was that we made producer regulation effective and
eliminated the possibility of legislation that would repeal it. That *was* a possibility if the system bogged down." That is a roseate view of the past. In fact,
the FPC never made producer regulation "effective."

The commission chaired by Lee White (1966–69), who followed Swidler,
was still relatively consumer-oriented. But the White era was one of transition,
with all the elements of chaos that attend transition.

By the time White quit (resigning eight months early because "I felt like a
fifth wheel and didn't feel I should be there, because I wasn't part of the Administration. That speeded me along. And besides, it had got a little sticky."),
the use of natural gas was sharply increasing and the claimed gas reserves
were beginning to decline.

The increase in use was not anticipated by the Swidler commission, or, for
that matter, by the White commission. All the early predictions were nullified
by the new national concern over air pollution. Freeman: "The industry projections in the early sixties were that this terrific growth that took place in the
fifties, which was accounted for by gas coming in and taking away markets
from coal and oil, would all be over as soon as all the virgin territory was
served. As soon as all the pipeline systems were laid out throughout America,
the projections were that gas use would drop off in the late sixties and start
growing at 3 or 3.5 percent a year, just a little more than the population. What
happened that no one predicted was that America woke up to the fact that
coal and some oils were fouling the air with sulfur. And we passed these antipollution laws that really outlawed coal and some oils. So instead of the
demand for gas tapering off, it really began to accelerate, because all the
industries that had to meet air quality laws had to switch from coal and oil. So
gas use grew twice as fast as they had anticipated. It grew at seven percent a
year."

White: "When Los Angeles was concerned about smog, they passed an ordinance saying you can't use any fuel that has more than 1 percent sulfur content. Now, what fuel falls beautifully into that category? Gas. It has some
problems, but compared to the other fuels it is mighty appealing. New York,
St. Louis, and other cities began passing the same kind of ordinances. The
L.A. ordinance was in 1965 or 1966. It really shot up gas use. Moreover, this
is an aggressive industry. They were advertising. And there was another fac-

tor. In the early 1960s, the pipeline network had finally spread across the country. The last outpost in New England was served with gas.

"Now you ought to ask the question: Why the hell didn't somebody foresee this? Or did they foresee it? After all, this is one of the things the FPC is supposed to do. Well, one reason we didn't foresee it was that we weren't too goddamn smart. We just weren't as good as we should have been."

With the coming of Nixon, the FPC was turned over to John Nassikas and others who were not enthusiastic about regulating private industry. But even if they had been, the combination of accelerating gas use and the decline in gas reserves would have made rate setting much harder than in the past. Also, President Johnson's foolish effort to support a war without raising taxes had triggered a much heavier inflation rate than the nation had previously experienced. That also made rate setting more difficult. It certainly guaranteed an increase in rates, for the FPC is obliged to give increases where producers can show costs have reduced their profits below the level of "fairness." And even though there is no statutory authority for giving higher prices as an "incentive" to finding more gas and therefore bolstering the reserves, there would naturally be a tendency for the FPC to allow such rates—sneaking in a few pennies per Mcf here, a little old nickle increase per Mcf there, to give the boys encouragement to step up their explorations. (Bear in mind that even one penny per Mcf equates to hundreds of millions of dollars over the life of a gas field.)

If the Nassikas commission did that sort of thing, White was sympathetic. He said (this interview was in 1971, after Nassikas had been in power a couple of years):

"It's a hell of a lot easier to be a regulator when prices in general are staying level or declining . . . It's only when inflation and other factors like environmental precautions that are costly come along that the price—the cost—begins to go up and then the poor regulator is in a hell of a spot. He senses it is time to go up, but he doesn't know how much to go up. He doesn't know how to grab hold of these issues called 'rate of return' and 'a just and reasonable rate.' If I had stayed on, I would have been forced up." (Q. So Nassikas et al. wasn't completely an ideological change?) "That's the way I would call it. Now, having said that, you get to the sticky question of how far he should allow the rates to climb. How do you hold the pendulum from swinging too far? It's a much harder job to be a regulator today than it was four or five years ago."

His sympathy, however, was apparently wasted. From all outward signs, the Nassikas commission did not seem to think the pendulum could swing too far toward higher prices. They seemed to enjoy raising prices, and they only regretted certain restrictions on their raising them much higher than they did. Indeed, the Nassikas commission favored deregulating gas prices altogether, and by a 4-to-1 majority told Congress, in March 1975, that deregulation would be the best way to ease the gas shortage.

The same attitude prevailed, in spades, at the FPC chaired by Nassikas' successor, Richard L. Dunham, who was appointed by President Ford in September 1975. By that time, the FPC had moved as far as it legally could—and some critics felt it had gone even farther than the law allowed—toward price deregulation. Dunham came to the FPC from his post as deputy director of the Domestic Council. Prior to that, he had been an aide to Vice-President Rockefeller. One of his duties had been to work on some of the presidential statements and speeches urging deregulation.

But, by that time, the whole notion of the FPC as a consumer-protection agency had evaporated, and within a couple of years the FPC itself would disappear, surrendering what token regulatory duties remained to that dismal, Dantean pit the Department of Energy.

Looking back for a historical judgment of the FPC, can it be said that at any time during its life it imposed effective and sensible regulation? The temptation is not only to say no but hell no, or to somehow embellish the negative response with curses. But when one considers the enormity of the problem, tolerance prevails. Setting prices fair both to gas producers and consumers was probably the toughest job ever handed a federal agency. But the FPC failed in other ways too. It also had the authority (supported by Supreme Court rulings) to allocate gas among customers. Why did it permit so much gas to be used by industry; not only permit it, but encourage it by allowing the industrial prices to be so much lower?

Patricia E. Starratt, then a special assistant for legislation in the Federal Energy Administration, wrote in 1974: "Generally, mention of 'natural gas consumers' calls to mind Mrs. Jones cooking on her gas stove and paying the bills for her gas service, but the bulk of natural gas consumed in the United States is not used in homes. The 1972 Bureau of Mines Mineral Industry Survey showed that industry used 41.6 percent of all gas consumed; electric generating facilities used 20.3 percent; residential consumers used 25.3 percent; and commercial establishments used 11.1 percent. While the number of consumers in one category or another differs regionally, it is noteworthy that bulk industrial and electric utility users together accounted for 61.9 percent of natural gas consumption."

It should be noted that *this* was going on even after the natural gas industry was claiming shortages. Why was industry allowed to consume the lion's share when coal or oil would have served it just as well? Why were electric utilities permitted to use so much natural gas when, as Dave Freeman said, "in the process of converting fuel to electricity, the efficiency is only about 33 to 35 percent. Two thirds of the fuel becomes waste heat. So a lot of people think it is pretty stupid to take gas and make electricity out of it and then heat your home with electricity." Why didn't the FPC recognize these stupidities earlier, and take action to stop them? Instead of being stopped, they were continued and expanded as a result of rates that favored the wasteful customers. In 1969, for example, the average delivered cost of natural gas per Mcf to residential customers was $1.05. Commercial customers were receiving it for 78 cents. The wasteful industrial customers got gas for a mere 35 cents, and the most wasteful of all customers, the electric utilities, were receiving it at the giveaway price of 27 cents.

But, however much the household consumer was ultimately abused by the FPC, it is really surprising that the abuse was not more extensive, considering the atmosphere in which the Commission operated—an atmosphere almost totally conditioned by big business, whether on the producing or on the consuming end. It has been an accepted fact of life in Washington for as long as regulatory commissions have existed that they owe their primary allegiance to the industry or industries they are supposed to be regulating. This was certainly true of the FPC. Writing in 1969 (and therefore including the supposedly "proconsumer" FPCs of recent Democratic administrations), *Wall Street Journal* reporter Kohlmeier claimed: "The test of competence to which a candidate for initial appointment is subjected consists of the submission by the White House of his or her name to industry executives before sending it on to the Senate for confirmation. CAB appointees are cleared with airline executives, FPC appointees with gas and electric companies . . . Every President in recent history has run some sort of check with industry before appointing or reappointing a regulator."

If commissioners with subtle proconsumer leanings have sometimes slipped through this precautionary net, they have then been subjected to constant pressures from industry while on the job. This does not mean corrupt pressures, but simply the normal intense pressures that special interests exert from every direction. And they are especially focused on the chairman, who in turn sets the mood of the Commission. Dave Freeman appraised the situation rather realistically, and with understandable sympathy, in this 1971 interview:

"Because the Power Commission handles matters of grave importance to the power industry and the general public pays practically no attention, the man who is sitting in the chairman's chair is really sitting in a hotbox, and nobody seems to give a damn.

"Go through a commissioner's life. He comes to his office in the morning and what does he have on his desk to read? He has the *Oil & Gas Journal,* he has *Electrical World,* he has an industry poop sheet. Who comes to see him? The presidents of power companies and the presidents of gas companies. If the president of the League of Women Voters ever set foot in that building, she'd get lost. If a reporter from the New York *Times* comes by to see you, that's got to be because of some extraordinary event. You don't get the general press coming by over there unless somebody in your agency has committed theft, or the lights have gone out. But, day in and day out, you're over there all by yourself.

"And I think I know why. The Power Commission is dealing mostly with wholesale. They are dealing with matters one step removed from the consumer. They never handle retail rates. There are so many things the average citizen has to be concerned about, and there are so many government agencies, and the FPC is so mysterious. To participate in an FPC proceeding is a very time-consuming, expensive, complicated thing. Almost every lawyer who practices before the FPC used to work there. You've really got to be an expert in all this rigmarole and gobbledygook to be able to participate. It's not a place where a little old lady walks in off the street and is made very welcome. Not that they are discourteous, it's just that the place is set up for experts. It's set up for the industry. The key to how much consumer orientation there is depends on who is sitting in the chairman's chair, and what the White House policies are. It's just that simple."

Charles R. Ross, another proconsumer commissioner of the Swidler-White era, adds his chilling memories of life at the Commission: "Once on the scene, the regulator is confronted by sweet-talking executives, tough, hard-hitting lawyers, and experts, even including experts in bugging . . .

"The doors of exclusive clubs are opened . . . The lure of life in the lap of luxury . . . becomes not just a dream but an actuality if one does not get too smart. On the other hand, if one does get too smart, it is back to the farm for our country bumpkin.

"The flattery, the press releases, the respect afforded an official regardless of performance, the cocktail parties, the utility and regulatory conventions at which comradeship between regulator and regulated is the No. 1 business . . . the prospect of important legal clients, the thoughts of large political donations"—all of these things work to "ensure the 'right decision' or, if not, at the very least, the industry lawyer starts off with the dice loaded in his favor."

SANTA BARBARA.   The people living in Santa Barbara never have liked the oil industry. Eighty percent of Santa Barbara's income was from the tourist business. It was a place of beauty, of languor—an upper-class lotus land. And that's the way they wanted to keep it.

Which isn't to say that the people of Santa Barbara didn't realize they were sitting on one of the potentially most productive oil basins on the West Coast. Some estimates place one and a half billion gallons of crude under the Santa Barbara Channel. Awareness of this was, in fact, the source of great unease. The people knew that rapacious oil companies would fill their marvelous beaches and their bay with oil wells, and they also knew that the California legislature would let them get by with it—if some special protection wasn't forced through the legislature to safeguard their coast. The threat was obvious when, in 1938, the California legislature legalized the awarding of oil leases out to the 3-mile limit and, in fact, subsequently did award several leases. (These were slant-drilled from the mainland, however.) Before the oil industry could push its drilling rigs into Santa Barbara's waters, the citizens of that town raised such a fuss that the legislature, in 1955, after a terrific fight, was finally forced to create (the Cunningham-Shell Act) a 16-mile-long sanctuary spanning the Santa Barbara area and reaching all the way out to the state's 3-mile limit.

No drilling would be permitted within the sanctuary area.

In 1958, Standard Oil Company was granted a state offshore lease just adjacent to the sanctuary. Almost immediately, the company struck a rich load of oil and gas. Within eight years, *all* the state tidelands in that region, except for the sanctuary, were under lease to the oil companies.

Having stripped the state of all they could, the companies then, in 1966, went after the federal largesses, and in that year Santa Barbara County officials were told that the Department of the Interior, then under the secretaryship of the "conservationist" Stewart Udall, was going to start leasing federal offshore lands to the oil companies. Interior officials excused their action by saying that the Standard Oil well on the state lease was "draining" the oil from nearby federal lands.

In December 1966 a federal lease was awarded Phillips Petroleum to offset the alleged "drainage" by Standard. But federal officials made it plain that this was just the beginning. Santa Barbara begged the feds not to do anything to ruin its tourist business. Specifically, local officials asked for a 5-mile buffer zone in the federal waters beyond the state sanctuary. This would have outlawed drilling for a total of eight miles from shore. The Interior Department refused to go for five miles but did set up a 1-mile-wide buffer strip alongside the outer boundary of the sanctuary—thus giving Santa Barbara a total of four miles of offshore protection from drilling.

Four miles sounds like quite a stretch, but where oil is concerned, it isn't much protection at all. An oil slick can cover four miles of water and move across a beach in a matter of hours.

So Santa Barbara officials kept pressing the feds to go slow on their leasing, and when Secretary Udall visited Santa Barbara in November 1967, he told local officials and the press that he agreed the leasing program should move slowly and cautiously.

That assurance notwithstanding, three months later the Interior Department opened the entire offshore area to bidding for leases.

George Clyde, then a member of the Santa Barbara Board of Supervisors and Channel Oil Advisory Committee, said, "It was obvious to all of us involved in the long discussions during 1967 that everyone in the mineral resources section of the Interior Department was hellbent to lease this channel and get drilling started. Whether it was the desire to get the money for the federal government, to establish a good record on the fiscal side, or pressure from the oil companies, I do not know, but the attitude was there from the beginning . . . I do know that we all had the impression that the oil industry, and this may be an understatement, had great influence in the Department." (pp. 281–82, Part 2, Water Pollution Hearings, 1969) ". . . I do know that within a matter of minutes after we said anything to the Department of the Interior, the oil industry knew exactly what we said verbatim."

One of the strongest antidrilling arguments made by local officials was that the offshore area might not be environmentally safe. Although the last major earthquake in Santa Barbara had been in 1925, almost every intervening year had felt a few; not severe ones, but enough to notice. During the previous year, 1968, University of California scientists had recorded sixty-six earthquakes epicentered in the Santa Barbara Channel. When local officials raised this point, and they raised it repeatedly, ". . . always Interior Department and oil industry officials led us to believe we had nothing to fear," said Clyde. "They said they had perfected shutoff devices that were foolproof even in such disasters as a ship running into the platform, or an earthquake. We asked what if an earthquake knocked down one of these [drilling] platforms. The answer we got invariably was, 'We have shutoff devices. There would be no problem.'"

Which may have been true. But what Interior and their buddies in the oil business should have known (and in fact may have known but were willing to risk) was that the earthquakes had left the earth's strata in that area riddled with fissures. Even if an earthquake never came to the Santa Barbara area again, past shakings of the earth's crust had made it a dangerous place to drill —dangerous, that is, for the environment.

On February 6, 1968, the Department received bids totaling $603 million for seventy-five of the hundred and ten lease blocks offered. The feds were so eager to comply with the oil companies' wishes and lease the offshore blocks that Interior officials made no serious effort to discover if they could not have gotten much more than $603 million. In secret testimony before a House Appropriations subcommittee on March 3, 1969, William T. Pecora, director of the U.S. Geological Survey, a branch of the Interior Department with close ties to the oil industry, conceded that government officials had been "flying partly blind," because they did not know the mineral value of the tracts before they leased them. Nor did USGS officials make much of an effort to get this kind of information, or data relating to drilling safety. They admitted to Senate investigators that they often relied, for that information, on informal contacts made at cocktail parties.

The highest bid, of $61.4 million, came from a combine of Union Oil, Gulf, Texaco, and Mobil, for parcel No. 402.

It was on this parcel that the disaster would occur. Thus Union Oil was assured a place in history. Not only was it the indirect (or hidden) owner of the *Torrey Canyon*, which a few months earlier had been responsible for the largest tanker spill in history, but now it would produce the largest spill from an offshore well up to that time.[1]

On January 28, 1969, trouble started on Union's Platform A, a 15-story structure standing out five and a half miles from the California shore.

Union had brought in three wells from Platform A; they were hooked up to the shore production system. Now Union was bringing in its fourth well from Platform A. Everything had gone without a hitch. Drilling had reached the 3,500-foot production level successfully, and now the crew was taking the drilling bit and the drilling strings out of the hole. It was all routine, until they brought the drill bit up about seven hundred feet. At that point, suddenly gas and oil mud came tearing up through the drill pipe and poured over the top of the derrick.

According to the official report of the U.S. Geological Survey, what had

---

1. Later, Udall would admit that the leases had been granted even though department experts knew the channel was geologically unstable. Looking back on it, he called Santa Barbara "an ecological Bay of Pigs." Why, then, did he give his consent to the leasing? It was believed that he had been under intense pressure from President Johnson to provide money to help keep a war-inflated budget under control. Congressional investigations turned up a letter from the Budget Bureau to Interior Under Secretary Charles F. Luce on July 11, 1967, in which Luce was told, ". . . we are particularly interested in the presidential decision to generate additional revenues from the leasing of the Nation's mineral resources," including the outer continental shelf. On November 20, 1967, Budget Director Charles L. Schultze wrote Udall to discuss possible revenues, including those from the Santa Barbara Channel. Udall, however, claimed he felt no particular pressure from the Budget Bureau. (Washington *Post*, March 9, 1969)

happened was this: As the crew was pulling up the drill bit, they lost control of the pressure within the casing.[2] The pressures exerted upward by gas within the well are usually counteracted by a sufficient column of drilling mud imposed from above to keep the oil and gas under control. (Drilling mud—used as a lubricant as well as a pressure control—is a mixture of water, chemicals of various kinds, and plain clays of various kinds. Oil-field workers can make mud —according to the needs of the moment—with weight of anywhere from slightly heavier than water, which is 62½ pounds per cubic foot, all the way up to 100-pound mud.) When the upward pressure of the gas overcame the downward pressure of the mud, the crew lost control of the well.

Ordinarily, however, that sort of problem can be easily handled. The Union crew did just what they were supposed to do. After working for fifteen minutes in a heavy hydrocarbon mist that made it impossible for them to see what they were doing, the workers realized they couldn't stop the flow from the pipe, so they dropped the drill piping back into the hole and closed the blind rams on the blowout preventer (a spring-loaded hydraulic valve that closes the top of the well when an abnormal flow activates the valve). Under ordinary circumstances, this would have done the trick.

Fred Hartley, president of Union Oil Company, said later, "In all my experience that I am aware of, that would have been a security measure and would have been the end of the problem, other than bringing in special equipment to complete the well after such a thing as that had happened."

But it wasn't the end of the problem. It was only the beginning.

As the crew was congratulating itself for having successfully controlled the casing blowout, they happened to look out about eight hundred feet into the channel from the drilling rig and saw . . . at first small bubbles and then a giant oil and gas bubble, a kind of boil that lifted the ocean about two feet above its normal horizon. The bubble moved slowly toward the drilling platform.

Hartley, notified around 11:30 A.M., "knew immediately, of course, that we had a problem."

What a problem! Gas and oil freed by the drill at thirty-five hundred feet was coming up the shaft and escaping via a fissure in the ocean floor. The well itself was closed completely—at the top—but far into the earth, the well had opened a natural outlet that could not easily be closed again. Oil and gas were coming up through the drilled opening and then veering off into a stratum of porous sands, through which they traveled in numerous directions before escaping into the water.

The Coast Guard, which has primary jurisdiction over such problems, was notified around 1 P.M. But Santa Barbara County officials weren't notified for another twenty-four hours, and might not have been notified then had it not

---

2. This was a misleading report. The USGS had, at Union's request, suspended ordinary well-casing requirements. After drilling 239 feet, and sinking a casing that distance, Union had received permission to go all the way to 3,500 feet before putting in any more casing. It was the only company drilling in the Santa Barbara Channel to get this favored treatment. If normal regulations had been followed, the blowout might not have occurred.

been for an anonymous telephone call to the local newspaper. When local officials asked a Union vice-president what the hell was going on, he told them not to worry, that the flow could be stopped by the next day.

Meanwhile, Union Oil's crew was going crazy with frustration. One of the standard methods for stopping a blowout of that sort is to pump drilling mud down the hole and plug it up. On the first day, Union pumped four thousand barrels of mud into the hole, thinking this would be far more than enough—but the mud kept escaping through the same fissure that the oil was escaping through. Desperately, they installed larger and higher-pressure pumps, and they brought together all the drilling mud they could get their hands on on the West Coast—about ten thousand barrels—and they started cramming it down the hole at the rate of about thirty barrels per minute.

On the seventh day, Hartley announced that "It is the feeling of the experts that this will be adequate to build up mud going down the well . . . to the point where we will build up a level of mud with gas bubbling through it and slowly the gas will be reduced and we will get a shutoff against the bottom hole pressure."

That was just more wishful thinking by the experts. The flow of oil did slow, but significant seepage would continue for years.

Four days before the blowout occurred, Walter Hickel had been sworn in to replace Udall as Secretary of the Interior. Hickel flew out on the Sunday after the spill to meet with the county supervisors and to look over the mess. At this meeting Supervisor Clyde put it to him flatly: "We only ask that you prohibit further holes being punched into this faulty, weak, gaseous crust until valid guarantees against a recurrence can be given. This will and should take time because the regulations should be thoroughly studied and revised and the guarantees soberly and sincerely given—for if guarantees can't be given, no further drilling should be allowed until such time as they can be given."

Hickel replied, "Yes, this is a reasonable request."

But no sooner had Hickel left that conference than he met with the press and said he would ask the oil companies to "voluntarily" cease drilling operations until new regulations were established. It took Hickel only three days to whip up the "new" drilling regulations. The dazzling speed with which he performed left Clyde and many others convinced that Hickel had simply adopted a set of rules proposed by the oil companies—rules under which, in fact, Humble Oil Company was already operating. "I say publicly," raged Clyde, "that in my opinion it is tokenism in its worst form—in fact, it smacks of cold cynicism and hypocrisy. This view, I am sure, is shared by virtually all Santa Barbarans." The locals' opinion was not improved by later rumors that Hickel had spent a relaxing week at the rich folks' retreat Bohemian Grove as the guest of Union Oil president Fred Hartley.

It was an old practice for the Interior Department to allow the oil companies to set their own rules, so Hickel was no softer than his predecessors had been on this point. In fact, the previous September 4 (1968), Interior's West Coast Regional Oil and Gas supervisor, D. W. Solanas, had met with California state safety experts and had admitted "our regulations are . . . nothing more than what are standard industry practices to begin with. So that's why we get as much cooperation as we do from the federal lessees. This is their company policy to begin with."

When the Senate Public Works Committee held hearings on the spill, Solanas gave other eloquent admissions that although his agency was well aware that the Santa Barbara Channel presented special perils, the only extra precaution taken was to give safety-oriented pep talks to the oil drillers.

Senator Joseph Montoya: "The geological surveys which you made . . . and the history of this particular area—did it not indicate to you that there were fissures down below and that there was an area susceptible to earthquakes? There had been tremors in this area before, and did that not trigger in your mind the greater concern than ordinary for the possibility of spillage and, therefore, require you to impose stricter adherence to safety precautions?"

Solanas: "Yes, sir; I believe in comparison with other operations being conducted that we were very cognizant of these problems in the Santa Barbara Channel, not only based on the geology, but based on the aesthetic importance of this area. We fully understood . . . that we had to be even better safety conscious and pollution control conscious than any place that we have ever operated, either on federal lands, state lands, or private lands . . ."

Montoya: ". . . [Y]ou state that you required more precautions in this drilling operation here at Santa Barbara than you ordinarily do. Then I asked you what specific additional precautions did you prescribe and I have not been able to get an answer."

Solanas: "More alertness and more caution in every person's mind that was involved in this operation in the Santa Barbara Channel."

Montoya: "In other words, you tried to exhort these people to go into a more active mental alert about the situation, but no additional equipment?"

Solanas: "That is good phraseology, sir. I would agree that that is what I meant to say."

Montoya, clearly not too impressed, asked Solanas if aside from "alertness" he had any suggestions as to how to prevent future seepage. Solanas was ready with a solution: "I have a pet philosophy that the best thing . . . that can be done is if the federal and state lessees get in there and drill these shallow sands and produce them as fast as can be and deplete these sands, so that if we do have a future earthquake we will no longer have the threat that there would be any oil that would be bled into the ocean."

He admitted that it might take forty to fifty years of heavy pumping to get rid of the peril.

That remarkable solution would soon surface again.

In June, President Nixon formed a cabinet-level Environmental Council and assigned an investigation of the Santa Barbara blowout. The President's science adviser, Dr. Lee DuBridge, formerly head of the California Institute of Technology (a school that had benefited greatly from oil company connections), was responsible for selecting the panel.

It held only one meeting—closed to public and press—and heard testimony only from the Union Oil Company, and the U.S. Geological Survey (many of whose officials had come from the oil industry). Based on this testimony, the panel concluded that drilling in the Santa Barbara Channel should proceed, because—echoing Solanas' "pet philosophy"—the best way to stop the seepage was to let the companies pump out all the oil even if it took half a century to accomplish, which some experts in fact thought it would take. Senator Alan Cranston protested that the panel shouldn't be taken seriously, since its members had recommended the leasing of the ocean bottom in the first place.[3]

How much oil escaped into the Santa Barbara Channel, and how much damage was done?

For the first five days, Santa Barbara was in luck. The wind kept the oil from reaching the beaches, except for a 1-mile stretch south of town. Then—on the very day that Secretary Hickel told the oil companies they could resume drilling—the winds changed. Soon the beaches were fouled, in some places with oil four to five inches deep, for more than thirty miles. At its worst, the slick covered an area of about eight hundred square miles. Hundreds of boats were tarred so heavily that they could never be completely cleaned. About 30 percent of the seabird population died from being coated with oil. Santa Barbara's tourist trade was, of course, temporarily wiped out. Seven months after the first spill, ". . . at noon on Sunday of the Labor Day weekend not a single swimmer could be seen in the ocean off East Beach, formerly one of the most popular public beaches in California." ("Santa Barbarans Cite An 11th Commandment: 'Thou Shalt Not Abuse the Earth,'" Ross Macdonald and Robert Easton, New York Times Magazine, October 12, 1969)

Union Oil president Hartley claimed that at its worst the pollution was between one hundred barrels and five hundred barrels a day. Scientists from General Research Corporation, on the other hand, estimated the minimum flow at five thousand barrels a day for the first ten days. After Union claimed to have brought the wild well under control, on February 8, oil continued to flow. Sometimes the seepage was via fissures that divers hadn't previously discovered. Sometimes there were splits in the pipe. A year after the original blowout, in mid-December, Platform A was suddenly the source of another giant spill, producing a slick ten miles long and five miles wide. A pipe had broken. By this time there were sixteen wells on Platform A. All were shut down while repairs were made, and during this brief shutdown the leakage went up to five hundred barrels a day (that is, up from the "normal" seepage

---

3. Two California Republican politicians—Senator George Murphy and Representative Charles M. Teague—came up with a bizarre proposal to end the quarrel over Santa Barbara Channel drilling. They suggested that the channel be set aside as a navy petroleum reserve, to be tapped only during national emergencies, and that the companies who held leases there be allowed to swap them for comparable tracts in the Elk Hills Naval Reserve, a 46,000-acre preserve in Kern County, California, a lush pool where dry holes were virtually an impossibility. Any company that didn't want to swap would have to give up its leases for cash compensation.

Nixon liked the idea and began pushing it. But the proposal died of embarrassment a few months later, when cynics pointed out that what the Republicans were suggesting was that the federal government compensate the oil companies for bad guesses. The government would pay $178 million to get back twenty leases that extensive exploratory drilling had shown were virtually worthless. One of the leases, which cost $45 million, had only yielded two dry holes and had already been given back to the government. On the other hand, the Nixon plan would allow companies that had struck oil to go on pumping for several years, as a "safety factor."

of ten barrels). Company officials argued that this was because when the wells weren't being pumped, the pressure built up and forced the oil through fissures. Their moral: "Better let us keep pumping, because the seepage will get worse if you close us down."

The oil companies came through the Santa Barbara disaster a bit embarrassed but generally unscathed financially.[4]

Much of their embarrassment had resulted from their pitifully inept public relations. Master of the foot-in-mouth technique was Union president Hartley, who became notorious for his talent for doing just the thing to make environmentalists hate him.

He seemed incapable of saying simply that he was sorry. He would say, instead, that "Mother Nature had let us down" by allowing the fissures in the ocean floor to exist. He said he wouldn't call the 3 million gallon spill a disaster, because "I think of a disaster in terms of people being killed."

Trying to butter up the local tourist industry, the oil companies paid for a regional ad campaign with the slogan "Santa Barbara is as enjoyable today as it was last year." The ads only made most Santa Barbarans more furious, and the local newspaper, the Santa Barbara *News-Press*, wrote that the truth of the situation was that "there are many days when oil or oily debris makes bathing and strolling along some beaches decidedly unpleasant."

The Santa Barbara spill radicalized not only citizens of California but citizens everywhere to the need for protecting the environment from commercial exploitation. Oil companies were never again able to move into an area with total disregard for the feelings of the natives.[5]

SHAH OF IRAN. Persia (Iran) was the first Middle Eastern country to be set upon by the oil exploiters of the West. Its mineral resources were opened on July 25, 1872, when Shah Nasr ed-Din granted a concession to a British national, Baron Julius de Reuter, founder of the British news agency. It was the most sweeping concession ever made, giving him access to—at least theoretically—the oil resources of all Persia; it was a 70-year monopoly, for which De Reuter made a 40,000-pound deposit.

---

4. In November 1971, the four oil companies who operated Platform A—Union, Gulf, Mobil, and Texaco—agreed to pay $4.5 million to settle a $105-million damage suit filed by 1,560 beachfront property owners. In addition, Union had spent about $16 million for cleanup costs.

5. But there was a negative side to this as well. Many in the oil industry and in government, observing their unpopularity, came to believe that the critical issue was not environmental protection, but public relations. They decided that the way to win future battles was not to treat the public's property with compassion but to figure out a way to brainwash the public. Thus in 1975, the West Coast manager of the Interior Department's Bureau of Land Management asked his superiors to earmark environmental research money for "educational thrusts" to soften opposition to offshore drilling for oil. He wrote, "The identification of the composition of the community power structure will assist in educational thrusts toward those officials at a later time, with a possible softening of their present opposition to offshore oil development . . . Identification of these elements will be invaluable in the development of a public affairs program designed to soften negative public opinion."

Unfortunately for him, the 70-year concession lasted only one year. The Shah, pressured by his Russian neighbors, canceled it in 1873.

The British Government, which looked upon De Reuter's business as its own, refused to acknowledge the cancellation. One must remember that, to Britain in those days, the most important eastern outpost of the Empire was India. It was willing to go to almost any limit, including war, to protect India and to maintain unrestricted access by land and sea. Persia was a crucial part of the land approach from the west. For a Britisher to have such a marvelous concession as De Reuter's was simply one more guarantee of the safety of the western approach.

Pressure from the British was so intense that in 1889 the Shah granted a new concession to De Reuter, this time for sixty years. But still he could not find oil, and once again, in 1899, the Persians canceled his concession.

Now William Knox D'Arcy, another British national, enters the picture. D'Arcy had become rich in Australia's Mount Morgan gold rush. Edouard Cotte, one-time secretary to Baron de Reuter, was convinced that Persia had oil, and it was his persistence and lucky fanaticism that got D'Arcy interested. In 1901 D'Arcy obtained an oil concession to all Persia except the five major northern provinces (which were excluded to keep peace with the Russians).

In 1908 D'Arcy struck his first oil. But, by that time, he had gone through so much of his own money that he had had to turn to other investors. When, on April 14, 1909, the Anglo-Persian Oil Company was formed, D'Arcy was merely a director. And in 1914 the British Government itself became the major stockholder and controlling partner in the company.

The Persians, needless to say, were much abused in all this. They were treated as if they hardly counted even in their own country. Going over their heads, the British and the Russians split up the country into three spheres of interest: the northern third going to Russia, the southern third to England, and the middle zone, "neutral" to the two great nations. A treaty outlining those divisions was signed in 1907. Britain and Russia did not exactly control their respective spheres, but they gave each other freedom to exploit the Persians without interference. For ten years, Persia's nationalism shriveled under the terms of this treaty, which had been arrived at without consultation with or consent of Persia's rulers.

The treaty ended for all practical purposes in 1917 with the Bolshevik revolution. The civil war in Russia made the British feel free to move throughout Persia, including the previously Russian "sphere of influence" in the North.

An anti-Persian spirit had pervaded the founding of the Anglo-Persian Oil Company, in 1909. It was actually a merger of two companies, First Exploitation Company and Bakhtiari Oil Company. Persian nationalists were virtually excluded from both; they owned 12 percent of the First Exploitation stock, 3 percent of the Bakhtiari Oil stock. Persians had nothing to say about the operation of these two companies or of their successor, the Anglo-Persian Oil Company.

That was plain enough in the royalties. Despite the fact that Persian oil significantly contributed to the Allied victory in World War I, the British showed no economic gratitude. Their contractual arrangement was to give Persia what amounted to 16 percent of Anglo-Persian Oil Company's net profits, and the net profits were arrived at only after inflating "costs" in a shameful fashion.

Persians did not take such treatment indifferently. They resented both the Russians and the British, but especially they resented the British, because they were the more successful at exploitation. But, to put their resentment into action, the Persians needed a strong leader—a dictator, in fact. Despite their sometime longing for republicanism, the Persians at that time were too badly shattered along tribal lines to develop a cohesive republic.

The strong leader who emerged was Riza Khan, a person of towering physique and harsh temper who worked himself up through the army ranks to become, in 1921, with intrigue and political muscle, Persia's Minister of War. That put him within easy striking distance of the Palace, and he did not miss the chance. In 1924 he issued a proclamation that the Persians should stop even discussing republicanism; and to drive his point home, he declared himself dictator in 1925. He ousted the Shah, assuming that title for himself as well as a new name: Pahlevi.

Thus was born the political dynasty that would last, with one brief interruption, until 1979.

A proud, tough Persian, and certainly no patsy for foreigners, Pahlevi waited only long enough to solidify his rule before canceling, in 1932, the contract with Anglo-Persian. A new contract was hammered out and signed the next year—a contract slightly better for Persia (henceforth it would get 20 percent of the net) but still overwhelmingly to the advantage of the British.

Meanwhile the Shah had tried to bring in American oilmen to develop the five northern (previously Russian-zoned) provinces as a counterbalance to the British influence.

The first effort was made in 1921—the year Riza Khan moved into, and began to dominate, the Persian Cabinet—when a preliminary contract was made with Standard Oil to develop the northern area. But hardly had the signatories finished toasting each other before Standard Oil took steps to betray the Persians. It entered into a secret agreement to develop the area on a fifty-fifty basis with the British—thereby frustrating the Persians' purpose for bringing in Americans. When the Persians learned of this betrayal, they canceled the Standard Oil contract (in 1923) and opened the territory to offers from other U.S. oil firms. Harry F. Sinclair, of the Sinclair Oil Company, stepped forward with an offer that the Persians were ready to accept. They signed a preliminary agreement with him on December 20, 1923. But, within a month, Sinclair's world began crumbling. First came the revelation that he had bribed Secretary of the Interior Albert Fall with $100,000 for access to the navy petroleum holdings at Teapot Dome, Wyoming (see the Appendix entry on *TEAPOT DOME*). Then one newspaper in Tehran accused him (never proved, but it didn't sound unreasonable) of bribing the Persian prime minister with $275,000. Exit Mr. Sinclair.

This left the British once again in unchallenged control. But, knowing that Riza Shah was thoroughly fed up with being cheated and would cancel their concession again at the first opportunity, the British were only too glad to depose him, in 1941, on the grounds that he was dangerous to the Allied effort in World War II. He was shipped under guard first to Mauritius and then to South Africa, where he died on July 26, 1944.

His son, Muhammad Riza Pahlevi, was elevated to the Peacock Throne. Prime Minister Winston Churchill declared in the House of Commons: "We have chased a dictator into exile, and installed a constitutional Sovereign pledged to a whole catalogue of long-delayed, seriously needed reforms and reparations." What he meant, and what the oil companies thought, for a long time with seeming good reason, was that they had installed on the throne a weak, vacillating chap whom the oil exploiters would be able to manipulate indefinitely.

They were correct in all their expectations but one. The new Shah was not exploitable forever, or at least not exploitable forever in the same way. Spoiled and arrogant, he was at first interested only in becoming the oil world's foremost playboy. But gradually he was consumed by another passion: he would become a new Cyrus the Great, who brought together twenty-seven nations to found an empire stretching from India to Greece, an empire whose glories burst across the Middle East twenty-five centuries ago. But that passion —madness, some felt—would not consume the young Shah for still some years, and then only after he was smitten, as virtually all Middle Easterners are sooner or later, by the passion of nationalism.

It was a passion that by the end of World War II had raised Iran's fever to a very high level. Officials of the Anglo-Iranian Oil Company failed to sense the depth of this new sentiment, but in 1951 they learned. Their lesson took place when they opened negotiations for a renewal of their oil concession as though nothing had changed. They offered merely a slight increase in the per-ton royalty, although Iranians knew that foreign oilmen just across the Persian Gulf were offering a fifty-fifty split of the profits to Saudi Arabia. By the time the British got wise to the hatred Iranians felt for them, and began offering a fifty-fifty split, it was too late.

By that time, the forces of rebellion had unified behind Mohammed Mossadegh and pushed him to power, on April 29, 1951, as head of the National Front government. He immediately persuaded the Iranian parliament to nationalize the Anglo-Iranian Oil Company. Though the Iranians now for the first time in half a century actually owned their own oil, they were frustrated in disposing of it profitably. Mossadegh chased the Shah from the country in 1953 and took total control for himself in a final desperate effort to make his revolution succeed, but the CIA within a few days put together a successful countercoup that overthrew Mossadegh and put the young Shah back on the Peacock Throne.

The American spy agency was, in effect, the flying wedge that opened Iran to U.S.-based oil companies. The Anglo-Iranian Oil Company was forced to pay for being restored to its former holdings by sharing them, especially with a group of U.S. firms. The British monopoly was ended. Iranian oil would now be produced by an international consortium consisting of:

British Petroleum (as Anglo-Iranian would henceforth be known), holding 40 percent of the consortium's equity;

Royal Dutch-Shell, 14 percent;

Gulf, 7 percent;

Standard Oil of California, 7 percent;

Exxon (Standard of New Jersey), 7 percent;

Texaco, 7 percent;

Mobil, 7 percent;

Compagnie Française des Pétroles, 6 percent;

The Iricon Group, 5 percent.

It will be seen from that list that the same companies controlling the oil concession in Saudi Arabia were now ensconced in Iran, too.

A word should be said about the strange-sounding "Iricon Group." Originally, the Iran consortium consisted only of the major oil companies. The arrangement was made with the blessing of the U.S. Justice Department, which officially stated that in splitting up the Iranian booty the U.S. companies would be exempt from all antitrust laws. But pressure from the independent oil lobby forced the Justice Department to change its mind. For appearances' sake, it ruled that before the exemption would apply, some independents must also be permitted a slight share. So 5 percent of the total was set aside for them, and this 5 percent was divided among sixteen smaller American companies. Over the years, mergers cut these sixteen down to six: American Independent Oil Company, Atlantic Richfield Company, Charter International Oil Company, Continental Oil Company, Getty Oil Co., and Standard Oil Co. (Ohio)—which is how things stood in 1973, when Iran nationalized its fields.

The Shah launched his "White Revolution," in 1963, to industrialize and modernize Iran. There is good reason to suspect that the idea for the "White Revolution" was put in his bonnet by the major oil companies themselves, for something had to be done to get the Middle Eastern oil price level started upward.

For two decades, the posted Mideast price had been stuck at between $1.25 and $1.50 a barrel, and by the early 1960s the oil companies, because of a glut, feared the real price—not the posted price—might sag to the dollar level. Consider this dilemma: The companies were paying the host countries half of the posted price: say, 75 cents a barrel. In Iran it cost the companies between 10 cents and 20 cents to produce a barrel. If the time came when the oil companies were forced to peddle oil at only one dollar a barrel on the world market, it would mean earnings of only 5 to 15 cents a barrel: terribly slim pickings by oil-company standards.

So the oil companies were desperate to find some strategy for rigging the market at a higher level. What better way than to inspire greed among the oil-producing nations by enticing them into an orgy of spending? The more they spent, the more they would want to spend or (because of debts) need to earn. Therefore, they would be eager to keep prices going up.

The Shah was the perfect mark. Not only was he easily excited by dreams of imitating Cyrus the Great and returning Iran to empire status, but he was also easily frightened by the bugaboo of Russia, looming, as he was persuaded, over Iran's future—and indeed the future of the entire Middle East—with lust in its heart. Dreams of empire could be developed in Iran more than in other Middle Eastern nations, because of its relatively large population (35 million) and several urban centers. It was not, like Saudi Arabia and Iraq, a nation of Arabian camel and goat herders. It was not Arabian at all, and though still largely oriented toward agriculture, clearly had a real place for big industry in its future. Thus came the "White Revolution." And with it came the Shah's determination to defend his to-be-industrialized nation against Communist predators by developing the largest and best-equipped armed forces in the Middle East.

His ambitions worked on the price of oil as expected. Although he had little empathy for the Arab members of OPEC and indeed felt strong political hostility toward some (especially Iraq), he worked closely with them in strong-arming increasingly profitable contracts from the oil companies (contracts which were, of course, equally profitable for the companies). Although during the 1960s there was a glut of oil, by the end of the decade something resembling a sellers' market had again developed. Seizing the initiative, OPEC forced an agreement, on February 14, 1971 (the so-called Tehran Agreement, because it was made in the Iranian capital), raising posted prices one third and guaranteeing additional increases over the next three years. Two months later, the Shah broke the agreement and kicked prices skyward again. Other OPEC countries were, of course, looting right along at his side, though no other quite so greedily.

With the inflation of oil prices and the squandering of money on ill-formed industrial plans, the Shah's fantasy of developing a great military empire also soared to unrealistic levels. He became the United States' best arms customer, buying $20 billion worth of military supplies from us from 1972 to 1978 and placing orders for billions more. New military doodads were like drugs to him; he had to have every new one as soon as it was developed. His airmen were just learning to fly our F-4s when the Shah began placing orders for billions of dollars' worth of F-5s. And before his pilots had discovered where the F-5's cockpit was, he was buying a batch of F-14s.

His plans for a self-sufficient, industrial Iran were also pressed too fast and too sloppily. His mistake was in trying to establish Iran in a world role based on qualities that at that point in history it was spectacularly devoid of. All the wealth of Persia could not make up for a shortage of training and experience. Most of the giant U.S. corporations that set up branches in Iran had to bring along their own personnel to run things, because Iran had few technicians, engineers, and scientists. The Shah was short an estimated half million skilled workers. He wanted to build two dozen atomic plants (looking to the day when his oil would run out), but he had only a dozen homegrown atomic technicians. When he bought airplanes or tanks or heavy construction equipment or computers or television gear, he had to hire foreigners—primarily American, German, and French—to come in to operate the equipment and to try to train Iranians to take over the job later on. (It cost an estimated average of $190,000 a year to support each outside expert.)

The Shah decided Iran needed more trucks, so he ordered an armada of trucks; but when the ships arrived, there wasn't dock space, so they lay at anchor for months. When the trucks were finally unloaded—two thousand of them—it was discovered that there weren't that many trained truck drivers in Iran. Frantically, drivers were imported and others were trained locally. Months later, when the trucks finally got rolling, it was discovered that there weren't enough trained mechanics to keep them rolling. Indeed, in 1976 a third of the nation's cars and trucks were laid up, waiting for mechanics to get around to repairing them.

Power shortages closed more than two hundred factories in the Tehran area for months at a time, and the factories that remained open had to curtail work for two to six hours daily. As a whole, industry was running at about half the production rate that the Shah had anticipated. Some new plants were operating at only 40 percent of capacity.

His engineers built mammoth irrigation dams—without canals to distribute the water. Fifteen years after the "White Revolution" had set forth to turn the vast desert into modern farms, most farmers were still tilling their lands with the same techniques used twenty-five centuries ago. Hunger was common; the diet of most Iranians was bread and vegetable oil. There were nearly seven million families, but only slightly more than five million housing units; many Iranians lived in holes, under cloth sheeting.

The mansions—castles, really—of the privileged class sprang up like sunflowers throughout Tehran, but the city's sewage was still handled by cesspools, and the streets were filled with garbage, fluid filth, and the debris cast up from potholes.

With two thirds of the population illiterate, the Shah decided to get his people educated via TV classrooms—apparently forgetting that many of the nation's villages had no electricity to operate the sets. The number of Iranians of high school age actually in high school declined from 30 percent in 1976 to 20 percent in 1978.

Iran's oil wealth disrupted the old way of life, luring millions from the farms to the cities, where they were confronted with intense inflation (up to 30 percent, some years) and frequent unemployment. The average citizen, if not hurt by the oil wealth, benefited little from it. But the privileged class lived in a euphoria of corruption. Foreign corporations doing business in Iran quickly learned that the standard kickback was 15 percent. The corruption was especially lavish among the Shah's family and closest friends, one of whom indulged himself in building a replica of Marie Antoinette's Petit Trianon for a mere $15 million and outfitting it with furnishings such as the $440,000 desk once owned by a czarina.

But the loot flowed outward, too. Early in 1972, President Nixon and Henry Kissinger went into secret conference with the Shah—a conference so secret that not even the U.S. ambassador to Iran was permitted to attend—in which they promised that the Shah could make unlimited purchases of U.S. arms. In return, the Shah funneled money through Mexico, with the assistance of CIA money laundries, into the Nixon campaign treasury. When the FBI began tracing the crooked money back to its source, the CIA protested that the investigation could "jeopardize a CIA operation." Richard Helms, who was then director of the CIA, was later appointed ambassador to Iran by Nixon.

Though the Shah had failed to raise the common people's standard of living an appreciable amount, he had raised their expectations so high that the resulting frustrations left him with a nation of enemies. Opposition was especially strong from leaders of the Shi'ite Moslems, some of whom he banished but failed to quiet. (A full 98 percent of the population are Shi'ite Moslems.) The Shah imprisoned and tortured thousands of political opponents and outspoken citizens (some estimated as many as forty thousand political prisoners in Iran's jails in 1977). According to Amnesty International, an organization that keeps a census of political torture around the world, there were numerous reports of Iranian prisoners whom the Shah's secret police subjected to "weighted handcuffs, insertion of electric cosh or bottle into the rectum, and placing the prisoner on an electric grill which is then heated. The last method is alleged to have paralyzed some of those subjected to it, so that they were unable to walk, but could only move about by crawling on all fours." Another of the Shah's favorite techniques for making dissidents love him was to have them beaten on the soles of their feet with rubber hoses, until their feet blew up to the size of basketballs.

Despite frequent reports of deep unrest in Iran, U.S. spy agencies failed to read the trouble correctly, and President Carter praised the Shah as a "stabilizing influence." The Shah was equally ignorant of his true predicament. In the June 26, 1978, issue of *U.S. News and World Report* he boasted, "Nobody can overthrow me. I have the support of 700,000 troops, all the workers and most of the people . . . I have the power."

Less than seven months later, his troops would desert him, Iran would be in total rebellion, and the Shah would escape only with his life and plenty of money. The Shah left Iran in his $115-million plane, including $2 million in gold-plated bathroom fixtures, on January 16, 1979, for a "vacation." He did not go home again.

The effect of the Shah's departure on the welfare of the oil industry was difficult to appraise. The Shah had been the major oil companies' most cooperative raiser of prices. But, on the other hand, he had been spending so wildly, and his need for more money had become so excessive, that he was no longer considered reliable or even stable.

The Shah's juggling of massive income and massive outgo could not have gone on much longer. The income balls were already beginning to fall. First signs of Iran's decline came in 1975, when it decided it could not afford to lend $300 million to Pan American Airways, which was in trouble because of soaring fuel costs. Shocked by the Shah's backing out of this deal, money experts began looking more closely at the supposed wealth of Iran. They found that the nation owed about $3 billion in unilateral and multilateral loans—debts for farm produce, for arms, for machinery—and that debt was rising much faster than income. In 1973, the Shah had set up a five-year plan calling for the expenditure of $123 billion. It was a jerry-built plan, for although his oil income jumped from $4.5 billion in 1973 to $20 billion in 1975, by the latter year he was already borrowing on the Eurodollar market and beginning to cut back on industrial expansion. Iran's growth rate, which had been a heady 40 percent in 1974, dropped to 10 percent in 1977.

There was one additional chilling cloud in the Shah's future. Experts predicted that he was pumping so madly that Iran's oil production would peak in the 1980s and begin to play out in twenty years or so.

Where would the Shah have gotten the money to pay off his mounting debts, with the end of Iran's great oil era in sight (in the 1970s it was second only to Saudi Arabia as an oil exporter)? Not from the rickety new industries that the Shah had been betting on.

Inevitably, when Iran's pumps began to suck air, the Shah would have contemplated aggression. Having wasted his own riches, perhaps he would have sought to loot a less prodigal member of OPEC—Saudi Arabia, just thirty minutes away, being the expected target. Saudi Arabia, with a population only about one fifth the size of Iran's and with a military force not even remotely comparable, would have been a pushover for him.

It was action that U.S. officials anticipated as a real possibility. On December 19, 1977, the Senate Committee on Energy and Natural Resources had issued a report warning of the possibility of war between America's two most important oil-producing allies—Iran and Saudi Arabia—and had concluded that if it came about, the United States would have to stand by and let Iran have its way, because "it must be recognized in advance by the United States that this is the role for which Iran is being primed. Blame cannot be assigned for Iran's carrying out an implied assignment." The committee report made Iran's motivation sound reasonable: Saudi Arabia's oil reserves are at least three times larger than Iran's, it pointed out. Iran at that time had the capability of producing up to 6.7 million barrels a day, compared to more than 10 million barrels a day for Saudi Arabia. And more important, Saudi Arabia would be capable of producing up to 20 million barrels a day in the 1980s, after Iran's oil production had peaked.

It is very likely, however, that the major oil companies that ran both Aramco and the Iranian consortium did not approve of either the Shah's tempestuous pumping of Iranian oil or of his brooding ambition to seize Saudi Arabia's fields. They had no desire to speed their way through the Middle Eastern oil supplies. Much more profitable over the long haul would be contrived shortages and sharply controlled production. In these respects, the end of the Pahlevi Dynasty served their purpose. Even the momentary disruption of a major source of Middle Eastern supplies was made to pay off. For a few weeks after the Shah's exile, in 1979, the Iranian fields were closed down entirely. This reduction, the significance of which was grossly exaggerated by the major oil companies, became their chief propaganda tool in trying to persuade the American people to accept decontrol of domestic oil prices. They argued that in order to escape from "unreliable" foreign imports, domestic producers should be encouraged, with higher prices, to hunt for more oil.

STANDARD OIL AND THE NAZIS. (The following is drawn mostly from Joseph Borkin's *The Crime and Punishment of I.G. Farben*, The Free Press, 1978.)

When the Nazis were rising to power in Germany, the world's principal manufacturer of tetraethyl lead, the gasoline additive, was the Ethyl Gasoline Corporation, owned jointly by General Motors and Standard Oil. The Nazis knew that they had to have tetraethyl lead for their war machine—primarily for the Luftwaffe—so they asked Standard Oil to help them out.

In 1927, Standard Oil had gone into cartel partnership with I.G. Farbenindustrie, the German chemical company. Now Farben suggested to Ethyl Gasoline Corporation that they go into partnership in a company, to be called Ethyl GmbH, to build tetraethyl-lead plants in Germany. At the time these negotiations were underway, an official of the Du Pont Corporation, which was the chief stockholder in General Motors, wrote to E. W. Webb, president of Ethyl Gasoline Corporation (the letter was dated December 15, 1934), warning: "It has been claimed that Germany is secretly arming. Ethyl lead would doubtless be a valuable aid to military aeroplanes. I am writing you this to say that in my opinion, under no condition should you or the Board of Directors of the Ethyl Corporation disclose any secrets or 'know-how' in connection with the manufacture of tetraethyl lead in Germany."

It is unlikely that Standard Oil or Ethyl officials needed to be told that they were aiding the Nazi movement. That was obvious. Nevertheless, Ethyl and Farben did form a joint company, Ethyl GmbH, to produce tetraethyl lead in Germany. Before these plants were completed, however, the Nazis felt that they needed to buy tetraethyl lead from American sources for Hitler's planned move into Czechoslovakia, in 1938. The Ethyl GmbH production plants would not be ready before 1939. So Nazi officials got Farben to buy five hundred tons of tetraethyl lead from Ethyl Export Corporation, a Standard Oil affiliate, to have on hand. Nothing was said about its being used in war, but there would hardly have been any other reason for a rush order for $20,000,000 worth of the gasoline additive. Some high Nazis were uneasy about this close relationship between I.G. Farbenindustrie, the most important military contractor in Germany, and a Standard Oil affiliate. But as August von Knierim, Farben's top attorney, wrote later in defense of the relationship: "Without tetraethyl lead, the present method of warfare would have been impossible. The fact that since the beginning of the war we could produce tetraethyl lead is entirely due to the circumstances that shortly before, the Americans presented us with the production plans, complete with their know-how."

Standard Oil's alliance with I.G. Farben had begun in the late twenties, when they cooperated in the development of a process for turning coal into oil. Farben was already well along in perfecting the synthetic oil process; what it needed most from Standard, and got, was lots of money.

In 1930, Standard and Farben formed and owned equally the Joint American Study Company (Jasco), through which they shared all new processes developed by either party. It was an arrangement that profited the Nazis more than it did the Americans. After Hitler's troops marched into Austria, in 1938, and it was evident that war was at hand, Standard turned over to Farben the patent rights and production data for a new synthetic rubber called Butyl. But Farben, which had developed a process for making a synthetic rubber called Buna, from oil, did not turn this formula over to Standard, despite Standard's requests that it do so, until late in 1940. The result of this delay, writes Joseph Borkin, "was a major military setback for the United States. On December 7, 1941, Japan attacked Pearl Harbor, and the United States was suddenly faced with a monumental rubber crisis. It was blocked from its main source of natural rubber, in Southeast Asia . . . The United States would have to rely on synthetic rubber for tires. However, the American rubber and chemical companies were completely unprepared to mass-produce a synthetic.

"While feverish work was going on among the rubber and chemical companies to develop a synthetic rubber out of which to make tires, there seemed to be no prospect for immediate success as far as Buna was concerned. I.G. [Farbenindustrie] had successfully kept the know-how for its production from reaching the United States. For the United States . . . the results were calamitous."

But such was the power of Standard that this government did not punish it at all for its cooperation with the Nazi war machine, and "punished" it to a ludicrously insignificant degree for suppressing the development of synthetic rubber in this country. In late 1941, the Justice Department was ready to indict the Standard Oil companies, I.G. Farbenindustrie, and their top executives for conspiring to create a worldwide monopoly in restraint of trade in the oil and chemical industries, including synthetic rubber and synthetic gasoline.

But President Roosevelt and his advisers decided that such a lawsuit would not be in the best interests of the war effort, so Standard and its officers were allowed to plead *nolo contendere* to a civil complaint, and all parties were fined a total of $50,000—averaging only $5,000 per individual—instead of the $1.5 million that the Justice Department had originally wanted the court to assess them. Nobody went to jail.

If Standard had cause to cheer, so, for other reasons, did the Nazis. "For five and a half years," Borkin notes, "Hitler's tanks, trucks, and planes were propelled by I.G.'s gasoline, their wheels made of I.G.'s rubber"—all developed in collaboration with Standard Oil.

Under a fraudulent, predated agreement signed in 1940 (it was made out to appear that the agreement had been signed two days before Great Britain and France officially declared war on Germany, rather than, as was actually the case, two weeks after the declaration of war), Standard and Farben tried to set up an arrangement by which they could resume their cooperative arrangement after the war had ended. This agreement was struck down in 1948 by a court that implied in its judgment that Standard Oil might be considered an enemy national because of its cooperation with I.G. Farbenindustrie. However, ultimately the patents once held by Jasco, the Standard-Farben company, were returned to Standard's ownership.

STRATEGIC PETROLEUM RESERVE. Even before the Arab embargo, of 1973–74, some members of Congress, including key energy spokesmen such as Senator Henry Jackson, had pushed for the establishment of an emergency oil stockpile, but President Richard Nixon had brushed aside the idea as being too costly. Then came the energy panic of '73–'74, and President Gerald Ford joined Congress in supporting the idea. It was the only important part of the

Energy Policy and Conservation Act of 1975 that wasn't controversial; to the last member of Congress, they favored that portion of the Act that declared it "to be the policy of the United States to provide for the creation of a strategic petroleum reserve for the storage of up to one billion barrels of petroleum products, but not less than 150 million barrels of petroleum products, by the end of the three-year period which begins on the date of the enactment of this act"—in short, by the end of 1978.

On paper, the Federal Energy Administration had things moving smartly along within a few months. On December 15, 1976, FEA bureaucrats trotted up to Capitol Hill with the big plan: The oil would be stored in salt dome caverns (formed millions of years ago when an ancient sea evaporated) along the Gulf Coast. The FEA figured it could have 500 million barrels in storage by 1982 at a cost of no more than $8 billion. That was a promise.

The plan turned out to have virtually no relationship to reality.

The next big idea came from Jimmy Carter. In his celebrated moral-equivalent-of-war energy program, presented in April 1977, he promised to have not a mere 150 million barrels (as Congress had originally ordered) but 250 million barrels in storage by December 1978. And by heck he wasn't going to settle for the FEA's promised 500 million barrels, either. He would *double* that amount, because "this reserve is the best kind of insurance the United States could buy." And in June 1978, Carter's energy planners officially asked Congress to start pumping money into the billion-barrel plan, because "the expansion of the reserve is essential in meeting the President's national energy objective of reducing U.S. vulnerability to . . . supply interruptions." Carter said he intended to step up the schedule. He would have the 500 million barrels in place by 1980, two years ahead of the FEA's proposal, and he would have one billion barrels in place by 1985.

All pipe dreams.

Throughout 1977 and 1978, the Department of Energy (as the caterpillar had by now become) and the Office of Management and Budget squabbled over how much money should be spent on the reserve. The OMB's stinginess and the DOE's inefficiency resulted in a catastrophic shortfall.

Came December 1978 and the salt mines contained not 250 million barrels, not 150 million barrels, but 60 million barrels—less than half the legal requirement set by Congress as a matter of "national policy" and about one-fourth Carter's rosy prediction.

By this time, Iran was falling apart, there was all sorts of wild talk about worldwide shortages, prices were shooting through the heavens—and the need for the strategic oil reserve was at hand. But it was useless. The caverns were mostly empty.

In a February 1979 article, "Where Is the Strategic Oil Reserve Now That We Need It?" *National Journal* writer Richard Corrigan pointed out sourly:

"Just as the department is getting its caverns and pipelines and terminals and assorted hardware in shape, the world oil market has gone dry.

"When oil was plentiful over the past two years, the department had no room for it; now it has the holes in the ground, but can't find oil to fill them."

What's more, the insignificant amount that was in storage was a mockery, because no pumps had yet been installed to get it out.

The strategic reserve's budget, meanwhile, was getting out of hand. The cost of storage alone had more than doubled since the original estimate, and the price of oil had increased more than 300 percent. A significant amount of the budget—many millions—was being wasted on inadequate pipelines, on defective drill rigs, on services that were never performed, on equipment that was stolen from the government by contractors and later resold to the government. Such antics would continue at least into 1981.

It was plain that the Department of Energy, being run mostly by executives drawn from the oil industry, was not trying to keep prices down. If they had wanted to do that, they would not have bought oil for the reserve on the open market.

In February 1977, the General Accounting Office had suggested that the caverns be filled either by what is called "royalty oil" or by oil from the Elk Hills Naval Petroleum Reserve. "Royalty oil" is oil the government can take in lieu of money royalties from the oil companies that hold leases on federal lands. The energy bureaucrats refused to do this, saying it would "disrupt" the industry. The GAO said, Well, if you don't like that idea, why don't you at least consider buying the Elk Hills oil from the Navy? The energy experts again rejected the idea, arguing that although the Elk Hills oil was cheaper than oil on the world market, it was still too expensive. At that time, they could have bought the Elk Hills oil for $12.31 a barrel. By 1980, that same oil was selling on the spot market for more than $40 a barrel.

Insult was added to injury in the spring of 1979, when Saudi Arabia notified the United States that it (Saudi Arabia) would increase its production level from a normal daily 8.5 million barrels to 9.5 million barrels, thereby making up for some of the oil lost by the Iranian revolution, *only* if the United States stopped stockpiling oil in its national reserve. In short, Saudi Arabia demanded veto power over an Act passed by Congress—and it got by with the demand. U.S. officials stopped adding to the strategic reserves.

By January of 1980, however, Carter apparently felt that the world oil supply had risen to such a surplus that he could safely sneak past the Arabians. So he stuck a $1.1 billion request into the 1981 budget for more oil for the reserves.

The Saudis spotted the request and began to threaten again. Increase your storage, they said, and we'll cut our production by one million barrels a day. Carter sent Energy Secretary Charles Duncan to Arabia to see if personal diplomacy would change their minds. This time, the Administration tried to sound tough. One State Department official said, "We [in the Administration] used to fight over whether the stockpiling should be resumed. Now, in the wake of Afghanistan, the only real issue is one of timing of the resumption." The Energy Department's Office of Policy and Evaluation issued a study recommending that our reserve capacity be expanded to perhaps as much as *four billion* barrels.

But all grandiose plans and tough talk evaporated when Duncan got to

Arabia. He found the Saudis adamant as ever. Further stockpiling, they said, would be viewed as a hostile act.

Obviously, the reason they felt that way, as Richard D. Lyons, of the New York *Times,* pointed out, is that "with a billion barrels of oil in the reserve, the United States would be more reluctant to go to the aid of Saudi Arabia if that nation were threatened. In addition, the less oil that the United States has in its reserve, the greater the power the Saudis might exercise over American foreign policy. Thus, a greater amount of oil might translate into a greater reluctance by the Carter administration to put pressure on Israel to moderate its stand in its dealings with the Palestine Liberation Organization and Arab countries in general."

The Administration backed down once more. On March 5, 1980, Secretary Duncan called a press conference in Washington to announce that the Administration was calling off stockpiling for the nonce, and that although they intended to someday follow the law passed in 1975, "to do so will take many years—perhaps all of this decade."

Congress, apparently less frightened of the Saudis than Carter was, mandated in the summer of 1980 that token stockpiling at the rate of one hundred thousand barrels a day be resumed; Carter was told that if he wanted Congress to pass his synthetic-fuels program, he would have to take that amount from the naval fields at Elk Hills and stick it into the salt domes.

So the program went limping on. Although under President Reagan another round of space, cost, and corruption problems developed, and although he was niggardly in his budget for the program, the fill rate did increase sufficiently that by the middle of 1983 the reserve was nearly half full. Half a dozen more years and who knows?

TEAPOT DOME. The foundation for this, the most famous political scandal up to the time of Watergate, was laid with the election of Warren G. Harding to the presidency, in 1920. Harding was, in the words of William Allen White, "almost unbelievably ill-informed." He was stupid in his handling of politics. He was, if possible, even stupider in his handling of men. In an effort to make his administration appear respectable, he filled his Cabinet with the purest of capitalists: none was purer on that score and none was a more unrelenting ally of Big Oil than Albert B. Fall, Secretary of the Interior.

Fall turned out to be a thief; but he was not a selfish thief. He believed that others, too, especially those engaged in exploiting natural resources, should have the same opportunity to steal. Before he reached Harding's Cabinet, he was firmly on record as opposing any government supervision or control over the development of timber, minerals, grass, water, or other resources to be found on or under the federal domain in the western states. It was Fall's belief —stated in public many times before 1920—that the West should be "developed" by lumber companies, oil companies, copper and other mineral companies, cattle barons, and electric utility companies, without the slightest interference from Washington bureaucrats.

Fall had shown his friendship for oil companies when he was in the Senate. As chairman of the Senate Subcommittee on Mexican Affairs, he had always

sided with the oil companies against Mexico's efforts to control its own resources. He had also favored a plan to partition the world into British and
American oil zones, with the Western Hemisphere staked out for U.S. oil companies.

He continued to act on his beliefs. No sooner had he been sworn in as Interior Secretary than he persuaded President Harding to transfer jurisdiction
over certain parts of the federal oil domain in California and Wyoming from
the Navy Department to the Interior Department. There were three oil fields
reserved by previous Presidents for emergency use by the Navy: Reserve No.
1 was thirty-eight thousand acres at Elk Hills, California, set aside by executive order on September 12, 1912; Reserve No. 2 was thirty thousand acres in
Buena Vista, California, set aside on December 13, 1912; Reserve No. 3 was
ninety-five hundred acres at Teapot Dome, Wyoming, about fifty miles north
of Casper, set aside April 30, 1915.

Then, in 1922—secretly—Fall leased Teapot Dome to Harry F. Sinclair's
Mammoth Oil Company and Elk Hills to Edward L. Doheny's Pan-American
Company. Except that he had taken this step without opening the land to
competitive bidding, there was nothing on the surface to indicate that Fall had
committed a crime. Both Mammoth and Pan-American contracted to deliver
oil where the Navy needed it delivered, and both agreed to pay the federal
government royalties of between 12.5 percent and 50 percent, depending on
the amount pumped. It was a fairly standard contract. The dirty work would
emerge later.

The deal between Fall and Doheny and Sinclair was not discovered until
April 1922, when some oil producers who were already working a part of
Teapot Dome became angry with the government for trying to evict them so
that Sinclair could move in and take over. When one company absolutely refused to budge, Fall sent in marines with orders to throw them out.

The Interior Department at first tried to pretend that there was no contract
with Sinclair; then, a week later, Fall admitted there was a contract. When the
Denver *Post* began digging into the background of the contracts, Sinclair
bought off its publishers with a quarter of a million dollars. Sinclair spent another three quarters of a million dollars to quiet the protests of the oilmen who
had felt pushed out.

Secretary Fall brushed aside the early criticism of his action by saying that
"national security" required him to make the leases in secrecy. For virtually all
the press, that was explanation enough. There was no stampede of reporters to
dig out the facts. Most of their publishers were Republicans.

In Congress, too, Fall's action stirred mostly indifference. Few seemed terribly offended, and not the least bit suspicious, when, in October 1923, Secretary Fall resigned from the Cabinet to go to work for none other than Harry
Sinclair. (That wasn't so unusual. Edward Doheny, who had won the Elk Hills
leases, hired *four* members of President Wilson's Cabinet.) At his last press
conference, Fall told reporters: "I have tried to impress upon my friends and
associates that my leaving Washington is not a case of saying 'goodbye,' but
'until we meet again.'"

He couldn't have known how right he was. Within the month, he was back in Washington, subpoenaed to start testifying about his handling of the Teapot Dome oil. His appearance was a victory for Senator Robert M. La Follette of Wisconsin, who had first introduced a Senate resolution, on April 21, 1922, calling for the investigation. But it didn't get underway for more than a year, and of course it then ran into enormous opposition. Republicans controlled both houses of Congress, and they were not eager to uncover scandals in the Republican presidency.

The chairman of the Public Lands Committee, Republican Reed Smoot of Utah, had no interest in handling the investigation, so he fobbed it off on Senator Tom Walsh, a Democrat from Montana.

Walsh didn't merely run the investigation. He *was* the investigation. Indeed, he was veritably a one-man inquisition. He got little assistance from other senators on the committee; he got research help from one law clerk, a student. But the contest was not pitifully one-sided: Walsh was no beginner. He had been in reform battles before. His efforts were crucial in passing legislation to improve factory working conditions, passing woman suffrage, and at least moderating the crookedness on Wall Street. He was a dour, unbending, relentless Irishman who simply would not quit—despite several threats on his life and constant harassment of his family—until the full story was out.

This, in brief, is what his investigation found:

After giving them the leases, Fall had accepted gifts and "loans" (for which no interest or security was asked) of more than $400,000 from Sinclair and Doheny, which Fall spent on his ranch in New Mexico.

Sinclair also was very generous with the Republican party. In 1920 he had given $75,000 to the Republican campaign. A couple of years later, Republican National Committee Chairman Will Hays finished toting up the party's campaign expenses and found that it was still heavily in debt, so he went back to Sinclair. This time Sinclair "loaned" the Party $185,000 in Liberty Bonds (the bonds had been purchased with money Sinclair defrauded from his own shareholders).

Hays (who would in the 1930s become morality czar of Hollywood) "laundered"—as the technique would come to be called in Watergate days—the Liberty Bonds through wealthy Republicans. Treasury Secretary Mellon refused to launder $50,000 in bonds sent to him, for which he gets less credit for morality than prudence. Mellon knew what the bond racket was all about but kept silent and didn't try to stop what was going on.

The scandal ended with the usual mishmash of justice and farce. Secretary Fall was convicted of accepting bribes from Sinclair and Doheny and went to prison (the first cabinet member to be imprisoned for crimes committed while in office), but Doheny and Sinclair were acquitted of offering bribes to Fall. Sinclair did go to prison briefly, however, for contempt of court when it was discovered that he had tried to influence the jury in his trial. It seems that he had had Burns detectives following some of the jurors. One juror claimed— though it was never proved—that Sinclair had indicated that his cooperation would result in the juror's becoming the lucky recipient of an automobile "long as this block."

WILD, CLAUDE C., JR.   As we pointed out in our entry for Mark Hanna, it is not easy for an oil company to pay its financial respects to politicians without the services of an intermediary. Hanna was Standard Oil's great disburser of money for persuasion in the nineteenth century. Claude C. Wild, Jr., served the same function for Gulf Oil Corporation in the 1960s and early 1970s.

In September 1958, Gulf Corporation informed its stockholders that "in the future the Corporation will take an increasingly active interest in practical politics." In June 1959, stockholders received a pamphlet, *A Political Program for Gulf Oil Corporation,* from Archie D. Gray, then a senior vice-president, in which Gray complained about the "creeping encroachment" of government toward the oil industry and decried the lack of a "fair hearing" for oilmen. The new political program envisioned beefing up Gulf's lobbying staff in Washington.

From 1958 until 1964, Gulf's Washington office was run by Kermit Roosevelt, famed for his part in overthrowing Mossadegh and reinstating the Shah of Iran (see Appendix entries on *EARLY FRIGHT CAMPAIGNS* and *SHAH OF IRAN*). Instead of using Roosevelt as its bagman, Gulf hired a new lobbyist, Wild, who previously had been employed by Mid-Continent Oil and Gas Association as an attorney, to distribute the money. He moved to Gulf in late 1959. He was told that, in addition to his salary, Gulf would make two hundred thousand dollars a year available to him for dealing with politicians. His first pass-through was fifty thousand dollars to Walter Jenkins, top aide to then Senate Majority Leader Lyndon Johnson.

The money used by Wild was laundered by Gulf through a Gulf subsidiary known as Bahamas Exploration Company Ltd., in Nassau. When Wild needed more money, he would get in touch with Bahamas Exploration and a delivery would be made to him in the United States; the places of delivery varied, but they were never in a Gulf office.

Apparently it is no easy job to secretly disburse millions of dollars to the crowd of politicians who line up for handouts: from time to time, Wild needed the assistance of others, because, as he put it, it was "physically impossible for one man to handle that kind of money." At various times, he used seventeen couriers to deliver money to politicians. Some of the couriers were Gulf's regional vice-presidents.

Gulf's most faithful retainer in the Senate was Senator Hugh Scott of Pennsylvania, minority leader, who annually received between ten thousand dollars and twenty thousand dollars from the oil company. Among the many others to whom Wild admitted giving large sums were Senator Hubert Humphrey and, ironically, every member of the Senate Watergate Committee except its chairman, Senator Sam Ervin.

In November 1973, Wild pleaded guilty to making an illegal contribution of one hundred thousand dollars to President Nixon's reelection campaign. (Actually, Gulf gave more than a million dollars to CREEP—the popular acronym for the Committee to Re-elect the President.)

The Senate Ethics Committee voted five to one in 1976 against taking action against Scott or any other senator who took Gulf money.

In 1974, the IRS ordered an investigation into the Gulf slush fund. But the

IRS agent put in charge of the investigation reported back to his bosses that only "several hundred thousand dollars" had moved through the secret slush fund in a since-liquidated Gulf subsidiary in the Bahamas, and he recommended that the investigation be "ceased and terminated." Later it was discovered that in fact more than $12 million was involved, not "several hundred thousand," and that the agent who had given the misleading information had, on the very day he filed his report, been vacationing in Pebble Beach with a couple of Gulf executives—at their expense. Also, it was discovered that the IRS agent had let Gulf pick up the tab for vacations in Las Vegas and at country clubs in New Jersey and Florida.

The disclosure of Gulf's and Wild's outlawry did not come about easily. It began with a lawsuit by Common Cause against the Committee to Re-elect the President. That dislodged a statement from Wild that he had given one hundred thousand dollars to CREEP. But the corporate source of the money was still unclear. That was squeezed into view by pressure from U.S. attorneys connected with the Watergate probe. On August 10, 1973, Gulf admitted that Wild had been handling corporate money. On November 13, 1973, both Wild and Gulf were charged with violating federal election laws, and on the same day both pleaded guilty.

But the probe wasn't over. In October 1974, the Securities and Exchange Commission ordered its staff to investigate the use of Gulf funds for contributions, gifts, and other outlays related to influencing politicians. Following negotiations between the SEC and Gulf, a consent judgment was handed down by Judge John Sirica on March 11, 1975, as the result of which Gulf's board of directors agreed to appoint a Special Review Committee to bring together details of Gulf's political dirty work. On the surface, the makeup of the Committee did not seem promising of candor. The chairman was John J. McCloy, a partner in the New York law firm of Milbank, Tweed, Hadley & McCloy, probably the most oil-saturated law firm in the world. McCloy, a former president of the World Bank and former chairman of Rockefeller's Chase Manhattan Bank, was the preeminent lawyer for the oil majors. The other two members of the Committee were Nathan W. Pearson, financial adviser to the Paul Mellon family interests and a director of Gulf since 1969; and Beverley Matthews, an influential Canadian lawyer and a director of Gulf since 1958.

The result of their investigation was not exactly a whitewash, though they did manage to keep any direct guilt from falling on any official of the Gulf Corporation who was not by that time dead or retired (Wild was retired by the time the report was issued).

Actually, the Committee was much more candid than skeptics had expected it to be. It acknowledged that the company's political activities were "shot through with illegality," being "generally clandestine and in disregard of Federal as well as a number of state statutes." The Committee went into detail not only about the domestic payoffs but also about the "gray fund" bribery in South Korea and the "black fund" payoffs to Italian journalists, and payoffs in Bolivia in collusion with the CIA. It acknowledged that while some Gulf officials were not exactly guilty of participating in the political chicanery, they were probably aware that something unsavory was going on and were certainly less than diligent in trying to prevent it. The Committee said Gulf's chairman, Bob Rawls Dorsey, "perhaps chose to shut his eyes to what was going on."

If the Gulf administration was anything more than moderately embarrassed, it was hard to discover. As window dressing, the board of directors asked for the resignation of chairman Dorsey and then "punished" him with a retirement income of about half a million annually.

The McCloy report would probably not have received much circulation had it not been for Chelsea House, a small New York trade publisher, which printed in 1976 half a million paperback copies under the title *The Great Oil Spill: The Inside Report: Gulf Oil's Bribery and Political Chicanery*. An official at Chelsea said that one of Gulf's lawyers phoned a threat to sue if the book was published and that he had urged them to sue, "for the health and sake of the book." But nothing came of it.

INDEX

Abadan refinery, 17
Abourezk, James, 182, 274–76, 275–76 n, 277, 278, 290 n, 304, 305, 311, 319, 359 n, 360–64, 385, 386, 388, 392, 394, 401, 403, 507
Adams, Brock, 270, 430, 527
Adams, F. J., 514
Adams, Henry, 537
Adams, Stanley, 37 n
Adams, Walter, 310
Adelman, Morris A., 105, 298
Aegean Captain (tanker), 456–57
AFL-CIO, 265, 278, 299, 309, 399, 401, 508
Agnew, Spiro, 296
Akins, James E., 96, 100, 168–69, 192, 227
Alaska Interstate, 29
Alaska pipeline, 2, 7, 26–33, 88–91, 137 n, 154–62, 183–87, 212, 285, 334–38, 371–73, 438; environmentalists and, 29, 30–33, 89–90, 91, 183–87, 334; federal courts and, 158; Interior Department's impact statement, 154–58, 159, 161–62; oil discoveries, 27–29; TAPS operation, 29–30, 163; trans-Canada debate, 158–62
Albert, Carl, 258, 261, 270, 292, 293, 321–22
Albright, Joseph, 428 n
Alderson, George, 143
Algeria, 193, 465 n; oil nationalization, 131, 133 n
Allen, Clifford, 341
Allen, Corbett, 122
Allen, George E., 512
Allen, James B., 403
Allied Chemical Corporation, 417
Alm, Alvin L., 416
Alyeska Pipeline Service Company, 30, 334–37, 373
Ambro, Jerome, 259, 262
Amerada Hess Corporation, 30, 99, 152, 165, 212 n, 331, 417; diversification (ranked by assets), 86; Nixon campaign contributions, 163; stockholders of, 492 n; Vietnam leases, 121
American Association of Petroleum Geologists (AAPG), 154, 475 n
American Association of Petroleum Landmen, 127
American Association of State Colleges and Universities, 297
American Electric Power Company, 249–50
American Enterprise Institute, 496
American Express, 418, 505
American Federation of State, County and Municipal Employees, 396 n
American Gas Association (AGA), 49, 52, 53, 70 n, 84, 125, 126, 127, 128, 129, 293–94, 296, 323, 328, 353, 389 n
American Home Products, 505
American Independent Oil Company, 561

American Institute of Merchant Shipping, 526, 528
American Oil Company (Amoco), 166–67, 213, 342, 442, 445, 478 n, 521; offshore leases, 341; price fixing, 111–12; profits, 429; projected crude oil needs (1972), 150
American Paper Institute, 358
American Petroleum Institute (API), 32, 37 n, 38, 40, 57, 58, 65, 69, 70, 79, 140, 141, 142–43, 154, 174, 180, 187, 188, 188 n, 198, 210, 211, 226, 257, 258, 258 n, 266, 276, 304, 305, 308, 348, 352, 389 n, 431, 435, 437, 445, 451–52, 460, 486, 507, 522, 528
American Public Gas Association (APGA), 53
American Public Power Association, 83, 87
American Society of Newspaper Editors, 424
American Telephone and Telegraph Company (AT&T), 417, 418, 505
Amini, Dr. Ali, 20
Aminoil U.S.A., 342
Amoco. *See* American Oil Company
Amoco Cadiz spill, 526
Amouzegar, Dr. Jamshid, 100, 102, 103, 195, 207
Ampex Corporation, 418
Anaconda Company, 409; uranium production, 348
Anderson, Carl, 479 n
Anderson, John B., 349–50
Anderson, Robert B., 512–16
Anderson, Robert O., 3, 27, 28, 35–36, 64 n, 213 n, 512
Anderson, Wendell R., 164, 403
Andrus, Cecil D., 117, 341, 342, 348, 392, 457
Angermueller, Hans, 467
Anglo-Iranian Oil Company (British Petroleum), 13 n, 16–17, 19, 20, 560
Anglo-Persian Oil Company, 558–59
Antitrust, 176–77, 241–43, 494, 516–24; cartel case (1953), 523–24; FTC study, 522–23; Standard Oil's success and, 516–21
Antitrust immunity, 132–33 n
Arab embargo, 186–87, 191, 195, 195 n, 196–201, 197 n, 203, 215, 408; end of, 223; Iran and, 200–1; reaction to, 196–201; State Department and, 196–97
Arabian American Oil Company (Aramco), 12–16, 13 n, 24, 133, 134, 192–93, 213, 214, 220, 226, 228, 417, 445, 461–62, 535; Arabian concession, 12–13; owners of, 103 n; royalty payments, 16; tax break, 15–16
Archbold, John, 530, 537–38
Areeda, Phillip, 41
Argo Merchant spill, 339, 524–26, 527
Arizona Public Service Company, 47
Ash, Roy L., 230